CHRISTIANIZING EGYPT

MARTIN CLASSICAL LECTURES

The Martin Classical Lectures are delivered annually at Oberlin College through a foundation established by his many friends in honor of Charles Beebe Martin, for forty-five years a teacher of classical literature and classical art at Oberlin.

John Peradotto, *Man in the Middle Voice: Name and Narration in the* Odyssey
Martha C. Nussbaum, *The Therapy of Desire: Theory and Practice in Hellenistic Ethics*
Josiah Ober, *Political Dissent in Democratic Athens: Intellectual Critics of Popular Rule*
Anne Carson, *Economy of the Unlost: Reading Simonides of Keos with Paul Celan*
Helene P. Foley, *Female Acts in Greek Tragedy*
Mark W. Edwards, *Sound, Sense, and Rhythm: Listening to Greek and Latin Poetry*
Michael C. J. Putnam, *Poetic Interplay: Catullus and Horace*
Julia Haig Gaisser, *The Fortunes of Apuleius and the* Golden Ass: *A Study in Transmission and Reception*
Kenneth J. Reckford, *Recognizing Persius*
Leslie Kurke, *Aesopic Conversations: Popular Tradition, Cultural Dialogue, and the Invention of Greek Prose*
Erich Gruen, *Rethinking the Other in Antiquity*
Simon Goldhill, *Victorian Culture and Classical Antiquity: Art, Opera, Fiction, and the Proclamation of Modernity*
Victoria Wohl, *Euripides and the Politics of Form*
David Frankfurter, *Christianizing Egypt: Syncretism and Local Worlds in Late Antiquity*

Christianizing Egypt

Syncretism and Local Worlds in Late Antiquity

David Frankfurter

PRINCETON UNIVERSITY PRESS
PRINCETON AND OXFORD

Copyright © 2018 Trustees of Oberlin College

Requests for permission to reproduce material from this work
should be sent to Permissions, Princeton University Press

Published by Princeton University Press
41 William Street, Princeton, New Jersey 08540

In the United Kingdom: Princeton University Press
6 Oxford Street, Woodstock, Oxfordshire OX20 1TR

press.princeton.edu

Cover and page vi art: Female figurine in orans position, with accentuated eyes and hair. Holes in headdress for adding threads. Painted terracotta, H. 14.6 cm. 6th–7th century CE. Probably from the Faiyum region, Egypt. Collection of the Newark Museum, # 38.161. Gift of Mrs. John D. Rockefeller, Jr., 1938

All Rights Reserved

First paperback printing, 2021
Paperback ISBN 978-0-691-21678-2

The Library of Congress has catalogued the cloth edition as follows:

Names: Frankfurter, David, 1961– author.

Title: Christianizing Egypt : syncretism and local worlds in late antiquity / David Frankfurter.

Description: Princeton : Princeton University Press, 2017. | Series: Martin classical lectures | Includes bibliographical references and index.

Identifiers: LCCN 2017018421 | ISBN 9780691176970 (hardcover : alk. paper)

Subjects: LCSH: Egypt—Religion—332 B.C.–640 A.D. | Christianity and other religions—Egyptian. | Syncretism (Religion)—Egypt.

Classification: LCC BL2455 .F725 2017 | DDC 200.932/09015—dc23 LC record available at https://lccn.loc.gov/2017018421

British Library Cataloging-in-Publication Data is available

This book has been composed in Arno Pro

For Anath

CONTENTS

List of Illustrations   xi
Preface   xiii
Acknowledgments   xvii
Abbreviations   xix

1 *Remodeling the Christianization of Egypt*   1

   I Overture   1
  II Historical Setting   3
 III The Problem of "Pagan Survivals"   7
 IV Syncretism and Purification   15
  V Agency, Gesture, and Landscape   20
 VI Social Sites and Religious Worlds of Syncretism in Late Antique Egypt   24
VII Postscript on Comparison and the Scope of Argument   31

2 *Domestic Devotion and Religious Change*
   Traditions of the Domestic Sphere   34

   I Overture   34
  II Defining the Domestic Sphere and Its Religious Character in Late Antique Egypt   38
 III Christianization and the Imagination of New Boundaries   44
 IV The Domestic World as Site of Religious Bricolage   48
  V Domestic Ritual, Domestic Agents, and the Syncretic Construction of Christianity   54
     A Lamp-lighting   55
     B Bread Stamps   55
     C Domestic Charms and Their *Dramatis Personae*   56
     D Female Figurines and the Ambiguity of Representation   58
     E Amulets, Curses, Saintly Blessings, and Votive Donations   61
 VI Agents of the Domestic Sphere: Gender and Creative Independence   64
VII Conclusion   68

CONTENTS

3 *Controller of Demons, Dispenser of Blessings*
   Traditions of the Holy Man as Craftsman of Local Christianity ... 69

   I Introduction: Saints and Syncretism ... 69
   II Implications of Classification: From "Saint" to "Regional Prophet" ... 74
   III Exorcism and the Reordering of Tradition ... 76
      A Reordering Perceptions of Evil ... 78
      B Exorcism and Charisma ... 80
      C Demonology as Preservation ... 85
   IV Holy Men in the Egyptian Landscape ... 87
      A Divination and the Definition of New Centers ... 87
      B Ritual and the Egyptian Environment ... 90
      C Syncretism and the Dispensing of Materials ... 92
   V Conclusion ... 100

4 *A Site of Blessings, Dreams, and Wonders*
   Traditions of the Saint's Shrine ... 104

   I Introduction ... 104
   II The Saint's Shrine as Social Site ... 108
   III Gestures ... 111
   IV Collective Expressions: Festivals and Their Gestures ... 114
      A Festival Hilarity and Control ... 114
      B Processions ... 118
      C Animal Slaughter and Feasting ... 120
      D Dance ... 122
   V Individual Expressions: Imprecation, Contact, Votive ... 126
   VI Divination ... 130
   VII Possession and the Performance of Spirits and Saintly Power ... 138
   VIII Conclusion ... 144

5 *The Magic of Craft*
   Traditions of the Workshop and the Construction of Efficacy ... 145

   I Introduction: Art and Efficacy ... 145
   II Workshops in Late Antique Egypt ... 151
   III Examples ... 160
      A Stonecarvers ... 160
      B Potters and Terracotta Artisans ... 162
      C Painters ... 167
      D Textile Weavers ... 171
      E The Mortuary Craft ... 176
   IV Conclusion ... 181

CONTENTS

6 *Scribality and Syncretism*
Traditions of Writing and the Book ... 184

  I Introduction ... 184
  II Scribality at the Shrines of the Saints ... 186
  III Monastic Scribes and the Mediation of Christianity ... 189
    A Monastic Libraries and Eclectic Scribes ... 190
    B Monastic Settings of Scribal Mediation ... 192
  IV Scribes and the Magic of Word and Song ... 197
  V The Recollection of Literary Traditions through the Scribal Craft ... 211
    A The Land of Egypt Oracle ... 212
    B Images of Amente and Its Demons ... 218
      1 The Media of Amente in Late Antique Egypt ... 219
      2 The Coptic Amente Mythology: Earlier Egyptian and Jewish Apocalyptic Traditions ... 222
      3 Apocalyptic Interpretation in Egypt and the Integration of Egyptian Traditions ... 226
  VI Conclusion ... 228

7 *Whispering Spirits, Holy Processions*
Traditions of the Egyptian Landscape ... 233

  I Introduction: Religious Landscape and Christianization ... 233
  II Temples and Churches ... 237
  III Habitats and Haunts of Spirits ... 242
  IV Procession and the Perception of Landscape ... 248
  V Inventing and Envisioning a Sacred Landscape ... 253
  VI Conclusion ... 256

Afterword ... 257

Bibliography ... 263
Illustration Credits ... 309
Index ... 311

ILLUSTRATIONS

PLATES

PLATE 1. Female figurine molded and painted to accentuate pregnant belly, with holes in headdress for jewelry.
PLATE 2. Female figurine, dressed in fabric.
PLATE 3. Mural of warriors' dance before the Virgin Mary (standing with Christ child to right).
PLATE 4. Detail of warriors' dance before the Virgin Mary
PLATE 5. Votive plaquettes of body parts and image of Daniel in lions' den from St. Colluthus shrine.
PLATE 6. Textile shoulder band(?) with medallion of cross surrounded by birds, flanked by medallions displaying warriors or heroes.
PLATE 7. Textile rectangular panel with *ankh*-cross, or *crux ansata*, set amid vases and flowers, with a face in the center.
PLATE 8. Panel painting of god Heron.
PLATE 9. Mural painting in monastic chapel of St. Sissinios mounted on horse and spearing the female demon Alabasdria, with various demonic and apotropaic figures added to the space around him.

FIGURES

FRONTISPIECE. Female figure in *orans* position.	vi
MAP. Egypt in late antiquity.	xxii
FIGURE 1. Female figurines found at Apa Mena site.	35
FIGURE 2. Female figurine molded to accentuate jewelry.	36
FIGURE 3. Female figurine with painted eyes and necklace.	36
FIGURE 4. Standing woman in long dress with fabric remains, child in arms.	36
FIGURE 5. Seated *mater lactans*.	59
FIGURE 6. Standing nude female figurine holding breasts, with the name *Phib* mold-pressed into the abdomen.	59
FIGURE 7. Standing nude and bejeweled *mater lactans* in aedicula.	60

ILLUSTRATIONS

FIGURE 8. Archaeological plan of Apa Mena pilgrimage city, showing main processional road, basilica and courtyard, and rounded building supposedly for incubation practice. 116–17

FIGURE 9. Coptic limestone frieze with bound antelopes. 146

FIGURE 10. Textile tunic front with cross on beaded necklace below nude satyr figure; border of marine monsters. 158

FIGURE 11. Textile panel with lobed cross resembling a lotus blossom, surrounded by lions, dogs, baskets, and tendrils. 159

FIGURE 12. Round amulet showing a saint on horseback spearing a crocodile. 170

FIGURE 13. Textile segment showing a mounted hero, his left arm raised, in a square surrounded by *putti*, vases, and plants. 174

FIGURE 14. Square textile segment showing two saints spearing serpents at their feet while holding crosses, surrounded by floral designs. 175

PREFACE

In my earlier book *Religion in Roman Egypt: Assimilation and Resistance* I tried to conceptualize Egyptian religion in the centuries leading into Christian rule in such a way as to suggest ways it *could* have continued alongside of, despite, or under the aegis of Christianity. My argument was that a culture's religion, properly understood, is a complex of places, practices, dispositions, charismatic roles, and traditions, and some elements of this complex may continue through—and often by means of—new religious or institutional idioms like Christianity. A number of critics, perhaps distracted by the term "resistance" in the subtitle, misunderstood the book as an argument simply for the timeless persistence of a monolithic "Egyptian paganism," but this was far from my goal or the book's actual contents. The culture obviously changed in important ways through Christianity, then Islam, and now modernity, but my main questions remain: What does it mean for a religion to "end," for a culture to Christianize, for temple cults to close? How do we conceptualize "religion" to answer those questions? And are there *comparanda* that might shed light on this issue of the "end" of religions?

In the almost two decades since it appeared, and enlightened by a spate of superb scholarship in many of the areas where I offered speculation, I have abandoned, adjusted, but also defended some of my arguments: how to make use of (rather than peremptorily dispose of) saints' lives in reconstructing historical religion; whether we can really talk about a Christian iconoclasm at all; whether churches actually replaced traditional cults in temples; the importance of the historical situations behind religious change in Panopolis, Philae, and Abydos; and how priests engaged Hellenism as a route to continued cultural authority. But a larger question emerged from these discussions, both for Egypt and for the broader world of late antiquity: If religion is to be conceptualized in local or regional terms (as I argued in *Religion in Roman Egypt*); if religion is mediated through gestures and material forms and performed in particular landscapes, through social roles, and through traditions and customs; and if religion thus conceived has a certain resilience in everyday life, then how should we understand Christianization itself? Obviously, old-fashioned notions of "conversion" that presuppose some new religious interiority across the Mediterranean world will not do, nor will approaches that simply deduce a state of "Christianness" from the closure of temples, the erection of churches and *martyria*, or the activity of a bishop—for what exactly would these occurrences mean for ordinary people?

Thus *Christianizing Egypt* came about as my effort to look at a later period of Egyptian religious transformation, this time in terms of how Christianity developed up to the time of Islamization (ca. fourth to seventh centuries CE). There are overlaps between this work and *Religion in Roman Egypt*, to be sure, in some topics (the ticket oracle) and primary sources (Shenoute on the monk who makes amulets). But the interests I have in this book and the theoretical perspective I offer in it are quite different. In that sense, this book is not so much a sequel as a turn of the kaleidoscope.

Most of the data I examine in this book are the kind once collected under the rubric of "pagan survivals," a term of curiosity, if not disapproval, that has tended to justify historians' dismissal of their historical worth. Yet increasingly, scholars like Ramsay MacMullen and Christopher Jones are reckoning with these data's value as windows into Christianity as it was actually lived in late antiquity. My contribution here is to move beyond the distorting categories of "pagan" and "survival" to try to frame their value in new ways: as, for example, local expressions of how Christianity itself could be assembled as a framework for meaningful action. And the term "syncretism," which for some readers will be a bright red flag, has struck me increasingly over the last fifteen years as an important and justifiable category for the developments that have taken place within Christianization. Chapter 1 should go far in explaining my use of this category, although it may not suffice for some.

This book is not organized chronologically, but according to a series of discrete religious worlds or "social sites" in which, I describe, Christianity was constructed—that is, made recognizable, sensible, indigenous, and authoritative. Within each chapter I take a largely synchronic approach within a period from roughly 350 to 700 CE, bringing in diachronic developments when they are observable and drawing on materials outside this period when they can elucidate religious processes within it. In choosing the religious worlds I do, I do not intend to be exhaustive—certainly one could imagine others: the merchant's villa, for example, or the ecclesiastical council—but rather to model an *approach* to Christianization that seeks out the specific contexts in which the religion could be assembled. The religious worlds on which I choose to focus here are those I have found most compelling in terms of stimulating regional creativity and agency in the construction of Christianity: the domestic sphere, the worlds of holy man and saint's shrine, workshops and artisans, monastic scribes, and the landscape itself. As will be clear, I approach these religious worlds as overlapping rather than separate in their activities and their creativity, even as I acknowledge that each has its own spatial center(s). Consequently, the chapters proceed from the home out to the holy man; then to that other regional cult site, the saint's shrine; then to the institutions that maintained both centers, the worlds of craftsmanship and monastic scribal culture; and finally conclude with a broader discussion of places within the landscape that stimulated Christianization. In the afterword I address a larger historical/definitional problem that my book presents: If the construction of Christianity comes down to idiosyncratic local efforts, and if syncretism as I explain it is an inevitable and perennial force in that construction everywhere, how should we talk about a "Christianity" at all?

Overall, my goal in this book is to model an approach to the process of Christianization that focuses on the discrete social worlds (and their various religious and ritual traditions) that have produced the various textual, documentary, and material data for Christianity—the "stuff" from which we extrapolate the religion's cultural currency in a region. And it is my hope that this approach (if not the specific religious worlds I address in this book) might be critically applied to other periods and places in history.

ACKNOWLEDGMENTS

The lengthy process of writing this book began with fellowship support from the John Simon Guggenheim Memorial Foundation and the Radcliffe Institute for Advanced Study at Harvard University during the 2007–2008 academic year and concluded with a fellowship from the Boston University Center for the Humanities in the fall of 2016 to complete manuscript revisions. In between, I was honored to give the 2013 Martin Classical Lectures at Oberlin College, to which I devoted four in-process chapters of the book. I am exceedingly grateful to all these sponsoring organizations, and especially for the vibrant and encouraging environments I found at the Radcliffe Institute, the BU Center for the Humanities, and Oberlin College.

Over the years I've been working and reworking chapters, I have depended on the particular generosity and critical acumen of late antiquity scholars David Brakke, Lucy Grig, AnneMarie Luijendijk, Arietta Papaconstantinou, Thelma Thomas, and Laura Nasrallah and the Casablanca Group of yore, all of whom read and annotated chapter drafts along the way, to my enormous benefit. In addition, a great number of colleagues have offered essential consultation, vital conversations, and the occasional letter of support, exemplifying the collegiality that makes academia, and especially the study of late antique religions, so rewarding: Roger Bagnall, John Baines, Betsy Bolman, Glen Bowersock, Béatrice Caseau, Malcolm Choat, Magali Coudert, Stephen Davis, Françoise Dunand, Jaś Elsner, Stephen Emmel, Barry Flood, Fritz Graf, Johannes Hahn, Sabine Huebner, Sarah Iles Johnston, Karen King, Chrysi Kotsifou, Magdalena Łaptas, Noel Lenski, Blake Leyerle, Tom Mathews, Christina Riggs, and Gesa Schenke. Not all of these colleagues knew exactly what I was doing with the information they were sharing, so I hope that this book will not come as too much of a surprise. My colleagues in the Department of Religion at Boston University welcomed this project with singular engagement when I arrived in 2010, and it has been a pleasure to develop ideas in the company of Jennifer Knust, Andrea Berlin, Jonathan Klawans, Deeana Klepper, and so many other smart scholars of religion here.

I also want to thank a number of colleagues from other, contiguous fields for sharing their research, both published and unpublished: Nicola Aravecchia, Adi Erlich, Helen Evans, Stephanie Hagan, Raz Kletter, Rita Lucarelli, Colleen

Manassa, Kerry Muhlestein, Janet Timbie, and Agnes Mihálykó. I am grateful to the American Society for the Study of Religion, in particular Peter Gottschalk, for devoting a whole weekend to the testing and clarification of the term "syncretism." Many of the valuable illustrations in this book appear only through the generosity and collegiality of Nicole Amaral (Rhode Island School of Design Museum), Sofia Asvestopoulos and Ulf Buschmann (Liebighaus Museum and Artothek), Michelle Fontenot (Kelsey Museum), Peter Grossmann, Joni Joseph (Dumbarton Oaks Museum), Włodzimierz Godlewski and Magda Łaptas (Polish Centre of Mediterranean Archaeology), Daniela Manetti and Giovanna Menci (Institute of Papyrology "G. Vitelli"), Daniel Maury (Ashmolean Museum), Gabe Moss (Ancient World Mapping Center at the University of North Carolina–Chapel Hill), Kerry Muhlestein (Brigham Young University Egypt Excavation Project), and Henrique Simoes (Musée des Beaux-Arts, Lyon). For organizing and operationalizing the bibliography for this project, I am indebted to Ryan Knowles.

I had the privilege of workshopping chapters or portions of chapters at various institutions over the years I was writing this book, a process that brought both more precision to some areas and, I hope, greater readability. Besides the Martin Lectures at Oberlin (chapters 1–2, 4, and 7), I presented chapter 1 at the Ohio State University (2009), Yale University (2010), Oxford University (2011), and University of Texas (2014); chapter 2 at the Radcliffe Institute (2008) and the College of William and Mary (2009); chapter 3 at Amherst College (2012); chapter 4 at Washington University (2010), Dartmouth College (2013), and University of Virginia (2016); chapter 5 at University of Pennsylvania (2014), the Ohio State University (2015), and Yale University (2015); chapter 6 for the Boston Patristics Group (2014); and chapter 7 at the University of Münster (2011) and Duke University (2015). I profited considerably from these invitations and opportunities, and I express my sincere gratitude to all my hosts and their colleagues.

A few parts of this book contain material previously published, and I thank the publishers for permitting their reuse here. Chapter 3 is a revision and expansion of "Syncretism and the Holy Man in Late Antique Egypt," which appeared in volume 11 of the *Journal of Early Christian Studies* (2003), and for whose permission to reprint I thank the Johns Hopkins University Press. A portion of chapter 4 first appeared in my article "Where the Spirits Dwell: Possession, Christianization, and Saint-Shrines in Late Antiquity," in volume 103 of the *Harvard Theological Review* (2010), for whose reuse I credit Cambridge University Press. My translation of portions of the Coptic *Apocalypse of Elijah* in chapter 6 first appeared in my 1993 book *Elijah in Upper Egypt* (pp. 301–28), now published by Trinity Press International, an imprint of Bloomsbury, for which I thank Bloomsbury Publishing Plc for its use. Chapter 7 uses material from my essay "The Vitality of Egyptian Images in Late Antique Egypt: Christian Memory and Response," from *The Sculptural Environment of the Roman Near East*, edited by Yaron Z. Eliav, Elise A. Friedland, and Sharon Herbert (Leuven, 2008), pp. 659–62, for which I thank Peeters Press.

ABBREVIATIONS

Note: Papyri are cited according to Duke University's Checklist of Editions of Greek, Latin, Demotic and Coptic Papyri, Ostraca and Tablets, edited by Joshua D. Sosin, Roger S. Bagnall, James Cowey, Mark Depauw, Terry G. Wilfong, and Klaas A. Worp, http://library.duke.edu/rubenstein/scriptorium/papyrus/texts/clist.html.

ACM   *Ancient Christian Magic: Coptic Texts of Ritual Power*, ed. Marvin Meyer and Richard Smith (San Francisco: Harper, 1994). Numbers refer to reference numbers in text.
PDM   *Papyri Demoticae Magicae*, trans. in *GMPT*
GLM   *Gospel of the Lots of Mary*, ed. A. Luijendijk, *Forbidden Oracles?* (Tübingen: Siebeck, 2014)
GMPT *The Greek Magical Papyri in Translation*, ed. H. D. Betz (Chicago: University of Chicago Press, 1986)
PO   Patrologia Orientalis
PG   *Patrologia Graeca*
PGM   *Papyri Graecae Magicae*, 2nd ed., ed. K. Preisendanz (Stuttgart: Teubner, 1973–1974)
SC   Sources chrétiennes

CHRISTIANIZING EGYPT

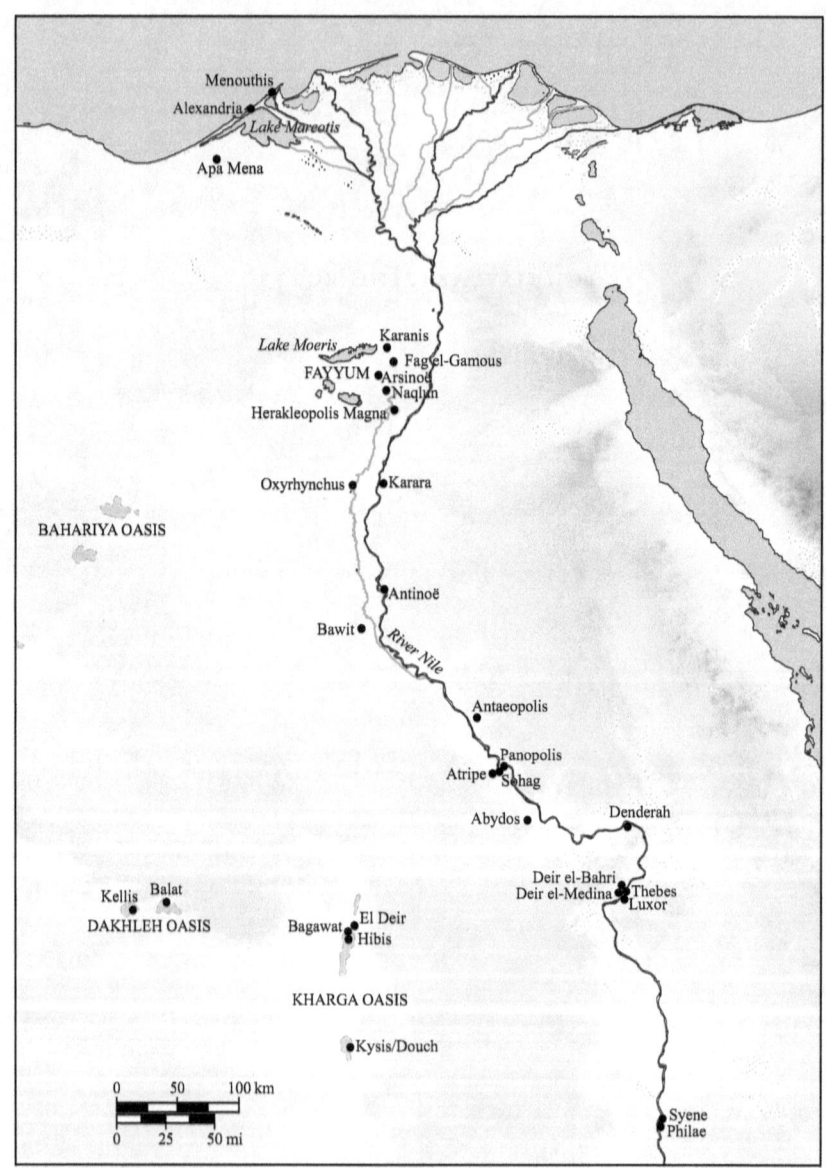

MAP. Egypt in late antiquity.

CHAPTER 1

Remodeling the Christianization of Egypt

I. OVERTURE

Sometime in about the seventh century CE, an Egyptian monk recorded two healing charms on either side of a piece of papyrus. At this point the temples of Egypt were in ruins, silent enclosures for the occasional Christian chapel or private devotions, and for impressive architecture one looked to the great saints' shrines, the churches with their colorful wall paintings, or the great estates outside the towns. Christianity and its images and leaders fairly permeated the culture of Egypt. The stories and songs that people shared revolved around the saints and the Holy Family. And so the first spell the monk took down, introducing it with a series of holy titles to evoke church liturgy, told a story of Jesus's and the apostles' encounter with a doe in labor, how the doe appealed to Jesus to help her through childbirth, and how Jesus sent the Archangel Michael to ease the pain. But in the second charm the monk shifted to another set of figures, whose story he continued onto the other side of the papyrus:

> Jesus Horus [ⲓ̅ⲥ̅ ϩⲱⲣ] [the son of Is]is went upon a mountain in order to rest. He [performed his] music, [set] his nets, and captured a falcon, ... a wild pelican. [He] cut it without a knife, cooked it without fire, and [ate it] without salt [on it].
>
> He had pain, and the area around his navel [hurt him], and he wept with loud weeping, saying, "Today I am bringing my [mother] Isis to me. I want a messenger-spirit [ⲁϩⲙⲟⲛ] so that I may send him to my mother Isis.
>
> ...
>
> [The spirit] went upon the mountain of Heliopolis and found his mother Isis wearing an iron crown and stoking a copper oven.
>
> ...
>
> [Isis] said to him, Even if you did not find me and did not find my name, the true name that the sun bears to the west and the moon bears to the east and that is borne by the six propitiatory stars under the sun, you would summon the three hundred vessels that are around the navel:

CHAPTER 1

Let every sickness and every difficulty and every pain that is in the belly of N, child of N, stop at this moment! I am the one who calls; the lord Jesus is the one who grants healing![1]

Sandwiched between invocations of Jesus as healer emerges an extensive narrative about the ancient Egyptian gods Horus and Isis—at a time when no temples and no priesthoods were still functioning to sustain their myths and no one could still read the Egyptian texts in which such traditional stories had been recorded. And yet this charm for abdominal pain, and the four others like it (for sleep, for childbirth, and for erotic success), replicate many of the basic features of charms from many centuries earlier. As in those ancient Isis/Horus spells for healing, we note here the drama of Horus's suffering far from his mother Isis, the repetitive, almost singsong structure, and—as in the preceding legend of Jesus and the doe—its application to some specific real-world crisis.[2]

What is this text doing in Christian Egypt? What does it tell us about Christianization, about abandoned rites and traditions, about the folklore that might stretch between these two religious periods? Is it "pagan" or "Christian" to record or recite such spells? And what of the scribe, whose investment in the authority and magic of Christian ritual speech is apparent from the very beginning of the document? How did he understand these ancient names? And how many others copied similar spells—in monastic cells, at shrines, or in villages?

It is such cases that this book examines, those in which seemingly archaic religious elements appear in Christian form, not as survivals of a bygone "paganism," but as building blocks in the *process* of Christianization. And while I will focus on the Christianization of Egypt over the fourth through seventh centuries, the arguments I make and the models I propose about the conglomerate nature of Christianization should apply to other parts of the Mediterranean and European worlds as well.

In fact, it is rare that we find such overt examples of the recollection of archaic religious traditions in ongoing folklore and practice as appear in this magical text with Isis and Horus. More often we find, in the vague and hostile testimony of Christian bishops and abbots, references to local practices that may strike us, in their independence from church teaching and their suggestion of another sacred landscape entirely, as reflecting a more archaic religious order:

> ... it is said that some of them ablute their children in polluted water and water from the arena, from the theater, and moreover they pour all over themselves water with incantations (spoken over it), and they break their clay pots claiming it repels the evil eye. Some tie amulets on their children, hand-crafted by men—those (men) who provide a place for the dwelling

---

1 ACM 49 = Berlin 8313b; Beltz, "Die koptischen Zauberpapyri."
2 See Frankfurter, "Narrating Power," 457–76; and, more specifically on these magic spells, Frankfurter, "Laments of Horus in Coptic."

of demons—while others anoint themselves with oil that is evil and incantations and such things that they tie on their heads and necks.[3]

The author does not accuse his subjects of visiting temples, making sacrifices, or praying to ancient gods (although similar testimonies from Gaul and Iberia often did make these accusations).[4] But what is this realm of practice, with its pollution and demons, that the author is describing? Is it Christianity? "Paganism"? Is it "popular religion," and if it is, from what "proper religion" might it be distinct?

It is in these kinds of testimonies, and their echoes in the archaeological record, that we begin to find religion as it was lived, Christianity in its local constructions, and the *syncretism* that characterizes any religion as it is negotiated in time and space. Christianity in Egypt of the fifth, sixth, and seventh centuries amounted to a framework within which mothers and scribes, artisans and holy men, priests and herdsmen experimented with diverse kinds of religious materials and traditions, both to make sense of the institution and its teachings and to conceptualize efficacy—the magic without which life couldn't proceed.

II. HISTORICAL SETTING

My 1998 book *Religion in Roman Egypt: Assimilation and Resistance* was intended to explore and model how Egyptian religion was able to continue in various ways, despite economic, legal, and social pressures (and albeit in diminished forms), into the fourth, fifth, and even sixth centuries in particular regions, then particular villages, then particular households. The underlying thesis, that religions don't just disappear over a few centuries but transform and shift in orientation, required a different concept of "Egyptian religion" than that held by many Roman historians raised to think of a monolithic "paganism" or a romantic era of great temples. Part of the work of the historian of religions is to think critically about what terms and models most productively cover the evidence one has.

While I also delved into types of continuity and preservation of Egyptian traditions in Christian guise (like the ticket oracle, to be addressed in more detail in chapters 4 and 6), it was not my goal then to address Christianization per se except in a series of preliminary observations at the end of the book proposing the religion's integration in Egypt as idiom, as ideology, and as license for iconoclasm. But since 1997 I have had the opportunity to rethink these observations in terms of new archaeological evidence and new discussions of Coptic literature as data for continuing traditions.[5] This book thus turns to the problem of Christianization indicated by *Religion in Roman Egypt*: Was this a "conversion" or a synthesis

---

3 Pseudo-Athanasius, *Homily on the Virgin* 95, in Lefort, "L'homélie de S. Athanase," 35–36.
4 Dowden, *European Paganism*, 149–91.
5 E.g., Hahn, Emmel, and Gotter, *From Temple to Church*; and Dijkstra and Van Dijk, *Encroaching Desert*.

CHAPTER 1

of religious traditions? How, and in what contexts, should we answer this question—through documents of ecclesiastical order, monastic or imperial administration, or even "degrees" of Hellenism? That is, what are the proper data for Christianization: The amount of churches or monasteries built?[6] The amount of people showing up at these places?[7] Their assimilation of "Christian" names?[8] A growing diversity of material objects that imply some association with the religion? Or, conversely, the functional end of all traditional religious infrastructure, perhaps implying people's concomitant absorption of Christianity?[9] Is there a point at which we can say that a "Christianity" has come to exist or that people "are Christian" or even hold a Christian "identity" in any sense?[10] Does the mere existence of Christian clergy—owning property, sending letters—signify the Christianization of culture or simply the growth of an autonomous institution?[11] These are all signs, to be sure, of an institution (or the decline of something in the culture), but do these types of documentation reflect cultural transformation, and if so, how?

My preference has always been for documents that illustrate "popular," "lived," or local religion: the cultures of pilgrimage and shrine, ritual expertise and magic, and domestic ritual concerns. These dimensions of the process of Christianization do not exclude or stand apart from the "institution," broadly defined. People of these cultures—the laity, members of the lower clerical ranks—can pay close attention to sermons and ecclesiastical instructions, but that still leaves us far from knowing the influence of those sermons and instructions.[12] At the same time, the various worlds of lived or local religion also exert their own innovations and self-determination—their own agency, as I will explain. And so the documents of lived or local religion do not tend to show a Christianity familiar to the modern historian (even if they do so to the anthropologist). They show a Christianity in gradual, creative assemblage, whose principal or most immediate agents may have been local scribes, mothers protecting children, or artisans, not priests or monks.

---

6 In his detailed study of the Christianization of the Philae region, Dijkstra takes the position that Christianity is in effect when the trappings of its institution, from ecclesiastical leaders to infrastructure, are evident; Dijkstra, *Philae and the End*, 45–63, 341–42. It is unclear, however, the extent to which the existence of the institution (or, for that matter, the sporadic adoption of Christian names; ibid., 47) reflects peoples' actual religious practices.

7 See MacMullen, *Second Church*.

8 See Bagnall, "Religious Conversion and Onomastic Change"; idem, "Conversion and Onomastics"; Depauw and Clarysse, "How Christian Was Fourth Century Egypt?"; Frankfurter, "Onomastic Statistics"; Depauw and Clarysse, "Christian Onomastics."

9 Bagnall, "Combat ou vide."

10 Rebillard, *Christians and Their Many Identities*; Jones, *Between Pagan and Christian*.

11 See in general Luijendijk, *Greetings in the Lord*.

12 On the ineffectiveness of one particularly well-spoken bishop (Augustine of Hippo) to influence his church audiences to think of themselves as Christian, see Rebillard, "Late Antique Limits of Christianness."

But where do such materials leave us in gauging degrees or depths of Christianness or even the means of Christianization? In fact, as with most of the late Roman world, we have no data to explain how Christianity spread in Egypt. It certainly did not happen simply by virtue of churches built and priests in residence. Hagiographical legends of saints motivating allegiance through the destruction of idols are so idealized as to be useless as documentation, and there is little actual evidence beyond the mere texts of sermons how public preaching occurred and to what effect. Most scholars have argued that Christianity spread by village rather than individual. Ramsay MacMullen suggested that the process must have involved miracles in some way, since hagiographies assume this, but it is unclear how these performances would have taken place.[13] Peter Brown's scenario, based generally on hagiography, in which holy men represented the face, charisma, and ideologies of Christianity by virtue of their social functions in the culture, seems quite likely (and is developed further in chapter 3),[14] although we have little notion of what teachings these figures would have taught as Christian or what ideas communities might have assimilated: One God or the powers of angels? One Bible or their own prophetic powers? The saving power of Jesus's crucifixion or the material efficacy of the cross symbol? The material signs of Christianization from the fourth century on—from personal names to decorated tombs, from monastic complexes to scripture fragments—do not tell us what ideas this religion involved for its diverse local adherents. We cannot, that is, infer a system of one Bible, one God, the power of the Eucharist, the authority of the church, and the rejection of idols, except in the most abstract sense, when the little data we have for lived religion show the power of martyrs and angels, the apotropaic nature of scripture, the use of oil as a vehicle of church authority, and an utterly fluid concept of idolatry. We must conclude that Christianity arose and developed as a local phenomenon.

Of course, by the sixth century, Egypt was probably at least as Christian as any premodern culture could be. Except for a few lingering shrines and isolated expressions of private or local devotion to the old gods, the traditional temple religion of Egypt had largely disintegrated, the result of internal economic decline, Christian imperial pressure, and many other factors. At the same time, the evidence gleaned from papyri, inscriptions, and archaeology shows the increasing influence of the Christian institution in many parts of life. In the domestic sphere we see a rise in Christian names (whether biblical or saints'), suggesting families' inclinations to endow their children with the blessings of the new heroes and holy beings.[15] In the urban sphere we see a shift in the topography of monumental centers, from temples to churches and saints' shrines, with those institutions'

---

13 Wipszycka, "La christianisation de l'Égypte"; and MacMullen, *Christianizing the Roman Empire*, 59–64.

14 Brown, "Rise and Function of the Holy Man"; and idem, *Authority and the Sacred*, 55–78.

15 Bagnall, "Religious Conversion and Onomastic Change"; Papaconstantinou, *Le culte des saints en Égypte*; Frankfurter, "Onomastic Statistics."

CHAPTER 1

liturgical calendars and processions now distinguishing public culture.[16] Christian offices seem to have provided civic reward for the local elite, and the schooling of those elite came to include Christian texts as well as classical.[17] Monks and monasteries also became central players in the social and economic lives of many regions of late antique Egypt, both as producers and as unofficial administrators. And the literary output in these monasteries was in full spate by the fifth century, offering a veritable library of documents describing the fantasies, ideals, pious models, scriptural exegeses, and often-conflicting ideologies embraced by Egyptian monks in late antiquity.[18]

In all these respects Egyptian culture—public, administrative, monastic—showed the influence of Christianity: Christianity as a context for prestige, as an extension of learning, as a framework for blessing one's children, and certainly as an idiom of imperial authority. But did these elements of influence amount to Christianization in the pervading sense that church historians usually mean it? How do we accommodate Peter Brown's important observations about the *function* of monks in their social environments, not as teachers of doctrine and exemplars of virtue, but as charismatic administrators of local tensions, conveyers of blessings, curses, and exorcisms?[19] And how do we accommodate the kinds of data with which this chapter began: the devotions, practices, texts, and visual materials that seem to belie simplistic labeling of the culture as "Christian" or "pagan," and that suggest that people at every level, in every social world, were actively engaged in working out what "Christian" meant in an ancient landscape, amid an ancient economy, and in the context of familiar gestures and the memories they bore?

This book starts from the position that "Christianity" describes not a state of cultural or religious accomplishment or "identity" but an ongoing process of negotiation—of syncretism (a term that I shall explain shortly). Indeed, this book is about how people in their various social worlds of home and shrine, workshop and cell, constructed Christianity as something both authoritative and recognizable. These various kinds of negotiation that allowed Christianity to take shape in culture did not amount to some national project of acculturation. This is why I use the term "Christianization," which suggests a process—or, as I describe in this book, multiple simultaneous processes that affected local traditions in discrete ways—rather than a historical achievement or monolithic cultural institution. It is also why I avoid the term "conversion," which carries the sense of a radical psy-

---

16 Alston, *City in Roman and Byzantine Egypt*, 277–322; Papaconstantinou, "Cult of Saints."

17 See Cribiore, "Higher Education in Early Byzantine Egypt"; and Wipszycka, "Institutional Church."

18 See, e.g., Pearson and Goehring, *Roots of Egyptian Christianity*; Brakke, *Demons and the Making*; Frankfurter, "Legacy of the Jewish Apocalypse."

19 Brown, "Rise and Function of the Holy Man"; idem, *Authority and the Sacred*. See also Frankfurter, *Religion in Roman Egypt*, 184–93; idem, "Syncretism and the Holy Man"; idem, "Curses, Blessings, and Ritual Authority."

chological shift at the level of the individual *even when* applied to the Roman Empire.[20] Christianization and syncretism both, I will argue, took place differently in different social worlds. How a grandmother integrated saints and blessings with family needs differed considerably from how a stonecutter deployed crosses on a traditional grave stela or from a ritual specialist combining magical names and prayers in a healing charm. While such social worlds and roles inevitably overlapped, their differing strategies and traditions led to different combinations of Christian and Egyptian symbols, ideas, and media. In these many linked social worlds and their active, creative agents, I argue, Christianity was constructed as a meaningful and authoritative framework for religious practice.

The different relationships to institution, authority, and tradition that people in these different social worlds cultivated emerge, in fact, through that startling range of materials—magical texts, bishops' sermons, and so on—in which modern historical scholarship finds "pagan survivals." But this term, with its latent assumptions about "paganism" and "conversion," has long distorted the nature of the religious practices and materials it is supposed to cover, as well as the very historical process of engaging Christianity. Indeed, all three of these terms force complex evidence into apologetic narratives of "true Christianity" or "pagan decay."

III. THE PROBLEM OF "PAGAN SURVIVALS"

Many of the materials that I use in this book as documents of the local process of Christianization, like magical texts, figurines, and apocryphal depictions of hell, have carried an unfortunate (if exotic) reputation as "pagan survivals"—that is, as persisting remnants of a pre-Christian religion. What is denoted in this term "pagan survival"?

One of Christianity's early conceptual innovations as a religious movement was the construction of an alternative, improper system of cult practice as a clear and demonic Other. Derived more from biblical depictions of improper cult than from actual observation of the cultural environment, "paganism" [*pagan-, hellēn-*] quickly became a standard term of censure, revolving around a purported affiliation between some implicated custom (a festival, a gesture) and the actual worship of demons.[21] Whether for Justin Martyr in the second century, John Chrysostom in the fourth, or local charismatic missionaries in Africa in the twentieth, the term "pagan" has always cast certain practices and customs at best as parochial and uncultured, and at worst as worship of the Devil—even when those practices and customs are intrinsic to local social life, community fortune, and the integrity of heritage.[22] Indeed, anthropologists and historians have tended to find that the

---

20 James, *Varieties of Religious Experience*, lectures IX–X; Nock, *Conversion*.
21 On the use of "paganism" as a discourse of censure, see Rothaus, "Christianization and De-Paganization"; and Frankfurter, "Beyond Magic and Superstition."
22 On the use of "pagan" in Roman antiquity, see O'Donnell, "Paganus"; and Remus, "End of

censure of a demonic "paganism" has usually masked a far more fluid sense of religious tradition in communities.[23]

A word with such archaic theological resonance and specific ideological force as "pagan" should properly have little utility for historians. As one scholar astutely noted in a review, "I do not see how it is possible to use the word at all without implicitly accepting that the Christians had it right about the world and its organization."[24] Still, the plain ease that "pagan" affords the historian in designating everything religious and cultic apparently outside (or prior to) Christianity and Judaism has maintained the term's currency in modern scholarship. Its value becomes, perhaps, greater for the study of late antiquity, when the term *Hellēn* came to signify for many non-Christian elites not just traditional modes of ceremony but culture, heritage, modes of social comportment, and familiar images of delight.[25] Shouldn't, then, the promotion of *Hellēn* as a religious alternative to Christianity by apparent insiders like Emperor Julian and the late fifth-century intellectual Damascius justify its use by modern historians? Or would we then be turning a rarefied rhetorical self-identification into a broadly descriptive category? What alternative to "paganism" do we even have for referring to non-Christian (and non-Jewish) religion, especially if we want to discuss wide currents in Mediterranean or regional cultural change? Might "polytheism" be a substitute, or does the increasing evidence for monotheism among non-Jews and non-Christians make this term too improper and even overtly theological—classifying religions by number of gods?[26] Ultimately, shouldn't the historian be able to use an inadequate word like "paganism" in a responsible way?

The problem with maintaining this convenient word to denote such a wide swathe of culture and religious experience in antiquity lies in the ways it ends up influencing discussion. Even the most objectively minded historians inevitably fall into the same traps of *imprecision* (what cultural features does "pagan" cover that would not have included "Christians"?),[27] *reification* (did non-Christian religions really constitute "-isms," or systems?), and—most classically—*triumpha-*

'Paganism'?" For contemporary examples of the same broad demonizing capacity of such terms, see Douglas, "Sorcery Accusations Unleashed"; Meyer, "Beyond Syncretism"; idem, "Modernity and Enchantment"; and Dulue Mbachu, "Christianity vs. the Old Gods of Nigeria," Associated Press, September 4, 2007.

23 A point made effectively by both Bonner, "Extinction of Paganism"; and Künzel, "Paganisme, syncrétisme."

24 James J. O'Donnell, review of *The Making of a Christian Aristocracy*, by Michelle R. Salzman, *Bryn Mawr Classical Review*, June 4, 2002.

25 See Chuvin, *Chronicle of the Last Pagans*; and Bowersock, *Hellenism in Late Antiquity*.

26 See Athanassiadi and Frede, *Pagan Monotheism in Late Antiquity*.

27 "Sacrifice," for example, is often viewed as "paganism's" definitive characteristic. Yet for most of the late antique world offerings to gods involved not bloody animal slaughter but wine, oils, or cakes, and animal slaughter persisted at Christian festivals, whether or not it was designated as sacrifice. See, e.g., Paulinus of Nola, *Carmen* 20, on the St. Felix festivals; and Sozomen, *Hist. Eccl.* 2.4.3-4, on the Mamre festivals. See Frankfurter, "Egyptian Religion and the Problem," 86–87.

lism. "Later paganism," claimed the historian Harold Bell, "died with a kind of mellow splendor, like a beautiful sunset, but dying it was. It had been conquered by the truer and finer religion, for which it had itself prepared the way, a religion which at last brought the solution of problems which paganism had posed but to which it had found no answer."[28] Even Marcel Simon, the otherwise discerning scholar of early Christianity, considered "the inability of the old religion which—still partly caught in the paralyzing trammels of monotheism—cannot reorganize and rejuvenate itself around a central figure. . . . [So,] after having in some sort opened the way to Christianity by lending it a vocabulary and some concepts to define itself, paganism was reduced to a pale copy of the rival cult."[29] Both authors illustrate how imagining the religious landscape and the religious narrative of the Roman and late antique worlds in terms of three—or, more often, two—*different* entities in interaction and conflict *invariably* leads to the assumption of "pagan" decadence and Christian inevitability (or some variation on this story), which proceeds to color all subsequent historical discussion. In fact, as I argued in *Religion in Roman Egypt*, the decline of some traditional cults, the establishment of Christianity, the persistence of other traditional cults and practices, and the Christianization of other practices were all far more complex processes than could possibly be captured under the rubric of "decline of paganism/rise of Christianity." The term "paganism" itself was never meant as a term of scholarly convenience; quite to the contrary, as a Latin or Greek insider's term it always signified Christianity's invented foil—a polemical category with little relationship to the many local cults, traditions, and religious expressions that existed around the Mediterranean world. "Paganism" implies its own insufficiency and replacement.

Of course, to the degree that we need a word to capture the full prejudicial color of *paganus* or *Hellēn*, as Christian writers wielded these terms, it may be more accurate to use something like "heathen" (which no modern reader would mistake as neutral) to describe the recalcitrant, infidel Other who engages in bloody sacrifices and worships idols, trees, and demons.[30] But accuracy in interpreting and characterizing the traditional religious forms of the late antique Mediterranean world demands that we find alternatives to "pagan," whether we are framing ideologies, practices, shrines, or cultural displays. At the very least, we should be wary of a terminology that assumes more of a dichotomy between religious worlds and identities—"Christian" and "pagan"—than could possibly have existed in a premodern culture.

Bell's and Simon's evocative depictions of the twilight of the old religions highlight not just the inherent bias of "paganism" but also the problem of conceptualizing Christianization and religious change itself. Was a heathen culture in fact

28 Bell, *Cults and Creeds*, 105.
29 Simon, "Early Christianity and Pagan Thought," 398.
30 I find encouragement in Jones's essay "The Fuzziness of 'Paganism.'"

"converted" to become Christian? How and where does conversion happen—in the individual, true-thinking soul, as Bell, Nock, and their Protestant forebears suggested, or in the complexities of village and urban life, as anthropologists would argue? Since well before William James, "conversion" has usually signified a private shift in spiritual allegiance from one religious identity to another.[31] In this sense the term has carried with it distinct theological overtones inherited from Protestant Christianity, a religion that offers individual salvation from sin and an intimate savior who symbolizes that process, culminating in a decisive shift from darkness to light. The very rupture or decisive shift in religion that we associate with conversion may be historically unusual, the post hoc construction of hagiography or modern psychology. Apart from certain rarefied and idealized testimonies, the shift to Christianity in antiquity and the Middle Ages, as in early modern Latin America and modern Africa, appears to have involved complex social dynamics, from elite interests in prestige to the public charisma of holy men and the erection of new shrines. Christianization could come about simply in the course of people's embrace of a new ritual medium (like a cross or oil) in their familiar landscape, or it could symbolize a new economic order or a broader cultural cosmos. In general, religious transformation was a group, not an individual, phenomenon and therefore involved much diversity among and across communities in terms of negotiating the relationship between the new religious system and the older traditions.[32]

Indeed, the decisiveness and completeness that the term "conversion" inevitably implies as a category has tended to run up against the evidence for "survivals"—appearances of older religious traditions within the new religious order—like those that began this chapter. How do we factor into our concept of conversion or Christianization all the many archaic-seeming folk customs that have punctuated local Christianities from late antiquity through today? The magical text and the condemnation of popular uses of "polluted" water quoted earlier thus become part of a curiosity cupboard of so-called "pagan survivals" that extends to "sacrifices" of animals for St. Felix in fifth-century Italy, the lighting of candles at crossroads in sixth-century Iberia, and rituals dedicated to fairies and elves in other parts of the medieval world. Even today we retain Christmas trees and Easter eggs, Catholics in Haiti and Brazil invoke *loa* and *orixas*, and an avid Red Sox fan might seek to magically hamper the success of the rival Yankees by burying a team jersey in the cement under the Yankees' new stadium—a ritual strategy akin to those in the Roman Empire for "fixing" chariot races.[33]

---

31 See, e.g., Nock, *Conversion*; the historiographical discussions by Papaconstantinou, "Introduction"; and Cameron, "Christian Conversion in Late Antiquity."

32 See MacMullen, *Christianizing the Roman Empire*; and, more generally, Fernández-Armesto, "Conceptualizing Conversion in Global Perspective." For modern religious change, see Goody, "Religion, Social Change"; and van der Veer, "Introduction."

33 On the binding spell against the baseball team, see Sushil Cheema, "The Big Dig: The Yanks

What does the persistence of these kinds of traditions mean? The term "pagan survival" in fact proposes its own intrinsic narrative: that these traditions all belonged to, and had greater meaning in, the ancient "pagan" religion—some putative organized religion that predated Christianity. Following Christianization, so the story goes, these various practices of the ancient "pagan cults" remained as random *superstitions,* or magic, or, in the words of the august antiquarian Alphonse Barb, "the syncretistic, rotting refuse-heap of the dead and dying religions of the whole ancient world."[34] "Pagan survival" implies both a *heritage* in a vague but historically prior religious system and a *resilience* in the face of true Christianity. At the same time, the continuity of these "pagan survivals" implies incomplete doctrinal instruction or lax missionizing, and certainly uncomprehending village folk.[35] Indeed, the portrayal of a Christian culture as rife with "pagan survivals" has long served as a kind of propaganda for proper missionizing and reform. Protestant histories and evangelists have often depicted idiosyncratic folk practices as evidence of an incomplete Christianity, a kind of whitewashed heathenism, and thus as a warrant for evangelization of these degenerate cultures outside of history. As the nineteenth-century archaeologist William Ramsay wrote:

> The introduction of Christianity into the country [of Asia Minor] broke the continuity for the moment. But the old religious feeling was not extirpated: it soon revived, and took up the struggle once more against its new rival. Step by step it conquered, and gradually destroyed the real quality of Christianity. The old local cults took on new and outwardly Christianised forms; names were changed, and outward appearance; a show of Christian character was assumed. The Iconoclasts resisted the revival for a time, but the new paganism was too strong for them. The deep-seated passion for art and beauty was entirely on the side of that Christianised paganism, into which the so-called Orthodox Church had degenerated.... There is little essential difference in religious feeling between the older practice and the new: paganism is only slightly disguised in these outwardly Christianised cults.[36]

Catholicism and the Greek and Russian Orthodoxies at one time or another have all been regarded as thinly veneered heathenisms on account of their inclusion of practices—folk and official alike—that seemed pre-Christian. Unique, culturally distinctive, or "excessive" religious movements within Christianity have likewise been understood as resurgences of some native "pagan" impulse.[37] But

---

Uncover a Red Sox Jersey," *New York Times,* April 14, 2008; cf. Gager, *Curse Tablets and Binding Spells,* 53–74.
  34 Barb, "Survival of the Magic Arts," 104.
  35 Dennis, "Popular Religious Attitudes."
  36 Ramsay, *Pauline and Other Studies,* 130–31.
  37 See, e.g., Frend, *Archaeology of Early Christianity,* 117–18, on Numidian Christianity.

the rhetoric of "pagan survivals" has also enjoyed a positive, even nationalist spin, in the sense that surviving (or simply old) practices are viewed as artifacts of some "authoritative cultural heritage." For some modern Greeks and Irish, the strange festival practices of their rural compatriots bespeak the transcendent power of cultural heritage and provide cause to celebrate an unbroken lineage with the ancient Greeks or the Celts.[38] Likewise for modern Copts, the apparent wealth of "pharaonic" or ancient Egyptian imagery in early Egyptian Christian art demonstrates their proper inheritance of the glory of the pharaohs, so that Coptic Christianity is seen as actually maintaining that heritage instead of obliterating it. From this perspective it is the Coptic Church, not Islam, that preserves and conveys Egyptian heritage.[39]

But if the term "pagan survival" inevitably imposes these theological or nationalist narratives on materials that seem to harken back to a pre-Christian stage, the *materials themselves* remain complex and intriguing challenges to all our assumptions about Christianization, "paganism," and conversion—and all the more so because they were inevitably preserved or reported on by agents who considered themselves exemplary Christians. This chapter opened with a magical text invoking Horus and Isis that was inscribed and edited by someone literate and, we might infer, capable in others' eyes of healing by the power of liturgical formulations. He was thus most likely a monk. A Coptic saint's life of the sixth century mentions two distinct ranks of heathen priests, recalling their Egyptian titles (ϩⲟⲛⲧ, ⲟⲩⲁⲁⲃ). The same text recounts the exorcism of a temple haunted by "an evil demon named Bes"—a popular god throughout the Roman Empire whose famous oracle inhabited a temple in the same area.[40] Collectors of Coptic survivals look especially to the appearance of such names and stories long after the decline of the temples as evidence of continuities (in whatever form), and although many alleged survivals end up being misunderstandings of biblical themes or medieval archaisms, the evidence for persisting traditions is quite extensive.[41]

The writings of the great abbot Shenoute of Atripe, an important Christian reformer in the region of Panopolis during the late fourth and early fifth centuries, offer another type of apparent "survival." In one text, Shenoute mocks the private pieties of a local dignitary who—it has been reconstructed—was only claiming to be Christian. Shenoute reveals him publicly as a "crypto-*Hellēn*" by

---

38 See, e.g., Piggott, *Druids*; also see Hobsbawm, "Introduction."

39 See, e.g., Meinardus, "Some Theological and Sociological Aspects," 10–11. See also the trenchant remarks by Mayeur-Jaouen, *Pèlerinages d'égypte*, 33–56; and Van der Vliet, "Copts."

40 *V. Mosis*, in Moussa, "Abba Moses of Abydos"; Moussa, "Coptic Literary Dossier"; Till, *Koptische Heiligen- und Martyrerlegenden*, 2:46–81; Amélineau, *Monuments pour servir*, 2:680–706.

41 See Behlmer, "Ancient Egyptian Survivals." Classic formulations of Egyptian survivals include Budge, *Coptic Apocrypha*, lix–lxxii; Hallock, "Christianity and the Old Egyptian Religion"; Burmester, "Egyptian Mythology in the Coptic Apocrypha"; and Hammerschmidt, "Altägyptische elemente im koptischen Christentum." Important critiques include Zandee, "Traditions pharaoniques"; and Papaconstantinou, "Historiography, Hagiography."

enumerating the various ways he belied his public Christian identity: how he would pray toward the west, the land of the dead; how he would "pour out (libations) to Kronos over the waters"; how he would collect sacred images in an interior room in his house, which Shenoute and his monks invaded and pillaged; and how he was caught asperging the temple of Atripe with various scented plants after the Christians had gutted it.[42] Here, presumably, we have a more deliberate, self-conscious form of maintaining older religious traditions, involving secrecy and a sense of ideological discontinuity between public and private religious practices. Evidence of secret devotion to traditional cult has been found in many parts of the late antique Mediterranean world, including the remains of a domestic pig sacrifice in sixth-century Athens and a sixth-century Syrian report of a Christian icon that could be reversed to display an image of the god Apollo.[43] Across cultures, such secrecy has usually resulted in a change in the concept of the older traditions that were preserved. The traditions become idealized and idiosyncratic links to a mythic past, or the secrecy becomes such a part of the traditions that they cannot be performed in public at all.[44] In this regard, we cannot really call these practices "survivals"—in any continuous sense—of older cult practices.

The far more common repository of survivals from which historians have drawn is exemplified in the other text with which this chapter opened: a complaint about popular local practices among Christians, practices that the author associates with pollution and demons and that recall much older religious traditions. Abbot Shenoute echoes such complaints in some of his sermons, likewise indicating the presence of Christians in his region:

> Woe to any man or woman who gives thanks to demons, saying that "Today is the worship of *Shai*, or Shai of the village or Shai of the home," while burning lamps for empty things and offering incense in the name of phantoms.... Accursed be he who worships or pours out (libations) or makes sacrifice to any creature, whether in the sky or on the earth or under water! ... Woe upon those who will worship wood or stone or anything made by man's handiwork (with) wood and stone, or (molded by putting) clay in-

---

42 Shenoute of Atripe, *Not Because a Fox Barks*, in Leipoldt, *Sinuthii Archimandritae Vita*, 3:82; Turin cod. IV, "On the Last Judgment," fol. XLIr-v, in Behlmer, *Schenute von Atripe*, 91–92, trans. 248. See also idem, "Historical Evidence from Shenoute," 2:13; Van der Vliet, "Spätantikes Heidentum," 108–9; Emmel, "From the Other Side of the Nile"; idem, "Shenoute of Atripe"; and Brakke and Crislip, *Selected Discourses of Shenoute*, 193–265, with translations of some of the relevant texts.

43 Pig sacrifice: Karivieri, "'House of Proclus,'" 133–36; and Lazaridou, *Transition to Christianity*, 79. Reversible image: John of Ephesus, *Hist. Eccl.* 3.29, in Smith, *Third Part of the Ecclesiastical History*, 214. Additional literary images of "crypto-devotion": Sophronios of Jerusalem, *Miracles of Ss Cyrus & John*, ch. 32, in Gascou, *Sophrone de Jérusalem*, 110–14; Cyril of Alexandria [attr.], *Sixth Miracle of the Three Youths*, in De Vis, *Homélies coptes de la Vaticane*, 2:185–89.

44 See Caseau, "Le Crypto paganisme," 541–72.

side them, and the rest of the kind, and (making from these materials) birds and crocodiles and beasts and livestock and diverse beings![45]

How do we categorize practices that seem prima facie to stand outside the penumbra of Christian piety yet do not apparently relate to any central cult or shrine to an ancient Egyptian god? Such lists of arcane local traditions that seemed to their authors to deviate from proper Christian practice appeared in many places in the Christianizing Roman Empire of the fourth through sixth centuries, especially in the Latin West. The sixth-century Iberian bishop Martin of Braga laments to churchgoers the "light[ing] of candles beside rocks and beside trees and beside fountains and at crossroads," as well as peoples' tendency "to put up laurel wreaths [at Kalends], to watch the foot, to pour fruit and wine on a log in the hearth, to throw bread into a fountain," and "for women at their weaving to call on the name of Minerva," all of which he labels Devil worship.[46] Caesarius of Arles, who more freely labels such rites *paganus*, attacks the "fulfilling of vows at trees or the adoring of fountains" by Christians, as well as "those wicked sacrifices which are still offered according to the custom of the *pagani*" and "those devilish banquets which are held at a shrine or fountains or trees."[47] In all such cases the subjects are viewed as part of an implicitly Christian audience—they are not imagined as adherents to some full-scale heathen cults—and the practices identified rarely involve any sort of sited or organized cult to a traditional god. They consist instead of traditional festivals, banqueting customs, and domestic gestures; of quotidian divination (in Caesarius) and amuletic protection; and, consistently, of visits to sacred places in the local environment. Do we call these "survivals"—and if we do, of what, exactly?—or are they elements of some "folkloric" or "popular" substratum of culture?[48] What models of "survival" or even of religion can help us to comprehend these reports from an officially Christianized region?

We need an approach to these materials and reports that both acknowledges their context in Christianized environments, and even the Christian identity of their subjects, and at the same time recognizes that a Christianizing culture depends on traditional forms of religious expression in order to make sense. How can we describe these traditional forms of religious expression in such a way as not to deny the "Christianness" of their agents? Here is the theoretical question that motivates this book. How do we draw on notions of folk agency, ritual fixity, *habitus*, and socially inscribed gesture to talk about, not survivals of some puta-

---

45 Shenoute of Atripe, *The Lord Thundered*, in Amélineau, *Oeuvres de Schenoudi I*, 66–70. See also Timbie and Zaborowski, "Shenoute's Sermon," 113–15.

46 Martin of Braga, *De corr. Rustic.* 16, in Barlow, *Iberian Fathers 1*, 81–82.

47 Caesarius of Arles, *Sermon* 54.5–6, in Delage, trans., *Césaire d'Arles*, 460–63; Mueller, *St. Caesarius of Arles*, 69–70.

48 On uses of the category "folklore" to designate a dimension of culture outside the Christian institution through which pre-Christian traditions are maintained, see Schmitt, "'Religion populaire'"; and Jolly, *Popular Religion*, 10–11.

tive old religion, but, rather, the very construction of Christianity in local worlds through traditional practices and expressions?[49]

IV. SYNCRETISM AND PURIFICATION

My aim here is to shift the focus from collections of isolated "pagan survivals" to the ways that people in Christianized cultures maintain religious forms as components of tradition and social interaction, often in the service of expressing Christianity. Thus we can see how religious forms of every sort involve ongoing *bricolages*, combinations and recombinations of symbols, conducted in the home and the workshop, at the shrine and by the ritual expert. This term, introduced by Claude Lévi-Strauss to describe a culture's recourse to a diverse range of materials in order to convey mythic truths, offers an invaluable metaphor for the assemblages that make up religious systems, and I will use it throughout this book to depict syncretism as a creative process, the work of agents.[50] Christianization as bricolage taking place in particular spaces involves, alternately, the domestication of *institutional symbols* (like liturgical formulations or crosses) and the revitalization and sanctioning of *traditional practices* (like festivals or iconographic forms). In these ways we can speak of Christianization and the perpetuation of indigenous religious traditions together as *syncretism*.

"Syncretism" as a notion of cultural process has come under as much criticism as have the concepts of "fetish" or "paganism" in the modern study of religion. Where once one could speak confidently of monolithic institutions in struggle or collusion with each other, now we speak of contested regional identities, competing discourses of authority or modernity, and local religious self-determination. Because of its earlier assumptions of coherent theological systems, irresistible religious teachings, and native passivity and ignorance, "syncretism" has been largely abandoned for such terms as "hybridity," "heterogeneity," and "acculturation" as historians and anthropologists try to approach the mixture of traditions with more critically astute sensibilities about power, discourse, and identity and with the realization that "mixture" is normative to religions, while "purity" is rare and often invented.[51]

For antiquity, the scholarly interest in syncretism has addressed three areas in particular: pharaonic Egypt, where priests habitually recombined the powers and names of gods[52]; the Greco-Roman Mediterranean, where priests, intellectuals, artists, and prophets creatively assimilated deities of different heritages through iconography and new languages of invocation[53]; and the problem of survivals in

---

49 For an unusually incisive discussion of these theoretical problems, see Pina-Cabral, "Gods of the Gentiles."
50 Lévi-Strauss, *Savage Mind*, 16–22.
51 See Johnson, "Migrating Bodies"; and idem, "Syncretism and Hybridization."
52 See, e.g., Bonnet, "On Understanding Syncretism"; and Baines, "Egyptian Syncretism."
53 See discussions in Dunand and Lévêque, *Les syncrétismes dans les religions*; Pearson and

Christianity, especially during late antiquity and the early Middle Ages. The term "syncretism" has been historically applied to each of these areas of religious combination, with the result that it has assumed an inappropriately self-evident meaning across the study of ancient religions, even while scholars have discovered how different each of these "syncretistic" endeavors could be: the Theban priest invoking Amun as Re, the terracotta image of the Syrian Magna Mater as Venus, and the maintenance of ancestral altars in Christian homes in Egypt. Like "pagan survival," "syncretism" often implies that the elements combined, or ostensibly combined, in some religious expression belong to pure and mutually exclusive religious systems—Egyptian and Greek, Jewish and Roman, Christian and heathen—when in fact all these alleged "systems" are themselves endlessly mutating and shifting bricolages taking place in many different regional and local contexts.[54]

But in recent years anthropologists have begun to rectify the notion of syncretism. This field has grown particularly attentive to how subjects and opponents each describe syncretistic phenomena and what the consequences of their different perspectives might be for our—the observer's—interpretation. Is a particular phenomenon, in fact, an ancient tradition or really a modern one? Do subjects consider it Christian? And what might "non-Christian" or "heathen" have actually meant for one or another historical community—in late antique Egypt or Gaul, say, or in modern Guatemala? From these questions has come a more nuanced sense of syncretism as not just religious combination but discourse *about* religious combination and purity. Thus it is useful to bring the term "syncretism" back into interpretive scholarship as a category not only sufficient for describing the diverse bricolages to which religions are perennially disposed but vital specifically because of its history of misapplications and distortions, as Charles Stewart and Rosalind Shaw proposed in 1994.[55] This rectified use of syncretism involves a multidimensional approach to cultures in transformation, recognizing their often-simultaneous tactics of embracing and eschewing modern religious idioms, inventing "authentic traditions," and appropriating new ideas to sanction old ones, all of which bear manifest political and economic implications.

Of course, as a condition of being readmitted, "syncretism" must imply not the weaving together of two theological systems or institutions, but rather an assemblage of symbols and discourses; not the reversion to a "semi-Christianity" or "Christianized paganism" among "converted" peoples, but rather cultures' inevitable projects of interpreting and assimilating new religious discourses; and not the leaving of "pagan survivals" in the wake of a people's uniform devotion to a

---

Widengren, *Religious Syncretism in Antiquity*; Bonnet, *Les syncrétismes religieux*; Assmann, "Translating God."

54 See critiques of "syncretism" as applied to religions of the Greco-Roman world in Cassidy, "Retrofitting Syncretism?"; esp. Lincoln, "Retiring 'Syncretism.'"

55 Shaw and Stewart, "Introduction"; cf. Gellner, "For Syncretism"; Stewart, "Syncretism and Its Synonyms," esp. 55; and cf. Pye, "Syncretism Versus Synthesis."

new creed, but rather the inevitable use of traditional imagery and landscape to articulate a new religious ideology—Christian or, for that matter, Buddhist or Muslim.

The models underlying the notion of syncretism should not assume external missionary coercion and passive native absorption of religious ideas but rather *indigenous agency* in the development of meaning, and sometimes even the assertion of native culture within or against the new religious discourse.[56] The creative sources of this indigenous agency have often initially been prophets and ritual experts within the culture, not missionaries from without. Syncretism should be understood as equivalent to the creative, synthetic process by which any idea, symbol, or idiom is appropriated and embraced by a culture: a cross inscribed over a doorway, for example, or the procession of a book of gospels around a field.[57] But it should also be understood as an indication of the subtle attitudes and practices through which cultures *perpetuate* tradition, even in the use of new idioms and centers: a local shrine preserved through identification with a saint or angel, for example. Finally, syncretism must be understood as an experimental assemblage, not a fixed and harmonious melding of ideas. This process is inevitably incomplete and often carries a tension or irony, which may itself lead to controversy rather than the simple preservation of tradition.[58]

The study of syncretistic phenomena in late antique Egypt or Syria or Gaul, much as in early modern Mexico, involves not simply the haphazard collection of things that seem archaic or superstitious, but, more precisely, the examination of how these things are embedded in culture, serve as Christian media, or, alternately, are picked out of local culture by missionaries and reformers as "heathen." On what basis does the reformer isolate a practice as heathen—according to what models, memories, or even manuals? Who it is that identifies heathen practices or symbols in a Christian culture and whether the identification serves the aim of censure or of proving cultural heritage make a big difference historically and for insiders. Is such an identification something the *scholar* performs on a culture that itself sees everything religious as Christian? Is it the accusation of some bishop or scribe trying to make sense of anomalies in some region's ritual practice? Or does this kind of classification—heathen/Christian—actually stem from the culture itself—that is, does the labeling (or recalling) of certain practices as "heathen" function as an "ethnoclassification," in the same way that some cultures label practices as sorcery or wizardry?[59]

---

56 See, e.g., Keane, "From Fetishism to Sincerity."
57 See, e.g., Flint, *Rise of Magic*, 254–328; and Roukema, "Early Christianity and Magic."
58 Compare Hugo Nutini's proposal of three "stages" of syncretism, progressing from confusion to integration in a new religious system; Nutini, *Ritual Kinship*, 7–9; this work is cited approvingly by Turner and Turner, *Image and Pilgrimage*, 105–6, but the model is far too teleological, since in real culture and history, authenticity and authority will always be contested.
59 Stewart describes these problems of gauging who is assessing and interpreting syncretism as the problem of framing in "Syncretism and Its Synonyms," 56. See in general Johnson, "Syncretism

CHAPTER 1

The term "antisyncretism" has been proposed to describe the latter two circumstances, in which indigenous or alien reformers pick out certain practices as heathen (or otherwise as contaminants of an ostensibly pure religious system) and allow others as legitimate. As we have seen in the sermons of Shenoute of Atripe, Caesarius of Arles, Martin of Braga, and many other vexed observers of popular Christian practice, diverse local traditions can be identified and censured through *discourses* of idolatry, demon worship, and blood sacrifice—discourses that demand purity and the elimination of pollution.[60] While these purifying discourses historically were rooted explicitly in biblical texts, the practices thereby condemned varied considerably among the reformers, the "antisyncretists," who were themselves an idiosyncratic and inconsistent bunch. Shenoute might, as we saw earlier, have condemned Shai devotions in one sermon, but in another he celebrates the incorporation of Nile symbols into church processions.[61] And while Shenoute railed against dream incubation as a heathen practice, a Christian scribe at the sixth-century shrine of Sts. Cyrus and John outside Alexandria acclaimed the dreams that came from these saints as *superior* (and, hence, analogous) to those delivered by the goddess Isis.[62] If the fourth- to fifth-century Paulinus of Nola encouraged the dedication of animals to St. Felix for slaughter and distribution, the fifth- to sixth-century Caesarius of Arles attacked public animal slaughter for banquets and encouraged the demolition of traditional shrines, while in the late sixth century, Gregory the Great instructed his emissaries to encourage both festive animal slaughter and the preservation of temple structures.[63] In the East, the late seventh-century John of Damascus endorsed the worship of icons even while acknowledging their "foul" use by heathens.[64] And further afield the antisyncretist rhetoric of idolatry that Spanish missionaries used to sanction iconoclastic purges in the Andes gradually shifted to a rhetoric of accommodation that has preserved Andean religious forms as Christian to this day.[65] Paulinus, Gregory, John, and the later Spanish missionaries served thus as "syncretists" for their religious worlds, acknowledging the importance of preservation, combination, and resacralization for maintaining the vitality of the religious system in its local milieu.

---

and Hybridization," whose recommendations for a rectified use of "syncretism" (766–67) resemble my use of the category in this book.

60 See esp. Markus, *End of Ancient Christianity*, chs. 7–9; Frankfurter, "Beyond Magic and Superstition"; Hen, "Converting the Barbarian West," 48–52.

61 Shenoute, *Let Our Eyes*, 2.5–6, in Emmel, "Shenoute of Atripe," 188.

62 Pseudo-Cyril of Alexandria, *Homily 3 on Ss. John and Cyrus*, in PG 77:1105A. On the context of the Cyril attribution, see Gascou, "Les Origines du culte"; and ch. 7 of this book. On diversity of Christian leaders' attitudes toward incubation, see Stewart, "Ritual Dreams and Historical Orders"; and Graf, *Roman Festivals*, 241–67.

63 Caesarius of Arles, *Sermon* 53–54; Paulinus of Nola, *Poem* 18 (also see ch. 4 of this book); Gregory the Great, *Ep.* 76 to Mellitus.

64 John of Damascus, in PG 94:1256–57.

65 MacCormack, "Gods, Demons, and Idols," esp. 642–47.

Given the diversity, idiosyncrasy, arbitrariness, and often-genuine modernity (as opposed to archaism or apparent traditionalism) of the historical reformers and purifiers—the "antisyncretists"—in their attacks on local practice, it becomes difficult to credit their anxious attention to heathenism and mixture as somehow representing a real orthopraxy, some "essential Christianity." Nor should a book like this one presume the existence of an essential Christianity from which a culture *claiming* Christian identity could so diverge as not to merit its own label from a historical perspective.

While antisyncretism captures the occasional idiosyncratic efforts that have been made to distinguish or purify a Christianity from heathen practices, "syncretism" refers to the whole dynamic process of religious acculturation and bricolage—the very process of interpreting, editing, and enacting a religious system in the local milieu.[66] The term also, as we have just seen, pertains to the politics of authenticity, the indigenous discourses of combination, or the ways in which religious leaders like Gregory the Great or Paulinus of Nola have self-consciously sanctioned or elided traditions. But I am most interested in syncretism as something the historian or ethnographer notices and seeks to understand. Let us consider, for example, the syncretism involved in a peculiar ritual that took place at some early Christian saint shrines in Egypt. A visitor would deliver a question to the entombed saint written in the form of two possible answers. One matched pair that was discovered read: "Oh God Pantokrator, if you command me, your servant Paul to stay under the roof of the monastery of Apa Thomas, command me in this ticket" and "Oh God Pantokrator, if you command me, your servant Paul to go to Antinoë, command me in this ticket."[67] The shrine attendants would return the answer chosen by the saint, according to some hidden rite we cannot reconstruct. This practice is attested at four major saints' shrines that were active in fifth- and sixth-century Egypt.

What is especially remarkable, however, is the ticket oracle's antiquity in Egyptian religion, attested at numerous shrines active since the New Kingdom and especially prominent in Egypt during the Ptolemaic and early Roman periods. It was a thoroughly Egyptian practice, an extension of the temple's authority into the legal and social life of a region, oriented toward individuals' concerns and enacted through the medium of writing. And now, in late antiquity, it became part of the communications of Christian saints. Yet there are no records that the ticket oracle was ever censured as a heathen practice. When we study it as one particular feature of the overall process of Christianization, this oracle practice could be described as a kind of syncretism. That is, as we shall see in chapter 7, the ticket

---

66 "Syncretism" as used here and as developed in Stewart/Shaw, Keane, Pye, and others (see notes 56–57) is *not* equivalent to "hybridity," the phenomenon of self-fashioning that in colonized cultures combines, exploits, and critiques prevailing discourses of dress, economy, and power. On this phenomenon, see Bhabha, *Location of Culture*, 113–22.

67 De Nie, "Een Koptisch-Christelijke Orakelvraag"; Papini, "Domande oracolari"; Papaconstantinou, "Oracles chrétiens."

CHAPTER 1

oracle procedure represents not a holdover from the age of the pharaohs but a traditional Egyptian form of *Christian* practice—a kind of gesture basic to the region, part of the repertoire of communication at a holy site.[68]

Used in this way, not as a static assumption of pure sources, but as a dynamic *process* in religious transformation and historical perpetuation, syncretism can serve as a productive theoretical model for examining the materials and reports of religious mixture. No longer the peripheral detritus of rudimentary missions or the natural superstitions into which rustic cultures devolve—no longer "pagan survivals," that is—the materials and reports we have been reviewing, from magical texts and ticket oracles to the popular practices enumerated in antisyncretist sermons, all emerge as central documentation of the *process* of incorporating Christianity into society and landscape.

V. AGENCY, GESTURE, AND LANDSCAPE

This rectified model of syncretism turns our attention to the actual contexts of religious combination—those life settings in which syncretism takes place in culture and history. This book will attend particularly to three basic dimensions of religious syncretism: *agency, gesture,* and *landscape*.

Attention to agency in syncretism has probably led to the most important reorientation of the term in recent years, for agency takes us from abstract notions of religious merging into the sphere of practice and creative experiment, what I here call bricolage. In its most basic sense, agency comprises *self-determination* and *creativity*, demonstrated by real historical individuals in real historical communities proposing different media and different places for imagining a new religious system—what the medievalist Julia Smith offhandedly called "do-it-yourself Christianity."[69] We may think of an Andean villager locating a shrine to Jesus at a site where community members previously claimed to have seen an apparition, or a Voudoun mambo placing an image of the Virgin of Czestochowa in the middle of her altar to the *loa* Ezili Danto. These individuals would be acting creatively and with self-determination within social conventions, in the interest of collective tradition, and often in an extension of traditional social roles. (Agency in this sense is not simply individualistic but works within social structure and conventions.[70]) Attention to agency consequently rejects a model of syncretism that casts the process as the passive perpetuation of tradition, even while we accept that agency will be expressed (or mediated) through multiple forms of cultural and gestural conventions (a mountain shrine, an altar). Indeed, it is the interplay of agency and tradition that concerns this book. Whether it is manifested as indi-

---

68 See in general Husson, "Les questions oraculaires chrétiennes"; Frankfurter, *Religion in Roman Egypt*, 193–95; and idem, "Voices, Books, and Dreams."
69 Smith, *Europe after Rome*, 237.
70 Emirbayer and Mische, "What Is Agency?"

vidual action (like the mambo's eclectic altar) or that of a group (like the dances of a village's pilgrims at a mountain shrine to Jesus), agency involves some degree of choice and effort. It may well be that participants impute their own agency to sources beyond themselves, a phenomenon we will see in chapter 4, in the case of magical efficacy and the crafting of amulets, and chapter 7, when we examine forms of spirit possession at saints' shrines.[71] But we must allow agency to play a role in the mediation of religious traditions and symbols even when it is credited to other sources.

The concept of syncretistic agency must also allow for a range of degrees of deliberate or self-conscious action. The most explicit examples of syncretistic agency are those people who resolutely maintain or even revitalize older traditions against or alongside newer ones—processes that we have already seen problematically labeled as "crypto-pagan." There were people who, following the repressive religious edicts of the Emperor Theodosius, whether for reasons of deliberate dissimulation or simply to continue traditional devotions under cover, kept traditional altars and observed festivals in secret while professing Christianity. These were unusual cases, and in late antiquity they provided bishops with especially graphic stories for sermons on proper Christianity, but they do illustrate the wide range of private efforts that were made to engage a new religious system alongside older traditions. Some people embraced the one by means of the other—Christ as a new form of hero or earth spirit or god—while others, accepting missionary discourse about Christian exclusiveness or imagining the systems as complementary, saw alternate ritual fields between which they were compelled to oscillate; still others created secret traditions behind the closed doors of the domestic sphere.[72] Many others, of course, conceptualized Christian saints, shrines, and ideas as a religious system with authority and efficacy; but they "performed" that system through the traditions and gestures passed down in local religious culture. Each strategy demonstrates agency, and by focusing on this idea we allow syncretism to cover all the ways that people act deliberately and creatively: choosing to maintain an ancestor shrine, add a cross to it, or burn it down; choosing to participate in a pilgrimage to a local spring, erect a cross there, or privately leave offerings.[73]

A final point regarding the application of syncretistic agency to the local worlds in which Christianity was assimilated concerns the actual artifacts or materials of religious bricolage: the votive deposits, crafted images, and amulets that constitute religious economy and practice. Through these objects—whether they are created, personalized, arranged, sold, exchanged, or deposited—one's agency is "distributed" throughout society and the environment. Thus, as the

71 Keane, "From Fetishism to Sincerity."
72 On the conceptualization of complementary ritual systems, distinguished spatially, linguistically, and otherwise, see McIntosh, *Edge of Islam*.
73 See in general Barasch, "Visual Syncretism," 52–54; and for antiquity, Graf, "Syncretism (Further Considerations)," 8934–38.

CHAPTER 1

anthropologist Alfred Gell explained, the world of objects, images, and tools—especially those related to the performance of religion—is a social world in itself, where each piece or assemblage extends and refers back to the agency of a historical or mythic being.[74]

To the extent that agency is shaped by convention and that syncretism itself involves a historical dimension, in the sense of the preservation of practices and associations over time, we must look at gestures—those made at festivals or upon leaving the house, before a sick child, or inside a shrine—as having the capacity to maintain traditions and attitudes. I refer here to the deep sense of "gesture" as a medium of social affiliation, embodied communication, and memory developed by Marcel Mauss and Pierre Bourdieu under the term *habitus*.[75] How does someone know what to do at a sacred tree or a healing shrine, how to approach a saint, how to react to a neighbor's unsafe word, or how to dance at a festival? Whence comes the impulse, recorded in a photograph in a newspaper some years ago, for a man from Dedham, Massachusetts, to pour whiskey on a friend's grave in an action reminiscent of, but certainly unconnected to, ancient Mediterranean customs of *profusio* during family visits to an ancestor's grave?[76] Gestures seem right and customary on given occasions and engage the body in commemoration or devotion or acknowledgment. Gestures embody memory and local tradition; they involve the individual in collective practice and the collective in religious institutions. Gestures like the *orans* hand position, so distinctive of embodied Christian devotion in early images (and presumably practice), could distinguish a soul in transit, signify communication with gods, or link oneself to an official image, like that of a saint.[77] Facility with gestures identifies one person as a ritual authority and another as a devotee, as we saw in the passage at the beginning of this chapter, in which people are said to "tie amulets on their children, handcrafted by men—those (men) who provide a place for the dwelling of demons."[78] This scenario of an amulet crafter or ritual specialist would have been distinguishable to a parent or grandparent through the use of distinctive gestures—through habitus. Communal gestures allow the perpetuation and adjustment of memories, whether those memories concern spirits of a pond, the power of an archaic image, or the necessity of some ritual for family prosperity, like the Shai lamp rites that Shenoute of Atripe described in the passage earlier.[79]

---

74 Gell, *Art and Agency*; this idea is elucidated with regard to ancient magical objects by Gordon, "From Substances to Texts."

75 Mauss, "Techniques of the Body"; Bourdieu, *Outline of a Theory of Practice*; for an application to syncretism theory, see Rey and Richman, "Somatics of Syncretism." See also Connerton, *How Societies Remember*.

76 Cemetery *profusio*: see the photograph accompanying Jenna Russell, "Bonded in Life and Death," *Boston Globe*, November 11, 2006; cf. Toynbee, *Death and Burial*, 51–52.

77 Barasch, "Visual Syncretism," 45–46.

78 See pp. 2–3.

79 See p. 13. See esp. Rey and Richman, "Somatics of Syncretism."

Much of the evidence we have for so-called pagan survivals in fact depicts popular gestures of response to places, times, and events. The same complaint just cited about popular practices in late antique Egypt also describes how people "*ablute* [ⲉⲩϫⲱⲕⲙ̄] their children in ... water from the arena [or] the theater, and ... *pour all over themselves* [ⲉⲩⲡⲱϩⲧ̄ ⲉϫⲱⲟⲩ] water with incantations [spoken over it] and *break* [ⲉⲩⲟⲩⲱϭⲡ̄] clay pots, claiming it repels the evil eye ... [and] *tie amulets* [ⲉⲩⲙⲟⲩⲣ ⲛ̄ϩⲉⲛⲫⲩⲗⲁⲕⲧⲏⲣⲓⲟⲛ] on their children."[80] In a text from about the same time in Gaul, Caesarius of Arles describes communal responses to a lunar eclipse, which the people "imagine they can overcome by the sound of a trumpet or the ridiculous tinkling of bells that are violently shaken," and common ritual responses to illness: "Let us," he parodies his audience, "sacrifice a garment of the sick person, a girdle that can be seen and measured. Let us offer some magic letters, let us hang some charms on his neck."[81] Again, what he here deems heathen are gestures of response that involve some measure of vital community tradition. Yet the Syrian holy man Simeon, who famously ascended a pillar on a rural mountaintop in the early fifth century by himself, invited great renown (as well as criticism) for this spectacular gesture, which resonated with pillar gestures and symbols common to Syrian religion of the Roman period. None of these practices points to holdovers from larger religious systems. Rather, each reflects gestures, habitus, and ways of acting socially that were embedded in life and directed at particular places, times, events, and even children. They are gestures that ecclesiastical witnesses may have picked out as anomalous or even heathen but participants regarded as necessary and congenial.[82]

These kinds of witnesses depict agency—one might even say assertiveness—in the maintenance of those gestures as part of the repertoire of safeguarding family members, marking time, addressing crises, and (in the case of Simeon) signifying holiness. But they also depict people negotiating forms of the new religious system within particular landscapes: rocks, trees, fountains, and even urban sites like the arena. Other sources show people conceptualizing Christianity, its saints and powers, in terms of particular mountains, rivers, marshes, boundaries, and even structures. We think with what surrounds us—with what we see, walk through, and steer away from. Social transition itself is invariably played out across territory, and dangers are invariably imagined according to pools, deserts, swamps, and crossroads. Anthropologists have long noted the capacity of landscape features to forbid or invite particular social groups, to symbolize liminality and center, to call for rites of passage and reentry, and to conjure both memory and emotion.[83] In his brilliant study of the Christianization of the Andes, Michael

---

80 Pseudo-Athanasius, *Homily on the Virgin* 95, in Lefort, "L'homélie de S. Athanase," 36.
81 Caesarius of Arles, *Sermon* 52, in Mueller, *St. Caesarius of Arles*, 260–62.
82 This is a point made by Pina-Cabral, "Gods of the Gentiles"; Künzel, "Paganisme, Syncrétisme et culture religieuse populaire," 1062; and Béatrice, "La christianisation des campagnes," 38–39. On Syrian stylitism, see Frankfurter, "Stylites and *Phallobatēs*"; and Eastmond, "Body vs. Column."
83 See, e.g., Stewart, *Demons and the Devil*.

Sallnow noted that power itself "was always spatial, mapped out across the variegated natural environment and thus appearing to issue from the landscape itself. Social relations became spatial relations, conceptualized through an energized landscape.... Political control was extended and consolidated by gaining control of the landscape, by annexing and reenergizing sacred sites."[84]

In these ways, as chapter 7 will explain, landscape serves as the fundamental context for the religious authority of a system like Christianity—the primary medium for recalling gestures, encountering spirits, and conceptualizing religious systems.[85] Landscape, including its miniature enclosed forms at saints' shrines, the cells of holy men, and domestic structures, channels social experience (processions, family workshops) and frames the agency of social subjects as they move between ritual consultations, shrines, villages, and domestic spaces.

Agency, gesture, and landscape are the most basic dimensions in which we can begin to make sense of the syncretism behind our witnesses, for they frame what people are doing as sensible and meaningful without recourse to notions of "pagan survival." All three dimensions also amount to a model of Christianization itself, inasmuch as a novel religious system—in whatever form it has been historically introduced—depends on popular agency, traditional habitus, and the framework of landscape to be sensible.

VI. SOCIAL SITES AND RELIGIOUS WORLDS OF SYNCRETISM IN LATE ANTIQUE EGYPT

All three dimensions of syncretism—agency, gesture, and landscape—bring us into the practiced, lived world of people in space and time; and they also invite us into the particular social worlds in which people *express* agency, *develop* or *maintain* gestures, and *act* in the landscape. These social worlds encompass such religious agents as mothers and grandmothers, craftsmen, monastic scribes, ritual experts, and even pilgrims at shrines. All such social worlds, or what Theodore Schatzki calls "social sites," involve different configurations of activity and personal engagement, social bonding, social identity, and movement through fixed spaces.[86] And consequently, in the course of Christianization of a region, different social sites will involve different motivations, attitudes, materials, and creative innovation in the area of religion. One might say that each social site constitutes a kind of laboratory of religious symbols.

Creators of media—terracotta figurines, say, or written amulets—may exemplify the most vivid forms of agency, while those who assert their demands on saints' shrines or on ritual experts may contribute in other ways to the syncretistic

---

84 Sallnow, *Pilgrims of the Andes*, 97–98; Frankfurter, "Introduction"; idem, "Espaces et Pèlerinage."

85 See Béatrice, "La christianisation des campagnes," 30–32.

86 Schatzki, *Site of the Social*; this work is usefully applied to religious creativity by Stowers, "Ontology of Religion."

construction of Christianity, as audiences, clients, tellers of stories, and collective shapers of tradition. In late antique Egypt both craftsmen and clients made up particular, if interconnected, social worlds: the clients impressed on craftsmen their demands for efficacious objects (figurines, vials), and the craftsmen developed from molds or traditional prototypes ritual materials that conveyed efficacy through their creative evocations of tradition or authority. Thus the project of describing religious syncretism—indeed, of locating the Christianization of Egypt or any other culture—becomes one of identifying the individual social sites at which religious agency was expressed.[87] In this way the locus of religious syncretism and Christianization shifts by necessity from the total culture—Egypt writ large—to individual social worlds that might have differed considerably in their agency and media of syncretism, their range of practices, and their sense of Christianity as a system of ideas. Neither the craftsman nor the grandmother nor the ritual specialist in his or her bricolages "represents" the culture and its Christianization; they simply stand for the exigencies and creative efforts of their respective social worlds in time and space. A sixth-century amulet invoking Isis and Horus, such as the one with which this chapter began, characterizes not Egyptian Christianity as a whole, but rather the social world of the ritual expert—or the scribe in his capacity as ritual expert—and the oral reservoir of charms from which he drew to create and edit this spell.

The subsequent chapters of this book investigate the social world, religious character, magical needs, and syncretistic impulses of a variety of contexts in which Christianization took place in late antique Egypt: the domestic sphere (chapter 2); the holy man (chapter 3); the saint's shrine (chapter 4); the workshop (chapter 5); the world and productions of monastic scribes (chapter 6); and the landscape itself, as a performative and social framework for acting, remembering, perpetuating, and erasing (chapter 7). Each social site involved a particular range of people and social roles, in ongoing or temporary interaction; a particular type and layout of space; and differing types of agency and creativity—all of which framed agency and habitus in the negotiation of Christianity. Each social world consisted of traditions that motivated and shaped creative action. The actual organization of each chapter will differ in order to capture the particular problems and character of each social site, its traditions, and the actual artifacts— archaeological, hagiographical, and magical—that illustrate it.

Most importantly, none of these social sites was entirely discrete; each naturally extended outward to overlap with others. As we will see in chapter 2, agents of the *domestic sphere*, the home, brought their needs and concerns to *holy men* and to *saints' shrines* for resolution through vows or by oracles, while the saint's shrine depended on *workshops* to produce images and amulets to commemorate devotees' visits and on *scribes* (often from monasteries) to develop legends for

---

[87] This point was made most significantly by Graf, "Syncretism (Further Considerations)," 8937.

CHAPTER 1

public reading.[88] *Landscapes*, both rural and urban, linked private and public experiences and gestures (e.g., the reciprocal domestic sites of house and tomb) and involved a diversity of extra-institutional holy places (e.g., dilapidated temples and statues) for local devotions. There were essential overlaps linking the various worlds of Christianization, and yet individually each site had its own traditions—its own distinctive needs, gestures, and social contexts—in which Christianity was interpreted and constructed.

The domestic sphere (chapter 2)—including house, tomb, and sometimes shop—involved particular concern for the perpetuation of the family, for procreative fertility, for commemoration of ancestors, and for protection. Across cultures, the ritual gestures particular to the home and its concerns tend to be embedded in everyday gestures, from threshold crossing to hearth keeping, from hair combing to water fetching. Everything may be brought into ritual application. A vignette from a Coptic saint's life introducing a story of violent Christianization depicts a Christian scribe's view of domestic ritual in a village that had so far retained its traditional cult as follows: "There was a village on the west side of the river in which they worship an idol called Kothos, which is mounted in the niches of their houses. And when they go inside their doors, they are accustomed to bow down their heads and worship him."[89] The scribe describes the niche-altar, with its simple domestic image and specific devotional gestures, much as Abbot Shenoute in the earlier text describes verbal celebrations of the local fortune spirit 'Shai over domestic lamps. Indeed, it is no surprise that most antisyncretist accusations of heathen practices in early Christianity list gestures that occurred in and around the home and were concerned with the protection of family members and the propitiation of spirits related to the home. In many ways, the home became a kind of axis of ritual agency, stimulating family members to go out, to discover or perpetuate holy places, and to prevail on shrines and holy men for protective water, oil, sand, amulets, and the like. Syncretism, as the historian and archaeologist find it here, comprises simple gestures, often-local holy sites, and an openness to the most eclectic bricolages of Christianity and folk traditions for the sake of family security and the negotiation of crises. If traditional, avowedly non-Christian spirits were propitiated, as Abbot Shenoute describes regarding the lamps lit for Shai, it was rarely as "cult" and more often as a function of calendrical observance, protection, and ancestral commemoration.

Another social site vital for the regional articulation of Christianity—for situating Christian teachings in the Egyptian landscape—can be found in the holy man (chapter 3). Most historians agree with Peter Brown's proposition that it was such indigenous charismatic leaders who spearheaded the process of Christian-

---

88 Frankfurter, "Interpenetration of Ritual Spaces."

89 Pseudo-Dioscorus, *Panegyric on Macarius of Tkow* 5.1, in Johnson, *Panegyric on Macarius*; see also Frankfurter, "Illuminating the Cult of Kothos," 180–82.

izing villages and regions in the eastern Mediterranean world.[90] The implication of their importance, however, is that Christianity itself—from the definition of its demonic world to the manipulation of its saving symbols—was subject to their synthetic visions. The same charismatic figures who saw demons in the images on temples might craft amulets of crocodile teeth; the same figures who were said to chat regularly with Christ in their caves might claim power over the Nile or deliver oracles in the possession of some spirit.

In what sense would the holy man have been a "social site," however? In fact, holy men in Egypt were embedded in society, the objects of plaintive letters and desperate regional supplicants, and often acted as "fathers" to an intimate band of acolytes. The archaeology of hermits' dwellings has revealed areas deliberately laid out for supplicants and for acolytes.[91] The syncretism of the holy man involved the integration of quite absolutist messages about the centrality of Christ with archaic Egyptian images of the demonic, like crocodiles and scorpions: it is Christ who repels the dangers you have always known in the landscape. Even in the amulets they distributed, holy men seem to have cleaved to some traditional media and gestures along with the inevitable sign of the cross. Holy men were both *prophets*—with a liminal role in society, representing a radical Christianity—and syncretistic *bricoleurs*, drawing on the gestures and symbols of the immediate culture to articulate Christian power.

Most of the social sites to which we can attribute syncretistic forms in late antique Egypt are distinctive for their dedication to the production of *Christian* materials: texts, figurines, lamps, vials, and even Christian legends and liturgical speech. Whether from the world of monks or craftsmen, these materials do not reflect some archaic world of belief and representation outside Christianization; instead, syncretism was the vehicle for the production of Christianity. We thus come in chapter 4 to the social world of the saint's shrine, a veritable crucible for the production of a lived Christianity and for the perpetuation of traditional religious forms. Saints' shrines served as regional religious centers for villagers and townspeople—agents of the domestic sphere—and as sites of creativity in ritual and craft. The space of the saint's shrine enveloped workshops, ecclesiastical performers, devotees, monks, and literate experts.

The central function of the saint's shrine in Christian Egypt—as, of course, elsewhere in the Christian world—was to offer the vital, healing presence of the saint him- or herself. Toward that end, and as a social site, the shrine involved various media, attendants, and ritual performances to construct that presence, ranging from iconography and the craftsmen who created it to the architecture that channeled devotees' activities and created a sense of center; the texts and scribes that permitted the collection of miracle stories and hagiography for public

---

90 Brown, "Rise and Function of the Holy Man"; and idem, *Authority and the Sacred*, 55–78. See as well Kaplan, "Ethiopian Holy Man"; Howard-Johnston and Hayward, *Cult of Saints*.

91 Brooks Hedstrom, "Divine Architects," esp. 376–77.

reading; the shrine attendants who interpreted the dreams of incubants and facilitated the placing of messages and votive offerings; the priests who devised and led processions from and around the shrine; and, of course, the workshops that manufactured the souvenir vials and figurines so central to the pilgrim's experience in Christian Egypt. At the same time, the shrine involved devotees, pilgrims, and the creative agency and traditions that they themselves brought to the shrine and its personnel. And out of this confluence of groups, attendants, and leaders there arose at different saints' shrines certain sanctioned forms of ritual interaction: stational processions; feasting and dance; incubation in some designated space near the shrine in order to receive the saint's direct vision; the removal of sand or oil as "blessings" in a souvenir vial; votive deposits of female figurines near the central crypt; and, most interesting for the study of syncretism in Christian Egypt, the submission of oracular questions in positive and negative forms, as we saw earlier, for the saint's divine choice.

While each of these forms of ritual interaction had pre-Christian precedents, they were not "pagan survivals" but basic gestures in the devotional interaction with a Christian shrine. Yet even in their essential function these gestures could be quite elaborate. The repertoire of embodied customs for interacting with the sacred comprised not just hand positions and utterances but sleep, the phrasing of questions, and the positioning of dolls. Of course, the religious world of the saint's shrine involved *peripheral* or unsanctioned forms of ritual interaction as well. There was feasting, for example, sometimes on the stamped cakes that were made locally as part of the pilgrim economy, and there was dancing. Both modes of interaction with the shrine expressed the traditions and agency of the domestic world, and, at least outside of Egypt, both modes could earn the censure of antisyncretists like Caesarius of Arles. But the religious world of the shrine, especially at festival times, called forth these expressions and these responses, and people ate and danced and sang as part of the celebration of the saint. "Syncretism" therefore lies not in the recycling of "heathen" ideas out of some uncatechized ignorance, but in the very acclamation of Christian power at a shrine or festival.

We might speak of a "magic" in the material presence of an amulet or holy man's blessing, but there was similarly a magic in the terracotta, stonework, woodcrafts, textiles, and carvings that workshops produced to decorate or protect homes, bodies, shrines, and gravesites—the subject of chapter 5. Considerable evidence of workshops in Roman and late antique Egypt reveals their great diversity in size and clientele, from large-scale urban stonecarving centers to local family-based pottery shops, some of which were attached to shrines and churches and some of which were entirely independent. It is therefore difficult to generalize about workshops as a single type of social site or religious world. Some stonecarvers maintained lively iconographies for tomb decoration based on classical mythology well into the fifth century, only occasionally adding crosses at clients' request.[92] The terracotta female figurines produced at Apa Mena and many other local ceramics workshops both for pilgrims' votive deposits and for domestic use clearly were a continuation of some type of pre-Christian ritual tradition, and yet each workshop developed its own distinct type of figurine, even adding *orans* or cross details to reflect Christian contexts. This chapter looks at five types of workshops or crafts (stonecarvers, terracotta artisans, painters, textile weavers, and mortuary specialists) to examine the ways that *efficacy*—a ritual functionality beyond decoration or mere representation—was constructed and involved traditions embedded in the workshop habitus. Mummification and burial in late antique (Christian) Egypt tends to be discussed in specific archaeological terms, and we know little about the sites and social contexts of those who carried out these services. Indeed, earlier assumptions that Christianity as an institution had an interest in, and effect on, mortuary traditions in the ancient world have been the subject of increasing skepticism, so we cannot assume that mortuary craft in late antique Egypt was practiced under church direction or in some other institutional context.[93] But even if it was not organized in guilds or institutions, mortuary preparations did constitute a craft, and a craft maintained for the purpose of ensuring an effective transition of the deceased, regardless of actual belief system.

The persistence and transformation of all these crafts, rather than representing a passive continuity of archaic tradition, involved the full agency and investment of craftsmen and clients. In the service of composing *efficacious* images for private devotion or spatial protection, mortuary safety or mythic heritage, workshops articulated the power and authority of the cross and saints (and, in the case of some tomb carvings, classical mythology as well) through traditional iconographic strategies—strategies that were handed down as part of the culture of the workshop and its clientele, not as dictates of the church.

In the case of texts and writing, the topic of chapter 6, syncretism appears to have occurred less through deliberate efforts at mixture and more often through attempts to articulate Christian verbal efficacy and stories for the various circumstances in which people engaged with writing, from liturgy to village crisis. Christian magical texts, for example, some of which combine Christian and Egyptian names (like the one at the beginning of this chapter), point not to some amorphous heathen underworld of magic but to scribes, literate specialists in the collection, editing, and construction of magical spells for everyday crises. These scribes seem to have had some sorts of monastic affiliations but operated across the worlds of monastery, church, shrine, and even village.[94] In addition, they had

92 On the versatility of stonecarvers' use of Christian motifs, see Thomas, *Late Antique Egyptian Funerary Sculpture*, 28–55; and Török, *Transfigurations of Hellenism*, 196–97, 208.

93 Rebillard, *Care of the Dead*; Dunand and Lichtenberg, "Pratiques et croyances funéraires," esp. 3242–43, 3248–49; and Dunand, "Between Tradition and Innovation."

94 Frankfurter, *Religion in Roman Egypt*, 257–64; and Jacques van der Vliet, review of *Testi della magia copta* by Pernigotti, *Bibliotheca Orientalis* 62, nos. 3–4 (2005): 278–79.

the responsibility of copying biblical texts, editing festival encomia, and composing apocryphal books for the purpose of maintaining a culture of holy narrative and legend through texts. This overlap in monastic literary culture is apparent in the extant Coptic and Greek magical spells, which draw on liturgical language and esoteric lore about angels and demons, features that imply some affiliation with ecclesiastical and monastic culture.[95] In their readiness to reorient liturgical or ecclesiastical language and lore in order to protect homes, invite angelic powers, and bind people's rivals, literate experts evidently worked independently from strict institutional oversight. In that sense we credit them with considerable agency in their reorientation of Christian efficacious speech.

In addition to monastic scribes' role as literate ritual specialists mediating between an eclectic world of apocryphal and apocalyptic texts and a broader folk world of charms and veneration for the inscribed word, the chapter addresses two types of literature that arose within monastic Christianity: a type of oracle that embraced the totality of Egypt and texts that imagined the underworld in gruesomely attentive detail. Both types of literature seem to have revitalized earlier Egyptian literary forms. Indeed, some of the most challenging examples of "pagan survivals" have come from Coptic apocryphal books and martyrologies that were progressively compiled over late antiquity and the Islamic period. These books contain numerous elaborate depictions of afterlife demonology, reminiscent of the ancient *Book of the Dead*, and gruesome narratives of the distribution of martyrs' body parts, inviting analogies to the distribution of the god Osiris's body in earlier Egyptian mythology, although the late dates of their final editing challenge any simple notion of continuity. Still, the books must be factored into any model of Christianization, and their composition and editing point both to a public culture of martyr commemoration (at which many such texts were read aloud) and to a particular scribal culture in which certain older literary forms were recalled, in a kind of scribal habitus, in the course of composing and elaborating texts.[96]

I earlier described the principles for considering religions and religious transformations like Christianization within the context of local landscapes, which structure movement, give place to collective memory, and draw out values and dispositions through legends. Chapter 7 thus addresses ways in which landscape allowed the persistence of some traditions and the growth of an indigenized Christianity. Dilapidated temples might have provided the monumental framework for churches; villagers might have continued to visit fallen statues and mutilated iconography for ritual interventions; and the two orientations might have clashed in space and time, if some abbot deemed intolerable popular devotional practices at a heathen site. Elsewhere, innovative processional routes effectively rooted Christian traditions in the local landscape and offered calendrical struc-

---

95 See Frankfurter, "Demon Invocations."
96 See Kotsifou, "Books and Book Production."

ture and collective commitment as well. And, of course, the landscape enshrined the stories of martyrs and holy men, Christian heroes whose exploits (and dismemberments) were played out across familiar territories. Landscape is not understood as a social site in the ways that the subjects of the other chapters are. Rather, it serves here as the larger performative framework in which craft and text take on meaning, in which holy men and shrines were imagined as particular sites to get to, and in which the local world of domestic concerns played out in space.

The process of Christianization in late antiquity can no longer be said to have involved the encounter or conflict between two mighty worldviews, Christian and heathen, or one mighty worldview and the inconsequential detritus of Greco-Roman religions. There was always, in some form, religious mixture and contestation—at the local as well as the trans-local, "discursive" level. The Christianization of Egypt, and the rest of the Mediterranean world, can no longer be imagined in terms of the definitive impact of ideologies and theological teachings. We now recognize the importance of miraculous claims linked to holy men and shrines in the evolving landscape; we grasp the *utility* of Christianity for expressing patronage and competition. That is, we have begun to turn to more performative, expressive, *social* contexts for understanding Christianization. And in this shift we must consider again that rich but misunderstood field of data once called "pagan survivals." What I consider in this book is not what these "survivals" say about "paganism," but what they say about *Christianity*. They teach us that Christian symbols, ideas, authority, names, and saints were imagined and negotiated at the local level—not just in particular regions, but, variously, in home and workshop, at saints' festivals, and by ritual experts. These were the social sites, the religious worlds, of Christianization—the *crucibles* of religious agency.

VII. POSTSCRIPT ON COMPARISON AND THE SCOPE OF ARGUMENT

This book focuses on the Christianization of Egypt from the fourth through the seventh centuries, using the literature, papyri, and archaeology of Egypt of this period. Egypt is particularly rich in these materials, and it is a culture and period in which I claim some expertise. However, many of the larger phenomena that I discuss in this book, from the status of the ritual expert to the culture of the saint's shrine, were part of broader historical developments in the Mediterranean world. It is thus instructive to draw on pertinent examples of similar phenomena from late antique Syria or Gaul (for example), as many historians since Edward Gibbon have done in producing general, synthetic studies of the transformation of the ancient world. Comparison across multiple Mediterranean, European, and Levantine cases of Hellenization, Romanization, and Christianization has allowed historians to make constructive generalizations about each of these cultural processes.⁹⁷ In making reference to ritual experts or saints' shrines (for example) in late antique cultures beyond Egypt in the course of *focusing* on Egypt and its distinctive situations, I provide a means for readers (and specialists of other parts of the ancient and medieval world) to test more broadly the models I have developed for late antique Egypt. The economic, political, and cultural differences between Egypt and Syria, Egypt and Iberia, are quite clear, but the models of looking at Christianization and syncretism in terms of social sites ought to work for the study of other cultures too (though presumably, I would suggest, they would require the definition of additional social sites, like royal courts or private estates).⁹⁸

While Egyptian materials provide unusually rich documentation for late antique life and experience, the questions I am asking about the social contexts of Christianization and syncretism go beyond the capacity of the extant papyri, miracle legends, and monastic archaeology to answer. Many historians and classicists insist that one can say only as much as the data allow, and yet, as the history of scholarship on late antiquity shows, those same historians tend to draw lavishly on their own unspoken (and generally theological) assumptions about religion, Christianity, and some sort of "paganism," in cleaving—they claim—to the data alone. Their (allegedly) theory-free attention to texts ends up simply perpetuating nineteenth-century conclusions about religion, society, and ritual. Today, we try to be more aware of our assumptions about religion and cultural change as well as about the categories we use—religion, magic, sacrifice, conversion—and the models that underlie those categories. Instead of relying on the triumphalist or nationalist narratives that dominated historiography throughout much of the twentieth century, we try to frame our language, terms of discussion, and larger arguments according to theoretical models—say, about religious violence, or the nature of procession, or charisma, or demon possession.

And where do we get these models? Through reading in the anthropology, sociology, and, in particular, the *comparison* of religions. Studies of syncretism and Christianization in particular have been carried out with regard to numerous historical and living cultures—colonial Latin America, medieval Europe, West Africa—with such richly documented and modeled results that they cannot but be mutually beneficial, even though they reflect quite different political worlds and missionary strategies.⁹⁹

It is important to recognize that comparison does not involve the arbitrary or gratuitous lining up of grossly different cultural entities to show similarity or con-

---

97 Lane Fox, *Pagans and Christians*; Brown, *World of Late Antiquity*; MacMullen, *Christianizing the Roman Empire*.

98 Kim Bowes has provided an excellent outline of how private estates in the late antique Latin West could themselves have been social sites for the construction of Christianity; Bowes, *Private Worship, Public Values*.

99 *Inter alia*, see Saunders, *Culture and Christianity*; Hefner, *Conversion to Christianity*; van der Veer, *Conversion to Modernities*; Greenfield and Droogers, *Reinventing Religions*.

trast. Comparison involves refiguring the historical situation under study as an *example* of some larger phenomenon, some pattern, and then seeking out other, more richly documented examples of that phenomenon in order to refine and add nuance to what that *phenomenon* actually means. Comparison, that is, directs our attention to a category ("amulet") or to a *type* of dynamic historical phenomenon ("iconoclasm") rather than to the peculiarities of specific events.[100]

For example, how do we make sense of various reports from late antiquity—in letters, sermons, and literary texts, many from Egypt—that before they were expelled by the power of the saint, demons were providing oracular services at saints' shrines? How could demons act so ambiguously, even helpfully, in a Christian world? The ethnography of spirit possession introduces a broader pattern in the history of religions in which traditional spirits, "demonized" under the ideology of a new religious system (like Christianity), retain some ambiguous powers in local religion. Stories that describe their oracular services followed by their exorcism (and the healing of their human vessels) reconcile the two views of spirits, possession, and the new status of the saint in the spiritual universe (see chapter 4, part 7). There is thus reason to expect that many of the testimonies from late antiquity—even those in hagiographical texts—may have reflected real historical situations: local efforts to negotiate, through possession, the new Christian "pantheon."[101]

Comparison among the different late antique reports and the ethnography of spirit possession configures all the various cases as potential examples of a broader historical phenomenon. Indeed, it is out of a sense of larger social or cultural phenomena, of patterns, that we develop the models that allow us to study history and to understand religion in the first place.

The appropriateness of a comparative example (say, from colonial Mexico or modern Sudan) depends on its ability to elucidate the situation, data, or witness under discussion *as* an example of a larger phenomenon—to show that more may be going on in our primary case (e.g., in late antique Egypt) *much as* we see more going on in our comparative case (e.g., in early modern Mexico). Comparison does not "prove" anything but simply points, through the relative richness of the *comparanda*, to the hypothetical likelihood that a particular kind of scenario might lie behind a reference or a witness. One can certainly debate the applicability or relevance of certain comparanda and the patterns they present, but such debate requires an involvement in the process, the method. It assumes some agreement that any comparative case points the primary case toward the definition of some larger pattern and the refiguring of the primary case as an *example*. These are the basic assumptions of the comparative method as I use it in this book.

100 See esp. Frankfurter, "Comparison and the Study of Religions."
101 See further Frankfurter, "Where the Spirits Dwell."

CHAPTER 2

Domestic Devotion and Religious Change

TRADITIONS OF THE DOMESTIC SPHERE

I. OVERTURE

Of the various material artifacts of Christianity in late antique Egypt, perhaps the most curious is the great number of terracotta figurines of women—pregnant or nursing infants, or standing with arms raised in the *orans* position (see figs. 1–7; plates 1–2). While most of these figurines are unprovenanced, exhibited in museums as examples of post-pharaonic religion, many do come from archaeological sites, found in private homes, cemeteries, and, more significantly, Christian pilgrimage shrines like the great complex devoted to St. Menas southwest of Alexandria, where even some of the figurines' molds were found (see fig. 1).

The figurines are extraordinarily diverse in their craftsmanship and representation of the female figure. Some are nude, some dressed modestly; some hold babies, others are in the *orans* position; some are freestanding, others can be hung or laid down in some space; some are crudely hand-modeled, others are products of molds. The diversity is regional: those from Apa Mena (fig. 1) are different from those found in Thebes or in the Fayyum (see figs. 2–4; plates 1–2). This extraordinary diversity suggests that their manufacture and use were stimulated in local, indigenous contexts rather than as the result of the marketing of a new ritual device or image, as happened with images of Egyptian gods in earlier Roman Egypt, where specific iconographic developments had spread through the influence of molds and archetypes. Here, in late antique Egypt, it is almost as if the figurines served some purpose general to the people.

So who are these figurines supposed to represent? They bear no explicit identities or symbols, either as saints (or the Virgin Mary) or as earlier Egyptian goddesses. Their various attested find sites—homes, tombs, shrines—might even suggest a flexible identity: sometimes a saint; sometimes an extension of a principal saint's blessing; sometimes the "extended person" of a pilgrim herself, to be left *ex voto* in some designated corner of a shrine; sometimes an image associated with a house *jinn*. No written documents of the period—neither miracle collections nor sermons nor saints' lives—even mention such figurines. And yet, in their varying emphases on breasts, bellies, infants, and even vulvas, the figurines clearly are meant to communicate—in the home or to a saint in his shrine—a

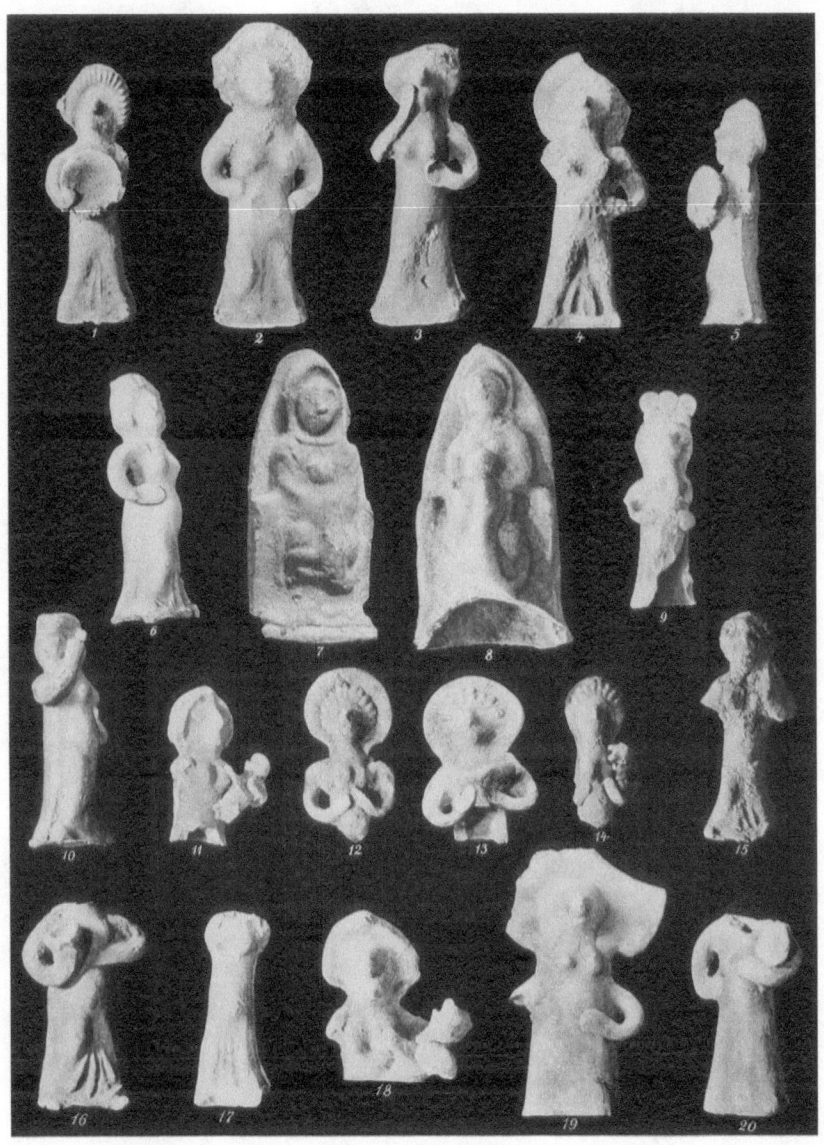

FIGURE 1. Female figurines found at Apa Mena site. Molded terracotta. Fifth to seventh centuries CE.

CHAPTER 2

FIGURE 2. Female figurine molded to accentuate jewelry. Molded terracotta with paint. Egypt, from Oxyrhynchus. Sixth to seventh century CE. Height: 14.2 cm.

FIGURE 3. Female figurine. Terracotta with painted eyes, necklace. Egypt, from Karanis. Fourth to fifth century CE. Height: 14.6 cm; width: 6.8 cm; depth: 2.1 cm.

FIGURE 4. Standing woman in long dress, holding child in arms. Molded terracotta with traces of paint, woolen cloth, and remains of bronze earring. Egypt, from cemetery at Antaeopolis. Sixth to seventh century CE. Height: 18.1 cm.

concern for procreative fertility, the bodily capacity to produce and safeguard a new generation. And as artifacts modeled and used across Egypt up into the Muslim period, they reflect a determination and agency, predominantly on the part of women, to assert this concern within their environments, whether by carrying the figurines out to shrines or back to homes or by stimulating craftsmen at shrines to produce familiar forms to sell to pilgrims. Certainly, they must also have inspired stories and a ritual culture in which such figurines served as potent devices.[1]

My interest in this book lies in the agency, the independent and assertive creativity, that these figurines imply and that embraces Christian landscape and shrine culture in one dimension while negotiating needs and traditions in another. To no Christian leaders of the period (that we know of) did these figurines and the ritual practices around them appear "heathen"—dangerously reminiscent of the deposed, demonic religious order—and yet it is difficult to place the figurines within our crudely delimited field of early Christian iconography. They point to a world of ritual action, of orientation in the landscape, of imagining the body, that took place outside the church and the monastery yet actively contributed to the assimilation of Christianity and Christian shrines into the culture of the everyday. This is the same world of quotidian agency of which an anonymous

---

1 See, further, Frankfurter, "Terracotta Figurines and Popular Religion"; idem, "Female Figurines in Early Christian Egypt."

fifth-century monk (quoted in the last chapter) complained, although he focused on different practices:

> Some of them ablute their children in polluted water and water from the arena, from the theater, and moreover they pour all over themselves water with incantations (spoken over it), and they break their clay pots claiming it repels the evil eye. Some tie amulets on their children, hand-crafted by men—those (men) who provide a place for the dwelling of demons—while others anoint themselves with oil that is evil and incantations and such things that they tie on their heads and necks.[2]

Here the author complains about those who, in ignorance or repudiation of proper Christian ritual practice, set out into a landscape they view as replete with powerful places and people and systematically collect protective materials for their bodies and their children's bodies. The need for apotropaic power is seen to extend well beyond the household, even if the protection of bodies, especially children's bodies, is an area of concern we typically associate with the domestic sphere. But these concerns generate and shape agency—in this case, ritual agency, the creativity and self-determination of individuals in developing or maintaining protective gestures and symbols. This is an agency, as I explained in chapter 1, that functions within social roles, traditions, and even structures of identity (e.g., as mother, as devotee of St. Menas, as resident of Karanis) but that extends beyond rote habitus to redefine or revitalize traditions in new, Christianizing ways.[3]

When it comes to the figurines (and their ritual contexts) and the polemical description of people's search for protective materials in the landscape, one thing is clear: in neither case are the categories "pagan" or "Christian" particularly relevant, at least in any dichotomous sense. Presumably every ritual practice of this time should be imagined as "Christian" to the degree that the prevailing religious culture was constructed according to ecclesiastical and monastic institutions. It therefore means little to speak of "pagan*ism*" as a viable religious system. But by the same token the category "Christian" means little beyond some larger religious framework or strategy through which people imagined their ritual practices to be meaningful and effective.

What is important here is the social context of the particular ritual practices evident in the figurines and the sermon: the domestic sphere, the locative and cultural setting in which family is defined, protected, reproduced, and communicated across generations. As I argued in *Religion in Roman Egypt*, this social setting becomes, in its inevitable commitment to reproduction and tradition across generations, the last redoubt of ritual practices eliminated from institutional and civic culture, which shift centrifugally to the locale, the village, and then individ-

---

2 Pseudo-Athanasius, *Homily on the Virgin*, 92, 95, in Lefort, "L'homélie de S. Athanase" (my translation).
3 See Emirbayer and Mische, "What Is Agency?"

ual homes.[4] But this centrifugal shift of practices—and even, sometimes, of ritual expertise and priestly traditions—does not take place inevitably but rather occurs through the interests and agency of those people within the domestic environments. The domestic sphere is a *social site* in which members—fathers, mothers, grandparents, siblings, youth—select, substitute, and assert old and new symbols, materials, images, gestures and prayers. They draw on local tradition and new institutional images of authority, as well as the pronouncements and blessings of local holy men. The perpetuation of the domestic sphere and its religious interests involves an ongoing process of synthesis and reinterpretation that is the very definition of syncretism itself.

II. DEFINING THE DOMESTIC SPHERE AND ITS RELIGIOUS CHARACTER IN LATE ANTIQUE EGYPT

Between archaeological remains and papyrus documentation, historians have a good idea of the *diversity* of domestic arrangements that existed in late antique Egypt, as well as the kinds of patterns running across them that might have impacted religious practices and ritual agency. In many ways, the house, with its walls, rooms, and inhabitants, constituted the primary "social site." Scholars have long identified the house as a place in which family is defined and articulated over generations through habits and customs and in which gender roles, social hierarchy, status, and economic tasks are defined and expressed, often through room partitions themselves. As the historian Richard Alston has argued, the architectural arrangement of a dwelling operates at least as much as a channel for social relationships as it does a reflection of those relationships: "Social structure is represented spatially but also reinforced and naturalized by that spatiality."[5] Here he builds on Pierre Bourdieu, who declared inhabited domestic space the "principal locus for the objectification of the generative schemes" of social structure (e.g., pure and impure, male and female, virtuous and criminal)—that is, where the links between social ideas and social practices are inculcated.[6] The social site of the home simultaneously contains and is a product of both social habitus—culturally ingrained gestures and bodily practices—and social agency, negotiated within and across the particular architectural boundaries of the dwelling.

Thus, one of the most interesting gauges of Christianization in Egypt, the increase in names of saints and biblical figures given to infants, reflects both child-rearing and child-protective practices in the household and the agency of family members to choose, or (perhaps) seek out, a saint's advice for naming a baby.[7]

---

4 Frankfurter, *Religion in Roman Egypt*, 143–44.

5 See Alston, *City in Roman and Byzantine Egypt*, 51 and, in general, 50–52; as well as Boozer, *Late Romano-Egyptian House*.

6 Bourdieu, *Outline of a Theory of Practice*, 89.

7 Bagnall, "Religious Conversion and Onomastic Change"; Wipszycka, "La valeur de l'onomastique"; Bagnall, "Conversion and Onomastics"; Depauw and Clarysse, "How Christian Was

If we do not know exactly the various procedures used to choose names in late antique Egypt, at least we can infer from the range of names given—drawn from martyrs, emperors, traditional gods, Hellenic and Roman gods and heroes, biblical heroes, and constructions on *noute* ("God")—that naming could carry vital significance, from a concern for the protection of a child to a dedication of gratitude to a sign of cultural affiliation, and hardly represented some abstract gift transcendent of the household itself.[8]

A town like Karanis, in the Fayyum, shows the many types of domestic layouts that people used to channel social activity, while papyri show that households of related people might have extended over several structures in a village or town, and a single dwelling might have involved unrelated groups in a "houseful."[9] This kind of diversity prevents any kind of generalization about the domestic sphere based on the modern nuclear family, and yet it is clear that across these various domestic arrangements some practices and dispositions would have remained consistent. For one thing, papyrologists have found that unrelated groups in a house might have been linked by—and therefore have celebrated—common relations or ancestry.[10] For another thing, Egyptian houses of this period did effectively divide a private space from a public sphere of action, rather than adopting the graduated interiority of houses found in other parts of the Mediterranean world,[11] and there is even evidence that this division of private and public space extended to individual rooms in the late Roman period.[12] Such developments in architectural arrangement would have translated into developments in social movement and role—perhaps an increased valuation of individual privacy or a shift away from the chaotic "houseful" of the Greco-Roman period. At the same time, there is much evidence that the Egyptian house of the later Roman period functioned *not* as a site for the seclusion of family members but as a particular anchor point in village relationships (e.g., across households) and regional activities like festival participation.[13]

Within, around, and beyond these physical parameters of the domestic sphere we find a welter of stories and artifacts like those with which this chapter began,

---

Fourth Century Egypt?"; and esp. Frankfurter, "Onomastic Statistics" (cf. Depauw and Clarysse, "Christian Onomastics").

8 See, e.g., Papaconstantinou, *Le culte des saints en Egypte*, 364–67; and Davis, *Cult of Saint Thecla*, 201–8.

9 Alston, *City in Roman and Byzantine Egypt*, 52–78.

10 Hobson, "House and Household," 221–23.

11 See Alston, *City in Roman and Byzantine Egypt*, 78–85; Huebner, *Family in Roman Egypt*, 40–41; idem, "Egypt as Part of the Mediterranean?," 157–64; and Abdelwahed, *Houses in Graeco-Roman Egypt*, 1–15. See also Nevett, *Domestic Space in Classical Antiquity*, ch. 5.

12 Alston, *City in Roman and Byzantine Egypt*, 104–27. On late antique conceptualizations of the *cubiculum* as a separate private space within the home, see Sessa, "Christianity and the Cubiculum," 184–86.

13 See Alston, *City in Roman and Byzantine Egypt*, 86–87; and Abdelwahed, *Houses in Graeco-Roman Egypt*, 16–25.

CHAPTER 2

which suggest both the vitality and the importance of religious practices and concerns related to this sphere. The deep concern for a successful pregnancy and a child's safe infancy that is reflected not only in figurines but also in magical texts and saints' legends can be related to the repressive social structure of the *virilocal* household, in which young brides found themselves under the general control of their mothers-in-law. As Sabine Huebner has argued, the situation new wives faced in late antique Egypt was very similar to that found in India: the husband often worked away from the home, and the wife had to gain status and social solidarity as a secondary female and outsider. Producing children not only provided status and demonstrated allegiance to the household but also provided a woman security for her own future. As one Egyptian woman's letter to a local god from the first century reads: "I hav[e] no power, I hav[e] no protector-son. I am unable to help (myself), I am childless(?)."[14] Thus a woman's motivations, in the broader context of domestic habitus and ritual traditions, could be translated into a remarkable, if canny, assertiveness in securing what she needed through direct, indirect, and ritual means.

Hagiographies and miracle cycles refer often to women making their way to shrines to obtain a pregnancy and to how the woman's social status and the family's fortune rely on these efforts.[15] The domestic *sphere*, as I am describing it, would have encompassed those places to which family members went in the service of maintaining the safety, concord, and continuance of the family, places including saints' shrines as much as numinous local ruins. One such text, pertaining to the St. Menas shrine, indicates that a festival for the Virgin was the particular time to make such an appeal.[16] Similarly, a woman with a deaf-mute son whose subsequent pregnancies ended in miscarriage is instructed in another text to sleep in the shrine of the Three Hebrew Youths in Alexandria on the night of their invisible arrival (when, of course, the demons responsible would also be expelled).[17] Meanwhile, the home itself served as a complex of protective boundaries whose supernatural penetration might bring ill effects on these efforts to maintain a family. As archaeologists have found elsewhere in the Roman and late antique Mediterranean world, a great range of apotropaic symbols, images, and inscriptions were used to guard the borders of houses, just as people seeking to bind or control their neighbors would place power objects or charms "at the door and the pathway" of their victims' homes, as one spell instructs.[18] A protective

14 Helmut Satzinger, "Old Coptic Schmidt Papyrus"; Frankfurter, "'It Is Esrmpe Who Appeals!'"

15 See Behlmer, "Women and the Holy," 410–12.

16 *Encomium on Apa Mena* (M590) f. 53v–54r, in Drescher, *Apa Mena*, 42–43, 132–33 (translation).

17 Pseudo-Cyril, *Encomium on the Three Youths*, in De Vis, *Homélies coptes de la Vaticane*, 189–93.

18 Apotropaia for homes: John Mitchell, "Keeping the Demons Out"; Bailliot, *Magie et sortilèges*; Choat and Gardner, *Coptic Handbook of Ritual Power*, 13.

incantation from a late antique Coptic manual specifies that supernatural defense should be applied to "the entrance and the exit and all [the client's] dwelling places, and his windows, and his courtyards, and his bedrooms, and his open rooms, and the lands which belong to him, and his foundations, and his orchards, and his wells, and his trees that bear fruit, and those that do not bear fruit."[19] The home, by this twofold evidence, was a place of vulnerability, whose safety required regular ritual vigilance.[20]

But more than a space of vulnerable bodies and economic pursuits, the home was a space of tradition, of habitus, even if some traditions might have struck outside reformers as un-Christian. Shenoute of Atripe, for example, in a passage quoted in chapter 1, excoriates "any man or woman who gives thanks to demons, saying that 'Today is the worship of Shai, or Shai of the village or Shai of the home,' while burning lamps for empty things and offering incense in the name of phantoms."[21] The complaint concerns a type of calendrical rite ("today is the worship of Shai") that was based in the home and located with lamps. Shai had been an Egyptian form of the well-known god of civic fortune *Agathos Daimon*, and here Shenoute's depiction of various dimensions of Shai suggest that the name was used to refer to fortune in general, and at most represented a kind of domestic spirit.[22] So while these domestic gestures might imply the persistence of explicit devotion to a traditional god, they might equally (and more simply) reflect the endurance of traditional practices of local Christians, for whom celebrating Shai with lamps was simply integral to domestic fortune and not in any way outside the spectrum of local Christianity. Lamps, after all, offered both an essential technology for the home and, from the evidence of their iconography, diverse ritual opportunities, from festival commemoration to divination.[23]

---

19 ACM 134 = Leiden, Anastasi 9, ms. p. 1v.

20 Alston, *City in Roman and Byzantine Egypt*, 85–86. Huebner, "Egypt as Part of the Mediterranean?" notes the structural fragility of most houses in Roman Egypt, which were capable of lasting only a few generations before collapse and rebuilding, and suggests on this basis that "the material house held little significance for the individual," that "it was the household as the community of residents that was significant" (169). Yet cultures living with such fragile or temporary dwellings nevertheless do invest borders and boundaries with supernatural significance—especially, perhaps, if certain components are more pronounced or permanent, as wooden frames and doors were in Roman Egypt.

21 Shenoute of Atripe, *The Lord Thundered* 45, in Amélineau, ed., *Oeuvres de Schenoudi I*, 379 (my translation).

22 See Quaegebeur, *Le dieu égyptien Shaï*; Frankfurter, "Illuminating the Cult of Kothos," 178–80.

23 Cf. Abdelwahed, *Houses in Graeco-Roman Egypt*, 26–38; see also Ballet, "Ceramics, Coptic," 494–97, on variety of domestic-style lamps; and Boozer, *Late Romano-Egyptian House*, ch. 7. While lamp lighting also indicates improper domestic devotions in Shenoute's sermon against Gesios, "Let Our Eyes" 1.21, 33 (in Emmel, "Shenoute of Atripe," 185; see also Frankfurter, *Religion in Roman Egypt*, 80–81, 185–86), Shenoute refers to this practice in more accepting, metaphorical terms in the Vienna K9313 sermon fragment (in Young, *Coptic Manuscripts*, 146–49).

Likewise, Shenoute, in an attempt to portray the heathen sympathies of his nemesis Gesios, lists in one text a series of devotional practices that he alleges Gesios had been conducting before the heathen images kept in his inner chambers: "He worships [his gods] by lighting a lot of lamps for them, and offering up incense to them on the altars, with what they call *kuphi*, and breaking bread before him."[24] In trying to delegitimize Gesios—unveil him as a "crypto-heathen," perhaps—Shenoute lists a series of domestic cult practices that were meant to be recognizable to his audience in the late fourth century as familiar gestures of domestic devotion.

These testimonies to the ongoing enactment of domestic and domestically oriented ritual practices seem to represent a continuation, in general terms, of those attested from the early Roman period, when doorposts were sometimes affixed with an image of the apotropaic and fecundity god Bes, and houses included one or another type of altar in or by the wall.[25] It is useful to go through some of this evidence from the earlier Roman period, not to propose that the same devotions continued in late antiquity, but to elucidate how the domestic social and architectural world *had* served as a ritual site with distinctive iconographic and gestural interests.[26] Niche-altars, for example, seem to have served as one of several visible sites for the placement of the various terracotta figurines that have been found in such abundance in Egypt.[27] A plethora of such figurines was available: Bes with a sword, the child-god Harpocrates on a horse or with a goose, the great goddess Isis nude or enthroned in robes, the serpentine Agathos Daimon as a coiled snake or with the head of Asclepius, eroticized scenes, and lamps in the shape of Isis's head. Most of these popular images of gods correspond to familiar areas of domestic religious orientation, like protection, procreative fertility, and festival observance, but with such a variety available through the beginning of the fourth century, the act of choosing a divine image for one's home would have involved family tradition, local identity, and personal needs. Images of Isis, for example, might have stressed her powers of fecundity in the household or field, but might also have been used to lend authority to a local goddess, like the Fayyum's agricultural snake-goddess Renenoutet/Thermouthis. A series of terracotta images of Isis with a snake's tail produced in the vicinity of

---

24 Shenoute, *Let Our Eyes* 21, in Emmel, "Shenoute of Atripe," 185, 193. See Frankfurter, *Religion in Roman Egypt*, 80–81, 135–38, on other such depictions of Gesios's devotional gestures.

25 Husselman, *Karanis Excavations*, 36; Husson, *OIKIA*, 63–65; Alston, "Houses and Households in Roman Egypt," 37–38; idem, *City in Roman and Byzantine Egypt*, 93–96. Huebner notes the particular value of wood components in Roman Egyptian homes, offering a partial context for lintel or doorpost apotropaia; Huebner, "Egypt as Part of the Mediterranean?" 161–62.

26 Though ranging quite widely in time, Abdelwahed, *Houses in Graeco-Roman Egypt*, offers a useful image of the home as a social site.

27 See, e.g., Allen, "Terracotta Figurines from Karanis"; Nachtergael, "Les terres cuites 'du Fayoum'"; Boutantin, "Production de terres cuites."

shrines to Thermouthis for domestic display served both to exalt Thermouthis and to localize the "national" Isis. By including such an image on a home altar, a family would have been able to link the home with the divine guardian or patron of regional agriculture, whose veneration would have been shared by many other homes and whose festivals would have regularly brought the concerns and traditions of the domestic sphere into a communal setting.[28]

Along with such material evidence as figurines and altars, papyri of the first three centuries reflect many features of a thriving domestic cult. In one letter, Aelius Theon writes to his prospective father-in-law that "every day I make devotion on [my fiancée's] behalf before the god ... the lord Sarapis, and yours and her mother's," while Didymarion mentions in her letter to Paniskos that "I pray for your health and I make devotion on your behalf to the lord Petesouchos," one of the chief crocodile gods of the Fayyum. In an illustration of the spatial gestures of domestic religion, two women write that their sisters should "please light a lamp for the shrines and spread the cushions." Domestic investment in the concern of particular deities is reflected in Serenus's letter to his brother Diogenes, which notes that "with the assistance of the gods our sister has taken a turn for the better, and our brother Harpocration is safe and well; for our ancestral gods continually assist us, granting us health and safety." An individual named Pausanias indicates his devotion to local Egyptian gods in a letter to his father in which he describes himself "mak[ing] devotion on your behalf before the gods of the region."[29]

Overall, there were a range of religious expressions in Roman Egypt that we can recognize as associated with the domestic sphere and that can be used to model the household as a crucible of Christianization after the third century as well. Given the culture's concern for the ritual protection of (or, sometimes, assault on) boundaries, its interest in domestic iconographic forms that correspond to (or even derive from) those in regional shrines, its concern for the benefits and crises of procreative fertility and economic fortune, and its rich local traditions of commemoration and festival, we can productively imagine that, as households began to integrate Christian ideas and sites, the larger interests of the domestic sphere continued to address the same concerns and benefits. This range of religious expressions may serve as a background to the scarcer evidence that the Christian period offers for domestic devotional practices. These general outlines of domestic religious interests in earlier Roman Egypt can frame the religious parameters within which agents of the domestic sphere during late antiquity worked to integrate and construct Christianity as well as the traditional expressions (e.g., lamp-lighting, figurines, apotropaic symbols) that might have remained salient in domestic life after the fourth century.

28 See esp. Frankfurter, *Religion in Roman Egypt*, 97–106.
29 Respectively, from P. Oxy 59.3992; P. Petaus 29; P. Athens 60; P. Oxy 6.935; and P. Oxy 6.936.

CHAPTER 2

III. CHRISTIANIZATION AND THE IMAGINATION OF NEW BOUNDARIES

One principal change in the religious parameters of the domestic sphere that occurred over the later Roman period revolved around the imagination of that sphere *from the outside*. In literature and sermons, the separate world of the home came increasingly to be conceptualized as a site of religious independence and deviance, especially in regard to heresy and heathenism, the perpetuation of rejected religious practices. This was a preoccupation of Christian leaders throughout the new empire, and it represented a shift from earlier attempts to influence the "Christian household" to a general suspicion of ritual activities within the home.[30] In one sense this ecclesiastical suspicion of a domestic sphere reflects the intrinsic privacy that a house affords its members to maintain traditions, to cultivate new religious groups separate from the civic space, or even to form the basis for a new local religious institution that can bring in participants from other households.[31] In this case we may regard the Christian authorities as rhetorically exacerbating architectural boundaries that had never been imagined as absolute in either a social or a religious sense and that had traditionally allowed connections beyond the household with cults or religious identities.[32]

But in another sense we might imagine that this exacerbation of the home's interiority and privacy over the fourth century might have stimulated a popular sense that separate domestic practices were necessary for, corollary to, or even in tension with public liturgy, or even that such practices involved some intrinsically covert features. For example, in late antique Egypt, following such Theodosian laws as the prohibition "to venerate, by more secret wickedness, [one's] *lar* with fire, his *genius* with wine, his *penates* with fragrant odors ... to burn lights to them, place incense before them, or suspend wreaths from them," all of which were constitutive gestures of Roman domestic cult, a series of narratives and sermons came to describe private homes as dangerous interior spaces whose invasion by righteous Christian authorities was warranted.[33] Abbot Shenoute of Atripe celebrates his late fourth- or early fifth-century invasion of the local dignitary Gesios's house, describing his penetration to an inner chamber where he discovered Egyptian images, and his desecration of those images by tossing them in the gutter outside.[34] Zachariah of Mytilene describes the final iconoclastic drama that oc-

---

30 See esp. Bowes, "Personal Devotions and Private Chapels," 205–9; idem, *Private Worship, Public Values*; and, on the cubiculum as increasingly suspect inner space, Sessa, "Christianity and the Cubiculum," 188–89.

31 See Maier, "Heresy, Households, and the Disciplining of Diversity"; BeDuhn, "Domestic Setting"; and, on the cultivation of new cults based in houses in Greco-Roman Priene, Murray, "Down the Road from Sardis."

32 See Frankfurter, "Interpenetration of Ritual Spaces."

33 *Cod.Th.* 16.10.12, in Pharr, *Theodosian Code and Novels*, 473.

34 Shenoute vs. Gesios: see primary text and discussion in Emmel, "Shenoute of Atripe."

TRADITIONS OF THE DOMESTIC SPHERE

curred in Alexandria following monks' early fifth-century invasion of a small temple to Isis in the town of Menouthis: the mob "eagerly brought all the graven images of the pagan gods, from the baths as well as from the houses, and placed them in the centre and set them on fire."[35] A sixth- or seventh-century legend about the destruction of a temple of Shai/Agathos Daimon begins with a depiction of heathen domestic cult performed behind closed doors, drawing a comparison with a child-sacrifice cult that—the story relates—took place behind the local temple's closed doors: "There was a village on the west side of the river in which they worship an idol called Kothos, which is mounted in the niches of their houses. And when they go inside their doors, they are accustomed to bow down their head and worship him."[36] And a story from the (likely) seventh- to ninth-century miracle collection of the Alexandrian shrine of the Three Hebrew Youths depicts "a very rich *Hellēn* who hated our people" who tried to steal wood from the Christian shrine and subsequently went blind. Salvation arrived only when a holy man came to his house, entered the "chamber ... where his gods stood [ⲕⲟⲓⲧⲱⲛ ... ⲡⲓⲙⲁ ⲉⲧⲉ ⲛⲉϥⲛⲟⲩϯ ⲭⲏ ⲙ̄ⲙⲁⲩ]," and uttered an exorcistic spell. "At that moment," the text declares, "[the images] fell (over and) broke against each other, (and) the demon that dwelled in them cried out, 'Woe to us, for they have cut us off today through John the Physician with the power of the Three Holy Youths!'"[37] In all these cases the drama of secrecy, Christian invasion, and purification revolves around the independence and secretive interiority of domestic space. Indeed, the ideology behind these literary—and sometimes historical—invasions represented the boundaries and religious functions of domestic space as akin to those of a temple, especially the traditional Near Eastern temple, whose architecture involved strict boundaries that protected a sacred interior.

Obviously, one result of this exacerbation of domestic religious boundaries through ecclesiastical rhetoric and local enforcement would have been the sense, on the part of some households, that the domestic sphere had to be guarded as a safe space for ritual tradition *against* Christian public hegemony: that is, that secretive traditional practices had to be cultivated within the home. The Syrian church historian John of Ephesus offers one striking example of such secretive domestic cult: a householder whose domestic icon of Christ could be reversed to show "a likeness of Apollo, so carefully done as not to be visible without looking closely at it."[38] But such examples are rife in the evidentiary record. At the end of

---

35 Zachariah of Mytilene, *V. Severi*, in Kugener, "Sévère, patriarche d'Antioche," 33–35; Ambjörn, *Life of Severus*, 30.

36 Pseudo-Dioscorus of Alexandria, *A Panegyric on Macarius of Tkow* 5.1, in Johnson, *Panegyric on Macarius*, 29–30; Frankfurter, "Illuminating the Cult of Kothos"; idem, "Iconoclasm and Christianization," 149–54.

37 Cyril of Alexandria [attrib.], "Sixth Miracle of the Three Holy Youths," in De Vis, *Homélies coptes de la Vaticane II*, 185–89.

38 John of Ephesus, *Ecclesiastical History* 3.29, in Smith, *Third Part of the Ecclesiastical History*, 214.

the fourth century, Shenoute's nemesis Gesios apparently retrieved images from desecrated temples, including "the images of priests with shaven heads and altars in their hands, everything that was in the temples [before Theodosius]," as well as some kind of Nile measure, which he "brought before the likenesses of the demons, just as we [found] it standing at their feet in the midst of them." Given that these would not have been customary domestic ritual materials even in the early Roman period, it would seem that Gesios had *extended* his conception of domestic religion to encompass temple images in an effort to address the destruction that Shenoute was wreaking in the area and to maintain the favor of the gods on his own.[39]

Christian authors like Shenoute tended to focus on the arrogant deceptions of elite householders, but the cultivation of secrecy around domestic cult—or the bringing of rival traditions into the domestic sphere—was probably more widespread.[40] And what is important to consider is how ritual action and religious tradition might have mutated as a result of external persecution and secretive performance. This is an issue not only of the domestic sphere's internalization of boundaries between Christian and traditional practices but also of the transformation of the traditional practices themselves under the pressure of secrecy and the exigencies of persecution. Which ceremonies *had to* be performed, and why, and when, and how? How could ceremonies once performed by a priest at a temple now be performed in domestic space, and who should officiate in the home? Which ritual elements or symbols were essential in the domestic or private sphere or under secretive conditions? Could a festive pig slaughter and meal count as a *thusia*, or did such a ceremony require a priest and his blessings?[41] The concealment of religious practices that were once continuous with civic space can invite individual choices and innovations in the private realm, and yet a reduction in communication and exchange among households and practitioners can lead to the atomization of domestic worlds, with their own hybrid interpretations of religious tradition and their own often-conflicting concepts of authority. The restriction of religion to the domestic sphere thus invites, as Paul Johnson has described, a *secretism*, wherein "secrets may become a form of value in and of themselves completely apart from the question of content, since the discourse of those claiming to hold secrets entails the creation of prestige. And these novel

---

39 Shenoute, "Let Our Eyes," in Emmel, "Shenoute of Atripe," 182–97; see also this source on evidence that Gesios came to affect some Christians' self-presentation. On Gesios's performance of traditional religious practices in some form, see Van der Vliet, "Spätantikes Heidentum in Ägypten"; Behlmer, "Historical Evidence from Shenoute"; and Shenoute, Sermon A26, in Brakke and Crislip, *Selected Discourses of Shenoute*, 238–39.

40 See Caseau, "Le crypto paganisme."

41 On this question, see the references to a donkey sacrifice in fourth-century Theban temple inscriptions: Łajtar, "Proskynema Inscriptions"; and idem, *Deir El-Bahari*, 96–104. On pig slaughters and feasts among Christians, see P. Oxy 56.3866, l. 3 (ca. sixth century CE), and possibly P. Oxy 10.1299 (fourth century CE).

forms may then, via a feedback loop, come to inform and reconstruct traditional practice at the level of the individual and the single temple again."[42] This is the phenomenon John of Ephesus depicts in his description of the reversible icon and Shenoute implies in his portrayal of Gesios's much more expansive scope of domestic cult; to some extent, it is also what the intellectual Hellene author Damascius describes in the late fifth century as the hybrid religious expressions of the priestly scions Heraiscus and Asclepiades. By then, the ritual world of the household and family had changed to address diminishing priestly authority and the hostility of the religious public sphere.[43] This is not to say that every effort to guard and maintain essential traditions results in "secretism," but that some transformation will inevitably occur through the efforts of the agents.

But the other result of ideologically exacerbated boundaries pertains to traditions and rituals performed in the home under the aegis of Christianity: the veneration of saints and Christ (as well as household spirits); the arrangement of material *eulogia* from pilgrimage; the lighting of lamps for saints' festivals; and the use of amulets, figurines, and even spoken charms linked to the Christian institution.[44] It is quite evident, not only from Egyptian witnesses like Shenoute of Atripe, but also from observers from elsewhere in the late Roman world, like Martin of Braga and Caesarius of Arles, that late antique villagers understood a wide range of practices to be acceptable (or not forbidden) within a Christian framework.[45] What would such a division between public and private ritual spaces in ecclesiastical ideology have meant for their homes and their sense of meaningful traditions? What would it have meant that clerics encouraged public forms of Christian practice rather than the domesticization of Christian ritual and most often condemned the religious expressions of the domestic sphere? In many parts of the late antique Mediterranean, Kim Bowes has shown, elite landowners established their own Christian shrines (and often officiants as well), whether for private or local use. To the extent that these chapels could emulate major churches in the area, whatever ceremonies took place within them must have involved idiosyncratic combinations of local religious traditions and prevailing Christian teachings.[46]

It may be that in Egypt, too, the rhetorical construction of borders around a suspect domestic sphere left the negotiation of domestic religion to individual households or local tradition, whose agents might consequently have combined local spirits, paraphernalia from saints' shrines, and magical verses of scripture and liturgy in innovative ways, shaping them according to both local exigency and new ecclesiastical expressions until some reforming bishop or abbot intervened to try to reframe Christian practice. This may be one reason why the domestic use

---

42 Johnson, *Secrets, Gossip, and Gods*, 30.
43 See Athanassiadi, "Persecution and Response in Late Paganism."
44 Leyerle, "Pilgrim Eulogiae and Domestic Ritual."
45 See esp. Pina-Cabral, "Gods of the Gentiles"; Klingshirn, *Caesarius of Arles*.
46 Bowes, *Private Worship, Public Values*; idem, "Sixth-Century Individual Rituals."

CHAPTER 2

of the female figurines with which this chapter began fell under the radar: there was a general disinterest in (if not suspicion of) the forms and material expressions of Christianity that domestic agents were creating in late antique Egypt.

Across these data for the domestic sphere as social site and space for religious agency I want to emphasize two points. One is the ambiguity we encounter in the boundaries of the domestic sphere. In one sense a house structure presented protective and socially insulating and channeling walls, a sense certainly appreciated and symbolized using apotropaic symbols like the cross or "suffering eye." And yet the people of that sphere may have extended across several houses or included unrelated people. Even more importantly, in late antique Egypt, as elsewhere, the religious practices of that sphere—or, rather, their creative agents—engaged, interpreted, and appropriated liturgical practices of ecclesiastical Christianity, local festival life, and the shared traditions of neighborhood and cultural landscape. At the same time, as we have seen, late antiquity saw an ideological tension between the religious world of the domestic sphere and that of the ecclesiastical institution: a definite boundary that may well have shaped domestic ritual agency in Egypt, as it did in the western Mediterranean.

The other point concerns the environmental expansiveness—the multiplicity of locations—of the "domestic sphere," that is, those places beyond the immediate space of the dwelling itself. It is this topic to which I turn in the next section.

IV. THE DOMESTIC WORLD AS SITE OF RELIGIOUS BRICOLAGE

So far in this chapter I have been focusing on ritual practices and religion (broadly conceived) within the confines of the household, elaborating the notion of the domestic sphere as both an architectural and a social site. But religion in the domestic sphere clearly and regularly extends beyond the walls of the home: to local and regional shrines, to tombs, and to the various sites in the environment that pose dangers or offer supernatural benefits. It is more useful, then, to consider religion of the domestic sphere as a cluster of concerns and orientations, rather than as simply practices performed within the home.[47]

Agents of the domestic sphere typically pursue the ritual resolution of these concerns in a variety of places. For example, as we saw earlier in the testimony of our fifth-century anonymous complainant, people in late antique Egypt went out to places "in city and village. For it is said that some of them ablute their children in polluted water and water from the arena, from the theater...." Such places promised material sources of apotropaic protection for children. So too people made pilgrimage to holy men and martyrs' shrines. In chapters 3 and 4 I will explore these sites as phenomena—as crucibles of Christianization—in their own

---

47 See Olyan and Bodel, "Comparative Perspectives," 276–78; and Frankfurter, "Spaces of Domestic Religion."

rights. But as I am defining the domestic sphere of religion, these sites beyond the home should also be conceptualized as part of a "domestic" topography of ritual spaces.[48] A domestic shrine or altar (such as we infer to have existed in many homes in late antique Egypt) did not anchor a solitary and aloof piety separate from the wider world but rather served as a node in a reciprocal relationship with some local or regional shrine.[49] It was from this regional shrine's festivals and ritual or iconographic innovations, for example, that the images and offerings on the domestic shrine could be perpetually renewed.[50] It was in the alternation between shrines and experiments with new shrines in the landscape that a domestic altar might have grounded a process of domestic Christianization.

But how, then, should we think about the concerns and orientations of domestic religion if it can exceed the bounds of the household? Jonathan Z. Smith's 2003 essay "Here, There, and Anywhere" emphasizes three major interests distinctive of religion in the domestic sphere in Greco-Roman antiquity, all of which are interwoven with places, stories, and meal customs: (1) preservation of contact with ancestors, (2) protection from nefarious forces, and (3) procreation.[51] This reasonable set of components can be helpfully expanded in order to frame the ways in which Christian ideas and symbols could have been integrated into traditional domestic life. I would propose eight features of domestic religion, properly conceived, which I find it helpful to frame comparatively—that is, by reference to more richly documented examples of domestic practices in the history of religions—in order to demonstrate the dynamic nature of religion in the domestic sphere:

1. *Concern for family perpetuation and procreative fertility.* This concern can be viewed both in the most physical sense, through sexuality and conception, and in the most abstract sense, with respect to wedding rites and the protection of children. The commitment is to the very endurance of the particular family as a social entity. This concern encouraged the revitalization of female figurine practices throughout Egypt beyond the fourth century.
2. *A concern for ancestors, ancestral spirits, and their continual communication.* The social boundaries of the family by nature extend beyond those who dwell together in this life to include the departed. Family (and clan) identity may itself be rooted in the recollection of particular ancestors. The recollection of ancestors and communication with their

---

48 See, e.g., Papaconstantinou, *Le culte des saints*, 348–67, on the appropriation of saints, their names, and associated materials within domestic areas.

49 This observation, of course, does not hold when the household becomes a protective enclosure for the self-conscious and secret perpetuation of prohibited ritual practices, as described earlier.

50 Feuchtwang, "Domestic and Communal Worship in Taiwan"; Bodel, "Cicero's Minerva"; Frankfurter, "Interpenetration of Ritual Spaces."

51 Smith, "Here, There, and Anywhere."

spirits are thus maintained physically—through the location of graves or images—and symbolically, through story and performance. In this way identity is maintained, and the ancestors' intervention in family fortune (including procreation) is assured. At the same time, proper devotions to the dead ensure the proper placement and function of the deceased in the world in the hopes that they will not improperly impinge on the family's affairs. This feature emerges most vividly in the local maintenance of mortuary customs, as we will see in chapter 5, as well as in local pilgrimages to haunts of ancestral spirits in the landscape, as chapter 7 describes.

3. *The use of apotropaic protection of children, thresholds, domestic health and livestock from particular spirits, from the evil eye, and from general misfortune.* Documented by amulets, the placement of symbols and objects around the house, and various gestures made over children and animals, the work of apotropaia is among the best documented of domestic ritual performance and religious concerns.[52] The reconceptualization of malicious spirits—*jinn, daimones, liliths,* elves, fairies, and so on—that new religions like Christianity and Islam offered audiences itself led to a new desperation for protection from those spirits: a divorce, for example, in fifth-century Egypt was attributed by the parties to "an evil demon."[53]

4. *An investment in calendrical ritual observance.* Whether or not the calendar itself is fixed by some religious institution, there is an effort characteristic of the domestic sphere to incorporate household ritual activities into some kind of larger cycle of ritual observance linked to other homes or to the broader culture or subculture, often through the creation of a special altar or the performance of special activities—the preparation of certain foods or hanging of certain objects—at specific times of the year. Of course, this investment in coordinating observances in time and space links the domestic and civic or institutional spheres and is therefore not unique to the domestic sphere. Yet the investment is expressed through domestic activities (baking, arranging, decorating *in the home*) and historically often continues regardless of the existence of any public dimension.

5. *Attention to mundane domestic activities as the basis for and source of domestic ritual action and religious expression.* Rather than revolving around some "altogether sacred" area of experience—a distinctly religious or awed state—domestic ritual is layered into food production and sharing, candle- or lamp-lighting, and the entering and exiting of spaces. In fact,

---

52 Vikan, "Art, Medicine, and Magic"; Bailliot, *Magie et sortilèges*; Mitchell, "Keeping the Demons Out."

53 P. Lond. 5.1713, ll. 18–21. On the demonization of local spirits and the cultivation of a world of hostile spirits, see in general Frankfurter, *Evil Incarnate,* chs. 2–3; idem, "Illuminating the Cult of Kothos"; idem, "Where the Spirits Dwell."

any domestic act may be drawn into symbolic expression. Smith describes the meal itself as the domestic rite *par excellence*, uniting family and ancestors (and often held at the grave itself), while folklorists have noted the use of everyday acts like pot stirring, hair combing, and mirror gazing for divination and spell construction.[54] The baking of specific breads and cakes—whether festally shaped or stamped—represents one central form of domestic participation in (sanctioned or unsanctioned) large-scale festivals.[55]

6. *The attribution of a sacred or ritually demarcated quality to the very topography of the house.* Roof and door, window and shrine, bedroom and kitchen assume sacred significance as the dwelling or gateway of certain spirits, as places to be kept pure or to be exorcised, or as the loci of key rituals.[56] The comparative value of wooden building materials in Roman Egypt—doorposts, doors, lintels, windows, and such—may have led to people's investing them with apotropaic or other powers, as some wood fragments have been found inscribed with magical writing.[57] In one sense the house may be demarcated as a microcosm of village and region, but in another sense, the demarcation, consecration, and purification of rooms and other domestic features may relate to concerns about the beneficence of ancestral spirits, the protection of procreation, and family endurance rather than to broader village concerns.[58]

7. *The context-specific nature of domestic belief systems.* Religious beliefs of the domestic sphere about gods, saints, demons, spirits, ancestors, and bad luck are based in concrete, traditional activities and gestures—opening doors, seeing the moon, healing a wound, swaddling a child, celebrating a holiday, traversing the neighborhood—rather than deriving from abstract systematizing. It is in this "lived," immediate context, for example, that local gods and saints assume familial, quasi-ancestral roles and characters, born out of memory and intimate story rather than general speculation.[59]

---

54 Smith, "Here, There, and Anywhere," 327–28; Flint, *Rise of Magic*, 286–89; Golopentia, "Towards a Typology of Romanian Love Charms," esp. 181.

55 Cf. Exodus 12:14–20; Jeremiah 7:18, 44:19; Ackerman, "Household Religion, Family Religion" 143–48.

56 See, e.g., Lecouteux, *La maison et ses génies*; Meskell, "Memory's Materiality"; Sessa, "Christianity and the Cubiculum."

57 On the value of wooden building accoutrements, see Huebner, "Egypt as Part of the Mediterranean?" 161–64. Inscribed wooden amulets (probably parts of lintels or window frames): Préaux, "Une amulette chrétienne"; Warga, "Christian Amulet on Wood." Compare the early Roman faience Bes image set in wood, also probably originating in domestic architecture: Schneider et al., *Small Masterpieces of Egyptian Art*, 77, #97.

58 Cf. Maximus of Turin, *Sermon* 91.2, in Dowden, *European Paganism*, 8, whose reference to "the heads of cattle fixed to [the heathens'] doorways" implies that such sacrifices (probably) performed publicly were brought back to the domestic space to function as a demarcating symbol.

59 See Graziano, *Cultures of Devotion*, 10; Orsi, *Thank You, St. Jude*.

8. *The expression of agency in the assertion of religious needs and traditions.* The self-determination and creativity involved in every household in addressing and maintaining religious traditions and traditional perspectives point to a distinctive agency on the part of the principal actors and experts of the domestic sphere, who are often (but not always) women. This agency is especially apparent in the selective mediation of the influence of religious institutions, which try to assert authority over domestic religious expression by defining models of domestic purity and allegiance. Ultimately these models must be interpreted and negotiated in the home, and it is here that we find evidence of agency.[60]

This assertiveness on the part of agents of the domestic sphere is synthetic, dedicated to a combination of household, family, and ancestral needs as well as to the authoritative frameworks and symbols of institutional religion. In that sense it is important not to juxtapose domestic religion with institutional religion. There is a continual interpenetration, as "official" symbols are appropriated and interpreted for use in the home and appeals are brought from the home to the temple or church, and as ecclesiastical authorities seek to exert influence over domestic activities and families demand blessings and other interventions from those same authorities. Religious institutions come to permeate domestic life through the sanctioning of festivals, the construction of pilgrimages, the organization and sanctioning of religious experts (scribes, priests, holy men), and the setting of ritual calendars.[61] Indeed, religious institutions are often invoked in the household to sanction ritual practices.

And yet, out of its own interests in protection, procreation, ancestral communication, and so on, domestic religion is historically self-determining and innovative, asserting needs, demanding relevance, and reinterpreting the deities or saints of the institution, even redefining the religion that the institution establishes. We find this assertive element, for example, in people's selection of shrines and saints to visit, and in the local and domestic traditions that supplicants bring with them to saint shrines at festivals, as we will see in chapter 4: dance styles; foods; expectations for divination, healing, and other resolutions of domestic crisis; and the selection of votive items to leave at shrines, which intrinsically extend domestic interests. And we find it as well in the forms of sanctification brought back to the local and domestic sphere to give institutional authority to saints and places at home.

But the agency of domestic religion carries an independent element as well, which is especially well illustrated in modern Latin American Christianity and Afro-Caribbean traditions. The household and neighborhood often observe festivals that the main institution ignores, such as celebrations of particular folk

60 See Kent, "Secret Christians of Sivakasi" on gendered features of this separate ritual agency.
61 See Feuchtwang, "Domestic and Communal Worship in Taiwan"; Frankfurter, "Interpenetration of Ritual Spaces."

saints. The household may venerate official gods or saints in unapproved local manifestations, unapproved gods or spirits under the guise of approved images, or sometimes even separate gods entirely, like the popular Latin American figure of San La Muerte: a skeleton bedecked in holy robes.[62] The figure of San Simon, a "cool guy" on a chair smoking a cigarette, has little connection with ecclesiastical saint lore, yet he is understood as a saint both intimate and powerful throughout Mexico and Guatemala, and devotion to him is expressed as a form of Christianity.

The axis of this agency in religious bricolage is often some kind of altar, a specific site where ritual action is regularly focused and where the iconography of institutional religion is variously miniaturized, imitated, and even critiqued.[63] Early Christian literature attests to the importance of some kind of household shrine in many homes for signifying domestic spatial divisions. We have seen the example of the Coptic saint's life that describes heathen villagers who keep images of their god "mounted in the niches of their houses. And when they go inside their doors they are accustomed to bow down their head(s) and worship him."[64] A tenth-century Byzantine saint's life mentions a place where a woman keeps her icons, along with a lamp, and how they might be turned in different directions and even, at one point, desecrated by a sorcerer, who smears them with excrement.[65] The site where such holy things are collected thus becomes the object of diverse ritual attentions.

Placed in different rooms (kitchens, bedrooms, congregation spaces) according to cultural or family tradition and used as the site of incense, food offerings, and particular images, domestic altars ensure spirits' and ancestors' intimacy with family activities. On such altars, as we understand them from both contemporary religions and those of antiquity, meaning is created through spatial focus and juxtaposition, and intimacy with spirits and ancestors is objectified through the choice and shifting of images. In the domestic sphere images assume local, even intimate, associations that are often quite different from those intended by the prototype: rather than "Mary the *Theotokos*," such a figure might be "the Woman who brings children" or "preserves the ancestors" or "stimulates the Nile spate."[66] The altar thus becomes a stage for mediating family concerns, regional identity, and institutional symbols. It serves as a *lieu de mémoire*, where images recall thoughts of past interactions and tokens recall the fulfillment of vows, acting as embodied dedications to a spirit at a time of special duress. Through the choice of special images and offerings to spirits and ancestors, the altar's "expert"—

---

62 Cf. Graziano, *Cultures of Devotion*, 34 on San La Muerte.

63 See Frankfurter, *Religion in Roman Egypt*, 138–42; Beezley, "Home Altars"; Pinney, "Paper Gods"; Graziano, *Cultures of Devotion*, 94.

64 *Panegyric on Macarios* V.1, in Johnson, *Panegyric on Macarius*; Frankfurter, "Illuminating the Cult of Kothos," 180–82.

65 *Life of Saint Andrew the Fool* II.2461–62, 2626–28, in Rydén, *Life of St. Andrew the Fool*.

66 Cf. Stresser-Péan, *Sun God and the Savior*, 15, 30–31, 59, 174–75, 241–44.

whether father, mother, or grandmother, according to cultural and family tradition—demonstrates his or her relationship with those beings.

Religion in the domestic sphere comprises both *spatial dispositions* (various religious practices that take place in, around, and beyond the home, that signify and sacralize the home, and that direct attention to specific sites in the home) and a *cluster of concerns and orientations* peculiar to family and home that yet exists on a continuum with local and institutional religious dimensions. It involves a range of *agents* who pursue these concerns actively, festively, and sometimes desperately, for the sake of protection, procreation, and fortune.[67]

V. DOMESTIC RITUAL, DOMESTIC AGENTS, AND THE SYNCRETIC CONSTRUCTION OF CHRISTIANITY

The reason for laying out a model of religion of the domestic sphere in general, comparative terms is so that we might appreciate the very real concerns and dispositions that preoccupy people in this social sphere, that motivate a variety of ritual efforts (often occurring beyond the home itself), and that transvalue the home from a complex structure for social interaction to a series of symbolic zones of vulnerability or protection and channels for social performance.[68] But the model of domestic religion I have laid out does not translate into one simple scenario of religious continuity. While the evidence for domestic cults and activities in earlier Roman Egypt shows a considerable autonomy in households' choices of symbols and practices, this does not imply the household's disinterest in the changing forms of religious authority and civic cult within the broader culture. It is important to examine the interaction among the different dimensions of local religion—the domestic sphere, the village sphere, regional cults, the institutional church or "great tradition"—that are combined, signified, or rejected in the household's bricolage of traditions, ritual gestures, altar arrangement, and varying attention to shrines in the landscape. Even more importantly, if more difficult to gauge, are the *agents* of this bricolage: it is not a household that selects symbols, maintains rites, or invites more devout engagement with an official religious institution, but individuals in the household: mothers, fathers, children, grandparents, uncles, aunts, and other household members of status or ritual authority.

In this penultimate section I highlight five ways that local or ancestral, rather than "pagan," traditions in late antique Egypt were perpetuated or reconceived in the domestic sphere in connection with Christian authority, and vice versa—that is, five modes of syncretism within the domestic sphere. The motivations for syncretism in each case would have followed from the interests of the domestic sphere described in the last section—*in nuce*, protective magic, assurance of re-

---

67 This two-dimensional definition obviates some of the problems involved in conceptualizing "family" and "household" religious spheres raised in Bodel and Olyan, *Household and Family Religion in Antiquity*; and especially acutely in Ackerman, "Household Religion, Family Religion."

68 See Hodder, "Domus."

production, contact with ancestral spirits—rather than from some modern notion of spiritual allegiance. The artifacts of domestic religion speak to practice, disposition, and anxiety, not orthodoxy.

A. Lamp-lighting

Abbot Shenoute's complaint about the lighting of lamps for Shai more likely reflects a traditional gesture of domestic ritual expression than it does the domestic lamp-lighters' self-conscious veneration of a non-Christian god, for a great range of papyrus documents and terracotta lamps from the early and late Roman period attest to lamp-lighting as a basic habitus of devotion both at shrines and in the home.[69] Shenoute himself elsewhere uses domestic lamp-lighting as an instructive parable for determining which divinity to worship and which not.[70] But the prosaic nature of lamp-lighting does not mean it lacked religious meaning in the late fourth-century Egyptian home. Such basic acts were inevitably endowed with significance in the ritually attentive world of the household. For example, John Chrysostom alludes to a practice from Antioch of choosing babies' names—and hence the protection of specific saints—by lighting household lamps. In this ritual, a holy name was assigned to each lamp whereby the correct sacred name could be divined according to whichever lamp burned the longest; in this way, the quotidian lamp turned into a source of revelation.[71] In the case to which Shenoute alludes, then, lamp-lighting at a particular time of the year may well have linked those present through ceremony and the memories it conjured to the traditions of the beneficent fortune spirit Shai. But these binding practices and their associations in the social context did not take place in opposition to or tension with the Christian system. Indeed, we should imagine lamp-lighting as a mundane but ritually laden domestic practice whose syncretistic elements revolved around the material form of the lamp itself: the many terracotta oil lamps from late antique Egypt with crosses, faces, or—strangely—frogs incised or stamped on top.[72]

B. Bread Stamps

A small cache of bread stamps from the Geneva and Budapest museums bearing the face of the folk-god Bes and dating roughly to the fourth century CE might

---

69 See Dunand, "Lanternes gréco-romaines d'Égypte"; Frankfurter, *Religion in Roman Egypt*, 136–38; Jordan, "Inscribed Lamps from a Cult"; Boozer, *Late Romano-Egyptian House*, ch. 7; and Abdelwahed, *Houses in Graeco-Roman Egypt*, 26–34.

70 Shenoute of Atripe, "The Lord Thundered," Vienna K9313 = Codex GG 69/70, in Young, *Coptic Manuscripts*, 148–49; cf. Timbie and Zaborowski, "Shenoute's Sermon," 117–18.

71 Chrysostom, *On 1 Corinthians* 12.13. See further on candle divination, PGM VII.593–619.

72 A representative selection of late antique Egyptian domestic oil lamps can be found in *Ägypten: Schätze aus dem Wüstensand*, 219–28, ##231–47.

reflect veneration of the god and his local cults (which did persist, at Abydos at least, through the fourth century)—that is, as a persisting tradition during the time of the Christian institution's ascendancy.[73] But it is important here to consider the medium in which such faces were impressed: not icons or wall-plaques, but bread, most likely baked for some festival time.[74] When we focus on the specific anomaly of the "heathen" image, we miss the larger material context in which the faces were supposed to make sense, to provoke feelings and memories and social connection. Such a context is essential for imagining the meaning of a Bes image in the fourth century. The bread stamps should thus be understood in terms of the symbolic meaning bread assumed at certain times of the year, as a medium for older religious traditions as well as new, Christian traditions. Indeed, bread stamps became common in Christian public culture as well, indicating an institutional source, a blessing on the household, or even protection of the bread from demonic subversion.[75] At the same time, in some areas of the late antique world, bread stamped with crosses might well have been the Eucharist itself, "reserved" and brought home for various purposes (including domestic protection), illustrating another way in which agents of the domestic sphere prevailed on a Christian institution for materials that served their own ritual interests.[76] Thus, with the Bes image on bread, it is not that a traditionally potent image here turned into an empty anachronism (as we often imagine when archaic religious symbols turn up as seeming decoration in Christian-era art), but rather that the perpetuation of meaningful ritual and symbolic traditions was located in everyday phenomena around which custom had invested religious memory.

C. Domestic Charms and Their Dramatis Personae

A more explicit example of perpetuation of older traditions appears in a cluster of Coptic charms from the sixth or seventh centuries that contain songs of Isis, Horus and other ancient Egyptian gods and that were designed for sleep, for erotic success, and for intestinal pain. Each of the songs depicts a situation in which Horus is in distress and in need of his mother Isis's aid (a common motif of ancient Egyptian magical charms). Their resemblance to laments seems to bear on their appearance so late in the Christian period. Indeed, I have argued, the two charms directed for sleep point to the social-performative setting of the lullaby, whence the other functions may have been improvised by the ritual experts who

---

73 Bes bread stamps: Hirsch, "Spätantike Brotstempel mit der Maske"; Török, *Hellenistic and Roman Terracottas*, 187, #315. See also Frankfurter, *Religion in Roman Egypt*, 124–31.

74 On evidence for a *Bēsia* in Roman Egypt, see Perpillou-Thomas, *Fêtes d'Égypte*, 73–74; on a terracotta image of bread offerings next to a Bes image in the Museum of Fine Arts, Budapest, see Török, *Hellenistic and Roman Terracottas*, 33–34, #11.

75 Caner, "Towards a Miraculous Economy"; Caseau, "Magical Protection and Stamps in Byzantium."

76 See Bowes, "Sixth-Century Individual Rituals."

edited the charms.⁷⁷ One of the sleep charms, dated to the fifth or sixth century, reads as follows:

> I send you to NN, that you may bring sleep upon him, and slumber, until the sun of Chousi (?) arises.
> Say [ⲭⲉ]: The true name is Papleu.
> Say [ⲭⲉ]: This is Isis, this is Nephthys, the two sisters, who are troubled within, who grieve within, who have wandered through heaven and earth, who are in the abyss.
> Say [ⲭⲉ]: Look, Horus the son of Isis was in distress. She is far from him..., since she turned to the sun, (she) turned to the moon, to confine them (?) in the middle of heaven, to the Pleiades, in the middle of heaven. Isis and Nephys are the two sisters who are troubled within, who grieve within, who are in the abyss.
> Say [ⲭⲉ]: You are Ax, you are Abrasax, the angel who sits upon the tree of Paradise, who sent sleep upon Abimelech for seventy-five years. You must bring sleep upon NN, now now, quickly quickly.⁷⁸

We will return to these songs in chapter 6 in connection with the syncretistic activities of the Christian scribe, but here it is worth considering their nature given that the cults and priesthoods of the gods they mention were no longer part of the landscape. Such a lullaby or other type of folk song would not have been an expression of devotion to institutional religion, or to bygone religion, or to some Egyptian heritage outside of Christianity. Rather, in this case, the circumstances of the fussy baby (or the erotically bereft youth) would have *called forth* a range of traditional songs or charms in which archaic myths were recalled ad hoc.⁷⁹ That is, social-performative circumstances would have involved habitus no less than lamp-lighting and bread-baking would have, and that habitus would have extended beyond simple gesture to the recollection of lore—familiar verses, images, and tunes. There was no assumption of an established cult or nostalgic projection of an alternative religious world, just a song with paradigmatic characters pertaining to the crisis at hand, a crisis quintessentially domestic in sphere.

Of course, we know from other Christianizing cultures and from the evidence for secret adherence to religious traditions discussed earlier that households might well have maintained elements of traditional cult performed explicitly to invoke a temple cult or serve as its replacement. Yet, as late as the fifth and sixth centuries, materials like the gestures to Shai and the Isis/Horus charms remind us that domestic religion could have involved names inherited from earlier religious contexts that were then maintained as traditions within a Christian (or

---

77 ACM 47–48 (sleep), 72 (erotic control), 49 (intestinal distress); see also Frankfurter, "Laments of Horus in Coptic."
78 ACM 47 = Berlin Coptic 5655.
79 See Karanika, *Voices at Work*, ch. 6.

Christianizing) culture. That is to say, in no case—neither in the primary artifacts nor in the Coptic witnesses—do we see the agents of these gestures or songs self-consciously shifting from a "Christian" to a "pre-Christian" religious mode. Inasmuch as the culture was in the process of Christianization, we see the religion framing and sanctioning these various domestic traditions as part of life.

D. Female Figurines and the Ambiguity of Representation

The female figurines with which this chapter began tell a similar story (see figs. 1–7, plates 1–2). Their iconography clearly signals that they represented concerns and hopes associated with the domestic sphere, and that they would have involved a rich sequence of embodied ritual acts on the part of agents of the domestic sphere. Their very function was to convey the ritual agency of the subject—the visitor to a shrine or tomb—as well as a desired state like pregnancy or an idealized state such as holding a tambourine.[80] Some figurines retrieved from cemeteries were clothed in crude cloth, pointing to their agents' further investment in the figurine's capacity to work, to communicate, to index the agency of the depositing subject (see fig. 4, plate 2). Dressing the small feminine form with accoutrements (and even, in one example from Antaeopolis, adding a baby to the form; see fig. 4) would have ritually invested the figurine with identity and agency: the capacity to convey hopes for conception to the deceased.[81]

But where did their iconography come from? In one sense the figurines suggest some continuity with a type of nude female figurine attested from the early pharaonic through the early Roman period and normally deposited in tombs to invoke ancestors' concern for the fecundity of the living family.[82] The wide diversity of forms of female figurines that have been found reflects local traditions of craftsmanship and thus traditions concerning the efficacy of the female plastic form that were maintained in various regions and subcultures in late antique Egypt. Several from the pilgrimage site of Apa Mena seem to draw on a wider Mediterranean form of the *mater lactans* that gave rise to iconographies of both Isis and, by the fifth century, Mary (see fig. 1, nos. 7–8). But in the local ritual world of these figurines and the desires people sought to convey through them, the *mater lactans* iconography was simply a familiar image of successful maternity (cf. figs. 5, 7).[83]

---

80 See Weiss, "Consumption of Religion in Roman Karanis"; and Frankfurter, "Female Figurines in Early Christian Egypt."

81 See Frankfurter, "Female Figurines in Early Christian Egypt," 207–10; and Boozer, *Late Romano-Egyptian House*, ch. 10.

82 Waraksa, *Female Figurines*; Allen, "Terracotta Figurines from Karanis," 81–90; Pinch, "Childbirth and Female Figurines"; idem, *Votive Offerings to Hathor*, 198–234; Pinch and Waraksa, "Votive Practices"; and Frankfurter, "Terracotta Figurines and Popular Religion."

83 *Mater lactans* and Isis: Tran Tam Tinh, *Isis lactans*; Dunand, *Religion populaire en Égypte romaine*, 70; Török, *Coptic Antiquities I*, 33–34; Langener, *Isis Lactans-Maria Lactans*; Bolman, "Enig-

FIGURE 5. Seated *mater lactans*. Hand-modeled terracotta with traces of paint. Egypt, unprovenanced. Fifth to sixth century CE. Height: 16 cm; width: 8.5 cm; depth: 3.5 cm.

FIGURE 6. Standing nude female figurine holding breasts, with the name *Phib* mold-pressed into the abdomen. From cemetery in upper Egypt. Sixth century CE. Height: 16.2 cm; width: 7.4 cm; depth: 3.3 cm.

FIGURE 7. Standing nude and bejeweled *mater lactans* in aedicula. Molded terracotta with paint accentuating pubis and sides of body. Egypt, unprovenanced. Fourth to sixth century CE. Height: 14.4 cm; width: 5.9 cm; depth: 3.5 cm.

These late antique female figurines clearly belong to a different era from those used in pharaonic times for mortuary deposit and to represent goddesses. Many are demurely dressed, and one type of figurine molded in the nude has been inscribed in two cases with the Christian saint's name Phib on the belly (see fig. 6).[84] More significantly, as chapter 5 will discuss, a great number of such figurines were designed, molded, and distributed at the Apa Mena pilgrimage shrine. Thus, whatever their distant historical lineage, female figurines were being produced in late antiquity in order to facilitate and shape people's ritual practices at Christian saints' shrines, and even to encourage pilgrimage to these shrines. Brought back into the home as symbols of a saint's blessing, the figurines came to signify allegiance to Christianity as mediated through the pilgrimage shrine. The figurines became, in a way, vital media between the interests of the domestic sphere, locative claims to Christian authority (like the saint's shrine), and other places in the landscape (like tombs) where they traditionally served as instruments of communication and blessing.

---

matic Coptic Galaktotrophousa." Relationship to more widespread Mediterranean iconography: Budin, *Images of Woman and Child*.

84 Perdrizet, *Les terres cuites grecques d'Égypte*, 5–6; Bayer-Niemeier, *Bildwerke der Sammlung Kaufmann I*, 147–48; Papaconstantinou, *Le culte des saints en Égypte*, 55.

E. Amulets, Curses, Saintly Blessings, and Votive Donations

A fifth type of material indicative of syncretism in the domestic sphere involves domestic ritual practices that explicitly engaged the new media and social landscape of ecclesiastical Christianity to meet the express needs of the domestic sphere. Most illustrative is the range of inscribed amulets, blessings (*eulogia*) from saints, and other material devices that family members solicited and brought into the home as symbols of the authority and efficacy of the Christian religious system. In a text to which I shall return in chapter 3, Shenoute of Atripe refers censoriously both to a "great monk" who gave a healing amulet made of a fox claw to a local official and to "elders of the church [and] monks" who provided people with blessed oil for diverse remedies.[85] If Shenoute himself disdained the function and ritual eclecticism of Christian experts in providing such "deceptions," we should attend to the agency of their clients in requesting material blessings from such monks and elders, for it shows a readiness on the part of domestic social worlds to appropriate the thaumaturgical potentiality of Christianity and its experts.

A rich corpus of Greek and Coptic magical texts from the sixth century and later provides evidence of people seeking protection for their homes and bodies from scorpions, serpents, and demons:

> ΧΜΓ Hor Hor Phor Phor, Yao Sabaoth Adonai Eloe Salaman Tarchei, I bind you, Artemisian Scorpion, 315 times! Preserve this house with its occupants from all evil, from all bewitchment of spirits of the air and human (evil) eye and terrible pain and sting of scorpion and snake, through the name of the highest god, Naias Meli 7.... Be on guard, O Lord, son of David according to the flesh, the one born of the holy virgin Mary, O holy one, highest God, from the holy spirit. Glory to you, O heavenly king. Amen. Α+Ω +Α+Ω ΙΧΘΥΣ[86]

Using language evocative of scripture and liturgy, this text draws on the authority of Christianity and its textuality for domestic protection against poisonous vermin. Another text seeks the same protection by the power of a St. Phocas, whose name is preceded by magical names made powerful through their deliberate archaeism (Aphrodite, Horus):

> + The Door, Aphrodite
> phrodite rodite odite
> dite ite te te e Hor Hor
> Phor Phor Iao Sabaoth Adonē

---

85 Shenoute, *Acephalous Work* A14, in Orlandi, *Shenute*, 18–21 (my translation).
86 ACM 26 = P. Oslo 1.5

CHAPTER 2

> I bind you, Artemisian Scorpion
> Free this house
> from every evil reptile
> [and] deed—Now! Now!
> Saint Phocas is here!
> 13 Phamenoth, 3rd Interdiction.[87]

I will return in chapter 6 to the scribal experts who, in navigating between monastic and popular culture, developed their roles as mediators of the empowered word for the purposes of quotidian protection and and the resolution of crises. We will also see written supplications to holy men to provide blessings in many forms for the domestic sphere in chapter 3. It is such charismatic literate experts who should be considered to have been the ultimate composers of such amulets. However, the amulets are also evidence of a vital interaction between those concerned with the protection of the household from scorpions and snakes—that is, the ritual agents of the domestic sphere—and those who represented the scribal powers of Christianity. In that context the amulets show an assertive interest on the part of the domestic sphere in the integration of Christian words and text into household protection.

Another amulet, designed to protect a pregnant woman and her household and found in a ritual handbook, demonstrates scribal expertise in defending people against a wide range of domestic threats. That is, the scribe did not simply project a simple or monolithic demonic assault:

> Watch and protect the four sides of the body and the soul and the spirit and the entire house of N, daughter of N, and her child who is in her womb as well as every child born to her. Bring them to life yearly without any disease. Cast forth from her every evil force. Never allow them to approach her or any of her children until she bears them. Cast forth from her every doom and every devil and every Apalaf and every Aberselia and every power of darkness and every evil eye and every eye-shutter and every chill and every fever and every trembling. Restrain them all. Cast them away from her and away from all her children until she bears them, and away from all her dwellings, immediately and quickly! Do not permit them ever to visit her or the child with whom she is pregnant for approximately two hundred miles around. Yea, yea, now, now, at once, at once! Sura daughter of Pelca, she and the child with whom she is pregnant.[88]

Beyond the occasional magical name, these charms show little or no pre-Christian traditions and, in fact, a deep dedication on the part of clients and

---

87 ACM 25 = P. Oxy 1060
88 ACM 64 = London Or. Ms. 5255, ll.10–32

scribes to the authority of Christianity, both its texts and its liturgy. Yet they illustrate syncretism no less than do other types of domestic religious combination, for they show individuals' assertive efforts to integrate an official Christianity of text and exorcistic power with the quotidian concerns that preoccupied the domestic sphere.

It is in this context that I want to consider a more remarkable innovation in the ritual relationship between the domestic sphere and the monastery, with its associated scribal sphere: families' donations of their children to monasteries. This was an act that clearly showed the safety and well-being of the domestic sphere as subjects' primary concern. The arrangement, attested from the eighth century from one particular monastery in Thebes, involved the fulfillment of a vow in which the child was dedicated to a monastery for menial service (like lamplighting) in return for God's protection of that child:

> I [Kalisthene, the mother,] made a decision and donated my beloved son Merkoure to the holy chapel of the holy Apa Phoibammon of the mountain of Jeme in order that he become a servant in the holy place forever for the health of my sinful soul and that of my late husband. I will inform you precisely: When the merciful and pitying God gave the child to me, afterward, when the little one approached adulthood, the good God brought on him a very hard and heavy sickness, so that I should abandon him as dying. Then we called upon the God of the holy Apa Phoibammon: "If you will grace him with a cure, I will donate him to your altar, and he shall be a servant of God in return for the good things that you did for me."[89]

The child would evidently be brought at a quite young age to the monastery, where his presence would constitute a symbolic blessing on the donating family and, implicitly, a boon to the economic life of the monastery.[90] Not that this system always worked for every family, as one mother confesses in another document: after vowing to give her son to the monastery, she felt she could not hand him over and only relented when he (again) became mortally ill.[91] But the "theory" of the donation was not unlike that of other votive dedications: the child, delivered from illness, became an extension of the family's or parent's social agency—mediating for them, even as a servant, in a sacred space. Presumably the child's participation in—or perpetual proximity to—monastic liturgy would have made the donation of him that much more beneficial for the family than the placement of a figurine at a shrine.

---

89 P. KRU 79, 13–29, in Wilfong, *Women of Jeme*, 102.
90 See MacCoull, "Child Donations and Child Saints"; Thissen, "Koptische Kinderschenkungsurkunden"; Papaconstantinou, "Notes sur les actes de donation d'enfant"; idem, "THEIA OIKONOMIA"; Wilfong, *Women of Jeme*, 99–104; Richter, "What's in a Story?"
91 P. KRU 86, in Crum and Steindorff, *Koptische Rechtsurkunden des achten Jahrhunderts*.

CHAPTER 2

VI. AGENTS OF THE DOMESTIC SPHERE: GENDER AND CREATIVE INDEPENDENCE

The literate (and literary) nature of the child donation documents points to the major role of the monastic scribe in conducting and shaping the ritual of handing over the child, but the documents themselves are phrased as the testimonies of parents, and especially mothers, who acclaim the power of God in donating their children. And, in fact, most of the agents we see involved in developing and conducting rituals of appeal and vow, especially the innovative use of gesture and space out of desperation, are women concerned for their maternity or their children—two central orientations of domestic religion.

Hagiographical legend in particular illustrates this form of child- and procreation-related self-determination. When an ailing woman approached the holy man Apa Pisentius for a blessing and was refused, she collected some dust from his footprints and returned to her friend, who was lying on the path to the monk's cell in an even sicker state. "Did you reach the holy man?" her friend asked,

> "Did your receive a blessing [смоу] at his hands? If your hands have touched his holy hands (and you) lay them upon me, I believe that I will be relieved from the scourge of this disease that is upon me." And the [other] woman said to her, "He did not lay his hand upon me. He ran away until he reached his cell and shut the door. And when I saw that I could not overtake him, I took the sand that had been under his right foot, and I raised it on top of my head, and by the grace of God, I had relief from my illness." And the [sicker] woman through her great faith said, "Give me also a little of that sand." She took it; she swallowed some of it; it entered her organs; and then her belly ceased from swelling, and her whole body was healed. And they gathered up the [rest of the] sand into their houses, and kept it as a blessing for them.[92]

Indeed, many hagiographical legends emphasize this assertiveness on the part of female supplicants: a woman despised by her husband for her inability to conceive throws herself at St. Hilarion in Palestine; another, claiming her husband is avoiding her because of a rival's sorcery, demands that St. Aphrahat in Syria give her some blessed oil to recapture her husband's love and release the spell on him; and yet another, whose husband has been three years at sea, begs St. Stephen (deceased, in his martyrion) to direct her to wait or to remarry.[93] Shrine miracle collections in particular focus on women, their physical crises, and the creative

---

92 *Life of Pisentius* (Bohairic version), in Amélineau, *Étude sur le christianisme*, 87–88.
93 Respectively, Jerome, *v.Hil.* 13; Theodoret, *Hist. Rel.*, 8.13; and *Miracles of St. Stephen* 2.5, in Meyers, *Les miracles de saint Étienne*, 284–87.

lengths they go to in securing a saint's intervention. One Dorothea who brings her sick child to the shrine of John and Cyrus in Menouthis wails all night before getting a dream instruction to leave the main shrine and lay the boy in the middle of the outer atrium, an unusual (and unusually public) site for a supplicant to seek healing. Of course, he is cured—although by the direct ministration of a mother snake.[94] It is not so much these texts' attention to female supplicants that is important, since shrines with any claim to resolve issues of child safety and maternity have always tended to receive crowds of female supplicants. Rather, it is the women's assertiveness, their innovativeness, and their facility with gesture, appeal, and the very materiality of blessing that emerges in these stories as remarkable. Such ritual assertiveness also appears in several Coptic curse spells solicited by women to paralyze rivals, like one written by a mother against her daughter-in-law:

> I... call upon the Lord God almighty that you perform my judgment against Tnoute, [who has] separated my son from me so that he scorns me. You must not listen to her, O [God].... You must strike her womb and make her barren. You must make her consume the fruit of her womb. You must make a demon descend upon her, [that will cast] her into troublesome illness and great affliction.[95]

Similar sentiments arise in women's erotic spells, intended not so much for physical satisfaction as to restrain and redirect the wandering interests of the men who protected and maintained the women's well-being.[96] But at the same time this female ritual assertiveness reflects a larger social role of women as ritual agents both responsible for and capable of soliciting supernatural aid through a broad vocabulary of performative gestures and expressions.

One of these performances, with its attendant gestures and supplications, involved the terracotta figurines we have already seen. The gestures surrounding these figurines included not just the private depositing of the surrogate image but also, presumably, a far more convivial process of *choosing* the right figurine from a selection (such as was offered at the Menas shrine; see fig. 1) and then deciding the place to put it—perhaps at the instruction of shrine attendants, or perhaps with little regard for shrine custom, as in the case of Dorothea, who chose the atrium of the John and Cyrus shrine as the location for her child's healing. The explicit depiction of pregnancy, breasts, and even the sexually receptive nude body across the corpus of figurines means that women preparing for some type of ritual appeal would have seen ideal aspects of themselves in the figurines and at the same time, through the purchase and deposit of these objects, would have

---

94 Sophronius of Jerusalem, *Miracles of John and Cyrus* 34.
95 ACM 93 = London Or. Ms. 6172 (translation emended).
96 See Frankfurter, "Social Context of Women's Erotic Magic."

transformed the private body of anxious expectation into a publicly represented body. Whether deposited at a shrine or a tomb to solicit an ancestor's intervention or brought home as a fecundity blessing from the shrine for a domestic altar, the figurines provided the material context for active ritual engagement and innovation on the part of women and on behalf of their social status as married women.[97]

In the context of the domestic sphere, women's ritual agency had the capacity to maintain efficacious traditions—gestures, customs, habitus—and to engage new ones. As the figurines most likely served women's ritual expressions at shrines and in homes, so the Isis/Horus songs preserved in lullabies (and other folk songs) reflect a social context of childcare and oral charm in which tragic themes sung according to traditional structure not only conveyed magical efficacy but offered an opportunity for reverie for the singer.[98] Now, this discussion of syncretism and the perpetuation of traditions in the context of women's ritual assertiveness should not be taken as an echo of ancient Christian sermons that caricatured women's inevitable "heathen" tendencies; rather, in addressing women's syncretistic efforts I mean to emphasize how, *in the interests of* the domestic sphere and its salient concerns and ritual spaces, women associated with that sphere drew on everything at their disposal to ensure its successful maintenance.[99]

But then what of men? It is important to take account of both the hagiographical and the documentary images of men as ritual agents of the domestic sphere in order to gather a better sense of the diversity of social roles involved in domestic religion as it has been broadly defined. The role of men as conductors of household-based rites is clear as far back as the papyri of the early Roman period (second and third centuries CE): "Every day I perform devotion [*proskynēma*] on [the recipient's daughter's] behalf before the God ... Lord Sarapis—and your [behalf] and her mother's," writes Aelius Theon; similarly, a couple writes together to their children that they "perform devotion on your behalf before your ancestral gods." One Serenus, writing to his brother in the third century, does not describe his *proskynēma* but merely declares that "our ancestral gods always assist us, giving us health and safety [*sōtēria*]."[100] Such declarations of domestic devotional rites performed on the recipients' behalf have the ring of formality rather than testimony, but clearly the idea that men

---

97 On this process see idem, "Female Figurines in Early Christian Egypt."

98 Idem, "Laments of Horus in Coptic," 240; Del Guidice, "Ninna-Nanna-Nonsense?," esp. 279–80. Cf. the diversified gesture of cradling that Jennifer Scheper Hughes traces over the *longue durée* of religions in Mexico; Hughes, "Cradling the Sacred."

99 Cf. Mernissi, "Women, Saints, and Sanctuaries"; Cuffel, "From Practice to Polemic"; Gemzoë, "Feminization of Healing." On the development of separate religious traditions within women's domestic worlds as a function of women's roles in local culture, though not necessarily applicable to late antique Egypt, see Kent, "Secret Christians of Sivakasi."

100 Respectively, P. Oxy 59.3992, 3993; 6.935.

might engage in devotional acts before domestic images of ancestral gods seemed at least plausible to the recipients.

If these early Roman letters present men's *proskynēmata* as a public epistolary gesture, saints' lives show men acting as more desperate and creative ritual agents. One father, unable to extract a token *eulogion* from Abba Aaron, took some dirt from beside his door

> and tied it up in his neckerchief. And when they came into the house they found a large crowd of people gathered together and the man's wife and her child. The child's father uncovered the little bit of earth tied up in in his neckerchief and sprinkled it upon the dead child. Immediately he moved his body and opened his eyes. Those who were sitting beside the mother were astounded and they glorified the God of the holy man Abba Aaron.[101]

Here it is the father who devises the ritual of sprinkling earth from the vicinity of the holy man on his son's body, but often hagiographies depict the mother as being in such desperate straits that the husband must serve as mediator, both in arranging ritual resolution and in fulfilling the vow. Among the miracles associated with the shrine of the Three Hebrew Youths in Alexandria is the story of a woman afflicted by miscarriages: each time she gets pregnant and is about to give birth, a demon enters her breast and pounds on her chest like a hammer on an anvil, after which she expels the fetus, covered in blood, and spends the next month catatonic with grief. Her husband, an artisan, appeals to the Archbishop Theophilus, who tells him to bring his wife, when she next becomes pregnant, to the shrine of the Three Hebrew Youths. The husband then asks for a blessing for his one live son, who has been afflicted by a deaf-mute demon. "If the saints expel it from my son," he declares, "I will make three gold and mosaic images and offer them to the holy shrine." So the archbishop instructs him, "Bring your son with you on the ninth of Pachoms [the eve of their festival]. Leave him at the shrine overnight to the tenth. The favor of the saints will come to him by the will of God." Of course, the healing is successful, with a spontaneous and dramatic exorcism by the shrine's saints; the man brings his family home and provides the church with the votive images he had promised.[102]

A legend like this one was meant to encourage votive donation as the conclusion to a successful healing. In it, the husband assumes the role of supplicant because of his family's general crisis and because he, rather than his wife, could provide such finely crafted offerings. Men and women do not simply alternate as parallel ritual agents; rather, their creative capacities differ by gender, by social context, and by degree of enmeshment in the crisis itself.

---

101 Paphnutius, *Histories of the Monks of Upper Egypt*, trans. Vivian, *Histories of the Monks*, 125.
102 Pseudo-Cyril, *Encomium on the Three Youths*, in De Vis, *Homélies coptes de la Vaticane II*, 160–202. Cf. similar agency by the husband described in Theodoret, *Hist. Rel.* 13.16.

CHAPTER 2

VII. CONCLUSION

While the first parts of this chapter explored the separate—but not autonomous—integrity of the domestic sphere as a social site with its own intrinsic interests and characteristics, the last two sections indicated the interconnections of the domestic sphere with others to be covered in this book. Women's and men's ritual agency in the effort to resolve specific areas of concern vis-à-vis family and home distinguish the domestic sphere, but that agency impels them to travel outside that sphere to holy men, to saints' shrines, to scribal experts, to craftsmen, and to potent sites in the landscape, all of which serve as points of mediation for the ritual resolution of crisis or concern. But rather than conceptualizing all these religious spheres in a sort of Venn diagram, it is more useful to examine each in turn as an axis that joins with the others at nodes. Thus, while the next chapter will examine the independent syncretistic agency of the holy man, here I have asked: In what ways did the women and men who ventured out to him determine—or exert their own concerns and traditions on—how he performed, articulated, and distributed his charisma? That is, how did the very mass of supplicants influence the material forms of his "blessings"—whether letters, physical contact relics, oil, or fox claws? Similar questions can be asked of the crafting and purveying of female figurines at saints' shrines, the maintenance of mortuary crafts in the village, and the writing of oracle requests or charms: each served as the ritual expression of a distinctive religious sphere, but each responded to the concerns of the domestic sphere as I have modeled them in this chapter.

CHAPTER 3

Controller of Demons, Dispenser of Blessings

TRADITIONS OF THE HOLY MAN AS
CRAFTSMAN OF LOCAL CHRISTIANITY

I. INTRODUCTION: SAINTS AND SYNCRETISM

In one of his more meandering sermons the redoubtable Abbot Shenoute touches on some of the ritual practices in his vicinity that were being conducted under the aegis of Christianity—administered, in fact, through the expertise of monks and elders:

> At the time of suffering, those fallen into poverty or in sickness or indeed some other trial abandon God and run after enchanters or diviners or indeed seek other acts of deception, just as I myself have seen: the snake's head tied on someone's hand, another one with the crocodile's tooth tied to his arm, and another with fox claws tied to his legs—especially since it was an official who told him that it was wise to do so! Indeed, when I demanded whether the fox claws would heal him, he answered, "It was a great monk who gave them to me, saying 'Tie them on you (and) you will find relief.'"
>
> Listen to this impiety! Fox claws! Snakes' heads! Crocodiles' teeth! And many other vanities that people put on themselves for their own relief, while others deceive them. Moreover, this is the manner that they anoint themselves with oil or that they pour over themselves water while receiving (ministrations) from enchanters or drug-makers, with every deceptive kind of relief.... Still again, they pour water over themselves or anoint themselves with oil from elders of the church, or even from monks![1]

Shenoute's observations highlight several important aspects of the monk in late antique Egypt outside the lives of prayer and renunciation for which they are typically known in literature and historical discussion. First, the acts that he describes pertain to encounters between monks (and other Christian specialists)

---

[1] Shenoute, Acephalous Work A14, §§255–259, in Orlandi, *Shenute*, 18–20. On the independent nature of this section of Orlandi's text, see Emmel, *Shenoute's Literary Corpus*, 2:944 no. 570, 1010.

and laity—even, as Shenoute indicates here, elite laity. Second, we see the same liturgical materials with which monks and elders claimed some expertise here repurposed as *eulogia*—as blessings, in the form of healing or protective substances. This kind of repurposing of ecclesiastical substances, from oil to the Eucharist to candle wax, has been recorded across local Christianities for most of the religion's history. It demonstrates how officially designated materials are, in essence, *materials*—portable, moldable, concealable, insertable, wearable, edible—and how local people will inevitably demand their share of what the institution dispenses. Third, and most central to this chapter, is the fact that the "great monk" about whom Shenoute complains has used as his singular medium of blessing the claws of a fox. Whether the efficacy of this monk's innovation came from the "weirdness" of these animal parts (a kind of potent antithesis of the straightforward cross) or from some local associations with fox claws, this medium of blessing took advantage of the local environment and addressed local understandings of ritual efficacy, much as, a century later at the shrine of John and Cyrus, we find patients instructed to eat local peacocks and snakes, and to use crocodile flesh as an eye salve.[2] That is to say, it was an act of syncretism, combining the fox claw amulet with monastic charisma, popular associations with the physical thing, and social understandings of ritual healing. Syncretism here is equivalent to assemblage, using things from the environment to articulate the charisma of the saints.

But how can the term "syncretism" be used to characterize figures known in both legend and their own writings as consummate Christians who embodied biblical lives and were in perpetual combat against the demonic residues of the religious past?[3] I here intend the term to cover both the performative and social worlds of living holy men and the ways in which legends and devotional traditions grew up around them when they died. To the extent that "saint" covers living holy men and prophets who stand on the relative periphery of their cultures—or between traditional and modernizing worldviews—such figures are veritable workshops of syncretism, alternately translating new ideas, asserting traditional ways in new guises, violently opposing older practices, and innovating hybrid worldviews. Through this ambivalent dramaturgy, and within the traditional religious landscape, they act on the minds and practices of their devotees, asserting themselves against religious institutions, while at the same time being acted upon by both pilgrims, who seek perennial benefits, and institutions, which often try to circumscribe these figures with official status—or to quash them entirely.

---

2 Sophronius, *Miracles*, 12.18, 27, 24.5. Bronislaw Malinowski notes the "coefficient of weirdness" in the construction of potency in magical objects; Malinowski, *Coral Gardens*, 218–23. See also Frankfurter, "Fetus Magic."

3 Brakke, *Demons and the Making*.

What social model frames this range of acts? As depicted in both hagiography and their own correspondence (on papyrus and clay sherds), and with some help from archaeology, the social world of the holy man ranged from the solitary figure on the periphery of popular habitation (the anchorite proper) to the charismatic figure accompanied by a small group of acolytes who dwelled nearby and aided with the administration of blessing, the performance of liturgy, and the development of an ascetic order: the *laura* structure reflected in recent archaeological sites.[4] Although ordained clergy might have been involved in such arrangements, there was much variation in the degree to which clergy influenced holy men or promoted specific ideologies beyond liturgical practices.[5] Communication among hermits and acolytes in circumscribed regions amounted to the formation of "micro-societies" for the negotiation of material needs, the conduct of liturgy, and general interactions with the larger world. And indeed, archaeological and textual evidence has demonstrated the extensive interactions of holy men and their acolytes with people in the region:

> Great multitudes used to come to [Apa Moses] on the Sabbath, and they would stay until Sunday and take communion with him. Their women, on the other hand, and their daughters used to go before the virgins [in the adjoining convent located in the Temple of Seti I]. At Sunday night when they had finished meditating, they would carry out reading, and when they had stopped reading he would speak to them in the words of God. . . .
>
> On Sunday morning [Apa Moses] gave communion with his (own) hands to the people and the brethren, and he taught them in memory of the prophet Apa Shenoute of the monastery of Atripe.
>
> On the tenth day of Apip after this when he was praying, he descended into an *ekstasis*. He was taken away in spirit and shown dwelling. . . .[6]

Hagiographical texts may exaggerate the size of the crowds, but they do reflect the types of interaction, both ceremonial and, as we will see, supplicatory, that developed around holy men as these figures introduced their own charismatic presence into the context of hymn, prayer, incense, icon, and charismatic lineage.[7]

But to the extent that the saints around whom syncretism developed were deceased supernatural figures celebrated and accessed ritually at tomb-shrines and martyria, they served as orientation points for others' agency. Supplicants

---

4 Crum and Winlock, *Monastery of Epiphanius at Thebes*, 125–37; Heurtel, "Le petit monde de Frangé"; Brooks Hedstrom, "Divine Architects."

5 See esp. Crum and Winlock, *Monastery of Epiphanius at Thebes*, 151–53.

6 *V. Mosis* §§131, 142–143, in Uljas, "IFAO Leaves of the Life," 399, 410–11 (text); 414, 420–21 (translation emended).

7 See also Behlmer, "Visitors to Shenoute's Monastery"; Goehring, *Ascetics, Society, and the Desert*, ch. 2.

from near and far, hagiographers, and shrine attendants developed mythology and ritual practices (festivals, divination) that drew the saint and all he stood for into the landscape and its traditions—particularly traditions dictating relations with spirits.[8] Meanwhile, religious institutions and their own hagiographers drew the saint's story and cult into the role of exemplar for the broader religious ideology—not as a healer of camels' hooves but as a new John the Baptist and staunch opponent of heresy. Yet the expectations of devotees and the traditions that informed native hagiography pressed so closely on these cults that one can talk confidently both of the culture's appropriation of the saint and of syncretism taking place in the saint's very location "among us." We can see this appropriation quite vividly in an example not from Egypt but from late antique Syria. Within a century after the death of Simeon the Stylite, and following the construction of an immense basilica around his pillar, a church official beheld the local farmers dancing one night around the pillar and circumambulating it with their beasts of burden—drawing Simeon into their landscape, as it were.[9] The social models that cover these phenomena are first and foremost the culture of the saint's shrine, the topic of chapter 4, and to some degree the culture of monastic scribes, the authors of hagiography and the subject of chapter 6. The present chapter will revolve around the activities and heroic memories of the holy men themselves in their role as instigators of Christianization in late antique Egypt.

In both the case of the living holy man and that of the shrine of the deceased saint, the very construction of sainthood is a product of syncretism between local traditions and broader ideologies. Saints function both as religious exemplars and as sources of practical beneficence, as outposts for disseminating new religious ideas and as touchstones for new regional cults in the landscape, as assaults on ancient religious custom and as instruments of revitalization of such customs. Syncretism thus implies a process of interpretation, localization, and indigenization. It is a process of articulating power and holiness—especially new notions of holiness—through the environment and its inhabitants, denizens, and dangers. Christianity is seen as emerging from the very landscape in the form of apparitions, healing shrines, sacred rocks and trees, legends of the beneficent peregrinations of holy men, and the vanquishing of old dangers.

Syncretism as a model for the development of a religion in space and time also involves the culturally inscribed gestures, responses, habits, and even senses of "center" that inform supplicants' behavior before saints: those gestural codes by which members of a culture perform and repeat socially meaningful acts, from table manners to games to ceremonies. By these gestural codes—"habitus," in the terminology of Marcel Mauss and Pierre Bourdieu—actions gain meaning, group

---

8 See, for Egypt, Quaegebeur, "Les 'saints' égyptiens préchrétiens."
9 Evagrius, *Eccl. Hist.* 1.14, in Bidez and Parmentier, *Ecclesiastical History of Evagrius*, 24.

activities are coordinated, and collective memories are actualized.[10] With respect to the cultural and bodily reception of holy men in the late antique landscape, the concept of habitus bears on how individual visitors adjusted their bodies toward the saint, represented desperation or obeisance, or received bodily the sensory powers and materials of liturgy. But the same force of habitus that informed the articulation of religious modes informed the saint's own performance as well: his definition of evil and its vanquishing, his gestures, his concoction of substances to transmit power, his establishment of a shrine or center, and his development of mantic powers, all according to forms recognizable to his culture. As examinations of prophets and holy men outside early Christian Egypt have shown, the ostensibly most innovative acts—building mounds, standing on pillars—quite often carried a recognizability in the culture that allowed the holy man to stand out in a meaningful or "sacred" way. Here also is habitus, but as a determiner of the "new," not simply as the repetition of the old.[11]

Conceptualizing holy men—charismatic Christian monks—in this way presents something of a paradox, since Christian monks are often imagined as embodiments of a pure Christian spirituality and doctrine, given their (supposed) devotion to scripture and their protracted ascetic meditations on Christian text.[12] Imagined in this way, monks would seem to have lived and performed in absolute repudiation of past religious traditions and customs. Certainly this is the picture that hagiographers convey—or seem to the modern reader to convey. But the proposition that living saints in late antique Egypt were agents of syncretism, working within their respective cultures rather than simply transforming them from a separate Christian standpoint, follows a path blazed by Peter Brown's 1971 essay "The Holy Man in Late Antiquity" and continued in its 1995 postscript, "Arbiters of the Holy." In these works Brown showed that the social roles of saints in Egypt and Syria were instrumental to their religious authority and sacred powers.[13] In their roles as "charismatic ombudsmen," the hermits provided regional authority where it was needed; resolved issues of health and adversity, both supernatural and human; and offered a sense of center and a collective identity to communities disoriented in the later Roman world. Christianity in the late antique East, he argued, was an embodied phenomenon, located and visible in the holy man and imagined through his legends. Subsequently, Brown added nuance to this view of the saint's relationship with the traditional religious culture that hagiographers like Theodoret took pains to portray as in opposition to their sub-

---

10 See Mauss, "Notion of Body Techniques"; and Bourdieu, *Outline of a Theory of Practice*, esp. 81, 82–83.
11 See, e.g., Frankfurter, "Stylites and *Phallobatēs*"; Johnson, *Nuer Prophets*, 88–94, 137–38.
12 See, e.g., Burton-Christie, *Word in the Desert*.
13 Brown, "Rise and Function of the Holy Man"; idem, *Authority and the Sacred*, 55–78. On the roles of holy men in resolving legal and political crises, see also Kotsifou, "Monks as Mediators in Christian Egypt."

jects: "When we get close to a holy man, it is often possible to glimpse, in the penumbra of his reputation, a busy world of cultic experimentation which, though disapproved of in our sources as the work of rivals, had, in fact, incorporated crucial elements of the Christian saint's own thought world."[14] By formulating the holy man's roles in these terms, Brown invited fruitful comparisons with "saints" in other cultures and, hence, the possibility of speaking in general about saints in society.[15]

II. IMPLICATIONS OF CLASSIFICATION: FROM "SAINT" TO "REGIONAL PROPHET"

This discussion can move productively in both directions, however, so that observations gleaned from the late antique East can help illuminate modern situations of sainthood at the same time that the problematization of sainthood in modern transitional cultures can help inform our understanding of late antiquity, at least in pressing the question, What social role would have been implied in calling someone a saint? To the extent that we can peer through the theological distortions of hagiography, the "literary construction of sainthood," to a kind of historical Christian charismatic leadership, how can we construct a role for these figures that villagers *would* have understood enough to engage meaningfully with them? If meaningful habitus is engaged through recognition in a social context, then how did saints in their historical settings construct their recognizability?

Many of the saints discussed in modern ethnographic work are in fact types of *regional prophet*. Across modern transitional cultures one finds a type of religious leader who arises to supplant or integrate local cults, defines broad new allegiances in times of political upheaval, responds dramatically to popular fears of sorcery, or lays claim to Christian power and ideology in regional terms; often, these figures combine several of these functions.[16] Such figures show the establishment of a regional cult in a *person*, who replaces and often rejects local shrines. The prophet thus independently defines a new system of divine powers, "true" versus hostile, around himself. The prophet conveys dramatically—through symbols, divination, trance, preaching, amulets, and exorcism—a new religious order, which is often Christian, but usually carries a sense of "modernity."[17] What if we

---

14 Brown, *Authority and the Sacred*, 68.

15 Brown's work on saints influenced Kaplan, *Monastic Holy Man*; and Stirrat, *Power and Religiosity*.

16 See, e.g., Johnson, *Nuer Prophets*; Werbner, *Regional Cults*; idem, "Regional Cult of God Above." Millennialist prophets in Melanesia and North America also embody some of these patterns in linking tradition and innovation: see, e.g., Burridge, *New Heaven, New Earth*; Overholt, *Prophecy in Cross-Cultural Perspective*.

17 Cf. Colson, "A Continuing Dialogue," with Brown's depictions of the holy man in the same vein in "Rise and Function of the Holy Man"; and further on the comparison, Frankfurter, *Religion in Roman Egypt*, 189–93.

were to approach Egyptian Christian holy men likewise as regional prophets—as agents of religious transformation and the remapping of sacred authority? To be sure, the holy man phenomenon saw a much slower development over the fourth and fifth centuries than did the prophet movements studied in Africa or Melanesia, which could overtake regions in less than a decade. But what might this approach allow us to learn about the religious functions of holy men in an Egyptian, rather than a Christian institutional, context?

In many ways the category of regional prophet improves on "saint" or "holy man," both in giving more *specificity* to his or her relationship to the religious context and in allowing more productive *general* comparison across those cultures in which new, charismatic figures have wielded universalizing ideologies against local traditions and become known as miracle-workers. Such comparisons are inevitable if one seeks to move beyond literary constructions and understand more generally the function of the holy man in ancient society. In moving to the category of "regional prophet" to describe Christian charismatic figures in late antique Egypt, we are able to extend Brown's work on the social context of the holy man, focusing on the agency of religious transformation and the remapping of sacred authority. Rather than examining these figures' intellectual or scriptural mastery of Christian theology, we can turn to their supplicants and their predispositions and catchment areas. Regional cults were distinctive in their embrace of multiple religious subcultures and their redefinition of the scope of divinities' actions, and these late antique holy men in many ways hybridized functions classically provided in their regions by great temples—Baalbek in Syria, Philae or Abydos in Upper Egypt. The allure of the new center, with its new, expansive divinity, mediated dramatically through a prophet and promising concrete benefits, would have drawn people regardless of their allegiance to the divinity's ideological demands.[18]

Warrant for this kind of approach appears in the hagiographical sources themselves, which occasionally depict folk from well *outside* the Christian fold appealing to Christian holy men. Literary evidence attests to Arab tribes flocking to Simeon the Stylite in Syria and Nubians visiting the fifth-century hermits Macedonius and Aaron in Upper Egypt and attending a liturgy in Shenoute's church in Atripe.[19] The saints' power was a function of their "being there," as prophets in the landscape, rather than of their being servants of Christ specifically. People of the surrounding regions noticed a new sort of religious authority and a new font of thaumaturgy:

---

18 On the social topography of local and regional pilgrimage cults, see esp. Turner, "Pilgrimages as Social Processes."

19 Simeon: Theodoret, *Hist. Rel.* 26.13, 5–16; Macedonius and Aaron: Paphnutius, *Histories of the Monks of Upper Egypt*, in Vivian, *Histories of the Monks*, 44–47, 98–100. See also evidence for non-Christian pilgrims to saints' shrines in Papaconstantinou, *Le culte des saints en Égypte*, 340. Shenoute of Atripe refers to Nubian visitors among his apparently non-Christian church audience in Discourses 4: "As We Begin to Preach," in Brakke and Crislip, *Selected Discourses of Shenoute*, 191.

Often our father [John the Little] would also go to the village, moved by God who especially worked through him many healings of every kind, especially for the purification of the villagers' souls from the mange of the abominable worship of heathenism, causing, as a result, the light of his virtue to shine in that place like a star. For he became to all of them a guide to salvation, and they partook of safety from our father. When they would hear that he had come up from the mountain, all the villages, crowds of them of all ages, would come to him to receive a blessing from him since he did good to all of them.[20]

John's allure to folk in the vicinity revolved around the blessings and *oujai* [ⲟⲩϫⲁⲓ]—"salvation" *or* "healing"—he conveyed, and this draw apparently extended beyond those identifying themselves as "Christian." Yet in John's case (and that of regional prophets more generally), these benefits were apparently often accompanied by quite stringent demands—indeed, he called occasionally for the wholesale repudiation of tradition. There was a totalism in the new religious order, along with a sharply defined demonology—sorcery, "idols," heathen practices, local cults and their priests—over whose nature and eradication the prophet alone presided. We must take seriously the polarizations that regional prophets project onto landscape and behavior if we are to understand their relationship to culture. They truly exemplify the new, but then how do they maintain the old? How do they produce syncretisms if they and their followers experience repudiation and replacement?

III. EXORCISM AND THE REORDERING OF TRADITION

This paradoxical combination of repudiation and syncretism becomes more understandable when we examine the discourse of repudiation itself: in this case, demonology and exorcism. The distinctive interest in demons among Egyptian monks and their hagiographers reveals a dynamic effort to reorder a world of active spirits.

With varying adherence to hagiographical conventions, Coptic authors describe fourth- and fifth-century saints' often quite violent assaults on the traditional religious practices still abiding in their regions. The demonizing caricatures these authors project over what we know to have been a rather vibrant local religiosity all serve to frame these monastic assaults as the final extirpation of Satan's order—sometimes in rather ludicrous guise: "Woe unto me," says the Devil in the *Life of Moses of Abydos*, "for I have been cast out of every place, even this house [Abydos] that was left for me. See how I have been thrown out of it and left outside like a beggar. In Shmin Shenoute threw me out. He took away my temples

---

20 *Life of John the Little* 78, in Amélineau, *Histoire des monastères de la Basse-Egypte*, 393; translation adjusted from Mikhail and Vivian, "Life of Saint John the Little," 51–52.

and converted them into churches. Even my heathen children, he took from me. And he was not satisfied with this, but chased me out of the region."[21]

The *Vita* of Abbot Shenoute, woven from a series of encomia and legends of his acts in the vicinity of his monastery, tells how he and some other monks attacked a village that maintained its traditional cults and invaded a landowner's house to ransack his domestic shrine. Shenoute's own sermons hammer repeatedly at the morality of this landowner, the evils of temple priests, and the many popular domestic devotions that did not, apparently, disappear with the official establishment of Christianity.[22] An anonymous writer describes the hermit Moses's destruction of a temple of "Apollo" in Abydos and his exorcism of the popular god Bes from his old oracle shrine there.[23] The hagiographer of Macarios of Tkow describes how this holy man brought his monks in an assault on a temple still held in great reverence by villagers and priests.[24] Apollo of Hermopolis is described as conquering the prevailing cult of his own region by magically halting a religious procession.[25] Other stories of saints demonstrate, in these figures' encounters with heathen priests and cults, a distinct competition with the traditional religious world of temples and offerings, especially as the efficacy of their saintly blessings invariably required supplicants' prior or eventual acceptance of Christ.

Such episodes—fictional, yet filtering local monastic memories of charismatic holy men—make clear that holy men did not in any way consider themselves as restorers of Egyptian religious traditions.[26] They sought, with varying force and effect, the obliteration of the old sacred landscape as a habitat of demons, and its replacement with the rule of the new gods *P-Noute*—"God"—and Christ and the memories of prior heroes. It is hard to imagine syncretism applying to charismatic performances conducted in this vein—the execrations, demolitions, and exorcisms that occupied these holy men in their encounters with native religion.

---

21 Ed. Till, *Koptische Heiligen- und Martyrerlegenden*, 2:50–51; translation (emended) from Moussa, "Abba Moses of Abydos," 34. Hagiographical traditions both East and West imagined this large-scale battle with Satan as proceeding through the extirpation of local religion: Price, "Holy Man and Christianization," esp. 217–20.

22 Besa, [attrib.] *V. Sin.* 83–86, 125–126, on which see Van der Vliet, "Spätantikes Heidentum in Ägypten"; Frankfurter, *Religion in Roman Egypt*, 77–82, 131–42; idem, "'Things Unbefitting Christians'"; idem,"Iconoclasm and Christianization." On the development of the *Vita Sinuthii* out of local encomia, see Lubomierski, "Coptic Life of Shenoute." New manuscripts discussed by Stephen Emmel show not only that the landowner was pretending to be a Christian, but also that Shenoute was obsessed with revealing and exposing the images that he had hidden in his house: Emmel, "From the Other Side of the Nile"; idem, "Shenoute of Atripe."

23 Texts in Moussa, "Abba Moses of Abydos"; see in general Coquin, "Moïse d'Abydos"; and Frankfurter, *Religion in Roman Egypt*, 129–30.

24 Texts in Johnson, *Panegyric on Macarius*; see also Frankfurter, *Religion in Roman Egypt*, 69–70, 131–32; idem, "Illuminating the Cult of Kothos."

25 *Hist. mon.* 8.25–29.

26 On hagiographical perspectives on monks, see Frankfurter, "Hagiography and the Reconstruction"; and idem, "Iconoclasm and Christianization."

But such polarizing discourse and its performances had somehow to be sensible and captivating to Egyptian audiences, including other monks. Perhaps, then, it is worth approaching this discourse as a reordering of native religious concepts rather than as their replacement.[27] In what ways can we see holy men in cultural memory *reorienting* traditional concepts of ritual speech, action, and even demonology for the promotion of Christianity?

A. Reordering Perceptions of Evil

In hagiography, when Christian regional prophets oppose Egyptian religion, the gestures and pronouncements they use serve not so much to reject superstition as to overwhelm one ritual form with another. It was a war of ritual experts, in which the opponent—the heathen—represented the forces of maleficence. "I was the son of a priest of the heathens," one monk testifies before describing how he used to watch as his father sacrificed to Satan and all his army and as demons reported to him what kind of misfortune they had wreaked on land and sea.[28] In Atripe, legend had it, temple priests would regularly slaughter twelve children over a bronze cauldron and await the disappearance of the blood. But when a group of Christian ascetics at the behest of the Archangel Michael sent forth their prayers, the blood remained, and the ritual was ruined.[29] Even more graphically, one text imagines an appeal from the Christians of a mixed village to Macarius of Tkow claiming that their heathen neighbors and cult priests were kidnapping Christian children, ritually slaughtering them in the temple, and gutting them to use their intestines as harp strings for treasure hunting.[30] If in the first example the normal priestly cult of yore emerges (ex post facto) as a veritable "center" for Satan's subversion, so in the latter two examples do resilient temple cults represent real, predatory evils that infect the surrounding villages and must be stopped or cleansed. But in the ensuing narratives, these evils are matched by the aggressive thaumaturgical force of holy men. Macarius of Tkow brings fire down from heaven against the child-sacrifice cult, causing the high priest to be roasted and his heathen devotees to be scattered. In contrast, the anonymous ascetics of Atripe, from an earlier age, notably do not erase the cult but only interrupt the efficacy of its rituals.

Indeed, saints' lives display the overwhelming supernatural power of the monks as working against the heathens' own rites. When Apollo of Hermopolis stops a temple procession in its tracks, the priests and villagers, unable to move

---

27 This approach represents a revision of the arguments in *Religion in Roman Egypt*, 273–83.
28 *Apophth. Patr.* (anon.), in Nau, "Histoire des solitaires égyptiens," 275–76.
29 *Coptic Synaxarium*: 7 Kihak, in Basset, *Le Synaxaire arabe jacobite II*, 315–16. Serge Sauneron derived this image of the sacrificial cauldron from curse iconography found on the walls of many Egyptian temples; Sauneron, "Le chaudron de Sohag."
30 Pseudo-Dioscorus, *Panegyric on Macarios*, 5.1–2, in Johnson, *Panegyric on Macarios*, 2: 21–22. See discussion of this passage in Frankfurter, "Illuminating the Cult of Kothos," 184–87; and, more broadly, Schroeder, "Child Sacrifice in Egyptian Monastic Culture."

from their places, understand that it is a holy man who has bound them and that he will have to be appeased. When they swear to renounce their god and temple, he releases them from the spell, and the whole village declares its allegiance to the Christian pantheon. Shenoute of Atripe, about to invade the heathen village of Plewit (according to a legend in his *Vita*), detects apotropaic substances that the villagers have placed in the road to keep him away. He digs them up with the intent of hanging them around the villagers' necks, thus turning the execration forces back on them. At another point, he sinks a heathen's vineyard in the Nile through the force of his curse.[31]

To be sure, these images of saints combating native religion are all hagiographical reminiscences, and it is often difficult to extract historical kernels (that is, beyond the historical context of a festival encomium, a public reading on a saint's day and the crowd's attendant enthusiasm for narrative drama). Yet we can recognize elements of charismatic performance in these stories that probably did take place and, more importantly, that would have been widely recognizable forms of efficacious gesture in rural Egypt: public cursing, manipulation of binding spells, and calling one god down upon another.[32] That is to say, even if the saints' god and moral system were new to the landscape, the means of articulating the god's power through speech and gesture were part of familiar tradition, perhaps all the more so in the world of legend.

If the prophet and his competing local cults shared much in the way of handling supernatural power, then how radical in effect would the demonic polarization of those cults' gods have been? As holy men demonized these gods and engaged them in dramatic combat in the temples' very corridors, they in no way would have reduced them to mere idols but simply would have located them differently.[33] Even the declarations of monks recalled in some accounts of temple robbery that holy temple images were "idols" or "mere wood" can be seen as *illocutions*, ritual acts of verbal neutralization, rather than descriptions of the images' real cultural status.[34] Chased from shrine to image to priest to desert, the gods of the landscape may have been demonized and harrassed, but their powers were respected.

Scholars might once have viewed this kind of reordering and the violence to which it occasionally gave rise as a total shift in worldview, but there are many ways in which this kind of demonological reordering can actually preserve as-

31 Apollo: *Hist. mon.* 8.25–29; Shenoute. *v. Sin.* 84, 86.

32 See Frankfurter, "Curses, Blessings, and Ritual Authority"; and, more generally on reconstructing cultural details from hagiography, idem, "Hagiography and the Reconstruction."

33 See discussion of these battles in Brown, *Authority and the Sacred*, 3–26; Price, "Holy Man and Christianization," 217–18.

34 See, e.g., Socrates, *Hist. Eccl.* 5.16; Zachariah of Mitylene, *V. Severus*, in Kugener, "Sévère, patriarche d'Antioche," 28–30; with Frankfurter, "'Things Unbefitting Christians,'" 282–84. On *illocutions*—ritually contextual pronouncements meant to accomplish what is said via the utterance itself—see esp. Tambiah, "Magical Power of Words"; following ideas of Austin, *How to Do Things with Words*.

pects of tradition. We might draw such lessons from modern cases of Christian competition with traditional religions, in which the rhetoric of demonology is often much starker and consequent acts of purification sometimes quite violent. Anthropologists who have followed the course of such conflicts have found several related patterns: (1) traditional spirits tend to be preserved and respected, albeit in demonic guise; (2) Christian evangelism often polarizes a traditional class of spirits seen as *ambivalent or capricious* to God and Christ, turning those spirits uniformly dangerous—indeed, making them *evil* spirits, whose eradication can only be accomplished through Christian exorcism; and (3) the focus on demonic evil may not simply transvalue a traditional pantheon but, rather, raise to the cultural forefront more general anxieties about intimate subversion, like the threats posed by witches. In each case, the devotee's experience of the supernatural world is substantially altered, polarized, and rendered frightening. But the denizens of that world, and even their places and habits, remain potent; indeed, some older hostile spirits reemerge in more dangerous guise. The regional prophet or evangelist thus recognizes and *reorders* the traditional spirits according to a system that polarizes a diabolical pantheon against Christ; in this way, concerns about demonic affliction, which have often been exacerbated prior to missionary activity, become the chief idiom for expressing and experiencing Christian power.[35]

B. Exorcism and Charisma

If the impact of demonology is a reordering of spirits and fears, then what is its reciprocal effect on those who identify and project a coherent image of threatening evil? With a rich grasp of the environment and a wide range of strategies to accommodate misfortune, local cultures' recourse to demonology was not the main or most obvious route to making sense of affliction. Late antique folk did not *expect* holy men to exterminate the hostile spirits of the landscape, nor did holy men cast every misfortune brought to them as satanic in essence.[36] The discernment of demonic powers at work in village or family life and the dramatic claim of having vanquished these powers represented one possible discourse of charisma, along with healing, teaching, and the crafting of blessings. But it was a powerful discourse, bringing together popular familiarity with local spirits, popular frustration with an immediate calamity, and more subtle anxieties about su-

---

35 See esp. Meyer, "Beyond Syncretism"; idem, "Modernity and Enchantment"; and idem, *Translating the Devil*, esp. chs. 4, 6; Douglas, "Sorcery Accusations Unleashed"; Stirrat, *Power and Religiosity*, 89–91; Caplan, "Popular Culture of Evil." Cf. Roberts, "Lumpa Church of Alice Lenshina." On the invention of a new class of afflicting spirits, see Lewis, *Ecstatic Religion*, 116–18; with examples of subsequent demonological classifying in Hastings, "Emmanuel Milingo as Christian Healer," esp. 163, 166; MacGaffey, "Kimbanguism and the Question of Syncretism"; and, in Western urban context, Hunt, "Managing the Demonic." In general, see Frankfurter, *Evil Incarnate*, ch. 2.

36 Horden, "Responses to Possession and Insanity," esp. 184.

pernatural evil. Even in modern Africa, Jack Goody observed, "when any cult is heard of that gives hope of banishing witchcraft, or at least of modifying its effects, it is likely to receive a warm welcome, even though it is of foreign extraction and carries with it theological and conceptual aspects that do not altogether conform to local custom and belief, to the world view of the hosts."[37]

What such modern studies show us is the dialectic between a prophet's charisma and his or her ability to identify and eradicate some type of subversive evil.[38] The most important differences among these various modern cases, as well as among late antique Egyptian cases, revolve around the nature of the evil that the prophet identifies—witchcraft, sorcery, rival or heathen cult practices, or Satan and his demons. Other differences, like the demonic materials over which the prophet demonstrates control, like charms, idols, and books, often themselves reveal important patterns in prophetic dramaturgy. Shenoute of Atripe, for example, made a public point of carrying out the "idols" preserved by a local landowner to expose them, and even taking "idols" and "books of magic" from a nearby village back to his monastery, as if by so doing he could consolidate his own authority through the physical capture and subordination of the material of the religion he opposed, "from the 'Pan' that is (actually the god) Min ... [and] the book full of every (sort of) sorcery [ⲙⲁⲅⲓⲁ], even to their idols and all the many offerings to them, and the container full of bread beneath them as 'first-fruits' [ἀπαρχή], as well as the lamp-stand in front of (the idols)."[39] Across the various historical cases of witch-finders, exorcists, and Christianizing prophets, a distinct pattern can be seen in the acts of depicting evil and establishing the authority to expel it. And this pattern emerges particularly vividly when Christian demonology is the dominant discourse and heathenism the immediate realization of that discourse in the prophet's teaching.[40]

---

37 Goody, "Religion, Social Change," 96. Cf. Johnson on Nuer views of prophets' apotropaic capacity: "The suppression of magic is never complete, but whenever a prophet is active public anxiety about the threat of magic is reduced"; Johnson, *Nuer Prophets*, 155.

38 See, e.g., Roberts, "Lumpa Church of Alice Lenshina," 522–38; Redmayne, "Chikanga"; Willis, "Instant Millennium"; and Frankfurter, *Evil Incarnate*, ch. 3.

39 *Only I Tell Everyone Who Dwells in This Village*, in Leipoldt, *Sinuthii Archimandritae Vita*, 89, #26. Compare similar testimony in the sermon "Let Our Eyes," in which Shenoute enumerates the holy objects that he stole from the landowner's house and exposed in the streets of Atripe, including various images of gods and a ritual object connected with Nile rites, with the exorcistic exposure of "heathen" images described by Zachariah of Mytilene in Menouthis and Alexandria circa 484 ce; Emmel, "Shenoute of Atripe; Zachariah, v.Severi, in Kugener, "Sévère, patriarche d'Antioche," 27–35; Watts, *Riot in Alexandria*, 238–41. Similar acts have been performed by African prophets: Ngundeng (Nuer, late nineteenth century) demanded that sorcerers bury their power-objects in his mound in order to express his own power to establish peace (Johnson, *Nuer Prophets*, 96–98); while Alice Lenshina (Zambia, 1950s) demanded that church initiates hand over all amulets—protective and hostile—that they might possess: "Piles of these charms accumulated in a hut near Lenshina's house at Kasomo, testifying both to her success in extracting them and to her immunity from any malevolence which they might have contained"; Roberts, "Lumpa Church of Alice Lenshina," 530.

40 In general see Frankfurter, *Evil Incarnate*, ch.3. On the late antique demonization of tradi-

When we look more closely at this discourse as it emerges in the legends of Egyptian Christian holy men, we note above all a preoccupation with demonology and exorcism, born out of Christianity's scriptural inheritance but certainly shaped in culturally distinct ways.[41] We are, of course, somewhat hindered in reconstructing these holy men's demonological discourse by the broader agendas of their hagiographers. In his *Life of Antony*, for example, Athanasius emphasizes his hero's combat with demons to the point that it subsumes most other dramatic interactions. But Antony too seems to have addressed demonology in his own work, and two of his disciples, Pityrion and Paul the Simple, seem to have been regarded particularly as exorcists.[42] Indeed, enough holy men are picked out in the literature for their exorcistic powers that we can conclude that the regional reputations of many holy men arose from their abilities to define and combat demonic threats.[43] Wielding sand, oil, water, and scripture before families and terrified disciples, they had the unique ability in society to *identify* the signs of demonic affliction, *dramatize* the spirit's expulsion, and then *seal* the cure by securing pilgrims' allegiance to this new Christian order that could vanquish demons.[44] Tales of these prophets/holy men stress their regional reputations, illustrated by the lengths people were willing to travel to appeal to them. Occasionally, they made house calls, as when Posidonius came to the home of a mute pregnant woman to expel a demon. Other exorcisms, such as that of a sailor's child, only required sand from the proximity of Abraham of Farshut and the uttering of his name.[45]

Their authority in matters demonological led also to ritual innovations by holy men in the domains of cursing and protection. These innovations were syncretistic not in the simplistic sense of identifiable older religious traditions reasserted

---

tional local religion, see Ries, "Cultes païens et démons"; Flint, "Demonisation of Magic and Socrery"; and Frankfurter, "'Things Unbefitting Christians'." On the impact of Christian demonology on traditional witch-finding patterns in modern cultures, see Bourdillon, "Witchcraft and Society," 188–91; Meyer, "Beyond Syncretism"; Douglas, "Sorcery Accusations Unleashed"; MacGaffey, "Kimbanguism and the Question of Syncretism in Zaire." Stirrat has observed similar effects in a Christian exorcistic cult in Sri Lanka: Stirrat, *Power and Religiosity*, ch. 5.

41 On the importance of demonology in Egyptian monasticism, see Festugière, *Les moines d'Orient I*, ch. 1; Timbie, "Dualism and the Concept of Orthodoxy," 113–59; and Brakke, *Demons and the Making*, esp. 236–39 on exorcism, although note his caution (129) on the relationship between hagiographers' presentations of monks' demonological expertise and the late fourth-century influence of demonological manuals.

42 Antony's own demonology: see Rubenson, *Letters of St. Antony*, 86–88, 139–40, and esp. Antony's *Ep.* 6 (216–24). Pityrion: *Hist mon.* 15.1, in Paul the Simple: Palladius, *H.L.* 22.

43 See, e.g., the fragments of a hagiography for one Apa Herouoj that mention several exorcisms: Hedrick, "Monastic Exorcism Text."

44 Note the preponderance of protective spells among the Egyptian Christian "magical" corpora, most of which were issued by monks, monasteries, and saint shrines as a typically expected service: e.g., ACM 19–24, 26.

45 Posidonius: Palladius, *H.L.* 36.4–5; Abraham of Farshut: Amélineau, *Monuments pour servir*, 2:750; and Goehring, *Politics, Monasticism, and Miracles*, 97.

behind a Christian veneer but in the sense of charismatic powers performed in a publicly recognizable (or intentionally recognizable) form. In one text, an anonymous holy man reassures a supplicant, inscribing an ostracon with the words, "Know the manner in which God has hindered (the Devil). Don't be drawn away! Be in Peace. Amen."[46] In a contrasting vein, in a written spell of the sixth century, one Apa Victor offers incense and calls down the "curse of God" upon a woman and her family, perhaps on behalf of a client.[47]

Shenoute himself claims to have enacted a series of ritual curses against his nemesis Gesios, whom the abbot condemns for maintaining a cache of Egyptian devotional images in his house. In a sermon, Shenoute declares that "I took your gods secretly and because I caused your disgrace and shame, written on papyri, tied to the doorposts of your house, (and) your urine, which was in jars like wine, was smashed on the doorstep of your house and into your door and the door of those like you."[48] Whether these jars of urine were placed there deliberately for the use of local fullers or were intended to be purely metaphorical, referring to Gesios's wine (which Shenoute elsewhere deems "foul"), the act of smashing them was implicitly reminiscent of prophetic dramas in biblical legend and, we might imagine, locally recognizable as an Egyptian curse gesture.[49] More interesting is the abbot's use of inscribed condemnations on doorposts as a way of reifying and directing a curse, for this innovation turned Shenoute's own public utterances into physical instruments of his authority. And his written words of condemnation could indeed be wielded and redirected as material assaults. Fragments of an amphora excavated from a sixth- or seventh-century monk's cell in Thebes are inscribed with "a *logos* of Shenoute" that condemns "the ones who persist in their sins and their pollutions ... the *hellēns* and heretics" and calls to "the man of God [to] run away from the evils." Like the ostracon assuring its recipient of the Devil's defeat, the abbot's condemnation of religious deviants was here apparently treasured as an apotropaic force against evils of diverse sorts.[50]

Along with, and substantiating, such examples of exorcistic drama, there are also testimonies about the powers of discernment into the demonic world claimed by (or attributed to) the most powerful holy men.[51] Exorcists will often

---

46 O.Theb.IFAO 3, in Calament, "Varia Coptica Thebaica," 43.

47 ACM 104 = Michigan 3365.

48 Shenoute, Discourse 4: *Not Because a Fox Barks*, in Chassinat, *Le quatrième livre*, 39; for a translation, see Brakke and Crislip, *Selected Discourses of Shenoute*, 201; cf. Timbie, "Jesus and Shenoute," 3.

49 Robert Ritner discusses aggressive pot-breaking rites in pharaonic Egypt in *Mechanics of Ancient Egyptian Magical Practice*, 144–53. On the uses of urine for cleaning materials in Roman antiquity, see Flohr, "Uses and Value of Urine."

50 Hasznos, "A Shenoute Homily."

51 David Brakke makes the important point that, by the late fourth century, as evidenced in the works of Athanasius and Evagrius, the association of demonological discernment and the monastic endeavor had been systematized in widely read texts, and thus one cannot exclude the possibility that legends describing such discernment did not depend somehow on the influence of such texts;

claim a kind of clairvoyant capacity to perceive the demonic in the environment and to understand its ways. The hermit Aaron is remembered as knowing the voices and appearances of demons as well as the specific biblical verses that could expel them. Macarius was said to know of a class of demons called "fiery" that could afflict people through fevers. To be sure, much of this exorcistic wisdom arose around the problem of ascetics' own temptations, like Pityrion's classification of demons by human passion, Evagrius Ponticus's codification of the scripture verses known in the monastic world to repel various demons, and Shenoute's distinction between the Devil sui generis and the illusions through which he appeared to monks.[52] It may also reflect a concept of demonological categories from older apocalyptic traditions, as I will discuss in chapter 6: mortuary and hell demons, for example, came to be perceived diagnostically in the subjects of exorcism. But this esoteric wisdom—whether ascetic or apocalyptic—was regularly extended to the world at large, as we might infer from the numerous exorcistic spells in the Coptic magical corpus, which show a concerted effort to bring together apocryphal Christian lore and liturgical speech to resolve cases thought to be of demonic onslaught.[53] Exorcism and the powers that it assumed in the holy man became a central drama both in the performance of early Christian sainthood and in the realization of Christianity in the culture.

Thus, in their roles as discerners of demons and popular exorcists, Egyptian Christian holy men functioned as regional prophets, reordering supplicants' senses of religion—both practice and belief—in polarized terms: the demonic, evident in heathen cult and perennial misfortune, versus Christ and God as articulated through the gestures of the saint. This scheme preempted local devotions and centered both proper ritual and the definition of the supernatural world in the environs of the holy man. His charismatic authority worked in tandem with his projection of demonology.

"Prophet," as I have been using the term so far, represents a social type, generated out of ethnographic case studies to clarify the ostensibly contradictory relationship among regional charisma, ideological repudiation of certain religious traditions and places, and the definition of a demonic world from which the prophet offers deliverance. This is not Weber's ideal type of "prophet" (which he defined on the basis of various legendary religious founders in order to examine

---

Brakke, *Demons and the Making*, 127–29. My interest in this section, however, lies in the dialectic between public claims of demonological discernment and charisma, and this performative dialectic can take place with or without textual influence; see Frankfurter, *Evil Incarnate*, ch. 3.

52 Aaron: Paphnutius, *History of the Monks of Upper Egypt*, in Vivian, *Histories of the Monks*, 94–96. Macarius: Palladius, H.L. 17.12. Pityrion: *Hist.mon.* 15.2–3. Evagrius Ponticus, *Antirrheticus*, in Sinkewicz, *Evagrius of Pontus*, 73–90; cf. Brakke, *Demons and the Making*, ch. 3. On Shenoute's advice to monks on the Devil, see Van der Vliet, "Demons in Early Coptic Monasticism," 148–52; idem, "Chenouté et les démons"; and Brakke, *Demons and the Making*, ch. 5. On applications of demonology to ascetic struggles in general, see Valantasis, "Demons and the Perfecting"; Brakke, "Making of Monastic Demonology"; and idem, *Demons and the Making*.

53 See ACM 61–64, 70–71, 132, 134.8–11, 135.1–14.

issues of succession, routinization, and independence from priesthood), nor do I imply any intrinsic relationship to biblical prophets in observing that the late antique holy man was a kind of prophet. It is thus an illuminating coincidence that Shenoute (at least) came to regard himself in his sermons as a prophet in the biblical mold, and that this title and its supernatural senses were earnestly maintained in the legends of his acts compiled in the abbot's *Life*. "Prophet," as Shenoute embraced and cultivated it, pertained to the authenticity and authority of his visions, the clairvoyance he claimed regarding demonic activities as well as the lives of his monks, and his authority in delivering commandments and chastisements. It amounted to a claim "to know what God knows and to announce it to others."[54]

C. Demonology as Preservation

The very manifestations and habitats of demons—snakes, scorpions, crocodiles; in deserts and abandoned buildings—echoed much older classifications of the demonic in Egyptian tradition. Shenoute, for example, delivered an extended sermon on the Devil as a serpent, apprehensible in the beasts and delusions of the physical world.[55] To the extent that the perception of the demonic and its expulsion was a central performance of holy men, one that was critical to the development of their charisma, it is important to note their use of indigenous schemes of the liminal or dangerous to "place" the demons of the Christian cosmos. In this dimension, the Egyptian holy men were reconceptualizing traditional notions of demonic threat.[56]

The holy men regarded the old gods and their sanctuaries with both hate and awe, and certainly as potent forces in the landscape. As late as the fifth century, according to the *Life of Moses of Abydos*, the "demon" Bes was perceived as having the power to afflict Christian villagers from his ancient sanctuary in Abydos with all sorts of disasters, and in this account Moses only repels him after a terrifying night of curses and prayers in the company of seven other monks.[57] When the god Kothos demands child sacrifices, Macarius of Tkow and his monks incinerate his temple, returning it to a liminal, chaotic state, "with wild animals and serpents breeding in it."[58] In this way a deity representing central moral values in the vicin-

---

54 Brakke, "Shenoute, Weber, and the Monastic Prophet," 72; and idem, *Demons and the Making*, 100–24. See also, on the visionary tradition among Egyptian monks, Frankfurter, "Legacy of the Jewish Apocalypse," 170–85.

55 Du Bourguet, "Diatribe de Chenouté contre le Démon"; Frankfurter, *Elijah in Upper Egypt*, 138–39; Brakke, *Demons and the Making*, 104–10.

56 E.g., Palladius, *H.L.* 2.4 (Dorotheus); and Athanasius, *v.Ant.* 9, 12. In general, see Keimer, "L'horreur des égyptiens"; and Aufrère, "L'Égypte traditionnelle." See also further in sec. III of this chapter.

57 *V. Mosis* (Codex EL 111–12: K9555), in Till, *Koptische Heiligen- und Martyrerlegenden*, 2:52; translated in Moussa, "Coptic Literary Dossier."

58 *Panegyric on Macarius* 5.9, in Johnson, *Panegyric on Macarius*, 1:36–37.

ity or a local jinn with beneficial powers would be transvalued as a hostile spirit peripheral to the Christian system, and subsequently the deity's "place" came to be perceived as actively dangerous—the antithesis of human habitation.

The syncretistic potential of the holy man's radical demonologizing extended well beyond such iconoclastic episodes as well. For example, across the various stories and incidents of demonically transvalued local gods, the winning god of the Christian pantheon, *P-Noute*, maintained the old Egyptian word for "divinity," *ntr*. However, the same Egyptian word in plural (*ntr.w*) seems to have been used to denote a kind of demon, the *entēr* spirit: "Let NN become safe ... and his flesh become safe from all magic of people and all attacks of the demons of the day and the night, *whether fates* [ⲙⲉⲣⲣⲁ;, from Grk *moira*] *or gods* [ⲛⲟⲏⲣ from Middle Egyptian *ntr*]."[59] Thus even in the very vocabulary of replacement we find, in fact, *reordering*. The traditional pantheon and its variously central, amoral, capricious, and guardian spirits ultimately fell under the aegis of the newly ascendant *P-Noute*, his divine companions, and their primary mediators, the saints.[60]

Such demonization of local spirits could still make room for their beneficial powers, even in "satanic" guise. Coptic ritual manuals occasionally invoke demons in their negative sense—Tartarouchos, Mastema, Theumatha, Bersebour—but as available, even familiar, spirits rather than as princes of evil.[61] The preservation of indigenous spirits in the guise of helpful devils (or the invocation of devils as familiar ancestral figures) was a frequent form of syncretism in early modern cultures under Christianization, reflecting people's tendency to seek out alternative, familiar spiritual powers *apart from* Christ and the saints but *within* the framework imposed by evangelists. The revaluation of demons in this way followed from the radical polarization of Christian and indigenous supernatural domains, as a "folk" means of preserving the value and relevance of the demonized despite its maleficent appearance—a process of depolarizing the imposed pantheon of spirits.[62]

All these images of a demonic world—whether the still-potent old gods, the reaffirmed old demons, the persisting religious practices, or danger in some broader sense—ultimately stemmed from the prophetic activities and imagination of the holy man himself. In recognizing demons in all these aspects of culture (or in specializing in some class of demons), he substantiated his own dramatic

---

59 P. Heid. Inv. Kopt. 685, 4.18–25, in Meyer, *Magical Book of Mary*, 14–15. Cf. Rossi Tractate §19, in Kropp, *Ausgewählte koptische Zaubertexte*, 1:77; Meyer, *Rossi's "Gnostic" Tractate*, 26; with discussion in Erman, "Heidnisches bei den Kopten," 47–48; and Crum, *Coptic Dictionary*, 230b.

60 See esp. Aufrère, "L'Égypte traditionnelle," 77–83. On the reordering of indigenous religion to emphasize previously otiose high gods, see Horton, "African Conversion"; and Goody, "Religion, Social Change," 102–3. Cf. Meyer, *Translating the Devil*, 109–11, for adjustments to Horton's thesis.

61 ACM ##74 (Yale 1791), 75 (Berlin 8314), 78 (London Hay 10376), 79 (London Hay 10414). See Frankfurter, "Demon Invocations."

62 See Frankfurter, "Demon Invocations," 460–61; with useful comparative illumination in Sánchez Ortega, "Sorcery and Eroticism in Love Magic"; and Cervantes, *Devil in the New World*, 46–53.

ritual assertions of healing power, of power to clear away misfortune, and articulated deep cultural concerns about subversion, both supernatural and social. In dispelling demons, he demonstrated the apotropaic force of the new Christian order. "The saints," proclaims Shenoute in one text, "have recognized [Satan] even in the atmosphere, and they have instructed us that he is beneath the heavens, so that we might fight against him." Ancient apocalyptic tradition had taught that the atmosphere veritably seethed with demons, bent on restraining the ascent of the righteous and seducing everyone else away from piety, but only holy men like Antony and Shenoute were granted full discernment into their activities. Here the broad scriptural (or, in this case, apocryphal) inheritance of Christianity offered an ideological framework for the prophet's discernment of demons.[63]

Yet the claims of discernment and the overall synthesis of local needs and new religious order by Egyptian Christian holy men did not follow simply from that ideology (or from the hagiographers' imagination) but rather came about in performance itself: that is, the historical activities of real figures in a landscape of familiar and unknown powers, recognizing spirits that others could not, expelling them with ritual expertise and innovation, and announcing the spirits' ways and natures to devotees. The very image of Satan, demons, and Christian exorcism, insofar as they contributed to Egyptian people's interest in Christianity, revolved around the clairvoyance and technique of the holy man.[64] He was both interpreter of a new religious order and example of it. And in this way syncretism occurred through his very roles as regional prophet, opponent of heathen institutions and capricious spirits, reorganizer of the divine landscape, and emblem of purification.

Yet the habitus of Egyptian ritual culture—the traditions of religious orientation, gesture, and thaumaturgy—also emerged in the very acts of, and toward, holy men. Gesture and performance served as a kind of language for understanding or mediating sacred power. In the next section we look at syncretism as it affected the performance and definition of sainthood in its most concrete, embodied sense.

IV. HOLY MEN IN THE EGYPTIAN LANDSCAPE

A. Divination and the Definition of New Centers

Perhaps the most vivid way that holy men revitalized and redefined basic ritual functions in the culture was in the role of oracle. In Egypt and numerous premod-

---

63 Shenoute, *De certamine contra diabolum* = "Discourses 4: A Beloved Asked Me Years Ago," in Koschorke, Timm, and Wisse, "Schenute: De certamine contra diabolum," 70; translation, Brakke and Crislip, *Selected Discourses of Shenoute*, 180. On demons in the air, discernible by holy men in particular, see Athanasius, *v.Ant.* 65; and Daniélou, "Les démons de l'air."

64 See in general Van der Vliet, "Demons in Early Coptic Monasticism," 147–48; and Brakke, *Demons and the Making*.

CHAPTER 3

ern societies, divination allowed a religious system to show its authority and everyday relevance through the definition of a ritual "palette" of symbols through which a god might speak. Classically, divination involved a random context or set of materials—the palette—consisting of anything from birds in flight to star formations, to a heavy image held by eight priests in procession, or even an untrained individual in ecstasy. By setting in motion an event or spontaneous arrangement of the materials of this palette, a message pertaining to the most basic social or political issues (the fate of a ruler, the imminence of invasion), ecological events (the year's Nile surge), or everyday crises (where shall I sell my pottery?) could be detected (often, historically, through the expertise of certain priests). This message and—as we will see in chapter 4—the religious center where it was sought and interpreted cumulatively assured witnesses of a god's broader control of life and the cosmos.[65]

As basic as oracles were to the function of Egyptian temples in society, so Christian holy men as early as the fourth century were recalled and celebrated for their mantic authority as new oracles: John of Lycopolis is celebrated in the *Historia monachorum* for his gift of prophecy in predicting political events in the empire; Athanasius juxtaposes the Egyptian oracle and Antony's various clairvoyant gifts.[66] Shenoute, celebrated in hagiography for his prophetic knowledge of the Nile's surge, also was remembered as employing a rather esoteric mantic technique, gazing into a bowl of water, to contact the Virgin Mary.[67] Moses of Abydos was recalled as knowing "in spirit" that the nomadic Blemmyes were about to attack the city of Antinoë and urging the *Dux* of the region to set up defenses. Thus "people were amazed at [Apa Moses's] prescience which had been realized and the way in which God reveals things to come to his saints."[68]

But while it has become a commonplace to view the rise of the holy man as a shift in the locus of oracles from place to person, it is worth considering how "prophecy" may have itself represented a dramatic role for saints in Egyptian society—a habitus or cultural behavior that informed both visitors' expectations and saints' performative repertoires.[69] When a woman wrote to the sixth-century hermit Pisentius to let her know whether or not God intended to cure her

---

65 Frankfurter, *Religion in Roman Egypt*, ch. 4; and idem, "Voices, Books, and Dreams."

66 John of Lycopolis: *Hist. mon.* 1.1, 11; cf. Palladius, *H.L.* 35; and, on the reach and authority of John's interventions, Zuckerman, "Hapless Recruit Psois." Antony: Athanasius, *v.Ant.* 34, 62, 87–88; cf. 31–32 on Nile divination.

67 Besa [attrib.], *v. Sin.* 150. The technique is commonly indicated in Greek and Demotic ritual manuals from the third/fourth centuries: PGM IV.221–43; LXII.43–46; PDM xiv, 395–427, 528–53.

68 *V.Mosis* 129, in Uljas, "IFAO Leaves of the Life," 397, trans. 413. "Prescience": literally "knowledge [ⲥⲟⲟⲩⲛ]."

69 On the holy man as new oracle, see Frankfurter, *Religion in Roman Egypt*, 184–93; cf. Brown, "Rise and Function of the Holy Man," 132–34; and Dunand, "Miracles et guérisons en Égypte tardive," 243–46.

eyes, she did so on the assumption that he could function as such a mediator of divine knowledge.⁷⁰

Other monks entered the oracular role almost as a consequence of their pedagogical charisma, as if all public expressions of religious expertise somehow had to be translated or extended into divination. An anonymous fourth-century monk living outside the Arsinoite village of Boushem, for example, promulgated a radical lay celibacy associated with one Hieracas and apparently had some success in convincing people to break up their marriages to achieve holiness before the bishop called in Macarius the Great to oppose him.⁷¹ Early sources describe this monk of Boushem as having particular authority as a prophet-diviner of great renown:

> He would tell people about numerous events that were going to happen to them: he would say "they will happen," and they happened, and he spoke about the waters of the Nile and about many other worldly events that he learned about from the spirits.
>
> ...
>
> Indeed, they believed in him because he said that the Spirit had entrusted them to him, telling people events that had not yet taken place and they would take place. In a word, he controlled them through these predictions. Indeed, if all the people's possessions were lost, he would say to them, "Go to a certain place and you will find them," and they would go and find them. He would also tell them when war was going to take place and how many people were going to die and it happened just as he had said.⁷²

In issuing oracles on such traditional concerns, these prophets were both revitalizing Egyptian views of public divination and defining the authority of the Christian "pantheon" to pronounce on these matters. Both the fourth-century desert hermit Aaron and Shenoute were credited with powers to predict and control the Nile's inundations much like the monk of Boushem, but they did so as mediators of Christianity, insinuating the power of scripture, angels, and the Christian God into an agricultural cycle long regarded in mythic terms.⁷³

---

70 Crum, "Theban Hermits and Their Life," 164 (ST 360).

71 PG 34:207–16 and Coptic version of Palladius, *H.L.* 17, in Chaîne, "La double recension"; Vivian, "Coptic Palladiana III"; Brakke, *Athanasius and Asceticism*, 51; Goehring, *Ascetics, Society, and the Desert*, 125–30.

72 Chaîne, "La double recension," 245–46; Vivian, "Coptic Palladiana III," 96–97. Despite the fact that this account is missing from the Greek Palladius, I would suggest that the details of the monk's prophecy are early and were gradually subsumed in the theological dispute over Hieracas that dominates the Greek Macarius text; PG 34:209–12. Prophecy of this sort has nothing to do with Hieracite teaching and cannot be attributed to literary typology.

73 Paphnutius, *Histories of the Monks of Upper Egypt*, in Vivian, *Histories of the Monks*, 131–35; Besa [attrib.], *v. Sin.* 102–5, 122. On monks' control of the Nile, see Frankfurter, *Religion in Roman*

B. Ritual and the Egyptian Environment

Divination and "prophecy" involved a particularly dramatic use of native ritual forms and assumptions to establish the authority of the new Christian pantheon. But the holy man's concerted attention to the typical crises and tensions of peasant (and often urban) culture allowed even simpler forms of syncretism to take place. In his authority over village disputes and protectorship of the region, the holy man demonstrated the application of Christianity to mundane social realities.[74] In turn, his acts and his ideological claims were interpreted according to culturally inscribed notions of ritual expertise, as we saw earlier with the letters of request for blessings. It is nothing new to observe that cultures tend to classify new forms of religious leadership according to indigenous models, especially in regard to thaumaturgy.[75] Egyptian holy men seem likewise to have been understood in relationship to a range of models of ritual expertise, from temple shrines to regional patrons and itinerant priests. They further aided this association by attending to precisely the *kinds* of crises that the older shrines had traditionally addressed: divination, agriculture, health and procreation, and protection.

The female prophet-saint Piamoun, for example, was specifically hailed in her village for resolving an irrigation dispute during the Nile's inundation and for protecting her village from marauders. The prophet Apollo was also remembered for resolving agricultural boundary disputes through the use of divine power as much as through advice. Pior brought water to a well whose excavators had despaired of finding any, and both Patermuthius and Abraham of Farshut directed their holy powers against worms infesting the crops, restoring fertility after periods of famine. Aaron dispensed holy substances to ensure good vineyard production and a fishing harvest. Macedonius was remembered for healing a camel's leg with water, invocation, and gesture. Holy men in these ways can be seen to have functioned within a world of specific misfortunes and needs intimately connected to the Egyptian landscape and the livelihoods it offered. The Christianity apparent in their acts and legends thus served as a new configuration of power for the resolution of ancient and perennial crises.[76]

The saints' assimilation to their environments emerges even more vividly in their protective capacity to repel and control the various fauna once regarded as

---

Egypt, 45–46; cf. the monastic almanac oracles discussed by Wilfong, "Agriculture among the Christian Population."

74 Cf. Kaplan, *Monastic Holy Man*, 74–75.

75 See Perrone, "Monasticism as a Factor," 74–75. The same phenomenon has been observed in modern Africa: see Schoffeleers, "Christ in African Folk Theology."

76 Piamoun: Palladius, H.L. 31. Apollo: *Hist. mon.* 8.30, 36. Pior: Palladius, H.L. 39.4–5. Patermuthius: *Hist. mon.* 10.26–29. Abraham of Farshut: Coptic synaxarium, 24 Toubeh, in Basset, *Le Synaxaire arabe jacobite III*, 688. Aaron: Paphnutius, *Histories of the Monks of Upper Egypt*, in Vivian, *Histories of the Monks*, 118–22. Macedonius: ibid., 44–47, cf. 117. The foundations for this argument lie in Brown, "Rise and Function of the Holy Man," 121–29, 150–51.

"Sethian," that is, demonic in an archaic Egyptian sense: crocodiles, serpents, hippopotami, scorpions, and even antelopes. Even in the early Roman period one could find these animals clustered in apotropaic designs on tablets, either set up by temples or for domestic use; temple festivals might also celebrate the god's victory over chaos with priestly curses and the incineration of images.[77] These animals were certainly taken very seriously as threats throughout late antiquity: "If you see an asp and want to fix it in its place," instructs a recipe in a third- or fourth-century ritual manual, "say while turning around: 'Stay!' When the names are said it will stay."[78] Indeed, scorpions and snakes in particular served as the very image of the demonic—or even of the Devil himself, as monks came to believe. Amoun is said to have burst a giant serpent harrassing local villagers by invoking Christ and Leviathan. In his sermon on the Devil, Shenoute tries to diminish the supernatural threat his disciples perceived in snakes. The holy man Bes was said to use special commands and curses to drive off a rampaging hippopotamus and a crocodile.[79]

But other stories use these dangerous beasts—symbolic opponents of human civilization—as examples of the saints' power to tame hostile powers rather than eradicate them. When a crocodile grabs a peasant in front of John the Little, he calls down an angel to bind it and make it carry the man back to shore, after which the beast expires. But then the holy man prays for the crocodile's soul:

> Immediately the crocodile arose, alive; he went and made obeisance [ⲁⲫⲡⲣⲟⲥⲕⲩⲛⲓ] at the feet of Saint Abba John, and he slept at the feet of the holy one like a sheep and would not leave his side, traveling in the water beside the boat until it came into port in Alexandria, and Abba John would each day throw it three loaves of bread all the days that it followed him.[80]

So also in another story, when a giant crocodile grabs a little boy, Aaron gives the distraught father a piece of wood to throw into the Nile right where his son was taken. The crocodile appears, delivers the son unharmed, and swims away.

---

77 Apotropaic "Horus-*cippi*" in Roman period: see Sternberg-El Hotabi, *Untersuchungen zur Überlieferungsgeschichte der Horusstelen*, 1:159–70. See the beginning of ch. 5 for a stela in Dumbarton Oaks that inherited some of these traditional iconographic strategies. Ancient fears of these animals are evident in the rituals preserved in pharaonic Egypt for their repulsion: see Borghouts, *Ancient Egyptian Magical Texts*; Wilson, "Slaughtering the Crocodile"; and in general Keimer, "L'horreur des égyptiens"; and Frankfurter, *Religion in Roman Egypt*, 46–52.

78 PGM XIII.249–50, trans. *GMPT*, 179 (emended).

79 Amoun: *Hist. mon.* 9; Shenoute, *Diatribe Against the Devil* 12.35–13.9, in du Bourguet, "Diatribe de Chenouté," 32; Van der Vliet, "Chenouté et les démons"; Frankfurter, *Elijah in Upper Egypt*, 138–39. Pisentius also was said to have encountered a dragon: Amélineau, *Étude sur le christianisme*, 135–36; Budge, *Coptic Apocrypha*, 122. On the importance of apotropeia against harmful fauna in the Roman/Byzantine period, see PGM VII.149–54, 193–96, 370–73; XXVIIIa-c; ACM 25, 68; and Papaconstantinou, *Le culte des saints en Égypte*, 345.

80 *Life of John the Little*, Sahidic fragment 1, in Mikhail and Vivian, "Life of Saint John the Little," 60–62.

The prophet Helle, it was said, summoned an enormous crocodile "that had devoured many people" to ferry him back and forth across the Nile. Then, according to one text, "While [a priest] and the brothers who lived on the other bank watched, seized with dread, he crossed the ford with the beast, came ashore, and hauling the beast out of the water, said to it 'It is better for you to die and make restitution for all the lives you have taken.' Whereupon the animal at once sank onto its belly and died."[81] The deceased martyrs Eulogia and Arsenius, in contrast, send a crocodile to eat a shepherd who has misbehaved in their martyrion.[82] The crocodile in both cases signifies an aspect of the saints' taming powers—their status as masters of dangerous fauna, much like the crocodiles on which the god Harpocrates is represented standing in the magical reliefs that stood in temples and homes throughout the Roman period.[83] Indeed, just as the naked Harpocrates grasps antelopes in these reliefs to show his power over beasts of the desert, so the monk Paphnutius beholds the spectacle of a brother monk walking among a herd of antelope as if their master. And when they came near, Paphnutius recalls, he saw that the monk, Timothy, was "naked and his hair covered his shame and served as clothing over him."[84]

These legends of anchorites' intimacy with wild and dangerous beasts certainly participated in a broader literary theme whereby the monks were imagined as semibestial denizens of the periphery, much as ancient authors had depicted the inhabitants of the outer reaches of the known world.[85] But each legend also shows a familiarity with the Egyptian landscape and the particularities of its dangerous fauna. Arising for the most part in local contexts rather than from the perspective of the distanced ethnographer, they indicate the materials out of which local cultures constructed the charisma and thaumaturgical powers of saints.

C. Syncretism and the Dispensing of Materials

The stories that I have been discussing illustrate popular conceptions of holy men and what they could have meant as prophets, out there in the landscape. To take seriously the local idioms through which these figures constructed their charisma requires an openness to some models of cultural continuity with paradigms for articulating divinity from earlier centuries.[86] Thus I want finally to shift from

---

81 Aaron: Paphnutius, *Histories of the Monks*, in Vivian, *Histories of the Monks*, 98–99. Helle: *Hist. mon.* 12.9, in Russell, *Lives of the Desert Fathers*, 91.

82 Coptic synaxarium: 16 Kihak, in Basset, *Le Synaxaire arabe jacobite II*, 394.

83 See Mayeur-Jaouen, "Crocodiles et saints du Nil," in a very convincing application of Quaegebeur, "Divinités égyptiennes sur des animaux dangereux."

84 Paphnutius, *Life of Onnophrius* 3, in Vivian, *Histories of the Monks*, 146.

85 Merrills, "Monks, Monsters, and Barbarians."

86 See esp. Dunand, "Miracles et guérisons en Égypte tardive," 238–43; Quaegebeur, "Les saints égyptiens préchrétiens"; Cannuyer, "Saint Mina aux chameaux."

miracle legends to the material mediation of charisma: What did agents of the domestic sphere seek from holy men? How did they extend their concerns for protection, procreation, and general fortune? And how did holy men themselves construct material tokens of their prophetic powers?

The most basic "rituals of center" that brought saints together with devotees, of course, involved the fashioning of "blessings," or *eulogia* [Copt. ⲥⲙⲟⲩ], for the enduring benefit of each supplicant. In supplicants' letters to holy men asking them to resolve crises in the domestic sphere, we can begin to see, from the inside, how these charismatic figures were imagined as purveyors of fortune as well as innovators of a new religious system.[87] A letter to an unknown holy man in the Bawit monastery (dated to the sixth to eighth centuries CE) beseeches him "to guard for me the house (as) divinely preserved."[88] A letter from the same period from the nun Maria appeals to the holy man Abba Kyriakos to "send your blessing to me that I may place it in my home and it may be for me a beautiful fragrance of my soul and I may see it in my house and it may urge me toward the good." Maria seeks Kyriakos's material token, an extension of his charisma, to serve on (or as) a domestic shrine, and her words show how such a shrine could have served as a theater in miniature for the combining of holy things.[89] In another letter from about the same time, one Esther appeals to a holy man in the vicinity of the Epiphanius monastery in Thebes "to instruct me.... I bear my children.... They die. Perhaps (I) do something unfitting. Be so kind as to send a rule [*entolē*] whereby I may walk." Here it is not a physical token but a discipline, a new domestic habitus, that she envisions as the blessing she could receive (although the rule would doubtless have come in material, written form and served as a guarantee of the monk's protection).[90]

The ritual relationship with holy men and the institution they represented produced new media in the economy of gaining blessings. And these relationships could also involve the mediation of scribes, who both wrote and helped word these letters for supplicants, a process that itself produced new ways of articulating misfortune. For example, in her appeal to the holy man Apa Pson, a woman named Eudoxia must have been coached to attribute her illness not to demonic affliction but to her many sins and iniquities: "Have pity, then, and entreat God for me, that I may cease from this scourge that is upon me ... for it is you who entreat [God] on behalf of the whole world."[91]

Such letters would have supplemented or even replaced visits to the holy man in person (which, when involving women, seem occasionally to have been re-

---

87 Cf. also Kotsifou, "Monks as Mediators in Christian Egypt," on appeals to holy men that range into the area of legal intervention.
88 P. Brux. Inv. E.9416, in Delattre, *Papyrus coptes et grecs*, #36, 261–64.
89 O.B.M. copt. Add. 23, in Bagnall and Cribiore, *Women's Letters from Ancient Egypt*, 200, #A14.2.
90 O. Mon. Epiph. 194, in ibid., 247, #A20.5.
91 O. Mon. Epiph. 199, in ibid., 248, #A20.6.

fused as inviting temptation).⁹² The fourth-century Valeria, appealing to the monk Paphnouthis in the vicinity of Herakleopolis to heal her from "a great disease of terrible shortness of breath," explains that "even if in body I have not come to your feet, in the spirit I have come to your feet." She then appeals to ritual acts that he might conduct separately on her behalf: "I have believed and believe that if you pray on my behalf I will receive healing."⁹³ And farther afield, in Gaul, as recorded in the *Lives* of the sixth-century Jura Fathers, the holy man Eugendus sends one devotee, a demon-afflicted woman, a letter (*scripturum*) with an exorcistic incantation to evacuate the demon; to another woman, gravely ill, he sends a letter with healing invocations, which "she put ... in her mouth for awhile, gripping it with her teeth while praying."⁹⁴

Such letters give a sense of supplicants' conceptions of holy men from afar and the role writing played in mediating these conceptions, with scribes even correcting supplicants' assumptions and demands according to their sense of orthodoxy or proper wording. But the letters less often reflect the personal, gestural interactions of supplicant and holy man—interactions mediated not by scribes but by the material "blessings" exchanged. In the complaint that opened this chapter, for example, Abbot Shenoute lists a number of material tokens of charisma that holy men in his area had dispensed: not only consecrated oil but "the snake's head tied on someone's hand, another one with the crocodile's tooth tied to his arm, and another with fox claws tied to his legs," about which the high-ranking bearer declares, " 'It was a great monk who gave them to me, saying 'Tie them on you (and) you will find relief.' "⁹⁵

Shenoute's complaint about popular encounters with saints fills some gaps found in the numerous stories from hagiography about the various blessings that holy men would offer. Shenoute himself was said in legend to have given a military official his belt as a war-charm for repelling barbarians.⁹⁶ The author of the *Historia monachorum* recounts watching local peasants collect sand from the vicinity of the Patermuthius monastery to be consecrated by the monks there as a blessing for the fertility of their fields.⁹⁷ Likewise the hermit Aaron customarily distributed sand and water over which he had pronounced holy words for healing, protection, and fertility; if he did not, his visitors would simply take it for themselves:

> [T]he father of the child [took] a little earth from beside the door of Abba Aaron's home and tied it up in his neckerchief. And when they came into the house they found a large crowd of people gathered together and the

---

92 On monks' wariness of women as forms of the demonic, see Brakke, *Demons and the Making*, 199–205.
93 P. London 6. 1926, in. Bagnall and Cribiore, *Women's Letters from Ancient Egypt*, 205, #A14.10.
94 *V. Eugendi* 143–46, in Vivian, Vivian, and Russell, *Lives of the Jura Fathers*, 168–69.
95 Shenoute, Acephalous Work A14, §§255–59, in Orlandi, *Shenute*, 18–20.
96 *V. Sin.* 106–8.
97 *His. mon.* 10.26–29.

man's wife and her child. The child's father uncovered the little bit of earth tied up in his neckerchief and sprinkled it upon the dead child. Immediately he moved his body and opened his eyes. Those who were sitting beside the mother were astounded and they glorified the God of the holy man Abba Aaron. Now the people used to bring large numbers of the sick and diseased to Abba Aaron and he would heal them. He was like the apostles to whom God gave power over every kind of sickness.[98]

Should these gestures and performative expressions on the part of holy men and their visitors be considered syncretistic? In many ways these uses of dust, water, and other substances contiguous with the saint or holy site are simply examples of the principle of "holy contagion," the laws of sympathy that James Frazer imputed to a magical worldview, and certainly cannot be seen as distinctive of Egypt.[99] "A bit of dust from the church [of St. Martin] is more powerful than" all the local ritual experts, asserts Gregory of Tours in a much later miracle collection awash with sacred fluids and objects.[100] Early Christianization proceeded especially by means of thaumaturgical performances and claims, with such substances as *hnana*, the oil/dust mixture that Syrian saints dispensed, acting as international vehicles of thaumaturgy. These material vehicles of saints' charisma served as an important form of relic and aided the definition of new centers in the landscape. They became one principal way that Christianity, broadly defined, entered and influenced the domestic sphere.[101]

Yet to restrict the concept of syncretism to historically identifiable religious ideas or culturally unique phenomena rather than the established gestures and expressions that mediated people's relationships to new centers may repeat the problems of older "pagan survivals" research: as I described in chapter 1, that romantic search for timeless "national" symbols that are inevitably taken out of cultural context. As we get a better sense of how local cultures integrated new pantheons, new configurations of sacred authority, and modernity itself, we should be especially attentive to the forms through which power was acquired from shrines and taken into everyday life, as well as to the forms by which innovative ritual experts might themselves have transmitted authority and power into devotees' everyday lives. Religion, and especially conceptions of efficacious power in the world, had always involved materiality more than abstract beliefs: sand and water, oil and stones; and in many ways (as I will explore in the afterword) Christianity itself amounted to a cluster of strategies for the use of such

   98 Paphnutius, *Histories of the Monks of Upper Egypt*, in Vivian, *Histories of the Monks*, 125, 98–136.

   99 See, e.g., Vikan, "Art, Medicine, and Magic." Magical "laws" of sympathy: Frazer, *Golden Bough*, ch. 3, §3; cf. van der Leeuw, *Religion in Essence and Manifestation*, ch. 3.

   100 Gregory of Tours, *Life and Miracles of St. Martin*, 1.27, in Van Dam, *Saints and Their Miracles*, 220.

   101 The thaumaturgical basis of early Christianization is advanced in MacMullen, *Christianizing the Roman Empire*; and Flint, *Rise of Magic*.

CHAPTER 3

material vehicles. In the anonymous complaint about popular practices that we saw in chapter 2, for example, it is clear that people were seeking out waters and oils from specific sites in the environment, as well as specific people who could make amulets, all as vehicles of ritual power.[102] Such testimonies and stories show that, in the fifth and sixth centuries (as earlier) ordinary people had a repertoire of ritual procedures and "maps" that they used for the acquisition of power and protection in the landscape. Most importantly, this repertoire of ritual expressions informed both attitudes toward saints and saints' attitudes toward supplicants.[103] Indeed, it is precisely on the basis of this repertoire that we see the innovation, the bricolage, that defined syncretism on both sides—the agency of the domestic sphere, as I explored it in chapter 2, and the agency of the holy man as bricoleur of materials.

Thus a letter from the sixth or seventh century seeks "a little water of the feet of the holy men and a little blessing of our father.... Give them to Pamoute and he will bring them and they will be a healing to me."[104] Another text depicts one supplicant's realization that the bloody phlegm of the consumptive hermit Apollo might carry the power to heal his own illness: "At once when it had dropped upon the ground, the sick man took it in perfect hope and swallowed it. And suddenly the grace of faith became the healing of the believer through that holy spittle [ⲡⲧⲉϥ ... ⲉⲧⲟⲩⲁⲁⲃ]."[105] In chapter 2 we saw the legend of the two ill women who sought a healing blessing from Apa Pisentius. According to the more able woman, when he ran off, she collected

> "the sand that had been under his right foot, and I raised it on top of my head, and by the grace of God, I had relief from my illness." And the [sicker] woman through her great faith said, "Give me also a little of that sand." She took it; she swallowed some of it; it entered her organs; and then her belly ceased from swelling, and her whole body was healed. And they gathered up the [rest of the] sand into their houses, and kept it as a blessing for them.[106]

Thus a holy man, by the late fourth century a fixture in the cultural landscape, served primarily as a transmitter of blessings. One could make demands on him: "Send me a seal [ⲟⲩ[ⲥ]ⲫⲣⲁⲅⲓⲥ] for my children," Koletjew closes her letter to the monk Epiphanius, expecting that the "seal" would arrive in material form.[107] At

---

102 Pseudo-Athanasius, *Homily on the Virgin*, 92, 95, in Lefort, "L'Homélie de S. Athanase," 35–36.

103 See Brown, "Rise and Function of the Holy Man," 150–51; idem, *Authority and the Sacred*, 63. The seventh-century monk Frange, for example, seems to have had some expertise in the healing properties of pepper and an aromatic herb: see Boud'hors and Heurtel, *Les ostraca coptes*, #101.

104 P. Mich. Copt. 8, 15–18, in Worrell, *Coptic Texts*, 189–90.

105 Stephen of Heracleopolis Magna, *Panegyric on Apollo, Archimandrite of the Monastery of Isaac*, in Kühn, *Panegyric on Apollo*, 35.

106 *Life of Pisentius* (Bohairic version), in Amélineau, *Étude sur le christianisme*, 87–88.

107 Ostr. 336, in Crum and Evelyn-White, *Monastery of Epiphanius at Thebes*, 84, 242; see also the discussion in Crum and Winlock, *Monastery of Epiphanius at Thebes*, 164.

the same time, whatever their personal ascetic intentions, holy men acquiesced readily and creatively to the roles that supplicants defined for them. As one text records: "Before he died [Apollo] bade them bring water to him. He washed his face, his hands and his feet. He told them to pour it into the little cistern on the south side. O how many healings came to pass in that water which had received blessing!"[108] Likewise, the Coptic *Synaxarium* describes Joseph of Coptos discovering—at God's behest—a pitcher of oil that he could bless and leave in his monastery for supplicants to use for healing.[109] These are, to be sure, etiological legends for the reservoirs of holy water and oil kept in monasteries for popular use and to keep present the memories of their heroes, yet it is likely (given other witnesses) that they also reflect the holy men's own creative bequests to keep their "blessings" alive after their death.

Holy men's creativity extended well beyond water, sand, and oil, as we saw in Shenoute's complaint about amulets made of animal parts. The very written words of monks also carried the force of powerful charms: "Give what I have written [т]ι... ⲛⲧⲁⲓⲥϩⲁⲩ] to the one split in herself," instructs an anonymous holy man under two lines of magical names, apparently to aid some obstetrical crisis, while Shenoute's own written words of condemnation, we saw earlier, carried the force of curses or apotropaic charms.[110] One expects that the early seventh-century monk Frange fulfilled a brother's request that he "write (a blessing on) a large stone chip and send it to me to place before the animals," for in another letter he recommends that the recipient "put this cord on your mare and attach to it the blessings around the neck, so that the Lord blesses and protects her." Here too the blessings are a material thing, a written sign or passage of scripture that Frange has produced.[111]

To some extent the miraculous power of the holy man's writings participated in a wider "cult of the charismatic letter," epitomized in the apocryphal letter of Jesus that promised healing to King Abgar of Syria, a text copied for amuletic purposes throughout the late antique world (and especially in Egypt).[112] By the fifth century the charismatic letter constituted one of a number of traditional media that holy men were expected to provide. The *Bohairic Life of Maximus and Domitius* tells of a dragon that was terrorizing the far-off city of Iconium. When people approached Maximus for help, he wrote a letter: "In the name of the Lord Sabaoth, God of Abba Macarius and of our father Abba Agabus, men who bear Christ the Word of God, if someone carries this brief letter to your lair, you, serpent, come out with your mouth closed and go to sleep in the middle of the road

---

108 Stephen, *Panegyric on Apollo* 20, in Kühn, *Panegyric on Apollo*, 37 (translation 28).
109 Coptic synaxarium: 13 Hatour, in Basset, *Le Synaxaire arabe jacobite II*, 209.
110 Pregnancy spell: Coll. Moen inv. #107, in Sijpesteijn, "Coptic Magical Amulet."
111 O. Frange 190–91, in Boud'hors and Heurtel, *Les ostraca coptes*, 158–59.
112 Abgar letter: Eusebius, *Hist. Eccl.* I.13; in Egypt: P. Oxy 65.4469; Vienna K8302 (= ACM 61); Leiden Anastasy 9 (= ACM 134). On the view of holy men's charismatic writing in general, see Rapp, "Safe-Conducts to Heaven," esp. 199–203.

and do not move from there until the birds of the air eat your flesh." The people put it by the dragon's lair and, lo and behold, it lay still "as the people threw rocks at it and gave glory to God who works wonders through his saints."[113]

Some of the charms and magical texts from late antique Egypt may have been meant to convey some of this anchoritic charisma: one long spell to protect an individual with holy oil concludes with the words "Apa Anoup has sealed this oil."[114] While it is safer historically to attribute most of the magical texts to a more general model of monastic scribe (as I do in chapter 6), a curse like the following would have relied for its efficacy on the prior authority of its author, one Apa Victor:

> I write; I adjure you, Saot Sabaot, that you receive this incense from me (?) and speak a word to my advantage over Alo daughter of Aese.... You must bring loss and grief. May the adjuration go (up) to heaven until you act on my behalf against Alo daugher of Aese. Upon Alo shall (the) curse (of) God come. May the darkness take her, Alo, daughter of Aese.... The curses (of) the Law and Deuteronomy(?) will descend upon Alo daughter of Aese. May hunger and misery rule the body of Alo and Phibamon.... May furnace flame(s) come from the mouth of Alo daugher of Aese. May (the) curse (of) God descend upon Alo and her entire house(hold). May the fear of death be in Alo's house. May you make them bedridden. Amen, Amen, Sabao[t]. Apa Victor son of Thib[am]on.[115]

If the modern reader finds herself struck by the paradox of a Christian monk issuing a curse, it is instructive to recall that in antiquity the material potency of the blessing was seen as enveloping the material potency of the curse as well: holy men were hailed for conveying and directing all possible forms of power.[116]

In the end, devotion toward the saint as a physical center in the landscape continued even after the saint had died. The bodies of saints, asserts the *Life of Abraham of Farshut*, are buried

> like the bodies of all who have died; but they do not remain as corpses. Rather, they work wonders among the living, such as indeed the body of the blessed Elisha remained in the tomb as a corpse but raised the dead. In this way also our holy father, the prophet and archimandrite Apa Abraham, after the Lord visited him (and) he left the body, God worked cures and wonders through him in the place where he is now buried.[117]

---

113 *Bohairic Life of Maximus and Domitius*, in Vivian, "Bohairic Life of Maximus and Domitius," 43.

114 Apa Anoup spell: ACM 63 = Berlin 11347, in Kropp, *Ausgewählte koptische Zaubertexte*, 2:113–17.

115 ACM 104 = Michigan copt. 3565, in Worrell, "Coptic Magical and Medical Texts," 13–16; trans. ACM 211–12.

116 See Frankfurter, "Curses, Blessings, and Ritual Authority."

117 *V. Abraham*, fr. 4, in Goehring, *Politics, Monasticism, and Miracles*, 93.

Similarly, the relics of the hermit Ammonius, installed in a church in Chalcedon, were said to cure fevers.[118]

The creation of such shrines to deceased Egyptian hermits led to some jostling in a world where "places" were for martyrs and biblical heroes.[119] The desire to continue the cult of the prophet's body had to contend with the prophet's own wishes to the contrary, in the case of Antony or Shenoute, or, in the case of Macarios of Tkow, with ecclesiastical objections. For Macarios's body, the destination was the great Alexandrian church of Elisha and John the Baptist, a glory perhaps a bit beyond his station: "What are you doing with this unclean Egyptian," one text records the Alexandrian bishop saying to the holy man's disciples, "burying him in the sanctuary of the holy men?" But, the text continues, lightning immediately strikes him dead, Elisha and John themselves arrive to embrace their avatar Macarios, and everyone cheers the installation of his corpse.[120] These stories show that as holy men embraced the charismatic roles with which villagers and monks sought to endow them, they could no longer disappear into the desert like Antony, but rather, like the pillar of Simeon the Stylite, their presence had to persist in some physical form as a continual source of blessings. They would "become like rock," like the fugitive saints in the *Apocalypse of Elijah*: "No wild animals will eat [their corpses] until the last day of the great judgment."[121]

Monasteries aided in the preservation of their blessings. A century or so after his death, a nun procured a piece of Shenoute's mantle from the monks in order to expel a demon from another nun.[122] Along with a spectacular tomb-chapel that depicted the abbot-prophet as a heavenly intercessor in the company of angels and texts that referred to his powers over the Nile surge (see chapter 7), Shenoute's monks developed a stational liturgy in the vicinity of the monastery, taking devotees through the desert sites that bore his memories. A processional cross on which his glowering image was inscribed may well have led these memorial

---

118 Later appendix to Palladius, *H.L.* 11. See Butler, *Lausiac History of Palladius*, 34, 191–93. Ammonius's body was allegedly placed in a shrine dedicated to Peter and Paul, known locally as the Rufinian (cf. Sozomen, *Hist. Eccl.* 8.17). The martyrs Eulogios and Arsenios, from their martyrion at Akhmim, could send and dispel crocodiles and wolves, as well as retrieve stolen objects from robbers; Papaconstantinou, *Le culte des saints en Egypte*, 59; Coptic synaxarium: 16 Kihak, in Basset, *Le Synaxaire arabe jacobite II*, 393–95.

119 Frankfurter, "Urban Shrine and Rural Saint."

120 *Panegyric on Macarius*, 16.1–5, in Johnson, *Panegyric on Macarius*, 123–27.

121 *Apocalypse of Elijah* 4.26, on whose reflection of third-century martyr beliefs see Frankfurter, "Cult of the Martyrs," esp. 28–32. In a martyr legend from Edfu, local saints executed under Maximian were similarly hidden in the mountains until after the persecution ended, when a church was built over their (putative) remains. But even beforehand, the river water with which their blood had mixed was said to cure fevers; *Coptic synaxarium*: 7 Kihak, in Basset, *Le Synaxaire arabe jacobite II*, 317. On the postmortem miracles of holy men, see also Amélineau, *Étude sur le christianisme*, 12–13. On the necessity of transforming holy men into relics, see Kaplan, "De la dépouille à la relique."

122 Louvre E 7401 (sixth/seventh century CE), in Jördens, "Reliquien des Schenute im Frauenkonvent."

marches and stood by as his legends were read aloud on the way.[123] Another monastery offered the continuing efficacy of one Longinus against demons: "Even though he is in a faraway place, the demons suffer defeat through him, screaming with the pain which afflicts them as a result of his prayers," one manuscript records. "'Longinus has burnt me! [ⲁⲗⲟⲅⲅⲓⲛⲟⲥ ⲣⲟⲕϩ̄ⲧ]'" the demons are said to cry.[124] Elsewhere monks invoked "Deacon Victor" in a spell as one whom Christ had "joined with" and "raised up."[125] And somewhere in the vicinity of the monastery of Bawit—or maybe Oxyrhynchus—festival-goers could buy small terra-cotta figurines of naked women, on whose bellies they might find inscribed the name Phib, the companion of Apa Apollo of Bawit, both of whom had acquired healing reputations after their deaths (see fig. 6). Such figurines, as we saw in chapter 2, were believed to aid conception and childbirth, but here they conveyed the agency of Apa Phib in connection with his festival or tomb.[126] The holy men thus entered the Christian pantheon of holy beings alongside the martyrs, but as intercessors firmly accessible through places.[127]

V. CONCLUSION

How, then, were Christian holy men instruments of syncretism in late antique Egypt? How did these ascetic prophets themselves provide the crucial syntheses of Christianity such that the new religion could be understood, received, and assimilated? In one dimension, we have seen, saints "performed" the Christian worldview and scheme of authority within the traditional landscape, tapping into both its living realities, like the Nile, dangerous fauna, and agricultural or medical crises, and the culture's long-standing attitudes toward religious authority. Egypt was a land of centers, from whose shrines one might expect "blessings," oracles, advice, protection, and even kinship with other supplicants.[128] Gestures as old as

---

123 Tomb-chapel: Bolman, Davis, and Pyke, "Shenoute and a Recently Discovered Tomb Chapel." Stational liturgy: Timbie, "Liturgical Procession"; and idem, "Once More into the Desert." Processional cross: MacCoull, "Coptic Inscriptions on the Votive Cross." Stephen J. Davis discusses the efflorescence of a cult of Shenoute in liturgy, hagiography, and spatial devotions over the eighth through tenth centuries: Davis, "Shenoute in Scetis."

124 Pierpont Morgan Coptic codex M579, fol. 108v B (§9), in Depuydt, "A Homily on the Virtues," 274, 285.

125 Deacon Victor invocation: P. Mich. Inv. 4971, in Paul Allan Mirecki and Stephen H. Skiles, "A Vellum Funerary Amulet to Ensure the Resurrection of a Deceased Coptic Priest" (unpublished paper). On invocations of deceased holy men, see also Crum, "Theban Hermits and Their Life," 169–70.

126 Figurines with Phib inscribed: Perdrizet, Les terres cuites grecques, 5–6; Bayer-Niemeier, Bildwerke der Sammlung Kaufmann I, 147–48, #262, fig. 48.6. On early legends and evidence of cult, see Papaconstantinou, Le culte des saints en Égypte, 53–56; and Coquin, "Phib, Saint."

127 On graffiti invoking local saints, see Papaconstantinou, Le culte des saints en Égypte, 331–36. On these kinds of appeals to holy men as intercessors in general, see Rapp, "'For Next to God.'"

128 See Dunand, "Lieu sacré païen"; Frankfurter, "Introduction"; and Volokhine, "Les déplacements pieux en Égypte pharaonique."

the needs they sought to resolve still governed supplicants' approaches to shrines, but the saints, both living and dead, came now themselves to serve as the shrines: "I do obeisance unto the footprints of your angel, which removes us [from] all evil," reads a letter from an individual to a holy man near the monastery of Epiphanius, while another was said to have scattered a pack of marauding wolves by invoking the name of Pisentius.[129] At the same time, the holy men offered divination and material "blessings" in a landscape of river surges, scorpions, and ailing camels—that is, in the "language" of the region.

In another dimension, however, many holy men stood apart from this world, establishing their dwellings on the periphery of culture and overtly in opposition to the monuments and practices of the old religious order. The worldview they demonstrated through exorcism and curse consisted of the Christian God, his son, and the saints, allied against an aggressive demonic presence. To implore the holy man's assistance was supposed to involve some measure of embrace of this Christian worldview, and even its embodiment through the revaluation of misfortune in demonic terms. The syncretism in this kind of religious stance arose, we have seen, in the *preservation* of older demonic models (spirits and fauna of the desert), the *clarification* or *polarization* of other traditional ranks of spirits, and even the *demonization* of certain gods still remembered and located in the landscape (Bes at Abydos, Min in Akhmim). Syncretism took place also in the ritual techniques the saints used to repel the demonic: execration, the wielding of sacred texts, the invocation of names and powers, iconoclastic mutilation—all archaic gestures that temple priests had used to protect their regions from chaos.[130] And syncretism might be recognized in the holy man's discourse of danger, its identification and alleviation—a discourse that invariably crystallized widely shared anxieties about supernatural subversion that were often exacerbated in times of unclear authority.

In the great range of holy men I have surveyed in this chapter—from abbots to hermits, in villages and in caves—there were certainly those whose syncretistic expression belonged more to the former "positive" type than to the latter "negative" type. Yet the Egyptian Christian prophet had the potential to engage in expressions belonging to both types, and it is instructive to keep a figure like Shenoute in mind as one who crusaded against all explicit forms of native religion while drawing adroitly on execration traditions related to Egyptian priestly ritual. It is to deal expressly with this combination of types of religious continuity that I have argued for conceptualizing the late antique Egyptian holy men not primarily

---

129 O. Epiphanius #411, in Crum and Evelyn-White, *Monastery of Epiphanius at Thebes*, 260; cf. #113 (182). Cf. the Vatican ostracon (KSB I.292) hailing the "angel" of Apas Constantine, Ananias, and Victor, in Mallon, "Quelques ostraca coptes de Thèbes"; and Hasitzka, *Koptisches Sammelbuch I*, 111. Protection by invoking Pisentius: John the Elder (B.M. Or. 7026) f. 61b-62b, in Budge, *Coptic Apocrypha*, 109–10.

130 See Ritner, "Curses: Introduction," 183–86; Frankfurter, *Religion in Roman Egypt*, 279–80; and Hansen, "Ancient Execration."

as heirs of Christian scripture and ascetic theology but as examples of regional prophets such as have been noted in traditional societies undergoing modernization in more recent times. Such figures stand apart from their societies, developing new rites, pantheons, and worldviews, and often epitomize the "new" and efficacious in their societies at the same time as they participate completely in those societies' basic worldviews, landscape, and idioms of power and authority. The prophet, one anthropologist has described, "carries the interpretative role of the diviner out of an established framework into a quite new ambience of awareness.... He imposes certainty on a situation characterized by doubts.... He externalizes and articulates what it is that others can as yet only feel, strive towards and imagine but cannot put into words or translate explicitly into action." He stands between two worldviews, two frameworks for experience, and thus represents both uniqueness—the hermit in the tomb, the holy man who encourages a discourse of sin among his devotees—and the possibility of *synthesis*. Indeed, his acts, from form of dwelling to healing to exorcism to teaching, inspire people to begin the process of *embracing* that synthesis, whose very possibility he represents.[131]

In adopting this model for understanding the late antique desert saint, we are acknowledging first that landscape and habitus will determine the form that Christianity, its rituals, and its experts will take in a region, and second that religion *will* change under the leadership of such figures. The changes will often take place through an overt and aggressive discourse of replacement, yet in a way that maintains or revitalizes basic cultural forms.

What, finally, does syncretism mean in the social world of the holy man? What types of phenomena should the term cover? This chapter has focused on ritual forms: gestures, speech, the creative use of substances, and even performative genres like exorcism, divination, and healing. I have argued not just that holy men in Egypt addressed perennial human issues in timeless ways but rather that the particular performances of exorcism, divination, and healing took place according to Egyptian traditions of ritual expression. Furthermore, these ritual forms pertained both to actions *by* saints and actions *toward* and *about* saints: that is, the ways in which saints were approached and addressed, the forms of mediation they were expected to offer, and the powers that people imputed to them—all the various gestures and discussions by which people constructed sainthood around a person in their region.

---

[131] Burridge, *New Heaven, New Earth*, 154, cf. 155, 162. The two worlds to which Burridge refers in his analysis of Melanesian prophets are those of the colonial cash economy and of the traditional competitive, prestige-based barter economy. While this essential aspect of his analysis might militate against any exportation of this model of "prophet," other "prophets" in Africa and the Americas have likewise bridged cultural worlds, and it is worth considering how much *christianitas* represented a new "global" worldview, the translation of which into local terms required the actions of the holy man.

It would seem that the best model for understanding this notion of syncretism in ritual forms is the habitus or habit-memory, the culturally ingrained expressive act that continues to organize attitudes both personal and social even through institutional changes in a culture. One knows to collect sand from the saint's door, to address him as "lord" or "angel," to treasure—perhaps even eat—the scripture verse he writes out for you. The saint correspondingly knows to address the Nile's fluctuations and to fashion amulets from holy writing or fox claws.

CHAPTER 4

A Site of Blessings, Dreams, and Wonders

TRADITIONS OF THE SAINT'S SHRINE

I. INTRODUCTION

Sometime at the end of the third century CE, when the term "saints [ⲛⲉⲧⲟⲩⲁⲁⲃ]" was primarily used to refer to biblical heroes or dismembered martyrs, an author who imagined himself in both camps produced an extended apocalyptic timetable that carried his audience from "now"—a time beset with confusion and false prophets—until the return of Christ and his millennial reign. The prophecy, labeled in one manuscript the *Apocalypse of Elijah*, showed a rather extreme form of the many Christianities tussling in Egypt in the later third century: it was a Christianity attentive to scriptural tradition (particularly the Book of Revelation), enamored of the bloodiest types of martyrdom, and committed to severe fasting regimens. Such ideological stances would have placed the author himself at a strict remove from both the local religious culture of third-century Egypt and the learned urban conventicles that were developing more nuanced approaches to scripture, the body, and the world under the aegis of Christianity. And yet the landscape within which the prophecy's lurid eschatology proceeds is Egypt, with all of this land's supernatural capacity for order, peace, fertility, and holy places. Beneficence is linked to kingship in this text, and Christ arrives like a king; political and social breakdown are linked to terrestrial chaos (a bloody Nile, famine), and general order in society is linked to the activity of "holy places."[1] It is not from gods or their images that true beneficence flows forth in this landscape, however, as it would have in traditional Egyptian religion; rather, it is from the *saints*, whose flesh is preserved in the desert, whose blood provides "healing [ⲟⲩϫⲁⲓ] for the people," whose heroic diatribes unveil and cripple demonic powers, and by whose presence "the earth gives fruit, the sun shines upon the earth, and the dew falls upon the earth."[2] The promotion of saints in the *Apocalypse of Elijah* provides the link between a fundamentally terrestrial, even agricultural, sense of religious power and a radically sectarian image of apocalyptic utopia. Landscape—specifi-

---

1 *Apocalypse of Elijah*, in Frankfurter, *Elijah in Upper Egypt*, chs. 7–8; and below, pp. 212–15.
2 *Apocalypse of Elijah* 4.26, 4.7, 5.18, in Frankfurter, *Elijah in Upper Egypt*, ch. 5; and idem, "Cult of the Martyrs in Egypt."

cally the Egyptian landscape of Nile, desert, cities, and rulers—provides the context for imagining power. "Truly," a Coptic hymn would declare some five hundred years later, "the land of Egypt was worthy of great grace because of the blood of these martyrs Apa Victor and Claudius."[3] So also, another Coptic hagiographer asserts, the deceased hermit Pisentius "illuminated our poor nome, and even more was the protector of our whole country."[4]

Saints, then, become a way of thinking about a country with potent centers and the blessings they could emit. Christian bodies came to serve as the axis points between Egyptian peasant culture and the Christian pantheon of holy beings, both in imagination (e.g., the *Apocalypse of Elijah*) and practice. "Egyptians," Athanasius wrote, "love to honor with burial rites and to wrap in linens the bodies of their worthy dead, and especially of the holy martyrs, not burying them in the earth, but placing them on low beds and keeping them with them inside, and they intend by this practice to honor the deceased." Hence, he claims, Antony himself had insisted "not to permit anyone to take [his] body to [inhabited] Egypt, lest they set it in the houses."[5] By 369 CE the desperation for such holy bodies had expanded, perhaps as the security they radiated came to be understood as extending to whole communities: the heretics, as Athanasius now regarded the mass of relic devotees, "try to put [the martyrs' corpses] on stretchers and pieces of wood so that those who want to can view them. They do this with pomp, as if on account of the martyrs' honor.... For indeed they do not have the bodies of martyrs in their city, nor do they know which is a martyr.... In fact, those who have already been buried they exhume and carry out." By the following year, complained the anxious bishop, people were flocking to the martyrs' shrines (however we are to imagine these structures) to "give glory to them and ask them what was to take place"—all the while, Athanasius insisted, mistaking demons for the martyrs' spirits.[6]

Clearly a new scheme of sacred landscape was evolving under Christian aegis over the course of the fourth century that in many ways complemented the traditional religious landscape (still alive in the fourth century) of oracle shrines, temples, and speaking gods. Indeed, while Athanasius earnestly sought to shift the Christian "center" from corpses to scripture, his reports of the cult of martyrs do not suggest the same degree of competition between Christian and native religious worldviews. These cults were demonic, perhaps, but not heathen in the institutional sense that hagiographers liked to caricature. The sense of a cosmos

---

3 "Alphabetic Acrostic on Apa Claudius, the General," in Kuhn and Tait, *Thirteen Coptic Acrostic Hymns*, 54–55).

4 Codex Vat. Copt. 66, f. 128, in Amélineau, *Étude sur le christianisme*, 84.

5 *V.Ant.* 90, 91, trans. Gregg, *Athanasius*, 96–97. On the historical realities behind such descriptions, see Montserrat, "Death and Funerals"; and Römer, "Das Werden zu Osiris."

6 *Ep. Fest.* 41 (Copt), in Lefort, *S. Athanase*, 62–63; trans. Brakke, "Athanasius of Alexandria," 14; *Ep. Fest.* 42 (Copt), in Lefort, *S. Athanase*, 65. See in general Brakke, "Athanasius of Alexandria," 16–17; and Camplani, *Le lettere festali di Atanasio*, 272–75.

CHAPTER 4

held together with saints' bodies seems to have arisen along the same conceptual outline as that of the older cosmos, which integrated temple cults and their processions. In this way, the new religious order, even in its most apocalyptic or utopian forms, depended on "place" in much the same way as the old religious order.[7]

As Peter Brown famously described it, the erection of shrines to "the very special dead" across the Mediterranean world amounted to a fundamental remapping of territory, center, and periphery. Ritual centers shifted from city to necropolis; then, through the relic trade, back to urban centers or out to frontier churches; and then, in Egypt, onto the grounds of monasteries. Their importance for the popular conceptualization of Christianity cannot be understated. For a religion that first spread through legends and claims of miraculous healings and dramatic exorcisms, these buildings became the arenas for thaumaturgical display, places where people could experience the immanence of some heroic martyr, biblical prophet, or holy man. In crude wall paintings (and eventually sumptuous mosaics), incense, hymns and popular songs, and the great crush of devotees a saint's presence and power would be ritually conjured. Through the fourth century, it has been argued, gatherings at saints' shrines and their immediate environs vastly outnumbered the capacity of most churches of that time, which means that the Christianity of this period revolved around not scripture and liturgy, but rather martyrs' legends, festival encomia, dancing, and feasting.[8] By the fifth century, saints' shrines, often in the form of great basilicas, had become objects of civic identity and patronage, points on the routes of urban or regional processions, and locations for all the customary forms of celebration that a city or region held dear.[9] Yet the festivals and festival states that these buildings could host clearly continued: in Carthage, the city's Council of 419 complained, people were celebrating "heathen feasts" not only with "the most wicked leapings throughout the fields and open places," but "even upon the natal days of most blessed martyrs and in the very sacred places themselves."[10]

The "realization" of the cult of saints through buildings and organized festivals was largely a fifth-century phenomenon, even if the ideological groundwork as I described it earlier was laid in the late third and fourth centuries.[11] By the sixth century, the enshrined martyrs themselves were being asked to adjudicate the relic inventions: "O God of all the saints," reads an oracle request submitted to the thriving shrine of St. Colluthus in Antinoë, "if you command to put the two mar-

---

7 See, e.g., Borghouts, "Martyria"; and Dunand, "Lieu sacré païen." On the relationship between "utopian" and "locative" religious conceptual strategies, see Smith, "Influence of Symbols Upon Social Change."
8 See MacMullen, *Second Church*.
9 See Brown, *Cult of the Saints*; Yasin, *Saints and Church Spaces*.
10 Council of Carthage [419 CE] Canon 60 (Grk 63), in Percival, *Seven Ecumenical Councils*, 932.
11 Papaconstantinou, *Le culte des saints en Égypte*. See also Clarysse, "Coptic Martyr Cult."

tyrs together [in one shrine—St. Colluthus's?], send forth this [ticket]."[12] It was a *living* system, this cult of saints—an extensive network of sacred centers that variously resolved crises; defined communities; dispensed the blessings that were seen as fertilizing crops and raising the Nile; and mediated, through liturgy and ecclesiastical presence, the reality of the new religious order.

Egypt provides especially rich documentation of the life and social world of saints' shrines, from those that developed among cemeteries during the late third and fourth centuries through the urban edifices and regional cult complexes of the fifth and sixth centuries and then to the monastic grounds, a shift that occurred with the Arab conquest. The larger geographical ideology I introduced earlier was no abstract conception of heavenly mediators but the translation of a profoundly material sensibility into the image of saints. Such an investment in these saints' bodies and tactile presence in the landscape emerges in both the *Apocalypse of Elijah* and Athanasius's brief condemnation of popular practices. Written at the end of the fourth century, the monastic travelogue *Historia monachorum in Aegypto* describes a tomb-shrine, labeled a *martyrion*, in which several martyrs were supposedly buried after their bones washed up on the riverbank and that people in the area associated with miracles. According to the travelogue, the martyrion stood as a goal for travelers' prayers.[13] And sometime in the early fifth century, Abbot Shenoute of Atripe, while himself quite invested in the veneration of martyrs, complains in sermons about the free invention of martyrs' relics from just such scattered bones, protesting their incorporation into church spaces and the diverse, uncouth ways people were celebrating and accessing the saints.[14]

Recognizing the inherent materiality of such ritual devotion to martyrs and saints brings us closer to the social and architectural world of the shrine—the spaces, practices, and people that physically mediated their holy presence. The nature of tomb-shrines and how they could evolve into thriving regional centers has emerged in necropolis archaeology at Antinoë, in central Egypt, and at El Bagawat in the Kharga Oasis.[15] The addition of wall paintings of saints to the tombs in El Bagawat, and, in Antinoë, the addition of a larger structure than the traditional funeral chapel layout created actual Christian cult sites—places that could accommodate appeals, prayers, dance, and feasting within the funeral grounds. The development of urban shrines, on the other hand, is principally documented through miracle collections (such as that related to the cult of the Three Hebrew Youths in Alexandria) and papyri that make reference to the

---

12 Donadoni, "Una domanda oracolare cristiana."

13 *Hist. mon.* 19.11–12.

14 Athanasius, *Festal Letter 42*, in Lefort, *S. Athanase*; with Brakke, "'Outside the Places,'" 479–80; Shenoute of Atripe, *Those Who Work Evil*, in Amélineau, *Oeuvres de Schenoudi I*, 212–20; with Lefort, "La chasse aux reliques." On Shenoute's own investment in the cult of martyrs, see Horn, *Studien zu den Märtyrern*.

15 Fakhry, *Necropolis of El-Bagawât*, 100–11.

shrines' status in urban life and topography, as places to establish time in relation to saints' days, for example, or as sites for oath taking.[16]

Literary evidence, although occasionally drawn from quite late manuscripts, illustrates such features of the cultic life of the saint's shrine as the roles of attendants, devotees' lives and expectations about the saints' presence, and especially the social implications of architecture and the zones of shrine activity.[17] Discussing one particularly important fifth-century shrine, that of Sts. Cyrus and John at Menouthis, just east of Alexandria, in his seventh-century collection of their miracles, Sophronius of Jerusalem describes the large interior space where people would lie on cots or on the ground, awaiting the instructive dream of the saints. In one story, however, the saints appear to a woman and "order . . . her to remove [her] child from the *temenos*"—the main shrine—"and place him in the middle of the exterior atrium"; she herself is told to "sit some distance away." She does as they instruct, and "about a half-hour later a great crowd had gathered to see what would happen."[18] Thus action was envisioned as taking place across various spaces, each with particular types of social groupings or privacy and varying degrees of independence from or supervision by attendants.

Excavations of one such shrine complex, that of Apa Mena, located forty-five kilometers southwest of Alexandria, have revealed an extensive city with a crypt-shrine, a basilica and baptistery, workshops, a processional arcade opening onto a courtyard, and elaborate hostel facilities.[19] It is from this complex, which reached its apogee in the sixth century, that the famous Menas *ampullae*—molded vials of sacred oil—traveled to Alexandria and all over the late antique Christian world.[20] Local terracotta artisans molded many other objects as well, like the female figurines discussed in chapters 2 and 5, and these objects give us additional information about the devotional rituals that took place at saints' shrines.[21]

II. THE SAINT'S SHRINE AS SOCIAL SITE

Notwithstanding the particularities of Egyptian shrines and the many ways that the saint's shrine was interconnected with other religious worlds, we may say that

---

16 Papaconstantinou, "La liturgie stationnale à Oxyrhynchos"; idem, *Le culte des saints en Egypte*; idem, "Cult of Saints."

17 Baumeister, *Martyr invictus*; MacDermot, *Cult of the Seer*. On the variable arrangements of social, liturgical, and devotional spaces in late antique churches across the Mediterranean, see esp. Yasin, *Saints and Church Spaces*.

18 Sophronius, *Miracles* 34.9–10, in Marcos, *Los Thaumata de Sofronio*, 317. See also Gascou, *Sophrone de Jérusalem*. On shrine layout, see also Sophronius, *Miracles* ##24.4; 62.

19 Kaufmann, *Die Menasstadt und das Nationalheiligtum*; and idem, "Archäologische Miscellen aus Ägypten, I." See now Grossmann, "Pilgrimage Center of Abu Mina"; with Davis, "Pilgrimage and the Cult of Saint Thecla."

20 See Kiss, "Évolution stylistique"; and idem, *Ampoules de Saint Ménas*; with Vikan, *Early Byzantine Pilgrimage Art*, on broader context and functions.

21 See Caseau, "Ordinary Objects"; and Bangert, "Archaeology of Pilgrimage."

the saint's shrine *in general* did constitute a religious world of its own—a social site for the negotiation of Christianity according to local traditions.²² It housed the local or regional saint and his or her active presence, signified through images, incense, the spectacle of votive offerings, and the monumentality (or intimacy) of the building itself, and in these ways the shrine provided an axis for the full range of mediating gestures, dances, and devotional exchanges that would have appeared traditional to visitors, as well as a map for these various collective activities: incubation *here*, feasting *there*, dancing *out there*, votive deposits *in there*, liturgical drama *over here*.²³

While there was never consistency at saints' shrines in their respective orchestration of ecclesiastical liturgy, commemorative activities, and popular veneration of relics, we can say that the shrine complex provided a framework and axis for a number of important activities.²⁴ It served as the axis of *myth*—the festally rehearsed and informally retold stories of a martyr's bravery, dismemberment, transcendence, and localization *in this place* that gave devotees a sense of the saint's intimacy with their lives. The shrine also served as the axis of *literacy*, as miracle stories flowed in and out of written collections, and literate specialists were at hand to inscribe requests, votive testimonies, and even—as seems likely—healing amulets invoking the saint's powers, like the one quoted in chapter 2 that declared the presence of St. Phocas.²⁵ The shrine was also the axis of *processions*: to the shrine, around the shrine, among different shrines, all signifying through collective movement the saint's claim on urban identity, ecclesiastical sanction, relationship to other saints, and membership in the festival calendar. Finally, the shrine was the stage for *festivals*: the milling and dancing, order and *communitas*, animal slaughter and feasting that make up "time out of time" in all cultures and would have been accompanied by public readings of the saint's legends and favors to supplicants and homilies by local bishops.

In these ways we may well speak of the saint's shrine as a social site, one that varied between festival and normative periods. Shrine culture embraced various economic activities, like the crafting of votives and *eulogia*; particular social roles, such as *oikonomos* and *patēr*²⁶; and certainly zones of inclusivity and status- or gender-exclusivity. Women were sometimes excluded from holy spaces (as in some Syrian shrines), monks and nuns were sometimes prohibited from attend-

---

22 See Leemans, "General Introduction."

23 See Caseau, "Christian Bodies"; and idem, "Ordinary Objects." On the diversification of performative spaces in shrines, see Yasin, *Saints and Church Spaces*.

24 On the inconsistency in orchestration of ritual activities at saints' shrines, see Yasin, "Sight Lines of Sanctity."

25 ACM 25 = P. Oxy 1060; above, pp. 61–62. Cf. ACM 18 = Berlin 984, to St. Serenus; and in general Papaconstantinou, *Le culte des saints en Égypte*, 340–53.

26 *Oikonomos*: Shrine of Sts. Cyrus/John, Menouthis; see Sophronius of Jerusalem, *Miracles*, 1.9, 8.1–2, 9.3. *Patēr*: Shrine of St. Colluthus, Antinoê; see Devos, "Un étrange miracle copte." See also Christian, *Local Religion in Sixteenth-Century Spain*.

CHAPTER 4

ing public *panēgyreis*, and the elite were sometimes able to gain more privileged access to holy spaces (or more comfortable sleeping arrangements) than the poor.[27] Indeed, many shrines had the capacity to attract and serve members of different religious identities, and thus they provided a temporary social identity transcendent of official boundaries. At the same time, the coming together of diverse groups—Bedouin and Greek in Palestine; Nubian, Alexandrian, and Theban in Upper Egypt—could have resulted in competition or mutual influence, whether related to the legends that brought them there or the gestures they expressed when there.[28] In his account of the festival of Mamre in Palestine, the fifth-century historian Sozomen depicts discrete devotional groups, ignoring how they might have interacted:

> Here there is still held, annually each summer, a brilliant *panēgyris* of both local folk [ἐπιχώριοι] and those from further away: Palestinians, Phoenicians, and Arabs. Many also gather for the market, both as buyers and sellers. The festival [ἑορτή] is sought eagerly by all: (by) the Jews because they declare Abraham their patriarch; (by) the heathens [Ἕλληοι] on account of the visit of angels; (and by) the Christians as well because the one who appeared to that pious man was he who later, born from a virgin, manifested himself for the salvation of mankind. Everyone honors this place with appropriate religious observances, some praising the God of all, others invoking the angels, pouring out wine and offering frankincense or a bull or a goat or a sheep or a chicken.[29]

If Mamre in Palestine was the most famous of such "shared shrines," the stories of heretics, Jews, and heathens seeking benefits from saints in the annals of Christian shrines suggest that people laid claim to saints' powers regardless of professed religious identity.[30] That is to say, the saint's shrine and the saint's festival on shrine grounds offered a spatially (not just temporally) specific identity that subsumed the exclusive allegiances that bishops promoted.

Theodore Schatzki's notion of the social site, introduced in chapter 1, involves particular attention to the productive interaction of people among spaces. As comparative studies of pilgrimage shrines show, the sacred district generally encompasses mercantile arcades and subshrines, diverse stational routes, and exte-

---

27 Gender exclusivity at shrines: see Talbot, "Pilgrimage to Healing Shrines," 162–64; Smith, "Women at the Tomb." On arrangements for elite at shrines, see, e.g., Sophronius, *Miracles*, #24.

28 On such social tensions at pilgrimage shrines see Eade and Sallnow, "Introduction," esp. 5, 15; Kreinach, "Seductiveness of Saints."

29 Sozomen, *Hist. Eccl.* 2.4.2–4, in Grillet and Sabbah, *Sozomène*, 246 (my translation). See also Cline, "Two-Sided Mold."

30 Papaconstantinou, *Le culte des saints en Égypte*, 339; Drescher, *Apa Mena*, #16; Sophronius, *Miracles*, ##28–29, 31–32, 54, in Gascou, *Sophrone de Jérusalem*, 92–101, 107–14, 187–90. Cf. Cuffel, "From Practice to Polemic."

rior sites for purification and "arrival rites," as well as monastic orders, artisanal families, and locally inherited ranks of attendants and guides, all of which overlap in multiple (and often conflicting) social-spatial dimensions.[31] Hagiographical depictions of saints' shrines, like Sophronius's *Miracles of Saints John and Cyrus* (620 CE), often refer to various spaces of interaction, supervision, hierarchy, and *independent* agency at a single shrine, like the case quoted earlier of a woman who, independently (if by the saints' instruction), laid her son in the middle of an exterior atrium, away from the main healing chambers, to procure the saint's healing.[32] At Apa Mena, one must consider social interactions that would have occurred among the various rooms and buildings for craftsmanship, wine production, liturgy, retail, popular milling about, and personal imprecations. But the broad outlines of the social dynamics specific to saints' shrines are meant to ground my larger thesis: the development of practices suggestive to the *historian* as pre-Christian (even if never subject to ecclesiastical censure as heathen), and all those other devotional practices that seem peculiar to particular shrines or regions, followed from the social activities, gestures, and ritual activities that were particular to the saint's shrine as a discrete religious world.

This chapter will proceed to investigate several areas of ritual gesture that were distinctive of shrines and their festivals and that allowed the persistence of habitus and performative expressions distinctive of the region. However, as with all the chapters in this book, the isolation of the saint's shrine is a purely heuristic maneuver to highlight types of ritual expression that occurred in space and the social sphere. In fact, saints' shrines were deeply interconnected with the ecclesiastical and monastic worlds (which, for example, hosted processions and provided shrines with literary propaganda), the domestic world (from which, for example, supplicants came and brought their concerns for maternity and health), the worlds of workshops (which designed and manufactured souvenirs and votive materials), and the world of ritual experts, many of whom could be found at shrines, purveying scribal skills. It would be incorrect to take any of these religious worlds as fundamentally separate from the others.

III. GESTURES

The study of gesture, going back to the the work of the early nineteenth-century priest Andrea de Jorio, has revolved around its function in both augmenting and shaping verbal language, lending embodiment to communication.[33] Ritualized, expressive gestures shape mourning and lamentation, market exchanges, and all manner of group interactions. But as gesture enters the religious sphere it as-

---

31 See van der Veer, *Gods on Earth*; Bilu, "Inner Limits of Communitas."
32 Above, p. 108. Sophronius, *Miracles* 34.9–10, in Gascou, *Sophrone de Jérusalem*, 120.
33 Jorio, *Gesture in Naples*.

sumes *illocutionary* functions, lending efficacy to a curse or blessing, for example; *sacralizing* functions, indicating a supernatural audience and the means of communicating with such a being; and *assertive* functions, indicating one's desperation in appeal. The very range of gestures associated cross-culturally with what we call "prayer" illustrates how basic gesture is to religion: prostration, clapping, and, especially in late antiquity, the *orans* position of raised arms with elbows bent. Religious gestures engage the performer not only with a specific space or ceremony but also with family and local traditions of proper gesture. Gesture, in this sense, amounts to habitus, the socially prescribed and learned modes of carrying and applying the body in public that are felt to constitute one's humanness, one's gender, and one's family identity.[34]

In the late antique world gestures could be innovated too, perhaps to convey an expression of ritual identity or corporate charisma: in the fourth century, for example, Cyril of Jerusalem describes the manual cross gesture as an apotropaic "seal" for all transitions, food, travel, and arising from sleep that also terrifies demons and evokes Christ's exorcisms.[35] In Gaul, however, Caesarius of Arles complains that people would thus "sign themselves" before eating meat slaughtered for a festival and through this act considered themselves full, sanctioned participants in both the festival and Christianity.[36] Gestures signify identity and bring the performer into line with an identity, as at Mamre, a goal for Christians, Jews, and *hellēsi* (devotees of local cults): "Everyone honors this place with appropriate religious observances, some *praising* the God of all, others *invoking* the angels, *pouring out* wine and *offering* frankincense or a bull or a goat or a sheep or a chicken. For whatever each person held most dearly and beautiful, nourishing it carefully throughout the year in promise for provision at that festival, he guarded for himself and his household."[37]

At the same time, gesture communicates efficacy: both effective imprecation to a spirit or god and effective transmission of holy power from an image. Pilgrimage to a single thirteenth-century shrine in Spain would have involved circumambulation of the tomb, embracing columns, lying underneath the tomb for healing, and, of course, depositing votive tokens.[38] The body's movements, often augmented with ritual media like candles or paper notes or vials of oil, became the actual means of comprehending sacred space, or liturgy, or relics. The Apostle Paul's legendary companion Thecla is said to have "rolled herself upon the place where Paul taught as he sat in prison," an act portrayed as spontaneous in the *Acts*

---

34 Mauss, "Techniques of the Body"; Bourdieu, *Outline of a Theory of Practice*, 81–83; Connerton, *How Societies Remember*, 59, 79–88.

35 Cyril of Jerusalem, *Catecheses* 13.36; cf. *Apostolic Constitutions* 8.2.12; *Acts of Paul and Thecla* 3.22.

36 Caesarius, *Sermon* 54.6.

37 Sozomen, *Hist. Eccl.* 2.4.4–5, ed. Grillet and Sabbah, *Sozomène*, 246 (my translation).

38 Ameijeiras, "Imagery and Interactivity," esp. 27–30.

TRADITIONS OF THE SAINT'S SHRINE

of Paul but certainly reflective of practices in some holy places.³⁹ But if gesture also represents tradition, as I have argued, then it serves as people's *embodied* means of mediating sacred materials with tradition. In early Ptolemaic Egypt, for example, Herodotus reports that priestesses riding on sacred barges during the Bubastis festival would raise their robes to expose their genitals to people on the Nile banks, a gesture mirrored in terracotta images of Isis *anasyrmenē*—holding up her robe. As difficult as it is to reconstruct the meaning of this gesture, it clearly linked bodies, mythical bodies, and festival time through a gesture of exposure.⁴⁰

Operating between intentional function (e.g., interaction with holy space or liturgy) and habitus, then, religious gesture amounts to a vocabulary of sorts. *Expressive gestures* advance prayers and imprecations, from the raising of the hands in the *orans* position to candle-lighting and even remaining awake in a shrine all night. Paulinus of Nola depicts such activities at the late fourth-century St. Felix shrine: some "kindle light with coloured candles, and attach lamps with many wicks to the vaulted ceilings.... Others still can eagerly pour spikenard on the martyr's burial place, and then withdraw the healing unguents from the hallowed tomb" as potent relics.⁴¹ Here expressive gestures shift into *contact gestures*, which serve the direct, efficacious acquisition of supernatural benefits, and range from taking sand or wax or leaves from around a shrine to embracing, touching, or rolling over sacred ground, or even eating sanctified foods.⁴² *Collective gestures*, which span both functions, have a public feature even if performed individually: one thinks of feasting, drinking, dancing, walking in procession, and circumambulation. To the censorious bishops of the Council of Carthage in 419, people's way of honoring traditional festivals by "perform[ing] the most wicked leapings throughout the fields and open places" was doubly abhorrent for its transcendence of both proper civic and proper religious boundaries, yet it serves as one more example of the diversity of the collective gestures through which people engaged with the saints.⁴³

This vocabulary of gestures, representing both immediate cultural tradition and the encounter with a holy shrine itself, thus embraces times of individual or family pilgrimage as well as festival times, those regional pilgrimages that create

---

39 *Acts of Paul* 3.20, trans. Schneemelcher, *New Testament Apocrypha*, 2:242.

40 Herodotus II.60.2, Diodorus I.85.3, with figurines in Dunand, *Religion populaire en Égypte romaine*, ##60–61. See also Ameijerias, "Imagery and Interactivity," 33; Lloyd, *Herodotus*, 275–76; Frankfurter, *Religion in Roman Egypt*, 104. On later uses of this gesture, see Zeitler, "Ostantatio Genitalium," esp. 186.

41 Paulinus of Nola, *Poem 18*, in Walsh, *Poems of St. Paulinus of Nola*, 115. Cf. expressive acts in early modern Spanish local religion: Christian, *Local Religion in Sixteenth-Century Spain*, 101–2.

42 Cf. Mayeur-Jaouen, *Pèlerinages d'Égypte*, 187, on contemporary Egyptian examples; and Christian, *Local Religion in Sixteenth-Century Spain*, 100–1, on early modern Spanish shrine practices.

43 Council of Carthage [419], Canon 60 (Grk 63), in Percival, *Seven Ecumenical Councils*, 932.

concentrations of social activity when new gestures may be observed and modeled. But across this vocabulary of gestures we see people bringing their traditions of embodied communication *to* the shrine. Perhaps a gesture such as the *orans* posture, which had a wide tradition in Egyptian mortuary and votive art but also achieved popularity in Christian devotional practices, would have been shaped or directed by a priest or attendant. Perhaps what another visitor performed (or where she performed it) would have seemed more appropriate for one's problem, even seductive in its assertiveness.[44] But in general the shrine, especially one with a broad catchment area, would have served as a magnet for the importation of traditional gestures, group by group, dancing one way, feasting another, and leaving diverse votive objects according to custom.

It is in this broader context that we must understand syncretism in the most basic social features of saints' shrines and pilgrimage, in the process of people's very *recognition* of a shrine's authority. For in traditional cultures, such recognition intrinsically involves performance, gesture, and movement, not just mental assertions. The rest of this chapter will cover four areas of ritual action and public performance that, in one form or another, involved syncretism—in the sense of synthetic encounters between local traditions and ecclesiastical traditions—that led to the construction of a Christianity in a regionally meaningful form. Both festival activity, including ritual slaughter and dance, and the selection and ritual depositing of votive objects revolved primarily around the agency of the supplicants, the participants who were exporting traditions from their local and domestic domains. A third area, divination, including both dream incubation and written ticket oracles, required more involvement and encouragement from shrine attendants, while the fourth area, spirit possession, assumed both popular functions (when the possessed served as local oracles) and official functions (when the possessed dramatized the potency of the saint and of Christian authority).

IV. COLLECTIVE EXPRESSIONS: FESTIVALS AND THEIR GESTURES

A. Festival Hilarity and Control

The principal context in which traditional gestures, and even more elaborate performances of local religious tradition, took place around the saint's shrine was the festival or *panegyris*. Here ecclesiastical efforts to control and focus participants by leading processions or vigils were met by the collective effervescence and spontaneity of the crowds.[45] Festival hilarity became a topic of ecclesiastical censure throughout the empire; like today, clerics complained of profane dances,

---

44 Kreinach, "Seductiveness of Saints."
45 See esp. Vryonis, "*Panēgyris* of the Byzantine Saint." I also draw comparatively on the incisive ethnographic work of Bilu, "Inner Limits of Communitas"; and Weingrod, *Saint of Beersheba*.

debauchery, and drunkenness.[46] In our most vital witness to the life of the shrine festival in fifth-century Egypt, Abbot Shenoute complains of activity around

> those who sell their wares in the shrines [ⲛⲧⲟⲡⲟⲥ][47] of the martyrs. O great folly! If you come to the martyr's shrine to eat, drink, buy, sell, (and) do what you want, then what good is your house, what good is the *polis*, what good are the villages? (Is it not they that are the places) for selling and buying? Oh, such hardness of heart! If your daughters and their mothers apply their perfume to their head(s) and eye shadow to their eyes, adorning themselves to deceive those who see them, and moreover (if) your son and your brother and your friend and your neighbor (do) thus, by going to the martyr's shrine, then what good is your house?[48]

But festivals, for all their "antistructure," were an integral part of shrine Christianity and the cult of the saints in late antiquity, and we must take seriously the expressive forms that arose around them.[49] In its most basic, social dimension, a saint's festival involved the transformation of the *space* of the shrine in its established environs—cemetery, monastery, basilica—from a site of orderly, often-restricted comportment to a fair.[50] The sheer concentration of pilgrims imposed the milling physicality of a crowd upon the quiet, individual gestures of cemetery or monastery, creating a conflict in propriety that gave rise to tensions. How was this space to be treated?[51] "Go then to the martyrs' shrines," says Shenoute, "to pray, to read (aloud), to sing psalms, to purify yourself, to receive the offering [*prosphora*] in the fear of Christ. That is good. It is the type of the Church, the canon of the house of God. But to sing (profane songs), to eat, to drink, to laugh, and especially to fornicate and murder people out of drunkenness and lewdness and brawls in foolishness, it is complete chaos! [ⲛⲓⲙ ⲟⲩⲁⲛⲟⲙⲓⲁ]"[52]

To give order to these milling, expectant crowds, ecclesiastical and monastic authorities developed structured forms of collective participation. The Apa Mena shrine developed spaces for such organized ceremony (see fig. 8): an en-

---

46 Harl, "La denonciation des festivités profanes"; Vryonis, "*Panēgyris* of the Byzantine Saint," 210–13; Frankfurter, "Beyond Magic and Superstition," 255–66.

47 Amélineau notes that Shenoute alternates between ⲧⲟⲡⲟⲥ and ⲧⲁⲫⲟⲥ, "tomb," confirming that the shrines were, in fact, sites claimed as holy in necropolis areas; Amélineau, *Oeuvres de Schenoudi* I, 199 n. 4. On the growth of the cult of martyrs from tomb-cults, see in general Baumeister, *Martyr invictus*, 63–73.

48 Shenoute of Atripe, *Discourses 8: Since it Behooves Christians*, ed. Amélineau, *Oeuvres de Schenoudi* I, 201; Emmel, *Shenoute's Literary Corpus*, vol. 2.

49 See Leemans, "General Introduction"; MacMullen, *Christianity and Paganism*, 36–44; idem, *Second Church*, 29–32. Cf. Perpillou-Thomas, *Fêtes d'Égypte ptolémaïque*.

50 See Vryonis, "*Panēgyris* of the Byzantine Saint," 200–9.

51 On local traditions of gender and gestural propriety at saints' festivals, cf. the analysis of the North African Jewish *hillula* in Weingrod, *Saint of Beersheba*, 59–65.

52 Shenoute of Atripe, *Discourses 8: Since it Behooves Christians*, in Amélineau, *Oeuvres de Schenoudi* I, 199–200.

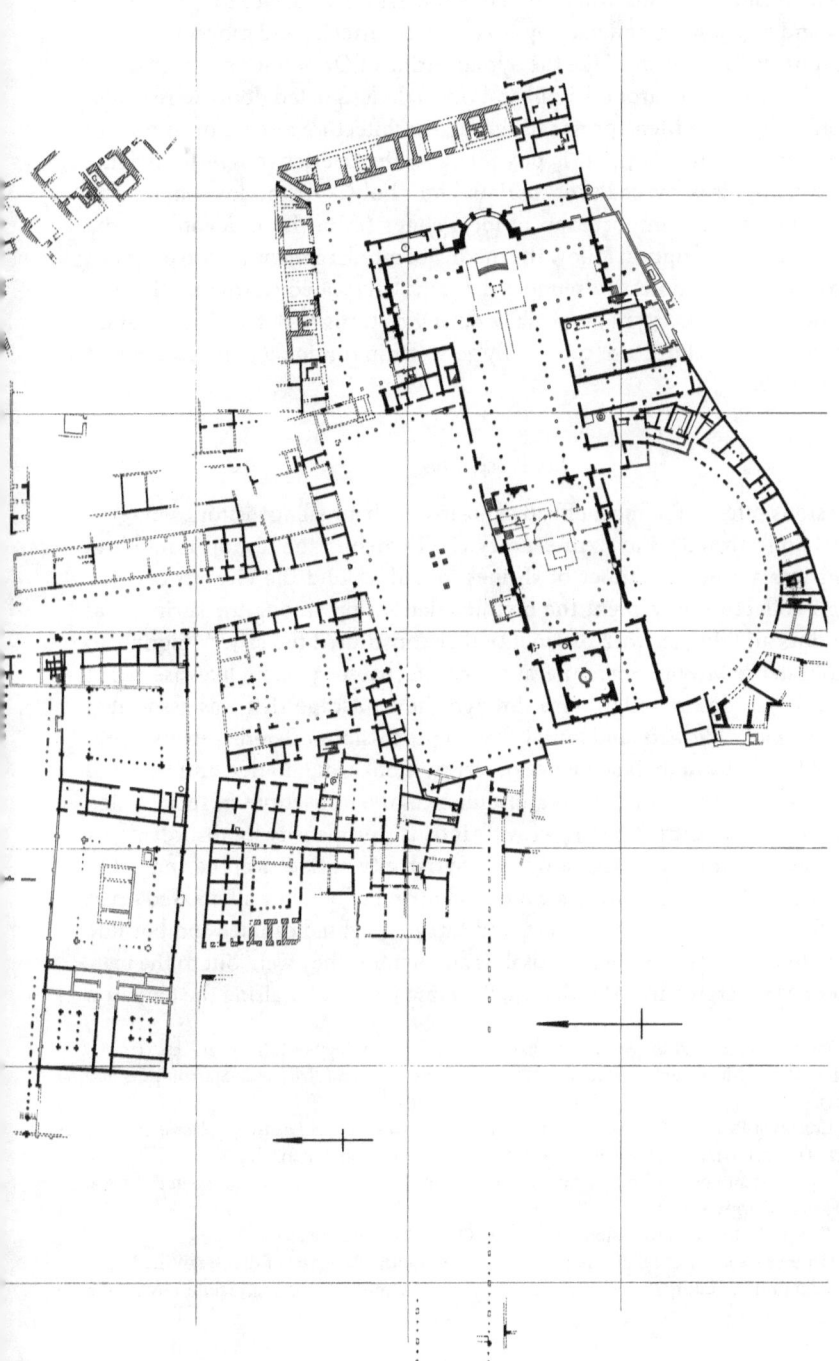

FIGURE 8. Archaeological plan of Apa Mena pilgrimage city, showing main processional road, basilica and courtyard, and rounded building supposedly for incubation practice.

trance road and courtyard to accomodate processions, a basilica to accomodate liturgy and vigils, stairs and hallways to channel curiosity and movement, hostels and baths for pilgrims. Like the Syrian shrine of Qalat Sim'an, which channeled pilgrims up and around a hill and through designated doors to reach St. Simeon's pillar, Apa Mena provided through architecture a sense of completeness to the pilgrim's visit.[53] It is possible also that clerics sought to channel collective impulses by chanting psalms and "holy"—orthodox—hymns in order to prevent the importation of local songs (even those devoted to the saint). And lest corruption follow the mixing of monks and nuns with pilgrims, the sixth-century canons of Pseudo-Athanasius advocated restricting the monastic orders from martyria, especially during festivals.[54] But such clerical interventions and architecture could only go so far in routinizing the excitement of pilgrimage.

B. Processions

Processions offered the most effective means of channelling visitors' energies. On certain festival days in sixth-century Oxyrhynchus, the bishop would lead participants among a number of shrines in and around the city, articulating through collective movement the mythic relationship among the shrines and their saints and the network of sanctity that constituted the city.[55] Pilgrims to the monastery of Abbot Shenoute, as we saw in chapter 3, might likewise be led on a stational "desert" pilgrimage through the landscape that was associated with the abbot's life, acts, and burial.[56] Such processions offered dramatic spectacles of hierarchy in their sequence of clergy, monks, dignitaries, and laity and thus impressed upon participants and audiences the restrictions of social order, even in the face of the processing crowd's intrinsic propensity for disorder.[57] As one witness describes a procession in the Syrian city of Edessa at the end of the fifth century (held in gratitude for imperial tax relief): "They all dressed up in white, from the greatest to the least, and carrying lighted candles and burning censers, to the accompaniment of psalms and hymns, they went out to the martyrion of Mar Sergius and Mar Simon, thanking God and praising the emperor.

53 Yasin, "Pilgrim and the Arch." Cf. also Mitchell, "Archaeology of Pilgrimage," esp. 175–82; Connelly, "Ritual Movement in Sacred Space"; and Christian, *Local Religion in Sixteenth-Century Spain*, 117.

54 *Canons of Pseudo-Athanasius*, ed. Riedel and Crum, *Canons of Athanasius of Alexandria*, §91 (singing of proper hymns during vigils), §92 (restrictions on nuns and monks).

55 Papaconstantinou, "La liturgie stationnale à Oxyrhynchos"; idem, *Le culte des saints en Égypte*, 354–55; Graf, "Pompai in Greece."

56 Timbie, "Liturgical Procession"; and idem, "Once More into the Desert."

57 On these features of religious procession, see Vryonis, "Panēgyris of the Byzantine Saint," 203–4; Humphries, "Liturgy and Laity"; Ashley, "Introduction"; Sheingorn, "Sainte Foy on the Loose."

There they held a eucharist, and on coming back into the city they extended the feast of joy and pleasure for a whole week, and decreed that they would celebrate this feast every year."[58]

Although bishops and abbots made considerable efforts to conduct such processions, separate monks or women from the rest of the crowd, encourage the use of proper music, and read the official martyrologies, we should not overestimate churches' control over festivals. All the evidence regarding festival liturgy in late antiquity shows its improvised, unpredictable character.[59] These occasions were very much a function of pilgrims, local visitors, and their gestural traditions. So what traditions did people bring with them to shape their sense of the saint?

While crowds of pilgrims at festivals may not have had the same propensity for *violent* disorder as crowds at games or urban processions (or at contested festivals, such as those for traditional gods in late antiquity), complaints like Shenoute's of drunkenness, immodesty, and hilarity certainly reflect real tendencies of festival behavior. In one sense they reflect the collective effervescence, the communitas (in the anthropologist Victor Turner's sense) of a crowd that has left its local, workaday social context for a liminal passage and a liminal time. In such an environment, aspects of social structure collapse; new forms of social order arise. Common devotion to the saint provides a transcendent identity. Devotion and liminality together inspire individuals' spontaneity, even impulsivity.[60] But the expressions and performances that ensue are not simply functions of communitas. They invariably consist of *importations* of local, even domestic, customs and gestures to the festival world: meats and breads, dress and music, and modes of socializing, even flirting: as Shenoute laments, "If your daughters and their mothers apply their perfume to their head(s) and eye shadow to their eyes, adorning themselves to deceive those who see them, and moreover (if) your son and your brother and your friend and your neighbor do thus, by going to the martyr's shrine, then what good is your house?"[61] In this complaint, the abbot argues that social gestures appropriate to village socializing should be left behind in visiting a shrine, but in fact they were not; they were brought quite readily to the shrine. Indeed, a woman visiting the Apa Menas shrine is said to have lamented her impoverished appearance: "She prayed and besought God with tears, seeing all the

---

58 *Chronicle of Pseudo-Joshua the Stylite* 31, trans. Trombley and Watt, *Chronicle of Pseudo-Joshua the Stylite*, 30.

59 See esp. Leemans, "General Introduction," 16–17; cf. Christian, *Local Religion in Sixteenth-Century Spain*, 118–19.

60 Turner, "Passages, Margins, and Poverty"; with application to the modern saint's festival in Weingrod, *Saint of Beersheba*, 47–68. As Leemans describes the late antique *panegyris*, the model fits well; Leemans, "General Introduction," 16–22.

61 Shenoute of Atripe, *Discourses 8: Since It Behooves Christians*, in Amélineau, *Oeuvres de Schenoudi I*, 201.

CHAPTER 4

women wearing gold and silver and diamonds and carrying their children, but she had no adornment of gold or silver because of the grief in her heart; and therefore she was filled with envious longing."[62]

In two particular areas we can speak of local gestures brought to the shrine in honor of the saint that involved a deeper mediation of traditional religious expression than food and cosmetics. The performance of animal slaughter and dances as indigenous expressions of devotion reflect the integration of a more complex habitus into Christian practice.

C. Animal Slaughter and Feasting

In the case of animal slaughter, performed ceremonially in honor of the saint and as an extension of domestic meal practice, historians have often been hampered by the application of the category "sacrifice"—*thusia*. Does the perpetuation of such practices indicate the continuity of a central Roman civic rite that was not only strictly forbidden in the Theodosian code but also the preeminent Christian symbol of repressive heathen dominion?[63] Certainly Shenoute viewed festival animal slaughter as linked to heathen sacrifice, criticizing "those who dare to do such things as building sacrificial altars [or braziers: ⲉⲥⲭⲁⲣⲁ] and slaughtering goats and such animals, vowing on them (and) eating them" at the martyr's shrine.[64] Yet despite his criticism, the practices continued. A century later, a letter from Oxyrhynchus declares that "we do not slaughter [σφάξομεν] on St. Parmouthios's day," suggesting a similar reticence about the performance of *thusia*-like practices in connection with martyrs' festivals.[65]

Popular animal slaughter was an integral component of festivals around the Mediterranean and certainly in Egypt, where pig slaughter had been a traditional part of extra-temple feasting since the Ptolemaic period, with varying degrees of ceremonial formality. At some festivals, it seems, the pig became identified with the celebration of Isis, but more often it was simply a popular component of the banquets of religious societies. In a letter from the fourth century CE, a couple who invoke "the Lord God" declare that "until now we have not ceremonially killed [ἐθύκαμεν] the pigs."[66] And even Shenoute refers approvingly to animal slaughter at wedding feasts [ⲉⲟⲩⲙⲁ ⲛ̄ϣⲉⲗⲉⲉⲧ], "when people, being of one family, some (of them) slaughter a calf [ⲁⲩϣⲱⲧ ⲛ̄ϩⲉⲛⲙⲁⲥⲉ] and prepare wine and

---

62 Ed. Drescher, *Apa Mena*, 43, 133 (translation).

63 See esp. Drake, "Lambs into Lions," esp. 33–36.

64 Shenoute of Atripe, *Discourses 8: Since It Behooves Christians*, ed. Amélineau, *Oeuvres de Schenoudi I*, 203; cf. ibid., 206, and Caesarius of Arles, *Sermon* 54.6

65 P. Harris 1.154; see Papaconstantinou, *Le culte des saints en Égypte*, 323.

66 P. Oxy X.1299, 6–7, which Malcolm Choat believes is *not* Christian (personal communication with author, October 31, 2008). See also P. Lugd.-Bat. 33 (#52) (II ce). On pigs at religious festivals in Egypt, see Perpillou-Thomas, *Fêtes d'Égypte*, 203–9; Nachtergael, "Un sacrifice en l'honneur"; Papaconstantinou, *Le culte des saints en Égypte*, 318.

other goods."⁶⁷ Categorizing a practice as "sacrifice"—and thereby as something both antithetical to Christianity and distinct from domestic animal slaughter—may distort its significance in a religious context.⁶⁸ The preparation of celebratory foods—meats as well as breads—was a basic component of festivals, and the preparation and consumption of the meat, from the animal's presentation to its slaughter and the sharing of its flesh, was typically assigned to the god or saint in ways ranging from the most formalized to the familial and intimate.⁶⁹ Bracketing the term "sacrifice" allows us to see ritual animal slaughter as a social gesture, an exportation of domestic and local practices of meal production for the sake of a saint.

An instructive comparandum from another late antique Christian region is provided by the poet Paulinus, who oversaw the shrine of St. Felix in the town of Nola, Italy, at the beginning of the fifth century. In his public homilies in honor of St. Felix, which sought to promote the active regional patronage of that saint's shrine, Paulinus tells a series of stories about animals that betake themselves to the shrine for the feeding of the poor and the fulfillment of their obstinate owners' vows. (In one case a horse returns to the shrine the butchered meat that his owner has secretly taken home.) Paulinus sets these legends in the spectacle of a bucolic and populous St. Felix fair, to which those benefiting from Felix's multifarious blessings bring all manner of gifts, including livestock for slaughter, and at which the poor gather to eat of these vowed and slaughtered animals. Scholars have noted the resemblance of Paulinus's fair to Gallo-Roman festivals that predate Christianization, which often revolved around public *thusia* and feasting. But as much as Paulinus exhorts the vowing, procession, and slaughtering of animals for food, he gives them a distinctive character in linking them to the poor and their relief. These practices should not, then, be seen as the "perpetuation of animal sacrifice" but rather as the sanctioning and rearticulation of rural feasting traditions that had always revolved around the choiceness of the animal.⁷⁰ Such traditions involved ritual focus, habitus rooted in domestic and local practices of food production, and an overall appropriation of the Christian shrine as a regional religious center and a site for festival feasting.

Of course, such practices are attested at other saints' shrines as well, both in late antiquity and today.⁷¹ At Mamre, we have seen, pilgrims from various religious traditions each offered "a bull or a goat or a sheep or a chicken or an ox, or

---

67 Shenoute of Atripe, *I Have Been Reading the Holy Gospels*, FZ 116ii, ed. Coquin and Emmel, "Le traité de Šenoute," 19, 38. See also Moussa, "I Have Been Reading," 133.

68 See Belayche, "Religion et consommation"; and Frankfurter, "Egyptian Religion and the Problem."

69 See in general MacClymond, *Beyond Sacred Violence*.

70 Paulinus of Nola, Poem 18; cf. ibid., 20, with trenchant analyses by Trout, "Christianizing the Nolan Countryside"; and Grottanelli, "Tuer des animaux."

71 Modern animal slaughter and feasting traditions at saints' festivals: Georgoudi, "Sanctified Slaughter in Modern Greece"; and Mayeur-Jaouen, *Pèlerinages d'Égypte*, 209–18.

CHAPTER 4

he-goat, a sheep, or a cock. For what each person deemed the most valuable and beautiful he carefully tended through the whole year in vow for feasting at that festival, designated for himself and his household."[72] In fifth-century Gaul, villagers made the meat of a festival animal slaughter suitably Christian by crossing themselves before eating, thus taking ritual conversion into their own hands.[73] But evidence from Nola, in which an ecclesiastical shrine director himself sanctioned the slaughter of festival meat through oratory, is especially helpful for making sense of the animal slaughters taking place at the Egyptian saints' shrines. That is, they were *not* "sacrifice" in the loaded sense used by Greek and Roman intellectuals and church authorities, but complex ritual gestures expressing the sanctity of space and time, the social status of the donor, the spectacle of benefaction, the extension of meal practice from the domestic sphere, and the sanctification of ritual action through the vow. Syncretism occurred through the integration of this complex gesture with the ideological framework and authority that Christianity represented to people. And in most cases, it seems, this integration came about through the efforts and the creative agency of the participants themselves.

D. Dance

Perhaps the most dramatic way that local cultures respond to holy places and integrate their most basic gestural traditions with the symbolism of the shrine is through dance. We see this function of dance throughout Latin America and southern Europe, where traditional dances have been developed to acknowledge Christ or a saint.[74] Sometimes dances are the spontaneous expressions of people at a saint's festival; sometimes they lead over time to the formation of dance troupes and guilds, in which case participation in such a guild becomes a means of engaging with Christianity itself. In dance, whether spontaneous or choreographed in troupes, bodies move simultaneously according to local habitus and to the architectural, temporal, and mythological authority of the church. It would thus be particularly useful to find evidence of any sort of dance at Egyptian saints' shrines in late antiquity.[75] The evidence, however, is sparse, even in the writings of such observant critics of popular devotion as Shenoute of Atripe. Yet dance is not the type of custom for which the absence of testimony can imply absence of practice. Thus I will approach festival dance in Egypt, a vital form of local habitus

---

72 Sozomen, *Hist. Eccl.* 2.4.4, in Grillet and Sabbah, *Sozomène*, 246.

73 Caesarius of Arles, *Sermon* 54.6: *Et quia solent aliqui dicere: Ego me signo, et sic manduco*, ed. Delage, *Césaire d'Arles*, 462.

74 See esp. Stresser-Péan, *Sun God and the Savior*, 248–52, chs. 12–13; Poole, "Rituals of Movement."

75 On types of archaeological evidence for dance in antiquity, see Connelly, "Ritual Movement in Sacred Space"; Naerebout, "Dance." Dances were clearly a component of ancient Egyptian religious life; see Brunner-Traut, *Der Tanz im alten Ägypten*; Meyer-Dietrich, "Dance"; Wild, "Les danses sacrées."

that was brought to saints' shrines and was involved in the construction of an embodied Christianity, in light of richer testimony from other parts of the late antique Christian world.[76]

Dances did take place at other shrines around the Mediterranean and Near Eastern worlds. The potential of dance to mediate the powers and authority of a saint's shrine first appears in the regular criticism of such practices in the sermons of early Christian leaders. John Chrysostom's abhorrence of dancing in martyria and churches in fourth-century Antioch could be distilled in his declaration that "where there is dancing, there is the Devil," while Caesarius of Arles resisted similar practices in fifth-century Gaul in more detail: "The unfortunate, miserable people who neither fear nor blush to execute dances and pantomimes [*ballationes et saltationes*] before the very churches of the saints, even if they come to church as Christians, return from it as heathens because that kind of dancing has carried over from heathen practice."[77] Yet bishops are consistently vague on what, if anything, dance had to do with pre-Christian religion. Their line of argument most often returns, as in Chrysostom's writings, to moral objection to dance's sensually flamboyant character, giddy spontaneity, and potential to bring participants to disorderly, Bacchantic heights of enthusiasm. Gregory of Nazianzus is quite specific on this point: "If you also must dance [ὀρχήσασθαι], because it is the *panēgyris* today and you love festivities, then dance, but not the indecent dance of (the daughter of) Herodias; . . . Imitate rather that of David at the resting of the Ark, which I consider the *mystērion* of fluid and twisting movement submitted to the will of God."[78] Proscribing dance at saints' shrines was always an effort to construct boundaries and establish gender propriety, sexual purity, and, ultimately, a strict form of *christianitas*.[79]

If dance was a topic of discussions about the regulation of the cult of the saints in most parts of the Mediterranean world, its absence in such conversations in late antique Egypt may indicate that it did not occupy Egyptian Christian leaders as much. We may presume some sort of dances were occurring when Shenoute refers to "those outside the martyr-shrines who cause the sound of horns and flutes to fill the whole place, (as if) in anger against those inside"—perhaps an incident the abbot or his agents overheard rather than observed directly.[80] But the topic still merits some general discussion because of its repeated occurrence in

---

76 See the excellent discussion of dance in late antique Christian contexts by MacMullen, *Christianity and Paganism*, 103–6; cf. Gougaud, "La danse dans les églises."

77 John Chrysostom, *Homily on Matthew* 48, PG 58: 491. Caesarius of Arles, *Sermon* 13, 4, trans. Mueller, *St. Caesarius of Arles*, 77–78. See also *Sermon* 55.2, relating dance to debauchery and the works of the Devil. See Klingshirn, *Caesarius of Arles*, 197–200, 224–26.

78 Gregory of Nazianzus, *Oration* 5.35, in Bernardi, *Grégoire de Nazianze*, 368 (my translation).

79 On the nature and implications of dance at saint shrines, see esp. Weingrod, *Saint of Beer-sheba*, 64–65. Erika Meyer-Dietrich notes the function of dance in ancient Egypt to establish gendered spaces, in "Dance," 8.

80 Shenoute, *Since It Behooves Christians*, ed. Amélineau, *Oeuvres de Schenoudi I*, 200.

CHAPTER 4

local forms of Christianity across cultures, where group dances of an indigenous character mediated local identity and tradition and the religious authority of the church, shrine, and holy figure. As a fourth-century homily on the martyr Polyeuctus declares, "What kind of gift should we present to the martyr as worthy? ... We will dance for him, if seemly, *according to (our) customs* [τα σύνηθη]."[81] Dance, that is, derives from and communicates custom.

Dance, then, can represent spontaneity and catharsis in religious settings, as church fathers so often feared, as well as transmit choreographies traditional to a culture in which social structure and crisis are acted out, worship itself is expressed, and communitas—the most embodied of devotional gestures—is achieved.[82] The more articulated of such traditional dances, which would have been performed as an integral part of collective devotion at shrines, are hardly discernible in late antiquity. However, an eleventh- to twelfth-century church in Old Dongola, Sudan, where a monastic Christianity notably continuous with that of late antique Egypt arose, may give us some idea of how cultures with elaborate dance traditions might have applied them to Christian festivals. On one wall of this church, archaeologists found a nativity scene augmented with the portrayal of an elaborate warrior dance in which rows of men with spears and shields, many with masks or castanets, move actively before Mary and the child (plates 3–4); the accompanying Old Nubian inscriptions are as yet indecipherable.[83] Presumably such dances took place in the painter's own Nubian world, a land distinctive for its diverse encounters of royal and nomadic cultures. Traditional dances maintained among these peoples as signs of strength and cultural identity were *brought to* the church, shrine, or procession.

The energy of the Old Dongola warrior dance reflects dance's capacity to shift participants from the everyday realm to one associated with spirits or saints, as well as with the communitas of heightened social bonds and collective enthusiasm. This capacity is most immediately apparent in elaborate choreographies, but even the simplest choreography can allow local communities to embrace a shrine, a saint, or a festival time through spontaneity and the rhythmic action and spatial focus of dance. Such practices are what Caesarius of Arles complains of in early sixth-century Gaul: peasants' "dances before the very basilicas of the saints."[84] And the mid-sixth-century historian Evagrius describes a nocturnal festival dance that he witnessed at the basilica of St. Simeon the Stylite (Qal'at Sim'an) as follows: "The rustics were dancing around [the remains of St. Simeon's] pillar [ἄγροικων πέρι τον κίονα χορεύοντων]," which stood at the center of the basilica rotunda, when he observed an astral prodigy—a shooting star—that apparently

---

81 Aubé, *Polyeucte dans l'histoire*, 79.
82 See Spencer, "Introduction."
83 Martens-Czarnecka, "Wall Paintings Discovered in Dongola"; and idem, *Wall Paintings from the Monastery*. See also below, pp. 170–71.
84 Caesarius, *Sermon* 13.4.

"only occurs at the commemoration of the saint [εν τοὶς του πανάγιου μνήμειοις]." Evagrius subsequently elaborates on the place of the pillar and rotunda in the devotional vocabulary of the local people: men, he reports, "repeatedly circumambulate [περινόστουντες] the pillar with their beasts of burden."[85]

Thus architecture, as much as sacred presence, invites embodied, choreographed response, and if the circumambulations of sixth-century Syrian pilgrims responded to the unusual layout of a pillar centered in a rotunda, other shrines and courtyards attracted other sorts of coordinated movement.[86] Dances at saints' shrines, some traditional and some spontaneous, expressed communal devotion to the saint and his building, the mutual understanding that "our" social solidarity and festive expressions might be reconstituted at this site for "our" saint.[87] Dancing, as historian of religions Sam Gill has observed, serves the localization of religion itself: it recognizes, from the perspective of culture and through embodied action, a physical place.[88]

References to dancing in or by churches and shrines can be found in such a wide array of ecclesiastical sources that we must regard dance as one of the principal ways that many local cultures around the empire integrated Christian structures into their expressive traditions. Such a process is a syncretism "danced out," to paraphrase the early anthropologist of religion R. R. Marett.[89] So can we apply this observation to late antique Egypt? If we have seen numerous witnesses to dance occurring at shrines elsewhere in the late antique Christian world, the evidence for Egypt has only been suggestive: the later paintings from the church at Old Dongola, and Shenoute's reference to the playing of horns and flutes outside martyrs' shrines amid feasting, drinking, and flirting. To these distant allusions we might add the fourth-/fifth-century letter from a woman requesting that her father send along her "leg ornaments [περισκελίδια] to wear at the festival"[90] and no doubt the terracotta figurines sold at the Apa Mena shrine that depict a woman standing with a large tambourine (see fig. 1). Recalling similar figurines of festival participants from Roman Egypt, these images must reflect the performative aspects of shrine devotion, as if to say, "I too will dance before you in gratitude for my request granted."[91]

---

85 Evagrius Scholasticus, *Eccl. Hist.* 1.14, in Bidez and Parmentier, *Ecclesiastical History of Evagrius*, 24.

86 Cf. Connelly, "Ritual Movement in Sacred Space."

87 Michael Psellos (eleventh century) describes a complex dance performed at the festival of Agathē in Constantinople by a women's clothworkers' guild. By this point, it was not local religious traditions that inspired dances but dance that served as its own inspiration: a response to festivals and expressive of social solidarity. See Laiou, "Festival of 'Agathe,'" esp. 112–13.

88 Gill, "Dancing and the Poetics of Place."

89 Marett, *Threshold of Religion*, xxxi.

90 SB 20.14226, trans. Bagnall and Cribiore, *Women's Letters from Ancient Egypt*, 237–38.

91 On dancing and tambourine figurines in Roman Egypt, see Dunand, *Religion populaire en Égypte romaine*, 96–100, with ##80–103. Cf. Kletter and Saarelainen, "Judean Drummers," 11–28; and Beck, "Human Figure with Tambourine," on a seventh-century BCE figurine. On dance and musical

All such materials point to the likelihood that dances were performed, probably in spontaneous fashion, at some Egyptian saints' shrines in late antiquity. Along with feasting and other collective gestures, dance should be considered a type of habitus that local people brought to saints' shrines from local and cultural traditions, situating the saint's shrine as a context for syncretism: that is, for the dynamic combination of traditions, space, and authority, motivated by communities themselves, yet *focused* on the mythology, the authority, and the *presence* of the Christian shrine, its holy beings, and its liturgies.

V. INDIVIDUAL EXPRESSIONS: IMPRECATION, CONTACT, VOTIVE

The documentation of saints' shrines in the lives of late antique Egyptian Christians shows a number of ways that individual pilgrims and local supplicants engaged the shrine for their own purposes through expressive and contact gestures. They appealed to the saint in inscriptions and stelae, which they placed near the holy *topos*: "God of St. Colluthus, doctor who cures souls and bodies, beseech God on behalf of the soul of the blessed Colluthos." This conventional wording of appeals, demoting the saint before God, also shows the mediation of local ecclesiastical attendants in expressing the visitors' desires, as I will discuss further in chapter 6.[92] But as shrine miracle collections imply, supplicants standing before the tomb or crypt more likely would have directed their appeals to the saints themselves, rather than the supreme Christian god. Here a woman laments that her child has ingested a snake during his visit to the shrine:

> Alas, my saints! In what way have you received my sacrifice? ... Other women, who have no children, give birth when they have had recourse to you, and for me, who arrived here flanked by two boys, it is (now) only with one that I leave here? Others come on the point of death and leave smiling. But for miserable me, my little boy who arrived playing and leaping is surely going to die if you do not save him![93]

Such direct appeals are still heard at Christian, Muslim, and Jewish saints' shrines today, demonstrating not an austere monotheism or crass polytheism but pilgrims' expectations—and verbal declarations—of the saints' intimate attentions. Accompanied by traditional gestures and weeping, these appeals illus-

---

instruments at modern *panēgyreis*, see Vryonis, "*Panēgyris* of the Byzantine Saint," 225. On musical instruments in artistic representations as an indication of dance, see Naerebout, *Attractive Performances*, 222.

92 *I. Ant. Munier* 2.3, in Papaconstantinou, *Le culte des saints en Égypte*, 327. On supplicants' inscriptions and written appeals, see in general ibid., 324–36, 354–57; and Cannuyer, "Des dieux aux saints guérisseurs," esp. 41–42.

93 Sophronios, *Miracles*, 34.6, in Gascou, *Sophrone de Jérusalem*, 119.

trate the self-determination of the pilgrim and a sphere of embodied engagement with the shrine in which customary gesture and speech engulf the religious center.[94]

Along with such evidence for verbal engagement with the shrine, archaeology reveals the use of objects: *ampullae* to collect potent oil; tokens to recall the saint's official image; molded (or stamped) body parts to leave as votive signs and requests (see plate 5); and figurines, especially of women, which served either as votive appeals in shrines or tombs, or as souvenirs of the saint's generative powers at home (see figs. 1–7, plates 1–2). These materials all stood at a dynamic nexus of individual supplicants' agency, craftsmen's agency, local and shrine customs, and the exigencies of space. They were, as we will see in chapter 5, designed and created in nearby workshops out of both official images and local traditions brought to the shrine. Shrine attendants would have indicated where such objects might be left, where oil or sand might be collected, and what in general supplicants ought to do at shrines, while individuals or family groups would have asserted themselves at the shrine with such objects to demand on their own terms the saint's attention. In the end, they might have returned home with souvenirs—*eulogia*, "blessings," like those bestowed by holy men, though in this case produced in larger numbers and with iconographic details that would have helped remind the bearer of the source of the blessing. Through that iconography, a saint's image, presence, shrine, and story might be regularly recalled from one's pocket or domestic altar.[95] Then, as now, the world in which supplicants expressed their agency through local and family traditions of efficacious gesture was a socially interconnected and spatially articulated one. What did my grandmother leave at this shrine? What are *those* women doing? What is available at shops, and therefore appropriate, to leave *ex voto*, and where should I leave it—what spaces are available or especially potent? Both social and mercantile contexts might have invited a visitor to engage in new devotional practices with new materials.

The miracle collections from specific shrines also show that, as much as there was an impulse to collect substances such as oil and sand, there was also an impulse to leave tokens of one's presence or hopes or thanks. While the collections' authors celebrate gifts of gold, mosaics, or beautiful epigraphy, promised in exchange for a saint's benefits, they record other types of votive deposits as well.[96] The seventh-century *Miracles of Saints John and Cyrus* by Sophronius refer to the display of bodily excrescences that had been expelled at the shrine. When a child is relieved of the scrofula in his neck, he reports, "those who then attended the

---

94 See, e.g., Betteridge, "Specialists in Miraculous Action"; Mernissi, "Women, Saints, and Sanctuaries."

95 Vikan, "Early Byzantine Pilgrimage Devotionalia"; Frank, "Loca Sancta Souvenirs"; Leyerle, "Pilgrim Eulogiae and Domestic Ritual."

96 Cf. P. Oxy 16.1925, a list of objects that seem to have been donated to a church *ex votos*.

sanctuary hung them for many days before the tomb of the saints, demonstrating the power of the martyrs and moving everybody to speak in a manner pleasing to God."[97]

The votive act—the gesture of depositing a particular object at a site in or near a shrine—appears here as a public act, one that communicates to others the saint's interventions and mobilizes them to celebrate the saint.[98] And as much as it signifies a private request (or gesture of gratitude) for a specific favor, the votive symbol—whether inscription, candle, figurine, or plaque—also reflects the customs of the particular shrine and its saint, assimilating the individual, in his or her particular state, to a social world of habitus.[99] At certain shrines of Isis in Egypt in the early Roman period, ear stelae were customary invocations to the goddess's attention; elsewhere, stelae of feet were left, signifying the goddess's desired presence (or the devotee's permanent adoration).[100] At an early Roman shrine in Sicily, a woman promises "to make a silver *spadika*" (palm frond?) if the goddess vindicates her by afflicting her enemy. Presumably this image was the token of exchange at this particular shrine.[101] Little boats, padlocks, and safety pins are today typical votive deposits at certain Muslim shrines, as are pairs of baby shoes at the shrines of Santa Niño de Atocha in New Mexico, small metal plaques with feet or weapons at some Indian shrines, and eyes at Sicilian shrines of St. Lucy. Clearly, the vocabulary of votive objects is rich and perennial. Attendants and supplicants both may offer legends to explain the specific symbols—why Santo Niño wants shoes, why a padlock is appropriate for this saint—but more important is the fact that these symbols and practices have become customary, creating traditions of what one *ought* to leave as appropriate to the saint. Thus, at the pilgrimage site of Apa Mena, it would appear that both female figurines and horses with riders came to serve as just such traditional votive deposits, representing not only the maternity, strength, or livestock that supplicants desired but also common symbols of votive ritual.[102] At the site of St. Colluthus in Antinoë, on the other hand, metalworkers contributed to the use of small metal plaques depicting body parts, a well-known shrine medium from around the Mediterranean world, or even biblical scenes (see plate 5).

97 Sophronius, *Miracles*, 1.9, ed. Marcos, *Los thaumata de Sofronio*, 245; Montserrat, "Pilgrimage to the Shrine"; Caseau, "Ordinary Objects," 648–49.

98 On this phenomenon in general, see Straten, "Gifts for the Gods," 75–77; Rousselle, *Croire et guérir*, 73, 77–80. On votive ritual across cultures in general, see Francis, *Faith and Transformation*; and Weinryb, *Ex Voto*.

99 On this feature of votive offerings across cultures, see Egan, *Mílagros*, 12–13; Faeta, "Physical Body," 55; idem, "Italian Ex-Votos," 58; and idem, "Ritual Context," 60–61; Betteridge, "Specialists in Miraculous Action," 203–6; Mayeur-Jaouen, *Pèlerinages d'Égypte*, 200–3.

100 On votive stelae and forms in pre-Christian Egypt, see Sadek, *Popular Religion in Egypt*, 245–67; Kayser, "Oreilles et couronnes"; Pinch, *Votive Offerings to Hathor*.

101 Syracuse Museum, inv. 39856, in Jordan, "A Survey of Greek Defixiones," 178.

102 At shared shrines, different groups would engage in different votive gestures and offerings, which can be apparent in the archaeology: see Ammerman, "Children at Risk."

It is also important to see votive deposits, especially those of an anatomical nature, not just as representative of personal affliction but also as mediating, through the space of the shrine, between a domestic or familial sphere in which affliction or insecurity becomes crisis and the saint himself. In Alfred Gell's terms, they serve as *agents* of the devotees in a complex interplay of communication with attending beings. This endowment of agency should apply to the metal plaques from Antinoë as well as to the figurines from Apa Mena that show women pregnant or holding or suckling infants (see plate 1; cf. figs. 1, 4–7). Procreative capacity and declining eyesight are highly personal crises in one sense. And yet, as individualized as any affliction or anxiety might appear, that affliction also involves—and the votive object acts within—the entire social world of the supplicant: his or her family, ancestors, and future children, as well as all the past and future supplicants at the shrine. At the same time, its placement in a specific site at the shrine—often restricted by shrine attendants—mediates the attention of the saint himself.[103]

The obvious derivation of the votive objects from workshops in the vicinity of the shrine means that the votive act itself extends beyond the actual deposit at the shrine to the workshop and the gestures of procurement that take place there. At the shop, of course, the figurine, plaque, or token representing the body part or condition (or, today, even miniature trucks or houses) is generic, even idealized—not particular to the supplicant's own circumstances or body. It is not her breast on the plaque, her face or shape in the figurine. Her investment in the mediating capacity of the votive object is progressive, mimetic, as it gradually comes to signify *her* body and circumstances—a process that probably takes place in the course of moving between the shop and the votive site itself.[104]

Finally, it is worth noting the variability with which votive objects function across cultures: as signs of request *or* of thanks; as signs declaring the supplicant's presence with the saint *or* the saint's presence with the supplicant; and even as signs taken away from the shrine as souvenirs or amulets, invoking the saint's perpetual attention through the placement of the votive symbol on clothing, animals, vehicles, or domestic altars.[105] If this variability might be less apparent in the limited selection of plaques from the St. Colluthus shrine, it would seem to explain both the great range of figurines molded for sale at Apa Mena and also the diverse archaeological sites at which female figurines have been discovered.[106] At

---

103 On shrine attendants' restriction of votive sites, see Christian, *Local Religion in Sixteenth-Century Spain*, 95–97.

104 I draw here on Alfred Gell's notion of the person "distributed" through created, owned, or otherwise personalized objects, found in *Art and Agency*, 16–27, ch. 7.

105 See Egan, *Mílagros*, 2.

106 Polaczek-Zdanowicz, "Genesis and Evolution of the Orant Statuettes"; Török, *Coptic Antiquities I*, 30–48; Grossmann, "Pilgrimage Center of Abu Mina," 298–300; Bangert, "Archaeology of Pilgrimage"; Frankfurter, "Female Figurines in Early Christian Egypt"; and Wilfong, *Women of Jeme*, 114–16.

CHAPTER 4

the Apa Mena complex, where molds and even terracotta workshops have been discovered, a cache of such figurines was found in the baptistery, and signs of hooks for their suspension were found near the crypt.[107]

As I discussed in chapter 2, the female figurines indicate a vibrant investment on the part of pilgrims in safe procreative fertility, which is also a dominant theme in women's shrine supplications recorded in Coptic miracle collections. Even today, women's shrine visits often involve quite elaborate contact gestures to gain a saint's blessings on womb or breasts.[108] Late antique gestures of supplication for procreative fertility that involved the purchase and placement of such figurines amounted, then, to a habitus: a traditional expression of one's family role and a traditional mode of shrine interaction that went *beyond* even the conventions of workshops. Do such complex votive acts and objects imply syncretism? Certainly not in the sense of a specific religious system's survival, but in our broader understanding of local gestures of shrine interaction, here facilitated by workshops and shrine attendants, pilgrims' assertions of such votive practices can indeed be seen to have contributed to the creation of synthetic and localized forms of Christianity and to have worked continually to acculturate religious ideas in body and practice. The Christianity at these saints' shrines was a Christianity of the figurine.

VI. DIVINATION

Another area in which local traditions were revitalized at saints' shrines occurred with the development of divination services, and here the two great Egyptian shrines of Apa Mena and Cyrus and John in Menouthis provide exceptionally good information. Divination, as I introduced it in the last chapter, was the ritual process by which a god or saint could be made to pronounce on a particular question of political, social, agricultural, or personal concern, and we saw that numerous holy men assumed some elements of this role in their capacity as seers or prophets. But saints' shrines became sites for these procedures as well, taking place in the forms of incubation, the experience of receiving the instructive and healing vision of the saint in a dream while sleeping in or near the sanctuary, and the ticket oracle.

The ticket oracle involved having one's question to the saint inscribed in both positive and negative versions of answers, a procedure that necessitated the participation and creative agency of local scribes. The saint would then "choose" one ticket by a procedure not yet known, and this ticket would be returned to the devotee as the saint's answer and promise. We have evidence of such oracles from

---

107 Grossmann, "Pilgrimage Center of Abu Mina," 300.

108 Procreative fertility sought in miracle collections: *Miracles of S. Menas*, in Drescher, *Apa Mena*; De Vis, *Homélies Coptes de la Vaticane I–II*. Modern appeals for conception and safe childbirth: Mayeur-Jaouen, *Pèlerinages d'Égypte*, 186–87; Betteridge, "Specialists in Miraculous Action."

> *Oracle Tickets from Lycopolis (shrine of St. Victor?)*
> *(sixth/seventh centuries CE)*
>
> | | A | B |
> |---|---|---|
> | Oh God Pantokrator, if you command me, your servant Paul to—

A: stay under the roof of the monastery of Apa Thomas;

B: go to Antinoë,

—command me in this ticket. | ☩ ⲡⲛⲟⲩⲧⲉ ⲡⲡⲁ
ⲛⲧⲱⲅⲣⲁⲧⲟⲣ ⲉ
ϣⲱⲡⲉ ⲕⲟⲩⲉϩⲥⲁϩ
ⲛⲉ ⲛⲁⲓ ⲁⲛⲟⲕ ⲡ
ⲉⲕϩⲙϩⲁⲗ ⲡⲁⲩⲗⲟⲥ
ⲉⲧⲣⲁϭⲱ ϩⲁⲧⲟⲩ
ⲉϩⲥⲟⲓ ⲛⲡⲙⲟⲛⲁⲥ
ⲧⲏⲣⲓⲟⲛ ⲛⲁⲡⲁ
ⲑⲱⲙⲁⲥ ⲕⲉⲗⲉⲩⲉ
ⲛⲁⲓ ϩⲓⲧⲛ ⲧⲓⲡⲓⲧ
ⲧⲁⲣⲛ ☩ | ☩ ⲡⲛⲟⲩⲧⲉ ⲡⲡⲁⲛ
ⲧⲱⲅⲣⲁⲧⲟⲣ ⲉϣⲱ
ⲡⲉ ⲕⲟⲩⲉϩⲥⲁϩⲛⲉ
ⲛⲁⲓ ⲁⲛⲟⲕ ⲡⲉⲕ
ϩⲙϩⲁⲗ ⲡⲁⲩⲗⲟⲥ
ⲉⲧⲣⲁⲃⲱⲕ ⲉⲁⲛ
ⲧⲓⲛⲟⲟⲩ ⲧⲁϭⲱ
ⲕⲉⲗⲉⲩⲉ ⲛⲁⲓ
ϩⲓⲧⲛ ⲧⲓⲡⲓⲧⲧⲁ
ⲣⲛ ☩[110] |

the fifth century onward at the shrines of St. Leontius of Arsinoë, St. Philoxenus of Oxyrhynchus, and St. Colluthus of Antinoë.[109]

Their concerns extend from relocation, as in the example from Lycopolis included here in the box,[111] to financial aspirations and pregnancy.[112] The questions are worded in ways that reflect a kind of clerical orthodoxy—"O God of St. Leontius"; "My Lord God Almighty and St. Philoxenus my patron"—and there is no record of the practice's censure by bishops or abbots. And yet, what has struck scholars of late antique Egypt for decades is that this very procedure of requesting an oracle from a supernatural patron using dual, pre-inscribed tickets was a standard form of shrine service in Greco-Roman Egypt and actually goes back to the New Kingdom.[113] Great numbers of oracle questions, written in both Demotic Egyptian and Greek, have been discovered at some crocodile-god temples in the Fayyum, while the Bes cult at Abydos, whose official closure in 359 Ammianus Marcellinus describes, had apparently developed its own ticket oracle of international renown, for an archive of questions people had sent there came to the attention of the Roman authorities, to the misfortune of some of the inquirers.[114]

---

109 De Nie, "Een Koptisch-Christelijke Orakelvraag"; Donadoni, "Una domanda oracolare cristiana"; Youtie, "Questions to a Christian Oracle"; Papini, "Biglietti oracolari in copto"; idem, "Domande oracolari."

110 Ed.De Nie, "Een Koptisch-Christelijke Orakelvraag."

111 Ibid.; Papaconstantinou, "Oracles chrétiens," 282; idem, *Le culte des saints en Égypte*, 295.

112 Financial aspirations: see, e.g., ACM 32 = P. Oxy 1926; ACM 33 = Harris 54. Pregnancy: ACM 65 = Rylands 100.

113 Frankfurter, *Religion in Roman Egypt*, 159–62; Ryholt, "Pair of Oracle Petitions."

114 Ammianus 19.3-4. Discussions of Christian ticket oracles: Papaconstantinou, "Oracles chrétiens," 281–86; idem, *Le culte des saints en Égypte*, 336–39; Husson, "Les questions oraculaires chré-

CHAPTER 4

Given this wealth of regional precedents, the ticket oracle might well be labeled a "survival." But does this represent accurately what was going on in the fifth century? No contemporaries seem to have regarded ticket oracles as heathen—indeed, not even hagiographers mention the practice—and the tickets' very phrasing ("God of St. Colluthus") seems to reflect not only the scribes' conscious endeavor to maintain an instructive monotheism but quite likely ecclesiastical supervision—a supervision well beyond, for example, what Coptic ritual manuals reflect (despite the fact that these writings too may have come from shrine milieux). By the fifth century it is doubtful that scribes and overseers affiliated with the cults had any memory of the old Egyptian ticket oracles (in contrast, as we shall see, to memories of traditional incubation oracles). It is up to the historian of religions, then, to explain a ritual continuity of which the subjects and observers themselves were apparently unaware.

This revitalization of an archaic literary form of mediating a god's authority can be attributed to three factors: (a) the role of *literate experts* as an integral social component of shrines; (b) the agency of *visitors* in demanding the mediation of saints' authority through writing; and (c) the culturally inscribed *ritual gesture* of articulating concerns in dual written form, revitalized in the context of the first two factors. By recognizing the dynamic interaction of these factors we obviate the need to fix the ticket oracle to particular gods, or temple religion, or "paganism." Rather, the ticket oracle constitutes a "shrine habitus"—an indigenous technology, even—operating at the nexus of certain social and spatial roles. The oracles, as institutionalized extensions of the shrines of Sts. Colluthus, Leontius, and others, were *Christian* practices in their context: like votives and *eulogia*, they were means of accessing the power and authority of the saints.

What about incubation? Sleeping in a shrine to gain a god's communication was a well-known practice in the ancient world and especially in Greco-Roman Egypt, where shrines at Abydos, Deir el-Bahri, and Saqqara became centers of incubation.[115] Incubation as a means of accessing a god's instruction goes back to both priestly and royal practices in pharaonic Egypt—the mantic dreams of kings, for example, made for a lively topic in ancient Near Eastern literature.[116] The popular use of incubation to contact traditional gods is attested at the Abydos Bes shrine as late as the fourth century CE, and quite likely beyond, and at the Isis temple of Menouthis, near Alexandria, into the late fifth century CE.[117] It is then perhaps no wonder that Shenoute of Atripe, from his vantage near Panopolis, disparages in his sermons "those who dream dreams like those in places for oracles" and elsewhere condemns those who "sleep in tombs to gain visions."[118] In-

---

tiennes"; Frankfurter, *Religion in Roman Egypt*, 193–95. On oracular practices in Roman and Christian Egypt in general, see idem, "Voices, Books, and Dreams."

115 See Renberg, *Where Dreams May Come*.
116 Frankfurter, *Religion in Roman Egypt*, 158–59, 162–74.
117 Dunand, "La consultation oraculaire"; Frankfurter, *Religion in Roman Egypt*, 162–74.
118 "Those who work evil," ed. Amélineau, *Oeuvres de Schenoudi I*, 220; see also Lefort, "La

deed, Christian incubation practices in Egypt seem to have developed in connection with cemeteries and the cults of the holy dead that developed there: the vibrant incubation and oracle center in Antinoë dedicated to the martyr St. Colluthus in fact grew out of the local cemetery.[119]

By the sixth century incubation was being celebrated in shrine miracle collections as a devout and proper means of beholding the saint at his shrine and was even seen as a point of competition between shrines. The *Miracles of Saints John and Cyrus*, for example, criticizes one supplicant who has abandoned the Menouthis shrine to be healed at the martyrion of St. Metras and likewise celebrates the geographical range of Cyrus's and John's powers in their rescue of a boat in trouble on Lake Mareotis—in the immediate vicinity of the Apa Menas shrine![120] Numerous architectural strategies were employed in Egyptian churches and martyria to incorporate incubation space into a shrine's overall arrangement, from the placement of beds along interior walls to, at Apa Mena, what the lead archaeologist has interpreted as an entire hostel for incubants, laid out in semicircular form near the crypt (see fig. 8).[121] To be sure, the shrines' miracle collections emphasize the use of incubation for *healing* rather than to resolve the diverse areas of life the ticket oracles address. But people probably brought other questions as well to the saints that are not recorded in miracle collections, which were often shaped with ideological motivations.[122] In general we ought to see healing in this ritual context not necessarily in a medical sense, but as providing the *pretext* and *context* for devotees—as well as the audiences of the collections—to encounter the presence, the glory, the image, and the authority of the saint.[123] The rites of healing provided, in the words of the historian William Christian, "a theater in which grace could plausibly be delivered."[124]

---

chasse aux reliques"; Canon 9: *God Who Alone Is True*, Vienna K9040, in Young, *Coptic Manuscripts*, 23–25; Emmel, *Shenoute's Literary Corpus*, 1:600–1; *Let Our Eyes* fr. 1, 10, in Emmel, "Shenoute of Atripe." Cf. Frag. US-NCD, P. Duke, inv. 244/Copt. Ms. 25 (uncertain authorship) in Emmel, *Shenoute's Literary Corpus*, 1:907; MacCoull, "Duke University Ms. C25."

119 See Grossmann, "Antinoopolis," esp. 268–69, 276–80.

120 Sophronios, *Miracles* 13.4–5 (vs. Metras cult); 8.3–5 (vs. Apa Mena).

121 Grossmann, "Pilgrimage Center of Abu Mina," 288–90; idem, "Late Antique Christian Incubation Centres"; and also, on the St. Colluthus site, idem, Antinoopolis," 242–45, 276–80. See also Baumeister, *Martyr invictus*, 68–71; and Frankfurter, "Voices, Books, and Dreams," 244–45. Cf. the specific (elite) use of the *ciborium* of the St. Demetrios church in Thessaloniki for incubation: Skedros, *Saint Demetrios of Thessaloniki*, 88–94.

122 See Maraval, "Fonction pédagogique."

123 In this sense, Gil Renberg's strict division between revelatory and therapeutic incubation does not capture the slippage between these types and functions on the ground; Renberg, *Where Dreams May Come*, 21–30.

124 Christian, *Local Religion in Sixteenth-Century Spain*, 98. See in general Stewart, "Ritual Dreams and Historical Orders." On healing at Menouthis, see Sansterre, "Apparations et miracles," esp. 72–73; and, in general, on healing as a discourse for interacting with gods and saints in late antiquity, see Rousselle, *Croire et guérir*, chs. 6–7.

CHAPTER 4

The growth of incubation at Egyptian saints' shrines thus provides a rich area for the discussion of the life of the shrine, the perpetuation of habitus, and syncretism itself as an integral part of Christianization. For not only does incubation strike the historian of religions as a continuing ritual form like the ticket oracle, but *unlike* the ticket oracle, it also struck contemporaries as theologically suspect and potentially heathen.[125] Shenoute, who rails against the practice in his sermons, never himself pronounced it heathen, but the establishment of the John and Cyrus cult in Menouthis, an area renowned throughout late antiquity as a place for Isis oracles, involved deliberate efforts to contrast the healing saints' powers to the goddess's.

Much has been written on the transition from Isis to John and Cyrus in this suburb of Alexandria, but the reconstruction of the sequence of events that occurred that I rely on in this book follows the work of Jean Gascou.[126] An Isis incubation temple with minimal staffing still persisted in Menouthis in 489 CE, when it was implicated in Alexandrian conflicts between Christian *philoponoi*, intellectual Hellenists, and the Alexandrian patriarch Peter Mongos, who sent monks to exorcise and then eliminate the small cult.[127] Soon thereafter the nearby monastery of the Metanoia imported the relics of the obscure martyrs John and Cyrus as part of its campaign to obliterate traditional religion, and these monks built a martyrion in Menouthis. This accomplishment seems to appear in a 531 CE mosaic in the Palestinian church of Gerasa.[128] And yet the shrine's authority (and the relics' authenticity) among Alexandrians and villagers in Menouthis seems to have remained a matter of contestation.[129] So, at some point in the sixth century, a series of homilies was written in the name of the early fifth-century Chalcedonian bishop Cyril of Alexandria. Ostensibly delivered as the relics were brought in procession from Alexandria to Menouthis, they explicitly contrast the healing powers of Cyrus and John with those of the Lady, *Kyra*, who "invents dreams" and "tells pilgrims [ἐρχομένοις] 'do this and that' "[130]—that is to say, with incubation oracles from Isis. Given the homilies' posthumous appearance, it is impossible to tell how real Isis remained to local

125 See esp. Graf, "Dangerous Dreaming."
126 Gascou, "Les origines du culte"; developing the thesis of Duchesne, "Le sanctuaire d'Aboukir." Cf. Takács, "Magic of Isis Replaced"; Montserrat, "Pilgrimage to the Shrine."
127 Zachariah of Mytilene, *v. Sev.* 14–37, in Kugener, "Sévère, patriarche d'Antioche"; trans. Ambjörn, *Life of Severus*. See Frankfurter, "Consequences of Hellenism," 188–91; Watts, *Riot in Alexandria*, 234–43.
128 Metanoia monastery's use of relics as part of Christianization is reflected in Eunapius, *v.Phil.* 472. Gerasa mosaic: Biebel, "Mosaics," 328; and McKenzie, *Architecture of Alexandria and Egypt*, fig. 413. See also Gascou, "Les origines du culte," 266, n.132.
129 See Sophronius, *Miracles*, #29, in Gascou, *Sophrone de Jérusalem*, 97–101, describing the skepticism of one Athanasia, a rich woman of Alexandria, toward the relics and their legend and citing "Cyril's" account (5).
130 Cyril of Alexandria [attrib.], Homily 3 on John and Cyrus, PG 77:1105A.

practitioners of religion by the sixth century, although clearly, in juxtaposing the powers of the saints to those of Isis, the author imagined the goddess to be quite functional in Cyril's time.[131]

These Cyril homilies promote the saints' healing powers, not incubation per se. But by 620, the first major hagiographical collection had been composed by the contemporary Alexandrian patriarch Sophronius celebrating incubation as the central means of interacting with sanctuary and saints:

> [Cyrus and John] took pity on (the woman) in such distress, wailing with piercing cries. They caused her to sleep and to have a dream or dream-vision.... (Then) she beheld men in monastic habits, of radiant appearance, who regarded her with a benevolent and sweet air. They approached her graciously and said to her, "With these wails you're going to wake up the sick people lying here—why?" She responded that she had pain in her abdomen.
>
> [The rich Alexandrian woman] presented herself [at the shrine]; and as she slept the night she saw the martyrs walking down the length of the rows of the sick. They attended to all of them, one by one, producing the remedy for each one, prescribing for one to do this, for another that. They began at the first, healing (as it were) each in his turn until they got to her. Arriving at her cot they turned their gaze as if she wasn't there, (then) left her without attending or prescribing a remedy.... [She complained to them, and they responded that they had no treatment, for she was going to die].[132]

This new Cyrus/John propaganda sought to promote the cult internationally—and certainly beyond the more successful pilgrimage center of Apa Mena some ninety kilometers to the southwest.[133] And yet this seventh-century miracle collection reflects a mainly local clientele, with local staffing and, in fact, suggestions of a rather diverse assortment of local ritual practices.[134] Clients take the saints as instructing them to eat a peacock and a live snake, and to use crocodile flesh as an eye salve. These kinds of dream communications, expressed through such particular local fauna, suggest that the Cyrus/John cult had been appropriated and assimilated into the local symbolic world and landscape of visitors from the region of Menouthis, including some who secretly maintained traditional

---

131 It is certainly conceivable that old gods would still have been quite real to Christian authorities in the fifth century, whether as competition or as demonic threats. In about 400 CE, for example, Shenoute refers to oracles deceptively produced through "Hekate": *Let Our Eyes* fr. 1, 10, in Emmel, "Shenoute and the Destruction," 184 (translation), 191–92 (text).

132 Sophronius, *Miracles*, #21.4, 62.4; ed. Marcos, *Los Thaumata de Sofronio*, 282–83, 379; trans. Gascou, *Sophrone de Jérusalem*, 79, 202.

133 Cf. Sophronius, *Miracles*, #8.3–12, in Gascou, *Sophrone de Jérusalem*, 40–43.

134 Local clientele: Montserrat, "Pilgrimage to the Shrine," 273–76; Gascou, "Les origines du culte," 275–76. Local staffing: Sophronius, *Miracles* 9.3, 10, in Gascou, *Sophrone de Jérusalem*, 45–48.

ritual practices.¹³⁵ The collection also refers to other modes of oracular dreaming that were seen as illegitimate, such as those "despicable apparitions of demons [τὰ τῶν δαίμονων φαυλότατα φάσματα]" mentioned by Sophronius whose "workings [δρώμενα] are kept secret [ἐν παράβυστω]." A subsequent miracle relates how one Theodoros, ordered by the saints to eat a live snake, fears the dream vision comes from a demon.¹³⁶ In light of the systematic effort over several centuries to replace the established Isis oracle with the Cyrus/John oracle,¹³⁷ these references to demonic dreams suggest that some sort of *illegitimate incubation* continued to be practiced, both to some traditional spirits ("demons") and perhaps in some traditional sites in the vicinity of the Cyrus/John oracle.¹³⁸ These factors in themselves would indicate that the rise of incubation in the Cyrus/John cult was not so much an official innovation as an established local form of interaction that developed at the shrine: a habitus, in the sense of the gesture of the body asleep and dreaming.¹³⁹

Of course, the Cyrus/John cult is only the most well documented of the shrines that developed incubation as a practice and as a hagiographical theme. Others, like Apa Mena, provided different arrangements for pilgrims who regarded their dreams and bodies, and especially their ailing bodies, as media for the appearance of saints.¹⁴⁰ In this sense incubation seems to have been understood as a perfectly proper mode of Christian healing at least as late as the sixth century. It would thus misrepresent the practice to label it a "survival." Rather, it was part of the cultural vocabulary of shrine gestures that were in play at Egyptian shrines, as surely as lighting candles, collecting sand, leaving votives, and verbally imploring the saint.¹⁴¹

---

135 On those described by Sophronius as secretly maintaining traditional forms of devotion (##31–32, 54), see Caseau, "Le crypto paganisme."

136 Sophronius, *Miracles*, 9.7, ed. Marcos, *Los thaumata de Sofronio*, 258, trans. Gascou, *Sophrone de Jérusalem*, 46.

137 See Sophronius, *Miracles*, 66.1, on memory of the defunct "Menouthē" temple; and ibid., #32, on a local Hellene who persisted in traditional devotions despite edicts; in Gascou, *Sophrone de Jérusalem*, 210, 110–14. Pace Gascou, "Les origines du culte," 265–66, 279–80, which rejects the idea that the Menouthis Isis cult remained vital in late antiquity.

138 Cf. the roughly contemporaneous ritual handbook Michigan ms. 593 (= ACM 133), which includes a spell "to cause an instruction to be given to you in a dream [ετρε-γ-τογνειατ-ⲕ ⲉⲃⲟⲗ ϩⲛ ⲟⲩ-ⲣⲁⲥⲟⲩ]. Take some rocksalt and place it under your head as you sleep, and you will be informed about everything [ⲥⲉⲛⲁⲧⲁⲙⲟⲕ ⲉϩⲱⲃ ⲛⲓⲙ]"; ed. Worrell, "Coptic Wizard's Hoard," 249; translation emended from Mirecki, in Meyer and Smith, *Ancient Christian Magic*, 307.

139 On the notion of the body as receiver of divine messages, see Struck, "Viscera and the Divine"; Stewart, "Ritual Dreams and Historical Orders."

140 Drescher, *Apa Mena*, 64–65, 122–23.

141 Cf. Graf, "Dangerous Dreaming"; and idem, *Roman Festivals*, 241–67, which argues for a starker difference in Christian attitudes to dreaming that obviates any model of continuity. His argument takes ecclesiastical objections to dreams, like Shenoute's and Tertullian's, as characterizing broader religious attitudes, such that "Christian incubation" amounts to an oxymoron. But the literary and archaeological evidence shows that incubation was a common practice at Christian shrines,

Both of these ritual traditions, the ticket oracle and incubation, were—notably—types of *divination*, an especially eclectic ritual field and one of particular importance for understanding ancient and traditional cultures. As I explained in chapter 3, divination always involves the preparation of some sort of controlled palette of random elements, the allowance of an active period for the random elements to assemble into an omen, and the presence of some interpretive authority to translate the omen into an oracle for social or personal utility. Historians and anthropologists are well aware of the immense diversity of such palettes, from *templa* in the sky to children playing in courtyards, the movement of animals or statues in procession, astral prodigies, and objects thrown from a cup. But even as divination was a common form of receiving official communication from cult deities in ancient times, it also covered a world of noninstitutional practices. In Roman Egypt alone there were divination books under the fictional authority of ancient wizards, and divination could occur using bowls of water and by children looking into mirrors. Christianization brought a more concerted sense of the mantic authority of the Bible, as well as holy men who functioned as speaking oracles.[142] Because divination comprises any means of getting socially or personally practical communications from any cult, or any authority, we should appreciate the development of ticket oracles and incubation at major Christian shrines not simply as an archaism, a reversion to ancient modes of ritual gesture, but also as part of the inevitable—popular *and* official—ritual innovation that occurred around shrines, temples, martyria, and churches, and even beyond such cult sites. Oracles were sought at sites in the landscape and even through domestic objects like lamps and mirrors. As one procedure instructs, "For an oracle [ⲘⲀⲚⲦⲈⲒⲞⲚ]: utter the prayer three times at the time when the morning star rises. The matter will be revealed [ⲚⲀϬⲰⲖⲠ] to you."[143] Like many such procedures, this one required no shrine. Overall, the popularity of divination traditions and technologies demonstrates that people wanted gods, saints, and spirits not only to hear, but to *answer*.

Both of these divination forms arose as functions of social interaction among local visitors, local shrine attendants and specialists, monks, and ecclesiastical officials, and they arose out of the nature of the shrine structure itself as an innovation in the landscape. Both constituted gestures of interaction with authoritative, sacred space: whether through the dreaming body or through the medium

---

so broad generalizations about Christian and "pagan" attitudes are not sustainable at the local level, where the impulse to incubate was generated as much from the devotees as from attendants.

142 Frankfurter, *Religion in Roman Egypt*, 179–97; idem, "Voices, Books, and Dreams"; idem, "Syncretism and the Holy Man"; Johnston, "Charming Children"; and, on the more refined bibliomancy promoted by the fourth-century church, Brakke, "Canon Formation and Social Conflict"; with singular Christian developments in the mantic use of the Bible in Wiśniewski, "Pagans, Jews, Christians."

143 ACM 128 = Cairo 45060, 39–40, ed. Kropp, *Ausgewählte koptische Zaubertexte*, 1.52. Cf. ACM 133 = Michigan 593, #27 (dream revelation).

of writing. Both came to operate as quintessentially Christian modes of shrine gesture, even if incubation was sometimes regarded as inappropriate or even demonic. But the popularity of both forms of divination point to the way that Christianization itself amounted to syncretism: that is, a locally negotiated process of selection and recombination performed in many different religious worlds.

VII. POSSESSION AND THE PERFORMANCE OF SPIRITS AND SAINTLY POWER

Divination assures audiences of the presence of a god or saint. Incubation and ticket oracles established the divine presence through direct, informative interventions: it is *this* that you should do; in your dream we provided *that* remedy. But some kinds of divination serve primarily to dramatize the divine presence and lend it nuance as a force in the world—to let us know that the spirit, whether saint or god, is *here*, in *this place*, right *now*. By their nature as "places" of holy beings, saints' shrines inevitably invited a range of divinatory indications of these figures' presence, especially at festival times. These indications might have involved celestial prodigies, like the shooting star that purportedly signified the arrival of the heavenly St. Simeon Stylites at his basilica in the fifth century, or even, at the shrine of St. Thecla in Seleucia (Asia Minor), an unusual vision of the saint riding through the sky:

> During the *panēgyris* that honours the Virgin (Thecla) . . . if one (seeks to) observe the night-vigil of the festival, one ascends to the summit of that mountain on the outskirts, and with one's back to the east one sets one's gaze to the west, remaining on the spot without sleeping; (and then at dawn) one beholds, in a flaming chariot rising high in the air, the Virgin (Thecla), driving the chariot, heading from one home to another.[144]

Expectations of such prodigies grow up around shrines and the miraculous nature of their festival times, and when they occur, all pilgrims can share in the certainty that the saint has arrived. But in ancient religions, more often than such collective indicators, the arrival of spirits was typically heralded by some kind of "speaking oracle," a person who entered a possessed state either by expertise (shamanism) or in apparently spontaneous response to historical circumstances, especially crises, when people often sought the reassuring presence and guidance of ancestral spirits.[145] It is this spontaneous oracular response, often communicated

---

144 *Miracles of Thecla* 26, in Dagron, *Vie et miracles*, 356. On Simeon Stylites, see above, pp. 124–25.

145 For antiquity, see Maurizio, "Anthropology and Spirit Possession"; for later Christian contexts, see Caciola, *Discerning Spirits*; Sluhovsky, *Believe Not Every Spirit*.

through the voice of a spirit other than the saint, that we find arising among devotees at saints' shrines as early as fourth-century Egypt, and across the Mediterranean world.[146]

From its earliest stages the Christian movement had provided legitimacy for the seer, prophet, or individual speaking oracle—the roles shade into each other—who could frame the times as urgent and perform the voice of the risen Christ or angelic spirit. Thus John of Patmos conveys his warnings and instructions in the Book of Revelation (chaps. 1–3, 22), and the New Prophecy movement that spread from Asia Minor to North Africa over the second and third centuries likewise cultivated ecstatic utterances.[147] In 256 CE Firmilian of Caesarea described how a woman in his congregation had begun to prophesy "as if stirred by the Holy Spirit," conveying signs and prodigies, assuming responsibility for liturgical acts like the Eucharist, and in the guise of the spirit describing its home in Judea. Subsequently, an outside exorcist showed up and denounced the spirit as, in fact, a demon. It was in full recollection of the spirit's *shift* in identity and function that Firmilian reported the episode.[148] It is thus clear that however outsiders, or even eventually insiders, evaluate the identity of such an authoritative spirit, the possessed person, as seer and speaking oracle, fulfills a vital function in manifesting, situating, and adding nuance to the divine presence for an audience.

What interests me here is how such ambiguous forms of spirit possession— spirits that are reevaluated as demons, demons that function as speaking oracles—became an important feature of saints' shrines in Egypt and elsewhere in the late antique world, maintaining for audiences the functional proximity of ambiguous spiritual powers while also dramatizing the power of Christ and the saints in local, embodied terms.

For example, in the early fifth century CE, Archbishop Theophilus of Alexandria instituted a building program designed to Christianize the very infrastructure of Alexandria and its surroundings. In this endeavor Theophilus reflected the growing sense in late antique Mediterranean culture that what distinguished a Christian city and gave it prestige was its saints—its protectors and conduits to heaven.[149] One particular edifice in this program, now lost in the palimpsest of Alexandrian topography, was a shrine to the three Hebrew youths who survived the furnace in the Book of Daniel (3:1–30). This shrine, however, seems to have suffered a significant handicap as a place for pilgrims to communicate with these saints: to wit, the Three Hebrew Youths' actual relics remained in Ctesiphon, in

---

146 The following condenses Frankfurter, "Where the Spirits Dwell"; and idem, "Urban Shrine and Rural Saint," 437–43.
147 Heine, *Montanist Oracles and Testimonia*. See also Origen, *c. Celsum* 7.9.
148 Cyprian, *Ep.* 75.10.2–5.
149 On Theophilus's building program, see Haas, *Alexandria in Late Antiquity*, 206–14; Caseau, "Sacred Landscapes," 36–38; Gauthier, "La topographie chrétienne," 207–9.

CHAPTER 4

Babylonia.[150] Thus the shrine of the Three Hebrews Youths in Alexandria would have presented a rather questionable degree of power, of saintly "presence," especially in a landscape already rich in real bones. If the heroes resided in Babylonia, what efficacy could they have in the shrine in Alexandria? Why would people come to an empty martyrion?[151]

This problem gave rise to two legends about the Three Youths' regular appearance at the shrine on their festival eve on the ninth of Pachons (May 17). In the first (but probably latest) legend, suggesting shamanic mediation, the fifth-century holy man John the Little is asked to intercede directly with the Three Youths themselves. He takes off on a cloud to Babylon and secures their promise that they will make an annual visit to the Alexandrian shrine, even while—the Youths insist—their relics would remain in Babylon.[152] In the second legend, which seems to reflect more closely shrine practices in the fifth and sixth centuries, the eve of their festival is regarded as the time of their actual arrival, accompanied by promises of healing and miracles. This belief consequently frames certain mantic practices meant to signify the Three Youths' presence in the shrine: lamps left unlit are miraculously illuminated, and—more pertinently—those lying in vigil at the shrine respond to their arrival as demons.

We see this belief underlying a miracle story that would have been recounted as a festival reading, one I used in chapter 2 to illustrate men's agency in religion of the domestic sphere.[153] In this tale the wife of an artisan repeatedly miscarries on account of a demon, each time descending into near-catatonic depression, and the couple's only son is himself afflicted by a deaf-mute demon. The husband is

---

150 Pseudo-Theophilus, "Sermon on the Three Hebrews," in De Vis, Homélies coptes de la Vaticane I–II, 2:121–57. According to an Armenian account of their invention, the cult of the Three Hebrew Youths in Ctesiphon seems to have started under the reign of Bahram V (early fifth century CE), perhaps with the relics' transfer from the Jewish community: see Garitte, "L'Invention géorgienne," esp. 69–75; and idem, "Le texte arménien." Chapter 92 of the Life of Daniel the Stylite attests to the relics' translation to Constantinople under Emperor Leo I (457–474) and their placement over Daniel's tomb at his burial in 493; see Dawes and Baynes, Three Byzantine Saints, 64–65.

151 See also Gascou, "Notes de papyrologie Byzantine (II)," esp. 333–37 ("Les sanctuaries dédiés aux trois saints jeunes gens en Égypte Byzantine"). It is conceivable that this rivalry with Babylon over important relics recalled Ptolemy I's claim of Alexander's body to sanction Alexandria. But rivalry among shrines to the same divinity over the divinity's "presence" is well known to have occurred elsewhere in the Mediterranean world: propagandists for the dominant shrine of Asclepius at Epidaurus asserted the god's *absence* from his shrine at Troizen, claiming that if one insisted on visiting Troizen, Asclepius would have to make a special trip *over from* Epidaurus: see Epidaurus B3, C5, in LiDonnici, Epidaurian Miracle Inscriptions, 71–73.

152 Life of John the Little, in Amélineau, Histoire des monastères de la basse-Egypte, 316–413; Pseudo-Theophilus, Sermon on the Three Hebrew Youths, in De Vis, Homélies coptes de la Vaticane I–II, 2:121–57. See also Mikhail and Vivian, "Life of Saint John the Little." On manuscripts behind the legend, see van Esbroeck, "Three Hebrews in the Furnace," 2257–59; and, in general, Frankfurter, "Urban Shrine and Rural Saint," 437–43.

153 See above, p. 40.

instructed to bring them both to the shrine of the Three Youths on the eve of their festival and to leave them there until morning.

It happened that at the ninth of Pachoms they led the woman with child to the holy shrine. And they prepared the lamps without oil, awaiting the arrival of the saints. During the night, the Lord manifested their arrival: the lamp (spontaneously) illuminated, and its flame brightened the entire city. Then the two demons—the one in the child and the one in the woman—cried out so that the whole crowd heard them: "Welcome, O Saints of God Ananias, Azarias, Misael, to the holy day of your festival. . . . By the order of God and by your (order) we leave and go into the river!" When the demons said this, they left and went into the river. Then the artisans took home those who were with them. The woman gave birth to a boy, and they called him Ananias. They gave an ex-voto [ⲛⲟⲩⲱϣ] and many gifts to the Shrine of the Three Saints.[154]

Thus the saints' advent and the commencement of their healing powers are indicated by the illumination of the unlit oil lamps and, more dramatically, by the verbal greetings of the "demons" in the bodies of those in vigil. Presumably the miraculous lighting of lamps and the greetings from the demoniacs were part of the culture of this shrine during its day.

Now, as stylized as this last image might appear to be (recalling, for example, the demons' recognitions of Jesus in the Gospel of Mark), the function of demon-possessed individuals in providing audiences with otherwise obscure information is well attested around the late antique Mediterranean world as a phenomenon of the saint's shrine itself. In Egypt we encounter it initially in the witness of Athanasius of Alexandria. In his festal letter of 370 CE Athanasius laments a new practice among Christians in the countryside of congregating in tomb-martyria for a curious ritual process. "Many people," notes Athanasius, " who had unclean spirits gain healing in the martyria, claiming that the martyrs' spirits come upon the demons [ϣⲱⲡⲉ ϩⲓϩⲉⲛⲇⲁⲓⲙⲱⲛⲓⲟⲛ] . . . and the demons cry out." However, he complains, people also "seek to see the demons [ⲥⲉⲛⲁϣⲓⲛⲉ ⲉⲩⲛⲁⲩ ⲉⲛ̄ⲇⲁⲓⲙⲱⲛ]," apparently through possession at these tomb-shrines. Then, with the demons manifest in devotees' bodies, "these people give glory to them and ask them about what will happen [ⲉⲧⲟⲩⲧⲉⲟⲟⲩ ⲛⲁⲩ ⲁⲩⲱ ⲉⲩϫⲛⲟⲩ ⲛ̄ⲙⲟⲟⲩ ⲉⲧⲃⲉⲧⲛⲁϣⲱⲡⲉ] . . . they dare to question the unclean spirits!" The people assume "the demons are the prophets of the martyrs. But the martyrs did not confess that they would speak through the demons! [ⲉⲩⲙⲉⲉⲩⲉ ⲉⲛⲇⲁⲓⲙⲱⲛⲓⲟⲛ ϫⲉ ⲙ̄ⲡⲣⲟⲫⲏⲧⲏⲥⲛⲉ ⲛ̄ⲙⲁⲣⲧⲩⲣⲟⲥ, ⲁⲗⲗⲁ ⲛ̄ⲧⲁⲙ̄ⲙⲁⲣⲧⲩⲣⲟⲥ ϩⲟⲙⲟⲗⲟⲅⲉⲓ ⲁⲛ ⲛ̄ⲛ̄ⲇⲁⲓⲙⲱⲛⲓⲟⲛ ϫⲉ ⲉⲩⲛⲁϣⲁϫⲉ ϩⲓⲧⲟⲟⲧⲟⲩ]."[155]

---

154 Pseudo-Cyril, *Encomium on the Three Youths*, Miracle 7, ed. De Vis, *Homélies coptes de La Vaticane I–II*, 2:189–93 (my translation).

155 Athanasius, *Festal Letter* 42, fr. 15, in Lefort, *S. Athanase*, 65; trans. Brakke, "'Outside the Places, Within the Truth,'" 479–80.

CHAPTER 4

Although he reports people going to tomb-shrines to experience demons, Athanasius is clearly not describing a simple cult of exorcism, the practice of *expelling* such spirits. There was some ambiguity in these Egyptian Christian possession forms. As Athanasius depicts the situation, it was demonic spirits that emerged at the shrines *due to* the awesome spirits of the martyrs. Once they became manifest, however, the "demons" became oracular voices—even "the prophets of the martyrs"—to which devotees could address their questions. The spirit possession Athanasius observed evidently involved some fluidity in function—that is, in social utility—between spirits deemed "demonic" and spirits deemed "martyrial."[156]

Less than a century later, around the mid-fifth century CE, Shenoute of Atripe echoes some of these complaints about the popular relic cult, but he aims his sermon at those who were illegitimately establishing *topoi*, "places" for relics in or by churches where people claimed to have seen lights appear.[157] After detailing how people "sleep in the tombs to gain visions and . . . question the dead about the living"—familiar and long-standing incubation practices—Shenoute refers to "other sorts of places—of divination [ⲙⲙⲁ ⲛϣⲓⲛⲉ] or of mediumship [ⲉⲅⲅⲁⲥⲧⲣⲓⲙⲩⲑⲟⲥ]." It would seem that the "places" were, again, shrines, while the word *eggastrimythos* denotes ecstatic speech, such as the medium of Endor provided for Saul in the Bible but was now being provided, Shenoute says, by "Christians and clerics (who serve) in the house of God."[158] While in the biblical account the medium of Endor was supposed to have channeled the spirit of a dead Samuel, Christian writers of the second and third centuries debated whether such a voice would have had to be intrinsically demonic, and Shenoute would certainly have been commenting on the ambiguity of possession by spirits in his time, asking whether they were dead martyrs or demons. Thus spirit possession of some sort appears to have arisen again ("in these times [ⲉⲃⲟⲗ ϩⲙ ⲛⲓⲕⲁⲓⲣⲟⲥ]") in connection with relic veneration and the founding of new martyr shrines.[159]

As we saw with the shrine of the Three Hebrew Youths in Alexandria, reports about demons with oracular functions were closely linked with the powers of specific saints and the authority of the saint's shrine in the landscape. Similar reports, for example, come from the shrine of St. Martin in Gaul and from shrines

156 It may be to this situation that Athanasius refers in *v.Ant.* 23.5, where the hermit Antony warns against demons' pretenses "to prophesy and foretell what is going to happen"; Bartelink, *Athanase d'Alexandrie*, 200.

157 Similar mantic practices for discovering martyrs' tombs and relics are reported for early fifth-century CE Carthage and were proscribed by the Council of Carthage (419 ce) in Canon 83.

158 ϩⲙ ⲡⲏⲉⲓ ⲙⲡⲛⲟⲩⲧⲉ does not necessarily mean that such acts take place in the church itself.

159 Shenoute of Atripe, *Those Who Work Evil*, in Amélineau, *Oeuvres de Schenoudi I*, 220. See Lefort, "La chasse aux reliques"; and, on the shortly post–431 CE date, Emmel, *Shenoute's Literary Corpus*, 1:649–50, 669–70. The term ⲉⲅⲅⲁⲥⲧⲣⲓⲙⲩⲑⲟⲥ is employed in Leviticus 19:31 and 1 Samuel 28:8 (LXX) to denote ecstatic mediumship and was a topic of considerable discussion in early Christian exegesis regarding the location of souls and the nature of demonic deception: see Smelik, "Witch of Endor"; and Greer and Mitchell, *"Belly-Myther" of Endor*.

of John the Baptist and St. Panteleemon in Constantinople. At the Italian shrine of St. Felix, described by Paulinus, and at an unnamed martyrion in Palestine described secondhand by Jerome, the elaborate, even acrobatic, performance of demon-possessed individuals signified the active presence of the resident saint.[160] In Antioch John Chrysostom observed that "if you grab someone who's demon-possessed and exhibiting manic behaviour and take him into that holy tomb where the martyr's remains lie, without a doubt you'll see him jumping back and fleeing."[161] A man visiting St. Artemios's shrine in Constantinople for a testicular condition, for example, turned out also to have an "evil spirit," which led him to hang suspended before the icon of Artemios "as though his hands were tied by chains, hovering one cubit above the floor, and yelling loudly, so that all [those supplicants likewise incubating in the shrine] were astonished by the sight and were cowed by fear."[162] Such performances served as authenticating spectacles at shrines, initiated through the centralizing experience of the shrine itself.

While the performances of possession ranged from responses to the saints' presence to oracular pronouncements, the "demons" were almost never identified with prior local gods. They were instead envisioned and enacted as *ambiguous* beings, responsive to the saint, to the audience's need to behold somehow the saint's presence, and to the audience's need for information or political assurance through supernatural authority—that is, for oracles. As ambivalent personalities, these spirits served as "loc[i] of historical specificity"[163]: from the ecstatic trances of devotees emerged voices—agencies—that recalled traditional spirits, addressed specific events, and reflected on the potency of the saint in space and time. In that particular sense, the possession phenomena maintained some traditional understandings and functions of local spirits and speaking oracles. But in a more general sense, we might say, these "demons" comprised the incoherent possession forms of a culture *conscious* of its abandoned gods but utterly *invested* in the power of the Christian saint in its shrine. And individuals' performative construction of these ambiguous beings developed in response to Christian demonology: the ecclesiastical assertion, disseminated through sermons and public readings, that there existed a rank of chaotic spirits that Christ and the saints *could* dramatically dispel. In that sense, these spirits were demons: the foils as well as the recognizers of the saints.

The syncretism of these possession phenomena pertains, then, to a range of functions: traditional roles for speaking oracles and the defining scripts provided by Christian demon tales, the authoritative presence of the saint's shrine as a theater of supernatural conflict, and the spontaneous role that some individuals will

---

160 Martin of Tours/Gaul: Sulpicius Severus, *v.Mart.* 18.1–2. John the Baptist/Constantinople: Sozomen, *Hist. Eccl.* 7.24.8–9. St. Felix Shrine/Nola: Paulinus of Nola, *Carmen* 14.25–33, 23:82–95. Jerome/Palestine: *Ep.* 108.13. See in general Mathisen, "Crossing the Supernatural Frontier."
161 Chrysostom, *Hom. In Jul. Mart.* 2 (PG 50: 669–70), in Leemans et al., *"Let Us Die,"* 133.
162 *Miracles of St. Artemios* 6, in Crisafulli and Nesbitt, *Miracles of St. Artemios*, 88–89.
163 Strathern, *Body Thoughts*, 154, 157.

inevitably assume for themselves as public indicators of the saints' presence. Spirit possession thus served as a dramatic, performative means by which people in the region could appropriate the shrine and the saint as active forces in the landscape, visible through spirits and the contorted bodies that channeled them.

VIII. CONCLUSION

The saint's shrine provided a new center for religion in the late antique landscape of Egypt: a place where a holy being who had lived and died in dramatic, fleshly fashion could continue to be accessible in every way. As scholars of pilgrimage across cultures have observed, these shrines served as axes of social activity, from their attraction of solitary supplicants to the great waves of pilgrims that flowed in at festivals. In fact, a theme of both excitement and censure in contemporary sermons was the behavior, the often-anomalous activities, of these festival crowds. Out of the *communitas* (to use Turner's felicitous term) of bodies concentrated outside of ordinary time, place, and social structure, there followed gestures of hilarity and dedication both: singing and dancing, animal slaughter and feasting, votive gestures and the use of objects of all sorts, buying and selling of food and souvenirs, and simple crowding at the holiest points. While church leaders and attendants sought everywhere to *channel* crowd impulses using processions, hymn singing, the reading of commemorative stories, and the assignment of spatial zones for different activities (like votive deposits and incubation), it is the religious expressions that people *brought to* shrines and festivals that have occupied our attention as indications of syncretistic agency. What some ancient authors and modern historians have labeled "pagan survivals" in festival behavior actually followed from the encounter between local gestural traditions and the shrine as axis and ideal place. Each traditional form—votive use of female figurines, choreographed dance, animal slaughter and feasting, possession and oracles—took shape in honor of the saint at his or her shrine. The syncretism of the saint's shrine is thus not a "balance" of religious heritages or a haphazard conglomeration of two religions but the steering of local gesture and agency to the Christian saint, a process facilitated by attendants and scribes. In the most remarkable performance of syncretism at these shrines, devotees in Egypt and elsewhere began to enact demons already associated with the landscape and local spirit traditions in preparation for the saint's dramatic exorcism. Thus, through the saint (and in his space), the earth spirits were affirmed—and even gave oracles—while the saint emerged preeminent.

CHAPTER 5

The Magic of Craft

TRADITIONS OF THE WORKSHOP AND
THE CONSTRUCTION OF EFFICACY

I. INTRODUCTION: ART AND EFFICACY

In the Byzantine collection of the Dumbarton Oaks Research Center hangs a limestone frieze depicting two antelopes harnessed tightly to a cross, under whose weight they strain and buckle (see fig. 9).[1] Now, it is common in late antique and Byzantine Christian art to depict deer grazing or posed "heraldically" next to a cross, or for the cross to be held between two contented animals or angels. Something else, however, was in the mind of this stonecarver: in representing the subduing of these antelopes by the cross he was demonstrating the cross's triumph over all that antelopes signified. But to get a sense of *what* antelopes signified in Egyptian relief sculpture, we have to consider artifacts from some centuries earlier: temple reliefs of the pharaoh spearing an antelope and a type of small stela, common for centuries in Egypt, that depicted the child-god Horus standing on crocodiles and grasping—among other hostile fauna—antelopes in his hands: the so-called Horus *cippi*.[2] What emerges from these artifacts is that antelopes in Egyptian art signified not the contented animals of Eden but the threat of the encroaching desert—a kind of demon, in fact, serving as a foil to the triumphant, apotropaic power of Horus in what we might call a traditional iconographic strategy.[3]

Like other ostensible "survivals" in this book, I want to shift the question so we are not left with some pharaonic anachronism but, instead, an anomaly that motivates inquiry into the process of Christianization itself. In this case I want to consider the agents behind the use of traditional iconographic strategies—craftsmen and workshops—and the ways in which they perpetuated or innovated such

---

1 BZ.1940.61; see Vikan, *Catalogue of the Sculpture*, 59; Bühl, *Dumbarton Oaks*, 122–23. Although this frieze, purchased before 1929, appears to be genuinely late antique and not part of the stream of "Coptic" fakes issuing from a few Egyptian workshops in the mid-twentieth century, another in the National Museum of Antiquities in Leiden, purchased in Cairo in 1970, seems to be a copy of the Dumbarton Oaks frieze (Leiden F 1984/4.1). See in general on the modern crafting of "Coptic" antiquities Bussmann, *Unearthing the Truth*.

2 Seele, "Horus on the Crocodiles"; Sternberg-El Hotabi, *Untersuchungen zur Überlieferungsgeschichte*; Gasse, *Les stèles d'Horus*.

3 Frankfurter, "Binding of Antelopes."

CHAPTER 5

FIGURE 9. Coptic limestone frieze with bound antelopes. Egypt, unprovenanced. Seventh century CE. Height: 34.5 cm; length: 65 cm.

iconographic strategies in the service of a Christianity, broadly defined. What lay behind the synthesis of tradition and innovation in the crafting of religious media—window friezes, clay figurines, images of saints, textile designs, and the proper preparation of a corpse? If in most cases, like that of the Dumbarton Oaks frieze, the pre-Christian models for an image are so widely removed chronologically from that image as to have had no direct historical influence on its creation, then what exactly can we mean by "traditional iconographic strategy" anyway?

The thesis I will be advancing in this chapter to answer these questions concerns the construction of efficacy. The Dumbarton Oaks frieze sought to express apotropaic power against demonic forces according to a strategy that had been used for such purposes in the past. The binding of antelopes—their harnessing to the cross—served the construction of the cross's apotropaic efficacy. Furthermore, while iconographic strategies were obviously shared across different media and their workshops, the repertoire of traditions and strategies of innovation involved in the construction of efficacy belonged to individual workshops. To put it differently, the agents of the construction of a visual and material Christianity, through traditional media and often using traditional strategies, were workshops. And to understand how the workshop played a part in the construction of a material Christianity and the perpetuation of older traditions, we have to focus on the construction of efficacy—the magic of craft.

I can hardly claim this formulation of workshop goals as altogether original. Art historian David Freedberg referred to the "efficacy" of images in his monumental study *The Power of Images*, and anthropologist Alfred Gell offered the term "technology of enchantment" to describe how traditional artisans endow objects with social meaning, and thus a kind of "social agency," through particular decorative elements that invite powerful responses.[4] Even Max Weber noted that, at least in ancient societies, "every specialized art that is uncommon and not widely disseminated is regarded as a magical charisma, either personal or, more generally, hereditary, the acquisition and maintenance of which is guaranteed by magical means."[5] One thinks of the mythic lore that surrounded metallurgy, weaving, and pottery in ancient Greece—the culture heroes and special gods that stood behind these crafts, the equipment and ritual elements involved in their manufacture, and their particular demonic threats.[6]

On the side of the completed objects, historians grappling with ancient discussions of and responses to statuary have described the various notions of *presence* that ancient peoples attributed to statues in their cities and temples and that, presumably, stone artisans themselves endeavored to represent in their works.[7] For example, an image's frontality—whether that of Medusa or the Egyptian Bes—was seen as having a particular potency in radiating protective force.[8] The corollary of the creation of such potent images can also be craft in its own way: the elimination or adjustment of presence through mutilation, sometimes carried out in a quite meticulous manner. The mutilation and destruction of images in antiquity involved a vocabulary of meaningful acts and responsive gestures, from incising a cross on a marble head to pulverizing or burying images, all of which served as ways of negotiating *presence* in a changing landscape.[9]

Art historians have noted that ancient peoples perceived a magical potency in the images incorporated into everyday life in Roman and Byzantine homes. From the depiction of faces on textiles to the phalluses, Medusa heads, knot work, and gospel vignettes that adorned bodies, mosaic floors, and walls, the "art" of everyday life involved a perennial conjuring of prosperity and warding off of demonic powers, especially the evil eye.[10] We are thus moving away here from a model of ancient crafts that emphasizes technical functionality or decoration to a model

---

4 Gell, "Technology and Magic," 160–62; clarified in idem, *Art and Agency*, 74–75; Freedberg, *Power of Images*, 3, 5.

5 Weber, *Sociology of Religion*, 97–98.

6 See esp. Scheid and Svenbro, *Craft of Zeus*; Blakely, *Myth, Ritual and Metallurgy*; Gillis, "Des démons dans l'atelier"; cf. also Faraone, "Collection of Curses against Kilns." On special gods, see e.g., Ovid, *Amores* 3.2.52 ("Minerva for artisans"). And as a context for Christianization cf. Winroth, *Conversion of Scandinavia*, chap. 5 and 134–35.

7 Freedberg, *Power of Images*; Stewart, *Statues in Roman Society*.

8 Volokhine, *La frontalité dans l'iconographie*; Bailliot, *Magie et sortilèges*; Elsner, *Roman Eyes*, 22.

9 Stewart, *Statues in Roman Society*, 261–99; Frankfurter, "Vitality of Egyptian Images"; Kristensen, *Making and Breaking the Gods*; with examples in Lazaridou, *Transition to Christianity*, 146–48. See also Freedberg, *Power of Images*, 378–428.

10 See esp. Maguire, Maguire, and Duncan-Flowers, *Art and Holy Powers*; Bailliot, *Magie et sortilèges*; and Bowes, "Christian Images in the Home," 178–81. On the apotropaic powers of knot work, see Kondoleon, "Gerasa Mosaics of Yale" 222–23.

that seeks to understand magical efficacy, especially in that most vulnerable sphere, the domestic. But this concern extended to workshops too: in ancient Greece, craftsmen placed crude apotropaic figures around kilns and forges to protect them from well-known demons; in late antique Rome and Antioch, artisans placed icons of St. Simeon the Stylite outside their workshops "to provide thereby some protection and safety for themselves."[11] Again, it is not the specific beliefs that concern us here but the people's dependence on representational crafts in everyday life that could *work*, somehow, to safeguard inhabitants and their activities. Thus, the agents behind such crafts considered the reproduction of such efficacy an essential function of their creativity.

Jaś Elsner's distinction between a "horizontal visuality" in beholding art and a "vertical" or "ritual-centered visuality" gets at another aspect of the efficacy of religious crafts. Elsner's concept of vertical visuality involves ritual interaction with an image to receive its gaze, much like the process of *darśan* in Hinduism, such that the image is regarded and constructed as a repository and medium of presence.[12] This visual goal became essential to the production of icons and other vehicles of intercessory presence in late antiquity, in which knowledge of paints and glass *tesserae* led to the production of vital, active images of martyrs and patriarchs.[13] Horizontal visuality, in contrast, involves deliberate projection into the image such that the image is appropriated into the social context of the viewer.[14] Yet both the "vertically oriented" image in its shrine and the "horizontal," socially functional image are the products of craftsmen, and both involve a kind of efficacy. Such horizontal images—garden statuary or jewelry, for example—gain efficacy as commodities, as "devices for reproducing relations between persons," as definers of value, and as creators of prestige.[15] The craftsman of religious representations might reproduce or innovate in his medium also with an eye toward this social dimension of efficacy; for example, in creating statuary or mosaic expanses that promote particular benefactors according to prevailing systems of prestige.[16] Our concept of efficacy—that is, of the magic of crafted material objects—must encompass these multiple dimensions. In using this general term "efficacy," then, I mean to capture a *continuum* in the utility and power of crafted things, from the most explicitly magical to those that signify prestige, gender, or tradition in a social sense. In confronting the syncretistic capacity of craftsmanship in antiquity, it is important not to draw hard

---

11 Theodoret, *Hist. Rel.* 26.11, trans. Price, *History of the Monks*, 165; Antioch: *Life of Simeon the Younger* 158, in Van den Ven, *Vie ancienne*, 2:164–65. Ancient Greek workshop apotropaia: Gillis, "Des démons dans l'atelier."

12 Elsner, *Roman Eyes*, 23–25.

13 See Miller, *Corporeal Imagination*, 166; and, on the phenomenon of the relief icon, Pentcheva, *Sensual Icon*.

14 Elsner, *Roman Eyes*, 289.

15 Appadurai, "Introduction," 25.

16 See, e.g., Stewart, *Statues in Roman Society*, 186–87.

distinctions between magical, religious, social, economic, and aesthetic domains of efficacy.[17]

For the broader purposes of this chapter I will also be eliding craftsmen and workshops—that is, places of production—with respect to agency, but it is important to note here that there were distinct cultural differences in late antiquity between them. Itinerant or independent craftsman (e.g., those hired to do mosaics or paintings in monumental structures) might have brought to their tasks a broader Mediterranean sense of prestigious and efficacious forms, borne out of travel and a broader geographical range of assignments, while workshops, embedded in communities and local cultures, tended to reflect regional, even local, traditions of representation and iconographic efficacy. The spectacular interior decorations of the fifth- to sixth-century CE Red Monastery Church near Atripe involved two groups of evidently freelance painters, who applied particular talents in their use of color, paint preparation, and the depiction of human figures to the walls, domes, and windows.[18] Workshops amounted to social sites comprising people interacting and moving through physical environment and social landscape, and in this sense they would have shared a need for efficacious materials and a conception of commodity with their clients. Both the perpetuation of tradition and innovative creativity responded to this kind of interaction between workshop and clientele. But workshops (and independent craftsmen as well) also would have preserved an intimate sense of the materials themselves and the efficacy that different media could convey: nails, for example, might have fastened boards for a barn or, as archaeologists have discovered, acted apotropaically in a burial to constrain the ghost of a corpse.[19] Workshops would also have cultivated and maintained a sense of magic in the very process of crafting, whether in the act of forming pots or forging tools or by simply stamping an image into some receptive material.[20]

Take color, for example. A common commodity in the Roman and late antique Mediterranean world was the so-called magical gem: a small colored stone, carved and inscribed with names, prayers, pseudo-letters, and images of Mediterranean gods, including Christ, the apostles, and Solomon.[21] Clearly these gems were created as concrete vehicles of efficacy, sometimes for identifiable ailments, sometimes for apotropaic protection, and sometimes to convey a social identity, and the range of images and names that they contain provides a perfect microcosm of the craftsman's capacity to combine traditional iconographies with new

---

17 My use of "magic" in this chapter is meant in its fluid, evaluative sense, denoting a charisma, agency, or potency in socially embedded materials, rather than a strictly defined area of religion.

18 See Lyster, "Artistic Working Practice."

19 Mortuary nails: Bailliot, "Autour des morts"; Villa, "Nails for the Dead."

20 Stamping: Caseau, "Magical Protection and Stamps in Byzantium"; Pentcheva, *Sensual Icon*, 28–33.

21 Bonner, *Studies in Magical Amulets*; Delatte and Derchain, *Les intailles magiques gréco-égyptiennes*; Schwartz and Schwartz, "Engraved Gems"; Mastrocinque, *Les intailles magiques*.

strategies of visual efficacy, often in consultation with a ritual expert.[22] Yet most research on the gems in the past few centuries has focused on their images, not the stones themselves. More recently, however, there has been increased attention to the efficacy imputed to the stones themselves and their colors, which (it has been argued) came subsequently to be ritually oriented by virtue of the craftsman's carving. That is, the potency of the gems came first from the stones, and then through the images and text inscribed on them.[23] And color itself, as the anthropologist Michael Taussig has proposed, inevitably signifies aspects of sacred presence or the control of spirits in culture. If *we* might tend to think of colors in terms of subtlety or loudness, spectacle or mystery, Taussig makes the cogent point that colors across many cultures and history have been viewed as conveying the presence of spirits—sorts of numinous power.[24] Such a principle is perhaps most familiar to travelers in such forms as the crimson of Chinese altars, the orange with which Indian images are painted, and the blues of Moroccan windows and doors—the first intended to appease spirits, the second to signify the holiness of the image, and the third to repel maleficent powers. The principle should also be familiar, Taussig argues, in its antithesis: the dark, muted clothing of Northern Europeans that has signified the avoidance of free-floating powers. But here let us turn that principle around to posit that the knowledge of colors and the techniques of coloring held by late antique craftsmen like these gem-carvers, as well as by ancient painters and mosaicists, amounted to a body of tradition concerned with the construction of efficacy—that is, with the creation of an object or a space that could mediate powers for ritual.[25] The same principle applies to the construction of efficacy through the details of knot work or facial frontality mentioned earlier. Craftsmanship presumed the ability to deploy these visual traditions and iconographic strategies to direct or avert powers.

Thus, from the interest in conjuring presence in images and statuary to the control of colors in painting and gems, from the creation of protective forces in domestic structures to the achievement of a "ritual-centered visuality" in liturgical spaces and amulets, workshops aimed at creating various kinds of efficacy in their crafts. They developed or reproduced iconographic strategies in such a way as to convey power, authority, prestige, protection, or presence. As Caroline Walker Bynum has noted with regard to medieval craftsmen of religious media, "the goal [was] not so much conjuring up or gesturing toward the unseen as manifesting power in the matter of the object."[26] More importantly for my purposes, a workshop's strategies of representation, whether perpetuating older traditions or innovating new ones, served this creation of efficacy. We may think about

22 Nagy, "Magical Gems and Classical Archaeology," 77–79.
23 Faraone, "Text, Image, and Medium," 57.
24 Taussig, *What Color Is the Sacred?*
25 Miller, *Corporeal Imagination*, 73–81, 176–78; cf. James, *Light and Color in Byzantine Art*.
26 Bynum, *Christian Materiality*, 28.

workshops' interests in functionality, decoration, beauty, or fame, but with this concept of efficacy we come closer to ancient artisans' actual motivations and the knowledge they brought to production, avoiding simplistic and anachronistic notions that they made "what sells." Of course there would have been a market, but the market would have been for what worked—what was successful—and the buyers would have tended to be like them.[27] Even in cases of commission—a panel painting, a mosaic floor—both client and artisan would have conceptualized the object according to traditions of efficacy, such as the devotional function of the painting, the apotropaic function of the mosaic floor, or simply the effective demonstration of prestige itself through color and theme. The very memory-objects and containers for blessings that were proffered near late antique shrines offer a case in point, capturing as they do key—perhaps the most potent—features of the shrine itself, the wondrous features of the cult image there, or the materials of ecclesiastical performance.[28]

Naturally, this model of the construction of efficacy I have been developing provides an important context for the perpetuation of iconographic strategies that seem to have come from earlier religious traditions. That is, they are not "survivals" but deployments of traditional iconographic strategies, often within the cultural context of Christianity.

II. WORKSHOPS IN LATE ANTIQUE EGYPT

What do we know about workshops in Roman and late antique Egypt? First of all, they functioned as extensions of families, temples, monasteries, and saints' shrines, sharing these institutions' spaces and economies. Papyri refer to workshops in, or connected to, homes in Roman Egyptian towns, with their handiwork involving the help of most family members and domestic dwellers.[29] Magical spells treat workshops as social entities in the urban or village landscape, subject to the same binding forces as homes: one Coptic spell invokes a long list

---

27 Cf. Naerebout, "How Do You Want Your Goddess?" In his 1986 essay on the social value of commodities, Arjun Appadurai points out that in premodern societies in which production is geared toward regional consumers, there are many more shared traditions and assumptions between craftsmen and consumers, and craftsmen have an understanding of their clients' usage that they would not have if the consumers were far away. Of course, when production and consumption are removed from each other, as with merchant middlemen, the efficacy constructed may not be the efficacy perceived. See Appadurai, "Introduction."

28 Cline, "Two-Sided Mold"; Vikan, "Early Byzantine Pilgrimage Devotionalia"; idem, *Early Byzantine Pilgrimage Art*. Cf. the Menas/Thekla ampule Louvre MNC 1926, with images of shrine paraphernalia flanking Menas instead of camels.

29 Workshops connected to dwellings: P. Oxy 46.3300, 16–20; P. Lugd.-Bat. 33.20 (P. Worp 20). See in general Wipszycka, *L'Industrie textile*, 56, 63–65, 70–71; and cf. Baker, *Rebuilding the House of Israel*, 39–40, 78–80; and, on the socially engaged character of workshops in Roman cities, Rockwell, "Sculptor's Studio at Aphrodisias."

of archangels to "gather together the people of this village into the *ergastērion* of NN.... Gather them all to NN, to the shop of NN."[30] It may be as the proprietor of such a private workshop that one Simos signed his line of Bes figurines in the early Roman Fayoum.[31] Another such private workshop, in early Roman Athribis, sprang up by the town baths, apparently to provide terracotta images of Isis-Aphrodite as ritual materials for women's purification and fecundity rituals. Another, using molds imported from Boeotia, operated near the Alexandria necropolis during the Hellenistic period to produce figurines for grave deposit.[32] And a recently excavated ceramics workshop of the fourth century CE in the Dakhleh oasis operated inside an abandoned temple, producing pots and the occasional female figurine.[33] Whether locally devoted to the molding of such terracotta images or regionally renowned for the production of fine stonework, workshops and their hierarchical social structures had the capacity to "form selves," raising individuals through their apprenticeships to think of themselves as specialists in a craft.[34]

In general, craftwork had its own culture of excellence and pride, as Nicolas Tran has shown using literary and epigraphical materials from the Latin West. Craftsmen of funerary inscriptions attached their specialties to their names. Technical knowledge and mastery, as well as an appreciation of materials, were understood as part of the perfecting of one's "art" and, by extension, one's capacity to produce efficacious materials. Apuleius's account of a wooden figure of Mercury he had commissioned from a famous local sculptor is a case in point. The client deferred to the craftsman, his excellence and sense of the potency of materials, "to carve a statuette of any god he wanted, to whom I could address my regular prayers, from any kind of material provided it was a type of wood" (which Apuleius ultimately provided).[35] Thus the efficacy of the figurine stemmed in large part from the agency of the sculptor himself rather than the particular god represented. Consequently, the figurine was used as evidence in Apuleius's trial for sorcery, during which the nature of its efficacy was redescribed as evil and the significance of the named sculptor was transferred to other, more nefarious types of agency: "They say I ordered [the figurine] to be made from a special kind of wood, in a secret workshop, for purposes of sorcery."[36]

---

30 ACM 117 = P. Moen 3, 1.8–10, 5.73–75, in Satzinger and Sijpesteijn, "Koptisches Zauberpergament Moen III." Cf. PGM IV.2373–440 and binding spells against a ceramics worker and some bronze workers in Gager, *Curse Tablets and Binding*, ##70–71. On workshops' predilection for magical curses and protection, see ibid, 153–54, citing Pliny 28.4.19.

31 Nachtergael, "Statuettes en terre cuite," 421.

32 Athribis: Szymańska, *Terres cuites d'Athribis*, 62–63. Alexandria: Tezgör-Kassab and el Fattah, "La diffusion des tanagréennes."

33 Ain el-Gedida: Aravecchia, "Church Complex of 'Ain El-Gedida."

34 Tran, *Dominus Tabernae*, 185.

35 On craftsmanship and personal identity see in general Tran, *Dominus Tabernae*. Apuleius, *Apol.* 61, trans. Harrison and Hunink, *Apuleius*, 84.

36 Ibid., 83.

At the same time, craftsmen's production of efficacy in such materials should also be understood in the context of the space of the workshop itself, its technology of creation and the vulnerabilities that hung over it. Both archaic traditions of workshop apotropeia (against demons that brought manufacturing catastrophes) and ritual efforts to protect the workshops at their inauguration (e.g., in Gaul, the practice of burying infants nearby) suggest that these spaces were often regarded as supernaturally vital and vulnerable in their own right.[37]

Christianity also opened up new social contexts for craft. The fifth-century Abbot Besa lists the many craftsmen (ⲛ̄ⲕⲉⲉⲓⲟⲡⲉ) who practiced in the White Monastery, from carpenters, shoemakers, and potters to linen and basket weavers, scribes, and bookbinders, and he even mentions an illicit private craft of garment embroidery. Subsequently he complains that the exchange and retailing of their products had gone on too freely, perhaps creating instability or discord. Instead, Besa insists, all commodities should go through overseers.[38]

Monasteries incorporated workshops for pottery and basket weaving, with one early urban monastery based in a mercantile district of Alexandria manufacturing glassware and small, classically themed ivory panels.[39] The monastic subculture also engaged in the transformation of certain crafts. Drawing on the earlier craft of figurative wood-panel painting for divine images, a new (post-fifth-century) practice of making wood-panel images of monks for memorial display responded to the distinctively monastic veneration of elders.[40]

Some craftsmen affiliated with monasteries or church institutions took a devotional attitude toward their creations, as we see in graffiti from the Egyptian monastery of Bawit. One reads: "I, John the painter, was deemed worthy to paint this vault and plaster it. Pray for me that God has mercy on me." John was likely a monk, as was Elias, another painter, and Joseph, a sculptor, who elsewhere inscribed their names in prayer at Bawit.[41] Like the Chinese Buddhist weaver who sewed into his small fabric shrine words of assurance that it was "respectfully made after bathing, offering incense, and worshipping," these rare declarations of piety speak to the sense of the created thing as a ritual and social extension of the craftsman—his "magic," as it were.[42] In Alfred Gell's useful terminology, these

---

[37] Workshop apotropaia: Gillis, "Des démons dans l'atelier." Infant burials in workshops: Baills-Talbi and Blanchard, "Sépultures de nouveau-nés," 189–91.

[38] Besa, *Ep.* 12.8, in Kühn, *Letters and Sermons of Besa*, 34–35.

[39] Monastic crafts: Ghaly, "Pottery Workshops of Saint-Jeremia"; Rodziewicz, "Reliefs figurés en os des fouilles"; Rodziewicz, *Les habitations romaines tardives*; Haas, *Alexandria in Late Antiquity*, 204–6; Török, *Transfigurations of Hellenism*, 264–65; Rodziewicz, "Remarks on the Domestic," 270–71; Goehring, *Ascetics, Society, and the Desert*, 89–109.

[40] Auth, "Brother George the Scribe"; see also Bolman and Szymańska, "Ascetic Ancestors."

[41] Maspero, *Fouilles exécutées à Baouît*, ##58, 60 (John, Elias); du Bourguet, "La signature sur son oeuvre." See also Rutschowscaya, *La peinture copte*, 23.

[42] Chinese inscription on cloth traveling shrine, Southeast Asia, seventeenth century CE, Peabody-Essex Museum 2001.E301682, in Proser, *Pilgrimage and Buddhist Art*, 128–29. See in general Dunbabin, *Mosaics of the Greek*, 270–76.

CHAPTER 5

especially pious creations served as the extension of the craftsman's inspired agency into society and religious practice.[43]

Finally, Christian saints' shrines and the pilgrimage economies that developed around them stimulated the development of crafts dedicated to pilgrims. A "pottery workshop [κουφοκεραμουργειον] of the Church of St. Thecla," for example, whose accounts are addressed in a seventh-century papyrus, would quite likely have produced—alongside the wine jars (κούφαι) in which it clearly specialized—Thecla-related lamps and ampullae, although there is no archaeology to prove it.[44] Several molds for lamps, pilgrims' ampules, and figurines associated with the saints Stephen and Theodore have been excavated at Elephantine, suggesting a shrine-related workshop there,[45] while the Apa Mena complex has revealed entire terracotta workshops, including molds, kilns, spaces, and products, dedicated to supplying visitors with souvenir ampules and votive figurines.[46] At a shrine for St. Phib, a holy man often paired in hagiography with the monastic founder Apa Apollo, terracotta artisans also seem to have developed the practice of molding female figurines with the name *Phib* printed on their bellies (see fig. 6), perhaps following an amuletic practice of invoking this saint's name.[47] Evidence of such cult-related workshops has been found in late antique Palestine as well (Caesarea, Beth Shean), while a mosaic from Antioch provides an amusing glimpse of "the *ergastēria* of the martyrion" in Daphne, Asia Minor, portraying its owner lying drunk by the door.[48] Some craftsmen of shrine souvenirs seem to have supplied more than one shrine with their wares. Some ampullae of St. Menas have an image of St. Thecla on the reverse, quite likely reflecting her nearby shrine, while a two-sided limestone mold at the University of Toronto was evidently used to make pilgrimage tokens for both the Mamre shrine and the Aphrodite temple at Aphaca (350 kilometers away). In this way craftsmen could themselves forge lines of association between different cult sites.[49]

43 Gell, *Art and Agency*; idem, "Technology and Magic."

44 P. Vindob. 2. 104. See Wipszycka, *Les ressources et les activités*, 57–63; Davis, *Cult of Saint Thecla*, 114–33.

45 Ballet and Mahmoud, "Moules en terre cuite"; MacCoull, "Christianity at Syene/Elephantine/Philae."

46 Kaufmann, *Die heilige Stadt der Wüste*, 197–207.

47 The Phib shrine might well have been at the Bawit monastery of Apa Apollo: see Papaconstantinou, *Le culte des saints en Égypte*, 55; Delattre, *Papyrus coptes et grecs*, 38–41. René-Georges Coquin discusses a gesture of prostration on the tomb of Apollo, called metanoia, that became part of the cult of these saints; Coquin, "Apollon de Titkooh." Phib figurines: Perdrizet, *Les terres cuites grecques*, 5–6; Bayer-Niemeier, *Bildwerke der Sammlung Kaufmann*, 1:147–48, #262. Amuletic invocation of name: P. Oxy 82. 5314.

48 Beth Shean: Agady et al., "Byzantine Shops in the Street," 441–42, where the clay indicates regional manufacture. Caesarea: Sussman, "Moulds for Lamps and Figurines." Martyrion workshop according to Megalopsychia mosaic; Kondoleon, *Antioch*, 114.

49 Thekla/Menas: Davis, "Pilgrimage and the Cult"; Aphaca/Mamre: Cline, "Two-Sided Mold."

Affiliation with a Christian institution, whether a monastery or a shrine, should not be taken to imply strict oversight of or even much influence over the design of ritual materials. We might better say that affiliation provided thematic inspiration for creating or designing in particular media (figurines, textiles), as well as offering centralized economies for their sale. A case in point, again, is the Apa Mena workshop, whose great range of female figurines—pregnant, seated, or playing the tambourine—bear no clear relationship to the Christian pantheon or liturgy.

What, then, impelled a workshop affiliated with a religious institution to create new objects from its repertoire, to innovate in the material expression of a mythic figure or ritual device? What, for example, precipitated the very range of female figurines available at Apa Mena, or, by the same token, the harnessing of the cross to an antelope (or the addition of crosses to other apotropaia on a mosaic floor)? It seems that workshops sought primarily to draw out particular features of the traditional iconography, sometimes to follow local shrine traditions that emphasized those features and sometimes simply to follow the creative innovations of a particular craftsman. This highlighting of preexisting features is most clearly observable in the range of terracotta figurines of Egyptian gods manufactured during the Roman period, which rarely had any relationship to the archaic iconographies of gods on temple walls beyond their crowns. Isis pulling up her dress, the fat toddler Harpocrates with a bowl of sweets, Bes dressed with a Gallic shield, Isis with the body of a serpent—all these images, molded and painted en masse for popular domestic usage into the fourth century, were envisioned and developed in workshops as ways of defining, clarifying, eliding, and embodying powers associated with these divinities. They did not serve theology or reflect mythology but mediated the presence of gods according to immediate contexts like festivals, desires for fecundity, or the aspirations of local shrines. In other words, the drawing out and material embodiment of iconographic features served the construction of efficacy.[50]

We see this context of workshop innovation—the highlighting of efficacious features—also in the development of funerary iconography: the treatment of the deceased. In ancient Egyptian tradition, mortuary workshops transformed the corpse visually and ritually into an Osiris or Hathor, otherworldly identities in which the dead could benefit the living. The Roman period, however, saw a diversification of these treatments: while some workshops crafted masks, for example, to indicate the subject's transformation to Osiris, some simply applied gold leaf to the faces of otherwise linen-bound corpses, while still others, located in the

---

50 See Dunand, *Religion populaire*; Nachtergael, "Les terres cuites 'du Fayoum'"; and Frankfurter, *Religion in Roman Egypt*, 132–41 on popular terracotta iconography. Cf. Freedberg, *Power of Images*, 92, on the function of *consecration*, the drawing out of an intrinsic quality rather than the imposition of that quality magically.

CHAPTER 5

Fayyum, shifted the emphasis from the divinely efficacious Osiris-self to the socially efficacious (though equally idealized) pre-mortem self through the preparation of the so-called portrait mummies.[51] Since we know that these portrait mummies were simply tossed into group tombs at the end of the funeral process, the workshops' innovation here probably served some new funeral practice: display of the mummy at home or perhaps a procession, practices that would have emphasized the living (or transitional) individual.[52]

Workshop innovations that integrated Christian symbols likewise served a magical potency, first and foremost as craftsmen sought to signify Christianity through local materials and technologies.[53] The assimilation of Christian symbols in late antique and early medieval metalwork provides important examples. In late antique (seventh- to eighth-century CE) Burgundy, in the Western Roman Empire, several bronze workshops developed a model of belt buckle that depicted Daniel in the lion's den, saints, angels, and crosses, often accompanied by magical writing. They were often hollow, as if to contain some protective substance.[54] In early medieval Sweden metalsmiths were creating amulets in the form of books, seizing on an iconic element in Christian ecclesiastical performance and reducing it to its pure, miniaturized (if illegible) form.[55] And a soapstone block from early medieval Denmark has molds for both small amuletic crosses and inverted T-shaped amulets ("hammer of Thor") that archaeologists believe came about as a counter-cross symbol, an indication of traditional identity during the Christianization of Scandinavia. Whether these amulets represented such assertions of identity, traditional religious images, or synthetic variations on the cross, the mold itself is evidence that the same metalsmith was crafting both symbols at the same time.[56] Through the innovations of metalworkers, Christianity took material form in such prestige objects. The buckles and amulets amounted to concrete, iconic interpretations of what the religion held: holy beings and the potent written word. In this way, artisans no less than church builders had a hand in the material construction of Christianity.

But of all the symbols that distinguished this religion in its encounter with local cultures from late antiquity through Byzantium and the Middle Ages, and that inspired a welter of regional interpretations in craft, it is the cross that elicited

---

51 Riggs, *Beautiful Burial in Roman Egypt*, ch. 3. Gold masks: Dunand, "Du séjour osirien des morts"; Dunand and Lichtenberg, "Pratiques et croyances funéraires"; cf. the distinctive iconography of Terenouthis mortuary stelae (Roman period), which likewise bore on the mortuary process and the commemoration of the deceased: el-Nassery and Wagner, "Nouvelles stèles," 232; el-Sawy, Bouzek, and Vidman, "New Stelae," 332.

52 On portrait mummies and domestic display, see Diodorus 1.91.1–2; and Athanasius, *v.Ant.* 90, with Borg, "Dead as a Guest at Table?"; Montserrat, "Death and Funerals"; Riggs, *Beautiful Burial in Roman Egypt*, 149–52.

53 See Ward Perkins, "Role of Craftsmanship."
54 Treffort, "Vertus prophylactiques et sens eschatologique."
55 Fabech and Näsman, "Ritual Landscapes and Sacral Places," 90–91.
56 See Winroth, *Conversion of Scandinavia*, 134.

special creativity. As early Irish cross carvings especially show, late antique and medieval craftsmen sought to conceptualize a simple mark within a great range of traditional decorative schemes, from faces to birds to knots, invariably to accentuate the triumphal or apotropaic efficacy of the symbol, as in the bound antelope relief with which this chapter began. Textile compositions like the "tunic front with marine motifs" (fig. 10) emphasize the cross alongside other classical motifs from the world of late antique Egyptian workshops: in this case, beneath a mysterious nude figure whose legs seem to be in the act of dancing, and amid borders full of mythical monsters. Another composition sets the cross among birds in a border alternating with images of heroes (plate 6), while another places it among protective beasts (fig. 11).[57] In domestic mosaic floors and textiles, the cross rarely serves as a central or identifying symbol but rather one among a range of apotropaic motifs. Conceptually, as a symbol conveying efficacy and indexing divine authority, the cross is a "seal [σφραγίς]," a term from early Jewish apocalyptic tradition that signifies a mark or image of divine origin, reproducible through gesture or craft.[58] The cross as reimagined in traditional workshops—on textiles, on stelae, on amulets, and painted on monastic walls—had little to do with Jesus's crucifixion, conveying rather the kind of efficacy that Athanasius captured in his *Life of Antony*, in which demons "are utterly terrified by the sign of the Lord's cross," and "where the sign of the cross occurs, magic is weakened and sorcery has no effect."[59] Indeed, for the composer of a small prayer-amulet, God would have been the "God of the ready crosses."[60]

But the cross was also an invitation to craftsmen to improvise, to demonstrate skill, and to capture in various ways the potency of that simple visual cue, which was supposed to materialize and direct supernatural power.[61] This process of indigenizing the cross through traditional iconographic strategies served as a way of acculturating the religion itself, as we see in the spread of the cross with an enlarged top-loop—the *ankh*-cross or *crux ansata*—over the course of the fourth century (see plate 7; cf. plate 5).[62] Its adoption, especially by stoneworkers and weavers, is given a curious etiology in the fifth-century *Ecclesiastical History* of

---

57 Brooklyn Museum 38.753, in Thompson, *Coptic Textiles in the Brooklyn Museum*, 82–83, #36. Victoria and Albert Museum 279–1891, in Kendrick, *Catalogue of Textiles*, 2:414, #313.

58 See, e.g., Ezekiel 9; Revelation 7.3–4, 14.1, 22.4; 4 Ezra 6.5; *Apocalypse of Elijah* 1.9. Cf. Clement of Alexandria, *Paedog.* 3.59.2, in Francis, "Clement of Alexandria on Signet Rings." The ca. sixth-century CE Coptic *Martyrdom of Apa Epima* calls the cross "the Seal of God, sealed in the face of Adam on the day when he was created", see 13, in Blumell and Wayment, *Christian Oxyrhynchus*, 694–95.

59 Athanasius, *v.Ant.* 35, 78. See Flint, *Rise of Magic*, 173–78.

60 P. Oxy 7.1058.

61 Cf. Fromont, *Art of Conversion*, 75–79. Note also the development of inverted-T-shaped amulets from crosses (or vice versa) in early medieval Denmark, represented in a stone block for molding metal amulets in both shapes, now in the National Museum of Denmark, Copenhagen. See Winroth, *Conversion of Scandinavia*, 134.

62 Bowen, "Crux Ansata"; Kendrick, *Catalogue of Textiles*, 2:5–19.

CHAPTER 5

FIGURE 10. Textile tunic front with cross on beaded necklace below nude satyr figure; border of marine monsters. Egypt, unprovenanced. Sixth century CE. Wool. Width: 33 cm; length: 113 cm.

Socrates Scholasticus: Christians, he reports, noticed the ankh symbol in the ruins of the Serapeum and took it as "the sign of Christ's saving passion," while local Hellenes took it as an Egyptian symbol. But then

> some of the heathen converts to Christianity, who were conversant with these hieroglyphic characters, interpreted the form of the cross and said

FIGURE 11. Textile panel with lobed cross resembling a lotus blossom, surrounded by lions, dogs, baskets, and tendrils. Wool/linen. Egypt, unprovenanced. Fifth to sixth century CE. Height: 49.5 cm; width: 56 cm.

that it signifies "Life to Come." This the Christians exultingly laid hold of, as decidedly favorable to their religion. Then other hieroglyphs were deciphered, with a prophecy that when the cross appears the Serapeum would fall. And all realized what had taken place.[63]

The story could only have developed after the use of the ankh-cross had been noticed and its resemblance to a hieroglyphic sign had led to some ecclesiastical consternation, for the story legitimates the resemblance (and even the meaning of the ankh) in the context of the Christian transformation of the Alexandrian cityscape. Yet the elaboration of the cross following the form of the ankh must have taken place in individual workshops and gained regional popularity from there.

63 Socrates, *Hist. Eccl.* 5.15, in Percival, *Seven Ecumenical Councils*, 2:126–27. Cf. Sozomen, *Hist. Eccl.* 7.15, and Rufinus, *Hist. Eccl.* 2.29, who links the scene of the recognition of the ankh as a cross prototype to an account of large-scale mutilations of Egyptian images across Alexandria. Françoise Thelamon suggests that "the ankh sign had been quickly adopted by Christians in Egypt as the equivalent of the cross" because of their "graphic resemblance" (Thelamon, *Païens et chrétiens*, 272, 271), but there is no evidence for this process of general adoption. The tradition seems to have arisen as a workshop innovation, especially in the areas of stonecarving and textile manufacture.

CHAPTER 5

Thus, with images like the cross, the book, and the saint, workshops innovated in their use of traditional models to draw out iconographically certain features or symbols and to achieve a new sort of efficacy in the image or symbol itself—just as in earlier times they had done with the transfigured ancestor and the Hellenized god. In what follows in this chapter I will approach the workshop strategies of stonecarvers, clay figurine modelers, textile workers, and mortuary preparers as they integrated Christian elements into traditional crafts and thereby became producers of Christianity itself through its material accoutrements.

III. EXAMPLES

A. Stonecarvers

With stonework, the richest area for examining the assimilation of Christianity—or the construction of a material Christianity—is that dedicated to mortuary monuments, where we find a tremendous creativity as early as the second century, and continuing through the fifth century, in the carving of both stelae that depict or call down blessings for the deceased and decorative niches for tombs. Like the mummy portraits, which I will discuss further later, this representational stonework mediates between ritually functional images of the deceased that conjure his or her presence and indications of the deceased's social status according to the customs of Hellenism: through dress, body position, accoutrements, and mythological references. Within these funerary stonework traditions, crosses and other expressions of Christian symbolic culture can be found, as products of the same workshops but as additions to and clarifications of the Hellenistic status constructed for all the other clients. That is, these symbols were applied much in the way that other special details requested by families, from animals and Egyptian gods to hand positions, were applied.[64]

These stonework traditions were local: examples include the shallow stelae from Terenouthis depicting the deceased as a transfigured being accompanied by Anubis and family members, the four-foot-high niches from Oxyrhynchus with deep-relief carvings of individuals in classical dress, the flat-relief stelae from Esna featuring birds and architectural elements, and the elaborate mortuary niche carvings from Herakleopolis Magna that feature mythic scenes among the acanthus leaves.[65] In fact, local stoneworkers would quite likely have engaged in other

---

64 See esp. Thomas, *Late Antique Egyptian Funerary Sculpture*, 35–38; Török, *Transfigurations of Hellenism*, 196–97. It is important to recognize that stone objects such as these became valuable commodities in the international museum trade in the early twentieth century, leading to local collectors' mutilation of certain types of stonework (like Oxyrhynchus funerary statues) for easier sale and to the manufacture of fakes; see esp. Bussmann, *Unearthing the Truth*.

65 On the diversity of funeral stelae in Roman Egypt: Schneider, *Beelden van Behnasa*, 42–47; D'Auria, Lacovara, and Roehrig, *Mummies and Magic*, 212; Thomas, *Late Antique Egyptian Funerary Sculpture*, 24–25; Török, *Transfigurations of Hellenism*, 205–11; Aly, "Some Funerary Stelae"; idem,

crafts besides the making of funerary stelae.[66] And consequently stoneworkers' integration of Christian symbols would have been pursued according to local styles and traditions, producing crosses held by *putti*, say, instead of Leda and the Swan in the Herakleopolis Magna niche carvings, or a *crux ansata* in the hand of a statue from Oxyrhynchus. The Christian symbols added apotropaic efficacy and an indication of religious allegiance, but they also, as I have discussed, offered stoneworkers the opportunity to explore the very placement of the cross within an overall strategy that emphasized Hellenistic prestige. The efficacy that stoneworkers conjured in these niches and stelae was very much a social efficacy—the declaration of status. The mythological vignettes in the Herakleopolis Magna niche carvings depicting Leda and the Swan, Dionysus, and sea nymphs suggest most of all the resident family's identification of its heritage with classical mythology, and perhaps even local associations with these myths.[67] But more fundamentally, the efficacy that was the stonecarver's achievement emerges in the overall medium of the funerary niche or stela as a site in the landscape to express presence, localize family devotions, signify memory, and concretize death and funeral in a pleasing monument.[68]

Beyond these particular stonework traditions, so evocatively analyzed by Thelma Thomas and László Török, there are great numbers of funerary stelae from other locales, especially the region of Thebes, that continued into the Roman period to display craftsmen's distinctive combinations of faces, animals, architectural motifs, different types of crosses, and inscriptions, all of which served as means of constructing effective monuments for the mediation of the deceased. The inscriptions themselves show the ritually *declarative* function of the stelae, comprising monotheistic slogans, commemorative formulae with the names of the deceased, and prayers and appeals on behalf of the deceased: "One is God!" "Lord, give rest to the soul of [this named person]!" "Do not grieve, [name of deceased]; no one is immortal!!"[69] We should presume that these stelae, whether inscribed or pictorial, were meant to integrate some funerary liturgy, family devotions, memories and expectations of the deceased, and even the landscape itself, all conveyed through the visual materiality of the carved stelae. It was in the mediation of so many values and concerns around family, heritage, Christian liturgy, and the status of the deceased, all expressed in the material me-

---

"More Funerary Stelae"; Hooper, *Funerary Stelae*; el-Sawy, Bouzek, and Vidman, "New Stelae"; el-Nassery and Wagner, "Nouvelles Stèles"; Abd el-Al, Grenier, and Wagner, *Stèles funéraires*. See photographs of stelae in situ in Bonner, "Ship of the Soul"; and Hooper, *Funerary Stelae*, pls. III–IV.

66 See Birk, "Carving Sarcophagi."

67 On local appropriations of Greek mythology for constructing a Hellenized identity, see Thomas, *Late Antique Egyptian Funerary Sculpture*, 59–70; Bowersock, *Mosaics as History*, 33–39, 63; and Belayche, "Foundation Myths in Roman Palestine."

68 See Thomas, *Late Antique Egyptian Funerary Sculpture*, 51–55.

69 Tudor, *Christian Funerary Stelae*, 139–40.

dium of the funeral stela, that these objects conveyed efficacy. And the particular strategies that carvers applied, whether out of innovation or tradition, served this efficacy and its local reception.

The value of this approach, I think, lies in the bracketing of the "Christian"/ "non-Christian" dichotomy and the reemphasis on the agents behind a visual Christianity, as well as on the social or ritual contexts of the media themselves. It is not that an authoritative Christian liturgy came to so dominate Egyptian life that stonecarvers had to reflect this domination, but that the stonecarvers themselves integrated elements of Christian symbolism and liturgy into traditional media, developing a material Christianity through the form of the funerary stela, or the niche, or the window frieze. It also allows us to move away from a preoccupation with particular graphic symbols—boats, ankhs, mothers with infants—as intrinsic bearers of Egyptian religious tradition.[70] We might say that all such symbols served as traditional iconographic strategies for various workshops, enhancing efficacy in some cases while being disposable in others, but overall their value lay in the creative choices of the artisans themselves in creating efficacious images and their consequent construction of a material Christianity that in many areas coexisted with material representations of mythic heroes as well as with the curious remains of bygone mortuary stelae. Indeed, the stonecarver's creativity might not even cease with the completed monument, as we learn from a well-known stela from the Roman period now in the Berlin Byzantine Museum, depicting a seated mother with her child. (The mother died at twenty-one, according to an inscription on the stela.) In the fifth century, in an act of veritable bricolage, a second carver added two crosses to the image of the deceased pair, such that it now suggested Mary and Jesus, perhaps as a devotional icon in some monastery. In this way the stonecarving craft served the material assimilation of Christian institutional symbols through the repurposing of a grave stela.[71]

B. Potters and Terracotta Artisans

The Roman period saw a veritable explosion in the design and manufacture of small molded and painted terracotta images in Egypt, purveyed from Aswan to Alexandria. I mentioned earlier the intense creativity dedicated in this medium to the interpretation of Egyptian gods in Hellenized guise, sometimes drawing on esoteric priestly formulations but more often simply evoking popular interests in a goddess's powers of fecundity or the delights of a festival. Other terracotta im-

---

70 Boat-symbol: Hooper, *Funerary Stelae*; Bonner, "Ship of the Soul"; Bonner, "Desired Haven"; Aly, "More Funerary Stelae," 129–30; Rassart-Debergh, "Quelques bateaux coptes"; Barasch, "Visual Syncretism."

71 Berlin, Staatliche Museen, inv.-nr. 4726; see Effenberger and Severin, *Das Museum für spätantike und byzantische Kunst*, 154, #66.

ages produced during this time included animals, festival celebrants, and nude, corpulent females in positions of supplication.[72]

It is these last types that continued to be manufactured with striking regional diversity through the fourth century and in some areas into the Muslim period: whether nude or robed, emphasizing sexuality, face, or hand position, these are the figurines with which chapter 2 began (see figs. 1–7, plates 1–2).[73] If most such figurines remain unprovenanced, enough come from specific sites that we know they were placed in homes, granaries, tombs, and sometimes temples. Archaeologists have even located a number of the workshops where they were made, which seem to have produced a diversity of clay objects for everyday use, including vessels and lamps.[74] We have evidence of their sites of manufacture around the Fayyum and Thebaid, up in Aswan, out in the decommissioned temple of Ein Gedidah in the Dakhleh oasis, and in several locations in the pilgrimage city of Apa Mena.[75] All these workshops functioned in the general context of an institutional Christianity—not as agents of the institution itself but rather as agents in the construction of a material Christianity by virtue of this religion's cultural domination.[76] Yet, given that female figurines are *not* what the modern historian typically associates with Christian ideology, it is worth considering the forms they took, their relationship to pre-Christian female figurines (which also continued to be manufactured into the fourth century), and the intentions behind their manufacture and use. What did terracotta workshops think they were doing, and how did they construct a material Christianity through the redefinition of a fairly archaic iconographic strategy for ritually mediating procreative hope?

Two ritual contexts seem to have determined these figurines' use as envisioned by their craftsmen: the shrine or tomb, where they would be left as votive symbols of the presence of a supplicant (e.g., fig. 4, plate 2) or in the hopes of gaining or assuring fecundity through the blessings of the saint in his shrine or ancestor in his tomb (e.g., fig. 6), and the domestic shrine, where they would be brought as "blessings" from a saint like Apa Mena.[77]

---

72 Ballet and Galliano, "Les Isiaques et la petite plastique"; Ballet, "Isis assise sur la corbeille"; Naerebout, "How Do You Want Your Goddess?"; Boutantin, *Terres cuites et culte domestique*.

73 See major corpora published by Perdrizet, *Les terres cuites grecques*; Dunand, *Religion populaire en Égypte romaine*; Török, *Hellenistic and Roman Terracottas*; Bailey, *Catalogue of Terracottas*.

74 See esp. Ballet, "Ceramics, Coptic"; cf. Ballet et al., "Artisanat de la céramique."

75 Elephantine: Ballet and Mahmoud, "Moules en terre cuite." Apa Mena: Kaufmann, *Die heilige Stadt der Wüste*, 203–4; Ballet, "Potiers et fabricants de figurines," 121. Fayyum: Allen, "Terracotta Figurines from Karanis"; Griggs, "Early Christian Burials," 192. Thebes. Wilfong, *Women of Jeme*, 114–16.

76 Cf. Foskolou, "Blessing for Sale?," who attempts to distinguish workshops for pilgrim tokens according to the orthodoxy of the images.

77 Frankfurter, "Terracotta Figurines and Popular Religion"; idem, "Female Figurines in Early Christian Egypt." Figurines apparently from the same Apa Mena molds have been found in Alexandrian excavations, suggesting their importation for domestic shrines (or, conceivably, burial) there: Martens, "Figurines en terre-cuite coptes"; and Parandowski, "Coptic Terra-Cotta Figurines."

CHAPTER 5

When I introduced these figurines in chapter 2 I considered their ritual usage as an extension and expression of the concerns of the domestic sphere. Their various regional styles, from Thebes to the oases to the Fayyum, indicate, I argued, their role not as an idiosyncratic commodity based on the availability of specific molds (as, for example, one sees with early Roman figurines of Isis and Bes) but as *autochthonous* traditions that addressed common ritual needs. Female figurines, that is, were simply components of life that potters provided or people made themselves according to local traditions of representing the female body in clay.

But terracotta workshops took the craft of providing these ritual materials into the realm of commodification and choice. Figurines were produced to represent a compelling ritual efficacy, often taking an array of different forms and certainly demonstrating an attention to details that contributed to the buyer's—the ritual subject's—hopes and sense of efficacy. Here the Apa Mena figurines (fig. 1), some of whose distinctive molds were also found at the site, provide the most extensive array of options: women carrying infants or tambourines, showing pregnant bellies, putting one hand to the mouth, or seated with a child. The act of choosing one figurine over another depended first on its ultimate destination (the home as a blessing or the Menas shrine as a votive deposit) but also on the buyer's family traditions, her companions' advice, and her personal identification with one or another form as capturing and communicating her hopes. It is likely that the Apa Mena array reflects the range of visitors who came to the shrine and the workshops' efforts to evoke their diverse notions of figurine efficacy.

On the other hand, the Theban and Fayyum figurines, which were produced for local use independent of saints' shrines, still seem to have been crafted as commodities, alongside items such as pottery vessels, and were designed, molded, and painted to attract buyers through their consistently extravagant features. Many Theban and Fayyum figurines, for example, stand in *orans* posture and, while sexual features are usually deemphasized, communicate elite status through extensive headdresses with holes for colorful threads, painted robes, and highlighted eyes (see figs. 2–3, plate 1).[78] Another type, of unknown provenance, depicts a nude female molded in relief inside a palm leaf arbor or *aedicula*, with genitals and pregnant belly highlighted and, in at least one case, holding a baby to her breast (see fig. 7).[79] In both cases we can perceive the development by craftsmen—through molds, painting, and the affixing of threads and cloth—of an image that could be used compellingly as a medium for the subject's hopes or as a blessing in the home, where it could act as a figure of mimesis (could this be me?) or of ritual materiality (where will I put this?). In some cases, it seems, the crafting of an effective image might have continued at home, with the domestic

---

78 Teeter, *Baked Clay Figurines*, 79–91; cf. Török, *Coptic Antiquities I*, figs. G18–29.
79 Cf. Török, *Coptic Antiquities I*, fig. G4.

agents—as we saw in chapter 2—"dressing" the figurine in cloth for deposit in a tomb or shrine (see plate 2, fig. 4).[80]

The attention to eyes and hairstyles across most of the extant figurines was apparently integral to their ritual value and their value as commodities—that is, as things bought with the presumption of efficacy.[81] Even in the crudest figurines the attention to these "cosmetic" features suggests that such details were crucial to their efficacy—they made the figurines "work." But why? What did they signify? Eye highlighting and hairstyle signified public self-presentation and could render a girl a woman. These adornments lent a woman social visibility and framed and emphasized her portals of communication.[82] For example, a story we have seen already from the *Miracles of St. Menas*, the principal public propaganda for the Apa Mena pilgrimage shrine, describes a barren woman lamenting that she bore no adornment to the shrine: "She prayed and besought God with tears, seeing all the women wearing gold and silver and diamonds and carrying their children, but she had *no* adornment of gold or silver because of the grief in her heart; and therefore she was filled with envious longing."[83] At about the same time, 350 miles south of the shrine, Abbot Shenoute complains that "your daughters and their mothers apply . . . perfume to their head(s) and eye shadow to their eyes, adorning themselves to deceive those who see them . . . [while] going to the martyr's shrine."[84] But highlighting the eyes must have meant more than an inclination to flirt. It signified public presence and status, and for women it may also have functioned to display a visual receptivity to the saint's presence, for a number of ritual spells from Roman Egypt prescribe various types of eye paint as part of the preparations to gain a "direct vision" of a god.[85] All these details endowed the figurines with the capacity to idealize the prospective buyer and supplicant, to represent her in a higher class with public finery, whether for social status or for authority with (or receptivity to) supernatural agents. These details were components of the craftsman's innovation.

If it is difficult to see the construction of Christianity in the manufacture of female figurines—beyond, of course, their molding and marketing at certain Christian saints' shrines—we can approach them as again exemplifying the transformation of indigenous iconographic strategies to "work" in Christian shrine contexts and Christianized domestic spheres. For example, art historians have often associated the nude figurines from this period with earlier Hellenistic-

---

80 Cf. also Cairo J 65699 (early fourth century CE), on which see Allen, "Terracotta Figurines from Karanis," 4446–47, #95. A photograph of the figurine in situ in Karanis Rm C 62B shows a fragment of cloth with which the doll was wrapped.

81 See Bailey, *Catalogue of Terracottas*, 45–46.

82 See Boozer, *Late Romano-Egyptian House*, ch. 7, on artifacts of hairdressing in an Egyptian domestic context of the Roman period.

83 Drescher, *Apa Mena*, 133, txt. 43 (quoted earlier, pp. 119–20).

84 In Amélineau, *Oeuvres de Schenoudi I*, 201.

85 PDM xiv.115–15, 304–8, 695–705, 875ff; cf. "Coptic eye paint" in PGM V.65, VII.335.

CHAPTER 5

Egyptian images of goddesses, especially Hathor, Aphrodite, and Isis.[86] The implication of this association is that workshops and some putative female heathenism maintained the images of goddesses and their functions over centuries.[87] But the workshops, especially those at Apa Mena, could not have been more removed, both historically and culturally, from those that produced images of goddesses in the early Roman period. So, rather than depending on notions of a perennial heathen iconography or deviant ritual traditions, we ought to make sense of the nude figurines as a comprehensible element of the total ritual world of a Christian pilgrimage shrine. In this regard, the figurines were evidently deemed by some producers and buyers as more efficacious when they represented the subject's prematernal body or some idealized "divine" body (perhaps to be put by the marital bed) than when they portrayed the more typical robed bodies. Workshop traditions and creative habitus led to further detailing of the nude body. Some late antique craftsmen designed molds that set the women's hands in the Aphrodite-like *pudica* position or set the body in a leafy *aedicula*, according to what seemed appropriate to the nude form, but without recalling in any direct way Aphrodite, Hathor, or Isis (see figs. 6–7).[88] Of course, the modern historian, with the benefit of archaeology, can appreciate (or imagine) the general legacy of earlier iconographic traditions. The workshops, however, aimed simply to convey efficacy in the votive representation of fecundity and maternity. In the context of the prevailing culture and the shrines where they were sold and used, the figurines must be understood as Christian.

The same approach can be applied to the figurines of a woman suckling a child—the *mater lactans* or *kourotrophos* form, found especially at Apa Mena.[89] The common temptation to link this form to a classical Egyptian *Isis lactans* iconography would seem to ignore their utility as a simple variation on the maternal fecundity figurine found throughout the Mediterranean world since the Bronze Age.[90] That is to say, in the range of fecundity figurines from the Bronze Age through late antiquity, which include many depictions of infants with mothers,

---

86 Török, *Coptic Antiquities I*, 32–33, 41–42.

87 E.g. Polaczek-Zdanowicz, "Genesis and Evolution."

88 On the significance of the female nude in popular ancient Near Eastern images, see Bahrani, "Hellenization of Ishtar."

89 See figs. 1 (##7–8, 11, 18), 4–5, 7. Some archaeologists have suggested that the enthroned figurines from Apa Mena (see fig. 1, ##7–8) and Alexandria include the remarkable detail of a crocodile crawling up the side: see, e.g., Parandowski, "Coptic Terra-Cotta Figurines," 305. If this detail could be shown definitively, it might represent a localized (Fayum) form of some divine female, as Tallet proposes for Roman Egyptian images of (male) divinities holding or "sprouting" crocodiles; Tallet, "Isis, the Crocodiles." But it is entirely unclear how such details would have been perpetuated in workshops so closely affiliated with a major Christian pilgrimage shrine.

90 On the dubious link between *Isis lactans* and *Maria lactans*, see Tran Tam Tinh, *Isis lactans*; idem, "De nouveau Isis Lactans," 1234–39; Langener, *Isis Lactans-Maria Lactans*; and Boespflug, "D'*Isis Lactans* à *Maria Lactans*." Cf. Mathews and Muller, *Dawn of Christian Art*, 164–68, who reassert the derivation. On the relationship of the late antique *mater lactans* figurines to either Isis or Mary, see Török, *Coptic Antiquities I*, 33–34.

breastfeeding scenes are well-represented variants and in no way require a particular mythological context or goddess figure as a template.[91] (In fact, the *lactans* type itself was only one of a number of sexual/maternal iconographies of the goddess Isis during the Roman period, and was hardly her most common image.[92]) The most likely explanation for the revitalization of the *mater lactans* image among terracotta figurines in late antiquity is that this image, with all it expressed about maternal hopes and fears, had long been a more general iconographic strategy in the ancient world than one linked to a particular goddess, and that it was from this general basis that the *Maria lactans* iconography developed. The *lactans* form, like the nude form or, for that matter, the *orans* or tambourine-playing form, represented a refinement and highlighting of womanly features in the interest of ritual efficacy. In this way we can read the figurines as Christian artifacts, objects that served the mediation and material construction of Christianity in everyday life. But we can also read these forms as efficacious by virtue of their traditional, even archaic, resonance, recognizable even when the figurines bore an ambiguous identity.

C. Painters

Painters, as masters both in the deployment of color and in producing the visual image, also sought efficacy—the power of an object to transform spaces and create "presence"—indeed, to instill power *in* an image. Colors and their juxtapositions, gestures, the detailing of eyes, and the general creation of otherworldly spectacle—the use of all these tools comprised the painter's craft as it came to integrate Christian themes with traditional strategies. Like the terracotta figurines of the early Roman period, portable panel paintings of Egyptian gods developed around the same time as alternative media for worshipping Egyptian gods and interpreting them within the domestic sphere.[93] The innovations in both cases came from workshops, which combined Greco-Roman styles of representation with locally valued gods to create more affordable and portable images for private shrines and votive offerings for temples.[94] The versatility of these second- and third-century painters was considerable. The panel paintings, which were set in wood frames for hanging on a wall in a house or temple atrium (see plate 8), are

---

91 On the widespread occurrence of *mater lactans* figurines, see Ammerman, "Children at Risk," 136–38.

92 On the incidence of *Isis lactans* among representations of Isis, see Dunand, *Religion populaire en Égypte romaine*, 70; Ballet and Galliano, "Les isiaques et la petite plastique," 200–1; Boespflug, "D'Isis Lactans à Maria Lactans."

93 Rassart-Debergh, "Plaquettes peintes d'époque romaine"; Rondot, *Derniers visages des dieux d'Egypte*; and Mathews and Muller, *Dawn of Christian Art*.

94 See Rondot, *Derniers visages des dieux d'Egypte*, 43–47, who notably avoids the category of *ex voto* as overused (31–32). The related painted murals were clearly for the domestic sphere: see ibid., 53–65. See also Mathews and Muller, *Dawn of Christian Art*, chs. 1–3; and Vikan, *Early Byzantine Pilgrimage Art*, 71–78.

complemented by a number of wall murals in the same style from houses in the Fayyum towns of Tebtunis and Karanis, and several of the panels seem to have functioned as doors to traditional shrine boxes, or *naoi*.[95] All these applications of the new medium show the interests of painters in extending this medium to different domains of religious practice and experience—domains in which devotions might have taken the form of hanging garlands, placing lamps, or lighting incense, all of which are mirrored in some of the panel paintings.[96] While mostly unprovenanced, the "pantheon" of painted images shows some consistency: Isis in her *lactans* pose with Harpocrates (an image found especially in Karanis), the military god Heron (plate 8), the crocodile god Soknebtunis as lord over other gods, a solitary Harpocrates, and several other divinities both Egyptian and Hellenistic all appear frequently. As other workshops were doing with images of the deceased (the so-called portrait mummies), the painters of these images depicted the gods in a Hellenistic style that emphasized the accoutrements of cultural prestige in dress, jewelry, crowns, hairstyles, and thrones, as well as the *frontality* that typically accentuated both familiarity and presence, contributing to what Elsner called a "ritual-centered" visuality.

It is in this frontality that we can begin to grasp the particular efficacy of the panel paintings as well as their likely role as the inspiration for the earliest Christian panel icons. If we recall the positions of Egyptian divinities represented outside temples, the potency of the body and of the frontal gaze was usually downplayed to stress ritual relationships, mythic accoutrements, and the presence of the pharaoh. (Relief images of Hathor and Bes offer notable exceptions.[97]) While the innovation of the molded terracotta figurines accentuated the body and its mysteries and potencies in the round, the panel paintings of gods brought forth the frontal gaze (even if the eyes of the subjects are often slightly averted). Indeed, except for a very few images seeking to mimic more narrative styles of painting, the vast preponderance of panel and mural paintings of gods from Roman Egypt offer their viewers the frontal gaze—inaccessible at traditional temples except during festival processions. And indeed, it is the frontal gaze, and later the focused eyes, that the earliest Christian painted icons, from the sixth century, emphasize for their viewers, even to the diminishment of bodies. The viewer's eyes are drawn to the face and its eyes gazing directly out.[98] Where—in the words of art historian Thomas Mathews—the panel paintings "document the living conversations that took place between gods and men, conveying the glance of gods toward their clients and the reactions of the devout in offering garlands," icons and their eyes served as vehicles of divine power and authority, often conveying the most concrete and dangerous of powers: an icon of the Syrian St.

---

95 Mathews and Muller, *Dawn of Christian Art*, chs. 1–3, with 103–17 on *naoi* doors, exemplified by the "Malibu panels" of Isis and Sarapis.
96 Ibid., 132.
97 See in general Volokhine, *La frontalité dans l'iconographie*.
98 Török, *Transfigurations of Hellenism*, 298–305.

Simeon, for example, worn by a devotee, served as such a vehicle for the saint when Simeon leapt out of it to foil a demon.[99] They also, like the older panel paintings of Egyptian gods, served as votive contributions to churches and shrines, and in the monastic world they served as memorial portraits of holy men for a different kind of veneration.[100]

Here, then, is a useful case of continuing workshop or artisanal innovation, both in the area of media and in the corollary area of devotional practice. This continuing innovation appears first in the development of painted images of Egyptian gods that conjured presence through frontality and that offered this material and visual presence to the domestic religious world; and then in the extension of this craft (and the frontal image) to Christian themes and functions, from the illumination of church structures to the cultivation of the portable icon.[101]

Painting's efficacy extended to the transformation of space. The remarkable wall painting of a mounted St. Sissinios spearing a demon, found in a chapel at the monastery of Bawit, turns the chapel into an exorcistic chamber (see plate 9). This image of a powerful and visually forbidding (or rescuing) soldier on a horse was assembled out of many regional iconographic traditions around the Mediterranean that were associated with Solomon; the gods Heron, Anubis, and Mithras; and various heroes, according to region and medium.[102] This "holy rider" became a regular motif in the depiction of Christian saints in Egypt and Ethiopia, although one can never be sure whether the rider was meant to be Christian or simply a heroic, apotropaic image. A small bone amulet from late antique Egypt seems to show such a rider saint spearing a crocodile, displaying the carver's integration of several traditions of apotropaic efficacy, including the saint's frontal gaze (see fig. 12). The painters of the Bawit St. Sissinios likewise positioned his face frontally, and they added further apotropaic symbols (e.g., the "suffering eye") next to the saint on his horse in order to show that the painting as a whole could work against hostile forces, not just recall a story.[103]

Another series of images of saints, painted on columns in the temple of Karnak in the fifth century, served to purify, declare triumph over, and establish the ecclesiastical space as Christian in this dangerously heathen monument.[104] As Abbot Shenoute declares in a sermon—possibly about this very installation—"at the

99 *Life of Simeon the Younger* 118, in Van den Ven, *Vie ancienne*, 2:119–20; cf. the use of a Simeon the Elder icon by a workshop in Rome recounted in Theodoret, *Hist. Rel.* 26.11.

100 Auth, "Brother George the Scribe"; on early Egyptian Christian panel paintings, see in general Rutschowscaya, *La peinture copte*, 34–37; and on the memorialization of holy men as ascetic/charismatic ancestors through iconography, see Bolman and Szymańska, "Ascetic Ancestors."

101 See in general Mathews and Muller, *Dawn of Christian Art*.

102 Perdrizet, *Negotium perambulans in tenebris*; Lewis, "Iconography of the Coptic Horseman"; cf. Johnston, "Riders in the Sky."

103 Compare the apotropaic painting programs in the monastery of Kellia and in a Cappadocian church of the ninth century; Rassart-Debergh, "Animaux dans la peinture kelliote"; Thierry, "Aux limites du sacré."

104 Coquin, "La Christianisation des temples de Karnak"; Rassart-Debergh, "L'Akh-Menou."

FIGURE 12. Round amulet showing a saint on horseback spearing a crocodile. Carved bone. Egypt, unprovenanced. Fifth to seventh century CE. Height: 4.2 cm; width: 3.2 cm.

site of a shrine to an unclean spirit, it will henceforth be a shrine to the Holy Spirit.... And if previously it is prescriptions for murdering man's soul that are therein... where these are, it is the soul-saving scriptures of life that will henceforth come to be therein, fulfilling the word of God with His name inscribed for them *and His son Jesus Christ and all His angels, righteous men and saints (portrayed)*."[105] But as other buildings in Shenoute's federation in the Panopolis region show, paintings applied within churches sought not just protection and triumph for visitors but the creation of spectacle and awe—another dimension in the creation of supernatural potency through colors and design.[106]

One of the most remarkable examples of painting as an act of religious synthesis comes from the monastery at Old Dongola in Nubia, in the chronological and geographical borderlands of late antique Egypt. First built in the seventh century, the monastery went through a series of decorative programs over the tenth to the fourteenth centuries, with the addition of dramatic depictions of biblical, apocryphal, and angelological themes that stylistically drew from both Byzantine iconography and Nubian traditions. One particular painting from the twelfth- to thirteenth-century phase, placed above a door, depicts a framed image of the Virgin and Child, before which a large group of warriors dance, some in masks and some holding clappers or maracas in various colorful dress (see plates 3–4).[107] The painter—perhaps one of the monks—was clearly responding to forms of African ceremonial dance in the region in a way that had been ignored in prior

---

105 Michigan ms. 158, in Young, "A Monastic Invective," 353–54. The association with Shenoute is based on his presence as Ur-Archimandrite in an inscription in the same church; see Coquin, "La Christianisation des temples de Karnak," 172–77.

106 See Bolman, "A Staggering Spectacle."

107 Martens-Czarnecka, "Wall Paintings Discovered in Dongola"; and idem, *Wall Paintings from the Monastery*, 233–38 (Room 5, images 108–9).

painting phases. Whereas in chapter 4 I invoked this mural as evidence of the importance and character of dances in the process of acculturating a shrine, its festivals, and its material accoutrements into local life, it is also worth considering the actual depiction of indigenous dance, especially as performed by elite warriors, as an artisanal strategy to recognize the local culture as receiving, welcoming, and integrating images of a new religion. In this way, this relatively late example of Christian painting might pertain to earlier materials that mediated Christianity and the celebration of Christian figures through details drawn from indigenous ceremonies, like the tambourines in the hands of terracotta figurines or the textiles (as we will see) that place the cross among mythical creatures. The warrior dance provides an idealized image of the Virgin Mary's (or her icon's) public acclamation. Yet an even deeper layer may be intended here. Analyzing a similarly conceived image of warriors dancing before a Christian missionary from eighteenth-century Congo, art historian Cécile Fromont highlights the function of such dances and their representations as demonstrating the power of the indigenous elite within a new system that has integrated Christian authority. Thus also at Old Dongola, the depictions of the warriors' dance may not illustrate local deference to Mary and Christ so much as the power of the warriors in a new royal system in which Mary and Christ *watch and approve* the warriors' preeminence—a preeminence customarily expressed in dance.[108] Overall, the depiction of such dances in paintings objectifies the process of acculturation and reception, of syncretism as an integral part of Christianization.

In general, paying attention to religious painting in late antique Egypt in terms of this quest for efficacy—through color, frontality, and the addition of magical accoutrements—allows us to make sense of the full range of works available without depending on essential "Christian" or Egyptian meanings. Both the Bawit St. Sissinios and the Karnak column paintings, both depictions of Isis and those of Christ on wood panels, were supposed to *work* in this world, and craftsmen dedicated their skills and knowledge of traditions to the achievement of this ritual functionality.

D. Textile Weavers

A large corpus of textile fragments from fourth- to seventh-century Egypt, comprising parts of tunics in which people were buried, many of which bear mythic or religious content, reflect the salient cultural symbols and mythological associations of the elite and those who aspired to that status in late antique Egypt. Like the elaborate burial niches of Herakleopolis Magna, the decorative segments from these tunics often depict Leda and the Swan, Dionysus, and sea nymphs. So, despite the increasing significance of Christian institutions and, more importantly, Christian story in popular culture, the imagery sought and crafted into

108 Fromont, *Art of Conversion*, 21–63.

CHAPTER 5

these tunics drew predominantly from classical mythology and only occasionally from Christian (including biblical) mythology.[109] As with stonework and painting, both Christian and Hellenistic textile designs came from the same workshops. Representations of Christian themes (e.g., saints, biblical scenes) show the same styles and arrangement as Roman mythological scenes, and even crosses are often decorated or complemented with mythical figures (see figs. 10–11, plates 6–7). In general, the range of textile images from the fifth through eighth centuries indicates, first, that Christians certainly commissioned tunics containing classical images, and second, that we need a better "theory" of these tunics as ritual objects to understand the context of their manufacture and the craftsmen's conception of these themes.

Clearly these late antique tunics meant more than just sumptuous public adornment, whether in life or in death. In his study of Indo-Arabic encounters in medieval south Asia, Finbarr Flood describes the highly charged symbolism of the gifting and donning of robes, as well as the adoption of foreign clothing, among this region's elite. Dress and special robes and tunics had "the ability to communicate political power, social status, personal wealth, and ethnic or religious affiliation" and "constituted the very categories they signified," in that one gained and embodied a particular status through wearing the robe associated with it.[110] The intrinsic value of such garments derived from the visibility and the cultural legibility through which they conveyed status and from the "radical translations in identity" they could provide to those who donned them.[111] That is to say, they had the capacity to affect one's self-presentation in gesture and mien, to saturate the wearer thoroughly with a new identity.

Likewise, from the evidence of papyri (and even some textiles imported from outside Egypt), we can regard the Egyptian tunics as commodities that bore in their very richness, color, detail, and overall design the legacy and notoriety of particular workshops.[112] Thus the production of these tunics, and the detailed segments that constituted them, involved the general goal of creating social efficacy—a performative efficacy in which the body was placed on display as something elite and cultured, and consequently the wearer himself came to be seen as elite and cultured. Asterius of Amaseia, for example, describes such displays in his region of Asia Minor in the late fourth century: "When they come out in public dressed in this fashion, they appear like painted walls to those they meet," he describes, providing delight to local children "who point their fingers at the pictures on the garments."[113] On the other hand, Abbot Besa of the White Monastery

---

109 See, e.g., Lewis, *Early Coptic Textiles*; Thompson, *Coptic Textiles in the Brooklyn Museum*; Maguire, "Garments Pleasing to God"; Stauffer, *Textiles of Late Antiquity*.

110 Flood, *Objects of Translation*, 62–63, and ch. 2 in general.

111 Ibid., 63.

112 On textile craftsmanship in late antique Egypt, see P. Mich. inv. 1050 (V-VI); and in general, Wipszycka, *L'industrie textile*; idem, "Textiles, Coptic"; and Gonosová, "Textiles."

113 Asterius of Amaseia, *Hom.* 1, PG 40: 165, in Mango, *Art of the Byzantine Empire*, 50–51.

specifically attacks "the embroidering of garments" among monks as a vanity, an abomination equivalent to "improper [i.e., vain] washing."[114]

Yet Besa's attack on embroidery should not be taken to imply that monks just wanted to make their otherwise dull robes flashier. They engaged in this ornamentation, he says, "with passion [ϩⲚϩⲈⲚⲠⲀⲐⲞⲤ]." Already in this monastery, as Rebecca Krawiec has argued, Shenoute had exhorted monks and nuns to regard their robes as resplendent in purity and evocative of biblical patriarchs.[115] So what is it that they were embroidering "with passion," especially when monastic robes typically involved, if anything, simply crosses? One might imagine they were adding symbols that endowed their wearer with prestige or even apotropaic power—both of which involved efficacy.

But even by themselves, and even if the more elaborate decorations of tunics were discouraged, robes assumed an important ritual value in Egyptian monastic communities. A story about the investiture of Shenoute of Atripe as Archimandrite tells how his monastic mentor, Apa Pjol, received a dream from heaven while they were together, foretelling that the prophet Elijah's own sheepskin cloak would appear beside them in the morning, destined for Shenoute himself. When they awoke, the cloak was there; Shenoute put it on, and a voice was heard from heaven: "Shenoute was appointed Archimandrite of the whole world on this day."[116] Here the handing on of garments endowed charismatic authority—as Flood puts it (vis-à-vis Muhammed's cloak), the mantle "conferred a degree of legitimacy on its possessor by virtue of an indexed relation to earlier owners and ultimately to the Prophet himself."[117]

Legends of Shenoute's cloak (which came to be preserved in the convent as a relic with exorcistic powers)[118] reflect other tales of magical garments and accoutrements: "the golden cord [ϩⲰⲤ] on the neck of Abraham," whose healing power [ⲞⲨⲬⲀⲒ] an esoteric liturgical text invokes; and the "three golden bands [Grk χόρδη; Coptic ⲀⲎⲖ]" that the patriarch Job gave to his daughters in the second- or third-century CE *Testament of Job*, a document that circulated among Egyptian monasteries in several recensions.[119] "It is not in [human] power to speak about their likeness," the author tells us, "for [the golden bands] were not [from] this world but from [heaven. They] threw out sparks of light." Job himself announces in this text that "these cords [will lead you] into the great [eternal] life [in] heaven. Do you [not know the value] of these cords with which I have adorned [your body]? . . . [I]f you gird yourselves with these [cords], the enemy will not

---

114 Besa, *Ep.*, frag. 12, 5.2, 6.5, 8.4, in Kuhn, *Letters and Sermons of Besa*, 1.33-35, 2.32-33.
115 Krawiec, "'Garments of Salvation,'" 143.
116 *V.Sin.* 8-9, in Amélineau, *Monuments pour servir*, 7.
117 Flood, *Objects of Translation*, 78; cf. Krawiec, "'Garments of Salvation,'" esp. 134-36.
118 See Jördens, "Reliquien des Schenute."
119 Golden cord: P. Macquarie 1, 7.14-15, in Choat and Gardner, *Coptic Handbook of Ritual Power*. Golden bands: *Testament of Job* 46-47, in Schenke, *Der koptische kölner Papyruskodex*, 176-83.

FIGURE 13. Textile segment showing a mounted hero, his left arm raised, in a square surrounded by *putti*, vases, and plants. Wool and linen. Third to fourth century CE. Height: 14.6 cm; width: 14 cm.

have power over you. [And also] no evil thought will capture [your] heart. For [these are] guards of the Father."[120] The efficacy of these cords is signified in their radiance and glitter, alerting us again to the fact that workshops that achieved such effects in any medium became catalysts in the performance of heavenly spectacle; significantly, Job himself is said here not to have crafted the bands but to have produced them from three golden boxes.

But what of the thematic content on textiles, whether gospel stories or images of Leda and the Swan? The classical mythological probably conveyed cultural participation—not in "paganism" but in Hellenistic heritage, which framed prestige. Certain motifs, like Dionysus and sea nymphs, might have had local resonance to the craftsmen and the wearers, whether or not they themselves participated in Christian liturgy,[121] and it is quite possible that some of the designs were also seen as having a protective function, like the armed equestrian figures in silk

---

120 *Testament of Job* (Coptic) 46.7–8; 47.3, 10–11, in Bauckham, Davila, and Panayotov, *Old Testament Pseudepigrapha*, 174 (emended).

121 Cf. Bowersock, *Mosaics as History*, 33–39; and idem, *Hellenism in Late Antiquity*, 48–52, on the diverse meanings of Dionysus iconography in late antiquity.

FIGURE 14. Square textile segment showing two saints spearing serpents at their feet while holding crosses, surrounded by floral designs, part of a tunic whose longer strips show armed heroes with fierce animals. Silk. Egypt (or Syria?), unprovenanced. Seventh to eighth century CE. Height: 12.5 cm; width: 13 cm.

from a workshop in Panopolis or the two saints spearing serpents in a segment in the Metropolitan Museum (see figs. 13–14).[122] Were Christian motifs—crosses or narrative scenes—conceived differently by weavers and clients? Given the mainly *apotropaic* function of the cross symbol in architecture and painting, it is likely that the intended efficacy of tunics bearing crosses lay in their protection of the wearer (rather than as an indicator of identity).[123] Some of the earliest crosses on tunics are designed out of, or within, more traditional motifs like leaves, birds, and circles, and some crosses have been magically enhanced by the placement of

---

122 Equestrian figures: Thomas, "Silks," 154–159; and further: Lewis, "Iconography of the Coptic Horseman"; Thompson, *Coptic Textiles in the Brooklyn Museum*, 56–57, #23. On protective designs in textiles in general, see Maguire, "Garments Pleasing to God"; and Ball, "Charms."

123 Maguire, "Garments Pleasing to God"; Davis, *Coptic Christology in Practice*, 168–69.

faces inside them (see plates 6–7, fig. 11).[124] Asterius of Amaseia (skeptically) imputes pious motivations to the wearing of Christian narrative scenes, noting that "the more religious among rich men and women, having picked out the gospel story, have handed it over to the weavers.... In doing this they consider themselves to be pious [εὐσεβεῖν] and to be wearing clothes that are agreeable to God."[125] Of course, Asterius's point is that such piety was indistinguishable from the performance of prestige—that the elite had simply appropriated Christian lore to demonstrate status, much the way they did with scenes of Leda and the Swan.

But an intriguing theory of the efficacy of tunics woven with gospel scenes proposed by the historian Stephen Davis holds that they allowed the (public or contemplative) "incorporation" of Christ's incarnation—"that, in late antique Egypt, discourses of 'putting on' Christ [from Pauline formulas] were not always restricted to the metaphorical realm." Rather, "such tunics became means by which christological realities were *performed* and *im-personated*."[126] The ingenuity of Davis's proposal is that it places the agency of interpreting and enacting the incarnation of Christ not in ecclesiastical performance but in the social worlds of craftsmen and wearers.

And yet the provenances of these tunics, our chief evidence for their actual use, point to their ultimate funerary function: as elements in the shrouding of the deceased. Considered in this way, their ritual function of effecting a transformation of the soul would have been quite apparent.[127] Like the mummy portraits of earlier Roman Egypt, the tunics would have used the cultural status of the living individual as a basis for constructing the transformative body, the self that would become a beneficial ancestor. Again, the goal of such craftsmanship lay in the *efficacy* of the funerary process as well as—and perhaps more than—the efficacy of the garment in public self-presentation. In one burial in Antinoopolis, linen and woolen shawls, some decorated, were carefully placed over various parts of a deceased woman's body, as if to convey particular care for each section: belly, breasts, shin, and a special woven wreath or crown for her head.[128]

E. The Mortuary Craft

This last aspect of the ritual efficacy intended in late antique tunics brings us finally to that most complex and evolving craft in Roman and late antique Egypt: the funerary preparation of corpses and the persistence of mummification. These

---

124 Kendrick, *Catalogue of Textiles*, 5–19.
125 Asterius of Amaseia, *Hom.* 1, PG 40: 168, in Mango, *Art of the Byzantine Empire*, 51 (translation emended).
126 Davis, *Coptic Christology in Practice*, 177, and, in general, 154–80. Cf. idem, "Fashioning a Divine Body."
127 See, e.g., Davis, *Coptic Christology in Practice*, 168–69.
128 Fluck, "Textiles from Antinoupolis," 118, 121.

remarkable types of continuing practice have long been considered under the separate rubric of mortuary "religion." Unfortunately, by the fifth century, we can no longer infer any particular beliefs from the mummification of corpses beyond families' (and monasteries') concern for the *efficacy* of mortuary ritual—that is, their concern that the treatments of and crafts surrounding the corpse should successfully transform the deceased into an ancestor or (for monks) intercessory figure, or at least should afford the deceased a measure of protection against mortuary demons, a concern attested by the elaborate inscription of some monks' tombs with apotropaic blessings.[129] These aims were fundamentally what funerals and interment practices, from mummification to its attendant application of amulets, wrappings, and wood coffins, were meant to accomplish.[130] Even funerary stelae, with their invocations to God and the saints to "give rest," likewise say less about actual afterlife beliefs than they do about the integration of text, especially liturgical text, into the overall transformative efficacy of the funerary process.[131]

From the early Roman period through late antiquity, what is especially noticeable about the range of mummies is their diversity, not only across Egypt but within individual cemeteries. There is wide variation in the types and levels of embalming that were performed, in the skills in wrapping employed, and in the use of coffins. For example, as late as the sixth and seventh centuries, cemeteries in Karara and Douch still included elaborately painted coffins with geometrically wrapped mummies, while some other cemeteries had abandoned much of their craftsmanship in mummy preparation.[132] At the monastery of Epiphanius in Thebes, monks wrapped their brothers' corpses in elaborate layers of cloth, with intricate binding patterns, after which "handfuls of coarse rock salt and juniper berries were poured between the legs and over the trunk, inside and outside the innermost wrappings—a reminiscence of ancient mummification which had but little effect on preserving the body."[133] At the monastery of Naqlun, in the Fayyum, one body was wrapped in eleven successive shrouds, with colored stripes in the outermost shroud and a wooden board placed under the body, cut to emphasize the shape of the head. The resulting anthropomorphic bundle was

---

129 See Krause, "Das Weiterleben ägyptischer Vorstellungen" (*pace* his theory of persisting beliefs); Dunand, "Between Tradition and Innovation"; and, on transformation of the deceased, Riggs, *Beautiful Burial in Roman Egypt*. Apotropaic tomb *dipinti*: Van der Vliet, "Literature, Liturgy, Magic."

130 An illuminating comparandum for the importance of the properly buried corpse for social felicity is the interment of infant corpses in the vicinity of workshops in Roman Gaul, which archaeologists Baills-Talbi and Blanchard argue were meant to bring fortune to the workshop in transitional periods; Baills-Talbi and Blanchard, "Sépultures de nouveau-nés."

131 Tudor, *Christian Funerary Stelae*; Dunand, "Between Tradition and Innovation," 180–81.

132 See Dunand and Lichtenberg, *Mummies and Death in Egypt*, 72–80; Dunand, "Between Tradition and Innovation"; Nauerth, "Pfauensarg und Mumienhülle"; Gessler-Löhr, "Mummies and Mummification."

133 Crum and Winlock, *Monastery of Epiphanius at Thebes*, 48.

CHAPTER 5

bound with tapes in a careful ornamental pattern.[134] Entire villages and monasteries maintained mummification practices without any apparent reflection on, or from, religious "identity."[135]

This diversity in practices suggests that we should think about mummification and its detailed work not as representative of "religious communities" or belief systems but as a locally based craft that, if originally maintained in professional guilds (like the *nekrotaphoi* in the oasis town of Kysis, who write of their receipt of a Christian corpse in a letter of the late third century),[136] devolved like so many other ritual practices into family- (and monastery-)based traditions, in which families or monks took care of some stages in the mortuary process and local specialists, working off inherited knowledge, took care of mummification, rudimentary mortuary rites, and burial.[137] This may be what Athanasius implied in his fourth-century *Life of Antony* in declaring that "the Egyptians" (as opposed to Egyptian priests, for example) "like to honour [the bodies of the special dead] with funeral rites and wind them up in linen strips; but they do not hide them underground but place them on beds and keep them in their homes with them."[138] Here the overall picture is of a domestic craft, as in the sixth-century Coptic *Story of Joseph the Carpenter*, which describes how Jesus himself washed and embalmed his father Joseph's corpse, although in this text the real efficacy in the preservation of the body comes from the power of Jesus's spoken words.[139] The burial itself is conducted by "corpse-buriers [ⲚⲒⲢⲈϤⲔⲰⲤ]"—presumably imagining community members who were versed in this rudimentary skill. Among these local forms of the craft, so clearly visible in late antique burials, a range of materials in mortuary preparation would have been considered vital or efficacious: the number of shrouds, the arrangement of strips and knots, or the use of particular salts or plant

---

134 Godlewski and Czaja-Szewczak, "Cemetery C.1 in Naqlun."

135 See Bowen, "Some Observations on Christian Burial Practices," 170–71.

136 P. Grenfell 73, with essential discussions in Dunand, "Les nécrotaphes de Kysis"; and Llewelyn and Nobbs, "P. Grenf. II 73."

137 On the range of crafts associated with funerary preparation, see Derda, "Necropolis Workers"; and Cannata, "Funerary Artists." Derda, "Necropolis Workers," 23–31, notes that the roles of *choachytes* and *nekrotaphoi* were inherited, so the traditions might have continued in families. O. Leiden 383 refers to a role of "embalmer," and the ingredients and materials of mortuary preparation seem to have been familiar in some homes: see P. Mich. inv. 3724 (III CE), a letter asking the sender's father to bring ῥιτίνην and σφατία for preparing the body of a servant; ACM 128 = P. Cairo 45060, l. 50, possibly from the sixth century, instructs preparers to use "embalming salt [ⲈⲘⲞⲨ ⲚⲔⲰⲤ]" in a ritual to deaccession or destroy a building. Possible embalming houses have been found at Kysis and perhaps El-Deir, notably between the Christian and traditional cemeteries; Dunand, "Les nécrotaphes de Kysis," 122–23; Dunand and Coudert, "Les débuts de la christianisation." Eva Subías Pascual discusses a Christian-occupied building by the Oxyrhynchus cemetery that was used for laying out corpses in *La maison funéraire*, 127.

138 Athanasius, *v.Ant.* 90.

139 ⲀⲒϢⲒⲞⲨⲒ ⲚⲞⲨⲘⲰⲞⲨ ⲈϪⲈⲚ ⲠⲤⲰⲘⲀ... ⲀⲒⲐⲀⲢϤ ϦⲈⲚ ⲞⲨⲚⲈϨ ⲚⲤⲐⲞⲒ ⲚⲞⲨϤⲒ; in Ehrman and Pleše, *Apocryphal Gospels*, 184–85. See also Boud'hors, "Histoire de Joseph," 27–28.

materials. It was in the addition (or virtuoso application) of these components that the craft was preserved.[140]

In the fifth century, mortuary preparation remained a skill not proffered by the church or monastic institution but passed down in families, although some families' exceptional craftsmanship earned them local renown, as the mummies from Karara suggest.[141] Only one document, an eighth-century bishop's will, associates the "covering [περιστολή]" of the body after death with "the holy offerings and memorial meals [ἀγάπας] and [observance of] the specific days of death," all "according to local custom [ἐπιχώριον νόμον]," although this extensive ritualization probably reflects the author's ecclesiastical status.[142] Generally we see little interconnection between mummification and funerary ritual, and funerary ritual itself appears to have been inconsistently and locally innovated.[143] For example, a baptismal font in the Antinoopolis cemetery seems indeed to have served the baptism of corpses, but this application of baptism would have been quite unusual in Egypt and the wider late antique world.[144]

The range of crafts associated with funerary preparations thus stand outside the sphere of institutional religion or even a broader mythology or ideology of the sacred. And yet they clearly served as a way of responding to death and to a potential relationship between the deceased and his or her family. Thus, whether through the application of gold leaf to the face, as we find in several early Roman cemeteries,[145] or simply through careful embalming or elaborate binding, people versed in the craft transformed the corpse into a condition in which it was ready to serve some postmortem state. New work on fourth-century mummies in the Kharga and Dakhleh oases has suggested the development of an Egyptian Christian mortuary tradition that eschewed evisceration, used salt crystals and herbs rather than natron to preserve the corpse, and oriented burials on an east/west axis. While modern efforts to connect these practices with Christian doctrines tend to be speculative at best, we can say that—to whatever degree they arose in connection with other Christian practices—they would have served the transformation of the soul, the family's investment in that transformation, and perhaps some community investment in the distinction of mortuary practices. The local integration of burial practices distinct to Christians may indicate an inclination on the part of local Christian authorities (or simply enterprising craftsmen) to offer new types of mortuary efficacy, whether or not these new types reflected

---

140 See above, n. 131. On the efficacy of knotting in earlier periods, see Wendrich, "Entangled, Connected or Protected?"

141 This describes at least the *chōra*. Alexandria and its burial topography involved different systems of mortuary belief and burial work that may sometimes have involved ecclesiastical influence: see Bond, "Mortuary Workers, the Church," 140–43.

142 P. Lond. 1.77, ll. 57–59.

143 As elsewhere in late antiquity; see Rebillard, *Care of the Dead*.

144 Grossmann, "Churches and Meeting Halls," 111.

145 Dunand, "Les 'têtes dorées' "; idem, "Du séjour osirien des morts."

ideas we might associate with Christianity.[146] If actually reflective of a Christian tradition, the east/west orientation might also express a new (or renewed) sense of geographical orientation in mortuary tradition and mythology that corresponded to other media in which the land of Egypt was envisioned as a sacred expanse (see chapter 6). As with other crafts addressed in this chapter, mortuary preparers aimed at *efficacy*—understood here in the sense of a "self" properly resituated in a new social status through the symbolic medium of the prepared corpse and its accoutrements. By late antiquity that efficacy was being conceived locally, so diversity in wrappings does not imply a decline in the tradition but simply perceptions of what was acceptable and pursued locally—that is, of what local craftsmen were capable.

But the local nature of the craft and the general disinterest on the part of the church in laying claim to mortuary ritual means also that the incorporation of Christian symbols and materials into these practices was quite idiosyncratic. Corpses were not regarded as "sites" of Christianization—as media between ecclesiastical tradition, family hopes, and the transition of the individual. Not even monastic corpses functioned in this way. The symbols of Christianity were applied instead to the more public medium of the funerary stelae, the work of stonecarvers. Only rarely does one find a cross attached to the body or magical scripture inscribed on wrappings, and the corpus of tunics with Christian symbols (and a few with Christian phrases) is small enough that it does not seem to reflect a cultural understanding of death as a Christian process.[147] In the Christian necropolis of El-Deir, archaeologists discovered two men with their right hands shaped in what might be a "benediction" gesture, and several more corpses with palm leaves possibly shaped as crosses placed on their bodies.[148] But these accoutrements are unusual and show the idiosyncratic ways that families and mortuary specialists endowed corpses with ritual meaning and efficacy. Even the churches excavated in necropoleis do not show evidence of a centralized mortuary craft or funerals but rather appear to have served as access points for the mediating powers of particular saints buried there.[149] Overall, it is difficult to see a Christianization of funerals in any consistent way in Egypt.

Thinking about funerary preparation and mummification in terms of craftsmanship instead of some more presumptive and abstract conception of death allows us to confront more readily the great diversity of local mortuary customs, in

146 East/west orientation: see esp. the work of Coudert on the El-Deir cemeteries, one of which has random orientations and the other strictly east/west ones; Coudert, "W99"; Dunand and Coudert, "Les débuts de la christianisation"; Bowen, "Some Observations." It is probably inappropriate to extrapolate the meaning of this orientation from the Syrian *Didascalia Apostolorum*, as in Bowen, "Some Observations," 169.

147 Cross: Smith and Dawson, *Egyptian Mummies*; amuletic scripture: Luijendijk, "Jesus Says"; Christian symbols: Kendrick, *Catalogue of Textiles*.

148 Dunand and Coudert, "Les débuts de la christianisation."

149 See Grossmann, "Churches and Meeting Halls." Cf. Subías Pascual, *Maison funéraire*, 127.

which one village might entertain a rudimentary "guild" for such procedures and others might share only the cemetery and burial team.[150] And thinking about the creation of efficacy as the goal of craftsmanship, especially in this case, allows us to consider comparatively the full range of mortuary practices that sought the effective transformation of the deceased: decorated tunics and mummy wrappings, amulets and crosses, embalming and incantations, burial orientation and funerary stelae. The integration of Christianity into this localized production of mortuary efficacy was thus a complex thing, a process that potentially impacted the protection of the deceased, a family's sense of custom or protocol, or even the local authority of baptism or liturgical chant. As challenging as it may be to generalize about the integration of Christian symbols and practices into local Egyptian mortuary procedures in late antiquity, we can be reasonably confident about the agents' goals, as well as about their motivations in maintaining traditional practices.

IV. CONCLUSION

Past approaches to religious conversion and "survival" have imagined broad, often-inchoate "religious communities" that threw off their heathen pasts, embraced Christian salvation, or tried naively to combine both. If scholars imputed *agency* to any of these shifts, they imagined it as oscillating between an individualistic rationality (why would I, as a Christian, want my mother mummified?) and a vague need for collective identity (how would the Christians there have expressed their religious difference?). But agency in Christianization, and especially agency in constructing Christianity in practice and landscape, has to be located more precisely in the social worlds that actually had their hands in it. When we confront the diverse artifacts that show seemingly non- or pre-Christian religious images coexisting with, or combined with, Christian images, we are looking at the social worlds of workshops and craftsmen. When we reconstruct the process by which a Christian materiality came into being in the context of Egyptian local culture, we must likewise reckon with these social worlds. And we are confronting not just questions of agency in the perpetuation of tradition but also questions of agency in the very construction of a material, visual, sensory Christianity—how "Christianity" came to be part of the physical world. That is, we are again confronting the syncretism that is essential to the acculturation and construction of any religion.

As the producers of media that expressed Christianity along with (and sometimes merged with) various religious and cultural traditions, workshops served as spaces for both the perpetuation and the innovation of forms. The principal goal

---

150 On mortuary guilds in the Roman period, see Dunand and Lichtenberg, "Pratiques et croyances funéraires," 3242–44. In P. Grenfell 73 (third century CE), Christians in Kysis (Kharga Oasis) represent themselves as "the elegant and trustworthy from among the corpse-bearers."

of such perpetuation and innovation was the creation of *efficacy*, whether in quotidian utility, social prestige, or supernatural protection. From both archaeological and documentary evidence we know that workshops in late antique Egypt comprised a range of social systems: not just masters and apprentices but family and monastic structures as well. Their interests in and strategies for creating efficacious media were thus sustained through craft traditions, community traditions about supernatural forces and prestige, and broader social bonds. They shared concerns about how to demarcate domestic borders or seek a saint's assurance of pregnancy or secure a corpse for the mortuary process. As participants in the culture, workshops and craftsmen knew well the needs for efficacy that their goods were meant to produce.

It is a delicate matter to generalize on the sources of symbols and iconographic strategies as they appear on materials like lamps, textiles, and stonework, since all the archaeological evidence shows a predominantly local reception and interpretation of such symbols. Certainly Christian churches, whose iconographic and ritual programs were more strictly governed by ecclesiastical authorities, provided sources for workshop themes, whether iconographic (gospel stories) or textual (liturgical phrases that could be woven into textiles or inscribed on funerary stelae). The potency of the cross in demarcating and protecting spaces certainly transcended the influence of churches, as we can see in the widespread appearance of the cross gesture and the creativity with which stoneworkers and textile artisans developed crosses in material culture. There was something captivating about the shape and its proffered powers that, I have argued, invited artisans to apply traditional strategies to innovating new forms of the cross.

Other symbols were also drawn into action to express a Christian efficacy. The "holy rider" image, for example, was produced in paintings, textiles, metals, and other media, sometimes to convey the more general apotropaic tradition associated with the mounted figure and sometimes to sharpen and advance a Christian iconography: the St. Sissinios painting in a monastery's chapel is one example, as is a textile segment with an (unmounted) bishop spearing a serpent (see plate 9, fig. 14; cf. fig. 12). And clearly some crafts, like female figurines, were maintained in workshops, not as "survivals" but as essential iconographic components, plausibly Christian media, in vibrant interaction between holy spaces and domestic spaces. The textile, stone, and other crafts associated with the mortuary process seem to have been maintained in workshops and families and to have developed only idiosyncratic interests in overt Christian symbols, yet there is no evidence (in Egypt or elsewhere) that bishops sought to reform the crafts per se.[151] The practice of aligning bodies on an east/west axis in some Egyptian cemeteries of the fourth and fifth centuries seems to have presumed some form of efficacy associated with Christianity, although it is difficult to determine how it came about. Overall, the routes by which various Christianizing symbols and practices en-

---

151 See also Rebillard, *Care of the Dead*.

tered workshops and craftsmanship were diverse and usually quite local in nature, ranging from the teachings of monks to stories brought by merchants.

What has interested me in this chapter, however, is the agency in innovation and bricolage that the workshops and craftsmen themselves expressed in producing religious materials—paintings, mummies, stelae, figurines—out of local traditions and habitus on the one hand and local impressions of Christianity on the other. These materials constituted a Christianity of practice, of the senses, of space, and of physical efficacy in the world.

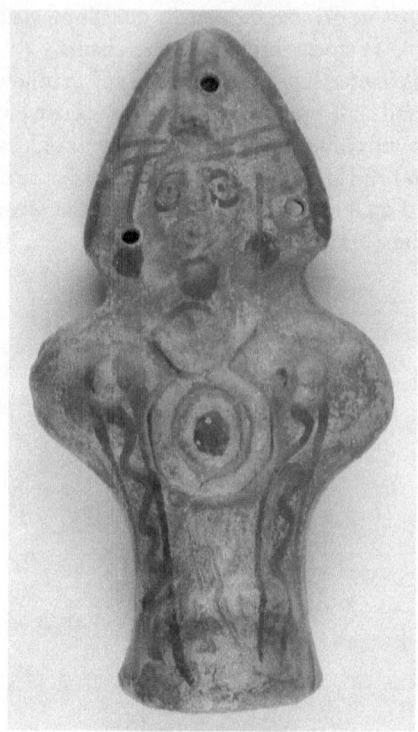

PLATE 1. Female figurine molded and painted to accentuate pregnant belly, with holes in headdress for jewelry. Molded terracotta with paint. Egypt, unprovenanced. Sixth to seventh century CE. Height: 13.4 cm; width: 7.8 cm; depth: 4.3 cm.

PLATE 2. Female figurine, seated, in *orans* position. Molded terracotta with three layers of linen and wool textile wrapping and belt to form clothing. Egypt, from Fag el-Gamous cemetery, next to male corpse, facing away. Third to fourth century CE. Height: 13 cm; width: 10 cm.

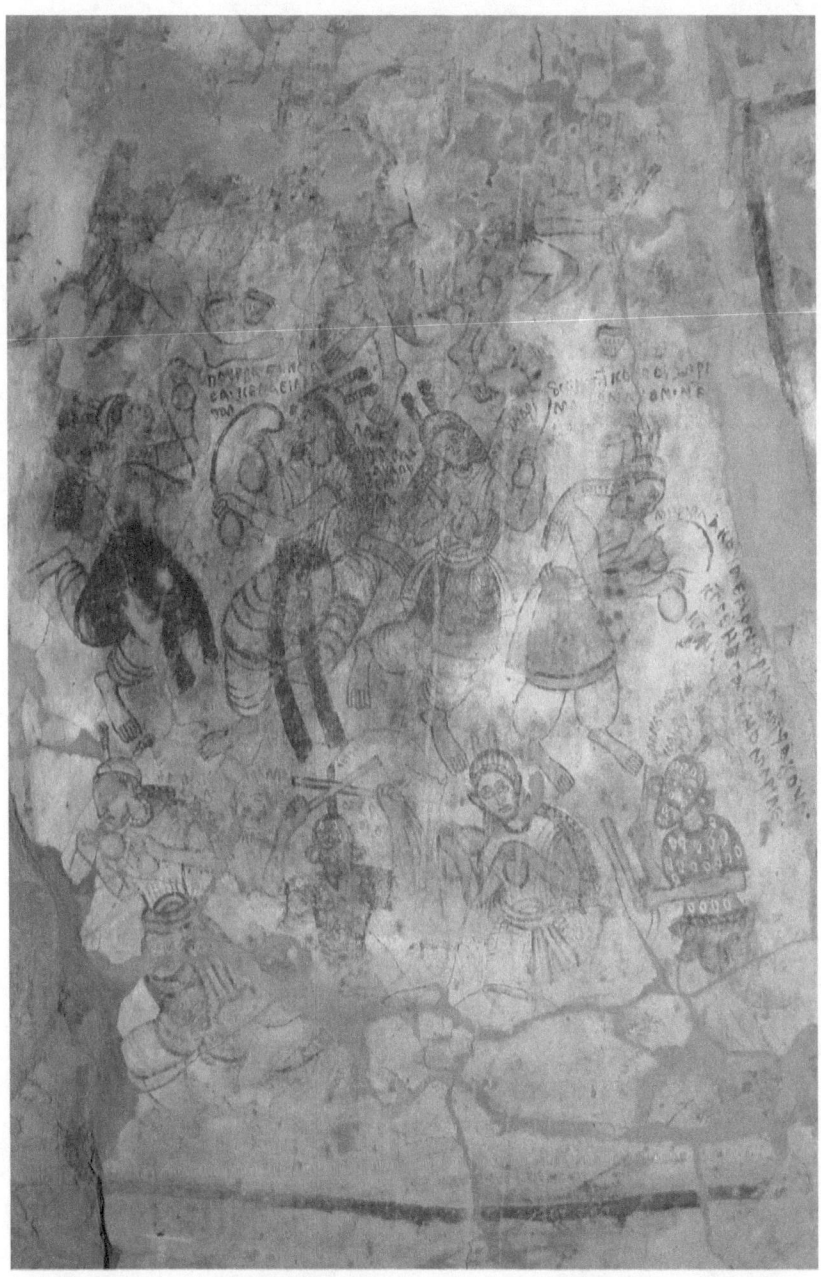

PLATE 3. Mural of warriors' dance before the Virgin Mary (standing with Christ child to right). Tempura on whitewash. Sudan, Dongola, Monastery of St. Anthony, Building SW, Room 5. Twelfth to thirteenth century CE.

PLATE 4. Detail of warriors' dance before the Virgin Mary.

PLATE 5. Votive plaquettes of body parts and image of Daniel in lions' den from St. Colluthus shrine. Bronze and copper, embossed. Egypt, excavated from St. Colluthus shrine precinct, north necropolis, Antinoë. Fourth to sixth century CE. Inv. 1231 (breast): 4.2 × 4.7 cm.; inv. 1217 (eyes): 8.6 × 3.1 cm.; inv. 1222 (nude woman): 2 × 3.5 cm.; inv. 1230 (thorax): 3.5 × 3.4 cm.; inv. 1234 (Daniel between lions and *ankh*-crosses): 3.3 × 3.0 cm.

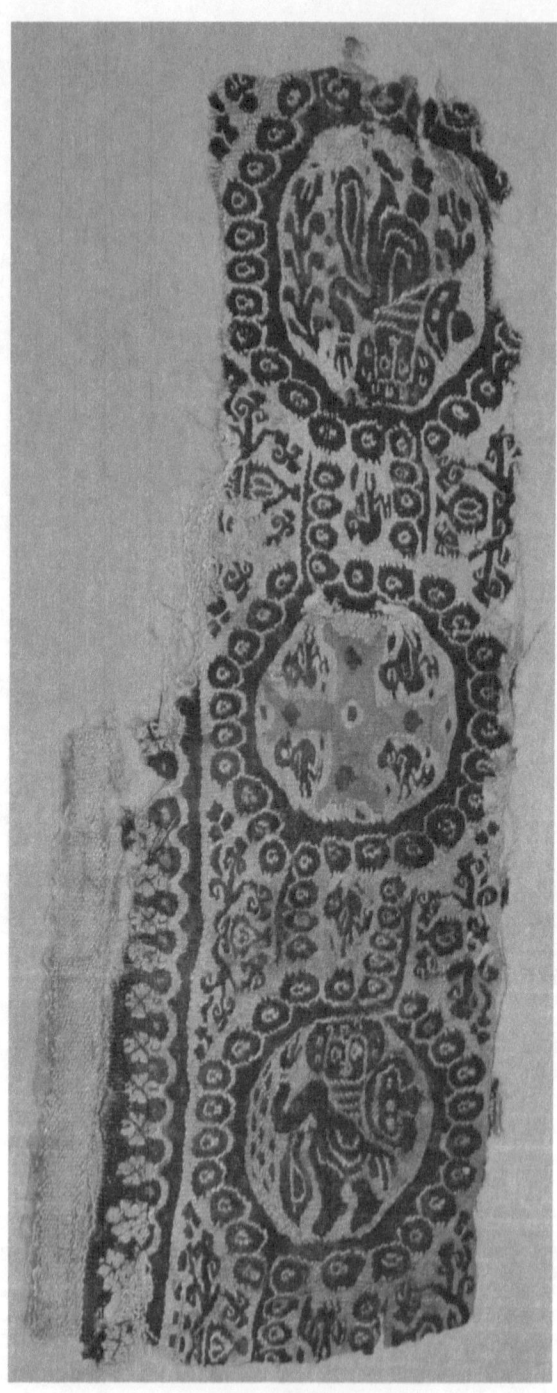

PLATE 6. Textile shoulder band(?) with medallion of cross surrounded by birds, flanked by medallions displaying warriors or heroes. Wool/linen. Egypt, unprovenanced. Fifth to seventh century CE. Height: 25 cm; width: 10.4 cm.

PLATE 7. Textile rectangular panel with *ankh*-cross, or *crux ansata*, set amid vases and flowers, with a face in the center. Wool/linen. Egypt, from Akhmim(?). Fourth to seventh century CE. Height: 22 cm; width: 16.5 cm.

PLATE 8. Panel painting of god Heron. Painted wood. Egypt, unprovenanced. Third century CE. Height: 58.1 cm; width: 48.7 cm (with frame).

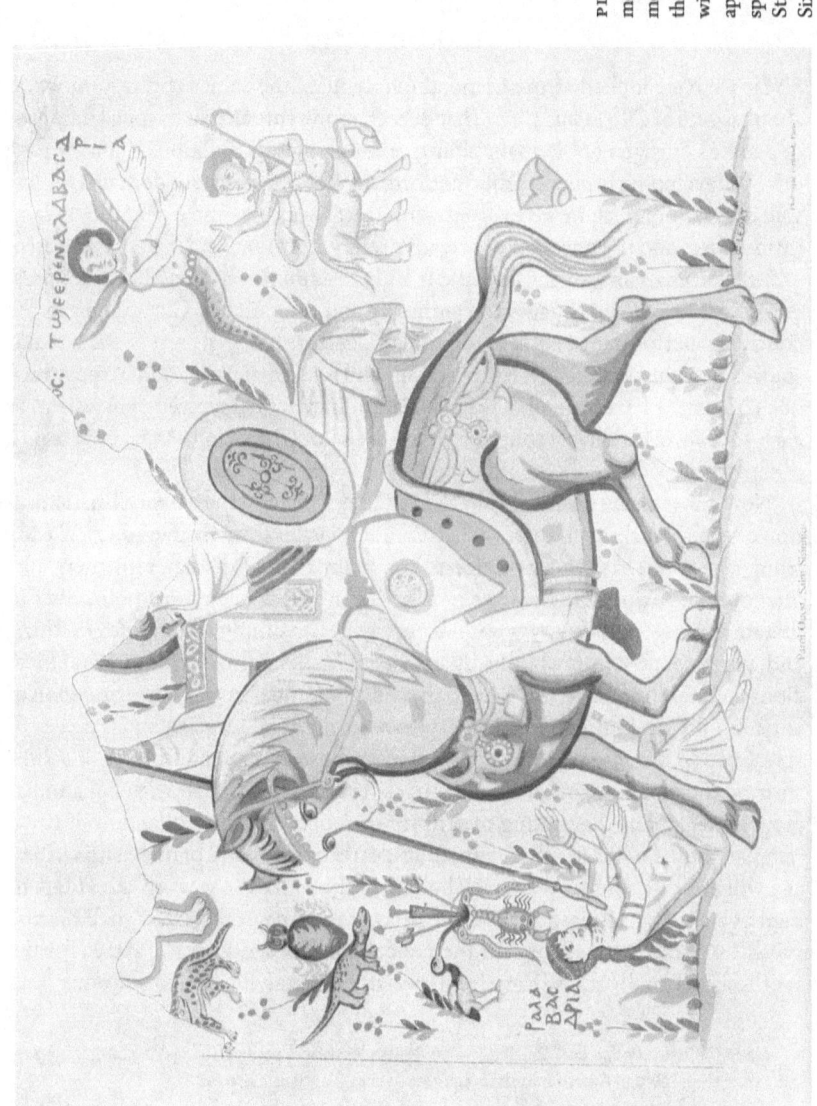

PLATE 9. Mural painting in monastic chapel of St. Sissinios mounted on horse and spearing the female demon Alabasdria, with various demonic and apotropaic figures added to the space around him. Egypt, Bawit, St. Apollo monastery, chapel 17. Sixth to eighth century CE.

CHAPTER 6

Scribality and Syncretism

TRADITIONS OF WRITING AND THE BOOK

I. INTRODUCTION

So far we have looked at the home, the holy man, the saint's shrine, and workshops as *sites of Christianization*. That is, each represents an axis of social interests, of people's engagement in maintaining certain religious traditions, transforming others, developing types of public performance, and seeking out domains for private expression. Each involves *agents* with their own roles and orientations: family members and the quest for procreative safety, holy men and the articulation of a Christian charisma, shrine attendants and the administration of the saint's presence. Each social site engages the authority and discourse of Christianity in the context of performance (liturgy, pilgrimage, gesture) as well as in social circumstances (consultation, festival, procession) and a sense of place. And in these various contexts, I have argued, Christianization inevitably involved syncretism, as each social world actively sought to make sense of Christianity in its own terms, idioms, and spaces.

Now, most of the resources I have used to understand the active Christianization of each social site have been texts: miracle cycles from shrines, magical texts from ritual experts, the occasional complaints of Christian reformers like Shenoute of Atripe, and the lives of monks. And texts of any sort point back to literate agents, "scribes," by whose expertise in (or simply capacity for) writing and, perhaps most importantly, by whose *understanding* of writing as an efficacious technology a variety of Christian media became part of the lived religion of laity, monks, and others. In this chapter scribality will serve as an *ideal type* of social expertise, covering the production and use of divination texts at saints' shrines, the composition of shrine miracle cycles as well as apocryphal and hagiographical texts, the writing of scripture amulets, and the collection of ritual manuals. Some of these activities belong clearly to the world of monastic scribes, as I will indicate, while others may belong to the functions or even the independent agency of ecclesiastical *literati*.[1] Among the "magical" texts I shall discuss (with "magical" a shorthand for the concrete use of writing or manuals for the synthesis of ritually transformative materials, *not* implying deviance from a "reli-

---

1 See Dijkstra, *Philae and the End*, 75–77, on ecclesiastical scribes as legal signatories, a role indicating their integral function in sixth-century Syene/Elephantine society.

gious" scribality), some suggest the authors' itinerant sphere of activity, while others point to service to clients from a central place, like a monastic *laura*. While most of our documents suggest that the scribe had some affililation with a monastic or ecclesiastical institution, broadly conceived, I cannot exclude the scribal services of figures not affiliated with a Christian institution in some way, especially given the diversity of ritual specialists in Egypt through the fourth century.[2] The experiment of this chapter, then, lies in the heuristic capaciousness of the terms "scribe" and "monastic scribe" as ideal types designating (a) a literate figure (of greater or lesser writing ability) (b) by whose familiarity with scripture, liturgy, and/or ecclesiastical discourse and (c) by whose interest in the technology of writing as an efficacious medium, functioned as (d) a mediator of Christian scriptural and institutional authority, integrating regional ritual traditions (like divination, song, amulet, blessing) or traditional compositional forms (in the service of apocrypha or liturgy, for example). This ideal type of scribe thus opens up another locus of agency in the syncretistic construction of Christianity in late antique Egypt.

The literary and "subliterary" productions of scribes were developed, copied, and edited amid a great range of texts that included biblical and apocryphal materials, public encomia on saints, and liturgical texts—the *libretti* of official Christian ceremonies.[3] These all made up the "scripture" of the Christian institution, that is, what constituted the religion *as* scriptural—as related to holy books. Magical texts imitate liturgy and refer to biblical scripture. Oracle tickets and divination manuals refer to orthodox theological formulas. Apocryphal texts and saints' lives expand on biblical narratives often in accessible, locative terms, and their tales cycle back through folklore and lived religion by means of magical texts and oral charms. The documents and fragments that have come down to us reflect a diverse world of literate specialists with eclectic interests in collecting, copying, editing, and composing various writings. And it is in this world that we see how the literary mediation of Christianity took place in remarkably "Egyptian" terms.

Past scholarship on Egyptian "survivals" used Coptic apocrypha and saints' lives to suggest that Christianity served as little more than a medium for ancient pharaonic mythology, highlighting the mythic treatment of martyrs' bodies; the depictions of Amente, the "western" land of the dead; and the gates (or ship) by which the soul got there.[4] If these claims to an ancient Egyptian heritage can be dubious, based more on modern impression than clear historical filiation, there

---

[2] Frankfurter, *Religion in Roman Egypt*, ch. 5; as well as the Manichaean letter conveying a magical charm in Mirecki, Gardner, and Alcock, "Magical Spell, Manichaean Letter."

[3] On the impact of liturgy on selection and editing of texts and shaping of manuscripts see Knust and Wasserman, "Biblical Odes."

[4] See, e.g., Budge, *Coptic Apocrypha*; Burmester, "Egyptian Mythology," 364–66; Hammerschmidt, "Altägyptische elemente im koptischen Christentum"; Kosack, *Die Legende im Koptischen*; Zandee, *Death as an Enemy*; Behlmer, "Ancient Egyptian Survivals"; Papaconstantinou, "Historiography, Hagiography, and the Making."

are other texts that do suggest various forms of maintaining ancient traditions in Coptic writing. For example, some Coptic magical texts preserve a range of Egyptian gods' names many centuries after the collapse of the temples that had maintained their myths[5] Other texts revitalize an archaic genre of poetic oracle that imagines the land of Egypt *tout court* as the site of cosmic distress and fortune. We might well ask, What did these scribes have in mind when they wrote such texts or preserved Egyptian names? Were they simply passing on the traditions of an Egyptian folk culture, or were they engaging those traditions deliberately, creatively, as part of the scribal craft? In what forms could such traditions have been passed down long after the temples: Through literary transmission (from Egyptian or Greek to Coptic)? As a perennial religious sensibility or "Coptic consensus"? Or through forms of expression and description that were somehow intrinsic to the writing and copying of texts on certain topics? And how can we comprehend the existence of these traditions amid—or *as*—Christian ideas illustrative of Christianization itself, rather than as evidence for some timeless romantic power of Egypt?

II. SCRIBALITY AT THE SHRINES OF THE SAINTS

The ticket oracles from the cults of Sts. Colluthus (Antinoë) and Philoxenus (Oxyrhynchus) provide a case in point. From at least the fifth through the seventh centuries, scribes at these shrines (among others) revitalized a type of divination ritual that, as we saw in chapter 4, went back to the New Kingdom and had been popular at many traditional temples during the Greco-Roman period into the fourth century. In this ritual clients would pass two alternative instructions on a practical matter, written out on papyrus by shrine attendants, to the saint (as it were), who would return the correct instruction following a divination procedure that has not been reconstructed.[6]

As in earlier times, one is struck by the tickets' pragmatic inquiries related to health or trips: "O God of our patron, St. Philoxenus, if you command us to bring Anoup to your hospital, show [your] power, and let the message come forth," or "God of the Christians: Is it your will [that] we give your handmaid Theodora to Joseph?"[7] It is as important that the shrine staff was extending itself to these everyday concerns of pilgrims as that the medium itself had been revitalized—somehow—from pre-Christian models. But lest we think that the participants in this exchange imagined themselves as engaging in "Egyptian religion," we should consider the orthodox character of the invocations: "O God *of* St. Colluthus"; "My Lord God Almighty *and* St. Philoxenus my patron"; or even, probably from

---

5 Kropp, *Ausgewählte koptische Zaubertexte*, 3:5–11. See above, pp. 1–2, 55–58.

6 See Frankfurter, *Religion in Roman Egypt*, 193–95; idem, "Voices, Books, and Dreams"; and above, pp. 19–20, 130–32.

7 Respectively: ACM 34 = Berlin 21269; ACM 31 = P. Oxy 1150. See also in general Valbelle and Husson, "Les questions oraculaires d'Égypte."

the Philoxenus shrine: "O God Almighty, holy, true, lover of humanity and creator, father of our Lord and Saviour Jesus Christ, show me your truth: Do you wish me to go to Chiout, and shall I find that you are of help to me and gracious? May it be so, Amen."[8] In contrast, in the hagiographical, festival, and miracle texts devoted to Sts. Colluthus and Philoxenus, the saints appear to and interact with devotees on their own (and quite personally) and are rarely described in such subordinate terms.[9] The mediators of oracular inquiry at their shrines were thus making a deliberate, if formulaic, effort to affirm the hierarchy of the Christian pantheon.[10] Further evidence from the St. Colluthus site points to a more orally based oracular exchange taking place there as well: archaeologists have found folded tickets with only the word συμφέρον ("useful") between two crosses, which would have been handed to a client in positive response to an oral inquiry.[11] But here too the process involved some kind of spatial association with St. Colluthus, such that the correct answer might be divined, and the crosses indicate an effort to bring the process under the general authority of the ecclesiastical institution. In brief, this was no "pagan" practice, nor even one marginal to some putative orthopraxy, but as central a feature of the administration of St. Colluthus's blessings as the incubation miracles hailed in the shrine legends.[12]

The ticket oracles provide immediate evidence for the availability of some kind of scribal services at saints' shrines. A nonliterate visitor would have found a literate specialist, a scribe, in the precinct of the shrine and explained his problem. The scribe would then have phrased that problem in positive and negative forms and would either have delivered the twin questions to a particular site regarded as mantic or have employed some device himself—a jar, dice—to produce the "right answer" from God and the saint. The orthodox character of the invocations noted earlier suggests these shrine scribes' investment in the language of ecclesiastical authority, even if the divination ritual might strike the modern church historian as a deviation from Christian practice.

The ticket oracle allowed scribes at these saints' shrines to sanction the most concrete interactions between supplicants and the saint and shrine space, using the written word in a way that might potentially have functioned as a talisman (or as a pharmaceutical script): "God of St. Colluthus, if it is your will that I place my daughter in your sanctuary [пектопос] (and) your mercy reach her, answer me," reads one, while another requests of Colluthus, "The true physician, if you order that your servant Rufus washes today in the healing bath, bring me the favorable

---

8 ACM 30 = P. Oxy 925.

9 Colluthus: see Palladius, *H.L.*, 60, along with incubation accounts in Devos, "Autres miracles coptes"; Papaconstantinou, *Le culte des saints en Égypte*, 122–28. Reverence for St. Philoxenus: see P. Oxy 11.1357, 24–27, for a prayer that invokes this and other saints directly.

10 Cannuyer, "Des dieux aux saints guérisseurs"; Delattre, "L'oracle de Kollouthos à Antinoé"; Luijendijk, *Forbidden Oracles?*, 35–37.

11 Delattre, "Nouveaux textes coptes d'Antinoé," 173.

12 On the multiple forms of divination taking place at the St. Colluthus shrine at Antinoë, see Frankfurter, "Voices, Books, and Dreams," 244–50.

CHAPTER 6

ticket."[13] Others refer to diverse foods that, presumably, were revealed in dreams or through other consultations at the shrine. The oracles clearly functioned—and were deployed—as a way of stretching Colluthus and his God over all the healing activities of the shrine.

Such shrine scribes seem to have revitalized other genres as well for the mediation of the saints. A type of divination book called the *Sortes* ("Lots") contained pages of preset answers that would have been indicated ritually through the casting of knucklebones or dice. The *Sortes* books go back to Greek versions from early Roman Egypt (the *Sortes Astrampsychi*), in which answers to such questions as "Will I open a workshop?" or "Is my wife going to miscarry?" could be found using a clever numerological procedure.[14] By the fifth century *Sortes sanctorum* books could be found (or their use attested) in the Latin West as well as in Egypt.[15]

The Christian *Sortes* books address the same perennial questions of economy, travel, and status as their precursors, as well as such issues of social mobility as "Will I become an Elder?" or "Will I become a monk?"[16] But one also finds references to specific shrine practices: "The Lord God *has* heard your request"; "Go make your vows, and what you have promised, fulfill it immediately"; or "Should I go to the holy place?"[17] These features give a sense of how the books might have complemented other devotional activities at shrines. And again, like the oracle tickets, these divination books frame their revelations in orthodox, monotheistic terminology that stands in important contrast to the independent powers and characters of the saints encountered in incubation visions and shrine propaganda.[18] "Do not harm your soul, for what has come to pass is from God," reads a fragment of such a text from Berlin[19]; another declares: "Walk and go immediately. Do not delay. Because it is God who fights for you. He will cause your enemies to subject to you. If you are patient for a little, you will receive the hope of your salvation and you will be at rest."[20] We might very well infer a didactic

---

13 PSI inv. Ant. N 66/110/A, in Papini, "20–21—Due biglietti oracolari cristiani," 250; Delattre, "Textes coptes et grecs d'Antinoé," 152–53; idem, "L'oracle de Kollouthos à Antinoé."

14 On the *Sortes* book tradition, see Frankfurter, *Religion in Roman Egypt*, 179–84; Van der Horst, "Sortes"; and Luijendijk, *Forbidden Oracles?* On new developments in book divination beyond the Sortes, including use of the *Apophthegmata patrum* for mantic guidance and randomized, direct use of bibles for divination, see Tovar, "A New Sahidic Coptic Fragment"; and Wiśniewski, "Pagans, Jews, Christians."

15 Klingshirn, "Defining the Sortes Sanctorum"; idem, "Inventing the Sortilegus." Papini, "Fragments of the Sortes Sanctorum"; on which see Frankfurter, "Voices, Books, and Dreams."

16 *Sortes Astrampsychi* 39, 55, ms. A., in Stewart, *Sortes Astrampsychi II*, xiv.

17 Respectively, GLM ##6, 25, in Luijendijk, *Forbidden Oracles?*, 107–8, 131; *Sortes Astrampsychi* 41, ms. A; see Stewart, *Sortes Astrampsychi*, 2:xiv.

18 Papaconstantinou, *Le culte des saints en Egypte*, 324–29; Luijendijk, *Forbidden Oracles?*, 35–38.

19 ACM 35 = Berlin 13232; see also Treu, "Varia Christiana," 120.

20 GLM #31 in Luijendijk, *Forbidden Oracles?*, 138; Papini, "Fragments of the Sortes Sanctorum," frag. B1. The same monotheizing character pervades the Vatican Coptic *Sortes* papyrus: Van Lantschoot, "Une collection sahidique."

function from this monotheizing character: that the oracular exchange between pilgrim-client and ecclesiastical or monastic diviner-scribe was meant not only to resolve questions and disclose divine will but to explicate God's providence, rather than that of other forces, in all aspects of life.[21]

The divination materials thus point to one kind of religious site in which scribes, functioning as diviners and mediums of Christian authority, aided clients through their literate capabilities. At these same sites, scribes also developed hagiographical materials like encomia and miracle collections for public reading, describing the dismemberment of a martyr, the accomplishments of a saint, or the visions of the holy man buried in this place, and promising rewards to those who visited and benefited the site:

> Whoso shall give an offering to your shrine, I [Christ] will fill his house with every good thing on earth; and I will cause My angels to protect their bodies and their souls in the aeons of the light.... And I will set My blessing and My peace in the place where your bodies shall be laid. And behold, I have set the angel Raphael to minister to your shrine; and great numbers of sick people suffering from diverse diseases shall come to your shrine, and obtain healing, and go home in peace.[22]

This kind of shrine literature tends to imagine a more elaborate pantheon than do the oracle tickets: here it is Michael or Raphael, St. Colluthus or Apa Shenoute, who represents the principal savior or focus of appeal.[23] In the service of promoting a shrine or sanctioning a festival, then, shrine scribes had the creative capacity to adjust the theological focus of the lived religion. The divination tickets and *Sortes* books contrast with these narrative materials in terms of theological focus, and yet they also show the ways in which scribes extended the capacity of writing—or, more specifically, the writing of Christian formulas—from "informative" to "performative" uses: here, to divination rituals that mediated the instructions of God and saint. We will see these performative extensions of writing further when we examine magical texts.[24]

III. MONASTIC SCRIBES AND THE MEDIATION OF CHRISTIANITY

The evidence of these last scribal activities at saints' shrines shows that the role itself was in no way passive, like the image of the professional letter writer of so many semiliterate cultures. Instead we see the independent agency of literate ex-

---

21   See Klingshirn, "Christian Divination in Late Roman Gaul," 106–10.
22   *Martyrdom of SS Paēse and Thekla*, Pierpont Morgan codex M591, T.28, fol. 85r, ii-85v, ii, in Reymond and Barns, *Four Martyrdoms*, 75–76, 181–82.
23   See also Papaconstantinou, *Le culte des saints en Égypte*, 340–48.
24   The evaluation of uses of text as "informative" vs. "performative" draws on Gill, "Nonliterate Traditions and Holy Books," esp. 238.

perts at work in their development and maintenance of divination rites as well as miracle records and saints' legends intended to be publicly read at festivals. And monastic scribes exerted the same agency, the same independence and creativity in choosing, composing, and editing texts for their own and others' edification: apocrypha and martyrs' legends, ritual texts and charms. The sheer variety of books held in monastery libraries, bound in codices, complained about by reformers, and invoked as sources of magical texts shows the rich field from which monastic scribes could draw biblical legends, Christian theological ideas, and local traditions.

A. Monastic Libraries and Eclectic Scribes

In the history of Christianity we commonly associate religious scribal activities with monasteries, whose book remains, evident reading habits, and library lists indicate quite eclectic literary worlds and copying activities. Monasteries also received regular visitors, and monks carried on regular correspondence with laypeople on the outside.[25] We might say, then, that monasteries represented social sites of Christianization that were distinctively textual—that is, distinctively interactive with books. And yet the Christianity that emerged from this monastic scribal enterprise of recording, collecting, exchanging, copying, editing, and composing texts was also a function of the types of literary materials that monks were reading or hearing. These materials were clearly not just biblical and patristic writings but, rather, all manner of apocryphal texts—apocalypses, acts, gospels, and what François Bovon once called "books useful for the soul"—as well as martyr legends, saints' lives, prophetic fragments, and magical texts.[26] Some monastic (or potentially monastic) collections were even more eclectic: the Bodmer and Nag Hammadi libraries, for instance, show scribal interests in copying and collecting books well outside the (albeit still disputed) boundaries of the canon.[27] Overall, the evidence of Christian manuscripts and library lists in late antique Egypt shows no gradual sloughing off of extracanonical materials in favor of the canon Bishop Athanasius declared in 367; rather, from the fourth century on, it demonstrates an increasing interest among monastic scribes in extracanonical, and especially apocalyptic, writings.[28]

---

25 Behlmer, "Visitors to Shenoute's Monastery"; Wipszycka, "Les formes institutionelles," 144–45.

26 Bovon, "Beyond the Canonical." On monastic libraries and their eclectic holdings in general, see Crum, *Catalogue of the Coptic Manuscripts*, 564–67 (library list); Evelyn White, *Monasteries of the Wâdi 'n Natrûn*, xxxi, 197–208; Coquin, "Le catalogue de la bibliothèque"; Krause, "Libraries," 5:1447–50; Orlandi, "Library of the Monastery," 225; Delattre, *Papyrus coptes et grecs*, 104–5. On the influence of apocalyptic literature in Egyptian Christianity, see Frankfurter, "Legacy of the Jewish Apocalypse," 150–200; and Golitzin, "Earthly Angels and Heavenly Men."

27 See Lundhaug and Jenott, *Monastic Origins*, esp. ch. 6.

28 The classic statement of the literary evidence is Bauer, *Orthodoxy and Heresy*, 44–60, which is unfortunately preoccupied with the dichotomy of orthodoxy and heresy rather than a more

Now, there were ecclesiastical and local monastic efforts to rein in or reshape the material that such scribes deemed authoritative, especially at historical crisis points like Chalcedon and during the spread of Islam. Diverse Christian leaders, from Athanasius to Shenoute and John of Paralos, complain about apocryphal writings and their influence. While Athanasius refers to the writing and circulation of pseudepigrapha of Enoch, Isaiah, and Moses (allegedly among the heretics of his day), John of Paralos (sixth to seventh centuries CE) reports a continuing creativity in the production of authoritative books: "Truly those blasphemers are worse than Jews and criminal, impure heathens. They have, notably, written books of every genre of blasphemy, to wit: the one they call 'The Investiture of Michael,' then 'The Proclamation of John,' 'The Jubilation of the Apostles,' 'The Teachings of Adam,' 'The Counsel of the Savior.' . . . They have forsaken the light of the holy writings of the prophets, the apostles, and all the Fathers."[29] But these testimonies simply add to the considerable evidence for literary diversity in the manuscripts and library lists. Far from being oriented toward consistency and canon, book reading and collecting were entirely eclectic activities among monks. We see monastic scribes embracing apocryphal traditions, from apocalyptic visions to accounts of the perambulations of the Holy Family and the correspondence of Jesus and King Abgar, as deeply resonant and even authoritative, if in a different sense from Psalms or the Gospels. The evidence of monastic interest in copying and composing these continuing revelations, and in keeping alive the dramatic angelologies and visions imagined in the texts, shows a different sense of scripture from what we are accustomed to associate with monks. It is a scripture of divine presence and revelation mediated through text—whether borrowed or recited, imagined or dreamt, discovered or invented. And it is in this world of monastic revelation that we find scribes expanding the lore and the media of Christianity.[30]

What we know of the production of Christian books from the second century through late antiquity shows less a coordinated, medieval scriptorium-styled factory for Christian books than quite localized and even private enterprises that may, indeed, have overlapped with intellectual circles and collectors beyond the monasteries. Borrowing a master text, procuring writing materials, copying select

---

nuanced picture of religious and literary eclecticism. See recent reconceptualizations of the evidence by Van der Vliet, "Coptic Gnostic Texts"; Kraus, "Lending of Books"; Stökl Ben Ezra, "Canonization—a Non-Linear Process?," 20.

29 Athanasius, *Festal Letter* 39, in Brakke, *Athanasius*, 326–32; John of Paralos, *Homily on Michael and on Heretical Books*, in van Lantschoot, "Fragments coptes d'une homélie," 303 (text), 319 (translation). See also Brakke, "A New Fragment," on Athanasius; and Orlandi, "A Catechesis Against Apocryphal Texts," on Shenoute.

30 On monks and "orthodoxy," see See Crum and Winlock, *Monastery of Epiphanius at Thebes*, 151–53; on the fluidity of the Old Testament canon, see Golitzin, "Earthly Angels and Heavenly Men," 127–28; Frankfurter, "Legacy of the Jewish Apocalypse," 174–96; and on diversity and esoteric interests in monastic reading, see Lundhaug and Jenott, *Monastic Origins*, ch. 6; and Brakke, "Scriptural Practices in Early Christianity," esp. 273–75.

books, binding the results, and then sharing and inheriting books involved individual efforts and choices at every stage, with no official oversight and great ranges in literacy and types of text ownership.[31] One distinctive codex collection that doubtless served some monk's particular interests combined a section of the Book of Enoch with parts of the *Apocalypse of Peter* and the *Gospel of Peter*.[32] Another collection, of martyrologies with apocalyptic features, is prefaced with an exhortation to potential copyists that suggests both a self-determination and a spiritual investment in the choice to commit oneself to a revelatory text: "Whoever shall write [ⲛⲉⲧⲛⲁⲥϩⲁⲓ] the book of [the main character's] martyrdom, I (Christ) will write his name in the Book of Life."[33] These artifacts give us a sense of a culture of scribal agency, in which copying—and, presumably, expanding—texts lay with the individual scribe, and apocalyptic interests might even elevate the status of the scribe.

It is in the context of this scribal eclecticism that we can grasp (a) the *range of traditions* and genres that might have been read and produced in monastic settings; (b) the *agency* of scribes in producing texts that integrated Christian traditions with local lore; and (c) the *range of lore*, written as well as oral, that scribes had at their disposal to deploy in new compositions, including magical texts. Both hagiographical and apocalyptic texts served as authoritative frameworks for recollecting earlier Egyptian scribal traditions. But even more, as I shall discuss further, the structure, cadence, and rhythms of *liturgy*—the foundation of monastic collective performance—inspired the elaborate invocations of magical texts. Apocalyptic texts rendered participation in heavenly liturgy conceivable for the righteous monk, and its powers transferrable to this world, like the fig that, in one legend, Apa Patermuthius brings back from Paradise and shows to all his visitors.[34]

B. Monastic Settings of Scribal Mediation

In conceptualizing monastic scribes as agents and monasteries as social sites for the syncretic construction of Christianity, we have to address both an internal—

---

31 On remodeling the context of writing and copying in Egyptian monasticism, see Mugridge, "What Is a Scriptorium?"; and esp. Crum and Evelyn-White, *Monastery of Epiphanius at Thebes*, 193–95; Wipszycka, "Le degré d'alphabétisation"; Kotsifou, "Books and Book Production"; and legendary examples in, e.g., *Apophth. Patr.* (Alph.) Abraham 3, in Ward, *Desert Christian*, 34. The *Life of Moses of Abydos* does refer to a "house of the calligraphers [ⲛϩⲓ ⲛⲕⲁⲗⲗⲓⲟⲅⲣⲁⲫⲟⲥ]" that the holy man set up at his monastery; see Uljas, "IFAO Leaves of the Life," 382 (text), 389 (translation). Scott Bucking publishes a monastic literary training book; see Bucking, *Practice Makes Perfect*. On nonmonastic scribal contexts, see Johnson, *Readers and Reading Culture*, 179–92; and Denzey Lewis and Blount, "Rethinking the Origins," 416–19. Cf. Haines-Eitzen, *Guardians of Letters*, regarding second- and third-century Christian scribal contexts.

32 See van Minnen, "Greek Apocalypse of Peter," which questions prior theories that it was buried with the monk as a kind of mortuary text.

33 *Martyrdom of Paēse and Thekla*, Pierpont Morgan Codex M 591, p. 85v, ii, in Reymond and Barns, *Four Martyrdoms*; see also MacDermot, *Cult of the Seer*, 677–82.

34 *Hist. mon.* 10.21–22.

literary and liturgical—culture and the ways in which monks creatively conveyed that culture to outsiders: through sermons, ritual performances, charismatic ritual expertise (e.g., the blessings of the holy man), and scribal services in the form of magical texts. I will leave some of the distinctive scribal combinations internal to monastic culture to the penultimate section of this chapter in order to focus first on the ways that monastic scribes mediated for outsiders forms of Christianity that were both local and thaumaturgical in nature. In keeping with the model of the creative social site, I want to lay out two spatial models for this kind of scribal mediation of Christianity: one in which people come to the monk, and another in which the monk or scribe is itinerant.

If the evidence for diverse tastes in monastic reading and copying comes from the libraries of larger monasteries, it is in the smaller *laura* and monastic settlements that we find evidence for an extension of scribal practices into ritual services through the dispensing of written blessings and the composition and use of magical texts. As we saw in chapter 3, the social structure of the *laura* involved a loose scattering of ascetic dwellings, often located in the vicinity of one holy man for whom junior monks might serve as disciples or acolytes. Senior monks' or holy men's cells sometimes included consultation rooms, where interactions between monks and laity might take place, facilitated by those acolytes.[35] Thus we find abundantly represented in hagiographical legends depictions of villagers and far-flung visitors bringing their concerns to the monks. The monks, as we saw, would offer "blessings" in the form of gestures, physical tokens, oil, talismans, and scripture amulets.[36] These textual blessings, like the (unprovenanced) slip instructing the bearer to "give what I have written [[т]ı . . . ⲚⲦⲀⲒⲤⲀϨⲀϤ] to the one split in herself," communicated the charisma of the holy man through his autograph.[37]

But it was not just the holy man who offered such textual blessings; other monks seem to have engaged in the crafting of potent texts by virtue of their knowledge of scripture, names, sounds, and writing itself as a ritual technology. Indeed, it is precisely from these smaller monastic environments that ritual handbooks have been uncovered, often from the actual cells.[38] For some time schol-

---

35 Drawing on archaeological and synthetic discussions in Crum and Winlock, *Monastery of Epiphanius at Thebes*, 125–33; Wilfong, "Western Thebes"; Wipszycka, "Les formes institutionelles"; O'Connell, "Transforming Monumental Landscapes"; Brooks Hedstrom, "Divine Architects"; and Godlewski, "Naqlun: The Earliest Hermitages." Palladius, *H.L.* 35.4 (comp. 18.19, 26) illustrates devotees stopping just outside the threshold of monastic dwellings. On minor roles in monastic environments, see Delattre, *Papyrus coptes et grecs*, 70–74.

36 See above, pp. 92–100.

37 Pregnancy spell: Coll. Moen inv. #107, in Sijpesteijn, "Coptic Magical Amulet."

38 A miscellany of spells was found in the Monastery of Epiphanius: see ACM 128 = Cairo 45060, ed. Kropp, *Ausgewählte koptische Zaubertexte*, 1:50–54; 2:31–40; and ACM 134 = BM 325 = Anastasy 9 = Leiden 441. On the character of this find, see Crum and Winlock, *Monastery of Epiphanius at Thebes*, 21, 207. Also from the Bawit monastery, see P. Brux. E6390/6391 = PGM LX; cf. Delattre, *Papyrus coptes et grecs*, 105 n.380. On texts from a sixth-century monk's cell at Naqlun, see Godlewski, "Naqlun: Excavations 1997"; and Van der Vliet, "Les anges du soleil." Amuletic scripture passages reflect a similar provenance: De Bruyn and Dijkstra, "Greek Amulets and Formularies."

CHAPTER 6

ars have observed important filiations between the language, mythology, and writing of Coptic magical texts and the world of monks.[39] The magical texts, for example, imitate (as we shall see) liturgical formulae, employ angels' names, and draw on apocryphal legends continuous with those prevalent in monastic culture. Often they interpose drawings of holy beings and para-alphabetic characters (the so-called *charakteres*) with the letters of incantations, suggesting that the scribes saw a continuity in magical technology between image and written word.[40] The archaeological finds make other magical texts' relationship to monastic culture all the more secure. Even more, we can infer that these magical compositions were not (or not only) monks' private or covert pursuits, since at least one ritual manual shows evidence of multiple hands, suggesting a kind of cooperation in the collecting and dispensing of ritual spells.[41]

The extant Greek and Coptic magical texts include a range of textual forms, from codices containing miscellaneous collections of spells to "loose-leaf" sets of master spells (with "DD" written wherever a client's name was supposed to be inserted)[42] to lone prayers or incantations with various quotidian applications. As diverse as it is, the corpus as a whole offers important evidence for the scribal process of reformulating traditions from a monastic culture of reading and retelling apocryphal legends and visions and then adapting those traditions for a lay culture with different needs but open to the authority of these traditions and especially to the power of the efficacious word. Thus a fifth-century fragment of a handbook found in Oxyrhynchus records two Jesus-charms between a series of concrete remedies:

> ... men met us in the desert and said to the Lord Jesus, what cure is there for the sick? And he said to them, I gave olive oil, poured out myrrh for those who believe in the name of the Father and the Holy Spirit and the Son. The angels of the Lord went up to the middle of heaven, suffering in (their) eyes and holding a sponge. The Lord said to them, why did you come up (here), holy all-pure ones? We came up to receive a remedy, Iaō Sabaōth, because you are mighty and strong.[43]

---

39 See Lexa, *La magie dans l'Égypte antique*, 1:139–53; Kropp, *Ausgewählte koptische Zaubertexte*, 3:314–71, 390–412; Richter, "Bemerkungen zu magischen"; Frankfurter, "Collections of Recipes"; idem, *Religion in Roman Egypt*, 257–64; Van der Vliet, "Literature, Liturgy, Magic."

40 See Frankfurter, "Magic of Writing," 205–11; cf. Van den Kerchove, "Livre du grand traité initiatique."

41 See ACM 133; with editions/discussions in Worrell, "A Coptic Wizard's Hoard"; Mirecki, "Coptic Wizard's Horde"; and idem in Meyer and Smith, *Ancient Christian Magic*, 295. Cf. Haines-Eitzen, *Guardians of Letters*, 94–104, on multiple scribes in one manuscript.

42 Loose-leaf spells from same hand: see, e.g., the London Hay collection (ACM 78–81, 127), a cache of master invocations and charms written on strips of leather that could be carried together in a bag. The Hay spells revolve around matters of quotidian crisis in village culture—erotic desire, gynecological maladies, and such—and instruct users to leave various preparations "at the door."

43 ACM 4 = P. Oxy XI.1384.

Such free-form tales of Christian mythical characters, called *historiolae*, work by setting up a dramatic, mythic form of a familiar crisis that is resolved in the legend. The "power" of the mythic resolution can then be transferred to the patient in this world by means of some substance (oil, myrrh, sponge) that crosses from the narrative to the performative dimension by means of the telling itself.[44] The composer here, who we can deduce from the theological details was a monastic scribe, derived the historiola from his familiarity with legends of Jesus circulating in his world and added to it a performative dimension that reflected the liturgical life with which he was associated. It is in such practical applications to social crises that monastic scribes mediated their own culture of efficacious speech and writing for village cultures in need of blessings and the directed efficacy that only the written charm could produce.

This model of scribal mediation of Christian monastic culture that I have so far been drawing is a "locative" model: that is, it proposes the scribes' affiliation with particular sites as well as with a particular world of Christian culture. These scribes functioned as mediators at the initiation of visitors and supplicants who flocked to monasteries and shrines for diverse purposes. But can we imagine a more itinerant model as well, one in which the social worlds of monks (or other ecclesiastical functionaries) consisted more in the villages they passed through and the layfolk with whom they interacted than in the more exclusive setting of the monastery?[45]

This model of the itinerant scribal expert would capture first the Manichaean presence in Egypt from the third century on, in which resolutely itinerant missionaries carried and instructed from books and produced amulets out of their own liturgical traditions.[46] So also do those shadowy figures on the margins of the Christian institution (about whom Shenoute and Pseudo-Athanasius complain in the texts I have quoted several times) have an itinerant cast—or at least seem to have been independent of specific sites of Christian culture: "[Folk receive ministrations] from *enchanters* or *drug-makers*, with every deceptive kind of relief," such texts complain. "Some tie amulets on their children, hand-crafted by men—those [men] who provide a place for the dwelling of demons."[47] And traditions preserved in the *Synaxarium* about John of Paralos tell of a "monk in Upper Egypt who told all sorts of things and said that the Angel Michael had instructed him. He acquired a considerable following.... Another (monk) pretended that the prophet Habbakuk had appeared to him and taught him secrets. A considerable crowd followed him.... There was, in [the same village] a priest who prac-

---

44 See Frankfurter, "Narrating Power"; and Bozóky, *Charmes et prières apotropaïques*, 36–45.

45 On itinerant monks in general, see Caner, *Wandering, Begging Monks*, 19–49; and Wipszycka, "Les formes institutionelles," 142–44.

46 See Mirecki, Gardner, and Alcock, "Magical Spell, Manichaean Letter"; Mirecki, "Manichaean Allusions to Ritual"; BeDuhn, "Domestic Setting."

47 Pseudo-Athanasius, *Homily on the Virgin* 95, in Lefort, "L'homélie de S. Athanase"; Shenoute, *Acephalous Work* A14, in Orlandi, *Shenute*.

ticed astrology and sorcery; this occupation brought him a great quantity of money."[48] These are plausible images of the charismatic ritual expertise that some monks embraced in late antiquity, and John of Paralos, a bishop well known for his opposition to heretical books, is celebrated here for expelling each one. One particular magical text, addressing a variety of domestic situations, includes a charm for keeping "the brother [from coming] to your house"—quite possibly a reference to an itinerant monk, whose powers of incantation, blessing, and cursing might have been regarded with fear.[49] These kinds of witnesses, as well as those discussed in chapter 3, offer a range of itinerant (or simply independent) ritual specialists, who are sometimes depicted as developing amulets, sometimes as drawing on prophetic claims or literary traditions that would have been associated with monastic culture, and sometimes as just purveying to those who appealed to them the materials that Christianity sanctioned and empowered.

In past discussions of ritual expertise in Egyptian cultures I introduced the example of the modern Ethiopian *däbtära* as illuminating, not only for understanding the nature of marginal scribal cultures in premodern African Christian societies, but also for examining the collective development of a "magical" culture of word, image, and incantation and the angelological and demonological lore that sustains it.[50] The *däbtäras* comprise a rank of itinerant church cantors responsible for the beautiful exorcistic scrolls, each inscribed for specific clients on the basis of demonological manuals, that entered the Western art market some decades ago.[51]

As ethnographers describe the role, the *däbtära* will travel to private homes in the countryside to perform exorcisms, healing ceremonies, and other rites, leaving amulets behind as guarantees of their performances. While regarded suspiciously as wizards and sorcerers by ordained priests (and more urbane Ethiopians), for their clients the *däbtäras*' ecclesiastical affiliation, self-definition, and authority are hardly deviant. Given the historical filiation and cultural similarities between the Ethiopian and Egyptian churches, the *däbtära* offers several key features for any model of an itinerant scribal ritual expert in late antique Egypt. As ecclesiastical figures *däbtäras* represent the Christian institution's broad authority in life and ceremony. Their special functions as ritual experts are grounded in an elaborate notion of the holy book, whether biblical, apocryphal, or liturgical, and they view themselves as specialists in the use of holy books. Indeed, their sense of religious role (and financial motivation) involves the *extension* of the institution and book to the quotidian needs of their clients.

---

48 *Synaxarium*: 19 Koiak, in Basset, *Le Synaxaire Arabe Jacobite II*; Müller, "John of Parallos, Saint."

49 P. Macquarie 1.1, p. 13, #9, in Choat and Gardner, *Coptic Handbook of Ritual Power*, 69.

50 Frankfurter, *Religion in Roman Egypt*, 212–17.

51 Young, "Magic as a 'Quasi-Profession'"; Mercier, *Ethiopian Magic Scrolls*; idem, *Art That Heals*; Shelemay, "Musician and Transmission"; Kaplan, "Magic and Religion in Christian Ethiopia"; idem, "Däbtära."

The *däbtära* thus offers one model for an itinerant ecclesiastical scribe engaged in the mediation of an esoteric, institutional Christianity for laypeople. He also illuminates how a culture of sorts might develop among such scribal experts from their mutual interest in extending apocalyptic, liturgical, and apocryphal traditions to practical ends. *Däbtäras* are distinctive in Ethiopian society for their scribal and liturgical training, to be sure, but also for their versatility in using that training for financial gain.[52] Out of this versatility with writing and chant have developed various autonomous *däbtära* cultures for the collection and circulation of amulets and spells, manuals for their composition, formulations of magical words and names, the assimilation of local traditions of demons and angels, and—most interestingly—the cultivation of a mysterious esotericism around their books, spells, and utterances, all with the aim of constructing efficacy and establishing boundaries to preserve an insiders' culture excluding the laity.

We might discern similar attributes in the culture behind the Greek and Coptic magical texts. In their florid angelology and demonology, their merging of text and image, and the established social role of ritual expertise they assume their owners to have, the Greek and Coptic texts point to a monastic (or possibly ecclesiastical) subculture along the lines of the *däbtära*. That is, the comparison offers an additional dimension to the world of scribality: not just the literate monk mediating his apocryphal books and liturgical culture to laypeople but a speculative, creative subculture formed among monks practicing such scribal mediation, a subculture that invited exchange with other such experts.

Constructing the monastic scribal world as a social site responsible for synthetic constructions of Egyptian Christianity thus involves particular attention to the work, services, and innovations of scribes "on the ground": from the holy man and his acolytes to the scribe writing a martyrology or copying the *Testament of Abraham*, from the itinerant monk or ecclesiastical functionary dispensing oil and writing out historiolae for domestic crises to the monastic scribe composing invocations to arcane angels to gain justice for some shopkeeper. Through the process of these exchanges between lay and monastic worlds, Christianity itself came together as a complex of local traditions, encompassing stories, songs, charms, a vast pantheon of supernatural beings, people skilled in their knowledge of these forms and beings, charismatic saints, and the various uses of the all-potent written word.

IV. SCRIBES AND THE MAGIC OF WORD AND SONG

Beyond its material, visual, and ritual expressions, Christianity in Egypt was distinguished by the authority of the book as well as by the authority of monks and

---

52 On liturgical training of *däbtäras*, see Shelemay, "Musician and Transmission"; Mercier, *Art That Heals*, 43–44. On financial incentives and trade, see Young, "Magic as a 'Quasi-Profession,'" 251–54.

ecclesiastical scribes as masters of the book and of writing.[53] So, we may say, Christianity in one important dimension took shape through the medium of scribes: through the whole range of social exchanges, consultations, festivals, pilgrimages, ceremonies, and appeals in which scribes interacted with the laity. For example, it is from social interactions like consultation, storytelling, and instruction that our extant magical texts ultimately derive. As documents of this interaction, the magical texts exhibit a *bricolage* of multiple skills and traditions: narrative materials cultivated in monastic settings, the particular circumstances—domestic, mercantile—that called for ritual negotiation, aural and incantational forms from both folk culture and liturgy, and techniques of mystifying the written word.

Scribal technology in late antique Egypt included various graphic traditions that mystified or added potency to the writing of certain words or phrases. Some of these traditions derived from more widespread magical writing, the *charakteres*—asterisks and signs the size of Greek letters—that suggested an alternate, sacred writing system much as Greeks had imagined Egyptian hieroglyphs.[54] Charakteres became so central to the inscription of charms and ritual manuals that one occasionally finds whole codex pages full of them, as well as figures made up of charakteres. The use of charakteres would have suggested that the scribe had control over nonsemantic writing forms that could be used for ritual purposes. Another early Christian form of sacred writing was the *nomina sacra*, which developed to signify the holiness of a divine name or attribute in the writing of a text and became a virtual convention in the writing or copying of certain names and terms.[55] The variety of practices that formed around the nomina sacra point to an internal culture of esoteric scribal convention.[56] But more broadly the use of the nomina sacra points to a practice peculiar to scribal self-consciousness: the transmission of an intrinsic magical potentiality to the scriptural or religious manuscript.[57]

Charakteres and nomina sacra both point less to clients' preferences in holy texts than to an internal scribal culture that cultivated not just simple conventions but a sense of the power in the craft itself—the conviction that writing was an efficacious medium that should involve the selective use of such techniques. The same sense of the potency of writing is evident in the development of *cryptographic* practices in Coptic monastic writing: letter substitution codes that make ostensibly nonsense sequences but, decoded, represent invocations of heavenly beings. Such practices served not to protect heterodox content but to create a second degree of magical efficacy through manipulation of the alphabet, some-

---

53 See Rapp, "Holy Texts, Holy Men," 208–19.
54 Frankfurter, "Magic of Writing." See also Gordon, "*Signa Nova et Inaudita*."
55 Roberts, *Manuscript, Society, and Belief*, 41–43, 47.
56 On variations in nomina sacra practice, see Hurtado, *Earliest Christian Artifacts*, 104–5; Choat, *Belief and Cult*, 119–25.
57 Nongbri, "Lord's Prayer and ΧΜΓ," 64–68.

TRADITIONS OF WRITING AND THE BOOK

times in magical texts and amulets, sometimes in apotropaic inscriptions or prayers on monks' cell walls.[58] Certainly not every use of cryptography (or nomina sacra) carried magical implications, and yet their use in writing always involved some reflection on the nature of names, writing, communication, and the letter itself as a symbol. Charakteres, nomina sacra, and cryptography all represent the magical sense of the written word and inscribed name that Christian scribes developed over the fourth and fifth centuries as components of the scribal craft. They "marked" a text as efficacious, as a vehicle of supernatural agency.[59]

Narrative traditions in monastic culture also influenced the composition of magical texts. In this case we must consider the ways that scribes regarded particular legends as especially conducive to ritual application. For example, three fifth- and sixth-century protective and healing amulets have been found that invoke the popular legend of Jesus's correspondence with the Syrian King Abgar. In the legend, Jesus writes to the king of Edessa to apologize for his inability to visit the ruler in his ailing state due to his imminent crucifixion. But, Jesus promises, he will send one of his disciples instead. This legend gained popularity around the eastern Mediterranean world for suggesting the existence of autographs of Jesus—relics of Jesus's own scribal charisma.[60]

The three Abgar charms adjust the tale in different ways according to the exigencies of particular patients and to stress different potencies in the myth. The salience of the Abgar letter tradition in late antique Egypt and beyond came from its reflection of holy men's practices of using "letters" in prayers, scripture, or simply writing as material vehicles of healing and protection.[61] A Greek amulet from Oxyrhynchus comprises only the letter from Abgar to Jesus requesting healing, but the scribe has inserted the name of his client patient ("Epimachus") and closes with holy names, charakteres, nomina sacra, and the concluding terms of ritual emphasis typical of Egyptian spells, "quickly, quickly, quickly."[62] A Coptic charm from Vienna concentrates on the letter from Jesus, surrounding the words of the legend with charakteres and phrasing the key text repetitively, as if in song: "The second letter that our Lord Jesus Christ, the Son of the ever-living God, wrote to him, to Abgar, the king, the king, at the city, the city, to give deliverance through Ananias, the messenger, the copyist, that it might give health."[63] The scribe thus

---

58 See Wisse, "Language Mysticism"; Doresse, "Cryptography"; Dieleman, "Cryptography at the Monastery"; idem, *Priests, Tongues, and Rites*, 80–101; Gordon, "Showing the Gods the Way," 165–72. See also Luijendijk, *Greetings in the Lord*, 219–21, on isopsephy, the Greek tradition of contemplating the numerical value of letters in words, akin to Jewish *gematria*.

59 Cf. Richter, "Markedness and Unmarkedness."

60 See the discussions of papyrological and epigraphical sources in Henry, "Apotropaic Autographs"; Given, "Utility and Variance."

61 See ch. 3 of this book and the sixth-century *Life of St. Eugendus* from Gaul, in which an exorcistic letter to a woman cures her of a demon (§§141–46), in Vivian, Vivian, and Russell, *Lives of the Jura Fathers*, 166–69.

62 P. Oxy 65.4469.

63 ACM 61 = Vienna Rainer 191; also in Stegemann, *Die koptischen Zaubertexte*, 70–73, and Taf.

CHAPTER 6

combines a common scribal technique for creating efficacious text through complex graphic layout and mysterious letters with the oral technique of repetition. Ananias is not the Coptic scribe of the charm but, rather, a minor figure in Eusebius's account of the Abgar legend. His invocation as both messenger (ⲕⲟⲣⲥⲟⲩⲛ = grk *koursōros*) and copyist (*kalligraphos*) suggests the Coptic scribe's own elevation of the scribal role, creating a kind of heroic prototype for himself as *kalligraphos*.[64] And a third charm, also in Coptic, is worded to emphasize Jesus's personal authorship—"It is I, Jesus, who have writ[ten this] letter with my (own) hand"— and then folded in such a way as to mimic a real letter of the fifth century.[65]

These applications of the Abgar legend to the immediate circumstances of spell composition exemplify scribes' mediation of the narrative culture of the monastery to create powerful written texts.[66] The spells involve the full arsenal of scribal techniques used to compound the potency of the written word, from charakteres to nomina sacra and graphic arrangement. But most importantly, they show the independent agency of monastic scribes in improvising narrative traditions for healing, cursing, protection, and other ritual purposes.

Another area of data that can be used to examine the creative agency of scribes in mediating between monastic and scriptural traditions and the world of everyday practices is the great number and variety of scripture passages and even gospel *incipits* copied out as amulets.[67] These materials, which come particularly from the fifth and sixth centuries, indicate how scribes were regarded as technical mediators of scripture—indeed, as performers of the very authority of scripture. For the bearer of Papyrus Oxyrhynchus 1077, whose scribal artisan cut and folded the sheet into fifteen linked octagons, each with a few words of the "curative gospel" of Matthew and a human face in the middle, the very meaning and value of scripture was a function of the scribe's special craft (which resulted in a piece of scripture folded into a single octagon with the face in the front).

Of course, such a product is scripture in its material—"performative" rather than "informative"—sense, embodying the power of the authoritative word inscribed on papyrus, which the client might physically wear or apply to places in need of its magic. While only some scripture passages on papyrus bear obvious marks of amuletic usage—folding, for example, or the inclusion of charakteres or closing prayers or crosses—scholars have noted the particular verses that scribes typically picked out of larger texts for inscription on slips of papyrus: Psalm

---

1,1. What others have claimed as scribal dittography I suggest are the repetitions of words characteristic of song.

64 See Eusebius, *Hist. Eccl.* 1.13.6. See also Stegemann, *Die koptischen Zaubertexte*, 73.

65 P. Mich. Inv. 6213, in Sullivan and Wilfong, "Reply of Jesus to King Abgar."

66 See in general Kropp, *Ausgewählte koptische Zaubertexte*, 3:40–103.

67 Judge, "Magical Use of Scripture"; Kruger, "P. Oxy. 840"; De Bruyn, "Papyri, Parchments, Ostraca, and Tablets"; De Bruyn and Dijkstra, "Greek Amulets and Formularies"; Sanzo, *Scriptural Incipits on Amulets*; and Jones, *New Testament Texts*. See also Wasserman, "P78 (P. Oxy. XXXIV 2684)"; Förster, "Christliche Texte in magischer Verwendung."

72:21–3, Psalm 90, John 1:5–6, Matthew 4:23, or even a combination of such passages.[68] Of course, what we denote as an "amulet" would have included and shaded into favorite or edifying scripture passages or powerful liturgical hymns. That is, a passage of scripture inscribed on papyrus—or, for that matter, on a monastic cell's walls—would have been seen as oscillating regularly between edification, liturgy, and protection/healing. Thus the evidence for scripture amulets covers many more examples of inscribed scripture than simply those with extra magical signs.

If often the scribe cleaved closely to what he imagined the precise words of scripture to be, at other times the goal of mediating the power of holy scripture for quotidian purposes required paraphrase and innovation:

> Holy, holy, holy, Lord . . . and who has healed again, who has raised Lazarus from the dead even on the fourth day, who has healed Peter's mother-in-law, who has also accomplished many unmentioned healings in addition to those they report in the sacred gospels: Heal her who wears this divine amulet of the disease afflicting her, through the prayers and intercession of the ever-virgin Mother, the Mother of God.[69]

In imagining the "sacred gospels" as a repository of reports of healings that might be drawn upon scribally for amulets and ritual healing, this text illuminates the very concept of scripture held by the laity and transmitted by scribes: the gospels were understood as, in the words of Papyrus Oxyrhynchus 1077 (quoted earlier), "curative." This concept bears on the frequent use of scripture *incipits*, or quotations of the opening verse of a gospel. As Joseph Sanzo has argued in an illuminating study of these amulets, such quotations were not meant to call to mind the entire salvific narrative of the particular gospel but rather referred to an image of the gospel as a practical repository of examples: a sequence of healing narratives that might be drawn upon for ritual application, like historiolae.[70]

Scripture amulets thus shaded into improvisations on scripture and on biblical and apocryphal legends, and perhaps especially into types of written text that reflected an oral or aural component, such as the Lord's Prayer or the *trisagion*. Depending on the literacy of the amulet's recipient, either of these features might have stimulated oral repetition or simply symbolized the aural charisma of the liturgy in which these components might have been heard.[71] But here the monastic scribe assumed a larger role, not simply as a technician of the written word

---

68 See, e.g., P. Oxy 73.4932 (Psalm 72:21–3); P. Oxy 78.5127 (Psalm 90); P. Vind. G 29831 (John 1: 5–6); ACM 9 = Berlin 9096 (collection of *incipits* and Psalm verses. Wasserman, "P78 (P. Oxy. XXXXIV 2684)," discusses the possible apotropaic use of a fragment of Jude.

69 ACM 13 = Florence/Vitelli 365.

70 Sanzo, *Scriptural Incipits on Amulets*, esp. 54–61.

71 See De Bruyn, "Use of the Sanctus," esp. 18–19; cf. Martinez, *P.Michigan XIX*, with a limited *Sitz-im-Leben* for the leather amulet ("post-baptismal," 23–28); Nongbri, "Lord's Prayer and XMΓ," 59–64; and, on ecclesiastical invocations in Coptic spells in general, Kropp, *Ausgewählte koptische*

CHAPTER 6

or as an interpreter and artisan of scripture but as the mediator of the larger ritual aesthetic of the monastery, liturgy itself. But with "liturgy" I mean not just the specific chants performed in churches at various times of the day or year but the very principles of liturgy as the official performative (incantatory, hymnic) context in which monastic choirs uttered sacred names and invoked divine beings. If anything signified Christianity's ritual power, it was liturgy and its particular psalms and chants, and monastic scribes knew well that the charisma they could purvey in inscriptions and incantations derived from the powers of liturgy.[72]

On the inside, even in *lauras* and hermitages, monastic culture was a liturgical culture in which monastic gatherings attuned monks to the cadences and image sequences of chant and ceremony, to the relationship of verbal description to the calling into being of angels, and even to the notion that through proper liturgy one might actually join with angels and other supernatural beings by the power of the chanted word. For one Apa Anouph, such liturgically styled apocalyptic visions typified his life in the desert: "I have often seen tens of thousands of angels standing before God. I have seen choirs of the just. I have seen companies of martyrs. I have seen armies of monks. I have seen the works of all those who praise God."[73] As sensory reinforcement of this experience of heavenly chant, monks' actual liturgical gatherings sometimes took place in chapels or churches decorated with images of saints, angels, transfigured monastic heroes, and esoteric heavenly beings that mirrored the invocations of liturgical chant and the apocalyptic lore of monastic culture.[74] Thus liturgical culture was also mirrored iconographically and reinforced spatially.[75]

It is in the context of this liturgical culture that we can begin to understand the composition of texts like the following, which carry such imagery and verbal power into new, often-private domains:

> Hail El Bathouriel, giver of power, as he replies to the angels!
> Hail Adonai! Hail Eloi! Hail Abrasax! Hail Yothael!
>
> Hail Mizrael, who has beheld the face of the father in the power of Iaō!
> KOK!

Zaubertexte, 3:183–196. On textual expressions of liturgy and popular Christian song in late antiquity see now Knust and Wasserman, "Biblical Odes."

72 See Page, *Christian West and Its Singers*, 147–50. Rather than depending on more traditional or confessional definitions of "liturgy," I here define it for the purposes of this book as prayers and chants performed aloud and ceremonially to represent an official language of devotion to the deity, *as well as* prayers and incantations composed to approximate such an official language of devotion through the use of traditional cadences, mythological figures, and strophic structures, *as well as* the larger performative circumstances of procession, music, iconographic media, and spatial movement within which such prayers and chants take place.

73 *Hist. mon.* 11.7, in Russell, *Lives of the Desert Fathers*, 88.

74 See Golitzin, "Earthly Angels and Heavenly Men," 136–37, 142–44; and Zanetti and Davis, "Liturgy and Ritual Practice."

75 See Bolman, "Depicting the Kingdom of Heaven."

I summon you (plur.) by the first seal put upon the body of Adam.
I summon you by the second seal—upon the limbs of Adam.
I summon you by the third seal, sealing the kidneys and the heart of Adam as
   he lies upon the earth, until Jesus the Christ guarantees him in the hands
   of his Father.
The Father established him; he breathed into his face; he filled him with the
   breath of life.
Send me your breath of life into this vessel!
AMEN AMEN AMEN! SOUSA SOUSA SOUSA!
I summon you by the three cries which the Son sent forth from the cross:
   ELOI ELOI ELEMA SABAKTANI, which means: God, my God, why
      have you forsaken me?
Holy Holy Holy!
Hail, David, (for) you are the father of Christ,
   who sings in the church of the first-born child of heaven!
Hail David, divine fa[ther, with] this ten-stringed cithara of joy,
   as he sings within the veil of the altar with joy!
Hail, Harmosiel, who sings within the veil of the Father,
   while echoing behind him (stand) those upon the gate, and those within
      the wall.
The tribes in the twelve worlds hear them, rejoice, and echo him:
Holy Holy [Holy]! One holy Father! Holy!
Amen Amen Amen!
Hail Ab[..]ais [in] heaven and earth! You praise! KOK!
Hail, O Sun!
Hail, twelve little children who shelter the body of the sun.
Hail, twelve bowls filled with water!
   They filled their hands (with it).
      They cast (it) toward the rays of the sun, so they shall not burn the
         fruits of the country.
Fill your hands! (Cast your) blessings downwards upon this chalice!
KOK! Hail, O four winds of heaven!
Hail, O four corners of the world!
Hail, O armies of heaven.
Hail, O earth of the inheritance!
Hail, O garden of the saints of the Father!
One holy Father!
[One] holy Son!
One holy Spirit ! Amen.[76]

---

[76] ACM 113 = Ostr. Cairo 49547 (my translation). See also the range of "liturgical fragments and prayers" collected in Wessely, *Les plus anciens monuments*, 2:428–37.

This incantation clearly stands apart from the official liturgical prayers of most monasteries, and yet the language also depends on experience with liturgical culture, which doubtless allowed such diversity.[77] Here the scribe has compounded the simple depiction of the heavens from orthodox liturgy to include esoteric angels' names, visionary declarations, and even ritual equipment (bowls, cithara) that would have been at home in the apocalyptic-liturgical environment of monastic scribes. Such expressly "invocational" texts were certainly developed for use within monastic culture.[78] Some of the larger manuals, produced in codex form, begin with a long liturgical incantation, followed by a list of ritual applications of that incantation: to protect a client from sorcery, to protect a ship, to protect a home, to cure a disease, and so on.[79] This compositional structure implies that the incantation was meant to "materialize" into the various substances stipulated: oil, water, and "amulets." It is likely that such extended invocations of divine beings and heavenly names represented some (or several) scribes' virtuoso compositions in the spirit of liturgy. In the world of these monastic scribes, such a composition must have conveyed tremendous potency and also, in the eyes of clients, invested the material media of the spell with considerable charisma (although, given its length, it is doubtful that the ritual specialist chanted the entire invocation for each application).

Most of the smaller, single-leaf spells, on the other hand, work the power of liturgical incantation into the circumstances of a particular client's pressing crisis. The following, for example, drawn from a "loose-leaf" collection of similar spells, applies liturgical tradition to the problem of attracting clients to a shop:

The gathering, the gathering of angels for the salutation of the Father:

I will sing and glorify and hymn: Holy, holy, God almighty, creator, invisible one, Horomosiel, the angel in whose hand is the trumpet, as he gathers the angels for the salutation {of the Father} of the whole council of the Father; Anaboel, the steward of the Father; the congregation, Pakothan Lerekiel. I ask, I invoke you today, Hormosel, the angel in whose hand are [the gath]erings, [that you might] gathe[r to]day the [whole] generation of Adam and [all] the children of Zoe, through the power of the [great] unseen names of terror:

Ariel, Oriel, Emiel, Thimiael, Thanael, Patriel, who gather the entire cos-

---

77 On liturgical elements in Coptic spells, see Kropp, *Ausgewählte koptische Zaubertexte*, 3:229–233. On liturgical diversity in late antiquity, see Page, *Christian West and Its Singers*, 93–95.

78 See Van der Vliet, "Les anges du soleil" (invocations of solar beings), and cf. also the extended protective spell of the so-called "Rossi tractate" (= ACM 71).

79 Multiple uses of liturgical incantations: see, e.g., P. Macquarie 1, with codex instructing different uses of the incantation that opens the codex, in Choat and Gardner, *Coptic Handbook of Ritual Power*, 1–11; ACM 135 = Heidelberg kopt. 686, where the incantation appears on pp. 1–14 and the applications on pp. 14–16. Cf. ACM 133 = Michigan 593, in which multiple uses precede the incantation (codex pp. 13ff).

mos, along with everything in it, from the region of the sunrise to its place of setting. I ask, I invoke!⁸⁰

As if to reinforce the liturgical authority of this spell, the reverse depicts nine figures in robes, each holding a processional cross and labeled with a magical name.⁸¹ Another spell applies the power of liturgical incantation to advance some client's aggressive need to curse several local families:

> I ask, I invoke, I worship, I lay my prayer and my request before the throne of God the almighty, Sabaoth....
>
> I appeal to you, Father, I appeal to you, Son, I appeal to you, Holy Spirit, the consubstantial Trinity, the good news of Gabriel the archangel, that you perform my judgment and my revenge and my violence with Tatore and Andres and Maria daughter of Tsibel, with their children. Bring upon them blindness to their two eyes. Bring upon them great pain and jaundice disease and burning fever and trouble and dispersion and ruin. Father, strike them; Son, strike them; God, who exists before the world had yet come into being, strike them. At once, at once!
>
> ...
>
> O four creatures who stand by the Father, the great God, strike Tatore and Andreas and Maria and her children and everyone who resides with them ... O twenty-four elders who are seated before the Father, strike Tatore and Andreas and Maria, quickly! ... O you who rescued Daniel from the lions' den, strike Maria and Tatore and Andreas with the anger of your wrath. Michael, strike them with your fiery sword. Gabriel, strike them with your fiery sword. Raphael, strike them with your fiery sword. Rakuel, strike them with your fiery sword. Suriel, strike them with your fiery sword. Amen!⁸²

If some modern scholars find paradoxical the application of Christian liturgical forms to explicit aggression, an understanding of small-scale village environments should give historians a more empathic approach.⁸³ Given that the performance or commissioning of such curses invariably followed or augmented efforts to negotiate social tensions more directly, the curse can be read as a response to extreme social crisis—exclusion or humiliation by several families, perhaps, that the client was unable to settle face-to-face. The client may well have gained the sympathy of the scribe who composed this curse, having expected that scribe to

---

80 ACM 81 = London Hay 10122r. New translation by D. Frankfurter.
81 See Meyer and Smith, *Ancient Christian Magic*, 173.
82 ACM 91 = Oxford Bodleian Coptic ms. C (P) 4, ll.1–10, 17–26, translated by Smith in Meyer and Smith, *Ancient Christian Magic*, 192–94.
83 See Frankfurter, "Social Context of Women's Erotic Magic."

deploy the full arsenal of incantatory efficacy in his capacity as mediator of monastic liturgical tradition.

For villagers knew the power of liturgy as well: "To the most pious and holy monks," a fifth- or sixth-century individual writes through a Greek-literate scribe, "I am writing to beseech and remind you . . . as you are supplicated and adjured by the mysteries of Christ that are celebrated in these holy days. . . . Look upon and pray for me [lit. "this one"] so that we will give thanks to the Lord to the fullest."[84] The sender asks here not for a material blessing, as we saw other supplicants request in similar letters in chapter 3, but for the favor of the monks in their capacity and charisma as performers of liturgy. Indeed, we should imagine that many Egyptians' regular and life-cycle encounters with an institutional Christianity involved some kind of liturgical performance.[85] It was liturgical formulations, for example, that were carried over from actual funerary rites and applied to inscriptions on gravestones in late antique Egypt, allowing a popular acquaintance with the efficacious formulas that liturgy produced.[86] It is thus understandable that monastic scribes constructed charms for such diverse purposes as increasing a store's clientele or cursing neighbors out of the formulaic structures of liturgy.

Scribes' expertise in liturgical traditions, such that they could improvise spells and everyday applications for liturgical phrases, seems also to have involved a sensitivity to other forms of efficacious song in late antique Egyptian culture. That is to say, scribal expertise in its Christian monastic form involved an acute awareness of the magic of chants, from the liturgical forms of monastic and church settings to what we would call "folk" varieties practiced in domestic, agricultural, and economic settings. In these settings, it seems, there was another range of songs that also conveyed performative efficacy and shared tradition.[87] And these songs are important to us, first, because monastic scribes seem to have integrated them into some Coptic magical spells, and second, because these songs served as vehicles for the perpetuation of stories of Egyptian gods well beyond the fifth century CE—that is, long after the temples that had sustained the stories had collapsed and their traditional writing systems had become unreadable.

Most of the late antique versions of these texts appear on single sheets of leather or papyrus as parts of loose-leaf ritual collections, but a sixth-century

---

84 SB 20.15192, in Bagnall and Cribiore, *Women's Letters from Ancient Egypt*, #A14.15 (translation emended).

85 Cf., for medieval Europe, Boynton, "Oral Transmission of Liturgical Practice."

86 See Tudor, *Christian Funerary Stelae*, 154–55, 160, 187–98, 210; and Van der Vliet, "Literature, Liturgy, Magic" on uses of funerary liturgy in late antique Egypt.

87 Several Coptic spells appeal to heavenly beings for excellent singing voices (although these seem to have been requested on behalf of those who performed publicly rather than in the context of liturgy): ACM 121 = Berlin 8318; ACM 122 = Yale 1791A; ACM 129 = London Or. 6794.

codex in the University of Michigan collection contains two such spells, placed one after the other:

[a]

Voice of winds when there are no winds,
voice of waves when there are no waves,
voice of Amun, the three deities.
Amun, where are you going in this way, in this manner?
I am going from the south wind northward—
neither reed nor rush nor—I am going to Abydos—nor these two mountains nor these two hills—
I am mounted on a silver horse with a black horse under me,
the books of Thoth with me,
those of the Great One of five in my hands.
I make those who are pregnant give birth,
I close up those who miscarry,
I make all eggs productive except infertile eggs.
Hail, Thoth!
He has come forth to me.
Amun, where are you going, the three of Isis?
Today she is in labor (for) four days of how many . . .
It is freed from the seals to give birth.
Let it happen.
You have not found me,
you have not found my name,
you have not found a little oil for disclosing . . .
and you put it against her spine toward the bottom,
and you say, young woman, young woman over there,

[b]

Cow, cow of Amun, mother of the cattle,
they have drawn near you.
In the morning you must go forth to feed (them).
They have drawn near you.
In the evening you must come in to let them drink.
Say, Watch out for these seven things that are bad for producing milk: the sheath, the lid, the worm of Paope that has not yet spread, the barley that has not yet produced shoots, the real weed that does not provide shelter (?) for a shepherd, does not provide a staff for a herder, does not provide a goad for a cowherd.
They have come to me, my shepherd, my herder, my cowherd, with their garments torn,
a strap in front of their shoe(s), fastened with . . . of reed.
What is it with you, that you are running, that you are in a hurry, my shepherd, my herder, my cowherd, with your garments torn?
What is it with you?
With a strap on the front of your shoe fastened with fibers of reed?
Seven white (?) sheep, seven black sheep, seven young heifers, seven great cows—
let every cow and every domestic animal receive its offspring,
for Yao Sabaoth has spoken!

restore yourself, restore your
  womb, serve your child,
give milk to Horus your son,
though the power of the Lord
  God.

Go north of Abydos, go south of
  Thinis,
until you find these two brothers
  calling and running north,
and you run after them and they
  run south.
Then say, Express the thoughts of
  your heart(s),
that every domestic animal may
  receive its offspring.[88]

Here the ancient Egyptian gods Amun, Thoth, Horus, and Isis appear in poetic, often-repetitive verses, punctuated with references to the Christian God. The poetic frames for their names are spatial (Abydos), woven into the experiences of cattle and of pregnancy, evocative of movement and discovery, and replete with second-person addresses—a type of speech that presumes and, one might say, brings into existence its supernatural interlocutors. These verses conform to a classical Egyptian ritualization of speech that includes "the structuring of recited texts in a rhythmic manner by employing the language's natural rhythm, caesuras, alternating speakers, choral passages, and refrains."[89] They do not resemble the Hellenistic styles of poetry or religious archaism that one finds in the late antique Greek works of Nonnos or Damascius, who sought to invoke an ancient heritage of old (Greco-Roman) gods. At the same time, they do not resemble temple prayers to these Egyptian gods, given their specific, even intimate applications.

Rather, these charms appear to derive from oral tradition, specifically *songs*, which have been lightly edited for inclusion in a ritual manual with Christian language otherwise typical of monastic scribal culture. The scribes who wrote down these verses preserved the names, paradigmatic acts, and historiolae of early Egyptian gods as verbal formulae based in performative situations: desire for pregnancy in (a) and blessing for the expansion of the herd in (b). It was these situations that would have provoked memories of these songs from one generation to the next, with varying adjustment to religious ideology. The formulae were thus embedded in perennial domestic contexts, so that—in some areas, at least—the quotidian practice of blessing one's herd would have intrinsically conjured ancient songs.[90] We might recall how oral formulae in Greek (and Balkan) epic

---

88 ACM 43 = Michigan 136, ll. 60–84, 85–110, ed. Worrell, "Coptic Magical and Medical Texts," 20–22, translated by Meyer in Meyer and Smith, *Ancient Christian Magic*, 85–87 (emended).

89 Meyer-Dietrich, "Recitation, Speech Acts, and Declamation," 5.

90 On cattle-blessing songs across cultures, see, e.g., Deng, *Dinka and Their Songs*, 96–158 (Dinka); Svoboda, *Cleaned the Crocodile's Teeth*, esp. 14 (Nuer); and Wallace, "Mongolian Livestock Rituals" (Mongolian). Another Coptic codex, ACM 135 = Heidelberg kopt. 686 ("The Praise of Mi-

recitation passed down cultic traditions and cultural conventions long after they were first practiced. The principle of continuity, of tradition, then, was not reverence for old gods (or nostalgic archaism) but simply the efficacy of sung formulae. It is for that reason that the text shows no evidence of the scribe's "editing out" the archaic names. Rather, he has added to the *textual* form the *additional* authority of the Christian god.

I am arguing, then, that magical songs preserved in folk culture as part of specific cultural pursuits came to be integrated into Coptic magical spells and codex formularies through the interests of scribes attuned to the powers of chant and incantation both in and beyond church settings. Scriptural names, phrases, and narratives have been integrated into all these songs, whether to sanctify them in liturgical terms or simply to compound their efficacy.

A similar phenomenon can be seen in five Coptic versions of a dialogue between the gods Isis and Horus, in which Horus is depicted in distress—from pain, loneliness, or sleeplessness—and Isis sends emissaries to heal him. We saw one such version of this dialogue in the beginning of chapter 1; here is another:

> Hear Horus crying,
> hear Horus sighing:
> "I am troubled, poured out (?) for seven maidens,
> from the third hour of the day
> until the fourth hour of the night.
> Not one of them sleeps,
> not one of them dozes."
>
> Isis his mother replied to him within the temple of Habin
> with her face turned toward the seven maidens
> (and) seven maidens turned toward her face:
> "Horus, why are you crying? Horus, why are you sighing?"
>
> [Horus:] "Do you wish that I do not cry,
> do you wish that I not sigh,
> from the third hour of the day
> until the fourth hour of the night,
> while I am poured out for seven maidens,
> not one of whom sleeps,
> not one of whom dozes?"
>
> "Even <if> [you] have not [found me] and have not found my name,
> take a cup [with] a little water;
> whether it is a small breath

---

chael the Archangel" codex, p. 16, #20), recommends a material form of the main spell to remove sorcery from a herd of cattle.

or the breath of your mouth
or the breath of [your nose],
call down to them."

You two angels, who imposed sleep upon Abimelech for seventy-two [years],
    impose upon NN and be a burden upon his head like a millstone,
upon his eyes like a sack of sand,
until I complete my request to accomplish the desire of my heart,
now now, quickly quickly.[91]

Here too the writing of the spell (seventh/eighth centuries) occurred long after the period when the cults of these ancient gods were in operation, and long after such texts could have been read in Egyptian hieroglyphs.[92] And yet, like the Michigan charms earlier, each version of the Isis/Horus spell lies formally closer to the ritualized speech of older Egyptian magical texts than to Hellenistic magical formulae.[93] Once again it seems that scribes drew these spells not from earlier manuscripts but from an oral culture of magical song, and in this case (given that two versions are for inducing sleep), a song for *lullaby*. This particular performative context makes sense of the alternating voices, the strophic format, and the pathos of the distressed Horus and helpful Isis—a detail that goes back to much earlier Egyptian narratives of Isis and Horus used for magical healing.[94] Given the relatively unusual function here of inducing sleep—rarely do curses, for example, call down insomnia on their victims (except in the context of general discomfort)—it is probable that the intended sleepless one would have been an infant. Lullabies often reformulate cult myths and maintain their names and stories well beyond the spaces and eras of the original cults.[95]

What does the editing of such oral charms in late antique Christian magical texts tell us about scribes and their roles as assemblers of a Christian culture—as syncretists by virtue of their regular practices? First of all, these practices show that at least some scribes conceived their professional expertise to involve the collection of efficacious speech forms from folk culture, and not simply the deliv-

---

91 ACM 48, ed. Kropp, *Ausgewählte koptische Zaubertexte*, 1:11–13, Taf. 1; trans. Kelsey in Meyer and Smith, *Ancient Christian Magic*, 94–95 (emended).

92 Paleography of Schmidt spells: Crum, in Kropp, *Ausgewählte koptische Zaubertexte*, 1: x–xi.

93 Other multiforms: ACM 72 = Kropp, *Ausgewählte koptische Zaubertexte*, 1:13–14; ACM 47 = Berlin 5565; ed. Beltz, "Die koptischen Zauberpapyri," 61–63; ACM 49 = Berlin 8313, ed. Beltz, "Die koptischen Zauberpapyri," 65–67. Another spell from the Michigan collection, ACM 82 = Michigan ms. 4932r (ed. Worrell, "Coptic Magical and Medical Texts," 184–87), which was meant for erotic binding, has a very brief historiola: "Oil! Oil! Oil! holy oil! Oil that flows from under the throne of Yao Sabaoth! Oil with which Isis anointed Osiris's bone(s)!"

94 See Frankfurter, "Laments of Horus in Coptic."

95 Pache, *Baby and Child Heroes*, 100–11; Karanika, *Voices at Work*, esp. 160–64, on the magic of song in multiple areas of folk culture. I know of only two spells for inducing insomnia: PGM VII.374–76; XII.376–96.

ery of efficacious speech and writing *to* folk culture *from* monastic culture.[96] As liturgical speech and biblical legend provided the basis for the composition of new spells for everyday purposes and for the direction of the authority of monastic textuality toward the crises of laypeople, so too did the oral charms of local, domestic culture represent an alternative "canon" of authoritative speech that was regularly extended to Christian figures.[97]

Moreover, the development of these oral charms illuminates certain scribes' roles as masters not only of the written word—the nomina sacra, the charakteres, and magical images—and of scripture as a material substance, but also of aural efficacy: the power of the oral invocation, of magical names, of repetition and sound and tune. Here the exploitation of liturgical formulae goes hand in hand with that of the folk charm: both types of text allow (or reflect) the scribes' movement beyond writing and text to incantation and song.

V. THE RECOLLECTION OF LITERARY TRADITIONS THROUGH THE SCRIBAL CRAFT

So far my analysis of scribal culture and syncretism has emphasized *locations* and *circumstances* of mediation: sites of convergence between monastery (or shrine apparatus) and village, between literate and oral worlds. We have seen monastic scribes' expansion of liturgical compositions to invoke solar beings and to address village animosities, as well as scribes' incorporation of oral charms, some addressing Egyptian gods, to redirect efficacious song in much the same way as liturgy. But the distinctive culture of Christian scribes also allowed the recollection of literary traditions more characteristic of the ancient priestly culture of the temples than of the village folk cultures of the fifth and sixth centuries CE. (I use this language—"more characteristic of"—deliberately, not to prejudge "survivals" in this case but to query whether what *seems* characteristic of temple traditions could actually be a substantive influence on the scribes under discussion.) These were predominantly textual traditions of an esoteric nature, and two shall concern us here. The first is a genre of literary prophecy that I will here call the "Land of Egypt oracle," in which key portents, catastrophes, and millennial triumphs, laid out in a prophetic chronological sequence, are explicitly set in the Egyptian landscape, suggesting an interest in Egypt as a sacred landscape above and beyond the particular sites of shrines or villages or the spatial parameters of Christian mythology. The second, a popular example of "pharaonic survival" to generations of Egyptologists, revolves around the depiction of Amente, the land of the dead in the "West," and the peculiar images of its demonic assailants in Egyptian Christian literature.

---

96 See Smallwood, "Transmission of Charms," on the relationship of monastic scribes to oral culture.
97 See Grey, "On the Christianity of the Incantations."

CHAPTER 6

A. The Land of Egypt Oracle

The Land of Egypt oracle is a fundamentally scribal genre that goes back to texts of the New Kingdom but enjoyed a particular resurgence in Greek during the Hellenistic and early Roman periods. Oracles were composed and re-edited, first as propaganda for various kings, then as general collages of chaos and redemption in the land, illustrating fertility and drought, civil concord and breakdown, security and invasion. The alternating fortunes reflected the effects of kingship and "antikingship" and articulated the nature of Egypt as a sacred landscape whose fortunes responded to divine presence.[98] This was not a "nationalism" but a literary genre pertaining to the effects of kingship, active for centuries after the last native rulers had controlled the land and exportable to many other types of writing about a macro-landscape.[99] It represented the professional efforts of temple scribes and those who inherited the genre from the temples through literary channels, steering the Land of Egypt oracle toward generalized lament, a kind of native messianism, or the advancement of new ideologies of apocalyptic certainty, like Hermeticism (the *Asclepius*) and Christian prophecy. These scribal efforts to imagine Egypt as a macro-landscape in relation to mythology or a particular god involved various genres and forms, even sometimes cartography, although the Land of Egypt oracle always had an impressionistic structure, warning or lamenting, that complemented its various oracular frames.[100]

The *Apocalypse of Elijah* is the first extensive use of this literary form in a Christian text. It is an extended prophecy about the endtimes, datable to the later third century and inspired partly by the Book of Revelation, a popular text in early Christian Egypt. It traces the signs of the eschaton through martyrdoms, the exposure of an Antichrist figure, and finally the return of Christ and millennial bliss. Two early Coptic manuscripts of this originally Greek composition actually came from Shenoute's monastery.[101] But for all its adamant Christian millennialism, the *Apocalypse of Elijah* frames its entire series of warning, portents, and false signs in the landscape of Egypt itself, following the earlier priestly genre of the Land of Egypt oracle:

---

98 The literature includes, from classical Egypt, the Prophecy of Neferti and Admonitions of Ipuwer; from Hellenistic Egypt (in Roman-era manuscripts), the Demotic Chronicle, the Oracle of the Potter, and the Oracle of the Lamb; from Roman and late antique Egypt, CPJ 520, P. Cairo 31222, Asclepius 24–27, the Tiburtine Sibyl, and the literature discussed in this section. See bibliographies of primary texts and historical discussions in Dunand, "L'Oracle du potier"; Assmann, "Königsdogma und Heilserwartung"; Frankfurter, *Elijah in Upper Egypt*, 159–238.

99 On problems with the category of nationalism as applied to these materials, see Frankfurter, *Elijah in Upper Egypt*, 250–57; Wipszycka, "Le nationalisme a-t-il existé."

100 On macro-landscape conceptions in ancient Egypt, see O'Connor, "From Topography to Cosmos"; and Baines, *High Culture and Experience*.

101 See Frankfurter, *Elijah in Upper Egypt*, for translation, manuscript character, dating principles, relationship to Revelation, and historical context.

2.9. At that time [the king] will command peace in Egypt and a worthless gift. 10. He will grant peace to the saints. He will proceed to say, "The name of God is One!" 11. He will give honor to the priests of God. He will exalt the holy places. 12. He will give worthless gifts to the house of God. 13. He will circulate among the cities of Egypt with deception, without (their) knowing. 14. He will take count of the holy places. He will weigh the idols of the *ethnos*. He will take count of their wealth. He will appoint priests for them. 15. He will command that the wise men of the land be seized, along with the great ones of the people, to be taken to a metropolis by the sea, as he says, "There is but one language!" ... 29. Woe to you, rulers of Egypt, at that time, because your time has passed! 30. The violence of the poor will turn against you, and they will seize your sons as plunder. 31. The cities of Egypt will groan at that time, and there will no longer be heard the voice of the buyer or seller in the markets of the cities of Egypt. They will collect dust.... 44. Blood will flow from Kos to Memphis: the river of Egypt will become blood, so that no one can drink from it for three days. 45. Woe to Egypt and to those who are in Egypt! 46. At that time a king will arise in the city which is called "The City of the Sun." At that time the whole land will tremble. 3.1 In the fourth year of that king there will appear someone saying "I am the Christ." But he is not—do not believe him! 2. For when the Christ comes he will come like a covey of doves, with his crown of doves surrounding him, as he traverses the clouds of heaven with the sign of the cross going before him. 3. The whole world sees him like the sun which shines from the east to the west.

Egypt and its cities thus provide the setting, the theater, for the vicissitudes of kingship and the portents of social breakdown—long-traditional motifs in the Land of Egypt oracle—leading up to premonitions of the return of Christ. Yet for this author, this return only follows a further series of portents, now revolving around the deceptions and depredations of an Antichrist figure, the "Shameless (or Lawless) One." These events are still framed spatially in a landscape cast in immediate, Egyptian terms, even when the narrative turns to the eschatological martyr Tabitha and her healing blood:

4.1. The virgin whose name is Tabitha will hear that the Shameless One has made his appearance in the holy places. She will put on her garment of linen, 2. and hurry up to Judea, reproving him as far as Jerusalem, saying to him, "O shameless one, O Lawless One, O you who are hostile to all the saints!" 3. Then the Shameless One will be angered at the virgin. He will pursue her towards the west. He will suck her blood in the evening 4. and toss her up onto the temple, and she will become a healing for the people. 5. At dawn she will rise up alive and rebuke him, saying, "You Shameless One—you have no power over my spirit or my body, because I live in the Lord always! 6. And even my blood which you cast upon the temple has become a healing for the people! ... 5.7. Then, in that time, the earth will tremble; the sun will darken.... The trees will be uprooted and topple over. Wild beasts and farm animals will die in a catastrophe. 8. Birds will fall on the ground dead. 9. The earth will parch and the waters of the sea will dry up.

The people complain to the Lawless One that the earth is in decline:

5.12. See, now we will die in a famine and tribulation. Indeed, where now is the footprint of a righteous person that we should worship you, or where is our teacher, that we might appeal to him? 13. Now we will be destroyed in wrath, because we disobeyed God. 14. We went to the depths of the sea and we found no water. We dug in the rivers and papyrus reeds and we found no water. 15. Then the Shameless One will weep in that time, saying, Woe is me, too, for my time has passed away! ... 18. Bring up the saints—For because of them the earth gives fruit, For because of them the sun shines upon the earth, For because of them the dew falls upon the earth! ... 32. After this Elijah and Enoch (will) come down. They (will) lay aside the flesh of this world (and) put on the "flesh" of the spirit. They (will) pursue the Lawless One. They (will) kill him without his being able to utter a word. 33. In that time he will dissolve in their presence as ice dissolves in fire. He will perish like a serpent with no breath in it.... 36. In that time the Christ (will) descend from heaven—the king with all his saints. 37. He (will) burn this earth. He (will) spend one thousand years on it, 38. because the sinners ruled it (before). He will make a new heaven and a new earth. There will be no devil ... in them. 39. He will rule with the saints, (and they will be) ascending and descending, along with the angels, with the Christ for a thousand years.[102]

The traditional motifs of terrestrial decline from the Land of Egypt oracle here serve to depict the uncertain political and social state of Egypt first under shifting kingships and then under the Shameless One, an eschatological adversary who instigates martyrdoms and social breakdown.[103] In the end, he too is dispatched before Christ's appearance, which happens "like the sun which shines from east to west" (3.3). Along the way we see references to the strange eschatological cult of Tabitha's healing blood (4.1–6) and the demise of the earth's fertility without the power of the saints (5.14–18).[104] In all these ways the text can be read as a deployment of an ancient genre to advance a Christian mythology. But it also rep-

---

102 *Apocalypse of Elijah* 2.6–3.3; 4.1–5; 5.7–18, 32–39 (privileging Sahidic recension), in Frankfurter, *Elijah in Upper Egypt*, 306–28.

103 A fourth-century martyrological fragment from Oxyrhynchus contains similar language about "a great persecution in the Land of Egypt," with signs reminiscent of the *Apocalypse of Elijah*: see P. Oxy 4 1B 74/K(a), in Blumell and Wayment, *Christian Oxyrhynchus*, #100.

104 On these subjects, see Frankfurter, "Cult of the Martyrs."

resents a revitalization of an ancient religious ideology (the priestly view of the land of Egypt's interaction with types of rulers) under the aegis of Christian millennial fantasy.

The real historical conundrum lies in *how* a historical scribe could have understood the perpetuation of these earlier, priestly traditions to advance a religious ideology that would, at least to the modern historian, seem at odds with those traditions and their religious perspective. The problem is somewhat resolved when we come to see scribal traditions and genres as capable of framing a diversity of ideologies, mysteries, and prophetic authorities. Over their many centuries of use, these oracles were directed to praise pharaohs and oppose Jews, support native revolts and lament social decline. For this scribe, the genre lay at hand as a fitting context for the articulation of Christian anxieties and fantasies of triumph in the late third century. As a composition of a period when temples were still functioning, the *Apocalypse of Elijah* may well have come from the pen of one formally versed in the traditions and genres of the temple scriptorium. During these early centuries of Christianization there was a lively continuum between Egyptian temple scribes and many other scribal groups, including Jewish, Hermetic, and—naturally—Christian writers.[105] But in its material form, in manuscripts of the fourth and fifth centuries, the text continued to demonstrate for later Christians (especially monks) the harmony of the Land of Egypt oracle with Christian eschatological hopes.

Another example of the Land of Egypt oracle comes from the same period as the *Apocalypse of Elijah*'s Coptic manuscripts, a period well after any kind of continuum with temple culture would have been possible. In this case we need a more nuanced social model to grasp the recollection of the Land of Egypt oracle as a genre of *Christian* scribality. The text itself, Papyrus Cologne 354, belongs to a more substantial document, an apocryphal post-resurrection discourse by Christ to certain apostles. Christian scribes had long used this framing device to present mysteries of the cosmos and salvation, implying their accessibility to a select few.[106] Within that frame the Cologne papyrus consists of a prophecy by some unknown biblical patriarch or angel about disturbances in Egypt and the mythological genesis of the Egyptian landscape. The "land [ⲭⲱⲣⲁ; or soil: ⲕⲉϩⲓ] of Egypt" is described as uniquely blessed by God and his angels, especially with regard to agricultural fertility (also an important matter in the *Apocalypse of Elijah*), and in this blessing Egypt stands unique among all other lands:

> But you, Land of Egypt, are the last to come forth from among the seventy-two lands [ⲛⲭⲱⲣⲁ]. You are destined through that which the Father wants. You shall be under the blessing of all those who are mine. My seventy-two sons shall visit you in a few months.... Those of the sceptres of the lands

---

105 See Frankfurter, *Elijah in Upper Egypt*, 100–101; idem, "Legacy of the Jewish Apocalypse," 146–50; Fowden, *Egyptian Hermes*.

106 Schenke, "P.Köln 354"; Boud'hors, "Manuscripts and Literature."

shall honor you. You shall become a footstool for me on the day of your inheritance through my Son. You shall not be thirsty under his blessing. (The blessing) shall be in your rivers. Fruit shall never cease in you.... Every sort of tree in Paradise will be planted in you, up to seven hundred and thirty-three. Twelve rays of the sun shall shine over you. For the other seventy-one (lands), (only) seven rays of the sun shall shine for them. Your light shall be greater than theirs by five rays.

But Egypt is also seen here as the "holy (landscape) where the 83,721 martyrs dwell, having poured out their blood because of my Son," and where the Holy Family—Joseph, Mary, and baby Jesus—once traveled, leaving their beneficent traces:

When he finished uttering these secret blessings over the soil of Egypt [ⲉⲡⲕⲉϩⲓ ⲛⲕⲏⲙⲓ], he took a seal and sealed his handful [ⲇⲣⲁⲭⲙⲏ] of soil [ⲛⲕⲉϩⲓ] with three seals. It is seventy-one handfuls of soil, however, that he sealed with only one seal. (9) For Michael was bringing forth all the lands [ⲛ̄ⲭⲱⲣⲁ]. He took only a small bit from each land, and he brought it up to the Father. (10) He (the Father) blessed each one according to its worthiness. When he had finished, and seventy-one angels had been summoned, he gave each of them a handful, so that (each angel) should take it and make the foundation of each land.... (Frag. C) (But) to me he gave the handful of Egyptian soil, and he let me write my name on it. He took it, and it came to be established (as that of) the land of Egypt. In Eden, in the regions of the east, where Adam was yet to be formed, one took again from the (4) hand[ful of Eg]yptian soil [ⲧⲉⲧⲣⲁ[ⲭⲙⲏ ⲙ̄ⲡⲕ]ⲉϩⲓ], while it was (still) in Eden. The Father has created (him), along with me, because it is my name that is on (5) it (the land of Egypt).... Therefore I also have came out to Adam, who has filled all lands.... Because one has brought forth (7) from all the lands and given to the land of Egypt. God therefore brought Adam forth from the land of Egypt and let him (8) to fill all [lands]. That one, then, who will be strong, in every land, his place of inheritance is the land of Egypt, (9) as an [inheritance] for all eternity.[107]

Like the *Apocalypse of Elijah* and its images of eschatological martyrdom and potent saints, the Cologne text reveals Egypt as a terrestrial entity distinctive for its prestige as the source of all things, for its saturation with divine powers, and for its staging of mythic events. The text's emphasis on fertility and soil harkens back to earlier Egyptian literature and gods' blessings of the fields. Yet the postresurrection framing story, the unusual story of Adam in Egypt[108] and the accompany-

---

107 P. Col 354, in Schenke, "P.Köln 354" (my translation, with gratitude to Gesa Schenke for her consultation and for sharing with me her own provisional translation, in preparation for the *Journal of Coptic Studies*).

108 On Adam apocrypha in Egyptian monastic circles, see Evelyn White, Sobhy, and Lythgoe, *Monasteries of the Wâdi 'n Natrûn*, text #1.

ing reference to the Holy Family's sojourn there, reflect a thoroughly *Christian* scribal milieu, with Christian heroes, myths, and local legends—the kind of milieu in which apocryphal legends of patriarchs, local traditions, and time-honored revelatory genres of dialogue were customarily woven in ever-new combinations.[109] Indeed, in a comparable combination of apocalyptic vision and ideologies of the vitality of the Egyptian land, a monk of Shenoute's monastery posthumously graced the abbot with an apocalyptic tour, during which the abbot beholds the angels responsible for irrigating the land of Egypt.[110] The mystery and essential value of the Nile's surges had already drawn the attention of Athanasius in his *Life of Antony*, and Shenoute in his own lifetime seems to have sought to integrate the surge into local liturgy.[111] In such diverse forms we see how some Christian scribes maintained a distinctly Egypt-centered scope in articulating the mythical powers of the new pantheon, so that the land of Egypt and its sources and fortunes came to be integrated into Christian literature.

Now, while the interest in Egypt and its blessings is explicit in both the *Apocalypse of Elijah* and the Cologne papyrus, we should not perceive their scribes' efforts as "archaizing"—that is, as making a deliberate effort to bring alternative religious traditions regarded as their cultural patrimony into Christian expression. Archaism presupposes a scribe's deliberate comparison between Christianity and an indigenous religious tradition in order to promote the indigenous one as authoritative. But these documents do not appropriate the Land of Egypt oracle as part of an *alternative* religious order. Both documents are fundamentally Christian, envisioning Egypt and the distinctive legends of its landscape as, in fact, extensions of the landscape, legends, and blessings of the Holy Land of Palestine: as surely as God blessed the land of Abraham, the texts imply, so too did he bless the land of Egypt and allow portents and heroes to arise there.[112] This Christian-Jewish "biblical" concept of sacred landscape provides the underlying ideology for these texts. But in developing this ideology and its relevance for terrestrial fertility in its most "earthly" dimension, the monastic scribe had access to a type of formulation, a genre of revelation, that recollected earlier Egyptian literary oracles and reflected ongoing interest in the fertility of the land of Egypt.

What then was the medium of these traditions? It is unlikely that the recollection of the Land of Egypt oracle was mediated directly through translations of ancient Egyptian documents. Christian texts like the *Apocalypse of Elijah* (which enjoyed considerable popularity in fourth-century Egypt) served as textual models or reminders of the genre in later Christian scribal contexts, and even hybrid

---

109 See, e.g., the "Apocalyptic Gospel" found at the Wâdi Natrûn monastery, bearing strong similarities to the *Apocalypse of Elijah*; Cairo ##7–8add, in ibid., 16–26).

110 See Roquet, "L'Ange des eaux"; Frankfurter, "Legacy of the Jewish Apocalypse," 191–93. Cf. ACM 112: "Ruphos, the Angel apponted over the Land of Egypt."

111 Athanasius, *v.Ant.* 32; Shenoute, "Let Our Eyes," fr. 2, 5–6, in Emmel, "Shenoute of Atripe," 197. See also below, pp. 250–51.

112 See Frankfurter, "Cult of the Martyrs."

CHAPTER 6

texts and fragments like the Hermetic *Asclepius*, included in one of the Nag Hammadi codices, were presumably in circulation, although it is hard to conceive of their use as authoritative literary models. Thus, rather than following a direct lineage of influence from Egyptian texts, it is more likely that the recollection of the Land of Egypt oracle took place in the scribal or compositional act itself—a memory of traditional formulae intrinsic to the very endeavor of drawing Christian authority over a landscape once *imagined* as holy and distinctive. In other words, the Land of Egypt oracle came to mind as an expressive genre when the scribe sought to articulate Egypt's holiness within a Christian mythic framework.

B. Images of Amente and Its Demons

Earlier we saw the influence of monastic liturgical culture, from hymn structures to biblical references and the names of angels, on the innovations of scribes, who carried these forms into the composition of charms and spells.[113] Above all, these forms brought authority, and therefore efficacy, to the sounds of novel ritual texts. But it was not just angels and hybrid angel names that monastic scribes invoked, for we also find a good number of demonic—or, perhaps better, "peripheral"—beings, sometimes associated with the Devil, but more often with Amente ("the West"), the land of the dead.[114] Most often these peripheral spirits were invoked for purposes like binding or punishing individuals, areas of crisis or conflict resolution that often required an alternative domain of spirits from that proffered by institutional Christianity as we usually imagine it.

Thus we find references in the Coptic texts to beings whose principal powers lie in punishing or even dismembering sinners: Theumatha, who dwells in Gehenna with fiery tongs; Temelouchos as "the one who ... tortures the lawless and the liars and the perjurers"; the six powers of death, "who bring every sickness down upon every person" and remove souls from bodies; Sourochchata, who is associated with dissolving "the sinews and ligaments and joints," presumably in some underworld capacity; "Tartarouchos of Amente, the ringlets of whose hair stretch out over the whole world, whose name is Sisinaei Amin"; and Aknator the Ethiopian, who seems both to lead souls to Amente and to decapitate them.[115]

Why would scribes have invoked such violent, demonic underworld denizens? In fact, as authorities over (or in) Amente, these beings served an ethical function, the maintenance of justice in the cosmos—that is, the just punishment of the wicked. This function is underlined in the spell that invokes Temelouchos:

---

113 This section is based on Frankfurter, "Demon Invocations"; and idem, "Amente Demons and Christian Syncretism."

114 In general, see Frankfurter, "Demon Invocations."

115 Theumatha: ACM 79 = London Hay 10414; Temelouchos: ACM 92 = Berlin 10587; Six Powers of Death: ACM 98 = Cairo bone texts A/B; Sourchchata: ACM 111 = Berlin 8321; Tartarouchos of Amente: ACM 66 = Michigan 1190, recto col. II. 20–21 (cf. ACM 75 = Berlin 8314); Aknator the Ethiopian: ACM 119 = Cairo, Coptic Museum 4959. See chart in Frankfurter, "Demon Invocations," 463–64.

revenge is sought against perjurers in this world by appeal to the being who destroys perjurers in Amente. Amente demons represent a greater justice, if a more dangerous and uncontrollable one. In these ritual spells we see scribes selecting powerful archons by name and activity for their combination of harsh justice, monstrosity, and authority: the very image of vindictive power in one mode, the servant of God in another.

Such references to Amente demons reveal two important aspects of a scribal culture adept at their invocation: first, the demons themselves were understood as participating in a greater order—a greater mythology, we might say—of Egyptian Christian monastic culture; second, the scribes' familiarity with this greater mythology, such that they could invoke it for everyday application, arose not only from literary sources but also from liturgical expressions, much like the ritual texts discussed earlier. Both contexts pertain to the most remarkable feature of this late antique Christian mythology of Amente demons: its resemblance to the mythology of underworld demons from pharaonic Egypt.

1. THE MEDIA OF AMENTE IN LATE ANTIQUE EGYPT

But how were these demons known to scribes? Through what media did they learn how to reference them in ritual contexts? The legacy of the apocalyptic tradition in monastic literature allowed such florid visions of the underworld as this one, which appears as the testimony of a heathen character in the eighth- to tenth-century *Life of Pisentius*:

> There were iron knives in their hands, and iron daggers with pointed ends as sharp as spear points, and they drove these into my sides, and they gnashed their teeth furiously against me.... I saw death suspended in the air in many forms. And straightway the Angels of cruelty snatched my wretched soul from my body, and they ... dragged me to Amenti.... When they had cast me into the outer darkness I saw a great gulf, which was more than a hundred cubits deep, and it was filled with reptiles, and each one of these had seven heads, and all their bodies were covered as it were with scorpions.... And [one] had in its mouth teeth which were like unto pegs of iron. And one laid hold of me and cast me into the mouth of that Worm, which never stopped devouring.[116]

The demons here carry a quite explicit ethical function, terrorizing and attacking the infidel. The Pisentius manuscripts are late, but the text exemplifies the unusually vivid focus of many late antique Coptic texts on the monstrous beings that threaten the soul on its departure from the body.

The image of "demonic" punitive angels was linked to another tradition that Coptic literature develops in its overall mythology of Amente: the demonic per-

---

116 *V. Pisentii*, in Amélineau, *Étude sur le christianisme*, 147–49; Budge, *Coptic Apocrypha*, 329.

sonification of Death itself. This personification appears in an early and elaborate form in the *Testament of Abraham*, a text preserved in multiple Egyptian Christian manuscripts that describes the patriarch's vision of the Last Judgment and then his final encounter with Death himself:[117]

> ... more fierce than all wild beasts and more unclean than all uncleanness. And he showed to Abraham seven fiery dragons' heads and fourteen faces—the face of a blazing fire and great fierceness, and the face of a horrible precipice, and the face of a murky darkness, and the face of a most gloomy viper, and a face more fierce than an asp, and the face of a fearful lion, and the face of a horned serpent and basilisk.[118]

Whatever its origins, the *Testament of Abraham* became the fountainhead of a variety of texts in the Christian tradition that tried to develop the pantheon of beings that preside over the extraction and judgment of souls at death, led especially by Death himself. The abundant manuscripts that address this topic show the popularity of such speculation among monastic scribes in the early centuries of Christianity.[119] In many texts Death becomes both heroic foil and monster, trying to claim souls for himself and occasionally incorporating attributes of the punitive demons or angels that were believed to control hell.[120] By the late fourth century this monstrous Death had become a standard component of Easter liturgies, vanquished annually through the power of liturgical narrative and procession, while the character was also picked up in new, "apocryphal" legends composed for liturgical reading, like the *Story of Joseph the Carpenter* and the *Book of Bartholomew*. While Death could assume in these texts the visible features of the punitive angels,[121] his role in narrative and liturgy differed from that of the Amente demons: rather than acting as an obstructer or destroyer, Death functions as an antagonist to the righteous hero, even (in some Byzantine hymns) assuming the role of a tragic victim.[122] There is an implication in the structure of

---

117 See 16–20, long recension. On the complex manuscript traditions, see Nickelsburg, "Eschatology in the Testament"; Allison, *Testament of Abraham*. Most scholars regard this text as having arisen in first-century (probably Egyptian) Jewish circles, but its development in two recensions in Greek and Coptic manuscripts suggests its importance in the Egyptian Christian monastic milieux under discussion. Note that in biblical tradition, the personification of Death has quite archaic Near Eastern roots (e.g., Jeremiah 9:21) but gains currency through its association with the so-called "harrowing of Hell" story in early Christianity. Cf. also 1 Corinthians 15:55; Acts 2:24.

118 17.13–14, long recension, in Allison, *Testament of Abraham*, 334.

119 A fifth-century protective charm (PGM P13: "apparently buried with a mummy") reveals a local scribal tradition that Death's name is Charon, whom God created "without offspring [ἄσπορος]" and whose "claw" was broken when Christ entered the world. See Mihálykó, "Christ and Charon."

120 See Gounelle, *La descente du Christ*; Frank, "Christ's Descent to the Underworld."

121 *Testament of Abraham* 17.13–15 (long recension), in Allison, *Testament of Abraham*, 333–34; *Story of Joseph the Carpenter* 21.1, in Ehrman and Pleše, *Apocryphal Gospels*, 178–79.

122 See, e.g., PGM P13, above, n. 119. See Frank, "Christ's Descent to the Underworld."

these texts that the oral performance of the liturgy itself bore the power to repel or vanquish Death through the description of his character and downfall.

The mythology of Amente and its demonic beings thus provided monastic and ecclesiastical liturgy with a rich cast of characters to display the efficacy of performance and incantation. For example, the elaborate account of Christ's descent to hell and subsequent enthronement in heaven compiled under the title of *The Book of Bartholomew* (fifth to eighth centuries) consists of dramatic speeches and dialogues between Christ, Death (known as Abbaton), and other inhabitants of Amente. The text culminates in eight angelic hymns, implying a liturgical provenance at least for later editions.[123] It is in this liturgical context also that we are meant to experience lists of demonic names, like the seven sons of Death and the thirty dragons that Christ sets on Judas. Liturgical settings, that is, would have prompted the scribe to elaborate certain details and draw out the efficacy of ritual speech.

We get a more explicit sense of performative context in the *Discourse on Abbaton by Archbishop Timothy* (tenth century CE, probably with earlier forms). One of the most vivid depictions of Amente demonology in Coptic literature, the *Discourse on Abbaton* establishes a feast day in celebration of the enthronement of Abbaton, the Angel of Death, whose teeth project from his mouth a half cubit, whose fingers and toes are like sharp reaping knives, and whose head is crowned with seven more heads, all of which can change shape.[124] This homily functions to sanction "the day wherein [God] established Abbaton, the Angel of Death, and made him to be awful and disturbing, and to pursue all souls until they yield up their spirits, so that we may preach concerning him to all mankind ... and also that when men hear of [him on] the day of his establishment they may be afraid, and may repent, and may give charities and gifts on the day of his commemoration, just as they do to Michael and Gabriel."[125] Working from earlier traditions and texts about this angel, the scribe constructs Abbaton as lord over Amente and as a monstrous judge of sinners in direct relationship to a public festival. A mythology of Amente is not only public in nature but binding collectively: "May God who has deemed us worthy to gather together in this place this day to commemorate Abbaton, the Angel of Death, whom God has made king over us," the text declares.[126] At the same time, the very monstrosity of Abbaton is said to reduce the performance of sin, while in his capacity as an Amente angel he mediates for the community.[127]

---

123 B.M. ms. Or. 6804, in Budge, *Coptic Apocrypha*, 1–47 (text), 179–230 (translation); on whose dating and liturgical characteristics see Bovon, Geoltrain, and Kaestli, *Écrits apocryphes chrétiens*, 1:300–302.

124 *Discourse on Abbaton*, in Budge, *Coptic Martyrdoms*, 227–49.

125 *Discourse on Abbaton* f. 7b-8a, in ibid., 231, 479–80 (translation adjusted).

126 *Discourse on Abbaton* f. 32a, in ibid., 248, 495 (translation adjusted). Mediation by Abbaton on behalf of righteous: see *Discourse on Abbaton* f. 24b-25a, in ibid, 490–91.

127 Two other Egyptian apocryphal texts from about the same period, the *Vision of Macarius*

It can be problematic to retroject textual circumstances of the tenth century into the formative period of Amente demonology in the fourth and fifth centuries. It might be suggested, for example, that these later documents reflect an archaizing tendency among ecclesiastical scribes under Muslim rule, representing a popular Christianity in more regular interaction with church belief systems—an authentically Egyptian Christianity, perhaps.[128] These texts about the underworld, however, reflect few ecclesiastical values or any broader "Egyptian" identity beyond what might have been consolidated in local rites and festivals. In fact, the embeddedness of hagiographical and apocryphal compositions in actual ritual settings has been widely observed throughout late antique Christian literature.[129] In this way the insights provided by these late documents may help add nuance to the performative context of Amente demonology and its texts in earlier times.

The scribal synthesis of an Amente demonology thus did not only take place in monastic settings, in the context of interpretation and literary composition. It also occurred in, or in anticipation of, public ritual settings where these compositions—legends, homilies, visions—would have both established images of Amente for popular reception and encouraged the development of a popular folklore of Amente that certainly cycled back into literary compositions. Scribes affiliated with churches or local monasteries effectively reimagined and rewrote for public performance earlier apocryphal texts depicting Death and "demonic" angels, from Revelation 9 and the *Testament of Abraham* to the elaborate hellscape of the *Apocalypse of Peter*. These liturgical performances involved not just drama but efficacy: the capacity to invoke supernatural powers and protect the community through hymn, command, and the uttering of names. And they extended, in at least one case, to iconography as well. A mural found in a tenth-century church in Tebtunis depicts the chief Amente demons Abbaton, Aftemeluchos, and a "Dekan who chews souls" in the grotesque process of punishing sinners.[130]

2. THE COPTIC AMENTE MYTHOLOGY:
EARLIER EGYPTIAN AND JEWISH APOCALYPTIC TRADITIONS

Egyptologists have long regarded this apparent proclivity on the part of monastic scribes to imagine Amente and its demons as a "survival" of ancient Egyptian af-

---

and the *Vision of Mark of Tarmaqa* (both preserved in Syriac), present the encounter of the departing soul with the angels and torments of Amente as a mythic reflection of the stages of funerary ritual, tracing what the soul encounters and how it benefits from liturgies at the third, seventh, thirtieth, and fortieth days after death. See van Lantschoot, "Révélations de Macaire"; see also Van der Vliet, "Literature, Liturgy, Magic," on the influence of funerary liturgy on other media of Coptic Christianity.

128 Orlandi, "Coptic Literature," 80; cf. Papaconstantinou, "Historiography, Hagiography, and the Making," 78–86.

129 See Rose, *Ritual Memory*; cf. Knust and Wasserman, "Biblical Odes."

130 Walters, "Christian Paintings from Tebtunis," 200–204.

terlife mythology.[131] Whether inscribed on tomb walls or copied out in mortuary texts like the *Book of the Dead*, the ancient Egyptian tradition did indeed imagine a series of gates through which the postmortem soul must safely pass; the animal-headed monsters that will threaten the soul's dismemberment and dissolution at each gate; and the passwords or spells the soul must utter at each gate so "he will not be driven off or turned away at the portals of the *Duat*. . . . He will be permitted to arrive at every gate according to what is written," and—in the words of a mortuary text written in the early Roman period—he will "not be handed over to the blades of the slaughtering demons at the execution of the damned through the words of any accuser."[132]

Here is certainly an elaborate tradition of postmortem dangers, monsters, and threats to the soul as it travels to the next world—a tradition that remains well attested into the Roman period. But the more one looks at the means of transmission and the ideologies of the texts involved, the less plausible a general continuity of ideas appears. For example, whereas the Coptic texts construct a rather polarized world—Christ or saint *versus* Death, Amente demon *versus* heathen or sinner—the Egyptian texts imagine the soul's passage through gates and monsters as occurring primarily through a knowledge of codes, that is, through the efficacy of the mortuary book and its spells.[133]

This "non-ethical" sense of otherworldly demons emerges most clearly in those hybrid texts in Greek and Coptic that lie closest to the Egyptian mortuary books in mythology, form, and historical period. The so-called *Mithras Liturgy*, from a third-century CE Egyptian ritual manual, notes the approach of asp- and bull-headed gods at different points in its ascending sequence of visions and instructions, but these are hardly demonic beings.[134] As in many Egyptian mortuary texts, they function not so much to hinder as to welcome the visionary into the divine world.[135] The two *Books of Jeu* (from about the same period), on the other hand, are intentionally Christian, framed as the revelations of Christ to his

---

131 See, e.g., Budge, *Coptic Apocrypha*, lxi–lxxii; Burmester, "Egyptian Mythology," 364–67; John Coleman Darnell, *Enigmatic Netherworld Books*.

132 *Book of the Dead*, ch. 144, in Faulkner, *Egyptian Book of the Dead*, 121; *Book of Glorifying the Spirit* (P. Sekowski, cols. 1–2), in Smith, *Traversing Eternity*, 460. On the Egyptian tradition of Amente demons, see Lucarelli, "Guardian-Demons"; idem, "Demonology During the Late Pharaonic"; and Spieser, "Avaleuses et dévoreuses."

133 See also the *History of Joseph the Carpenter* 21–28 and the *Discourse on Abbaton*, esp. fol. 5a, 7b-8a (harassing souls to give up spirits), and 22a (monstrous appearance), in Budge, *Coptic Martyrdoms*; Piankoff, "La descente aux enfers"; Zandee, *Death as an Enemy*, 328–41; Faulkner, *Egyptian Book of the Dead*, 121. Thus a "bad" person could be effectively presented as "good" through the spells of the *Book of the Dead*. In contrast, the punitive angels of the Jewish/Christian hell tradition *preside over* punishments; no barriers at all restrict the souls' entrance to their destined locations, and they simply land in each place, to receive their due rewards or punishments.

134 PGM IV.663–93.

135 See, e.g., *Book of Traversing Eternity*, in Smith, *Traversing Eternity*, 407; and *Book of Transformations*, in ibid., 648.

CHAPTER 6

disciples.¹³⁶ Like the earlier Egyptian mortuary texts, these two compositions were meant as guides or passports for the soul's ascent, enumerating the gates to be penetrated by the ascending soul, the guardians of each gate, and the "seals" and "characters" required to appease these guardians. The supernatural opponents to the soul's progression through these gates serve primarily not to eliminate sinners but to guard the purity of the heavenly world. The process of passing the gates and their guardians according to the instructions of the *Books of Jeu* highlights the very efficacy of the instructions—the teachings of the risen Christ—and the mysterious symbols that they involve.¹³⁷

These latter, hybrid texts are important historically for the sense they provide of how the archaic Egyptian afterlife passage traditions were mediated in Greek and Christian environments. Clearly the pictures these texts give of supernatural gates, guardians, and obstructors differs considerably from the elaborate Amente mythology of Coptic literary and liturgical materials, which emphasized the horrors of hell for sinners. But the *Mithras Liturgy* and the *Books of Jeu* also point to another textual/ritual tradition in operation that is similar to the Egyptian mortuary "books of Gates" but came together in Jewish milieux: a literature of ascent through a series of monstrous "toll collector" angels. A second-century *Apocalypse of Paul* in the Nag Hammadi library describes the apostle's ascent past "toll-collectors" of each heaven, who judge the worthiness of each passing soul, and in an *Apocalypse of James* from Nag Hammadi, Jesus provides the coded responses that his hearer must say to the "obstructers" by whom he seeks to pass.¹³⁸ The ethics of the obstructive archons, that is, lie between opposing the wise and prohibiting the invasion of the impure.¹³⁹ The texts promise the successful ascent of the saints at the same time as the punishment of the arrogant pretenders. The *Apocalypse of Elijah*, discussed earlier as an example of the Land of Egypt oracle, promises that God "will write [his] name upon their foreheads and seal their right hands" so that neither "the Lawless One will have power over them, nor will the Thrones hinder them, but they will go with the angels to my city. *But as for those who sin*, they will not pass by the Thrones, but the Thrones of death will seize them and exert power over them."¹⁴⁰ This notion of ascending past demonic op-

---

136 Schmidt and MacDermott, *Books of Jeu*.

137 See Van den Kerchove, "Le livre du grand traité."

138 *Apocalypse of Paul* = Nag Hammadi Corpus V, 2; *Apocalypse of James* = Nag Hammadi Corpus V, 3. On the diverse traditions informing this scene, see Pesthy, "Earthly Tribunal."

139 See esp. Himmelfarb, "Heavenly Ascent." There are also mortuary ascent traditions from well beyond Egypt: see, e.g., Irenaeus of Lyons, *c. Haer.* 1.21.5; and the *Acts of John* 114–15, in which the apostle John "seals himself in every part" in anticipation of death, calling on the "angels [to] be put to shame and demons be afraid; let the rulers be shattered and the powers fall; let the places on the right hand stand fast and those on the left be removed; let the devil be silenced, let Satan be derided.... And grant me to finish my way to [Christ] preserved from violence and insult"; *Acts of John* 114–15, in Schneemelcher, *New Testament Apocrypha*, 2:204.

140 *Apocalypse of Elijah* 1.9–11, in Frankfurter, *Elijah in Upper Egypt*, 303. Cf. Athanasius, *v.Ant.* 65, 22. In general see Frankfurter, *Elijah in Upper Egypt*, 35–37.

ponents in the subheavenly realms by virtue of one's magical "seals"—provided by God or in some type of manual—recalls the contents of the hybrid *Books of Jeu*, but it derives from Jewish traditions, in which the seal serves as a protective insignia in the endtimes.[141]

As for the details of Amente itself as an underworld of monstrous beings that flay and torture those they catch, these too most likely derive from Jewish and Christian apocalyptic traditions, in which the "order" of the land of just punishment serves as an extension of God's perfect (if secret) cosmos, and in which the agents of divine punishment correspond to his archangels. The range of manuscripts that attest to this tradition and its influence in early and late antique Christian Egyptian milieux is extensive: the Book of Revelation, the *Testament of Abraham*, the *Book of the Secrets of Enoch* (*2 Enoch*), the *Apocalypse of Peter*, and the *Apocalypse of Zephaniah*. In the *Apocalypse of Peter*, for example,

> The children [who were exposed or aborted] shall be given to the angel Temlakos. And those who slew them will be tortured for ever, for God wills it to be so. Ezrael, the angel of wrath, brings men and women with the half of their bodies burning and casts them into a place of darkness, the hell of men; and a spirit of wrath chastises them with all manner of chastisement, and a worm that never sleeps consumes their entrails.... And near to those who live thus were other men and women who chew their tongues, and they are tormented with red hot irons and have their eyes burned.[142]

This text was so widely read and influential as to have inspired a subsequent Egyptian monk (in the late fourth or early fifth century) to compose an even more extensive geography of heaven and hell in the *Apocalypse of Paul*.[143] But the earlier texts, most of which hover between "Christian" and "Jewish" orientations, excel in their depiction of the monstrous punishing angels that dwell in the underworld. One reads in Revelation of human-headed, iron-scaled, giant stinging locusts under the angel Abaddon and in *2 Enoch* of the Guardians of Hell, "their faces like those of very large snakes, their eyes like extinguished lamps, and their teeth naked down to their breasts." The *Apocalypse of Zephaniah* reveals the Accuser of Hades: "His hair was spread out like the lionesses'. His teeth were outside his mouth like a bear. His hair was spread out like women's. His body was like the serpent's when he wished to swallow me."[144] As horrific as they are described to

---

141 Revelation 7:3–4; 14:1; 22:4. Cf. *Pistis Sophia* 86, 98, 112–15, 138–44, in Schmidt and MacDermot, *Pistis Sophia*.

142 *Apocalypse of Peter* 8–9, in Schneemelcher, *New Testament Apocrypha*, 2:630–31.

143 On the influence of the *Apocalypse of Peter*, see Jakab, "Reception of the Apocalypse." On its use in the *Apocalypse of Paul*, see Schneemelcher, *New Testament Apocrypha*, 2:713–15; Bauckham, *Fate of the Dead*, 92–93; and Himmelfarb, *Tours of Hell*, 140–47. On the relationship of the *Apocalypse of Paul* to Egyptian monasticism, see Copeland, "Mapping the 'Apocalypse of Paul.'"

144 Revelation 9; *2 Enoch* 42 [ms. A], in Charlesworth, *Old Testament Pseudepigrapha*, 1:167; *Apocalypse of Zephaniah* 6.8, in ibid., 1:512. Darnell notes some filiations between the *Apocalypse of*

be, these punishers are identified as *angels* and as serving at the direction of God and the archangels to punish the sinful and none else.[145] That is, as we saw with the Amente demons of Coptic literature, they served an ethical function in an ordered cosmos.

It seems clear that the basic literary resources that late antique monastic scribes used to imagine Amente, its demonic tormenters, and the journey of the soul consisted of these early (first to second century CE) apocalyptic texts. And yet we must allow some influence from "Egyptian tradition," broadly defined, whether in the Amente demons' threats to the innocent soul, the particular details of dismemberment or dissolution, or the elevation of the Amente demons to ritual importance. The question is how to situate this influence within the normal compositional activities of monastic scribes in the fifth and sixth centuries. That is, if Christian monks could not read ancient Egyptian mortuary texts but were habitually reading biblical and apocalyptic texts, through what practices would they have recalled the earlier traditions?[146]

3. APOCALYPTIC INTERPRETATION IN EGYPT AND THE INTEGRATION OF EGYPTIAN TRADITIONS

Monastic scribes' various engagements with apocalyptic texts—reading, interpreting, expanding, composing—were themselves a synthetic dimension of Christianization, an assimilation of text and lore into culture, and scribes were *agents* in this process no less than they were in relation to magical texts, ticket oracles, and Land of Egypt oracles. The syncretism involved in scribes' developments of Amente demons was a fundamentally *interpretive* process. Scribes drew out the implications, powers, and images of the underworld angels of apocalyptic literature, but in such a way as *to invite the recollection of* indigenous traditions of Amente demons.

Abbot Shenoute provides an example of this "exegetical" synthesis of Amente demons. "I have said many times," he argues in one of a number of sermons on the topic of hell, that "if the place did not exist [in which] the Lord God will give

---

Zephaniah (incorrectly labeled the "Apocalypse of Elijah") and Egyptian cosmographical tradition in *Enigmatic Netherworld Books*, 125.

145 So, e.g., the mid-fourth-century *Confession of Cyprian of Antioch*, in which the character Cyprian, in Memphis during his sorcery stage, encounters the diverse forms of demons, dragons, and "Rulers of Darkness," including the monstrous forms of *hatred* ("blind, having four eyes in the back of its skull that always shunned the light and many feet which hung directly from its head"), *wickedness* ("thin, many-eyed, having arrows in the place of its pupils"), and *hooked-nose* ("having its entire body sharp like a sickle and the pupils of its eyes sunk together in abandonment"); *Confession of Cyprian of Antioch* 4, in Bailey, "Confession of Cyprian of Antioch," 40–43. The images of monstrous demonic afflictors here resemble those of the (roughly contemporaneous) *Testament of Solomon*, but the Cyprian text deliberately places them in an Egyptian underworld.

146 Cf. Nickelsburg, "Eschatology in the Testament," 31–40, on strained attempts to derive the Egyptian-sounding judgment scenes in the *Testament of Abraham* from Egyptian texts.

retribution to those who do these [sinful] things, the fallen would not [still] be kept in the cities, in the roads, in the streets, ... *pierced and slaughtered by the hidden powers who bear these axes*, just like those whom the prophet (Ezekiel) saw."[147] In the guise of invoking Ezekiel's vision (in chapter 9) of horrific angels of slaughter, Shenoute thus conjures a "place [where] God will give retribution" to sinners and where "hidden powers who bear ... axes" will slaughter the sinful. The abbot superimposes the eschatological scenario onto Ezekiel's vision, giving to the punishers of the underworld all the powers once attributed to Amente demons to dismember and dissolve (while still counting as angels of God). Thus even in public discourse the lore of Amente gathered biblical and "para-biblical" support and inspiration. Developing an image of the demonic tormenters was not so much an "Egyptianizing" process as a "revealing"—an apocalyptic—process, one that expanded on the biblical text or, more often, an apocryphal legend according to long-standing scribal traditions of Egyptian monasteries. Thus traditions of Amente—its structure and its denizens—from earlier Egyptian iconography and mortuary texts might be recollected as part of scribes' interpretations of scripture and related to the conceptualization of a Christian Amente.

Deriving the lore and mythology of Amente from ancient Egyptian mortuary tradition has long consumed scholars, but the very abstractness of the images, ideas, and structures that are claimed to have "survived" distorts any nuanced discussion of acculturation and syncretism and begs for grounding in some creative activity, as have all the materials approached in this book.[148] In this case, during the early Christian centuries in Egypt, the internal literary preoccupations of the scribes who developed the Amente mythology revolved not around "survivals" but rather around apocalyptic literature and the authority of books or holy men to reveal cosmic secrets. These preoccupations drove the perpetual copying and re-editing of apocalyptic materials (like Ezekiel or Enoch) and legends of holy men both biblical and monastic that revealed the esoteric realities (and divine justice) of the mortuary process.[149] And they also drove the composition of ritual spells as an extension of apocalyptic authority. Interpretation, copying, composition, and textual innovation thus served as intrinsically syncretistic practices, for they invited the recollection of ideas and images that followed sensibly from the materials while striking the modern scholar with the impression of continuity.

More important than isolating "pagan survivals," then, is the recognition that, for Egyptian monastic scribes, ritual experts, and their clients, (a) there existed a class of monstrous, bloodthirsty spirits belonging functionally *and topographically* to the periphery; (b) this realm—Amente—had a system of roles and hierarchy;

---

147 Shenoute, *I Have Been Reading the Holy Gospels* 12, 17, in Moussa, "I Have Been Reading," 138 (emended), 35 (text); cf. 145–46, 49 (text).

148 Cf. Behlmer, "Ancient Egyptian Survivals."

149 Cf. Zandee, *Death as an Enemy*; and Baumeister, *Martyr invictus*, 80–83.

(c) this realm, esoterically revealed, contributed to cosmic order; and (d) by his knowledge of the names and features of these beings, the ritual expert could call upon them and direct them to concerns in this world (often of a disruptive or personal justice type). By always grounding the Amente mythology in ritual applications (including liturgical and graphic expressions), Christian ritual experts were able to maintain this class of spirits from earlier Egyptian tradition and to keep them familiar, transforming them into a resource for ritual invocation.

VI. CONCLUSION

This chapter has tackled that anonymous world of authors and editors who were responsible for some of our most arresting examples of Egyptian tradition as it was preserved, reframed, or reimagined to situate Christianity. I have presented these figures as agents of the mediation of Christianity, operating between literate worlds of Christian ritual expertise and a semiliterate world of lay villagers and pilgrims—participants in shrines, festivals, church liturgies, and other public forms of Christianity. These villagers and pilgrims had come to regard the literate experts—monks, ecclesiastical or shrine scribes—as agents of a Great Tradition, to use Robert Redfield's term for an authoritative institution of books, liturgies, and powerful images and sounds, as well as the capacity to articulate that institution in the realm of ritual expertise.[150]

I have focused my discussion of this scribal mediation on monks, largely because those magical and apocryphal texts that have been provenanced come from monastic settings. I would also observe that the sheer diversity of monastic worlds in Egypt, their regular engagement with the laity through material "blessings" and liturgical performance, and their culture of angelological, demonological, and scriptural speculation all make the innovation, editing, and purveying of magical texts historically comprehensible. At the same time, the ticket oracles and *Sortes* books point to the presence of literate experts at saints' shrines, and the deep familiarity of some magical texts with liturgical traditions point to church clergy as likely authors, an argument supported by Shenoute's complaint that folk in his vicinity "anoint themselves with oil from elders of the church" as well as that from monks.[151]

Another, less institutionally grounded model for scribal expertise that has gained some scholarly interest is the literate figure who composed and exchanged charms, spells, and other innovations within Christian tradition as simply one who could write, had access to texts, and pursued certain esoteric predilections. A mid-fourth-century letter that includes a curse spell invoking "the One sitting

---

150 Redfield, *Peasant Society and Culture*. On the relevance of the Redfield model, see Frankfurter, "The Great, the Little."

151 See Kropp, *Ausgewählte koptische Zaubertexte*, 3:183–96, 229–33. On the evidence of *Sortes* books, see Klingshirn, "Inventing the Sortilegus"; and Luijendijk, *Forbidden Oracles?*, 65–69.

above the Cherubim and Seraphim" (and whose author states his intention to send another such spell, "should I find it"!) reveals a literate world of Manichaeans who may have exchanged such materials in a friendly way, without the distribution of personal or institutional charisma that accompanied the monastic materials.[152] And yet even with this document there is a shared sense of the authority of Manichaean prayer-language—the implication of religious community—as the basis for the spell.

A more general world of Egyptian *literati*, rather than monks, has also been proposed as the scribal context of the early fifth-century Nag Hammadi Library: "a kind of Egypt-wide network (more or less informal) of educated, primarily Greek-speaking ... philosophically and esoteric-mystically like-minded people, for whom *Egypt* represented (even if only somewhat vaguely) a tradition of wisdom and knowledge to be revered and perpetuated."[153] This scribal context would not have involved personal or institutional charisma or its transmission through manuscripts or magical compositions, although the context does presume the use of a far more eclectic range of books than the biblical, apocryphal, and occasionally folkloric materials that the authors of magical texts mediate in their spells. In these ways this model does not seem pertinent to the materials or dynamics of mediation addressed in this chapter. Even the Land of Egypt oracle and Amente demonology flourished first and foremost in monastic settings, not in this urbane world of esoteric Egyptianism. Thus, for the purposes of locating social contexts of scribality in which Christian traditions were constructed and mediated to pilgrims, villagers, and other non- or semiliterate laity, we do best with models that can embrace the local diversity of monastic scribes and shrine or ecclesiastical scribes.[154]

Scribes operated in a range of physical sites. At pilgrimage shrines they provided textual media and propaganda for the elaboration of a saint's authority and the book-based rituals for conjuring his presence. In monasteries and *lauras* they read, interpreted, and composed a great range of texts, from apocrypha to liturgy, and transmitted the potent features of such texts in charms and spells. In an itinerant capacity, such as we might infer from the activities of the modern Ethiopian exorcist-cantor, the *däbtära*, scribes brought a self-professed (and probably group-cultivated) ritual expertise into the village—into the domestic sphere itself. In all these social milieux we can see evidence of scribal creativity and engagement with Christian literary traditions, but also an independence, even idiosyncrasy, in the treatment of those traditions.[155]

---

152 P. Kell. copt. 35, in Mirecki, Gardner, and Alcock, "Magical Spell, Manichaean Letter."
153 Emmel, "Coptic Gnostic Texts," 48; see also Denzey Lewis and Blount, "Rethinking the Origins."
154 On the diversity of scribes, especially monastic scribes, see Lundhaug and Jenott, *Monastic Origins*.
155 Cf. Dijkstra, *Philae and the End*, 75–77, on ecclesiastical scribes' independent roles as legal signatories in fifth-century Syene/Elephantine.

CHAPTER 6

What were these literary traditions? What can we say was the "culture" of the Christian scribe in late antique Egypt? Library lists, manuscript remains, and papyri make clear the literature they read and exchanged as resources hardly ended with biblical texts, writings of the church fathers, and other institutionally canonical materials. Rather, we see tendencies toward (a) apocryphal works, some edited from earlier Jewish versions, others composed by monks *de novo*; (b) miraculous legends of holy men and martyrs; (c) apocalyptic visions and prophecies; and (d) liturgical and other public ceremonial works and their creative extensions for private ritual. This range of literature constituted the inner culture of monastic scribes, serving as the source of monastic visions, folklore, and mythic preoccupations with angels and demons. Monasticism itself—asceticism, the pursuit of holiness, intimacy with the angelic realm—lent a potential charisma to this scribal culture that enhanced the broader status of many monastic scribes and brought pilgrims to the places where they read and wrote. Renunciation, asceticism, and holy men provided sources of power that could be transmitted through scribal means such as letters and amulets, going beyond the material blessings of oil and sand. Monastic liturgies that laity witnessed or the legends they were told could be condensed in amulets and charms.

By definition, syncretism would embrace the whole creative process of mediation by which scribes conveyed the practices, ideas, and lore of the monastic and shrine worlds for active use and recombination in the everyday world of the laity. But a number of texts from the fifth and later centuries convey ancient Egyptian traditions that had been otherwise lost, at least from Christian institutional culture: ticket oracles at saints' shrines, songs about Egyptian gods in magical texts, the ancient literary form of the Land of Egypt oracle, and a preoccupation in many texts with the demons of the underworld and the transition of the postmortem soul. Are these apparent "survivals" in Christian literature a *particular* kind of syncretism, or a greater degree of it? Are they, in fact, "survivals"?

It fact, it is only the modern Egyptologist or historian who recognizes the peculiar "Egyptianness" of these materials and tries to disentangle them from their contexts to stand alone as "survivals," for the texts themselves show no awareness of engaging non-Christian or repudiated religious traditions, nor is there evidence of others'—reformers'—censure of these kinds of interests or texts. They appear entirely in the context of *Christian* writing and practice, even when the texts were intended to serve quotidian ritual purposes, as the magical texts were. Thus it is not really correct to call them either "survivals" or "Egyptianizing" texts, for their scribes composed them as extensions of liturgy or apocalyptic vision, or collected them as forms of verbal power equivalent to liturgy, or—in the case of the ticket oracles or the *Sortes* manual—used them to advance the laity's orthodoxy. We must be careful about isolating material as somehow "more Egyptian," as "survivals," when there is no evidence that the scribe himself thought he was moving into an archaizing or heathen mode of composition.

And yet the evidence of the ticket oracles tells us that the historian's diachronic perspective on such materials has value—that it does matter that *we* can recognize earlier traditions that have been revitalized or recombined. Indeed, there may be ways that we can understand scribes' agency in shifting to forms or genres or images that we can recognize as traditional—as *not* simply continuing along the same Christian compositional channels but engaging recollections of earlier literary traditions through the act of writing itself. In drawing out the nature of Amente for exegesis or liturgy, the scribe would have gained access to a memory that was not of the cognitive sort ("I remember . . .") nor the kind of gestural habitus described in chapters 2 and 4, but more like that of the craftsman: a recollection that pertained to how one ought to express one's craft in a particular medium.[156] As we saw in chapter 5, the eighth-century stonecarver of the Dumbarton Oaks frieze with the cross and antelopes sought to frame the exorcistic power of the cross by means of the popular motif of antelopes, but in this case he brought into play an archaic Egyptian strategy of efficacious juxtaposition, in which antelopes represented the chaos subordinated by their conqueror. The result was a fundamentally Christian form of apotropaic design whose closest iconographic analogue was the archaic Horus *cippus*, even if the image, concept, or memory of those *cippi* were the furthest thing from the carver's mind.[157] Much in the same vein, scribes engaged archaic literary strategies, genres, and images in the process of writing on certain themes. The recollection followed from the scribal or performative circumstances: funerary liturgy, apocalypse, exegesis of a biblical passage, or the use of text to mediate a saint's authority at a shrine. The adherence to structure or form may be clearer in the cases of the Land of Egypt oracle or the ticket oracle, but these cases merely demonstrate the natural tenacity of textual traditions and forms within scribal culture. The same model ought also be applied to frame the curiously rich speculation on Amente, its demons, and their capability to be conjured.

What then of the cases of the magical texts invoking Isis, Horus, Amun, and Nephthys centuries after their last cults had disappeared? Again, we have no evidence that these texts were collected or composed as subversive or heathen departures from a putative mainstream Christianity. Quite to the contrary, these texts are all interwoven with biblical, apocryphal, and other features of monastic Christian culture, and they were written in Coptic, the language of the monastery. I have proposed that these invocations of the old Egyptian gods were in fact *songs* that remained in circulation and performance in their everyday folk-worlds—used for quieting babies through lullaby, for blessing cattle, and so on—remaining in culture not only because they were traditional songs but also because they were means of verbal efficacy: songs as performative vehicles of power. Presum-

---

156 Cf. Connerton, *How Societies Remember*, 22–23, on cognitive vs. habit-based memories.
157 Cf. Frankfurter, "Binding of Antelopes."

ably these songs were imagined as aurally efficacious along the lines of Christian liturgy itself, which was likewise improvised and reimagined for charms and spells. Our literate agents, the scribes, did not simply transcribe the songs but, in the case of the Isis/Horus songs (or what had once been songs), revised and redirected their efficacy for erotic charms, to relieve intestinal pain, and for other purposes, much as liturgy might be redirected to various ends.

In all these practices and creative activities we see scribes standing *between* the monastic and ecclesiastical worlds, the worlds of villages and those of pilgrims; between the diverse media of folk blessing and ceremonial liturgy; between apocryphal legend and amulet; between an institutional Christianity of "One God" and the diverse traditions of monastic and lay Christianity, ever in formation, flux, and experimentation.

CHAPTER 7

Whispering Spirits, Holy Processions

TRADITIONS OF THE EGYPTIAN LANDSCAPE

1. INTRODUCTION: RELIGIOUS LANDSCAPE AND CHRISTIANIZATION

In the middle of the great south wall of the temple of the goddess Hathor at Denderah, there is an enormous relief of the goddess's head in typical frontal pose, which served as the principal shrine for ordinary, nonpriestly Egyptians in the vicinity from the beginning of the Roman period. Inaccessibly high off the ground and gilded to stand out from the other reliefs on the south wall, this face of Hathor offered laypeople magical access to a far more mysterious object stowed just on the other side of the wall, in the temple's innermost crypt: an ancient statue of Hathor in gilded wood—something that probably remained always within the temple's pure walls. The giant Hathor head, perhaps covered with a curtain or door, served as the main portal to her image, her physical embodiment, for all personal and festival appeals. And all along the lower wall people gouged out sand for healing and protection.[1]

This monumental public shrine to Hathor provides a useful overture to the transformation of Egypt's religious landscape in late antiquity because of what happened to it in the fifth or sixth century, perhaps about the time a large church was built in the temple precinct.[2] For, at some point in those years, the face of Hathor was hacked to the point of virtual unrecognizability. This was no pilgrims' zeal, gradually gouging out more and more sand for devotional purposes, since the mutilation of the Hathor head required ladders and scaffolding to reach. There is no explanation for the vehemence of destruction but that the image was still potent, active—"hot"—centuries after the temple cult itself had dwindled and the holy statue within had been hidden or stolen or burned. Indeed, for those engaged in such mutilation, the Hathor shrine was not the only image still brimming with demonic power: Hathor's face was knocked off some column capitals, while on others the smaller images of the popular god Bes were also meticulously

---

1 Daumas, *Dendara et le temple d'Hathor*, 70–71; Cauville, *Le temple de Dendera*, 51–52; Traunecker, "Manifestations de piété personelle"; idem, "Une pratique magique."

2 Date of south wall of Hathor temple: see Arnold, *Temples of the Last Pharaohs*, 221, 255–57. Erection of basilica: Grossmann, "Dandarah."

chipped away. As one wanders through the remains of temple precincts like Denderah one can see clearly which divine images in Christian times were regarded as defunct, neutral spolia and which remained potent—for local villagers, certainly, but even more for monks and bishops sensitive to the pervasive assaults of the Devil.[3]

Between the mutilation of the images and the building of the church, then, the Denderah precinct offers a microcosm of the transformation of the religious landscape that took place in Egypt between the legalization of the Christian institution in 323 CE and the establishment of Islam in the late seventh century. For one thing, the methodical iconoclasm and the devotional gouging of sand both responded to some sense of potency in the images, whether from specific spirits or a traditional, local sense of numinous presence. But how could sections of a vacant temple remain potent long after its abandonment? For another, the placement of the church neatly alongside the Hathor temple—rather than within, across, or well away from—illustrates one of the more challenging phenomena of late antiquity: the deliberate overlaying or juxtaposition of ritual structures. What did it mean to build a church within a temple precinct, or *inside* a temple, or on *top* of a *demolished* temple? And most importantly, how should we understand the Christianity that oriented itself by and through these structures?

Such remarkable juxtapositions of church and temple at Denderah, Karnak, Philae, Medinet Habu, and beyond Egypt, coupled with dramatic legends of temple conversions in the lives of various saints, for many years led scholars to presume two different scenarios in the so-called conversion of the Roman Empire. On the one hand, Christianization is said to have involved an intrinsically violent impulse that played itself out in iconoclastic acts across the countrysides of Egypt, Asia Minor, Gaul, and beyond, erasing all functional vestiges of the prior "heathen" order.[4] This is what we might call the "palimpsest" perspective, using the word for the erasure of a manuscript page in order to reuse its space. On the other hand, Christianization is said to have involved an intrinsically weak claim to hearts and minds that required a compensatory violence in the *appropriation* of prior sacred places, replicating the ancient sacred landscape under a new Christian veneer—what we might call the "sacred continuity" scenario.[5]

In the past few decades these two scenarios have been complicated by closer attention to the archaeology of the Christian buildings, the literary character of

---

3 These paragraphs were previously published in Frankfurter, "Vitality of Egyptian Images," here 659, 662. For further work on iconoclasm at Denderah, see Sauer, *Archaeology of Religious Hatred*, 89–101; Kristensen, *Making and Breaking the Gods*, 151–58; and Wong, "Raze of Glory." On late antique iconoclasm in general, see Saradi-Mendelovici, "Christian Attitudes Toward Pagan Monuments"; Jacobs, "Production to Destruction?"

4 See esp. Sauer, *Archaeology of Religious Hatred*. I endorsed this view in the last chapter of *Religion in Roman Egypt*, 277–83, before a spate of archaeological and historical studies suggested different scenarios of the Christianization of the landscape: see, e.g., Caseau, "ΠΟΛΕΜΕΙΝ ΑΙ-ΘΟΙΣ"; Hahn, Emmel, and Gotter, *From Temple to Church*; and Dijkstra, *Philae and the End*.

5 See, e.g., Rassart-Debergh, "Sacralité continue ou exorcisme."

the hagiographical sources—the saints' lives—and the tremendous regional variation in what was appropriated, what demolished, and where churches were built and when. Christianization certainly involved violence, demolition, and iconoclasm, especially under the reigns of the Emperor Theodosius and Bishop Theophilus, and certainly in the region of the notorious Abbot Shenoute of Atripe. But to what extent we can generalize about Christianization *and* violence has become much more fraught.[6]

Clearly the sources that allege violent rampages by monks come from long after the events they narrate and have demonstrable interests in imagining dualistic conflict, both to sharpen what was historically a far more ambiguous process of Christianization and to render a landscape of long-dilapidated temples a record of the triumphs of local saints.[7] But there are literary sources of greater fantasy and literary sources of greater verisimilitude,[8] and much depends on the predisposition of the modern historian to throw up his hands in frustration at patently invented stories or to persevere critically and comparatively in the task of modeling scenarios of Christianizing behavior in the vicinity of certain monasteries or holy men, or under the reigns of certain emperors or bishops.[9] In the latter sense it's less helpful to speak of "violence" in the abstract anyway than to discuss modes of purposeful behavior that responded destructively to things and places in the landscape: images, monuments, and landscape features, for example.[10] Some acts may have been devotional, some enthusiastic; some fearful and apotropaic; some hostile; some, at the rare extreme, destructive in the totalist way historians associate with conquests and millennialist movements; and some just "neutral"—although, as I will explain, the modern urban sense of neutral, meaningless zones and spaces really shouldn't be applied to antiquity or premodern societies. The point, then, is not to look for "Christian attitudes to heathen sites" or the interruption of continuing reverence to temples, or other such dynamics that overgeneralize what temples or images meant, but rather to examine a range of constructive, "agentive" responses to the landscape and its structures that helped Christianity to take shape there. If in prior chapters of this book I have tried to isolate individual social sites with their particular agents to see how Christianity took shape through their creative work, here I am interested in responses that involved a range of agents.

6 See in general Saradi-Mendelovici, "Christian Attitudes Toward Pagan Monuments"; Caseau, "ΠΟΛΕΜΕΙΝ ΛΙΘΟΙΣ"; Emmel, "Shenoute of Atripe"; Jacobs, "Production to Destruction?"; Watts, *Riot in Alexandria*; Shaw, *Sacred Violence*; Kristensen, *Making and Breaking the Gods*.

7 See Gaddis, *There Is No Crime*; Van der Vliet, "Bringing Home the Homeless"; Dijkstra, *Philae and the End*, 221–333; and Busine, "From Stones to Myth."

8 Frankfurter, "Hagiography and the Reconstruction."

9 Among more critically modelled scenarios of violence, see Frankfurter, " 'Things Unbefitting Christians' "; Caseau, "ΠΟΛΕΜΕΙΝ ΛΙΘΟΙΣ"; Watts, *Riot in Alexandria*; Hahn, "Public Rituals of Depaganization."

10 See esp. Stewart, *Statues in Roman Society*, 261–99; Kristensen, *Making and Breaking the Gods*.

CHAPTER 7

At the very least, a new religious landscape took shape over the fourth century in Egypt through the establishment of churches, monasteries, and saints' shrines—all visible and influential edifices. But what do we mean by "landscape" in the way that people used it and moved through it? Egypt had a particular, symbolically loaded topography that had long influenced social and religious experience: a radical contrast between the arable zone around the Nile and the desert, which provided an accessible zone for burial and commemoration; the river itself, which involved not only miraculously changing annual floods but the need to cross it or sail up or down it for social, political, and mercantile reasons; and marshlands that, while symbolically liminal, were associated with the arable zones, not the desert, and traditionally resisted the elite monumentalism of the near-desert areas.[11] Each of these zones and their symbolic associations continued to impact the lore of late antique Christianity, from the image of bandits dwelling in the marshlands to the tales of holy men crossing the Nile or martyrs disembarking along its banks to be further disemboweled. In addition, the late antique landscape included (as in prior times) ruined, abandoned, and repurposed structures, many of which had images of gods on them. In this sense the closing or dwindling of one temple or another would not itself have had the devastating cultural impact that some have imagined would have followed the enforcement of edicts in the later fourth century. The question is, rather, how local peoples would have engaged the ruin as a feature or facility of the local landscape.

Thus, at the most basic level, the consideration of landscape assumes that communities have a deep, traditional sense of the topography around them and beyond them, and furthermore that this sense of topography involves the ordering of values according to various zones, a spatialization of cultural propriety and difference. Landscapes, as Maurice Halbwachs famously outlined, also invite and maintain collective memory: one remembers things said and legends enacted through walking, seeing, and encountering particular landforms and spaces.[12] In the case of the ruined temple, for example, collective memory might have recalled the local saint's heroic purging of heathen priests or the ebullience of a fertility procession for the god Min—or both at different times, among different people. And intertwined with collective memory are the gestures, bodily dispositions, and habitus that real places demand from people and that maintain memories in embodied, socially shared form. To dwell in a landscape (or, for that matter, a cityscape) thus involves and also shapes habitus.[13] Finally, as I will discuss further, landscapes inevitably involve spirits, marginal beings, whose encounters, gracious acts, or assaults become stories that articulate local values, the nature of topographical zones, and a larger cultural sense of intimacy with the landscape.

11 I draw these observations from Baines, *High Culture and Experience*, 30–47.
12 Halbwachs, *On Collective Memory*.
13 Bourdieu, *Outline of a Theory of Practice*, esp. 81–83; Connerton, *How Societies Remember*.

By this model a landscape is not "converted" but, rather, *built (or performed) differently*, with different processions conducted through it, new holy sites identified as worthy of visiting, and some new calendrical details established—none of which replaces the older topography and its customs, but all of which invite local peoples to select and engage with them according to social exigency.[14] The dilapidation of a temple, the erection of a church or saint's shrine, or the legal proscription of traditional rites do not add up to a "Christian landscape" so much as signify the various *contexts* within which people constructed or perceived Christianity in their immediate worlds. These spatial contexts, as well as the social forces that lay behind them (like monastic orders and charismatic abbots) were hardly definitive in establishing Christianity or eliminating prior religious traditions, for they were matched in popular culture (and monastic culture as well) with a great variety of local traditions concerning the sites where personal appeals might be heard, the spirits that still dwelled nearby, and the manner in which devotions might still be directed toward the Nile. Our anonymous fifth-century monk, for example, complains about a landscape charted and crossed for the pursuit of potent substances to protect the family: "Some of them practice abominations in city and village. For it is said that some of them ablute their children in polluted water and water from the arena, from the theater."[15]

This chapter will explore four dimensions of the Christianization of the Egyptian religious landscape that stress the agency of the actors on the ground—bishops, townspeople, villagers, monks—in *constructing* an Egyptian Christianity: (a) the reconstruction of a religious infrastructure through the building of churches in explicit or implicit relationship to temples; (b) the memories of powerful ancestral or liminal spirits in the landscape and ways of negotiating their presence; (c) the use of *procession* to mediate stories and ideology with local social experience; and (d) various efforts to conceptualize a mythic landscape of martyr shrines.

II. TEMPLES AND CHURCHES

Any visitor to Egypt recognizes quickly the extent to which churches were built in relationship to temples. At Denderah one sees a church placed between the Birth temple and the Hathor temple. At Philae, Elephantine, Karnak, and elsewhere churches and shrines were built among the pillars of the temples, marked with incised crosses or paintings of saints. At Hermopolis Magna and throughout western Thebes sizeable church structures made use of Egyptian temple struc-

---

14 Cf. Dijkstra's observation that a "Christian" Philae began with newly built churches (fourth to fifth century CE), not a transformed temple; Dijkstra, *Philae and the End*, 315–38. The once-monumental temple of Isis, whose cult dwindled over the course of the fifth century, came to serve as a shrine to St. Stephen in the sixth century. Of course, liturgical structures and *topoi* of martyrs had quite different meanings in the landscape and religious practice.

15 Pseudo-Athanasius, *Homily on the Virgin* 92, 95, in Lefort, "L'homélie de S. Athanase," 35–36.

CHAPTER 7

tures and foundations.[16] In nearly every case the temple had ceased to function as a priestly establishment, sometimes recently, but often centuries earlier. And so the question follows: Why choose these ancient monuments at all for the site of Christian ritual structures?

It used to be thought that placing churches within or around temples sought to appropriate the temples' intrinsic sacred powers. This notion that churches could co-opt the more archaic or abstract sacredness of prior temples may have occasionally typified the ideology of Christianization in the western Roman Empire, as expressed by Pope Gregory in a letter to a bishop heading for England in 601:

> ... that the temples of the idols among that people should on no account be destroyed. The idols are to be destroyed, but the temples themselves are to be aspersed with holy water, altars set up in them, and relics deposited there. For if these temples are well built they must be purified from the worship of demons and dedicated to the service of the true God. In this way, we hope that the people, seeing that their temples are not destroyed, may abandon their error and, flocking more readily to their accustomed resorts, may come to know and adore the true God.[17]

This is a more irenic ideology than the Theodosian edict of 435, which decreed that various temples and shrines of prior religions "be destroyed and purified by the erection of the sign of the venerable Christian religion."[18] Gregory's letter conveys much of the ideological context for the Christianization of springs, for example: the view that a site retained such archaic centrality in local culture that Christian forces might profit through its co-optation.[19] But the churches built in Egyptian temples during the fifth, sixth, and seventh centuries seldom have any architectural relationship to those sections of the temples once associated with holy images.[20] Nor, as Ann Marie Yasin has argued with regard to church spaces and martyria, should the perceived sacredness of ancient ritual structures be imagined as somehow immutable and prior to the ceremonies that took place in and around them.[21] Without those ceremonies and their mobile sacra—relics in the case of Christian structures, images in the case of Egyptian temples—the buildings would not have been perceived to carry any intrinsic sanctity, although

---

16 On the diversity of Christian uses of temples for building ritual structures, see Jullien, "Le culte chrétien"; Nautin, "La conversion du temple"; Coquin, "La christianisation des temples"; Grossmann, *Christliche Architektur in Ägypten*, 446–65; McKenzie, *Architecture of Alexandria and Egypt*, 312–16; and Dijkstra, *Philae and the End*, 306–15.

17 Gregory I, Letter to Abbot Mellitus, in Bede, *History of the English Church*, 86–87.

18 *C.Th.* 16.10.25.

19 See esp. Stancliffe, "From Town to Country"; and Rousselle, *Croire et guérir*; Barnish, "Religio in Stagno"; and Sauer, "Religious Rituals at Springs."

20 See, e.g., Dijkstra, *Philae and the End*, 86–122.

21 Yasin, *Saints and Church Spaces*.

quite often they might have harbored a "ghostliness," a liminal numinousness, in the perspective of local folk.[22]

Indeed, it was this liminal numinousness, not abiding sanctity, to which installers or maintainers of churches in or near temples seem to have been responding in their efforts to *purify* and *exorcise* spaces of demonic spirits. We can infer church installers' efforts to eliminate the presence of local spirits from the extensive mutilation of images around the Denderah temple (and others) and the incision of crosses in key locations.[23] And Abbot Shenoute of Atripe, an important witness to and instigator of these Christianization efforts in the late fourth and early fifth centuries, himself lays out this radical approach to disruption and conversion, rather than continuation, of space:

> At the site of a shrine to an unclean spirit, it will henceforth be a shrine to the Holy Spirit. And at the site of sacrificing to Satan and worshipping and fearing him, Christ will henceforth be served there, and He will be worshipped, bowed down to and feared.... If previously it is prescriptions for murdering man's soul that are in there, written with blood and not with ink alone—[indeed,] there is nothing else portrayed ... except the likeness of the snakes and scorpions, the dogs and cats, the crocodiles and frogs, ... the likeness of the sun and moon ...—where these are, it is the soul-saving scriptures of life that will henceforth come to be in there ... and His son Jesus Christ and all His angels, righteous men and saints [will be portrayed on these walls].[24]

It is this kind of exorcistic ideology in the appropriation of Egyptian temples that dominates hagiographical texts, in which saints are pitted against various local and satanic spirits, sometimes in temples, sometimes in tombs, but which never lead to the reassignment of the same space to Christian liturgy.[25] Exorcism and its architectural expressions—graffiti, incised crosses, and even, as Shenoute says, the very installation of a church with its cult—signify triumph, the victory of Christ over a prior heathen or demonic order.[26]

But for whom? Shenoute's own role in declaring the conversion here, as well as the likely site of the sermon—a monastic chapel set among the columns of the temple of Karnak, complete with saints painted on the columns[27]—point not to

---

22 I use this term to denote a sense of power and presence after Michael Bell's discussion in "Ghosts of Place."

23 See, e.g., Nautin, "La conversion du temple," 21–24; with Dijkstra, *Philae and the End*, 313–14; and, more generally, Saradi, "Use of Ancient Spolia."

24 Shenoute, Acephalous work 158, Michigan ms. 158, in Young, "A Monastic Invective."

25 Frankfurter, "Iconoclasm and Christianization."

26 See Saradi-Mendelovici, "Christian Attitudes Toward Pagan Monuments."

27 On the Christian church in the Karnak temple, see Coquin, "La christianisation des temples"; and Rassart-Debergh, "L'Akh-Menou." Shenoute's name is included in a list of archimandrites on the wall; see I.Karnak 5, in Coquin, "La christianisation des temples," 175–76; Carnot, "L'Akh-Menou," 799.

popular, local interest in the triumph of Christian space, as Gregory desired, but rather to the interest of monks. It now seems likely that monks were also the ones to install churches in several Theban temples and that they did so to symbolize, among those grandiose ancient structures, the charisma of some founding abbot.[28] Likewise it seems to have been monastic interests and agency that led to the appropriation of a temple in Abydos for Christian ritual purposes: the remains of a convent installed under the authority of one Apa Moses seem to situate in real space the dramatic legend of this holy man's exorcism of a demon from the main temple in the precinct, the so-called Memnonion.[29] This part of the Abydos temple complex seems to have become a pilgrimage goal, perhaps one linked with the viewing of the rising of the Nile waters in the ancient subterranean temple behind the Memnonion. The miracle came now to be celebrated as the work of God and the saints, especially the deceased Apa Moses.[30]

But there may be a more general context in which we can read the intention and popular significance of the installation of churches by temples as a feature of the Christianization of the landscape. That is, it may be that such installations represented not a response to traditional religion but the securing and symbolic control of the *monumental* in the landscape: those buildings—active or (more typically) defunct—that most visibly and traditionally demarcated the landscape.[31] This effort to secure the monumental for the glory of Christianity took place most vividly in urban centers, as a project of bishops. In the late fourth century, for example, Bishop Theophilus took it upon himself to secure the monumental cityscape of Alexandria for a visible Christianity through a program of demolishing temples, leading processions, and erecting new saints' shrines.[32] Elsewhere in the Mediterranean world, Christian liturgical installations (like Justinian's Hagia Sophia) were clearly designed to dominate the cityscape. In Egypt, of course, temple structures had always been attractive for their monumentality, their imposing visibility in a landscape of minor shrines.[33] Perhaps no temple more epitomizes this attraction of the monumental than the sprawling Luxor complex, which the Emperor Diocletian appropriated in 302 for an imperial shrine, evidently due to its religious and monumental monumentality.[34] But

---

28 Boutros and Décobert, "Les installations chretiennes."

29 Till, *Koptische Heiligen- und Martyrerlegenden*, 2:46–81; Amélineau, *Monuments pour servir*, 2:679–706; Moussa, "Abba Moses of Abydos"; idem, "Coptic Literary Dossier"; and Uljas, "IFAO Leaves of the Life."

30 See Delattre, "Les graffitis coptes"; Westerfeld, "Monastic Graffiti in Context."

31 See Ward-Perkins, "Reconfiguring Sacred Space"; Sotinel, "La disparition des lieux," 40–41; Van der Vliet, "Bringing Home the Homeless," 51.

32 See Haas, *Alexandria in Late Antiquity*, 206–14; Watts, *Riot in Alexandria*, 190–215; cf. Tsafrir, "Christianization of Bet Shean"; Baynes, "Supernatural Defenders of Constantinople"; Gauthier, "La topographie chrétienne."

33 On temples' ancient function in demarcating the landscape, see Baines, "Temples as Symbols," 225.

34 See esp. McFadden, "Dating the Luxor Camp," 32–37.

then, over the next four centuries, at least four churches were built among and alongside the temples' pillars.[35] The temple represented "greatness" in the physical and cultural landscape.

Of course, an imposing basilica could also signify monumentality, either alone or in contraposition to a nearby temple whose cult had long ago ended. Thus we find, for example, with Denderah's basilica, built alongside the Hathor temple, and also at Philae, whose major Christian edifice, the late sixth- or early seventh-century so-called East Church, would have rivaled in spectacle the great Isis temple, some fifty meters away on the island. The Isis temple itself had been claimed in the mid-sixth century as the shrine of St. Stephen the protomartyr.[36] Thus monumentality could be achieved in different ways, even in one area.

To be sure, that monumentality might have had meaning only for a small group of monks, who saw it as a way to credit their founder. But as a governing theme in the reconstruction of the religious landscape, the effort to secure monumentality in an area ties together the violent programs of certain Alexandrian bishops, the diverse installations of churches in abandoned temples, the promulgation of saints' legends that imagined the wholesale conversion of buildings, and even the construction of more spectacular freestanding basilicas in Egypt, like the pilgrimage church of Apa Mena and Abbot Shenoute's own church, which itself was designed in size and shape to recall an Egyptian temple.[37]

As for agency in this resignification of temple structures, this monumentalizing of Christian spaces, historians tend to attribute the creative force in Christian infrastructure to particular bishops, like Theophilus in late fourth-century Alexandria and Theodore in sixth-century Philae. But when it comes to the appropriation of old temples as Christian monuments, it is likely that monks were the creative forces (at least initially) behind such programs, looking first to commemorate their own local saints and heroes and then actively locating and installing cult spaces with these motives in mind.[38] It was probably these interests, exclusive to the inner culture of asceticism, that most typically impelled the appropriation of temples, rather than the exorcism of the landscape, as Coptic hagiographies suggest, or demonstrations of triumph in order to promote Christianity in the broader society.[39] However, the wide-scale destruction of images at Denderah suggests that, when confronted with the continuing devotions of local people in the temple precincts, monks might well have responded with an iconoclasm

---

35 McKenzie, *Architecture of Alexandria and Egypt*, 314–15; Grossmann, *Christliche Architektur in Ägypten*, 448–54.

36 See Grossmann, *Christliche Architektur in Ägypten*, 47, 461–64; Dijkstra, *Philae and the End*, 315–24.

37 See Török, *Transfigurations of Hellenism*, 153–64; and Warner, "Architectural Survey," 50–51.

38 See esp. Boutros and Décobert, "Les installations chrétiennes." Cf. Haas on the Christianization of Ethiopia: "In almost every case, the new ascetic settlements were accompanied by the occupation of an earlier pagan site"; Haas, "Mountain Constantines," 119.

39 See Brakke, "From Temple to Cell," on the inner preoccupations of monks that were worked out through inhabiting temple spaces.

imagined as exorcism—an extreme form of the casual mutilations and carving of crosses that they carried out in other temple spaces.

III. HABITATS AND HAUNTS OF SPIRITS

Let us then move to the nature of these devotions at temple sites long after the temple cults had dwindled away. It was the persistence of such local devotions at Denderah that, I have argued, accounts for monks' systematic mutilation of the iconography around this shrine. At the Osiris temple of Abydos, local legends preserved in the *Life of Apa Moses* tell of this holy man's exorcism of a "demon" named Bes from one of the structures there. But this is no gratuitous heathen god's name, like "Apollo," whose temple suffers attack in another part of the *Life*.[40] It is the name of the very spirit that, according to Ammianus Marcellinus and graffiti on the exterior walls of the Memnonion, had issued oracles via incubation and letter at least until 359 CE, when his shrine was officially closed.[41] But imperial closures of shrines only halted large-scale administrative activity; they would hardly have interrupted the sense of the shrine and its functions in local culture. Here, in fact, the literary evidence shows that the name Bes itself was preserved into the fifth century or later, when the *Life* was first compiled, while the story preserved in the *Life of Apa Moses* implies that, more than just a name, the "demon" was well known to local people. According to the *Life*: "The citizens of these two villages came" and appealed to Apa Moses, claiming that the spirit "would come out and afflict those passing by. Some of them he blinded in one eye. In other cases, their hands would shrivel up. He would cripple others in the feet.... Indeed, many saw him leaping down from the temple and transforming his appearance many times."[42] As the *Life* recounts it, Moses exorcised the "demon" from the building after a dramatic night's battle (though whether such an exorcism ever took place—or was even carried out by Apa Moses—is anyone's guess). Thus, as I argued for Denderah, the spaces in the Abydos Memnonion (and, as we will see, the adjoining Osireion too) retained memories and associations of potency in local culture through the Christian period.[43] It is now time to investigate how not just memories, but spirits—active, haunting forces—might remain associated (or come to be associated) with dilapidated religious sites.

If for monks and bishops Egyptian temples often signified monumental structures, structures with an authority and dominating presence that could be appropriated for monastic or ecclesiastical glory, for those who lived in the vicinity they

---

40 *V. Mosis*, codex EL 49–50: K 9554, in Till, *Koptische Heiligen- und Martyrerlegenden*, 2:49–51; Moussa, "Coptic Literary Dossier," 79–80.

41 Dunand, "La consultation oraculaire"; Frankfurter, *Religion in Roman Egypt*, 128–31; idem, "Voices, Books, and Dreams."

42 *V. Mosis*, codex EL 111, in Till, *Koptische Heiligen- und Martyrerlegenden*, 2:52–53; Moussa, "Coptic Literary Dossier," 83.

43 See also Effland, "'You Will Open Up,'" 203–4.

were, first and foremost, marked sites in a traditional landscape long mapped in terms of local spirits. The contrast, of course, would not have been absolute, but this sense of the landscape as alive with spirits and punctuated with their haunts is a feature of traditional societies well documented in ethnography and that would have been largely independent of official cults in a region. Hills, valleys, ponds, rivers, and diverse liminal zones are associated with particular spirits, ghosts, or even gods. Their attacks or beneficial appearances are retold in legend, warned about in families, sought secretly, or mediated by local specialists: "Let no pregnant woman walk by that structure," one might say, or "let no husband nap by that pond"; if crisis occurs, one might be confident that "that woman" would go visit the spirit over on that hill. Such stories and memories do not so much articulate a worldview or belief system as put in topographic, narrative form the moral system, gender values, and even sense of identity held in the community—indeed, the general sense that meaning, guidance, and security can be interpreted in terms of landscape.[44] The landscape is a mnemonic for stories that encapsulate binding tradition. Even an old church might be haunted with mischievous spirits, as the fifth-century Cilician holy man Daniel the Stylite encountered (and then proceeded to exorcise).[45]

Well before the Christian period, this topography of supernatural forces and dangers was captured in amuletic texts issued by certain temples that promised their bearers protection "from any demon of (a pool) left (by the inundation), from any demon of a runnel, from any demon of a well, from any demon of a lake, from any demon of a hollow, from any demon of the mountains, from every demon of all swamps."[46] But even in the Christian period, images of the old gods preserved in Coptic ritual spells (as we saw in chapter 6) depict these beings not as occupying temples but as moving through the hills and up and down the Nile: Amun "is going from the south wind northward ... to Abydos"[47]; Horus, "upon a mountain to rest," sends to Isis "upon the mountain of Heliopolis ... stoking a copper oven."[48] As charms and songs passed down in communities beyond the temple cults, these Coptic texts illustrate how Egyptian gods might have been recalled in local culture: not as the salvific figures of cult ceremony but as storied beings haunting the landscape.

If so far my materials about the persistence of landscape spirits have applied chiefly to rural cultures, let it not be thought that city dwellers lacked this sense

---

44 See esp. Basso, "Stalking with Stories"; Stewart, *Demons and the Devil*. See also Meylan, "(Re)conversion of the Spirits," on the intertwining of landscape spirits and moral principles; Sotinel, "La disparition des lieux," 37–42, on the great variety of ritual and holy spaces in traditional Mediterranean religions; and Bell, "Ghosts of Place" on the more abstract sense of "ghosts of place" in modern culture.

45 *Life of Daniel the Stylite* 14–15, in Dawes and Baynes, *Three Byzantine Saints*, 14–16.

46 B.M. 10587r, in Edwards, *Hieratic Papyri*, 39; see also ibid., xxii.

47 ACM 43 = Michigan 135, p. 5.

48 ACM 49 = Berlin 8313; cf. PGM IV.1–25, 94–153.

CHAPTER 7

of potent sites, informal shrines, and spirits disconnected from any formal cult. Springs served very much as haunts in cities: centers of devotional action and appeals could be found in Rome, Corinth, Jerusalem, and elsewhere, and our fifth-century Coptic complainant himself picks out "water from the arena (and) from the theater" as especially potent for protective charms, even if not attributed to a particular spirit.[49] But the abundance of statuary that distinguished the Roman city still in late antiquity would have almost necessitated that some images acquire traditions of devotion and efficacious response.[50] Images, after all, could easily oscillate between a decorative, prestige-oriented, or (in Elsner's words) "horizontal visuality" and a "vertical" or "ritual-centered visuality" as the vehicle of a spirit's presence, so that a city full of such images—even when mutilated—would have constituted likewise a "landscape" of spirits, portals, and potent sites.[51]

Thus, when we talk about Egyptian gods being "remembered" in the fifth or sixth century, or about continuing reverence for or the performance of devotional acts for such gods at ostensibly ancient cult sites, the argument should not be taken to imply that discursive memories of gods—that is, from priestly mythologizing—persisted.[52] The memories, of whatever character, were attached to objects and places—a feature that Coptic literature picks up, although under the aegis of demonology. The *Life of Moses of Abydos* goes so far as to imagine Satan's lament that he has been exiled from all his habitats through the Christ-like force of holy men like Moses:

> Woe unto me, I, the wretched one, for I have been cast out of everyplace, even this house that was left for me. See how I have been thrown out of it and left outside like a beggar. In Shmin Shenoute threw me out. He took away my temples and converted them into churches. Even my heathen [ⲚϨⲈⲖⲖⲎⲚ] children he took from me. And he was not satisfied with this but chased me out of the region.[53]

This image of the evacuation of Satan and his beings from the landscape affirms the monastic composer's experience of a landscape full of potentially de-

---

49 Coptic complaint: see above, p. 237n15; Rome: Piranomonte, "Religion and Magic at Rome"; Corinth: Jordan, "Inscribed Lamps from a Cult"; Jerusalem: John 5:2–4; and, in general, Sauer, "Religious Rituals at Springs."

50 See esp. Stewart, *Statues in Roman Society*, 192–93.

51 Elsner, *Roman Eyes*. See my discussion of these categories above, p. 148. On a late antique urban "landscape" of spirits in the perspective of Christian bishops, see Kalleres, *City of Demons*.

52 This important distinction between priestly/cultic interests in a shrine, which can formally cease, and popular, lay, or independent forms of veneration of a site is discussed in detail in my *Religion in Roman Egypt*, 62–77, 97–144. Cf. Dijkstra's distinction between "the Ancient Egyptian Religion" and "certain groups [that] could have been attracted to the site for a long time"; Dijkstra, *Philae and the End*, 217.

53 *v. Mosis*, cod. EL50/K9554, in Moussa, "Coptic Literary Dossier," 81. See also Rufinus, *E.H.* II.28.

monic beings, especially in temples and tombs. The tendency of people to imagine such liminal areas as demonic and as sources of misfortune (or, for a monk, distraction) goes far—I have argued—toward explaining the aggressive Christianization epitomized at Denderah and in the fixing of hieroglyphic stelae in the floors of Shenoute's monastic church to signify their defeat or desecration. These acts, as well as those imagined in hagiography, presume the identification of traditional shrine spirits with Christian demons and thus constitute ritual—apotropaic—responses to those demons.[54]

But what happened to these toppled and mutilated remains? Even those objects that monks ritually reviled and mutilated as demonic tended to acquire an *ambiguity* in the local world, not the polarized danger of the satanic demons of scripture.[55] For example, spolia—remnants of pre-Christian iconography—were often recycled as potent apotropaia for the supernatural protection of buildings. Often the apotropaic spolia consisted of dangerous fauna—scorpions, serpents—or unusual faces or bodies, like the *sheila-na-gigs* of medieval Irish churches. Here too we are not dealing with the "survival of old gods" but rather with the maintenance of *images* that were—or could be deemed—potent for the control of local demonic spirits.[56] And here also we see local agency arising in response to acts of Christianization. Reutilizing archaic remains for apotropaic purposes—in the home, in a church, or in any other building—actively configured them as components in a local iconographic repertoire—a repertoire that in turn maintained the distinctive character of demonic beings in the local landscape, implying in the apotropaic image a type of demon repelled.

So Christian demonizing in practice masked, or alternated with, local understandings of ambiguous spirits in the landscape, as well as various iconographic strategies for controlling or dispatching them, often drawing on the archaic remains and spolia in the environment. But the topography of traditional spirits and potent sites carried positive valences as well, in which places were figured as sites of healing and sites of communication *associated with* archaic religious sites and images. I have argued that what impelled the mutilation of the Hathor image on the back of the Denderah temple at the time of the basilica's construction was some kind of continuing local devotions at that image as a place and an image of potency, even if not "lady Hathor."

But such devotions to ancient images need not be "continuous" either. They might involve a (re)discovery of an image as well as the agency of an individual or

---

54 Saradi, "Use of Ancient Spolia"; idem, "Christianization of Pagan Temples"; Frankfurter, "Iconoclasm and Christianization"; Jacobs, "Production to Destruction?" On *spolia* in Shenoute's monastery, see Klotz, "Triphis in the White Monastery"; cf. Haarman, "Medieval Muslim Perceptions," 612, on similar uses of hieroglyph-inscribed blocks in medieval mosques. On exorcistic graffiti at Abydos, see Grossmann, "Modalitäten der Zerstörung," 306.

55 Aufrère, "L'Égypte traditionnelle."

56 See Saradi, "Use of Ancient Spolia," 413–23; Flood, "Image Against Nature"; Papalexandrou, "Memory Tattered and Torn."

CHAPTER 7

family in investing a temple relief or statue with material potency and legend. The ancient spring shrine of the Abydos Osireion temple, where one could apparently witness the annual Nile surge in microcosm, was apparently rediscovered (and probably cleared) in the sixth century CE, around the time (so inscriptions imply) that annual visitors were attributing the Nile surge to the blessings of God and the local saint Apa Moses.[57] In modern cultures negotiating such landscapes, these responses have been regarded as a kind of "indigenous archaeology: local, vernacular discourses and practices involving things from another time" that constitute traditionally significant elements of a local culture's landscape.[58]

Such objects often gain a discursive context—an *interpretatio Christiana*—whether through folklore or through a kind of scripturalist "acculturation" to Christian dominion. During her tour of Egypt, for example, the late fourth-century Iberian pilgrim Egeria encountered "a single enormous stone on which are two very large carved figures, which are said to be of the holy men Moses and Aaron.... In addition there is a sycamore tree ... [and] those who are ill go there and take away twigs, and it helps them."[59] Here it was a local bishop who reinterpreted the statues by means of biblical mythology (although the unlikely proposition that Moses and Aaron could have been commemorated through statues suggests that the interpretation had a more indigenous basis), yet the persisting "life" of such images in the local landscape lies in the ritual responses to their materiality.

It is this material appropriation of archaic images, independent of priests or ritual specialists, that emerges in a remarkable Arabic legend from the thirteenth century. The legend tells of an Egyptian village's interaction with the statue of "a woman seated with a child in her lap as if she were suckling him." To the extent that this story recalls a type of local practice still ongoing in medieval Egypt, this image would presumably—at one time—have been a statue of Isis with the infant Horus, but the author himself does not know the figures' names, and he presents the statue as locally conceptualized in a more general sense: as a statue of a woman suckling a child.

> Any woman who, afflicted by a disease in her body, rubbed the (corresponding part of) the body of that statue, recovered her former state. In a likewise manner, if her milk diminished and she rubbed its breast, then it increased. And in the same manner, if she wanted that her husband feel af-

---

57 See Piankoff, "Osireion of Seti I," 130–31; Delattre, "Les graffitis coptes"; Westerfeld, "Monastic Graffiti in Context," 17–19. Strabo (17.1.42) mentions the spring as connected to the Nile by a canal.

58 Hamilakis, "Indigenous Archaeologies in Ottoman Greece," 49; Flood, "Image Against Nature," 146–47. Cf. Haarman, "Medieval Muslim Perceptions," 612, 621, on medieval Muslim veneration of the Sphinx as an apotropaic image. Nutini, *Todos Santos in Rural Tlaxcala*, 181–82, discusses ancient figurines discovered in the vicinity and incorporated into domestic religion in modern rural Mexico.

59 *Itin. Eg.* 8, in Gingras, *Egeria*, 62–63; Jacobs, "Production to Destruction?," 278–82.

fection towards her, she rubbed its face with good oil and told it: Make this and this. If her menstruation decreased and she became afraid of this, (she) rubbed it under its knees. If anything afflicted her son, she did the same to (its) son, and he recovered. If her delivery was difficult, she rubbed the head of (its) son and it became easy. In the same manner, it made deflowering easier for the virgin. If the adulteress put her hand on it, she (started) to tremble so that she renounced her dissolute life.[60]

This story reflects likely practices and attitudes toward statuary in a period centuries after the shift to Islam, and yet it offers a convenient picture of how local communities might still have "read" a classical Egyptian image when no names or myths remained. People interpreted the *Isis lactans* image according to domestic exigency, a repertoire of ritual gestures (like rubbing) for the use of such an image, and a sense of authoritative potency perhaps rooted in its monumental form and resemblance to temple images. Still today ethnographers have noted Egyptian villagers' embrace of temple sites and images—sometimes even in museums, and especially for issues of procreative fertility.[61] Attention to these places may be best understood in terms of the total landscape of power and collective memory with which traditional communities comprehend their surroundings and the *agency*—the self-determination and creativity—with which family members in such communities maintain ritual associations with particular sites. In Egypt of the fifth, sixth, and seventh centuries, these perspectives must have led, in some places, to a continuing reverence for temple remains and statuary of the prior religious system, once recalled by the name of the old god, and eventually by new stories simply about "the woman and her child." The story of the Abydos temple after its fourth-century closure by imperial decree may be a unique example of the persistence of a god's name in local culture in connection with a specific ruin such that it would be recalled in the fifth-century life of the holy man Moses of Abydos. But here there may have been a more obvious context for continuity, since the closure of the Bes oracle could not have led to the complete elimination of devotional activities and incubation there. More likely these activities simply shifted from priestly administration to the independent agency and traditions of local villagers. Something called "Bes" might still have been sought and encountered there, even when the traditions became part of regional folklore.[62]

Thus we can understand how archaic images and sites could have maintained power and authority in the landscape long after those images and sites ceased to be part of functioning religious cults. The landscape of late antique Egypt was

60 In Fodor, "Traces of the Isis Cult," 185, with useful commentary at 186–87.
61 See Wassef, *Pratiques rituelles et alimentaires*, 147–48; Inhorn, *Quest for Conception*, 218–38; Van der Spek, "Feasts, Fertility, and Fear," 185–86.
62 See Dunand, "La consultation oraculaire"; Frankfurter, *Religion in Roman Egypt*, 169–74; idem, "Hagiography and the Reconstruction," 24–25.

itself not just "Christian" but an integrated topography of potent and ambiguous (and sometimes aggressive) spirits within which churches, shrines, and monasteries required ongoing local assimilation as ritual centers. The relics of the old religion could, in the ways I have described, *complement* saints' shrines and churches—sometimes through their proximity, sometimes through their traditional associations with procreative fertility, sometimes by virtue of their liminality as dilapidated structures, and sometimes through their associations in collective memory with past religious practices. They might also have been acculturated to the Christian landscape as monuments of a new Christian past, as in Egeria's description of the two statues and their tree that had come to be identified with Moses and Aaron.

Other landforms became linked to the legend of the Holy Family in their flight through Egypt, based on a verse in the Gospel of Matthew (2:14). Stories about miraculous trees they visited, springs they tapped, or idols they toppled in the Egyptian landscape are attested as early as the fourth century and probably reflected at least some actual sites of veneration. A fragment of prophecy from the fourth or fifth century (discussed in chapter 6 as a late example of the Land of Egypt oracle) describes how "the childhood of my Son will take place in you [Egypt], three years and eleven [months] in length. When your enemies pursue him you will hear his mysteries. In those days, [he will give] you his spring as a pledge. You shall receive a blessing from it for fifty years. My Son shall visit it for seven days. My ministering spirits shall always remain in you, from now until eternity." Egypt is here depicted as a landscape blessed through its divine visitors (and the unusual fifty-year spring [ⲘⲈⲦⲂⲂⲒ] they left behind).[63] But as this tradition of the Holy Family's flight through Egypt developed between the fourth and twelfth centuries, the legends came to reflect closely the natural forms of the landscape as places establishing their trials, adventures, and resting points.[64] Thus, from the fourth century on, landscape became both a pretext and a context for the development of Christian legend: an opportunity to tell stories and a theater in which to place and indigenize a sacred history.

IV. PROCESSION AND THE PERCEPTION OF LANDSCAPE

Of all the features of the Egyptian landscape that impacted the construction of Christian belief and ritual in late antiquity, probably the most deeply entrenched

---

63 ⲘⲈⲦⲂⲂⲒ from ⲘⲈⲦ-ⲂⲈⲈⲂⲈ: see Schenke, "P.Köln 354," 196 (with gratitude for the use of her forthcoming English translation). Schenke suggests that the fifty-year blessing refers to the Nile inundation. Cf. *v.Sin.* 154–57 (in Leipoldt, *Sinuthii archimandritae*, S. coptici 1: 66–67; Bell, *Besa*, 85), in which a corpse testifies to Apa Shenoute that he met the Holy Family in the village of Šmoun.

64 *Hist.Mon.* 8.1; Sozomen, *Hist. Eccl.* 5.21; P. Col. VIII. 354, B. On the elaboration of this tradition by the seventh century, see MacCoull, "Holy Family Pilgrimage"; Valensi, *La fuite en Égypte*; Boutros and Boud'hors, "La sainte famille."

in culture was the Nile itself, with its mysterious annual surges.[65] For millennia temples had governed the regular integration of the Nile with regional mythology and cult by means of processions and hymns, structures linking temple and river, and Nilometers, which brought Nile observation into the larger temple cosmology. Even early saints' lives, which on the whole are critical of Nile veneration as heathen, recall various features of such rituals on a local scale.[66] One would be hard pressed to imagine that a landscape feature of such agricultural, economic, social, and spatial centrality could somehow lose its value, its religious implications, even if the broader discursive or mythological contexts might change with religious regimes and rulers.[67] And indeed, in the sixth century CE, church officials at the church complex installed within the temple of Isis at Philae continued the practice of the Nilometer, marking how "the most holy Nile rose ... up to the foot of the cross" on a particular date. Here was a new type of Nilometer: one that used the cross as measurement. Here, Christianity gained authority through the sacred observation of the Nile surge, which in turn acquired a new ceremonial authority through the church.[68] At about the same time (sixth century CE) people were still visiting the ancient spring shrine beneath the Osireion temple at Abydos, where the Nile surge had once been ritually welcomed by Osiris priests, yet now they watched the water rise to an interior pool "by the will of God and the prayers of the saints" on the day of the holy man of Abydos, Apa Moses.[69]

By the fifth century the observation and celebration of the Nile surge had acquired distinctly ceremonial forms. "I proclaim as good news," someone writes in a letter, using an explicitly Christian verb (εὐαγγελίζομαι), "that the sanctifying (and) fruitful River of Egypt has surged by the power of Christ," and he proceeds to give the measurements of its rise.[70] A Christian hymn "for the festival marking the rising of the most sacred Nile, the festival with its sacred rites of abundance" gives a more intimate sense of the public ceremony involved in greeting the Nile surge:

> The water has come. Hail to the streams at the rising of the freshet of Isis. Rule the streams, O Nile of many floods, of great name. From Meroe flow down to us, gracious and welcome, and spread the fruitful silt in your abundant freshets. May you sweeten the whole of Egypt, fertilizing it each year in due season. Look ye how golden is the flood for each and every one, and

---

65 See, e.g., P. Oxy 65.4473 (second/third century CE), a series of astrological predictions of the annual Nile surge.

66 Athanasius, v.Ant. 32; Hist.Mon 8.25; Firmicus Maternus, errores 2.

67 See Frankfurter, Religion in Roman Egypt, 42–46.

68 Kreuzsaler, "Ho hierōtatos neílos"; cf. Dijkstra, "Late Antique Inscriptions"; and idem, Philae and the End, 116–18.

69 See Delattre, "Graffitis coptes d'Abydos," esp. 134–38 (cf. 139, I.Abydos 44, mentioning Apa Moses); Westerfeld, "Monastic Graffiti in Context," 17–19; cf. Piankoff, "Osireion of Seti I," 131–33.

70 P. Oxy 16. 1830.

chorus ye thrice, in celebration of the flowing streams, "Rise, O Nile, mount up to the joyous six and ten cubits!"[71]

The inclusion of multiple voices and the reference to the Nile's measurement suggest that the context for this hymn was some kind of procession to or from the Nile's banks—originally, perhaps, in the context of a temple; now under the aegis of the church. (The hymn itself is preserved in a small codex, followed by a creed and Psalm 133, suggesting a liturgical collection for an ecclesiastical procession.) The references to Meroe and the "freshet of Isis [Ισειας ρειθροις]" would have given the hymn an archaizing, Hellenistic cast—metrical formulae harking back to an older landscape.[72] Thus, traditions of festal movement across the landscape to the Nile became integrated into Christian liturgy, as the fifth-century church historian Rufinus describes:

> Now it was the custom in Egypt to bring the gauge of the rising Nile River to the temple of Sarapis, as being the one who caused the increase of water and the flooding; so that when his statue was overthrown and burned, everyone of course unanimously declared that Serapis, mindful of this injury, would never again bestow the waters in their usual abundance. But so that God could show that it was he who ordered the waters of the river to rise in season, and not Serapis, . . . there began then such a succession of floods as never before recorded. And thus the practice of bringing that very measuring rod, or water gauge, which they call a *pēchys*, to the Lord of waters in the church.[73]

It is not just the ritual focus on the Nile's momentous surge that interests us in Rufinus's clever condensation of legend but the "bringing [*deferre*]" of this object—its processional oscillation between the Nile and the religious sanctuary—as the performative context. For in that procession, participants and viewers both drew out the polarity of these sites and connected them through ordered movement. An early stage in this Christianization of the traditional Nile procession emerges in a sermon of Abbot Shenoute, in the context of criticizing those who had kept traditional religious images in their homes. Such heathens, he thunders, might even have "the ell [ⲙⲁϩⲉ], measure of the water's rise. This object, which *we* bring in gratitude [ⲉⲧⲛ̄ϫⲓ . . . ϩⲛⲟⲩⲙⲛ̄ⲧ ⲣⲉϥϣⲡ̄ϩⲙⲟⲧ] to the holy church, *they* have brought [ⲁⲩϫⲓⲧϥ] before the likenesses of demons, just as we [found] it standing at their feet in the midst of them."[74] Thus what Rufinus declares in his narrative as a settled shift in the processional route from temple to church, here in

---

71 P. Lond. Lit. 239, in Lewis, *Life in Egypt*, 95; Bonneau, *La crue du Nil*, 410–13; idem, "Les hommes et le Nil"; idem, "Les courants d'eau d'Isis."
72 Bonneau, "Les courants d'eau d'Isis," 93–94.
73 Rufinus, *Eccl. Hist.* 11.30, in Amidon, *Church History of Rufinus*, 86–87.
74 Shenoute, "Let Our Eyes" 2.5–6, in Emmel, "Shenoute of Atripe," 197, 188 (translation).

Shenoute's world is still contested, as people were evidently carrying the Nile measures to both sanctuaries. In subsequent centuries, however, it was Shenoute himself who came to be celebrated in legend, invoked in prayers, and doubtless invoked in processions too as a heavenly mediator of the Nile surge—in this capacity replacing for many people the Archangel Michael.[75]

It was through such acts of procession, as we saw in chapter 4, that Abbot Shenoute also gained popular sainthood in the area of his monastery. A stational procession developed, no doubt from the processions the abbot himself had led, that stopped at various points in the landscape associated with his legendary activities and finally, perhaps, at his sumptuously decorated tomb-chapel.[76] Through such processions an occasional religious identity was forged among devotees through the linking of collective action, landscape, and the now-mythic value of the abbot's legends, fixed in particular sites. Memory, identity, ritual action, and even authority—Shenoute's in heaven, that of abbots or bishops in this world—came to be combined through the organized passage through a landscape and its features.

Indeed, we may say that the institution of processions, whether in the countryside of Upper Egypt or the streets of Alexandria or Oxyrhynchus, provided the principal *ritual* means of Christianizing the landscape—integrating topography with legend, ideology, and some kind of collective Christian identity, however ephemeral. Through processions and their articulated routes and orders, participants learned what sites were focal and which marginalized, what songs or prayers or legends corresponded to which stages along a route. The Nile might maintain its status, while some popular local shrine might be shunned through the order of the cortège. In sixth-century Oxyrhynchus, for example, a great variety of saints' shrines—to biblical saints, local martyrs, angels, and regional saints—were integrated into an annual sequence of stational processions, many of which corresponded to periods of the agricultural cycle. Through this festal calendar, moreover, the presiding bishop's authority and the celebration of the Eucharist gained a certain dramatic focus.[77]

The Egyptian landscape, of course, had been the theater of religious processions for millennia, as these were the principal means for temples and their images to interact with fields and villages.[78] (Indeed, one might say that the cult proces-

---

75 Herrmann, "Der Nil und die Christen," 43–47; MacCoull, "Stud. Pal. XV 250ab"; Bonneau, *La crue du Nil*, 435–37; Roquet, "L'ange des eaux"; Budge, *Miscellaneous Coptic Texts*, 520.

76 See Timbie, "Liturgical Procession"; idem, "Once More into the Desert." On pilgrimage to Shenoute's monastery in general, see Behlmer, "Visitors to Shenoute's Monastery"; and Blanke, "Allure of the Saint." On the tomb chapel: Bolman, Davis, and Pyke, "Shenoute and a Recently Discovered Tomb Chapel."

77 Papaconstantinou, "La liturgie stationnale."

78 See Finnestad, "Temples of the Ptolemaic and Roman Periods"; Frankfurter, *Religion in Roman Egypt*, 145–61; Baines, *High Culture and Experience*, 48–58.

CHAPTER 7

sion was as central to Egyptian religion as ritual animal slaughter was to Greek and Roman religions.) Yet the Christian institution's embrace of procession in late antiquity represents less an assimilation of indigenous ritual forms than an exportation of a distinctly urban practice. In Rome, Antioch, and Alexandria processions were the customary means of dramatizing the monumentality of a city (and, in the case of Alexandrian bishops like the late fourth-century Theophilus, dramatizing Christian control over that monumentality).[79] They were also the customary means of introducing the authority of some important personage.[80] In some cities a carefully mapped procession might interconnect the cityscape with its particular local landforms—hills, sea, rivers—or might revitalize a beneficial relationship between the city and some suburban shrine; in general, such processions would introduce or rehearse a new local history made up of new collective memories of Christian heroes and heathen antagonists. In situations of crisis, the procession to the suburban, regional shrine would have allowed a collective, spatial response. In Jerusalem and in many local stational processions around the late antique world (like the one dedicated to Abbot Shenoute), the order or stages of collective action might have had a mimetic character, immersing participants in sacred memories fixed to particular shrines. But whether these processions occurred in urban or rural worlds, it is important not to regard landscape as simply a backdrop to action. Landscape and cityscape both effectively shape, direct, and mediate processional action and all the ideological or mythological meanings they express. Landscape and cityscape—streets, squares, shrines, basilicas, paths through wadis and past temples and alongside rivers—provide the very symbols by which processional participants remember saints and gather a sense of liturgy or hierarchy.[81]

But the landscape in this case *was* Egyptian, and so ecclesiastical processions could not but have reinforced a religious sense of the landscape, addressing central features like the Nile, gathering the efficacy of shrines, and shaping the collective response to the agricultural cycle. Both by its ritual nature and in its various historical contexts, the procession provided participants a medium for collectively engaging Christianity as an institution, as well as specific local cult memories, through movement and song and gesture. Through processions landscape maintained its preeminence in guiding local memories and the popular comprehension of religion.

---

79 See Baldovin, *Urban Character of Christian Worship*, 254–59; Watts, *Riot in Alexandria*, 190–243.

80 See MacCormack, *Art and Ceremony*, 17–61; Baldovin, *Urban Character of Christian Worship*, 234–38; cf. Andrade, "Processions of John Chrysostom."

81 See useful remarks on procession in ancient and medieval religion by Baldovin, *Urban Character of Christian Worship*, 254–68; Graf, "Pompai in Greece"; and idem, *Roman Festivals*, 43–46, 232–38; Howe, "Conversion of the Physical World," 68–71; Boogaart, "Our Saviour's Blood," esp. 92–96; and, on the importance of procession in the Christianization of the late antique city, Busine, "Introduction," 10–11.

V. INVENTING AND ENVISIONING A SACRED LANDSCAPE

But where did one go in procession? We have seen examples of old statues that one rubbed and wells with magical water, dilapidated temples where a spirit might be contacted, the Nile, and the Christian shrines and churches. But Christian martyrological legend sanctioned the idea well into the medieval period that martyrs' bones and footprints lay potentially anywhere in city, village, or countryside; people had only to find them. Much as villagers in colonial Latin America claimed their own encounters with Christ and the Virgin in the mountains, so in late antique Egypt the recognition of the martyrs in the landscape came about as often through the agency of local people as from official *inventio*.[82]

Shenoute, for example, complains about local folk who would announce that martyrs had appeared to them and claim that the martyrs' own spirits had showed them where their relics lay.[83] Some people would discover remains in some building and take them to be martyrs' relics. Indeed, Shenoute says, they would go so far as to declare, "I will build a shrine [ⲙⲁ] for [the martyr]," sometimes inside the church itself, and proceed to light lamps over the relics and sleep there for healing.[84] In other words, the situating of holy martyrs had become a local, lay endeavor already by the fourth century, even while in urban worlds these relics might have served as political commodities. Coptic martyrologies attribute a similar agency to villagers in retrieving and enshrining relics. In one, a local holy man is led to the remains of Sts. Paēse and Thecla, where he wraps them up, takes them to a "high place," and buries them "until the day when it pleased God to reveal them."[85] The (implied) scribe of another martyrology claims that many imprisoned martyrs arrived at his house after Constantine's accession, and some even died there, whom he proceeded to bury in his "storehouses and workshops, that their blessing and their grace be with us."[86] The hagiographer of the holy man and martyr Apa Apoli celebrates a "dumb man ... (and devout!)" who builds "a small shrine-complex [ⲅⲱⲡⲣⲟ] in your honor and a church in honor of your name, and he will lay your pure body in it. And the village will grow great, and they shall call it Psenetai. . . . [And then] they shall remove your body to a village called Psobt-mp-hoi."[87]

---

82 Frankfurter, "Introduction." On Latin America, see, e.g., Sallnow, *Pilgrims of the Andes*.

83 The Council of Carthage (491) issued similar complaints about popular revelations of martyrs' relics and the shrines built in response to them (Canon 83).

84 Shenoute, "Those Who Work Evil," in Amélineau, *Oeuvres de Schenoudi* I, 212, 219–20, also 215, 217. See in general Lefort, "La chasse aux reliques."

85 *Martyrdom of Paēse and Thecla*, Pierpont Morgan Codex M591 t. 28, f. 88rii, in Reymond and Barns, *Four Martyrdoms*, 78–79, 184 (translation).

86 Martyrdom of S. Shenoufe, Pierpont Morgan Codex M 583, t. 41, f. 138r I, in ibid., 126–27, 221 (translation).

87 Martyrdom of Apa Apoli, frag. 5, in Evelyn White, Sobhy, and Lythgoe, *Monasteries of the Wâdi 'n Natrûn*, 92.

CHAPTER 7

This indigenous impulse to collect, enshrine, and ritually interact with martyrs' relics outside of ecclesiastical sanction often met with skepticism on the part of authorities. Shenoute argues that those newly "invented" relics may belong to perverts and criminals; Athanasius has St. Antony demand a secret burial lest his relics be improperly taken into homes, as Egyptians were supposed to do by custom; and even in Gaul, Martin of Tours reveals that the relics in a popular local shrine actually belong to a robber.[88] The indigenous invention of relics was hardly an Egyptian phenomenon, but it does illustrate the dedication with which local people situated Christianity in their own neighborhoods and landscapes, actively creating a sacred topography largely out of the frameworks that Christianity offered in the form of martyrology, biblical legend, and ascetic holy men.[89]

The result, as we come to see it in hagiography, was an ideology—shared between local worlds and ecclesiastical institutions—that envisioned a terrestrial network of saints' shrines, some along the road, some in domestic districts, some in churches, and many with dramatic legends that traced some martyr's lurid tortures en route to "this place here." The holy Victor is taken from the "emperor's palace" to Alexandria, then the Thebaid, and finally Hierakopolis, where he is decapitated.[90] Shenoufe and his brethren are brought from Alexandria to "Chortasa," then "Tilog," tortured all along the way, to wind up sanctifying the town of Poubaste.[91] St. Eusebius is sent up the Nile to Coptos, then to the village of Hnes, and to a valley just to the east, where he is finally beheaded.[92] Apa Macarius of Antioch is brought from Alexandria to Pshati, where the drama is set among the town's streets and theater, before being taken south, to be decapitated in the village of Chetnoufi.[93] "This is the place," says the Archangel Michael, "that the Lord has designated for your holy body to stay, and he will not allow (this village) to lack anything good, on account of your holy body that will be deposited among them.... Glory to the village that receives you!"[94] Through this literature of spatiality and etiology, continuously composed and expanded up through the twelfth century, villages gained prominence as stops in the martyr's journey or as the final resting spot of martyrs' heads, while entire regions became defined by their particular saints.[95]

88 Shenoute, "Those Who Work Evil," in Amélineau, *Oeuvres de Schenoudi*, 216. Antony: Athanasius, *v.Ant.* 90–91. Martin: Sulpicius Severus, *v. Mart.* 11.

89 See Van der Vliet, "Bringing Home the Homeless," 44–48.

90 B.M. Or. 7022, in Budge, *Coptic Martyrdoms*, 46–100 (text), 299–355 (translation).

91 Pierpont Morgan Codex M 583, in Reymond and Barns, *Four Martyrdoms*, 81–127 (text), 185–222 (translation).

92 Cod. Vat. 58, in Hyvernat, *Les actes des martyrs*, 1–39.

93 Cod. Vat. 59, in ibid., 40–77. See also Papaconstantinou, *Le culte des saints*, 140, on epigraphical evidence for the cult of St. Macarius of Antioch.

94 Martyrdom of St. Macarius of Antioch (Cod. Vat. 59, ff.75–76), in Hyvernat, *Les actes des martyrs*, 66–67.

95 Papaconstantinou, "Où le péché abondait," esp. 244–48.

TRADITIONS OF THE LANDSCAPE

As much as this shared ideology of a network of shrines came out of *indigenous* inclinations to map supernatural potency and to localize aspects of the Great Tradition, it also reflected the *scribal* tradition (described in chapter 6) of coordinating the Egyptian landscape as a geography of blessings. Some Egyptian texts from the late first millennium BCE, like the Book of the Fayyum and the Brooklyn Delta Papyrus, give a sense of the kind of sacred landscape that the medieval (twelfth- to thirteen-century) Coptic martyrologies were envisioning. Through such "cultic geographies" a designated landscape became more than just a sequence of shrines for processional visit; rather, it became the image of a body or even of the cosmos.[96] At an even broader geographical level, Egypt as a whole could be imagined as sanctified and maintained through the bodies of saints, which must be kept near, "for because of them the earth gives fruit; for because of them the sun shines upon the earth, for because of them the dew falls upon the earth!"[97] In these words the third-century *Apocalypse of Elijah* imagines the locative value of martyrs' bodies, anticipating the words of the Cologne prophecy (discussed in chapter 6) that pronounced blessings on Egypt: "You holy one, 83,721 martyrs shall exist throughout you, who have poured out their blood on account of my Son."[98] And by the ninth century such sentiments had become part of festival liturgies: "Truly, the land of Egypt was worthy of great grace because of the blood of these martyrs, Apa Victor and Claudius."[99] These *scribal* projections of an entire Egypt blessed through martyrs entirely transcended the real world of local landscapes, with their particular saints, spirits, and traditions of ritual movement. They followed both early literary traditions, as we have seen, and a scribal interest from the period following Islamization to articulate the value of Christian saints for a country incorporating another religion.[100]

Thus, in multiple dimensions and multiple social worlds, the landscape became narrated and memorialized as sacred, powerful, and linked to "us": *our* village, *our* hills, and the river that integrates *our* territory. Certainly these stories developed and maintained a vitality in local oral culture, and hagiography undoubtedly picked up on many of these local legends.[101] But hagiography also reflected its own authors' social worlds and literary traditions—not just in collect-

---

96 See Beinlich, *Das Buch vom Fayum*; with review by Derchain in *Bibliotheca Orientalis* 51 (1994): 42–50; Meeks, *Mythes et légendes du Delta*. On this geographical characteristic of martyrologies, see Baumeister, *Martyr invictus*.

97 *Apocalypse of Elijah* 5.18 in Frankfurter, *Elijah in Upper Egypt*, 324–25; see idem, "Cult of the Martyrs."

98 P. Col. Inv. 20912 A.2, 7–9, in Schenke, "P.Köln 354" (translation based on unpublished English translation provided graciously by Schenke).

99 "Alphabetic acrostic on Apa Claudius," 24, in Kühn and Tait, *Thirteen Coptic Acrostic Hymns*, 54–55.

100 Papaconstantinou, *Le culte des saints en Égypte*, 247–48; idem, "Historiography, Hagiography, and the Making."

101 See Décobert, "Un lieu de mémoire religieuse."

ing folklore but in constructing the regional landscape as a Christian microcosm: the martyr who sailed down from Alexandria to this village, the glorious network of saints housed in our entire district, the land of Egypt, and the legends that connected it all with Christian teachings.[102]

VI. CONCLUSION

In many ways the Christianization of the Egyptian landscape took place through the work of similar social worlds as sites of agency, and through the same ritual means as elsewhere in the empire. Indigenous structures, many used for prior cults, were appropriated for their spectacular prominence in the countryside, while bishops, priests, and monks created and led processions to link liturgical structures, healing shrines, and sites of sanctity in the countryside, all according to a calendar that allowed regular participation in this kind of synthesis of Christian topography. Belief in ancestral and earth spirits clearly persisted in many parts of the local landscape, sometimes with the memory of ancient names, but more often as a function of liminality, territorial features, or even the intrinsic power of certain images—as in the case of the maternal Isis or the two reliefs, "Moses" and "Aaron," that Egeria encountered. These spirits might have been warded off through the use of spolia, or even appropriated for protective or beneficial purposes. Engagement of such spirits in the landscape was no nostalgic "pagan survival" but very much part of life in the local community and the people's negotiation of its landscape, seasons, memories, and social structure. Indeed, the same local agency that led local Christians to rub a statue of Isis or light lamps by Hathor's head also led them to collect bones of martyrs, install them in shrines, and narrate their stories according to the hills and structures of the surrounding landscape.

---

102 See also Bitel, "Ekphrasis at Kildare"; Saradi, "Christianization of Pagan Temples," 123–25.

Afterword

In the end, what *is* Christianization? Does it not somehow presuppose a Christianity with a fixed belief system, books, and central rituals? Does it not imply some basic change in cultures—a "conversion" of sorts? What we understand by the term "Christianity" now is very much the product of the Reformation, just as Islam, Judaism, and now even Hinduism have assumed a modern guise of scripturalist orthodoxy that could not possibly have described these religions in their early centuries. Let me offer some models instead for thinking about "Christianity" as people would have conceptualized it in late antique Egypt.

As the chapters in this book have pursued it, Christianization amounts to an ongoing and historically contingent *process* without an endpoint; in late antique Egypt that process was a function of social agency, of material media like figurines and papyri, and of places in the landscape: the Nile on the one hand, a monumental church on the other. I have focused on social worlds of concern and of technological expertise, ranging from the domestic sphere, whose agents moved out to shrines and holy men for healing and fertility, to the textile workshop, whose agents crafted garments efficacious in life and in death out of Christian and other symbols. According to social world and locale, Christianity could be brought into play—into relevance and efficacy—in the context of a liturgical procession or through the funerary stela, through amulet or blessed oil, through figurine or oracle procedure. In many areas Christianity was apparent through its liturgical performances and the apparently unified hierarchy and economic system behind it, all of which gave the impression of "an artificial kin group," a more accessible empire, as it were.[1] Yet in other areas the strange collectivities of monks or the charismatic holy man might have been the face of the religion. Thus, in the vaguest formulation, Christianity amounted to a system of authority and a repository of symbols and stories, variously combined and recombined with local traditions according to the goals, crafts, and everyday circumstances of specific types of people.

This is the benefit of Robert Redfield's model of the Great Tradition in contradistinction to the "Local" tradition: the Great Tradition is not an a priori and immutable presence but an invention, the product of historical agency and

---

1 Brown, *Cult of the Saints*, 31.

exigency. For what reasons, we must ask, and in what senses do *which* people profess or invoke a Great Tradition?[2]

What does it mean, then, to imagine Christianity as a Great Tradition? We can use this concept not to project a true or orthodox system but to consider what may have been distinctive about Christianity in late antiquity (from the fourth century on) and as it was received by, for example, villages in Egypt. As a Great Tradition Christianity brought together not only meaningful collective action and ritual but also cosmic authority—*powers* to heal bodies and impact kingdoms. Those powers came in categories: ecclesiastial substances, a pantheon of martyrs and saints, the saintly fathers in the local monastery, and certainly bishops. Christianity as a Great Tradition signified a kind of *modernity* (to the extent that this term can apply to a sensibility in late antiquity), so that participating in Christianity and patronizing its infrastructure made you "modern" and aided economic success. It comprised a micro-society, a *hierarchy* of offices and roles, although we should be wary of reifying a Christian "institution" as if there were not—always—competing claims to authority over texts, "salvation," and other religious commodities.[3] For some this Great Tradition involved expressive and performative *codes*—for example, in the promulgation and use of letters, with their nomina sacra and codes of deference, between individuals and congregations.[4] Its central symbol, the cross, bore little reference to Jesus's execution by this time, but it was visible in ecclesiastical processions, church iconography, and potential demonic habitats, and it oriented and stimulated gesture, prayer, and funerary art. Its *pantheon* of God, Christ, Mary, angels, and saints was also cosmic in essence: transcendent of the local domain (even if intimately active there) but leaving impacts throughout the world and history. Its central medium was a *book*, a sacred scripture, whose stories and writing could be drawn upon for all manner of things in this world, and so the Christian institution put a high premium on the reading and interpretation of that book, both as a material object (a source of amulets) and as an authoritative ideal of truth (the codex from which one could read or divine).[5]

But did this mean you could travel anywhere and find the same texts being read, the same stories being told, and the same ceremonies being performed? No. Ultimately, late antique Egypt consisted of local cultures and cities made of localizing districts. A Great Tradition is not a real institution maintaining cohesiveness across time and space but a set of ideas and symbols imagined differently in different towns and differently by the layperson, the priest, the monastic scribe, and the elite lord. Religion is always a process of negotiation between *local* traditions,

---

2 Redfield, *Folk Culture of Yucatan*; idem, *Peasant Society and Culture*; Marriott, "Little Communities"; Srinivas, *Cohesive Role of Sanskritization*; Sallnow, *Pilgrims of the Andes*; Christian, *Local Religion in Sixteenth-Century Spain*; Frankfurter, "The Great, the Little."
3 See Brakke, "Scriptural Practices in Early Christianity," esp. 269.
4 See esp. Luijendijk, *Greetings in the Lord*, 102–23; and in general Choat, *Belief and Cult*.
5 See esp. Beard, "Writing and Religion"; and Lane Fox, "Literacy and Power."

often one deeply invested in claiming the *authority* of a Great Tradition and the ever-changing ideology—and its representatives—of that Great Tradition. In late antique Egypt, everybody was involved in this negotiation: the devout monastic scribe who composed a festival reading about John the Baptist, the bishop appalled with local holiday customs, the holy man who dispensed fox claw amulets, the bride so anxious to conceive that she left a figurine in the tomb of an ancestor, and the cowherd who would sing a song to bless his cattle by the powers of a few old gods and a couple new ones. In each case there is a set of symbols, ideas, and terminology that seems integrated and authoritative to the agent: "Christian." In some settings "Christian" consisted in names or stories that could be brought together with older, more familiar names and stories, like the Berlin papyrus's magical stories with which chapter 1 began, or the *Apocalypse of Elijah*, which chapter 6 discussed. In other cases "Christian" would have been invoked to imply a rejection of other (heathen) symbols and discourses, as in the sermons of Shenoute of Atripe. In some areas—or for some individuals—what signified "Christian" was to assume for oneself one of those names or to bestow one on a child, to *become* Paul or Elijah rather than just hear their stories. In still other settings, "Christian" simply designated new centers for familiar practices, like private devotional gestures at saints' shrines in the hope of conception. Those who built those centers had concepts of Christian authority that differed from those who staffed them and offered divination services there and from those who visited them and left ritual deposits.

It is the negotiation between these multiple notions of Christian authority and the traditions embedded in local experience and creative practices that has concerned this book: the kinds of people who engage in such negotiation, in what kinds of social spaces, and to what creative or ritual ends. For this process of negotiation between Great and Local traditions is not only inevitable, but the very synthesis of religion in life and culture. And it is syncretistic by definition: it consists of phrasing the new (or authoritative) in terms of the habitual, the traditional, and vice versa.

But let me offer two other, complementary models for thinking about Christianity in the contexts I have been describing: not as one ideology but as a range of possible strategies for action. This was the proposal of the sociologist Ann Swidler for how "culture" works in practice: not through fixed customs or maps for behavior, nor even through a "structure of identity," but through often-inconsistent ideas, stories, and symbols that we draw upon, improvise from, and select and reject according to circumstances.[6] Thus Christianity in late antiquity was drawn upon to sanction imperial militancy and ascetic poverty, magical curse spells and glorious monastic liturgies, almsgiving and the production of gold lampstands for churches, gospel stories and folk songs about martyrs. It was a

---

6 Swidler, "Culture in Action"; idem, *Talk of Love*; and, as applied to religious enculturation, Campany, "Religious Repertoires and Contestation."

series of possible strategies that one might, but not always, draw upon, and that more often than not integrated older traditions rather than excluding them. It is such strategies we see in Coptic scribes' reinventions of the Land of Egypt oracle, in craftsmen's quests for efficacy in corpse wrapping and textile design, in innovations in procession from the church through the local landscape, and in the ways people ventured out to places from their homes in the hope of "blessings" from holy men or martyrs.

But here Swidler's more intellectual sense of strategies might be augmented with a reemphasis on the *material media* by which people recognized Christianity and agents crafted it—the topic of chapter 5, but a theme that has run throughout this book. This is the sense in which the anthropologist Birgit Meyer has discussed the "sensational forms"—"configuration(s) of religious media, acts, imaginations, and bodily sensations"—that religious traditions present to participants in alternative, sometimes conflicting modes according to time, place, and relevance. "A sensational form," Meyer continues, "provides an authorized procedure to experience, in a structured manner, a movement towards a limit that evokes a sense of there being something more." A sensational form is a kind of regimen for interacting *through* material media, "shaping and framing... the body and the senses as harbingers and an index of the divine."[7] Here then is another dimension of the strategies that Christianity put in place for negotiation by individuals and communities: not just crosses but dispositions toward crosses; not just books or writing but a particular sensory awe of these materials; not just familiarity with liturgical chants and the invocation of angels but ways of hearing or smelling that made these verbal media all the more distinctive; and not just the social intuition of the holy man but the whole process of approaching him, beholding him, communicating with him, touching his body. The strategies and sensory forms that constituted Christianity extended to uses of text and sacred writing, the cross, figurines, and liturgical incantation, all of which would have been imagined by their agents as conveying Christian authority and would have been *experienced* by their lay and monastic users in intimate, tactile ways—as *things* with their own agency and force.

To speak of syncretism today requires more than just a repudiation of pure dual systems; it requires that we conceptualize processes and sites of bricolage and the particular elements that can be assembled in that bricolage according to the exigencies of particular religious worlds. Thus Christianity can be seen as entering the ongoing syncretistic process of Egyptian culture, not as a theological statement or creed but as a cluster of authoritative *strategies*—narratives of miracles, sanctions of ritual expertise, demonologies, asceticisms—and of *sensational forms*, ranging from basilica and martyrion to the body of the holy man and the image of the cross. This is what constitutes "Christianity"; these are the elements

---

7 Birgit Meyer, "Mediation and the Genesis of Presence," 26; and idem, "How to Capture the 'Wow,'" 20.

that local agents, from grandmothers to monks to shrine attendants, strived to make recognizable and central in the immediate environment. By focusing on the agency of people who selected particular religious strategies and engaged (or even appropriated) the sensational forms of Christianity, these final models again move us away from Christianization as "conversion," as the wholesale cultural embrace of a religious ideology, and toward the local introduction of certain stories and principles—principles, say, for thinking about one's ailing body, for seeking guidance about a trip, for walking behind a procession, for crafting a protective amulet, or for imagining that huge headless statue lying next to the field, where the women scratch sand to protect their children.

BIBLIOGRAPHY

Abd el-Al, Abd el-Hafeez, Jean Claude Grenier, and Guy Wagner. *Stèles funéraires de Kom Abu Bellou*. Mémoire (Éditions Recherche sur les civilisations) 55. Paris: Editions Recherche sur les civilisations, 1985.

Abdelwahed, Youssri Ezzat Hussein. *Houses in Graeco-Roman Egypt: Arenas for Ritual Activity*. Oxford: Archaeopress, 2016.

Ackerman, Susan. "Household Religion, Family Religion, and Women's Religion in Ancient Israel." In *Household and Family Religion in Antiquity*, edited by John Bodel and Saul M. Olyan, 127–58. Malden, MA: Wiley-Blackwell, 2008.

Ägypten: Schätze aus dem Wüstensand: Kunst und Kulture der Christen am Nil. Wiesbaden, Germany: Reichert Verlag, 1996.

Agady, S., M. Arazi, B. Arubas, S. Hadad, E. Khamis, and Y. Tsafrir. "Byzantine Shops in the Street of the Monuments at Bet Shean (Scythopolis)." In *What Athens Has to Do with Jerusalem: Essays on Classical, Jewish, and Early Christian Art and Archaeology in Honor of Gideon Foerster*, edited by L. V. Rutgers, 423–533. Leuven, Belgium: Peeters, 2002.

Allen, Marti Lu. "The Terracotta Figurines from Karanis: A Study of Technique, Style and Chronology in Fayoumic Coroplastics." Ph.D. diss., University of Michigan, 1985.

Allison, Dale C. *Testament of Abraham*. Commentaries of Early Jewish Literature. Berlin and New York: Walter de Gruyter, 2003.

Alston, Richard. "Houses and Households in Roman Egypt." In *Domestic Space in the Roman World: Pompeii and Beyond*, edited by A. Wallace-Hardill and R. Laurence, 25–39. Portsmouth, RI: Journal of Roman Archaeology Press, 1997.

———. *The City in Roman and Byzantine Egypt*. London and New York: Routledge, 2002.

Aly, Zaki. "More Funerary Stelae from Kôm Abou Bellou." *Bulletin de la société archéologique d'Alexandrie* 40 (1953): 101–50.

———. "Some Funerary Stelae from Kôm Abou Bellou." *Bulletin de la société archéologique d'Alexandrie* 38 (1949): 53–88.

Ambjörn, Lena, trans. *The Life of Severus by Zachariah of Mitylene*. Texts from Christian Late Antiquity 9. Piscataway, NJ: Gorgias Press, 2008.

Ameijeiras, Rocío Sánchez. "Imagery and Interactivity: Ritual Transaction at the Saint's Tomb." In *Decorations for the Holy Dead: Visual Embellishments on Tombs and Shrines of Saints*, edited by Stephen Lamia and Elizabeth Valdez del Alamo, 21–38. Turnhout, Belgium: Brepols, 2002.

Amélineau, Émile. *Étude sur le Christianisme en Égypte au septième siècle*. Paris: E. Leroux, 1887.

———. *Histoire des monastères de la Basse-Egypte: Vies des saints Paul, Antoine, Macaire, Maxime et Domèce, Jean le Nain: Texte copte et traduction française*. Paris: E. Leroux, 1894.

———. *Monuments pour servir à l'histoire de l'Égypte chrétienne aux IVe, Ve, VIe et VIIe siècles: Textes et traduction*. Paris: Leroux, 1895.

———, ed. *Oeuvres de Schenoudi I: Texte copte et traduction française*. Paris: E. Leroux, 1907.

BIBLIOGRAPHY

Amidon, Philip R., trans. *The Church History of Rufinus of Aquileia, Books 10 and 11*. New York: Oxford University Press, 1997.

Ammerman, Rebecca Miller. "Children at Risk: Votive Terracottas and the Welfare of Infants at Paestum." In *Constructions of Childhood in Ancient Greece and Italy*, edited by Ada Cohen and Jeremy B Rutter, 131–51. Princeton, NJ: American School of Classical Studies at Athens, 2007.

Andrade, Nathanael. "The Processions of John Chrysostom and the Contested Spaces of Constantinople." *Journal of Early Christian Studies* 18, no. 2 (2010): 161–89.

Appadurai, Arjun. "Introduction: Commodities and the Politics of Value." In *The Social Life of Things: Commodities in Cultural Perspective*, edited by Arjun Appadurai, 3–63. Cambridge and New York: Cambridge University Press, 1988.

Aravecchia, Nicola. "The Church Complex of 'Ain El-Gedida, Dakhleh Oasis." In *The Oasis Papers 6: Proceedings of the Sixth International Conference of the Dakhleh Oasis Project*, edited by Roger S. Bagnall, Paula Davoli, and Colin A. Hope, 391–408. Oxford: Oxbow Books, 2012.

Arnold, Dieter. *Temples of the Last Pharaohs*. New York: Oxford University Press, 1999.

Ashley, Kathleen M. "Introduction: The Moving Subjects of Processional Performance." In *Moving Subjects: Processional Performance in the Middle Ages and the Renaissance*, edited by K. M. Ashley and W.M.N. Hüsken, 7–34. Atlanta: Rodopi, 2001.

Assmann, Jan. "Königsdogma und Heilserwartung: Politische und kultische Chaosbeschreibungen in ägyptischen Texten." In *Apocalypticism in the Mediterranean World and the Near East*, edited by David Hellholm, 345–77. Tübingen: Mohr Siebeck, 1983.

———. "Translating God: Religion as a Factor of Cultural (Un)Translatability." In *The Translatability of Cultures: Figurations of the Space Between*, edited by Sanford Budick and Wolfgang Iser, 25–36. Stanford, CA: Stanford University Press, 1996.

Athanassiadi, Polymnia. "Persecution and Response in Late Paganism: The Evidence of Damascius." *Journal of Hellenic Studies* 113 (1993): 1–29.

Athanassiadi, Polymnia, and Michael Frede, eds. *Pagan Monotheism in Late Antiquity*. Oxford: Clarendon Press, 1999.

Aubé, E. B. *Polyeucte dans l'histoire: Étude sur le martyre de Polyeucte d'après des documents inédits*. Paris: Firmin-Didot, 1882.

Aufrère, Sydney. "L'Égypte traditionnelle, ses démons vus par les premiers chrétiens." In *Études coptes V: 6e journée d'études, Limoges, 18–20 juin 1993 et 7e journée d'études, Neuchâtel, 18–20 mai 1995*, edited by M. Rassart-DeBergh, 63–92. Paris: Peeters, 1998.

Austin, J. L. *How to Do Things with Words*. Cambridge, MA: Harvard University Press, 1975.

Auth, Susan. "Brother George the Scribe: An Early Christian Panel Painting from Egypt in Context." *Eastern Christian Art* 2 (2005): 19–36.

Bagnall, Roger S. "Combat ou vide: Christianisme et paganisme dans l'Égypte romaine tardive." *Ktema* 13 (1988): 285–96.

———. "Conversion and Onomastics: A Reply." *Zeitschrift für Papyrologie und Epigraphik* 69 (1987): 243–50.

———. *Early Christian Books in Egypt*. Princeton, NJ: Princeton University Press, 2009.

———. *Egypt in Late Antiquity*. Princeton, NJ: Princeton University Press, 1995.

———. "Religious Conversion and Onomastic Change in Early Byzantine Egypt." *Bulletin of the American Society of Papyrologists* 19 (1982): 105–24.

Bagnall, Roger S., and Raffaella Cribiore. *Women's Letters from Ancient Egypt, 300 BC–AD 800*. Ann Arbor: University of Michigan Press, 2006.

Bahrani, Zainab. "The Hellenization of Ishtar: Nudity, Fetishism, and the Production of Cultural Differentiation in Ancient Art." *Oxford Art Journal* 19, no. 2 (1996): 3–16.

Bailey, Donald M. *Catalogue of Terracottas in the British Museum IV: Ptolemaic and Roman Terracottas from Egypt*. London: British Museum Press, 2008.

Bailey, Ryan. "The Confession of Cyprian of Antioch: Introduction, Text, and Translation." M. A. thesis, McGill University, 2009.

Bailliot, Magali. "Autour des morts: Rites et croyances du paganisme au christianisme dans le département de l'Essonne." *Cartes archéologique de la Gaule* 91 (2004): 75–81.

———. *Magie et sortilèges dans l'antiquité romaine: Archéologie des rituels et des images*. Paris: Hermann Éditeurs, 2010.

Baills-Talbi, Nathalie, and Phillippe Blanchard. "Sépultures de nouveau-nés et de nourrissons du 1er âge du fer au haut Moyen Âge découvertes hors des contextes funéraires traditionnels sur les territoires carnute, turon et bituriges cube: Inventaire, synthèse et interprétations." In *Ensembles funéraires gallo-romains de la région centre, I, Tours*, 157–205. Tours, France: FÉRACF, 2006.

Baines, John. "Egyptian Syncretism: Hans Bonnet's Contribution." *Orientalia* 68, no. 3 (1999): 199–214.

———. *High Culture and Experience in Ancient Egypt*. Studies in Egyptology and the Ancient Near East. Sheffield, UK: Equinox Publishing, 2013.

———. "Temples as Symbols, Guarantors, and Participants in Egyptian Civilisation." In *The Temple in Ancient Egypt: New Discoveries and Recent Research*, edited by Stephen Quirke, 216–41. London: British Museum Press, 1997.

Baker, Cynthia. *Rebuilding the House of Israel: Architectures of Gender in Jewish Antiquity*. Divinations. Stanford, CA: Stanford University Press, 2002.

Baldovin, John F. *The Urban Character of Christian Worship: The Origins, Development, and Meaning of Stational Liturgy*. Orientalia Christiana Analecta 228. Rome: Pont. Institutum Studiorum Orientalium, 1987.

Ball, Jennifer L. "Charms: Protective and Auspicious Motifs." In *Designing Identity: The Power of Textiles in Late Antiquity*, edited by Thelma K. Thomas, 54–65. Princeton, NJ: Princeton University Press/Institute for the Study of the Ancient World, 2016.

Ballet, Pascale. "Ceramics, Coptic." In *The Coptic Encyclopedia*, edited by Aziz Atiya, 2:480–504. New York: Macmillan, 1991.

———. "Isis assise sur la corbeille, au sistre, au pot rond et au miroir: Essai d'interprétation." In *Hommages à Jean Leclant 3: Études isiaques*, edited by Catherine Berger, Gisèle Clerc, and Nicolas-Christophe Grimal, 21–32. Cairo: IFAO, 1994.

———. "Le moulage des terres cuites dans l'Égypte gréco-romaine: État des problématiques." In *Le moulage en terre cuite dans l'Antiquité: Création et production dérivée, fabrication et diffusion: Actes du XVIIIe colloque du Centre de Recherches Archéologiques-Lille III (7–8 déc. 1995)*, edited by Arthur Muller, 241–56. Lille, France: Presses universitaires du Septentrion, 1997.

———. "Les terres cuites romaines de Coptos: Du musée à l'atelier." *Bulletin des musées et monuments lyonnais* 4 (1999): 2–17.

———. "Potiers et fabricants de figurines dans l'Égypte ancienne." *Cahiers de la céramique égyptienne* 4 (1996): 113–22.

Ballet, Pascale, and Geneviève Galliano. "Les isiaques et la petite plastique dans l'Égypte hellénistique et romaine." In *Isis on the Nile: Egyptian Gods in Hellenistic and Roman Egypt: Proceedings of the 6th International Conference of Isis Studies, Liège, November 27–29, 2008: Michel Malaise in Honorem*, edited by Laurent Bricault and M. J Versluys, 197–220. Religions in the Graeco-Roman World 171. Leiden: Brill, 2010.

Ballet, Pascale, and Fatma Mahmoud. "Moules en terre cuite d'Éléphantine (Musée copte)." *Bulletin de l'institut français d'archéologie orientale* 87 (1987): 53–72.

Ballet, Pascale, Fatma Mahmoud, Michèle Vichy, and Maurice Picon. "Artisanat de la céramique dans l'Égypte romaine tardive et byzantine: Prospections d'ateliers de potiers de Minia à Assouan." *Cahiers de la céramique égyptienne* 2 (1991): 129–45.

Bangert, Susanne. "The Archaeology of Pilgrimage: Abu Mena and Beyond." In *Religious Diversity in Late Antiquity*, edited by David M. Gwynn, Susanne Bangert, and Luke Lavan, 293–327. Late Antique Archaeology 6. Leiden: Brill, 2010.

Barasch, Moshe. "Visual Syncretism: A Case Study." In *The Translatability of Cultures: Figurations of the Space Between*, edited by Sanford Budick and Wolfgang Iser, 37–54. Stanford, CA: Stanford University Press, 1996.

Barb, A. A. "The Survival of the Magic Arts." In *The Conflict Between Paganism and Christianity in the Fourth Century: Essays*, edited by Arnaldo Momigliano, 100–125. Oxford: Clarendon Press, 1963.

Barlow, Claude W., trans. *Iberian Fathers 1: Martin of Braga, Paschasius of Dumium, Leander of Seville*. Fathers of the Church 62. Washington, DC: Catholic University of America Press, 1969.

Barnish, S.J.B. "*Religio in Stagno*: Nature, Divinity, and the Christianization of the Countryside in Late Antique Italy." *Journal of Early Christian Studies* 9, no. 3 (2001): 387–402.

Bartelink, G.J.M. *Athanase d'Alexandrie, Vie d'Antoine*. Sources chrétiennes 400. Paris: Éditions du Cerf, 2004.

Basset, René. *Le Synaxaire arabe jacobite II: Les mois de hatour et de kihak*. Patrologia Orientalis 3.3. Paris: Firmin-Didot, 1909.

———. *Le Synaxaire arabe jacobite III: Les mois de toubeh et d'amchir*. Patrologia Orientalis 11.5. Paris: Firmin-Didot, 1915.

Basso, Keith H. "Stalking with Stories: Names, Places, and Moral Narratives among the Western Apache." In *On Nature: Nature, Landscape, and Natural History*, edited by Daniel Halpern, 95–115. San Francisco: North Point Press, 1987.

Bauckham, Richard. *The Fate of the Dead: Studies on the Jewish and Christian Apocalypses*. Supplements to Novum Testamentum 93. Leiden: Brill, 1998.

Bauckham, Richard, James R. Davila, and Alexander Panayotov, eds. *Old Testament Pseudepigrapha: More Noncanonical Scriptures*. Grand Rapids, MI: W. B. Eerdmans, 2013.

Bauer, Walter. *Orthodoxy and Heresy in Earliest Christianity*. Translated by Robert A Kraft and Gerhard Krodel. Philadelphia: Fortress Press, 1971.

Baumeister, Theofried. *Martyr invictus: Der Martyrer als Sinnbild der Erlösung in der Legende und im Kult der frühen koptischen Kirche*. Forschungen zur Volkskunde 46. Münster: Regensberg, 1972.

Bayer-Niemeier, Eva. *Bildwerke der Sammlung Kaufmann I: Griechisch-römische Terrakotten*. Melsungen, Germany: Bayer, 1988.

Baynes, Norman H. "The Supernatural Defenders of Constantinople." *Analecta Bollandiana* 67 (1949): 165–77.

Beard, Mary. "Writing and Religion: Ancient Literacy and the Function of the Written Word in Roman Religion." In *Literacy in the Roman World*, edited by Mary Beard, 35–58. Ann Arbor, MI: Journal of Roman Archaeology, 1991.

Béatrice, P. F. "La christianisation des campagnes pendant l'antiquité tardive dans les régions méditerrannéennes: Bilan de recherches et questions de method." In *La christianisation des campagnes: Actes du colloque du C.I.H.E.C. (25–27 août 1994)*, edited by Jean-Pierre Massaut and Marie-Élisabeth Henneau. Bibliothèque de l'Institut historique belge de Rome. Brussels, Rome, and Turnhout, Belgium: Brepols, 1996.

Beck, Pirhiyah. "Human Figure with Tambourine." In *Tel 'Ira: A Stronghold in the Biblical Negev*, edited by Itzhaq Beit-Arieh, 386–94. Tel Aviv: Tel Aviv University, 1999.

Bede. *A History of the English Church and People*. Translated by Leo Sherley-Price, revised by R. E. Latham. Harmondsworth, UK: Penguin, 1968.

BeDuhn, Jason D. "The Domestic Setting of Manichaean Cultic Associations in Roman Late Antiquity." *Archiv für Religionsgeschichte* 10 (2009): 259–74.

Beezley, William H. "Home Altars: Private Reflections of Public Life." In *Home Altars of Mexico*, edited by Dana Salvo, 91–107. Albuquerque: University of New Mexico Press, 1997.

Behlmer, Heike. "Ancient Egyptian Survivals in Coptic Literature: An Overview." In *Ancient Egyptian Literature: History and Forms*, edited by Antonio Loprieno, 567–90. Probleme der Ägyptologie 10. Leiden: Brill, 1996.

———. "Historical Evidence from Shenoute's De extremo iudicio." In *Sesto congresso internazionale di egittologia: Atti*, edited by G. M. Zaccone and T. R. di Netro, 2:11–19. Turin: International Association of Egyptologists, 1993.

———. *Schenute von Atripe: De Iudicio (Torino, Museo egizio, Cat. 63000, Cod. IV.* Monumenti e testi 8. Turin: Museo delle antichità egizie, 1996.

———. "Visitors to Shenoute's Monastery." In *Pilgrimage and Holy Space in Late Antique Egypt*, edited by David Frankfurter, 341–72. Religions in the Graeco-Roman World 134. Leiden: Brill, 1998.

———. "Women and the Holy in Coptic Hagiography." In *Actes du huitième congrès international d'études coptes*, edited by N. Bosson and A. Boud'hors, 2:405–16. Leuven, Belgium: Peeters, 2007.

Beinlich, Horst. *Das Buch vom Fayum: Zum religiösen Eigenverständnis einer ägyptischen Landschaft.* Ägyptologische Abhandlungen 51. Wiesbaden, Germany: O. Harrassowitz, 1991.

Belayche, Nicole. "Foundation Myths in Roman Palestine: Traditions and Reworkings." In *Ethnic Constructs in Antiquity: The Role of Power and Tradition*, edited by Ton Derks and Nico Roymans, 167–83. Amsterdam: Amsterdam University Press, 2009.

———. "Religion et consommation de la viande dans le monde romain: Des réalités voilées." *Food & History* 5, no. 1 (2007): 29–43.

Bell, David N. *Besa: The Life of Shenoute.* Cistercian Studies Series 73. Kalamazoo MI: Cistercian Publications, 1983.

Bell, Harold Idris. *Cults and Creeds in Graeco-Roman Egypt.* Liverpool: University of Liverpool Press, 1953.

Bell, Michael M. "The Ghosts of Place." *Theory and Society* 26 (1997): 813–36.

Beltz, Walter. "Die koptischen Zauberpapyri der Papyrus-Sammlung der staatlichen Museen zu Berlin." *Archiv für Papyrusforschung* 29 (1983): 59–86.

Bernardi, Jean, ed. *Grégoire de Nazianze: Discours 4/5, contre Julien.* Sources chrétiennes 309. Paris: Éditions du Cerf, 1984.

Betteridge, Anne H. "Specialists in Miraculous Action: Some Shrines in Shiraz." In *Sacred Journeys: The Anthropology of Pilgrimage*, edited by E. Alan Morinis, 189–209. Westport, CT: Greenwood Press, 1992.

Bhabha, Homi K. *The Location of Culture.* London; New York: Routledge, 1994.

Bidez, Joseph, and Léon Parmentier, eds. *The Ecclesiastical History of Evagrius, with the Scholia.* Byzantine Texts. London: Methuen & Co., 1898.

Biebel, Franklin Matthews. "Mosaics." In *Gerasa, City of the Decapolis*, edited by Carl H. Kraeling, 297–354. New Haven, CT: American School of Oriental Research, 1938.

Bilu, Yoram. "The Inner Limits of Communitas: A Covert Dimension of Pilgrimage Experience." *Ethos* 16, no. 3 (1988): 302–25.

Birk, Stine. "Carving Sarcophagi: Roman Sculptural Workshops and Their Organization." In *Ateliers and Artisans in Roman Art and Archaeology: Papers Based on a Session Held at the 109th Annual Meeting of the Archaeological Institute of America in Chicago, January 3–6, 2008*, edited by T. M Kristensen and B. Poulsen, 30–37. Portsmouth, RI: Journal of Roman Archaeology, 2012.

Bitel, Lisa M. "Ekphrasis at Kildare: The Imaginative Architecture of a Seventh-Century Hagiographer." *Speculum* 79, no. 3 (2004): 605–27.

Blakely, Sandra. *Myth, Ritual and Metallurgy in Ancient Greece and Recent Africa.* Cambridge: Cambridge University Press, 2006.

Blanke, Louise. "The Allure of the Saint: Late Antique Pilgrimage to the Monastery of St. Shenoute." In *Excavating Pilgrimage: Archaeological Approaches to Sacred Travel and Movement in the Ancient World*, ed. T. M. Kristensen and W. Friese, 203–23. London and New York: Routledge, 2017.

Blumell, Lincoln H., and Thomas A. Wayment, eds. *Christian Oxyrhynchus: Texts, Documents, and Sources.* Waco, TX: Baylor University Press, 2015.

Bodel, John. "Cicero's Minerva, Penates, and the Mother of the Lares: An Outline of Roman Domestic Religion." In *Household and Family Religion in Antiquity*, edited by John Bodel and Saul M. Olyan, 248–75. Malden, MA: Wiley-Blackwell, 2008.

Bodel, John, and Saul M. Olyan, eds. *Household and Family Religion in Antiquity.* Malden, MA: Wiley-Blackwell, 2008.

Boespflug, François. "D'*Isis Lactans* à *Maria Lactans*: Quelques réflexions sur deux motifs similaires."

In *Le Myrte et la rose: Mélanges offerts à Françoise Dunand*, edited by G. Tallet and Chr. Zivie-Coche, 179–97. Montpellier, France: Université Paul Valéry-Montpellier III, 2014.

Boin, Douglas. *Ostia in Late Antiquity*. Cambridge and New York: Cambridge University Press, 2013.

Bolman, Elisabeth S. "Depicting the Kingdom of Heaven: Paintings and Monastic Practice in Early Byzantine Egypt." In *Egypt in the Byzantine World, 300–700*, edited by Roger S. Bagnall, 408–33. New York: Cambridge University Press, 2010.

———. "The Enigmatic Coptic Galaktotrophousa and the Cult of the Virgin Mary in Egypt." In *Images of the Mother of God: Perceptions of the Theotokos in Byzantium*, edited by Maria Vassilaki, 13–22. Burlington, VT: Ashgate Publishing, 2005.

———. "A Staggering Spectacle: Early Byzantine Aesthetics in the Triconch." In *The Red Monastery Church: Beauty and Asceticism in Upper Egypt*, edited by Elizabeth S. Bolman, 119–27. New Haven, CT: Yale University Press/American Research Center in Egypt, 2016.

Bolman, Elizabeth S., Stephen J. Davis, and Gillian Pyke. "Shenoute and a Recently Discovered Tomb Chapel at the White Monastery." *Journal of Early Christian Studies* 18, no. 3 (2010): 453–62.

Bolman, Elizabeth S., and Agnieszka Szymańska. "Ascetic Ancestors: Identity and Genealogy." In *The Red Monastery Church: Beauty and Asceticism in Upper Egypt*, edited by Elizabeth S. Bolman, 164–73. New Haven, CT: Yale University Press/American Research Center in Egypt, 2016.

Bond, Sarah E. "Mortuary Workers, the Church, and the Funeral Trade in Late Antiquity." *Journal of Late Antiquity* 6, no. 1 (2013): 135–51.

Bonneau, Danielle. *La crue du Nil, divinité égyptienne, à travers mille ans d'histoire (332 av.-641 ap. J.-C.) d'après les auteurs grecs et latins, et les documents des époques ptolémaïque, romaine et byzantine*. Études et commentaires 52. Paris: C. Klincksieck, 1964.

———. "Les courants d'eau d'Isis (P. Lond. Lit. 239)." In *Miscellània papirològica Ramón Roca-Puig: En el seu vuitantè aniversari*, edited by Sebastià Janeras, 89–96. Barcelona: FSC, 1987.

———. "Les hommes et le Nil dans l'antiquité." In *L'eau et les hommes en méditerranée*, edited by André Réparaz, 187–98. Paris: CNRS Editions, 1987.

Bonner, Campbell. "Desired Haven." *Harvard Theological Review* 34, no. 1 (1941): 49–67.

———. "The Ship of the Soul on a Group of Grave-Stelae from Terenuthis." *Proceedings of the American Philological Society* 85 (1941): 84–91.

———. *Studies in Magical Amulets, Chiefly Graeco-Egyptian*. Ann Arbor: University of Michigan Press, 1950.

Bonner, Gerald. "The Extinction of Paganism and the Church Historian." *Journal of Ecclesiastical History* 35, no. 3 (1984): 339–57.

Bonnet, Corinne, ed. *Les syncrétismes religieux dans le monde méditerranéen antique: Actes du colloque international en l'honneur de Franz Cumont à l'occasion du cinquantième anniversaire de sa mort, Rome, Academia Belgica, 25–27 Septembre 1997*. Études de Philologie, d'archéologie et d'histoire anciennes 36. Brussels and Rome: Brepols, 1999.

Bonnet, Hans. "On Understanding Syncretism." Translated by J. Baines. *Orientalia* 68, no. 3 (1999): 181–98.

Boogaart, Thomas. "Our Saviour's Blood: Procession and Community in Late Medieval Bruges." In *Moving Subjects: Processional Performance in the Middle Ages and the Renaissance*, edited by K. M. Ashley and W.M.N. Hüsken. Ludus 5. Atlanta: Rodopi, 2001.

Boozer, Anna Lucille. *A Late Romano-Egyptian House in the Dakhla Oasis: Amheida House B2*. Amheida, 2. New York: NYU Press, Institute for the Study of the Ancient World, 2015. http://dlib.nyu.edu/awdl/isaw/amheida-ii-house-b2/.

Borg, Barbara. "The Dead as a Guest at Table? Continuity and Change in the Egyptian Cult of the Dead." In *Portraits and Masks: Burial Customs in Roman Egypt*, edited by M. L. Bierbrier, 26–32. London: British Museum Press, 1997.

Borghouts, J. F. *Ancient Egyptian Magical Texts*. Nisaba 9. Leiden: Brill, 1978.

———. "Martyria: Some Correspondent Motifs in Egyptian Religion." In *Die Entstehung der jü-*

dischen Martyrologie, edited by J. W. van Henten, B. Dehandschutter, and H. J. W. van der Klaauw, 197–203. Leiden: Brill, 1989.

Boud'hors, Anne. "Histoire de Joseph le charpentier." In *Écrits apocryphes chrétiens*, edited by François Bovon, Pierre Geoltrain, and Jean-Daniel Kaestli Bovon, 2:25–59. Bibliothèque de la Pléiade 516. Paris: Gallimard, 2005.

———. "Manuscripts and Literature in Fayoumic Coptic." In *Christianity and Monasticism in the Fayoum Oasis*, edited by Gawdat Gabra, 21–31. Cairo: American University in Cairo Press, 2005.

Boud'hors, Anne, and Chantal Heurtel. *Les ostraca coptes de la TT 29: Autour du moine Frangé*. Études d'archéologie thébaine 3. Brussels: CReA-Patrimoine, 2010.

Bourdieu, Pierre. *Outline of a Theory of Practice*. Translated by Richard Nice. Cambridge: Cambridge University Press, 1977.

Bourdillon, M.F.C. "Witchcraft and Society." In *African Spirituality: Forms, Meanings, and Expressions*, edited by Jacob K. Olupona, 176–97. World Spirituality 3. New York: Crossroad, 2000.

Boutantin, Céline. "Production de terres cuites et cultes domestiques de Memphis à l'époque impériale." *Chronique d'Égypte* 81 (2006): 311–34.

———. *Terres cuites et culte domestique: Bestiaire de l'Égypte gréco-romaine*. Religions in the Graeco-Roman World 179. Leiden: Brill, 2014.

Boutros, R., and Anne Boud'hors. "La sainte famille à Gabal Al-Tayr et l'homélie du rocher." In *Études coptes VII*, edited by N. Bosson, 59–76. Cahiers de bibliothèque copte 12. Louvain, Belgium: Peeters, 2000.

Boutros, R., and C. Décobert. "Les installations chrétiennes entre Ballas et Armant: Implantation et survivance." In *Études coptes VII*, edited by N. Bosson, 77–108. Cahiers de bibliothèque copte 12. Louvain, Belgium: Peeters, 2000.

Bovon, François. "Beyond the Canonical and the Apocryphal Books, the Presence of a Third Category: The Books Useful for the Soul." *Harvard Theological Review* 105, no. 2 (2012): 125–37.

Bovon, François, Pierre Geoltrain, and Jean-Daniel Kaestli. *Écrits apocryphes chrétiens*. 2 vols. Bibliothèque de la Pléiade 442, 516. Paris: Gallimard, 1997, 2005.

Bowen, Gillian E. "The *Crux Ansata* in Early Christian Iconography: Evidence from Dakhleh and Kharga Oases." In *Le Myrte et la rose: Mélanges offerts à Françoise Dunand*, edited by G. Tallet and Chr. Zivie-Coche, 291–303. Montpellier, France: Université Paul Valéry-Montpellier III, 2014.

———. "Some Observations on Christian Burial Practices at Kellis." In *The Oasis Papers 3: Proceedings of the Third International Conference of the Dakhleh Oasis Project*, edited by Colin A Hope and Gillian E. Bowen, 167–82. Oxford: Oxbow Books, 2003.

Bowersock, Glen. *Hellenism in Late Antiquity*. Ann Arbor: University of Michigan Press, 1990.

———. *Mosaics as History: The Near East from Late Antiquity to Islam*. Revealing Antiquity 16. Cambridge: Belknap Press, 2006.

Bowes, Kimberly. "Christian Images in the Home." *Antiquité tardive* 19 (2011): 171–90.

———. "Personal Devotions and Private Chapels." In *A People's History of Christianity*, Vol. 2: *Late Ancient Christianity*, edited by Virginia Burrus, 188–210. Minneapolis, MN: Fortress Press, 2005.

———. *Private Worship, Public Values, and Religious Change in Late Antiquity*. Cambridge and New York: Cambridge University Press, 2008.

———. "Sixth-Century Individual Rituals: Private Chapels and the Reserved Eucharist." In *Group Identity and Religious Individuality in Late Antiquity*, edited by Éric Rebillard and Jörg Rüpke, 54–88. Washington, DC: Catholic University of America Press, 2015.

Boynton, Susan. "Oral Transmission of Liturgical Practice in the Eleventh-Century Customaries of Cluny." In *Understanding Monastic Practices of Oral Communication: Western Europe, Tenth-Thirteenth Centuries*, edited by Steven Vanderputten, 67–83. Turnhout, Belgium: Brepols, 2011.

Bozóky, Edina. *Charmes et prières apotropaïques*. Typologie des sources du Moyen Age occidental 86. Turnhout, Belgium: Brepols, 2003.

Brakke, David. *Athanasius and the Politics of Asceticism*. Oxford: Clarendon, 1995.

———. "Athanasius of Alexandria and the Cult of the Holy Dead." *Studia Patristica* 32 (1997): 12–18.
———. "Canon Formation and Social Conflict in Fourth-Century Egypt: Athanasius of Alexandria's Thirty-Ninth 'Festal Letter.'" *Harvard Theological Review* 87, no. 4 (1994): 395–419.
———. *Demons and the Making of the Monk: Spiritual Combat in Early Christianity*. Cambridge, MA: Harvard University Press, 2009.
———. "From Temple to Cell, from Gods to Demons: Pagan Temples in the Monastic Topography of Fourth-Century Egypt." In *From Temple to Church: Destruction and Renewal of Local Cultic Topography in Late Antiquity*, edited by Johannes Hahn, Stephen Emmel, and Ulrich Gotter, 91–112. Religions in the Graeco-Roman World 163. Leiden and Boston: Brill, 2008.
———. "The Making of Monastic Demonology: Three Ascetic Teachers on Withdrawl and Resistance." *Church History* 70, no. 1 (2001): 9–48.
———. "A New Fragment of Athanasius's Thirty-Ninth Festal Letter: Heresy, Apocrypha, and the Canon." *Harvard Theological Review* 103, no. 1 (2010): 47–66.
———. "'Outside the Places, Within the Truth': Athanasius of Alexandria and the Localization of the Holy." In *Pilgrimage and Holy Space in Late Antique Egypt*, edited by David Frankfurter, 445–82. Religions in the Graeco-Roman World 134. Leiden: Brill, 1998.
———. "Scriptural Practices in Early Christianity: Towards a New History of the New Testament Canon." In *Invention, Rewriting, Usurpation: Discursive Fights over Religious Traditions in Antiquity*, edited by Jörg Ulrich, Anders-Christian Jacobsen, and David Brakke, 263–80. Early Christianity in the Context of Antiquity 11. Frankfurt: Peter Lang, 2012.
———. "Shenoute, Weber, and the Monastic Prophet: Ancient and Modern Articulations of Ascetic Authority." In *Foundations of Power and Conflicts of Authority in Late-Antique Monasticism*, edited by Alberto Camplani and Giovanni Filoramo, 47–73. Leuven, Belgium: Peeters, 2007.
Brakke, David, and Crislip, Andrew. *Selected Discourses of Shenoute the Great: Community, Theology, and Social Conflict in Late Antique Egypt*. Cambridge: Cambridge University Press, 2015.
Brooks Hedstrom, Darlene L. "Divine Architects: Designing the Monastic Dwelling Place." In *Egypt in the Byzantine World, 300–700*, edited by Roger S. Bagnall, 368–89. Cambridge and New York: Cambridge University Press, 2007.
Brown, Peter. *Authority and the Sacred: Aspects of the Christianisation of the Roman World*. Cambridge: Cambridge University Press, 1997.
———. *The Cult of the Saints: Its Rise and Function in Latin Christianity*. Chicago: University of Chicago Press, 1981.
———. "The Rise and Function of the Holy Man in Late Antiquity." *Journal of Roman Studies* 61 (1971): 80–101.
———. *The World of Late Antiquity: AD 150–750*. New York: W. W. Norton, 1989.
Brunner-Traut, Emma. *Der Tanz im alten Ägypten: Nach bildlichen und inschriftlichen Zeugnissen*. Ägyptologische Forschungen 6. Glückstadt, Germany: Verlag J. J. Augustin, 1958.
Bucking, Scott. *Practice Makes Perfect: P. Cotsen-Princeton 1 and the Training of Scribes in Byzantine Egypt*. Los Angeles: Cotsen Occasional Press, 2011.
Budge, E.A.W. *Coptic Apocrypha in the Dialect of Upper Egypt*. London: British Museum, 1913.
———. *Coptic Martyrdoms, Etc. in the Dialect of Upper Egypt*. Coptic Texts 4. London: British Museum, 1914.
———. *Miscellaneous Coptic Texts in the Dialect of Upper Egypt*. London: British Museum, 1915.
Budin, Stephanie Lynn. *Images of Woman and Child from the Bronze Age: Reconsidering Fertility, Maternity, and Gender in the Ancient World*. Cambridge: Cambridge University Press, 2011.
Bühl, Gudrun. *Dumbarton Oaks: The Collections*. Washington, DC: Dumbarton Oaks Research Library and Collection, 2008.
Burford, Alison. *Craftsmen in Greek and Roman Society*. Ithaca, NY: Cornell University Press, 1972.
Burmester, Oswald H. E. "Egyptian Mythology in the Coptic Apocrypha." *Orientalia* 7 (1938): 355–67.
Burridge, Kenelm. *New Heaven, New Earth: A Study of Millenarian Activities*. Oxford: Blackwell, 1980.

BIBLIOGRAPHY

Burton-Christie, Douglas. *The Word in the Desert: Scripture and the Quest for Holiness in Early Christian Monasticism.* New York: Oxford University Press, 1993.

Busine, Aude. "From Stones to Myth: Temple Destruction and Civic Identity in the Late Antique Roman East." *Journal of Late Antiquity* 6, no. 2 (2013): 325–46.

———. "Introduction: Religious Practices and Christianization of the Late Antique City." In *Religious Practices and Christianization of the Late Antique City (4th–7th Cent.)*, edited by Aude Busine, 1–18. Leiden and Boston: Brill, 2015.

Bussmann, Edna R. *Unearthing the Truth: Egypt's Pagan and Coptic Sculpture.* Brooklyn: Brooklyn Museum, 2009.

Butler, Cuthbert. *The Lausiac History of Palladius.* Texts and Studies 6. Cambridge: Cambridge University Press, 1898.

Bynum, Caroline Walker. *Christian Materiality: An Essay on Religion in Late Medieval Europe.* New York: Zone Books, 2011.

Caciola, Nancy. *Discerning Spirits: Divine and Demonic Possession in the Middle Ages.* Ithaca NY: Cornell University Press, 2003.

Calament, Florence. "Varia coptica thebaica." *Bulletin de l'institut français d'archéologie orientale* 104 (2004): 39–102.

Cameron, Averil. "Christian Conversion in Late Antiquity: Some Issues." In *Conversion in Late Antiquity: Christianity, Islam, and Beyond,* edited by Arietta Papaconstantinou, Neil McLynn, and Daniel Schwartz, 3–21. Farnham, UK: Ashgate, 2015.

———. *Christianity and the Rhetoric of Empire.* Berkeley: University of California Press, 1991.

Campany, Robert Ford. "Religious Repertoires and Contestation: A Case Study Based on Buddhist Miracle Tales." *History of Religions* 52, no. 2 (2012): 99–141.

Camplani, Alberto. *Le lettere festali di Atanasio di Alessandria: Studio storico-critico.* Corpus dei manoscritti copti letterari. Roma: CIM, 1989.

Caner, Daniel. "Towards a Miraculous Economy: Christian Gifts and Material 'Blessings' in Late Antiquity." *Journal of Early Christian Studies* 14, no. 3 (2006): 329–77.

———. *Wandering, Begging Monks: Spiritual Authority and the Promotion of Monasticism in Late Antiquity.* Transformation of the Classical Heritage 33. Berkeley: University of California Press, 2002.

Cannata, Maria. "Funerary Artists: The Textual Evidence." In *The Oxford Handbook of Roman Egypt,* edited by Christina Riggs, 597–612. Oxford and New York: Oxford University Press, 2012.

Cannuyer, Christian. "Des dieux aux saints guérisseurs dans l'Égypte pharaonique et copte." In *Deus Medicus: Actes du colloque organisé à Louvain-la-Neuve les 15 et 16 juin 2012 par le centre d'histoire des religions Cardinal Julien Ries,* edited by René Lebrun and Agnès Degrève, 21–48. Turnhout, Belgium: Brepols, 2013.

———. "Saint Mina aux chameaux: Autour des origines d'un iconotype copte." *Le monde copte* 27/28 (1997): 139–54.

Caplan, Lionel. "The Popular Culture of Evil in Urban South India." In *The Anthropology of Evil,* edited by David Parkin, 110–27. Oxford: Wiley-Blackwell, 1991.

Carnot, É. "L'Akh-Menou—Status Quaestionis II—Les Inscriptions." *Cahiers de Karnak* 12 (2007): 797–802.

Caseau, Béatrice. "Christian Bodies: The Senses and Early Byzantine Christianity." In *Desire and Denial in Byzantium,* edited by Liz James, 101–9. Aldershot, UK: Variorum, 1999.

———. "Le crypto paganisme et les frontières du licite: Un jeu de masques?" In *Pagans and Christians in the Roman Empire: The Breaking of a Dialogue, (4th–6th Century A.D),* edited by P. Brown and R. L. Testa, 541–72. Berlin: LIT Verlag Münster, 2011.

———. "Magical Protection and Stamps in Byzantium." In *Seals and Sealing Practices in the Near East: Developments in Administration and Magic from Prehistory to the Islamic Period,* edited by Kim Duistermaat, Ilona Regulski, and Peter Verkinderen, 119–37. Louvain, Belgium: Peeters, 2012.

———. "Ordinary Objects in Christian Healing Sanctuaries." In *Objects in Context, Objects in Use: Material Spatiality in Late Antiquity*, edited by Luke Lavan, Ellen Swift, and Toon Putzeys, 625–54. Late Antique Archaeology 5. Leiden: Brill, 2007.

———. "Sacred Landscapes." In *Late Antiquity: A Guide to the Postclassical World*, edited by Glen Bowersock, Peter Brown, and Oleg Grabar, 21–59. Cambridge, MA: Harvard University Press, 1999.

———. "ΠΟΛΕΜΕΙΝ ΛΙΘΟΙΣ: La désacralisation des espaces et des objets religieux païens durant l'Antiquité tardive." In *Le sacré et son inscription dans l'espace à Byzance et en Occident: Études comparées*, edited by Michel Kaplan, 61–123. Paris: Publications de la Sorbonne, 2001.

Cassidy, William, ed. "Retrofitting Syncretism?" Special issue, *Historical Reflections / Réflexions Historiques* 27, no. 3 (2001).

Cauville, Sylvie. *Le temple de Dendera: guide archéologique*. Bibliothèque générale 12. Cairo: IFAO, 1990.

Cervantes, Fernando. *The Devil in the New World: The Impact of Diabolism in New Spain*. New Haven, CT: Yale University Press, 1997.

Chaîne, M. "La double recension de l'*Histoire Lausiaque* dans la version copte." *Revue de l'orient chrétien* 25 (1925): 232–75.

Charlesworth, James H., ed. *The Old Testament Pseudepigrapha*. 2 vols. Garden City, NY: Doubleday, 1983–85.

Chassinat, E. *Le quatrième livre des entretiens et épîtres de Shenouti*. Mémoires publiés par les membres de la mission archéologique française au Caire 23. Cairo: IFAO, 1911.

Choat, Malcolm. *Belief and Cult in Fourth-Century Papyri*. Studia Antiqua Australiensia 1. Turnhout, Belgium: Brepols, 2006.

Choat, Malcolm, and Iain Gardner, eds. *A Coptic Handbook of Ritual Power (P. Macq. I 1)*. Macquarie Papyri 1. Turnhout, Belgium: Brepols, 2013.

Christian, William A. *Local Religion in Sixteenth-Century Spain*. Princeton, NJ: Princeton University Press, 1981.

Chuvin, Pierre. *A Chronicle of the Last Pagans*. Cambridge, MA: Harvard University Press, 1990.

Clarysse, Willy. "The Coptic Martyr Cult." In *Martyrium in Multidisciplinary Perspective: Memorial Louis Reekmans*, edited by M Lamberigts and Peter van Deun, 377–95. Leuven, Belgium: Uitgeverij Peeters, 1995.

Cline, Rangar. "A Two-Sided Mold and the Entrepreneurial Spirit of Pilgrimage Souvenir Production in Late Antique Syria–Palestine." *Journal of Late Antiquity* 7, no. 1 (2014): 28–48.

Colson, Elizabeth. "A Continuing Dialogue: Prophets and Local Shrines among the Tonga of Zambia." In *Regional Cults*, edited by Richard P Werbner, 119–40. London and New York: Academic Press, 1977.

Connelly, Joan. "Ritual Movement in Sacred Space: Towards an Archaeology of Performance." In *Ritual Dynamics in the Ancient Mediterranean*, edited by Angelos Chaniotis, 313–46. Heidelberger althistorische Beiträge und epigraphische Studien 49. Stuttgart: Franz Steiner Verlag, 2011.

Connerton, Paul. *How Societies Remember*. Cambridge: Cambridge University Press, 1989.

Copeland, Kirsti Barrett. "Mapping the 'Apocalypse of Paul': Geography, Genre, and History." Ph.D. diss., Princeton University, 2001.

Coquin, René-Georges. "Apollon de Titkooh ou/et Apollon de Bawit?" *Orientalia* 46, no. 4 (1977): 435–46.

———. "La christianisation des temples de Karnak." *Bulletin de l'institut français d'archéologie orientale* 72 (1972): 169–78.

———. "Le catalogue de la bibliothèque du couvent de Saint Élie 'Du Rocher' (Ostracon IFAO 13315)." *Bulletin de l'institut français d'archéologie orientale* 75 (1975): 207–39.

———. "Moïse d'Abydos." In *Deuxième journée d'études coptes, Strasbourg 25 mai 1984*, 1–14. Louvain, Belgium: Peeters, 1986.

---. "Phib, Saint." In *The Coptic Encyclopedia*, edited by Aziz Atiya, 6:1953–54. New York: Macmillan, 1991.

Coquin, René-Georges, and Stephen Emmel. "Le traité de Šenoute 'Du salut de l'âme humaine.'" *Journal of Coptic Studies* 3 (2001): 1–43.

Coudert, Magali. "W99: Un individu particulier de la nécropole byzantine d'El-Deir (Oasis de Kharga)." In *Le Myrte et la rose. Mélanges offerts à Françoise Dunand*, edited by G. Tallet and Chr. Zivie-Coche, 249–57. Montpellier, France: Université Paul Valéry-Montpellier III, 2014.

Cribiore, Raffaella. "Higher Education in Early Byzantine Egypt: Rhetoric, Latin, and the Law." In *Egypt in the Byzantine World, 300–700*, edited by Roger S. Bagnall, 47–66. Cambridge: Cambridge University Press, 2007.

Crisafulli, Virgil S., and John W. Nesbitt, eds. *The Miracles of St. Artemios: A Collection of Miracle Stories by an Anonymous Author of Seventh Century Byzantium*. Medieval Mediterranean 13. Leiden: E. J. Brill, 1997.

Crum, Walter Ewing. *Catalogue of the Coptic Manuscripts in the British Museum*. London: British Museum, 1905.

---. *A Coptic Dictionary*. Oxford: Clarendon, 1939.

---. "Theban Hermits and Their Life." In *The Monastery of Epiphanius at Thebes: Part 1*, 125–85. New York: Metropolitan Museum of Art, 1926.

Crum, Walter Ewing, and Hugh Gerard Evelyn-White. *The Monastery of Epiphanius at Thebes: Part 2—Coptic Ostraca and Papyri; Greek Ostraca and Papyri*. 2nd ed. New York: Metropolitan Museum of Art, 1926.

Crum, Walter Ewing, and Georg Steindorff. *Koptische Rechtsurkunden des achten Jahrhunderts aus Djême (Theben)*. Subsidia Byzantina lucis ope iterata 18. Leipzig: J. C. Hinrichs Buchhandlung, 1912.

Crum, Walter Ewing, and H. E. Winlock. *The Monastery of Epiphanius at Thebes: Part 1*. New York: Metropolitan Museum of Art, 1926.

Cuffel, Alexandra. "From Practice to Polemic: Shared Saints and Festivals as 'Women's Religion' in the Medieval Mediterranean." *Bulletin of the School of Oriental and African Studies* 68, no. 3 (2005): 401–19.

Dagron, Gilbert. *Vie et miracles de sainte Thècle: Texte grec, traduction et commentaire*. Subsidia hagiographica 62. Brussels: Société des bollandistes, 1978.

Daniélou, Jean. "Les démons de l'air dans la 'Vie d'Antoine.'" In *Antonius magnus eremita, 356–1956: Studia ad antiquum monachismum spectantia*, edited by Basilius Steidle, 136–47. Rome: Herder, 1956.

Darnell, John Coleman. *The Enigmatic Netherworld Books of the Solar-Osirian Unity: Cryptographic Compositions in the Tombs of Tutankhamun, Ramesses VI and Ramesses IX*. Orbis Biblicus et Orientalis 198. Fribourg, Switzerland: Academic Press, 2004.

Daumas, François. *Dendara et le temple d'Hathor*. Recherches d'archéologie, de philologie et d'histoire 29. Cairo: IFAO, 1969.

D'Auria, Sue, Peter Lacovara, and Catharine H. Roehrig. *Mummies and Magic: The Funerary Arts of Ancient Egypt*. Boston: Museum of Fine Arts, 1988.

Davis, Stephen J. *Coptic Christology in Practice: Incarnation and Divine Participation in Late Antique and Medieval Egypt*. Oxford: Oxford University Press, 2008.

---. *The Cult of Saint Thecla: A Tradition of Women's Piety in Late Antiquity*. Oxford and New York: Oxford University Press, 2001.

---. "Fashioning a Divine Body: Coptic Christology and Ritualized Dress." *Harvard Theological Review* 98, no. 3 (2005): 335–62.

---. "Pilgrimage and the Cult of Saint Thecla in Late Antique Egypt." In *Pilgrimage and Holy Space in Late Antique Egypt*, edited by David Frankfurter, 303–39. Religions in the Graeco-Roman World 134. Leiden: Brill, 1998.

———. "Shenoute in Scetis: New Archaeological Evidence from the Cult of a Monastic Saint in Early Medieval Wadi Al-Natrun." *Coptica* 14 (2015): 1–19.
Dawes, Elizabeth A. S, and Norman H. Baynes. *Three Byzantine Saints: Contemporary Biographies of St. Daniel the Stylite, St. Theodore of Sykeon, and St. John the Almsgiver*. Crestwood, NY: St. Vladimir's Seminary Press, 1977.
De Bruyn, Theodore. "Papyri, Parchments, Ostraca, and Tablets Written with Biblical Texts in Greek and Used as Amulets: A Preliminary List." In *Early Christian Manuscripts: Examples of Applied Method and Approach*, edited by Thomas J. Kraus and Tobias Nicklas, 145–89. Leiden: Brill, 2010.
———. "The Use of the *Sanctus* in Christian Greek Papyrus Amulets." *Studia Patristica* 40 (2006): 15–19.
De Bruyn, Theodore, and Jitse H. F. Dijkstra. "Greek Amulets and Formularies from Egypt Containing Christian Elements: A Checklist of Papyri, Parchments, Ostraka, and Tablets." *Bulletin of the American Society of Papyrologists* 48 (2011): 163–216.
De Nie, H. "Een koptisch-christelijke Orakelvraag." *Jaarbericht van het vooraziatisch-egyptisch Gezelschap: Ex Oriente Lux* 8 (1942): 615–18.
De Vis, Henri. *Homélies coptes de la Vaticane I–II*. Cahiers de la bibliothèque copte 6. Louvain, Belgium: Peeters, 1990.
Décobert, C. "Un lieu de mémoire religieuse." In *Valeur et distance, identités et sociétés en Égypte*, edited by C. Décobert, 247–59. Paris: Maisonneuve et Larose, 2000.
Del Francia Barocas, Loretta, ed. *Antinoe cent'anni dopo: Catalogo della mostra, Firenze, Palazzo Medici Riccardi, 10 luglio-10 novembre 1998*. Florence: Istituto papirologico "G. Vitelli," 1998.
Del Guidice, Luisa. "Ninna-Nanna-Nonsense? Fears, Dreams, and Falling in the Italian Lullaby." *Oral Tradition* 3, no. 3 (1988): 270–93.
Delage, Marie-José, trans. *Césaire d'Arles, Sermons au peuple (21-55)*. Sources chrétiennes 243. Paris: Editions du Cerf, 1978.
Delahaye, G.-R. "La diffusion des ampoules de Saint-Ménas en Gaule." *Le monde copte* 27/28 (1997): 155–65.
Delatte, Armand, and Philippe Derchain. *Les intailles magiques gréco-égyptiennes*. Paris: Bibliothèque nationale, 1964.
Delattre, Alain. "Inscription grecques et coptes de la montagne thébaine relatives au culte de Saint Ammōnios." In *"Et maintenant ce ne sont plus que des villages...": Thèbes et sa région aux époques hellénistique, romaine et byzantine*, edited by A. Delattre and P. Heilporn, 183–88. Brussels: Association égyptologique Reine Élisabeth, 2008.
———. "Les graffitis coptes d'Abydos et la crue du Nil." In *Études coptes VIII*, 133–46. Cahiers de la bibliothèque copte 13. Paris: Peeters, 2003.
———. "L'oracle de Kollouthos à Antinoé." *Studi e materiali di storia delle religioni* 79, no. 1 (2013): 123–33.
———. "Nouveaux textes coptes d'Antinoé." In *Proceedings of the Twenty-Fifth International Congress of Papyrology, Ann Arbor, July 29–August 4, 2007*, edited by Traianos Gagos, 171–75. Ann Arbor: University of Michigan Press, 2010.
———. *Papyrus coptes et grecs du monastère d'Apa Apollō de Baouît conservés aux Musées Royaux d'art et d'histoire de Bruxelles*. Mémoires de la classe des lettres 43. Brussels: Académie royale de Belgique, 2007.
———. "Textes coptes et grecs d'Antinoé." In *Antinoupolis I*, edited by Rosario Pintaudi, 131–62. Florence: Istituto papirologico "G. Vitelli," 2008.
Deng, Francis Mading. *The Dinka and Their Songs*. Oxford Library of African Literature. Oxford: Clarendon Press, 1973.
Dennis, George T. "Popular Religious Attitudes and Practices in Byzantium." *Proche-orient chrétien* 43 (1993): 273–94.
Denzey Lewis, Nicola, and Justine Ariel Blount. "Rethinking the Origins of the Nag Hammadi Codices." *Journal of Biblical Literature* 133, no. 2 (2014): 399–419.

Depauw, M., and W. Clarysse. "Christian Onomastics: A Response to Frankfurter." *Vigiliae Christianae* 69, no. 3 (2015): 327–29.

———. "How Christian Was Fourth Century Egypt? Onomastic Perspectives on Conversion." *Vigiliae Christianae* 67, no. 4 (2013): 407–35.

Depuydt, Leo. "A Homily on the Virtues of Saint Longinus Attributed to Basil of Pemje." In *Coptology: Past, Present, and Future: Studies in Honour of Rodolphe Kasser*, edited by Søren Giversen, Martin Krause, and Peter Nagel, 267–92. Orientalia Lovaniensia Analecta 61. Leuven, Belgium: Peeters, 1994.

Derda, Tomasz. "Necropolis Workers in Graeco-Roman Egypt in the Light of the Greek Papyri." *Journal of Juristic Papyrology* 21 (1991): 13–36.

Devos, Paul. "Autres miracles coptes de Saint Kolouthos." *Analecta Bollandiana* 99 (1981): 285–301.

———. "Un étrange miracle copte de Saint Kolouthos: Le paralytique et la prostituée." *Analecta Bollandiana* 98 (1980): 363–80.

Dieleman, Jacco. "Cryptography at the Monastery of Deir El-Bachit." In *Honi soit qui mal y pense: Studien zum pharaonischen, griechisch-römischen und spätantiken Ägypten zu Ehren von Heinz-Josef Thissen*, edited by Hermann Knuf, Christian Leitz, and Daniel von Recklinghausen, 511–17. Leuven, Belgium: Peeters, 2010.

———. *Priests, Tongues, and Rites: The London-Leiden Magical Manuscripts and Translation in Egyptian Ritual, 100–300 CE*. Religions in the Graeco-Roman World 153. Leiden: Brill, 2005.

Dijkstra, Jitse H. F. "Late Antique Inscriptions from the First Cataract Area Discovered and Rediscovered." *Journal of Juristic Papyrology* 33 (2003): 55–66.

———. *Philae and the End of Ancient Egyptian Religion: A Regional Study of Religious Transformation (298–642 CE)*. Orientalia Lovaniensia Analecta 173. Leuven, Belgium: Peeters, 2008.

Dijkstra, Jitse H. F., and Mathilde Van Dijk, eds. *The Encroaching Desert: Egyptian Hagiography and the Medieval West*. Church History and Religious Culture 86. Leiden: Brill, 2006.

Donadoni, Sergio. "Una domanda oracolare cristiana da Antinoe." *Rivista degli studi orientali* 29 (1954): 183–86.

Doresse, Jean. "Cryptography." *The Coptic Encyclopedia*, edited by Aziz Atiya, 8:65–69. New York: Macmillan, 1991.

Douglas, Mary. "Sorcery Accusations Unleashed: The Lele Revisited, 1987." *Africa* 69, no. 2 (1999): 177–93.

Dowden, Ken. *European Paganism: The Realities of Cult From Antiquity to the Middle Ages*. London: Routledge, 2000.

Drake, H. A. "Lambs into Lions: Explaining Early Christian Intolerance." *Past & Present* 153 (1996): 3–36.

Drehkhahn, Rosemarie. "Artisans and Artists in Pharaonic Egypt." In *Civilizations of the Ancient Near East*, edited by Jack M. Sasson, 1:331–43. New York: Scribner, 1995.

Drescher, James. *Apa Mena: A Selection of Coptic Texts Relating to St. Menas*. Cairo: Société d'archéologie copte, 1947.

Du Bourguet, Pierre. "Diatribe de Chenouté contre le démon." *Bulletin de la société d'archéologie copte* 16 (1961): 17–72.

———. "La signature sur son oeuvre d'un sculpteur copte du VIe siècle." In *Hommages à la mémoire de Serge Sauneron: 1927–1976, 2: Égypte post-pharaonique*, edited by Jean Vercoutter, 115–20. Cairo: IFAO, 1979.

Duchesne, L. "Le sanctuaire d'Aboukir." *Bulletin de la société archéologique d'Alexandrie* 12 (1910): 3–14.

Dunand, Françoise. "Between Tradition and Innovation: Egyptian Funerary Practices in Late Antiquity." In *Egypt in the Byzantine World, 300–700*, edited by Roger S. Bagnall, 163–84. Cambridge: Cambridge University Press, 2007.

———. "Du séjour osirien des morts à l'au-delà chrétien: Pratiques funéraires en Égypte tardive." *Ktema* 11 (1986): 29–37.

———. "La consultation oraculaire en Égypte tardive: L'oracle de Bès à Abydos." In *Oracles et prophéties dans l'antiquité: Actes du colloque de Strasbourg, 15–17 juin 1995*, edited by Jean-Georges Heintz, 65–84. Paris: De Boccard, 1997.

———. "Lanternes gréco-romaines d'Égypte." *Dialogues d'histoire ancienne* 2, no. 1 (1976): 71–97.

———. "Les nécrotaphes de Kysis." *Cahier de recherches de l'Institut de papyrologie et d'égyptologie de Lille* 7 (1985): 117–27.

———. "Les 'Têtes Dorées' de la nécropole de Douch." *Bulletin de la société française d'Égyptologie* 93 (1982): 26–46.

———. "Lieu sacré païen et lieu sacré chrétien." In *Le comparatisme en histoire des religions*, edited by F. Boespflug and F. Dunand, 239–58. Paris: Éditions du Cerf, 1997.

———. "L'oracle du potier et la formation de l'apocalyptique en Égypte." In *L'apocalyptique*, edited by Marc Philonenko, 41–67. Paris: Paul Geuthner, 1977.

———. "Miracles et guérisons en Égypte tardive." In *Mélanges Étienne Bernand*, edited by Nicole Fick-Michel and Jean-Claude Carrière, 235–50. Paris: Les Belles Lettres, 1991.

———. *Religion populaire en Égypte romaine: Les terres cuites isiaques du musée du Caire*. Études préliminaires aux religions orientales dans l'empire romain 77. Leiden: Brill, 1979.

Dunand, Françoise, and Magali Coudert. "Les débuts de la christianisation dans les oasis: Le cas de Kharga." In *Alexandrie la divine*, edited by Charles Méla, Frédéric Möri, Sydney Aufrère, Gilles Dorival, and Alain Le Boulluec, 2:796–801. Paris: Éditions de la Baconnière, 2014.

Dunand, Françoise, and Pierre Lévêque, eds. *Les syncrétismes dans les religions de l'antiquité: Colloque de Besançon, 22–23 octobre 1973*. Études préliminaires aux religions orientales dans l'empire romain 46. Leiden: Brill, 1975.

Dunand, Françoise, and Roger Lichtenberg. *Mummies and Death in Egypt*. Translated by David Lorton. Ithaca, NY: Cornell University Press, 2006.

———. "Pratiques et croyances funéraires en Égypte romaine." In *Aufstieg und Niedergang der römischen Welt* II.18.5, edited by Wolfgang Haase, 3216–3315. Berlin: de Gruyter, 1995.

Dunbabin, Katherine M. D. *Mosaics of the Greek and Roman World*. Cambridge and New York: Cambridge University Press, 1999.

Eade, John, and Sallnow, Michael J. "Introduction." In *Contesting the Sacred: The Anthropology of Christian Pilgrimage*, edited by John Eade and Michael J. Sallnow, 1–29. London: Routledge, 1991.

Eastmond, Antony. "Body vs. Column: The Cults of St. Symeon Stylites." In *Desire and Denial in Byzantium*, edited by Liz James, 87–100. Aldershot, UK: Variorum, 1999.

Edwards, I.E.S. *Hieratic Papyri in the British Museum: Fourth Series, Oracular Amuletic Decrees of the Late New Kingdom*. London: Trustees of the British Museum, 1960.

Effenberger, Arne, and Hans-Georg Severin. *Das Museum für spätantike und byzantinische Kunst*. Mainz, Germany: P. von Zabern, 1992.

Effland, Andreas. "'You Will Open Up the Ways in the Underworld of the God': Aspects of Roman and Late Antique Abydos." In *Egypt in the First Millennium AD: Perspectives from New Fieldwork*, edited by Elisabeth R. O'Connell, 193–205. Leuven, Belgium: Peeters, 2014.

Egan, Martha. *Milagros: Votive Offerings from the Americas*. Santa Fe: Museum of New Mexico Press, 1991.

Ehrman, Bart, and Zlatko Pleše, eds. *The Apocryphal Gospels: Texts and Translations*. Oxford University Press, 2011.

El-Nassery, S.A.A., and Guy Wagner. "Nouvelles stèles de Kom Abu Bellou." *Bulletin de l'institut français d'archéologie orientale* 78 (1978): 231–58.

el-Sawy, Ahmed, Jan Bouzek, and Ladislav Vidman. "New Stelae from the Terenouthis Cemetery in Egypt." *Archiv Orientální* 48 (1980): 330–55.

Elsner, Jaś. "The Origins of the Icon: Pilgrimage, Religion and Visual Culture in the Roman East as 'Resistance' to the Centre." In *The Early Roman Empire in the East*, edited by Susan E Alcock, 178–99. Oxford: Oxbow Books, 1997.

BIBLIOGRAPHY

———. *Roman Eyes: Visuality and Subjectivity in Art and Text*. Princeton, NJ: Princeton University Press, 2007.
Emirbayer, Mustafa, and Ann Mische. "What Is Agency?" *American Journal of Sociology* 103, no. 4 (1998): 962–1023.
Emmel, Stephen. "The Coptic Gnostic Texts as Witnesses to the Production and Transmission of Gnostic (and Other) Traditions." In *Das Thomasevangelium: Entstehung, Rezeption, Theologie*, edited by Jörg Frey, Enno Edzard Popkes, and Jens Schröter, 33–49. Berlin: Walter de Gruyter, 2008.
———. "From the Other Side of the Nile: Shenute and Panopolis." In *Perspectives on Panopolis: An Egyptian Town from Alexander the Great to the Arab Conquest*, edited by A. Egberts, B. P. Muhs, and Jacques van der Vliet, 95–113. Leiden: Brill, 2002.
———. "Shenoute of Atripe and the Destruction of Temples in Egypt: Rhetoric and Reality." In *From Temple to Church: Destruction and Renewal of Local Cultic Topography in Late Antiquity*, edited by Johannes Hahn, Stephen Emmel, and Ulrich Gotter, 161–201. Religions in the Graeco-Roman World 163. Leiden: Brill, 2008.
———. *Shenoute's Literary Corpus*. 2 vols. Corpus Scriptorum Christianorum Orientalium 599–600. Leuven, Belgium: Peeters, 2004.
Erman, Adolf. "Heidnisches bei den Kopten." *Zeitschrift für ägyptische Sprache und Altertumskunde* 33 (1895): 47–51.
Evans, Helen C., and Brandie Ratliff. *Byzantium and Islam: Age of Transition, 7th–9th Century*. New York: Metropolitan Museum of Art, 2012.
Evelyn White, Hugh G., G.P.G. Sobhy, and Albert M. Lythgoe. *The Monasteries of the Wâdi 'n Natrûn, Part I: New Coptic Texts from the Monastery of Saint Macarius*. Publications of the Metropolitan Museum of Art Egyptian Expedition 2. New York: Metropolitan Museum of Art, 1926.
Fabech, Charlotte, and Ulf Näsman. "Ritual Landscapes and Sacral Places in the First Millennium AD in South Scandinavia." In *Sacred Sites and Holy Places: Exploring the Sacralization of Landscape Through Time and Space*, edited by Sæbjørg Walaker Nordeide and Stefan Brink, 53–109. Turnhout, Belgium: Brepols, 2013.
Faeta, Francesco. "Italian Ex-Votos: Personhood and Society." In *Faith and Transformation: Votive Offerings and Amulets from the Alexander Girard Collection*, edited by Doris Francis, 58–59. Santa Fe: Museum of New Mexico Press, 2007.
———. "The Physical Body and the Imaginary Body." In *Faith and Transformation: Votive Offerings and Amulets from the Alexander Girard Collection*, edited by Doris Francis, 54–55. Santa Fe: Museum of New Mexico Press, 2007.
———. "The Ritual Context of Italian Ex-Votos." In *Faith and Transformation: Votive Offerings and Amulets from the Alexander Girard Collection*, edited by Doris Francis, 60–61. Santa Fe: Museum of New Mexico Press, 2007.
Fakhry, Ahmed. *The Necropolis of El-Bagawât in Kharga Oasis*. Cairo: Service des antiquités de l'Égypte, 1951.
Faraone, Christopher. "A Collection of Curses Against Kilns (Homeric Epigram 13.7-23)." In *Antiquity and Humanity: Essays on Ancient Religion and Philosophy, Presented to Hans Dieter Betz on His 70th Birthday*, edited by Margaret Mitchell and Adela Yarbro Collins, 435–49. Tübingen: Mohr Siebeck, 2001.
———. "Text, Image, and Medium: The Evolution of Graeco-Roman Magical Gemstones." In *"Gems of Heaven": Recent Research on Engraved Gemstones in Late Antiquity, AD 200–600*, edited by Chris Entwistle and Noel Adams, 50–61. London: British Museum Press, 2011.
Faulkner, Raymond. *The Egyptian Book of the Dead: The Book of Going Forth by Day—The Complete Papyrus of Ani Featuring Integrated Text and Full-Color Images*. San Francisco: Chronicle Books, 1994.
Fernández-Armesto, Felipe. "Conceptualizing Conversion in Global Perspective: From Late Antique to Early Modern." In *Conversion to Christianity from Late Antiquity to the Modern Age: Con-*

sidering the Process in Europe, Asia, and the Americas, edited by Calvin B. Kendall, 13–43. Minneapolis: Center for Early Modern History, University of Minnesota, 2009.

Festugière, André-Jean. *Les moines d'Orient I: Culture ou sainteté*. Paris: Éditions du Cerf, 1961.

———. *Historia monachorum in Aegypto: Édition critique du texte grec et traduction annotée*. Subsidia hagiographica 53. Brussels: Société des Bollandistes, 1971.

Feuchtwang, Stephan. "Domestic and Communal Worship in Taiwan." In *Religion and Ritual in Chinese Society*, edited by Arthur P. Wolf, 105–29. Stanford, CA: Stanford University Press, 1974.

Finnestad, R. B. "Temples of the Ptolemaic and Roman Periods: Ancient Traditions in New Contexts." In *Temples of Ancient Egypt*, edited by Dieter Arnold and Byron Schäfer, 185–238. London: I. B. Tauris, 1997.

Flint, Valerie I. J. "The Demonisation of Magic and Sorcery in Late Antiquity: Christian Redefinitions of Pagan Religions." In *Witchcraft and Magic in Europe*, Volume 2: *Ancient Greece and Rome*, edited by Bengt Ankarloo and Stuart Clark, 277–348. Philadelphia: University of Pennsylvania Press, 1999.

———. *The Rise of Magic in Early Medieval Europe*. Princeton, NJ: Princeton University Press, 1991.

Flohr, Miko. "The Uses and Value of Urine." In *Roman Toilets: Their Archaeology and Cultural History*, edited by Gemma C. M. Jansen, Ann Olga Koloski-Ostrow, and Eric M. Moormann, 148–54. Leuven, Belgium: Peeters, 2011.

Flood, Finbarr Barry. "Image Against Nature: Spolia as Apotropaia in Byzantium and the Dar Al-Islam." *Medieval History Journal* 9 (2006): 143–66.

———. *Objects of Translation: Material Culture and Medieval "Hindu-Muslim" Encounter*. Princeton, NJ: Princeton University Press, 2009.

Fluck, Cäcilia. "Textiles from the So-Called 'Tomb of Tgol' in Antinoupolis." In *Egypt in the First Millennium AD: Perspectives from New Fieldwork*, edited by Elizabeth R. O'Connell, 115–23. Leuven, Belgium: Peeters, 2014.

Fodor, Sándor. "Traces of the Isis Cult in an Arabic Love Spell from Egypt." In *The Intellectual Heritage of Egypt: Studies Presented to László Kákosy by Friends and Colleagues on the Occasion of His 60th Birthday*, edited by Ulrich Luft, 171–87. Budapest: Eötvös Loránd University, 1992.

Förster, Hans. "Christliche Texte in magischer Verwendung: Eine Anfrage." In *Proceedings of the 24th Congress of Papyrology, Helsinki, 1–7 August, 2004*, edited by Jaakko Frösén, Tiina Purola, and Erja Salmenkivi, 341–52. Helsinki: Societas Scientarum Fennica, 2007.

Foskolou, Vicky. "Blessing for Sale? On the Production and Distribution of Pilgrim Mementoes in Byzantium." *Byzantinische Zeitschrift* 105, no. 1 (2012): 53–84.

Fowden, Garth. *The Egyptian Hermes: A Historical Approach to the Late Pagan Mind*. Cambridge: Cambridge University Press, 1986.

Francis, Doris, ed. *Faith and Transformation: Votive Offerings and Amulets from the Alexander Girard Collection*. Santa Fe: Museum of New Mexico Press, 2007.

Francis, James A. "Clement of Alexandria on Signet Rings: Reading an Image at the Dawn of Christian Art." *Classical Philology* 98, no. 2 (2003): 179–83.

Frank, Georgia. "Christ's Descent to the Underworld in Ancient Ritual and Legend." In *Apocalyptic Thought in Early Christianity*, edited by Robert J. Daly, 211–26. Grand Rapids, MI: Baker Academic, 2009.

———. "Loca Sancta Souvenirs and the Art of Memory." In *Pèlerinages et lieux saints dans l'antiquité et le moyen âge: Mélanges offerts à Pierre Maraval*, edited by Béatrice Caseau, Jean-Claude Cheynet, and Vincent Déroche, 193–201. Paris: Centre d'Histoire et Civilisation de Byzance, 2006.

Frankfurter, David. "Amente Demons and Christian Syncretism." *Archiv für Religionsgeschichte* 14 (2012): 83–101.

———. "Beyond Magic and Superstition." In *A People's History of Christianity, 2: Late Ancient Christianity*, edited by Virginia Burrus, 255–66. Minneapolis, MN: Fortress Press, 2005.

———. "The Binding of Antelopes: A Coptic Frieze and Its Egyptian Religious Context." *Journal of Near Eastern Studies* 63, no. 2 (2004): 97–109.

———. "Collections of Recipes: Introduction." In *Ancient Christian Magic: Coptic Texts of Ritual Power*, edited by Marvin W. Meyer and Richard Smith, 259–62. San Francisco: Harper, 1994.

———. "Comparison and the Study of Religions of Late Antiquity." In *Comparer en histoire des religions antiques: Controverses et propositions*, edited by Claude Calame and Bruce Lincoln, 83–98. Liège: Presses universitaires de Liège, 2012.

———. "The Consequences of Hellenism in Late Antique Egypt: Religious Worlds and Actors." *Archiv für Religionsgeschichte* 2, no. 2 (2000): 162–94.

———. "The Cult of the Martyrs in Egypt Before Constantine: The Evidence of the Coptic 'Apocalypse of Elijah.'" *Vigiliae Christianae* 48, no. 1 (1994): 25–47.

———. "Curses, Blessings, and Ritual Authority: Egyptian Magic in Comparative Perspective." *Journal of Ancient Near Eastern Religions* 5, no. 1 (2005): 157–85.

———. "Demon Invocations in the Coptic Magic Spells." In *Actes du huitième congrès international d'études coptes*, edited by N. Bosson and A. Boud'hors, 2:453–66. Leuven, Belgium: Peeters, 2007.

———. "Egyptian Religion and the Problem of the Category 'Sacrifice.'" In *Ancient Mediterranean Sacrifice*, edited by Jennifer Wright Knust and Zsuzsanna Várhelyi, 75–93. New York: Oxford University Press, 2011.

———. *Elijah in Upper Egypt: The Apocalypse of Elijah and Early Egyptian Christianity*. Studies in Antiquity and Christianity 7. Minneapolis, MN: Fortress Press, 1993.

———. "Espaces et pèlerinage dans l'Égypte de l'antiquité tardive." In *Pèlerinages et lieux saints dans l'antiquité et le moyen âge: Mélanges offerts à Pierre Maraval*, edited by Béatrice Caseau, Jean-Claude Cheynet, Vincent Déroche, and Pierre Maraval, 203–21. Paris: Centre d'Histoire et Civilisation de Byzance, 2006.

———. *Evil Incarnate: Rumors of Demonic Conspiracy and Ritual Abuse in History*. Princeton, NJ: Princeton University Press, 2006.

———. "Female Figurines in Early Christian Egypt: Reconstructing Lost Practices and Meanings." *Material Religion* 11, no. 2 (2015): 190–223.

———. "Fetus Magic and Sorcery Fears in Roman Egypt." *Greek, Roman, and Byzantine Studies* 46 (2006): 37–62.

———. "The Great, the Little, and the Authoritative Tradition in Magic of the Ancient World." *Archiv für Religionsgeschichte* 16 (2014): 11–30.

———. "Hagiography and the Reconstruction of Local Religion in Late Antique Egypt: Memories, Inventions, and Landscapes." *Church History and Religious Culture* 86, no. 1–4 (2006): 13–37.

———. "Iconoclasm and Christianization in Late Antique Egypt: Christian Treatments of Space and Image." In *From Temple to Church: Destruction and Renewal of Local Cultic Topography in Late Antiquity*, edited by Johannes Hahn, Stephen Emmel, and Ulrich Gotter, 135–59. Religions in the Graeco-Roman World 163. Leiden: Brill, 2008.

———. "Illuminating the Cult of Kothos: The *Panegryic on Macarius* and Local Religion in Fifth-Century Egypt." In *The World of Early Egyptian Christianity: Language, Literature, and Social Context: Essays in Honor of David W. Johnson*, edited by James E. Goehring and Janet Timbie, 176–88. Washington, DC: Catholic University of America Press, 2007.

———. "The Interpenetration of Ritual Spaces in Late Antique Religions: An Overview." *Archiv für Religionsgeschichte* 10 (2008): 211–22.

———. "Introduction: Approaches to Coptic Pilgrimage." In *Pilgrimage and Holy Space in Late Antique Egypt*, edited by David Frankfurter, 13–18. Religions in the Graeco-Roman World 134. Leiden: Brill Academic Publishers, 1998.

———. "'It Is Esrmpe Who Appeals!': Place, Object, and Performance in the Quest for Pregnancy in Roman Egypt." In *Placing Ancient Texts: The Rhetorical and Ritual Use of Space*, edited by Mika Ahuvia and Alexander G. Kocar. Tübingen, Germany: Mohr Siebeck, forthcoming.

———. "The Laments of Horus in Coptic: Myth, Folklore, and Syncretism in Late Antique Egypt." In *Antike Mythen: Medien Transformationen und Konstruktionen*, edited by Ueli Dill and Christine Walde, 229–47. Berlin: Walter de Gruyter, 2009.

———. "The Legacy of the Jewish Apocalypse in Early Christian Communities: Two Regional Trajectories." In *The Jewish Apocalyptic Heritage in Early Christianity*, edited by James C. VanderKam and William Adler, 129–200. Compendia Rerum Iudaicarum ad Novum Testamentum III.4. Assen, The Netherlands: Van Gorcum, 1996.

———. "The Magic of Writing and the Writing of Magic: The Power of the Word in Egyptian and Greek Traditions." *Helios* 21, no. 2 (1994): 189–221.

———. "Narrating Power: The Theory and Practice of the Magical Historiola in Ritual Spells." In *Ancient Magic and Ritual Power*, edited by Marvin W. Meyer and Paul Allan Mirecki, 457–76. Religions in the Graeco-Roman World 129. Leiden: Brill, 2001.

———. "Onomastic Statistics and the Christianization of Egypt: A Response to Depauw and Clarysse." *Vigiliae Christianae* 68, no. 3 (2014): 284–89.

———. "The Perils of Love: Magic and Countermagic in Coptic Egypt." *Journal of the History of Sexuality* 10, no. 3/4 (2001): 480–500.

———. *Religion in Roman Egypt: Assimilation and Resistance*. Princeton, NJ: Princeton University Press, 1998.

———. "The Social Context of Women's Erotic Magic in Antiquity." In *Daughters of Hekate: Women and Magic in the Ancient World*, edited by Kimberly Stratton with Dayna Kalleres, 319–39. New York: Oxford University Press, 2014.

———. "The Spaces of Domestic Religion in Late Antique Egypt." *Archiv für Religionsgeschichte* 18 (forthcoming).

———. "Stylites and *Phallobatēs*: Pillar Religions in Late Antique Syria." *Vigiliae Christianae* 44, no. 2 (1990): 168–98.

———. "Syncretism and the Holy Man in Late Antique Egypt." *Journal of Early Christian Studies* 11, no. 3 (2003): 339–85.

———. "Terracotta Figurines and Popular Religion in Late Antique Egypt: Issues of Continuity and 'Survival.'" In *Le Myrte et la rose. Mélanges offerts à Françoise Dunand*, edited by G. Tallet and Chr. Zivie-Coche, 129–41. Montpellier, France: Université Paul Valéry-Montpellier III, 2014.

———. "The Vitality of Egyptian Images in Late Antique Egypt: Christian Memory and Response." In *The Sculptural Environment of the Roman Near East: Reflections on Culture, Ideology, and Power*, edited by Yaron Z. Eliav, Elise A. Friedland, and Sharon Herbert, 659–78. Interdisciplinary Studies in Ancient Culture and Religion 9. Leuven, Belgium: Peeters, 2008.

———. "'Things Unbefitting Christians': Violence and Christianization in Fifth-Century Panopolis." *Journal of Early Christian Studies* 8, no. 2 (2000): 273–95.

———. "Urban Shrine and Rural Saint in Fifth-Century Alexandria." In *Pilgrimage in Graeco-Roman and Early Christian Antiquity: Seeing the Gods*, edited by Jaś Elsner and Ian Rutherford, 435–50. Oxford: Oxford University Press, 2005.

———. "Voices, Books, and Dreams: The Diversification of Divination Media in Late Antique Egypt." In *Mantikē: Studies in Ancient Divination*, edited by Sarah Iles Johnston and Peter T. Struck, 233–54. Religions in the Graeco-Roman World 155. Leiden: Brill, 2005.

———. "Where the Spirits Dwell: Possession, Christianization, and Saints' Shrines in Late Antiquity." *Harvard Theological Review* 103, no. 1 (2010): 27–46.

Frazer, James George. *The Golden Bough*. 3rd ed. London: Macmillan and Co., 1913.

Freedberg, David. *The Power of Images: Studies in the History and Theory of Response*. Chicago: University of Chicago Press, 1989.

Frend, William H. *The Archaeology of Early Christianity: A History*. Minneapolis, MN: Fortress Press, 1998.

Fromont, Cécile. *The Art of Conversion: Christian Visual Culture in the Kingdom of Kongo*. Chapel Hill: University of North Carolina Press, 2014.

Gaddis, Michael. *There Is No Crime for Those Who Have Christ: Religious Violence in the Christian Roman Empire*. Transformation of the Classical Heritage 39. Berkeley: University of California Press, 2005.

Gager, John G. *Curse Tablets and Binding Spells from the Ancient World*. Oxford: Oxford University Press, 1992.

Garitte, G. "Le texte arménien de l'invention des Trois Enfants de Babylone." *Le Muséon* 74 (1961): 91–108.

———. "L'invention géorgienne des Trois Enfants de Babylone." *Le Muséon* 72 (1959): 69–100.

Gascou, Jean. "Les origines du culte des saints Cyr et Jean." *Analecta Bollandiana* 125, no. 2 (2007): 241–81.

———. "Notes de papyrologie byzantine (II)." *Chronique d'Égypte* 59 (1984): 333–45.

———. *Sophrone de Jérusalem : Miracles des saints Cyr et Jean*. Paris: Editions De Boccard, 2006.

Gasse, Annie. *Les stèles d'Horus sur les crocodiles*. Paris: Musée du Louvre, 2004.

Gauthier, N. "La topographie chrétienne entre idéologie et pragmatisme." In *The Idea and Ideal of the Town Between Late Antiquity and the Early Middle Ages*, edited by Gian Pietro Brogiolo and Bryan Ward-Perkins, 195–210. Leiden: Brill, 1999.

Gell, Alfred. *Art and Agency: An Anthropological Theory*. Oxford: Clarendon Press, 1998.

———. "Technology and Magic." In *Greek Magic: Ancient, Medieval and Modern*, edited by J.C.B. Petropoulos, 160–67. London and New York: Routledge, 2008.

Gellner, David N. "For Syncretism: The Position of Buddhism in Nepal and Japan Compared." *Social Anthropology* 5, no. 3 (1997): 277–91.

Gemzoë, Lena. "The Feminization of Healing in Pilgrimage to Fátima." In *Pilgrimage and Healing*, edited by Jill Dubisch and Michael Winkelman, 25–48. Tucson: University of Arizona Press, 2005.

Georgoudi, Stella. "Sanctified Slaughter in Modern Greece: The 'Kourbáni' of the Saints." In *The Cuisine of Sacrifice among the Greeks*, edited by M. Détienne and J.-P. Vernant, translated by Paula Wissing, 183–203. Chicago: University of Chicago Press, 1989.

Gessler-Löhr, Beatrix. "Mummies and Mummification." In *The Oxford Handbook of Roman Egypt*, edited by Christina Riggs, 664–83. Oxford and New York: Oxford University Press, 2012.

Ghaly, Holeil. "Pottery Workshops of Saint-Jeremia (Saqqara)." *Cahiers de la céramique égyptienne* 3 (1992): 161–71.

Gill, Sam D. "Dancing and the Poetics of Place (Revised)." Paper presented at the American Academy of Religion, Toronto, 2009. http://sam-gill.com/PDF/Dancing%20and%20the%20Poetics%20of%20Place.pdf.

———. "Nonliterate Traditions and Holy Books: Toward a New Model." In *The Holy Book in Comparative Perspective*, edited by Frederick M. Denny and Rodney L. Taylor, 224–39. Columbia: University of South Carolina Press, 1985.

Gillis, Anne-Catherine. "Des démons dans l'atelier: Iconographie et piété des artisans en Grèce ancienne." In *Perception et construction du divin dans l'antiquité*, edited by Philippe Borgeaud and Doralice Fabiano, 87–118. Geneva: Libraririe Droz S.A., 2013.

Gingras, George E. *Egeria: Diary of a Pilgrimage*. Ancient Christian Writers 38. New York: Paulist Press, 1970.

Given, J. Gregory. "Utility and Variance in Late Antique Witnesses to the Abgar-Jesus Correspondence." *Archiv für Religionsgeschichte* 17 (2016): 187–222.

Godlewski, Włodzimierz. "Naqlun: Excavations 1997." *Polish Archaeology in the Mediterranean* 9 (1997): 77–86.

———. "Naqlun: The Earliest Hermitages." In *The Oasis Papers 6: Proceedings of the Sixth International Conference of the Dakhleh Oasis Project*, edited by Roger S. Bagnall, Paola Davoli, and Colin A. Hope, 475–89. Oxford: Oxbow Books, 2009.

Godlewski, Włodzimierz, and Barbara Czaja-Szewczak. "Cemetery C.1 in Naqlun: Tomb C.T.5 and Its Cartonnages." *Polish Archaeology in the Mediterranean* 18 (2009): 247–60.

Goehring, James E. *Ascetics, Society, and the Desert: Studies in Early Egyptian Monasticism.* Harrisburg, PA: Trinity Press International, 1999.

———. *Politics, Monasticism, and Miracles in Sixth-Century Upper Egypt.* Studien und Texte zu Antike und Christentum 69. Tübingen, Germany: Mohr Siebeck, 2012.

Golitzin, Alexander. "Earthly Angels and Heavenly Men: The Old Testament Pseudepigrapha, Niketas Stethatos, and the Tradition of 'Interiorized Apocalyptic' in Eastern Christian Ascetical and Mystical Literature." *Dumbarton Oaks Papers* 55 (2001): 125–53.

Golopentia, Sandra. "Towards a Typology of Romanian Love Charms." In *Charms and Charming in Europe*, edited by Jonathan Roper, 145–87. New York: Palgrave Macmillan, 2005.

Gonosová, Anna. "Textiles." In *Beyond the Pharaohs: Egypt and the Copts in the 2nd to 7th Centuries A.D.*, edited by Florence D. Friedman, 65–72. Providence: Rhode Island School of Design, 1989.

Goody, Jack. "Religion, Social Change and the Sociology of Conversion." In *Changing Social Structure in Ghana: Essays in the Comparative Sociology of a New State and an Old Tradition*, edited by Jack Goody, 91–106. London: International African Institute, 1975.

Gordon, Richard. "From Substances to Texts: Three Materialities of 'Magic' in the Roman Imperial Period." In *The Materiality of Magic*, edited by Dietrich Boschung and Jan N. Bremmer, 133–76. Paderborn, Germany: W. Fink, 2015.

———. "Showing the Gods the Way: Curse-Tablets as Deictic Persuasion." *Religion in the Roman Empire* 1, no. 2 (2015): 148–80.

———. "*Signa Nova et Inaudita*: The Theory and Practice of Invented Signs (*Charaktēres*) in Graeco-Egyptian Magical Texts." *MHNH* 11 (2011): 15–44.

Gougaud, L. "La danse dans les églises." *Revue d'histoire ecclésiastique* 15 (1914): 5–22.

Gounelle, Rémi. *La descente du Christ aux enfers: Institutionnalisation d'une croyance.* Collection des études augustiniennes, série antiquité 162. Paris: Institut d'études augustiniennes, 2000.

Graf, Fritz. "Dangerous Dreaming: The Christian Transformation of Dream Incubation." *Archiv für Religionsgeschichte* 15 (2013): 117–42.

———. "Pompai in Greece: Some Considerations about Space and Ritual in the Greek Polis." In *The Role of Religion in the Early Greek Polis: Proceedings of the Third International Seminar on Ancient Greek Cult, organized by the Swedish Institute of Athens, 16–18 October 1992*, edited by Robin Hägg, 55–65. Stockholm: Pauil Aströms Förlag, 1996.

———. *Roman Festivals in the Greek East: From the Early Empire to the Middle Byzantine Era.* Cambridge: Cambridge University Press, 2015.

———. "Syncretism (Further Considerations)." In *Encyclopedia of Religion*, edited by Lindsay Jones, 13:8934–38. Detroit: Macmillan Reference USA, 2005.

Graziano, Frank. *Cultures of Devotion: Folk Saints of Spanish America.* New York: Oxford University Press, 2006.

Greenfield, Sidney M., and A. F. Droogers. *Reinventing Religions: Syncretism and Transformation in Africa and the Americas.* Lanham, MD: Rowman & Littlefield, 2001.

Greer, Rowan A., and Margaret M. Mitchell. *The "Belly-Myther" of Endor: Interpretations of 1 Kingdoms 28 in the Early Church.* Writings from the Greco-Roman World 16. Atlanta: Society of Biblical Literature, 2007.

Gregg, Robert C. *Athanasius: The Life of Antony and the Letter to Marcellinus.* Classics of Western Spirituality. New York: Paulist Press, 1980.

Grey, David Elton. "On the Christianity of the Incantations." In *Charms and Charming in Europe*, edited by Jonathan Roper, 32–46. New York: Palgrave Macmillan, 2005.

Griggs, C. Wilfred. "Early Christian Burials in the Fayoum." In *Christianity and Monasticism in the Fayoum Oasis*, edited by Gawdat Gabra, 185–95. Cairo: American University in Cairo Press, 2005.

Grillet, Bernard, and Guy Sabbah. *Sozomène: Histoire ecclésiastique, Livres I–II.* Sources chrétiennes 306. Paris: Éditions du Cerf, 1983.

Grossmann, Peter. "Abu Mina: Zehnter Vorläufiger Bericht, Kampagnen 1980 und 1981." *Mitteilungen des deutschen archäologischen Instituts, Abteilung Kairo* 38 (1982): 131–54.

———. "Antinoopolis: The Area of St. Colluthos in the North Necropolis." In *Antinoupolis II: Scavi E Materiali*, edited by Rosario Pintaudi, 241–300. Florence: Firenze University Press, 2014.

———. *Christliche Architektur in Ägypten*. Handbuch der Orientalistik 62. Leiden and Boston: Brill, 2002.

———. "Churches and Meeting Halls in Necropoleis and Crypts in Intramural Churches." In *Egypt in the First Millennium AD: Perspectives from New Fieldwork*, edited by Elisabeth R. O'Connell, 93–113. Leuven, Belgium: Peeters, 2014.

———. "Dandarah." In *The Coptic Encyclopedia*, edited by Aziz Atiya, 3:690–91. New York: Macmillan, 1991.

———. "Late Antique Christian Incubation Centres in Egypt." In *Salute e guarigione nella tarda antichità: Atti della giornata tematica dei seminari di archeologia cristiana, Roma, 20 maggio 2004*, edited by Hugo Brandenburg, Stefan Heid, and Christoph Markschies, 125–40. Vatican City: Pontifical Institute of Christian Archaeology, 2007.

———. "Modalitäten der Zerstörung und Christianisierung pharaonischer Tempelanlagen." In *From Temple to Church: Destruction and Renewal of Local Cultic Topography in Late Antiquity*, edited by Johannes Hahn, Stephen Emmel, and Ulrich Gotter, 299–334. Religions in the Graeco-Roman World 163. Leiden: Brill, 2008.

———. "The Pilgrimage Center of Abu Mina." In *Pilgrimage and Holy Space in Late Antique Egypt*, edited by David Frankfurter, 281–302. Religions in the Graeco-Roman World 134. Leiden: Brill, 1998.

Grottanelli, Cristiano. "Tuer des animaux pour la fête de Saint Félix." In *La cuisine et l'autel: Les sacrifices en questions dans les sociétés de la méditerranée ancienne*, edited by S. Georgoudi, R. K. Piettre, and F. Schmidt, 387–407. Turnhout, Belgium: Brepols, 2005.

Haarman, Ulrich. "Medieval Muslim Perceptions of Pharaonic Egypt." In *Ancient Egyptian Literature: History and Forms*, edited by Antonio Loprieno, 605–27. Probleme der Ägyptologie 10. Leiden: Brill, 1996.

Haas, Christopher. *Alexandria in Late Antiquity: Topography and Social Conflict*. Baltimore: Johns Hopkins University Press, 1997.

———. "Mountain Constantines: The Christianization of Aksum and Iberia." *Journal of Late Antiquity* 1, no. 1 (2008): 101–26.

Hahn, Johannes. "Public Rituals of Depaganization in Late Antiquity." In *Religious Practices and Christianization of the Late Antique City (4th–7th Cent.)*, edited by Aude Busine, 115–40. Religions in the Graeco-Roman World 182. Leiden: Brill, 2015.

Hahn, Johannes, Stephen Emmel, and Ulrich Gotter, eds. *From Temple to Church: Destruction and Renewal of Local Cultic Topography in Late Antiquity*. Religions in the Graeco-Roman World 163. Leiden: Brill, 2008.

Haines-Eitzen, Kim. *Guardians of Letters: Literacy, Power, and the Transmitters of Early Christian Literature*. New York: Oxford University Press, 2000.

Halbwachs, Maurice. *On Collective Memory*. Translated by Lewis A. Coser. Chicago: University of Chicago Press, 1992.

Hallock, Frank H. "Christianity and the Old Egyptian Religion." *Egyptian Religion* 2 (1934): 6–17.

Hamilakis, Y. "Indigenous Archaeologies in Ottoman Greece." In *Scramble for the Past: A Story of Archaeology in the Ottoman Empire, 1753–1914*, edited by Zainab Bahrani, Zeynep Çelik, and Edhem Eldem, 49–69. Istanbul: SALT, 2011.

Hammerschmidt, Ernst. "Altägyptische Elemente im koptischen Christentum." *Ostkirchliche Studien* 6 (1957): 233–50.

Hansen, Nicole B. "Ancient Execration in Coptic and Islamic Egypt." In *Magic and Ritual in the Ancient World*, edited by Paul Allan Mirecki and Marvin W. Meyer, 427–45. Religions in the Graeco-Roman World 141. Leiden: Brill, 2002.

Harl, M. "La dénonciation des festivités profanes dans le discours episcopal et monastique, en orient chrétien, à la fin du IV siècle." In *La fête, pratique et discours: d'Alexandrie hellénistique à la Mission de Besançon*, 123–47. Paris: Les Belles Lettres, 1981.

Harrison, John Hilton, and Vincent Hunink. *Apuleius: Rhetorical Works*. Oxford and New York: Oxford University Press, 2001.

Hasitzka, Monika R. M. *Koptisches Sammelbuch I*. Mitteilungen aus der Papyrussammlung der Osterreichischen Nationalbibliothek (Papyrus Erzherzog Rainer) 23. Vienna: Hollinek, 1993.

Hastings, Adrian. "Emmanual Milingo as Christian Healer." In *African Medicine in the Modern World: Proceedings of a Seminar Held in the Centre of African Studies, University of Edinburgh, 10 and 11 December, 1986*, 147–71. Edinburgh: Centre of African Studies, 1987.

Hasznos, Andrea. "A Shenoute Homily Found in Theban Tomb 65." *Enchoria* 30 (2006): 7–9.

Hedrick, Charles W. "A Monastic Exorcism Text." *Journal of Coptic Studies* 7 (2005): 17–21.

Hefner, Robert W., ed. *Conversion to Christianity: Historical and Anthropological Perspectives on a Great Transformation*. Berkeley: University of California Press, 1993.

Heine, Ronald E. *The Montanist Oracles and Testimonia*. Patristic Monograph Series 14. Macon, GA: Mercer University Press, 1989.

Hen, Yitzhak. "Converting the Barbarian West." In *A People's History of Christianity, 4: Medieval Christianity*, edited by Daniel E. Bornstein, 29–52. Minneapolis, MN: Fortress Press, 2009.

Henry, Andrew Mark. "Apotropaic Autographs: Orality and Materiality in the Abgar-Jesus Inscriptions." *Archiv für Religionsgeschichte* 17 (2016): 165–86.

Herrmann, Alfred. "Der Nil und die Christen." *Jahrbuch für Antike und Christentum* 2 (1959): 30–69.

Heurtel, Chantal. "Le petit monde de Frangé: Une microsociété dans la région thébaine au début du VIIIe siècle." In *"Et maintenant ce ne sont plus que des villages...": Thèbes et sa région aux époques hellénistique, romaine et byzantine*, edited by A. Delattre and P. Heilporn, 163–74. Brussels: Association égyptologique Reine Élisabeth, 2008.

Himmelfarb, Martha. "Heavenly Ascent and the Relationship of the Apocalypses and the 'Hekhalot' Literature." *Hebrew Union College Annual* 59 (1988): 73–100.

———. *Tours of Hell: An Apocalyptic Form in Jewish and Christian Literature*. Philadelphia: University of Pennsylvania Press, 1983.

Hirsch, Silvia. "Spätantike Brotstempel mit der maske des ägyptischen Gottes Bes." In *Coptic Studies on the Threshold of a New Millennium: Proceedings of the Seventh International Congress of Coptic Studies, Leiden, August 27–September 2, 2000*, edited by Mat Immerzeel and Jacques van der Vliet, 2:1259–72. Orientalia Lovaniensia Analecta 133. Leuven, Belgium: Peeters, 2004.

Hobsbawm, Eric. "Introduction." In *The Invention of Tradition*, edited by Eric Hobsbawm and Terence Ranger, 1–14. Cambridge: Cambridge University Press, 1983.

Hobson, Deborah. "House and Household in Roman Egypt." *Yale Classical Studies* 28 (1985): 211–29.

Hodder, Ian. "The Domus: Some Problems Reconsidered." In *Archaeology Beyond Dialogue*, edited by Ian Hodder, 99–109. Salt Lake City: University of Utah Press, 2003.

Hooper, Finley. *Funerary Stelae from Kom Abou Billou*. Ann Arbor, MI: Kelsey Museum of Archaeology, 1961.

Horden, Peregrine. "Responses to Possession and Insanity in the Earlier Byzantine World." *Social History of Medicine* 6, no. 2 (1993): 177–94.

Horn, Jürgen. *Studien zu den Märtyrern des nördlichen Oberägypten, 1: Märtyrerverehrung und Märtyrerlegende im Werk des Schenute. Beiträge zur ältesten ägyptischen Märtryrerüberlieferung*. Wiesbaden, Germany: Harrassowitz, 1986.

Hornung, Erik. *The Ancient Egyptian Books of the Afterlife*. Translated by David Lorton. Ithaca, NY: Cornell University Press, 1999.

Horton, Robin. "African Conversion." *Africa* 41, no. 2 (1971): 85–108.

Howard-Johnston, J. D., and Paul Antony Hayward, eds. *The Cult of Saints in Late Antiquity and the*

Middle Ages: Essays on the Contribution of Peter Brown. Oxford and New York: Oxford University Press, 2002.

Howe, John M. "The Conversion of the Physical World: The Creation of a Christian Landscape." In *Varieties of Religious Conversion in the Middle Ages*, edited by James Muldoon, 63–78. Gainesville: University Press of Florida, 1997.

Huebner, Sabine R. "Egypt as Part of the Mediterranean? Domestic Space and Household Structures in Roman Egypt." In *Mediterranean Families in Antiquity: Households, Extended Families, and Domestic Space*, edited by Sabine R. Huebner and Geoffrey Nathan, 154–73. Oxford: Blackwell, 2016.

———. *The Family in Roman Egypt: A Comparative Approach to Intergenerational Solidarity and Conflict*. Cambridge: Cambridge University Press, 2013.

Hughes, Jennifer Scheper. "Cradling the Sacred: Image, Ritual, and Affect in Mexican and Mesoamerican Material Religion." *History of Religions* 56, no. 1 (2016): 55–107.

Humphries, Mark. "Liturgy and Laity in Late-Antique Rome: Problems, Sources, and Social Dynamics." *Studia Patristica* 71 (2014): 171–86.

Hunt, Stephen. "Managing the Demonic: Some Aspects of the Neo-Pentecostal Deliverance Ministry." *Journal of Contemporary Religion* 13, no. 2 (1998): 215–30.

Hurtado, Larry W. *The Earliest Christian Artifacts: Manuscripts and Christian Origins*. Grand Rapids, MI: William B. Eerdmans, 2006.

Husselman, Elinor M. *Karanis Excavations of the University of Michigan in Egypt, 1928–1935: Topography and Architecture: A Summary of the Reports of the Director, Enoch E. Peterson*. Ann Arbor: University of Michigan Press, 1979.

Husson, Geneviève. "Les questions oraculaires chrétiennes d'Égypte: Continuités et changements." In *Akten des 21. internationalen Papyrologenkongresses, Berlin, 13.-19.8. 1995*, edited by Bärbel Kramer, Wolfgang Luppe, and Herwig Maehler, 482–89. Stuttgart and Leipzig: B. G. Teubner, 1997.

———. *OIKIA: Le vocabulaire de la maison privée en Egypte d'après les papyrus grecs*. Paris: Publications de la Sorbonne, 1983.

Hyvernat, Henri. *Les actes des martyrs de l'Égypte: Tirés des manuscrits coptes de la Bibliothèque Vaticane et du Musée Borgia: Texte copte et traduction française avec introduction et commentaires*. Paris: E. Leroux, 1886.

Inhorn, Marcia C. *Quest for Conception: Gender, Infertility, and Egyptian Medical Traditions*. Philadelphia: University of Pennsylvania Press, 1994.

Jacobs, Ine. "Production to Destruction? Pagan and Mythological Statuary in Asia Minor." *American Journal of Archaeology* 114, no. 2 (2010): 267–303.

Jakab, Attila. "The Reception of the Apocalypse of Peter in Ancient Christianity." In *The Apocalypse of Peter*, edited by Jan N. Bremmer and István Czachesz, 174–86. Leuven, Belgium: Peeters, 2003.

James, Liz. *Light and Color in Byzantine Art*. Oxford: Clarendon Press, 1996.

James, William. *The Varieties of Religious Experience*. Cambridge, MA: Harvard University Press, 1985.

Johnson, D. W, trans. *A Panegyric on Macarius, Bishop of Tkôw, Attributed to Dioscorus of Alexandria*. Corpus Scriptorum Christianorum Orientalium 415–416. Louvain, Belgium: Secrétariat du CorpusSCO, 1980.

Johnson, Douglas. *Nuer Prophets: A History of Prophecy from the Upper Nile in the Nineteenth and Twentieth Centuries*. Oxford: Clarendon Press, 1994.

Johnson, Paul Christopher. "Migrating Bodies, Circulating Signs: Brazilian Candomblé, the Garifuna of the Caribbean, and the Category of Indigenous Religions." *History of Religions* 41, no. 4 (2002): 301–27.

———. *Secrets, Gossip, and Gods: The Transformation of Brazilian Candomblé*. New York: Oxford University Press, 2002.

———. "Syncretism and Hybridization." In *The Oxford Handbook for the Study of Religion*, edited by Michael Stausberg and Steven Engler, 754–71. Oxford: Oxford University Press, 2017.

Johnson, William A. *Readers and Reading Culture in the High Roman Empire: A Study of Elite Communities*. New York: Oxford University Press, 2010.

Johnston, Sarah Iles. "Charming Children: The Use of the Child in Ancient Divination." *Arethusa* 34, no. 1 (2001): 97–117.

———. "Riders in the Sky: Cavalier Gods and Theurgic Salvation in the Second Century A.D." *Classical Philology* 87 (1992): 303–21.

Jolly, Karen. *Popular Religion in Late Saxon England: Elf Charms in Context*. Chapel Hill: University of North Carolina Press, 1996.

Jones, Brice C. *New Testament Texts on Greek Amulets from Late Antiquity*. London: Bloomsbury Academic, 2016.

Jones, Christopher P. *Between Pagan and Christian*. Cambridge, MA: Harvard University Press, 2014.

———. "The Fuzziness of 'Paganism.'" *Common Knowledge* 18, no. 2 (2012): 249–54.

Jordan, D. R. "Inscribed Lamps from a Cult at Corinth in Late Antiquity." *Harvard Theological Review* 87, no. 2 (1994): 223–29.

———. "A Survey of Greek Defixiones Not Included in the Special Corpora." *Greek, Roman, and Byzantine Studies* 26, no. 2 (1985): 151–97.

Jördens, Andrea. "Reliquien des Schenute im Frauenkonvent." In *Paramone: Editionen und Aufsätze von Mitgliedern des Heidelberger Instituts für Papyrologie zwischen 1982 und 2004*, edited by James M. S. Cowey and Bärbel Kramer, 142–56. Munich and Leipzig: K. G. Saur, 2004.

Jorio, Andrea de. *Gesture in Naples and Gesture in Classical Antiquity: Gestural Expression of the Ancients in the Light of Neapolitan Gesturing*. Translated by Adam Kendon. Bloomington: Indiana University Press, 2000.

Judge, E. A. "The Magical Use of Scripture in the Papyri." In *Perspectives on Language and Text*, edited by E. W. Conrad and E. G. Newing, 339–49. Winona Lake, IN: Eisenbrauns, 1987.

Jullien, Michel. "Le culte chrétien dans les temples de l'ancienne Égypte." *Les études* 92 (1902): 237–53.

Kalleres, Dayna S. *City of Demons: Violence, Ritual, and Christian Power in Late Antiquity*. Berkeley: University of California Press, 2015.

Kaplan, Michel. "De la dépouille à la relique: Formation du culte des saints à Byzance du Ve au XIIe siècle." In *Les reliques: Objets, cultes, symboles. Actes du colloque international de l'Université du Littoral-Côte d'Opale (Boulogne-Sur-Mer), 4–6 septembre 1997*, edited by Edina Bozóky and Anne-Marie Helvétius, 19–38. Turnhout, Belgium: Brepols, 1999.

Kaplan, Steven. "Däbtära." In *Encyclopaedia Aethiopica*, edited by Siegbert Uhlig, 2:53–54. Wiesbaden, Germany: Harrassowitz, 2005.

———. "The Ethiopian Holy Man as Outsider and Angel." *Religion* 15 (1985): 235–49.

———. "Magic and Religion in Christian Ethiopia: Some Preliminary Remarks." In *Studia Aethiopica: In Honour of Siegbert Uhlig on the Occasion of His 65th Birthday*, edited by V. Böll, D. Nosnitsin, T. Rave, W. Smidt, and E. Sokolinskaia, 413–20. Wiesbaden, Germany: Harrassowitz, 2004.

———. *The Monastic Holy Man and the Christianization of Early Solomonic Ethiopia*. Studien zur Kulturkunde 73. Wiesbaden, Germany: F. Steiner, 1984.

Karanika, Andromache. *Voices at Work: Women, Performance, and Labor in Ancient Greece*. Baltimore: Johns Hopkins University Press, 2014.

Karivieri, Arja. "The 'House of Proclus' on the Southern Slope of the Acropolis: A Contribution." In *Post-Herulian Athens: Aspects of Life and Culture in Athens, A. D. 267–529*, ed. Paavo Castrén, 115–39. Helsinki: Finnish Institute, 1994.

Kaufmann, Carl Maria. "Archäologische Miscellen aus Ägypten, I." *Oriens Christianus* 3 (1913): 105–10.

———. *Die heilige Stadt der Wüste: unsere Entdeckungen Grabungen und Funde in der altchristlichen*

Menasstadt weiteren Kreisen in Wort und Bild geschildert. Kempten-München, Germany: J. Kösel, 1918.

———. *Die Menasstadt und das Nationalheiligtum der altchristlichen Ägypter in der westalexandrinischen Wüste*. Leipzig: K. W. Hiersemann, 1910.

Kayser, François. "Oreilles et couronnes: À propos des cultes de Canope." *Bulletin de l'institut français d'archéologie orientale* 91 (1991): 207–17.

Keane, Webb. "From Fetishism to Sincerity: On Agency, the Speaking Subject, and Their Historicity in the Context of Religious Conversion." *Comparative Studies in Society and History* 39, no. 4 (1997): 674–93.

Keimer, L. "L'horreur des égyptiens pour les démons du désert." *Bulletin de l'institut d'Égypte* 26 (1944): 135–47.

Kendrick, A. F. *Catalogue of Textiles from Burying-Grounds in Egypt*. 3 vols. Victoria and Albert Museum Publication 153T. London: Victoria and Albert Museum, 1920.

Kent, Eliza F. "Secret Christians of Sivakasi: Gender, Syncretism, and Crypto-Religion in Early Twentieth-Century South India." *Journal of the American Academy of Religion* 79, no. 3 (2011): 676–705.

Kiss, Zsolt. "Alexandria in the Fourth to Seventh Centuries." In *Egypt in the Byzantine World, 300–700*, edited by Roger S. Bagnall, 187–206. New York: Cambridge University Press, 2010.

———. "Évolution stylistique des ampoules de St. Ménas." In *Coptic Studies: Acts of the Third International Congress of Coptic Studies, Warsaw, 20–25 August, 1984*, edited by Włodzimierz Godlewski, 195–202. Warsaw: PWN, 1990.

———. *Les ampoules de Saint Ménas découvertes à Kôm el-Dikka (1961–1981)*. Alexandrie 5. Warsaw: PWN, 1989.

Kletter, Raz, and Katri Saarelainen. "Judean Drummers." *Zeitschrift des deutschen Palästina-Veneins* 127 (2011): 11–28.

Klingshirn, William E. *Caesarius of Arles: The Making of a Christian Community in Late Antique Gaul*. Cambridge: Cambridge University Press, 1994.

———. "Christian Divination in Late Roman Gaul: The Sortes Sangallenses." In *Mantikê: Studies in Ancient Divination*, edited by Sarah Iles Johnston and Peter T. Struck, 99–128. Religions in the Graeco-Roman World 155. Leiden: Brill, 2005.

———. "Defining the *Sortes Sanctorum* : Gibbon, Du Cange, and Early Christian Lot Divination." *Journal of Early Christian Studies* 10, no. 1 (2002): 77–130.

———. "Inventing the Sortilegus: Lot Divination and Cultural Identity in Italy, Rome, and the Provinces." In *Religion in Republican Italy*, edited by Paul B. Harvey, Jr., and Celia E. Schultz, 137–61. Cambridge and New York: Cambridge University Press, 2006.

Klotz, David. "Triphis in the White Monastery." *Ancient Society* 40 (2010): 197–213.

Knust, Jennifer, and Tommy Wasserman. "The Biblical Odes and the Text of the Christian Bible: A Reconsideration of the Impact of Liturgical Singing on the Transmission of the Gospel of Luke." *Journal of Biblical Literature* 133 (2014): 341–65.

Kondoleon, Christine. *Antioch: The Lost Ancient City*. Princeton, NJ: Princeton University Press, 2000.

———. "The Gerasa Mosaics of Yale: Intentionality and Design." In *Roman in the Provinces: Art on the Periphery of Empire*, edited by Gail L. Hoffman and Lisa R. Brody, 221–34. Chestnut Hill, MA: McMullen Museum of Art, 2014.

Kosack, Wolfgang. *Die Legende im Koptischen. Untersuchungen z. Volksliteratur Ägyptens*. Habelts Dissertationsdrucke, Reihe klassische Philologie 8. Bonn: Habelt, 1970.

Koschorke, K., S. Timm, and F. Wisse, eds. "Schenute: De certamine contra diabolum." *Oriens Christianus* 59 (1975): 60–77.

Kotsifou, Chrysi. "Books and Book Production in the Monastic Communities of Byzantine Egypt." In *The Early Christian Book*, edited by William E. Klingshirn and Linda Safran, 48–66. Washington, DC: Catholic University of America Press, 2007.

———. "Monks as Mediators in Christian Egypt." In *Law and Legal Practice in Egypt from Alexander to the Arab Conquest*, edited by James G. Keenan, J. G. Manning, and Uri Yiftach-Firanko, 530–40. Cambridge: Cambridge University Press, 2014.

Kraus, Thomas J. "The Lending of Books in the Fourth Century C.E. P. Oxy LXIII 4365—A Letter on Papyrus and the Reciprocal Lending of Literature Having Become Apocryphal." In *Ad Fontes: Original Manuscripts and Their Significance for Studying Early Christianity, Selected Essays*, edited by Thomas J. Kraus, 185–206. Leiden: Brill, 2007.

Krause, Martin. "Das Weiterleben ägyptischer Vorstellungen und Bräuche im koptischen Totenwesen." In *Das römisch-byzantinische Ägypten: Akten des internationalen Symposions 26–30 September in Trier*, 85–92. Mainz am Rhein, Germany: Verlag Philipp von Zabern, 1983.

———. "Libraries." In *The Coptic Encyclopedia*, edited by Aziz Atiya, 5:1447–1450. New York: Macmillan, 1991.

Krawiec, Rebecca. " 'Garments of Salvation': Representations of Monastic Clothing in Late Antiquity." *Journal of Early Christian Studies* 17, no. 1 (2009): 125–50.

Kreinach, Jens. "The Seductiveness of Saints: Interreligious Pilgrimage Sites in Hatay and the Ritual Transformations of Agency." In *The Seductions of Pilgrimage: Sacred Journeys Afar and Astray in the Western Religious Tradition*, edited by Michael A. Di Giovine and David Picard, 121–43. Farnham, UK: Ashgate, 2015.

Kreuzsaler, C. "*Ho hierótatos neîlos*: Auf einer christlichen Nilstandsmarkierung." *Journal of Juristic Papyrology* 34 (2004): 81–86.

Kristensen, Troels Myrup. *Making and Breaking the Gods: Christian Responses to Pagan Sculpture in Late Antiquity*. Aarhus Studies in Mediterranean Antiquity 12. Aarhus, Denmark: Aarhus University Press, 2013.

Kropp, Angelicus. *Ausgewählte koptische Zaubertexte*. 3 vols. Brussels: Édition de la Fondation égyptologique reine Élisabeth, 1931.

Kruger, Michael J. "P. Oxy. 840: Amulet or Miniature Codex?" *Journal of Theological Studies* 53, no. 1 (2002): 81–94.

Kugener, M-A. "Sévère, Patriarche d'Antioche, 512–518, première partie: Vie de Sévère par Zacharie le scholastique." *Patrologia Orientalis* 2, no. 1 (1907): 3–115.

Kühn, K. H. *A Panegyric on Apollo, Archimandrite of the Monastery of Isaac by Stephen of Heracleopolis Magna*. 2 vols. Corpus Scriptorum Christianorum Orientalium 394–95, S. coptici 39–40. Louvain, Belgium: CSCO, 1978.

———. *Letters and Sermons of Besa*. 2 vols. Corpus Scriptorum Christianorum Orientalium 157–58, S. coptici 21–22. Louvain, Belgium: L. Durbecq, 1956.

Kühn, K. H., and W. J. Tait. *Thirteen Coptic Acrostic Hymns from Manuscript M574 of the Pierpont Morgan Library*. Oxford: Griffith Institute, 1996.

Künzel, Rudi. "Paganisme, syncrétisme et culture religieuse populaire au haut moyen âge. Réflexions de méthode." *Annales* 47, no. 4 (1992): 1055–69.

Laiou, Angeliki. "The Festival of 'Agathe': Comments on *The Life of Constantinopolitan Women*." In *Byzantium: Tribute to Andreas N. Stratos, 1: History—Art and Archaeology*, edited by N. Stratos, 111–22. Athens: Stratos, 1986.

Łajtar, Adam. *Deir El-Bahari in the Hellenistic and Roman Periods: A Study of an Egyptian Temple Based on Greek Sources*. Journal of Juristic Papyrology Supplements 4. Warsaw: Journal of Juristic Papyrology, 2006.

———. "Proskynema Inscriptions of a Corporation of Iron-Workers from Hermonthis in the Temple of Hatshepsut in Deir El-Bahari: New Evidence for Pagan Cults in Egypt in the 4th Cent. A.D." *Journal of Juristic Papyrology* 21 (1991): 53–70.

Lane Fox, Robin. "Literacy and Power in Early Christianity." In *Literacy and Power in the Ancient World*, edited by Alan Bowman and Greg Woolf, 126–48. Cambridge: Cambridge University Press, 1994.

———. *Pagans and Christians*. New York: Knopf, 1987.

Langener, Lucia. *Isis Lactans-Maria Lactans: Untersuchungen zur koptischen Ikonographie*. Arbeiten zum spätantiken und koptischen Ägypten 9. Altenberge, Germany: Oros Verlag, 1996.

Lazaridou, Anastasia D., ed. *Transition to Christianity: Art of Late Antiquity, 3rd–7th Century AD*. New York and Athens: Alexander S. Onassis Public Benefit Foundation, 2011.

Lecouteux, Claude. *La maison et ses génies: Croyances d'hier et d'aujoud'hui*. Paris: Imago, 2000.

Leemans, Johan. "General Introduction." In *"Let Us Die That We May Live": Greek Homilies on Christian Martyrs from Asia Minor, Palestine and Syria 350–450 AD*, edited by Johan Leemans, Boudewijn Dehandschutter, Pauline Allen, and Wendy Mayer, 5–22. London: Routledge, 2003.

Leemans, Johan, Boudewijn Dehandschutter, Pauline Allen, and Wendy Mayer, eds. *"Let Us Die That We May Live": Greek Homilies on Christian Martyrs from Asia Minor, Palestine and Syria 350–450 AD*. London: Routledge, 2003.

Lefort, L.-Th. "La chasse aux reliques des martyrs en Égypte au IVè siècle." *La nouvelle Clio* 6 (1954): 225–30.

———. "L'homélie de S. Athanase des papyrus de Turin." *Le Muséon* 71 (1958): 5–50, 209–39.

———. *S. Athanase: Lettres festales et pastorales en copte*. 2 vols. Corpus Scriptorum Christianorum Orientalium 150–51, S. coptici 19–20. Louvain, Belgium: Durbecq, 1955.

Leipoldt, Johannes. *Sinuthii archimandritae vita et opera omnia*. 3 vols. Corpus Scriptorum Christianorum Orientalium 41–42, 73, S. coptici 1–2, 5. Paris: Imprimerie nationale, 1906–13.

Lévi-Strauss, Claude. *The Savage Mind*. Chicago: University of Chicago Press, 1966.

Lewis, I. M. *Ecstatic Religion: A Study of Shamanism and Spirit Possession*. 3rd ed. New York: Routledge, 2003.

Lewis, Naphtali. *Life in Egypt under Roman Rule*. Oxford: Clarendon Press, 1983.

Lewis, Suzanne. *Early Coptic Textiles: Stanford Art Gallery, Stanford University*. Stanford Art Book 9. Stanford, CA: Stanford University Press, 1969.

———. "The Iconography of the Coptic Horseman in Byzantine Egypt." *Journal of the American Research Center in Egypt* 10 (1973): 27–63.

Lexa, François. *La magie dans l'Égypte antique: De l'ancien empire jusqu'à l'époque copte*. Paris: Paul Geuthner, 1925.

Leyerle, Blake. "Pilgrim Eulogiae and Domestic Ritual." *Archiv für Religionsgeschichte* 10 (2008): 233–37.

LiDonnici, Lynn R. *The Epidaurian Miracle Inscriptions: Text, Translation and Commentary*. SBL Texts and Translations 36. Atlanta: Scholars Press, 1995.

Lincoln, Bruce. "Retiring 'Syncretism.'" *Historical Reflections/Réflexions Historiques* 27, no. 3 (2001): 453–59.

Llewelyn, Stephen R., and Alanna M. Nobbs. "P. Grenf. II 73: A Reconsideration." In *Akten des 21. internationalen Papyrologenkongresses, Berlin, 13.-19.8. 1995*, edited by Bärbel Kramer, Wolfgang Luppe, and Herwig Maehler, 613–30. Stuttgart and Leipzig: B. G. Teubner, 1997.

Lloyd, Alan B. *Herodotus, Book II, Commentary 1–98*. Études préliminaires aux religions orientales dans l'empire romain 43. Leiden: E. J. Brill, 1975.

Lubomierski, Nina. "The Coptic Life of Shenoute." In *Christianity and Monasticism in Upper Egypt*, edited by Gawdat Gabra and Hany N. Takla, 91–98. Cairo: American University in Cairo Press, 2008.

Lucarelli, Rita. "Demonology During the Late Pharaonic and Greco-Roman Periods in Egypt." *Journal of Ancient Near Eastern Religions* 11 (2011): 109–25.

———. "The Guardian-Demons of the Book of the Dead." *British Museum Studies in Ancient Egypt and Sudan* 15 (2010): 85–102.

Luijendijk, AnneMarie. *Forbidden Oracles? The Gospel of the Lots of Mary*. Studien und Texte zu Antike und Christentum 89. Tübingen, Germany: Mohr Siebeck, 2014.

———. *Greetings in the Lord: Early Christians and the Oxyrhynchus Papyri*. Harvard Theological Studies 60. Cambridge, MA: Harvard Divinity School, 2008.

———. "'Jesus Says: "There Is Nothing Buried That Will Not Be Raised."' A Late-Antique Shroud with Gospel of Thomas Logion 5 in Context." *Zeitschrift für Antike und Christentum* 15, no. 3 (2011): 389–410.

Lundhaug, Hugo, and Lance Jenott. *The Monastic Origins of the Nag Hammadi Codices*. Studien und Texte zu Antike und Christentum 97. Tübingen, Germany: Mohr Siebeck, 2015.

Lyster, William. "Artistic Working Practice and the Second-Phase Ornamental Program." In *The Red Monastery Church: Beauty and Asceticism in Upper Egypt*, edited by Elizabeth S. Bolman, 97–117. New Haven, CT: Yale University Press/American Research Center in Egypt, 2016.

MacClymond, Katherine. *Beyond Sacred Violence: A Comparative Study of Sacrifice*. Baltimore: Johns Hopkins University Press, 2008.

MacCormack, Sabine. *Art and Ceremony in Late Antiquity*. Transformation of the Classical Heritage 1. Berkeley: University of California Press, 1981.

———. "Gods, Demons, and Idols in the Andes." *Journal of the History of Ideas* 67, no. 4 (2006): 623–47.

MacCoull, Leslie S. B. "Child Donations and Child Saints in Coptic Egypt." *East European Quarterly* 13, no. 4 (1979): 409–15.

———. "Christianity at Syene/Elephantine/Philae." *Bulletin of the American Society of Papyrologists* 27, no. 1–4 (1990): 151–62.

———. "The Coptic Inscriptions on the Votive Cross of the Monastery of Shenoute." *Cahiers archéologiques* 44 (1996): 13–18.

———. "Duke University Ms. C25: Dreams, Visions, and Incubation in Coptic Egypt." *Orientalia Lovaniensia Periodica* 22 (1991): 123–32.

———. "Holy Family Pilgrimage in Late Antique Egypt: The Case of Qosqam." *Jahrbuch für Antike und Christentum Supplement* 20 (1995): 987–92.

———. "Stud. Pal. XV 250ab: A Monophysite Trishagion for the Nile Flood." *Journal of Theological Studies* 40 (1989): 130–32.

MacDermot, Violet. *The Cult of the Seer in the Ancient Middle East*. London: Wellcome Institute for the History of Medicine, 1971.

MacGaffey, Wyatt. "Kimbanguism and the Question of Syncretism in Zaire." In *Religion in Africa: Experience and Expression*, edited by Thomas D. Blakely, W.E.A. van Beek, and Dennis L. Thomson, 241–56. London and Portsmouth, NH: J. Currey; Heinemann, 1994.

MacMullen, Ramsay. *Christianity and Paganism in the Fourth to Eighth Centuries*. New Haven, CT: Yale University Press, 1997.

———. *Christianizing the Roman Empire: A.D. 100–400*. New Haven, CT: Yale University Press, 1986.

———. *The Second Church: Popular Christianity A.D. 200–400*. Atlanta: Society of Biblical Literature, 2009.

Maguire, Eunice Dauterman, Henry Maguire, and Maggie J. Duncan-Flowers. *Art and Holy Powers in the Early Christian House*. Illinois Byzantine Studies 2. Urbana: University of Illinois Press, 1989.

Maguire, Henry. "Garments Pleasing to God: The Significance of Domestic Textile Designs in the Early Byzantine Period." *Dumbarton Oaks Papers* 44 (1990): 215–24.

Maier, Harry O. "Heresy, Households, and the Disciplining of Diversity." In *A People's History of Christianity, 2: Late Ancient Christianity*, edited by Virginia Burrus, 213–33. Minneapolis, MN: Fortress Press, 2005.

Malinowski, Bronislaw. *Coral Gardens and Their Magic*, 2 vols. New York: Dover Publications, 1978.

Mallon, Alexis. "Quelques ostraca coptes de Thèbes." *Revue de l'Égypte ancienne* 1 (1927): 152–56.

Mango, Cyril A. *The Art of the Byzantine Empire, 312–1453: Sources and Documents*. Toronto: University of Toronto Press, 1986.

Maraval, Pierre. "Fonction pédagogique de la littérature hagiographique d'un lieu de pèlerinage: L'exemple des Miracles de Cyr et Jean." In *Hagiographie cultures et sociétés: IV–XII siècles*, 383–97. Paris: Études augustiniennes, 1981.

BIBLIOGRAPHY

Marcos, Natalio Fernández. *Los thaumata de Sofronio: Contribución al estudio de la incubatio cristiana.* Madrid: Instituto "Antonio de Nebrija," 1975.

Marett, R. R. *The Threshold of Religion.* 2nd ed. London: Methuen, 1914.

Markus, Robert A. *The End of Ancient Christianity.* New York: Cambridge University Press, 1991.

Marriott, McKim. "Little Communities in an Indigenous Civilization." In *Village India: Studies in the Little Community*, edited by McKim Marriott, 171–222. Chicago: University of Chicago Press, 1955.

Martens, Małgorzata. "Figurines en terre-cuite coptes découvertes à Kôm El-Dikka (Alexandrie)." *Bulletin de la société archéologique d'Alexandrie* 43 (1975): 53–77.

Martens-Czarnecka, Małgorzata. *The Wall Paintings from the Monastery on Kom H in Dongola.* Translated by Barbara Gostyńska. Warsaw: Polish Centre of Mediterranean Archaeology and Warsaw University Press, 2011.

———. "Wall Paintings Discovered in Dongola in the 2004 Season." *Polish Archaeology in the Mediterranean* 16 (2005): 273–84.

Martinez, David G. *P. Michigan XIX. Baptized for Our Sakes: A Leather Trisagion from Egypt.* Beiträge zur Altertumskunde 120. Stuttgart and Leipzig: B. G. Teubner, 1999.

Maspero, Jean. *Fouilles exécutées à Baouît.* Edited by Etienne Drioton. Mémoires publiés par les membres de la mission archéologique française au Caire 59. Cairo: IFAO, 1931.

Mastrocinque, Attilio. *Les intailles magiques du département des Monnaies Medailles et Antiques.* Paris: Bibliothèque nationale de France, 2014.

Mathews, Thomas F., and Norman E. Muller. *The Dawn of Christian Art in Panel Paintings and Icons.* Los Angeles: J. Paul Getty Museum, 2016.

———. "Isis and Mary in Early Icons." In *Images of the Mother of God: Perceptions of the Theotokos in Byzantium*, edited by Maria Vassilaki, 3–11. Burlington, VT: Ashgate, 2005.

Mathisen, Ralph W. "Crossing the Supernatural Frontier in Western Late Antiquity." In *Shifting Frontiers in Late Antiquity*, edited by Ralph W. Mathisen and Hagith Sivan, 309–20. Aldershot, UK: Variorum, 1996.

Maurizio, Lisa. "Anthropology and Spirit Possession: A Reconsideration of the Pythia's Role at Delphi." *Journal of Hellenic Studies* 115 (1995): 69–86.

Mauss, Marcel. "The Notion of Body Techniques." In *Sociology and Psychology: Essays*, edited by Marcel Mauss, translated by Ben Brewster, 97–123. London: RKP, 1979.

———. "Techniques of the Body." In *Sociology and Psychology: Essays*, translated by Ben Brewster, 70–88. London: Routledge, 1979.

Mayeur-Jaouen, Catherine. "Crocodiles et saints du Nil: Du talisman au miracle." *Revue d'histoire des religions* 217, no. 4 (2000): 733–60.

———. *Pèlerinages d'Égypte. Histoire de la piété copte et musulmane, XVe–XXe siècles.* Recherches d'histoire et de sciences sociales 107. Paris: Éditions de l'École des Hautes Études en Sciences Sociales, 2005.

McFadden, Susanna. "Dating the Luxor Camp and the Politics of Building in the Tetrarchic Era." In *Art of Empire: The Roman Frescos and Imperial Cult Chamber in Luxor Temple*, edited by Michael Jones and Susanna McFadden, 25–37. Cairo: American Research Center in Egypt, 2015.

McIntosh, Janet. *The Edge of Islam: Power, Personhood, and Ethnoreligious Boundaries on the Kenya Coast.* Durham, NC: Duke University Press, 2009.

McKenzie, Judith. *The Architecture of Alexandria and Egypt, C. 300 B.C. to A.D. 700.* New Haven, CT: Yale University Press, 2007.

Meeks, Dimitri. *Mythes et légendes du Delta: D'après le papyrus Brooklyn 47.218.84.* Cairo: IFAO, 2006.

Meinardus, Otto F. A. "Some Theological and Sociological Aspects of the Coptic Mulid." *Bulletin de l'institut d'Égypte* 44 (1962): 7–25.

Mercier, Jacques. *Art That Heals: The Image as Medicine in Ethiopia.* New York: Museum for African Art, 1997.

———. *Ethiopian Magic Scrolls.* Translated by R. Pevear. New York: G. Braziller, 1979.

Mernissi, Fatima. "Women, Saints, and Sanctuaries." *Signs* 3, no. 1 (1977): 101–12.
Merrills, Andrew. "Monks, Monsters, and Barbarians: Re-Defining the African Periphery in Late Antiquity." *Journal of Early Christian Studies* 12, no. 4 (2004): 217–44.
Meskell, Lynn. "Memory's Materiality: Ancestral Presence, Commemorative Practice and Disjunctive Locales." In *Archaeologies of Memory*, edited by Ruth M. Van Dyke and Susan E. Alcock, 34–55. Malden, MA: Blackwell, 2003.
Meskell, Lynn, and Rosemary A. Joyce. *Embodied Lives: Figuring Ancient Maya and Egyptian Experience*. London and New York: Routledge, 2003.
Meyer, Birgit. "Beyond Syncretism: Translation and Diabolization in the Appropriation of Protestantism in Africa." In *Syncretism/Anti-Syncretism: The Politics of Religious Synthesis*, edited by Rosalind Shaw and Charles Stewart, 43–64. London and New York: Routledge, 1994.
———. "How to Capture the 'Wow': R. R. Marett's Notion of Awe and the Study of Religion." *Journal of the Royal Anthropological Institute* 22 (2016): 7–26.
———. "Mediation and the Genesis of Presence: Towards a Material Approach to Religion." Inaugural Lecture, University of Utrecht, 2012.
———. "Modernity and Enchantment: The Image of the Devil in Popular African Christianity." In *Conversion to Modernities: The Globalization of Christianity*, edited by Peter van der Veer, 199–230. London and New York: Routledge, 1996.
———. *Translating the Devil: Religion and Modernity among the Ewe in Ghana*. Trenton, NJ: Africa World Press, 1999.
Meyer, Marvin W. *The Magical Book of Mary and the Angels (P. Heid. inv. kopt. 685): Text, Translation and Commentary*. Heidelberg: Universitätsverlag C. Winter, 1996.
———. *Rossi's "Gnostic" Tractate*. Occasional Papers of the Institute for Antiquity and Christianity 13. Claremont, CA: Institute for Antiquity and Christianity, 1988.
Meyer, Marvin W., and Richard Smith. *Ancient Christian Magic: Coptic Texts of Ritual Power*. San Francisco: Harper San Francisco, 1994.
Meyer, Robert T. *Palladius: The Lausiac History*. Ancient Christian Writers 34. Westminster, MD: Newman Press, 1965.
Meyer-Dietrich, Erika. "Dance." In *UCLA Encyclopedia of Egyptology*, edited by W. Wendrich, J. Dieleman, E. Frood, and J. Baines. Los Angeles: University of California–Los Angeles, 2009. http://escholarship.org/uc/item/5142hodb.
———. "Recitation, Speech Acts, and Declamation." In *UCLA Encyclopedia of Egyptology*, edited by W. Wendrich J. Dieleman, E. Frood, and J. Baines. Los Angeles: University of California–Los Angeles, 2010. http://escholarship.org/uc/item/1gh1qomd.
Meyers, Jean. *Les miracles de saint Étienne: Recherches sur le recueil pseudo-augustinien (BHL 7860-7861) avec édition critique, traduction et commentaire*. Hagiologia 5. Turnhout, Belgium: Brepols, 2006.
Meylan, Nicolas. "The (Re)conversion of the 'Spirits of the Land' in Medieval Iceland." *Revue d'histoire des religions* 30, no. 3 (2013): 333–54.
Mihálykó, Ágnes T. "Christ and Charon: PGM P13 Reconsidered." *Symbolae Osloenses* 89, no. 1 (2015): 183–209.
Mikhail, Maged S., and Tim Vivian. "Life of Saint John the Little: An Encomium by Zacharias of Sakha." *Coptic Church Review* 18, no. 1–2 (1997): 17–64.
Miller, Patricia Cox. *The Corporeal Imagination: Signifying the Holy in Late Ancient Christianity*. Philadelphia: University of Pennsylvania Press, 2009.
Mirecki, Paul Allan. "The Coptic Wizard's Horde." *Harvard Theological Review* 87, no. 4 (1994): 435–60.
———. "Manichaean Allusions to Ritual and Magic: Spells for Invisibility in the Coptic Kephalaia." In *The Light and the Darkness: Studies in Manichaeism and Its World*, edited by Paul Allan Mirecki and Jason BeDuhn, 173–80. Leiden: Brill, 2001.
Mirecki, Paul Allan, Iain Gardner, and Anthony Alcock. "Magical Spell, Manichaean Letter." In

Emerging from Darkness: Studies in the Recovery of Manichaean Sources, edited by Paul Allan Mirecki and Jason BeDuhn, 1–32. Nag Hammadi and Manichaean Studies 50. Leiden: Brill, 1997.

Mitchell, John. "The Archaeology of Pilgrimage in Late Antique Albania: The Basilica of the Forty Martyrs." In *Recent Research on the Late Antique Countryside*, edited by William Bowden, Luke Lavan, and Carlos Machado, 146–86. Late Antique Archaeology 2. Leiden: Brill, 2003.

———. "Keeping the Demons out of the House: The Archaeology of Apotropaic Strategy and Practice in Late Antique Butrint and Antigoneia." In *Objects in Context, Objects in Use: Material Spatiality in Late Antiquity*, edited by Luke Lavan, Ellen Swift, and Toon Putzeys, 273–310. Late Antique Archaeology 5. Leiden: Brill, 2007.

Montserrat, Dominic. "Death and Funerals in the Roman Fayum." In *Portraits and Masks: Burial Customs in Roman Egypt*, edited by M. L. Bierbrier, 33–44. London: British Museum Press, 1997.

———. "Pilgrimage to the Shrine of Ss. Cyrus and John at Menouthis in Late Antiquity." In *Pilgrimage and Holy Space in Late Antique Egypt*, edited by David Frankfurter, 257–80. Religions in the Graeco-Roman World 134. Leiden: Brill, 1998.

Moussa, Mark. "Abba Moses of Abydos." M. A. thesis, Catholic University of America, 1998.

———. "I Have Been Reading the Holy Gospels by Shenoute of Atripe (Discourses 8, Work 1): Coptic Text, Translation, and Commentary." Ph.D. diss., Catholic University of America, 2010.

———. "The Coptic Literary Dossier of Abba Moses of Abydos." *Coptic Church Review* 24, no. 3 (2003): 66–90.

Mueller, Mary Magdeleine, trans. *St. Caesarius of Arles: Sermons, Volume I (1–80)*. Fathers of the Church 31. Washington, DC: Catholic University of America Press, 1956.

Mugridge, Alan. "What Is a Scriptorium?" In *Proceedings of the 24th Congress of Papyrology, Helsinki, 1–7 August, 2004*, edited by Jaakko Frösén, Tiina Purola, and Erja Salmenkivi, 781–92. Helsinki: Societas Scientarum Fennica, 2007.

Müller, C. Detlef G. "John of Parallos, Saint." In *The Coptic Encyclopedia*, edited by Aziz Atiya, 5:1367–68. New York: Macmillan, 1991.

Murray, Michele. "Down the Road from Sardis: Adaptive Religious Structures and Religious Interaction in the Ancient City of Priene." In *Religious Rivalries and the Struggle for Success in Sardis and Smyrna*, edited by Richard S. Ascough, 197–210. Waterloo, ON: Wilfrid Laurier University Press, 2005.

Nachtergael, Georges. "Les terres cuites 'du Fayoum' dans les maisons de l'Égypte romaine." *Chronique d'Égypte* 60 (1985): 223–39.

———. "Statuettes en terre cuite de l'Égypte gréco-romaine: Recueil des signatures de coroplathes." In *Tranquillitas: Mélanges en l'honneur de Tran Tam Tinh*, edited by Marie-Odile Jentel, Gisèle Deschênes-Wagner, Claude d'Aigle Tremblay, and Bruno Bernard, 413–32. Québec: Université Laval, 1994.

———. "Un sacrifice en l'honneur de 'Baubo': Scènes figurées sur un moule cubique de l'Égypte romaine." In *Egyptian Religion: The Last Thousand Years: Studies Dedicated to the Memory of Jan Quaegebeur*, edited by Willy Clarysse, Antoon Schoors, and Harco Willems, 159–77. Orientalia Lovaniensia Analecta 84. Leuven, Belgium: Peeters, 1998.

Naerebout, F. G. *Attractive Performances: Ancient Greek Dance: Three Preliminary Studies*. Amsterdam: J. C. Gieben, 1997.

———. "Dance." In *A Companion to the Archaeology of Religion in the Ancient World*, edited by Rubina Raja and Jörg Rüpke, 107–19. Malden, MA: Wiley-Blackwell, 2015.

———. "How Do You Want Your Goddess? From the Galjub Hoard to a General Vision on Religious Choice in Hellenistic and Roman Egypt." In *Isis on the Nile: Egyptian Gods in Hellenistic and Roman Egypt: Proceedings of the IVth International Conference of Isis Studies, Liège, November 27–29, 2008: Michel Malaise in Honorem*, edited by Laurent Bricault and M. J. Versluys, 55–73. Religions in the Graeco-Roman World 171. Leiden: Brill, 2010.

Nagy, Árpád. "Magical Gems and Classical Archaeology." In *"Gems of Heaven": Recent Research on*

BIBLIOGRAPHY

Engraved Gemstones in Late Antiquity, AD 200–600, edited by Chris Entwistle and Noel Adams, 75–81. London: British Museum Press, 2011.
Nau, François. "Histoire des solitaires égyptiens." *Revue de l'orient chrétien* 13 (1908): 47–57, 266–97.
Nauerth, Claudia. "Pfauensarg und Mumienhülle: Bestattungsformen im spätantiken Ägypten." In *Grab und Totenkult im Alten Ägypten*, edited by Heike Guksch, 227–39. Munich: Beck, 2003.
Nautin, Pierre. "La conversion du temple de Philae en église chrétienne." *Cahiers archéologiques* 17 (1967): 1–43.
Nevett, Lisa C. *Domestic Space in Classical Antiquity*. Cambridge: Cambridge University Press, 2010.
Nickelsburg, George W. E. "Eschatology in the Testament of Abraham: A Study of the Judgment Scene in the Two Recensions." In *Studies on the Testament of Abraham*, edited by George W. E. Nickelsburg, 23–64. Septuagint and Cognate Studies 6. Missoula, MT: Scholars Press, 1976.
Nock, Arthur Darby. *Conversion: The Old and the New in Religion from Alexander the Great to Augustine of Hippo*. Oxford: Clarendon, 1933.
Nongbri, Brent. "The Lord's Prayer and XMΓ: Two Christian Papyrus Amulets." *Harvard Theological Review* 104, no. 1 (2011): 59–68.
Nutini, Hugo G. *Ritual Kinship—Volume 1: The Structure and Historical Development of the Compadrazgo System in Rural Tlaxcala*. Translated by Betty Bell. Princeton, NJ: Princeton University Press, 1980.
———. *Todos Santos in Rural Tlaxcala: A Syncretic, Expressive, and Symbolic Analysis of the Cult of the Dead*. Princeton, NJ: Princeton University Press, 1988.
O'Connell, Elisabeth R. "Transforming Monumental Landscapes in Late Antique Egypt: Monastic Dwellings in Legal Documents from Western Thebes." *Journal of Early Christian Studies* 15, no. 2 (2007): 239–73.
O'Connor, David. "From Topography to Cosmos: Ancient Egypt's Multiple Maps." In *Ancient Perspectives: Maps and Their Place in Mesopotamia, Egypt, Greece and Rome*, edited by Richard J. A. Talbert, 47–79. Chicago: University of Chicago Press, 2012.
O'Donnell, James. "Paganus." *Classical Folia* 31, no. 2 (1977): 163–69.
Olyan, Saul M., and John Bodel. "Comparative Perspectives." In *Household and Family Religion in Antiquity*, edited by John Bodel and Saul M. Olyan, 276–82. Malden, MA: Wiley-Blackwell, 2008.
Orlandi, Tito. "A Catechesis against Apocryphal Texts by Shenute and the Gnostic Texts of Nag Hammadi." *Harvard Theological Review* 75, no. 1 (1982): 85–95.
———. "Coptic Literature." In *The Roots of Egyptian Christianity*, edited by James E. Goehring and Birger Pearson, 51–81. Philadelphia: Fortress Press, 1986.
———. "The Library of the Monastery of Saint Shenute at Atripe." In *Perspectives on Panopolis: An Egyptian Town from Alexander the Great to the Arab Conquest*, edited by A. Egberts, B. P. Muhs, and J. van der Vliet, 211–31. Leiden: Brill, 2002.
———, ed. *Shenute: Contra Origenistas*. Roma: C. I. M., 1985.
Orsi, Robert A. *Thank You, St. Jude: Women's Devotion to the Patron Saint of Hopeless Causes*. New Haven, CT: Yale University Press, 1996.
Overholt, Thomas W. *Prophecy in Cross-Cultural Perspective: A Sourcebook for Biblical Researchers*. Atlanta: Scholars Press, 1986.
Pache, Corinne Ondine. *Baby and Child Heroes in Ancient Greece*. Traditions. Urbana: University of Illinois Press, 2004.
Page, Christopher. *The Christian West and Its Singers: The First Thousand Years*. New Haven, CT: Yale University Press, 2010.
Papaconstantinou, Arietta. "The Cult of Saints: A Haven of Continuity in a Changing World?" In *Egypt in the Byzantine World, 300–700*, edited by Roger S. Bagnall, 350–67. Cambridge and New York: Cambridge University Press, 2007.
———. "Historiography, Hagiography, and the Making of the Coptic 'Church of the Martyrs' in Early Islamic Egypt." *Dumbarton Oaks Papers* 60 (2006): 65–86.

———. "Introduction." In *Conversion in Late Antiquity: Christianity, Islam, and Beyond*, edited by Arietta Papaconstantinou, Neil McLynn, and Daniel Schwartz, xv–xxxvii. Farnham, UK: Ashgate, 2015.

———. "La liturgie stationnale à Oxyrhynchos dans la première moitié du 6è siècle. Réédition et commentaire du P. Oxy XI 1357." *Revue des études byzantines* 54 (1996): 135–59.

———. *Le culte des saints en Égypte: Des Byzantins aux Abbassides: l'apport des inscriptions et des papyrus grecs et coptes*. Paris: CNRS Editions, 2001.

———. "Notes sur les actes de donation d'enfant au monastère thébain de Saint-Phoibammon." *Journal of Juristic Papyrology* 32 (2002): 83–105.

———. "Oracles chrétiens dans l'Égypte byzantine: Le témoignage des papyrus." *Zeitschrift für Papyrologie und Epigraphik* 104 (1994): 281–86.

———. "Où le péché abondait, la grâce a surabondé: Sur les lieux de culte dédiés aus saints dans l'Égypte des V–VIII siècles." In *Le sacré et son inscription dans l'espace à Byzance et en Occident: Études comparées*, edited by Michel Kaplan, 235–49. Byzantina Sorbonensia 18. Paris: Publications de la Sorbonne, 2001.

———. "THEIA OIKONOMIA: Les actes thébains de donation d'enfants ou la gestion monastique de la pénurie." *Travaux et mémoires* 14 (2008): 511–26.

Papalexandrou, Amy. "Memory Tattered and Torn: Spolia in the Heartland of Byzantine Hellenism." In *Archaeologies of Memory*, edited by Ruth M. Van Dyke and Susan E. Alcock, 56–80. Malden, MA: Blackwell, 2003.

Papini, Lucia. "20–21—Due biglietti oracolari cristiani." In *Trenta testi greci da papiri letterari e documentari: Editi in occasione del XVII Congresso internazionale di papirologia, Napoli, 19–26 maggio 1983*, edited by Manfredo Manfredi, 68–70. Florence: Istituto papirologico "G. Vitelli," 1983.

———. "Biglietti oracolari in copto dalla necropoli nord di Antinoe." In *Acts of the Second International Congress of Coptic Study: Rome, 22–26 September 1980*, edited by Tito Orlandi and Frederik Wisse, 245–55. Roma: C. I. M., 1985.

———. "Domande oracolari: Elenco delle attestazioni in greco ed in Copto." *Analecta Papyrologica* 4 (1992): 21–27.

———. "Fragments of the Sortes Sanctorum from the Shrine of St. Colluthus." In *Pilgrimage and Holy Space in Late Antique Egypt*, edited by David Frankfurter, 393–401. Religions in the Graeco-Roman World 134. Leiden: Brill, 1998.

Parandowski, Piotr. "Coptic Terra-Cotta Figurines from Kom El-Dikka." In *Coptic Studies: Acts of the Third International Congress of Coptic Studies, Warsaw, 20–25 August, 1984*, edited by Włodzimierz Godlewski, 303–7. Warsaw: PWN, 1990.

Pearson, Birger A., ed. *Religious Syncretism in Antiquity: Essays in Conversation with Geo Widengren*. Missoula, MT: Scholars Press, 1975.

Pearson, Birger A., and James E. Goehring, eds. *The Roots of Egyptian Christianity*. Studies in Antiquity and Christianity 1. Philadelphia: Fortress Press, 1986.

Pentcheva, Bissera V. *The Sensual Icon: Space, Ritual, and the Senses in Byzantium*. State College: Pennsylvania State University Press, 2010.

Percival, Henry R., ed. *The Seven Ecumenical Councils*. Nicene and Post-Nicene Fathers 14. Grand Rapids, MI: Christian Classics Ethereal Library, 1899.

Perdrizet, Paul. *Les terres cuites grecques d'Égypte de la collection Fouquet*. 2 vols. Nancy, France: Berger-Levrault, 1921.

———. *Negotium perambulans in tenebris: Étude de démonologie gréco-orientale*. Publications de la Faculté des lettres de l'Université de Strasbourg 6. Strasbourg, France: Istra, 1922.

Perpillou-Thomas, Françoise. *Fêtes d'Égypte ptolémaïque et romaine, d'après la documentation papyrologique grecque*. Studia Hellenistica 31. Leuven, Belgium: Universitas Catholica Lovaniensis, 1993.

Perrone, Lorenzo. "Monasticism as a Factor of Religious Interaction in the Holy Land During the Byzantine Period." In *Sharing the Sacred: Religious Contacts and Conflicts in the Holy Land: First-*

Fifteenth Centures CE, edited by Arieh Kofsky and Guy G. Stroumsa, 67–96. Jerusalem: Yad Izhak Ben Zvi, 1998.

Pesthy, Monika. "Earthly Tribunal in the Fourth Heaven (NH V,2 20,5–21, 22)." In *The Visio Pauli and the Gnostic Apocalypse of Paul*, edited by Jan N. Bremmer and István Czachesz, 198–210. Leuven, Belgium: Peeters, 2007.

Pharr, Clyde, trans. *The Theodosian Code and Novels, and the Sirmondian Constitutions: A Translation with Commentary, Glossary, and Bibliography*. Corpus of Roman Law 1. Princeton, NJ: Princeton University Press, 1952.

Piankoff, A. "La descente aux enfers dans les textes égyptiens et dans les apocryphes coptes." *Bulletin de la société d'archéologie copte* 7 (1941): 33–46.

———. "The Osireion of Seti I at Abydos During the Greco-Roman Period and the Christian Occupation." *Bulletin de la société d'archéologie copte* 15 (1958/60): 125–49.

Piggott, Stuart. *The Druids*. Ancient Peoples and Places. London: Thames and Hudson, 1985.

Pina-Cabral, João de. "The Gods of the Gentiles Are Demons: The Problem of Pagan Survivals in European Culture." In *Other Histories*, edited by Kirsten Hastrup, 45–61. London and New York: Routledge, 1992.

Pinch, Geraldine. "Childbirth and Female Figurines at Deir El-Medina and El-'Amarna." *Orientalia* 52, no. 3 (1983): 405–14.

———. *Votive Offerings to Hathor*. Oxford: Griffith Institute, Ashmolean Museum, 1993.

Pinch, Geraldine, and E. A. Waraksa. "Votive Practices." In *UCLA Encyclopedia of Egyptology*, edited by W. Wendrich, J. Dieleman, E. Frood, and J. Baines. Los Angeles: University of California–Los Angeles, 2009. http://escholarship.org/uc/item/7kp4n7rk.

Pinney, Christopher. "Paper Gods." In *Gods beyond Temples*, edited by Harsha V. Dehejia, 223–27. Delhi: Motilal Banarsidass Publishers, 2006.

Piranomonte, M. "Religion and Magic at Rome: The Fountain of Anna Perenna." In *Magical Practice in the Latin West: Papers from the International Conference Held at the University of Zaragoza, 30 Sept.–1 Oct. 2005*, edited by R. L. Gordon and Francisco Marco Simón, 191–213. Religions in the Graeco-Roman World 168. Leiden: Brill, 2010.

Polaczek-Zdanowicz, Krystyna. "The Genesis and Evolution of the Orant Statuettes Against a Background of Developing Coptic Art." *Études et travaux* 8 (1975): 135–49.

Poole, Deborah A. "Rituals of Movement, Rites of Transformation: Pilgrimage and Dance in the Highlands of Cuzco, Peru." In *Pilgrimage in Latin America*, edited by N. R. Crumrine and E. A. Morinis, 307–38. New York: Greenwood Press, 1991.

Préaux, Claire. "Une amulette chrétienne aux Musées Royaux d'Art et d'Histoire de Bruxelles." *Chronique d'Égypte* 10 (1935): 361–70.

Preisendanz, Karl. *Papyri Graecae Magicae: Die griechischen Zauberpapyri*. 2 vols. 2nd ed. Stuttgart: Teubner, 1973–74.

Price, Richard M. "The Holy Man and Christianization from the Apocryphal Apostles to St. Stephen of Perm." In *The Cult of Saints in Late Antiquity and the Middle Ages: Essays on the Contribution of Peter Brown*, edited by J. D. Howard-Johnston and Paul Antony Hayward, 215–38. Oxford: Oxford University Press, 2002.

Price, Richard, trans. *History of the Monks of Syria*. Cistercian Studies 88. Kalamazoo, MI: Cistercian Publications, 2006.

Proser, Adriana G. *Pilgrimage and Buddhist Art*. New Haven, CT: Yale University Press, 2010.

Pye, Michael. "Syncretism Versus Synthesis." *Method and Theory in the Study of Religion* 6, no. 1 (1994): 217–29.

Quaegebeur, J. "Divinités égyptiennes sur des animaux dangereux." In *L'animal, l'homme, le dieu dans le proche-orient ancien: Actes du colloque de Cartigny 1981*, edited by Philippe Borgeaud, Yves Christe, and Ivanka Urio, 131–43. Louvain, Belgium: Peeters, 1985.

———. *Le dieu égyptien Shaï dans la religion et l'onomastique*. Leuven, Belgium: Leuven University Press, 1975.

———. "Les 'saints' égyptiens préchrétiens." *Orientalia Lovaniensia Periodica* 8 (1977): 129–43.
Ramsay, William. *Pauline and Other Studies in Early Christian History*. London: Hodder and Stoughton, 1908.
Rapp, Claudia. "'For Next to God, You Are My Salvation': Reflections on the Rise of the Holy Man in Late Antiquity." In *The Cult of Saints in Late Antiquity and the Middle Ages: Essays on the Contribution of Peter Brown*, edited by J. D. Howard-Johnston and Paul Antony Hayward, 63–81. Oxford: Oxford University Press, 2002.
———. "Holy Texts, Holy Men, and Holy Scribes: Aspects of Scriptural Holiness in Late Antiquity." In *The Early Christian Book*, edited by William E. Klingshirn and Linda Safran, 194–222. Washington, DC: Catholic University of America Press, 2007.
———. "Safe-Conducts to Heaven: Holy Men, Mediation and the Role of Writing." In *Transformations of Late Antiquity: Essays for Peter Brown*, edited by Philip Rousseau and Emmanuel Papoutsakis, 187–203. Burlington, VT: Ashgate, 2009.
Rassart-Debergh, Marguerite. "Animaux dans la peinture kelliote." In *L'animal dans les civilisations orientales*, edited by Christian Cannuyer, Julian Ries, Alois van Tongerloo, D. Homès-Fredericq, and Francine Mawet, 183–96. Leuven, Belgium: Peeters, 2001.
———. "L'Akh-Menou—Status Quaestionis, I—Les peintures chrétiennes." *Cahiers de Karnak* 12 (2007): 745–96.
———. "Plaquettes peintes d'époque romaine." *Bulletin de la société d'archéologie copte* 30 (1991): 43–47.
———. "Quelques bateaux coptes et leur signification." *Bulletin de la société d'archéologie copte* 31 (1992): 55–73.
———. "Sacralité continue ou exorcisme chez les coptes." In *Aegyptus Christiana: Mélanges d'hagiographie égyptienne et orientale dédiés à la mémoire du P. Paul Devos, Bollandiste*, edited by Ugo Zanetti and Enzo Lucchesi, 287–308. Geneva: P. Cramer, 2004.
Rebillard, Éric. *The Care of the Dead in Late Antiquity*. Translated by Elizabeth Trapnell Rawlings and Jeanine Routier-Pucci. Ithaca, NY: Cornell University Press, 2009.
———. *Christians and Their Many Identities in Late Antiquity, North Africa, 200–450 CE*. Ithaca, NY: Cornell University Press, 2012.
———. "Late Antique Limits of Christianness: North Africa in the Age of Augustine." In *Group Identity and Religious Individuality in Late Antiquity*, edited by Éric Rebillard and Jörg Rüpke, 293–317. Washington, DC: Catholic University of America Press, 2015.
Redfield, Robert. *The Folk Culture of Yucatan*. Chicago: University of Chicago Press, 1942.
———. *Peasant Society and Culture: An Anthropological Approach to Civilization*. Chicago: University of Chicago Press, 1956.
Redmayne, Alison. "Chikanga: An African Diviner with an International Reputation." In *Witchcraft Confessions and Accusations*, edited by Mary Douglas, 103–28. New York: Routledge, 2004.
Remus, Harold. "The End of 'Paganism'?" *Studies in Religion/Sciences Religieuses* 33, no. 2 (2004): 191–208.
Renberg, Gil H. *Where Dreams May Come: Incubation Sanctuaries in the Greco-Roman World*. Religions in the Graeco-Roman World 184. Leiden: E. J. Brill, 2017.
Rey, Terry, and Karen Richman. "The Somatics of Syncretism: Tying Body and Soul in Haitian Religion." *Studies in Religion/Sciences Religieuses* 39, no. 3 (2010): 379–403.
Reymond, E.A.E., and John W. B. Barns, eds. *Four Martyrdoms from the Pierpont Morgan Coptic Codices*. Oxford: Clarendon Press, 1973.
Richter, Siegfried G. "Bemerkungen zu magischen Elementen koptischer Zaubertexte." In *Akten des 21. internationalen Papyrologenkongresses*, edited by Bärbel Kramer, 835–46. Stuttgart: B. G. Teubner, 1997.
Richter, Tonio Sebastian. "Markedness and Unmarkedness in Coptic Magical Writing." In *Écrire la magie dans l'antiquité*, edited by Magali De Haro Sanchez, 85–108. Liège, Belgium: Presses Universitaires de Liège, 2015.

———. "What's in a Story? Cultural Narratology and Coptic Child Donation Documents." *Journal of Juristic Papyrology* 35 (2005): 237–64.
Riedel, W., and Walter Ewing Crum, eds. *The Canons of Athanasius of Alexandria: The Arabic and Coptic Versions Edited and Translated with Introductions, Notes and Appendices*. London and Oxford: Williams & Norgate, 1904.
Ries, Julien. "Cultes païens et démons dans l'apologétique chrétienne de Justin à Augustin." In *Anges et démons: Actes du colloque de Liège et de Louvain- la-Neuve, 25–26 novembre 1987*, edited by Henri Limet, 337–52. Louvain-la-Neuve, Belgium: Centre d'Histoire des Religions, 1989.
Riggs, Christina. *The Beautiful Burial in Roman Egypt: Art, Identity, and Funerary Religion*. New York: Oxford University Press, 2006.
Ritner, Robert K. "Curses: Introduction." In *Ancient Christian Magic*, edited by Marvin W. Meyer and Richard Smith, 83–86. San Francisco: Harper San Francisco, 1994.
———. "Horus on the Crocodiles: A Juncture of Religion and Magic in Late Dynastic Egypt." In *Religion and Philosophy in Ancient Egypt*, edited by James P. Allen, 103–16. New Haven, CT: Yale Egyptological Seminar, 1989.
———. *Mechanics of Ancient Egyptian Magical Practice*. Studies in Ancient Oriental Civilization 54. Chicago: Oriental Institute, 1993.
Roberts, Andrew D. "The Lumpa Church of Alice Lenshina." In *Protest and Power in Black Africa*, edited by Ali Al'Amin Mazrui and Robert I. Rotberg, 528–32. Oxford: Oxford University Press, 1970.
Roberts, Colin H. *Manuscript, Society, and Belief in Early Christian Egypt*. New York: Oxford University Press, 1979.
Robinson, James M. *The Nag Hammadi Library in English*. San Francisco: Harper & Row Publishers, 1988.
Rockwell, Peter. "The Sculptor's Studio at Aphrodisias: The Working Methods and Varieties of Sculpture Produced." In *The Sculptural Environment of the Roman Near East: Reflections on Culture, Ideology, and Power*, edited by Yaron Z. Eliav, Elise A. Friedland, and Sharon Herbert, 91–115. Interdisciplinary Studies in Ancient Culture and Religion 9. Leuven, Belgium: Peeters, 2008.
Rodziewicz, Elżbieta. "Reliefs figurés en os des fouilles Kôm El-Dikka." *Études et travaux* 10 (1978): 318–36.
Rodziewicz, Mieczysław. *Les habitations romaines tardives d'Alexandrie: À la lumière des fouilles polonaises à Kôm el-Dikka*. Alexandrie 3. Warsaw: PWN, 1984.
———. "Remarks on the Domestic and Monastic Architecture in Alexandria and Surroundings." In *The Archaeology of the Nile Delta, Egypt: Problems and Priorities*, edited by Edwin C. M. van den Brink, 267–77. Amsterdam: Netherlands Foundation for Archaeological Research in Egypt, 1988.
Römer, Claudia. "Das Werden zu Osiris im römischen Ägypten." *Archiv für Religionsgeschichte* 2, no. 2 (2000): 141–61.
Rondot, Vincent. *Derniers visages des dieux d'Égypte: Iconographies, panthéons et cultes dans le Fayoum hellénisé des IIe–IIIe siècles de notre ère*. Paris: Presses de l'université Paris-Sorbonne, 2013.
Roquet, Gérard. "L'ange des eaux et le dieu de la crue selon Chenouté: Sur un fragment copte des visions de l'Apocalypsis Sinuthii." *Apocrypha* 4 (1993): 83–99.
Rose, Els. *Ritual Memory: The Apocryphal Acts and Liturgical Commemoration in the Early Medieval West (ca. 500–1215)*. Mittellateinische Studien und Texte 40. Leiden: Brill, 2009.
Rosenstiehl, Jean-Marc. "Tartarouchos-Temelouchos." In *Deuxième journée d'études coptes, Strasbourg 25 Mai 1984*, 29–56. Louvain, Belgium: Peeters, 1986.
Rothaus, Richard. "Christianization and De-Paganization: The Late Antique Creation of a Conceptual Frontier." In *Shifting Frontiers in Late Antiquity*, edited by Ralph W. Mathisen and Hagith Sivan, 299–308. Aldershot, UK: Variorum, 1996.
Roukema, Riemer. "Early Christianity and Magic." *Annali di storia dell'esegesi* 24, no. 2 (2007): 367–78.
Rousselle, Aline. *Croire et guérir: La foi en Gaule dans l'antiquité tardive*. Paris: Fayard, 1990.

Rubenson, Samuel. *The Letters of St. Antony: Monasticism and the Making of a Saint.* Studies in Antiquity and Christianity. Minneapolis, MN: Fortress Press, 1995.

Russell, Norman, trans. *The Lives of the Desert Fathers: Historia Monachorum in Aegypto.* Cistercian Studies 34. Collegeville, MN: Cistercian Publications, 2006.

Rutschowscaya, Marie-Hélène. *La peinture copte.* Paris: Musée du Louvre, 1992.

Rydén, Lennart. *The Life of St. Andrew the Fool.* 2 vols. Acta Universitatis Upsaliensis 4. Uppsala, Sweden: Almqvist & Wiksell International, 1995.

Ryholt, Kim. "A Pair of Oracle Petitions Addressed to Horus-of-the-Camp." *Journal of Egyptian Archaeology* 79 (1993): 189–98.

Sadek, Ashraf I. *Popular Religion in Egypt During the New Kingdom.* Hildesheimer ägyptologische Beiträge 27. Hildesheim, Germany: Gerstenberg, 1987.

Sallnow, Michael J. *Pilgrims of the Andes: Regional Cults in Cusco.* Washington, DC: Smithsonian Press, 1987.

Sánchez Ortega, Maria Helena. "Sorcery and Eroticism in Love Magic." In *Cultural Encounters: The Impact of the Inquisition in Spain and the New World*, edited by Mary Elizabeth Perry and Anne J. Cruz, 58–91. Berkeley: University of California Press, 1991.

Sansterre, Jean-Marie. "Apparitions et miracles à Menouthis: De l'incubation païenne à l'incubation chrétienne." In *Apparitions et miracles*, edited by A. Dierkens, 69–83. Brussels: Editions de l'Université de Bruxelles, 1991.

Sanzo, Joseph E. *Scriptural Incipits on Amulets from Late Antique Egypt: Text, Typology, and Theory.* Studien und Texte zu Antike und Christentum 84. Tübingen, Germany: Mohr Siebeck, 2014.

Saradi, Helen. "The Christianization of Pagan Temples from the Greek Hagiographical Texts (4th–6th C.)." In *From Temple to Church: Destruction and Renewal of Local Cultic Topography in Late Antiquity*, edited by Johannes Hahn, Stephen Emmel, and Ulrich Gotter, 113–34. Religions in the Graeco-Roman World 163. Leiden and Boston: Brill, 2008.

———. "The Use of Ancient Spolia in Byzantine Monuments: The Archaeological and Literary Evidence." *International Journal of the Classical Tradition* 3, no. 4 (1997): 395–423.

Saradi-Mendelovici, Helen. "Christian Attitudes Toward Pagan Monuments in Late Antiquity and Their Legacy in Later Byzantine Centuries." *Dumbarton Oaks Papers* 44 (1990): 47–61.

Satzinger, Helmut. "The Old Coptic Schmidt Papyrus." *Journal of the American Research Center in Egypt* 12 (1975): 37–50.

Satzinger, Helmut, and P. J. Sijpesteijn. "Koptisches Zauberpergament Moen III." *Le Muséon* 101 (1988): 51–63.

Sauer, Eberhard W. *The Archaeology of Religious Hatred in the Roman and Early Medieval World.* Charleston, SC: Tempus, 2003.

———. "Religious Rituals at Springs in the Late Antique and Early Medieval World." In *The Archaeology of Late Antique "Paganism*," edited by Luke Lavan and Michael Mulryan, 505–50. Late Antique Archaeology 7. Leiden: Brill, 2011.

Saunders, George R. *Culture and Christianity: The Dialectics of Transformation.* New York: Greenwood Press, 1988.

Sauneron, Serge. "Le chaudron de Sohag: Comment naît une légende." In *Villes et légendes d'Égypte*, edited by Serge Sauneron,160–64. Cairo: Institut français d'archéologie orientale, 1983.

Schatzki, Theodore R. *The Site of the Social: A Philosophical Account of the Constitution of Social Life and Change.* Philadelphia: Pennsylvania State University Press, 2002.

Scheid, John, and Jesper Svenbro. *The Craft of Zeus: Myths of Weaving and Fabric.* Translated by Carol Volk. Revealing Antiquity 9. Cambridge, MA: Harvard University Press, 2001.

Schenke, Gesa, ed. *Der koptische Kölner Papyruskodex 3221, 1: Das Testament des Iob.* P. Coloniensia 33. Paderborn, Germany: Verlag Ferdinand Schöningh, 2009.

———. "P. Köln 354: Über Ägyptens Sonderstatus vor allen anderen Ländern." In *Kölner Papyri (P. Köln): Bd. 8*, edited by Michael Gronewald, Klaus Maresch, and Thomas Corsten, 183–200. Opladen, Germany: Westdeutscher Verlag, 1997.

Schmidt, Carl, and Violet MacDermot, eds. *Pistis Sophia*. Nag Hammadi Studies 9. Leiden: Brill, 1978.

———. *The Books of Jeu and the Untitled Text in the Bruce Codex*. Nag Hammadi Studies 13. Leiden: Brill, 1978.

Schmitt, Jean-Claude " 'Religion populaire' et culture folklorique." *Annales* 31, no. 5 (1976): 941–53.

Schneemelcher, Wilhelm, ed. *New Testament Apocrypha*. Translated by R. McL. Wilson. Revised. 2 vols. Cambridge: James Clarke & Co., 1991.

Schneider, Hans D. *Beelden van Behnasa: Egyptische kunst uit de Romeinse keizertijd 1e-3e eeuw na Chr.* Zutphen, The Netherlands: Terra, 1982.

Schneider, Hans D., Stephen Spurr, Nicholas Reeves, and Stephen Quirke. *The Small Masterpieces of Egyptian Art: Selections from the Myers Museum at Eton College*. Leiden: Rijksmuseum van Oudheden, 2003.

Schoffeleers, Matthew. "Christ in African Folk Theology." In *Religion in Africa: Experience and Expression*, edited by Thomas D. Blakely, W.E.A. van Beek, and Dennis L. Thomson, 73–88. London and Portsmouth, NH: J. Currey; Heinemann, 1994.

Schroeder, Caroline T. "Child Sacrifice in Egyptian Monastic Culture: From Familial Renunciation to Jephthah's Lost Daughter." *Journal of Early Christian Studies* 20, no. 2 (2012): 269–302.

Schwartz, Frances M., and James H. Schwartz. "Engraved Gems in the Collection of the American Numismatic Society, 1: Ancient Magical Amulets." *American Numismatic Society Museum Notes* 24 (1979): 149–97.

Seele, Keith C. "Horus on the Crocodiles." *Journal of Near Eastern Studies* 6 (1947): 43–52.

Sessa, Kristina. "Christianity and the Cubiculum: Spiritual Politics and Domestic Space in Late Antique Rome." *Journal of Early Christian Studies* 15, no. 2 (2007): 171–204.

Shandruk, Walter M. "Christian Use of Magic in Late Antique Egypt." *Journal of Early Christian Studies* 20, no. 1 (2012): 31–57.

Shaw, Brent D. *Sacred Violence: African Christians and Sectarian Hatred in the Age of Augustine*. Cambridge: Cambridge University Press, 2011.

Shaw, Rosalind, and Charles Stewart. "Introduction: Problematizing Syncretism." In *Syncretism/Anti-Syncretism: The Politics of Religious Synthesis*, edited by Rosalind Shaw and Charles Stewart, 1–26. London: Routledge, 1994.

Sheingorn, Pamela. "Sainte Foy on the Loose. Or, The Possibilities of Procession." In *Moving Subjects: Processional Performance in the Middle Ages and the Renaissance*, edited by K. M. Ashley and W.M.N. Hüsken, 53–67. Atlanta: Rodopi, 2001.

Shelemay, Kay Kaufman. "The Musician and Transmission of Religious Tradition: The Multiple Roles of the Ethiopian Däbtära." *Journal of Religion in Africa* 22, no. 3 (1992): 242–60.

Sijpesteijn, P. J. "A Coptic Magical Amulet." *Chronique d'Égypte* 57 (1987): 183–84.

Simon, Marcel. "Early Christianity and Pagan Thought: Confluences and Conflicts." *Religious Studies* 9, no. 4 (1973): 385–99.

———. "Symbolisme et traditions d'atelier dans la première sculpture chrétienne." In *Le Christianisme antique et son contexte religieux: Scripta varia*, edited by Marcel Simon, 219–31. Tübingen, Germany: Mohr Siebeck, 1981.

Sinkewicz, Robert E. *Evagrius of Pontus: The Greek Ascetic Corpus*. Oxford: Oxford University Press, 2003.

Sizgorich, Thomas. *Violence and Belief in Late Antiquity: Militant Devotion in Christianity and Islam*. Philadelphia: University of Pennsylvania Press, 2009.

Skedros, James C. *Saint Demetrios of Thessaloniki: Civic Patron and Divine Protector, 4th–7th Centuries CE*. Harvard Theological Studies 47. Harrisburg, PA: Trinity Press International, 1999.

Sluhovsky, Moshe. *Believe Not Every Spirit: Possession, Mysticism and Discernment in Early Modern Catholicism*. Chicago: University of Chicago Press, 2007.

Smallwood, T. M. "The Transmission of Charms in English, Medieval and Modern." In *Charms and Charming in Europe*, edited by Jonathan Roper, 11–31. New York: Palgrave Macmillan, 2005.
Smelik, K.A.D. "The Witch of Endor: I Samuel 28 in Rabbinic and Christian Exegesis till 800 A.D." *Vigiliae Christianae* 33, no. 2 (1979): 160–79.
Smith, Grafton Elliot, and Warren R. Dawson. *Egyptian Mummies*. London and New York: Kegan Paul, 2002.
Smith, Jonathan Z. "Here, There, and Anywhere." In *Relating Religion: Essays in the Study of Religion*, edited by Jonathan Z. Smith, 323–39. Chicago: University of Chicago Press, 2004.
———. "The Influence of Symbols upon Social Change: A Place on Which to Stand." In *Map Is Not Territory: Studies in the History of Religions*, 129–46. Chicago: University of Chicago Press, 1993.
Smith, Julia M. H. *Europe after Rome: A New Cultural History 500–1000*. Oxford: Oxford University Press, 2007.
———. "Women at the Tomb: Access to Relic Shrines in the Early Middle Ages." In *The World of Gregory of Tours*, edited by K. Mitchell and I. N Wood, 163–80. Leiden: Brill, 2002.
Smith, Mark. *Traversing Eternity: Texts for the Afterlife from Ptolemaic and Roman Egypt*. Oxford: Oxford University Press, 2009.
Smith, R. Payne, trans. *The Third Part of the Ecclesiastical History of John, Bishop of Ephesus*. Oxford: Oxford University Press, 1860.
Sodini, Jean-Pierre. "L'artisanat urbain à l'époque paléochrétienne (IVè–VIIè S.)." *Ktema* 4 (1975): 71–119.
Sotinel, C. "La disparition des lieux de cultes païens en Occident: Enjeux et méthode." In *Hellénisme et christianisme*, edited by Michel Narcy and Éric Rebillard, 35–60. Lille, France: Presses Univ. du Septentrion, 2004.
Spencer, Paul. "Introduction: Interpretations of the Dance in Anthropology." In *Society and the Dance: The Social Anthropology of Process and Performance*, edited by Paul Spencer, 1–46. Cambridge: Cambridge University Press, 1985.
Spieser, Cathie. "Avaleuses et dévoreuses: des déesses aux démones en Égypte ancienne." *Chronique d'Égypte* 84 (2009): 5–19.
Srinivas, M. N. *The Cohesive Role of Sanskritization and Other Essays*. New York: Oxford University Press, 1989.
Stancliffe, C. E. "From Town to Country: The Christianisation of the Touraine, 370-600." In *The Church in Town and Countryside*, edited by Derek Baker, 43–59. Studies in Church History 16. Oxford: Blackwell, 1979.
Stauffer, Annemarie. *Textiles of Late Antiquity*. New York: Metropolitan Museum of Art, 1995.
Stegemann, Viktor. *Die koptischen Zaubertexte der Sammlung Papyrus Erzherzog Rainer in Wien*. Heidelberg: C. Winter, 1934.
Sternberg-El Hotabi, Heike. "Der Untergang der Hieroglyphenschrift: Schriftverfall und Schrifttod im Ägypten der griechisch-römischen Zeit." *Chronique d'Égypte* 69 (1994): 218–45.
———. *Untersuchungen zur Überlieferungsgeschichte der Horusstelen: Ein Beitrag zur Religionsgeschichte Ägyptens im 1. Jahrtausend v. Chr.* 2 vols. Ägyptologische Abhandlungen 62. Wiesbaden, Germany: Otto Harrassowitz Verlag, 1999.
Stewart, Charles. *Demons and the Devil: Moral Imagination in Modern Greek Culture*. Princeton, NJ: Princeton University Press, 1991.
———. "Ritual Dreams and Historical Orders: Incubation Between Paganism and Christianity." In *Greek Ritual Poetics*, edited by Dimitrios Yatromanolakis and Panagiotis Roilos, 338–55. Cambridge: Center for Hellenic Studies, Trustees for Harvard University, 2004.
———. "Syncretism and Its Synonyms: Reflections on Cultural Mixture." *Diacritics* 29, no. 3 (1999): 40–62.
Stewart, Peter. *Statues in Roman Society: Representation and Response*. Oxford and New York: Oxford University Press, 2003.

Stewart, Randy, ed. *Sortes Astrampsychi, Volume II*. Bibliotheca Scriptorum Graecorum et Romanorum Teubneriana. Leipzig: Saur, 2001.

Stirrat, R. L. *Power and Religiosity in a Post-Colonial Setting: Sinhala Catholics in Contemporary Sri Lanka*. Cambridge: Cambridge University Press, 1992.

Stökl Ben Ezra, Daniel. "Canonization—a Non-Linear Process? Observing the Process of Canonization Through the Christian (and Jewish) Papyri from Egypt." *Zeitschrift für Antike und Christentum* 12, no. 2 (2009): 193–214.

Stowers, Stanley. "The Ontology of Religion." In *Introducing Religion: Essays in Honor of Jonathan Z. Smith*, edited by Willi Braun and Russell T. McCutcheon, 434–49. London: Equinox Publishing, 2008.

Straten, F. T. van. "Gifts for the Gods." In *Faith, Hope and Worship: Aspects of Religious Mentality in the Ancient World*, edited by H. S. Versnel, 65–151. Leiden: Brill, 1981.

Strathern, Andrew. *Body Thoughts*. Ann Arbor: University of Michigan Press, 1996.

Stresser-Péan, Guy. *The Sun God and the Savior: The Christianization of the Nahua and Totonac in the Sierra Norte de Puebla, Mexico*. Translated by Claude Stresser-Péan. Boulder: University Press of Colorado, 2009.

Struck, Peter T. "Viscera and the Divine: Dreams as the Divinatory Bridge Between the Corporeal and Incorporeal." In *Prayer, Magic, and the Stars in the Ancient and Late Antique World*, edited by S. B. Noegel, J. T. Walker, and B. M. Wheeler, 125–36. University Park: Pennsylvania State University Press, 2003.

Subías Pascual, Eva. *La maison funéraire de la nécropole haute à Oxyrhynchos (El Minyà, Égypte): Du tombeau à la diaconie*. Nova Studia Aegyptiaca 5. Barcelona: Missió Arqueològica d'Oxirrinc, 2008.

Sullivan, Kevin P., and Terry G. Wilfong. "The Reply of Jesus to King Abgar: A Coptic New Testament Apocryphon Reconsidered (P. Mich. Inv. 6213)." *Bulletin of the American Society of Papyrologists* 42, no. 1–4 (2005): 107–24.

Sussman, Varda. "Moulds for Lamps and Figurines from a Caesarea Workshop." *'Atiqot [English Series]* 14 (1980): 76–79.

Svoboda, Terese. *Cleaned the Crocodile's Teeth: Nuer Song*. Greenfield Center, NY: Greenfield Review Press, 1985.

Swidler, Ann. "Culture in Action: Symbols and Strategies." *American Sociological Review* 51, no. 2 (1986): 273–86.

———. *Talk of Love: How Culture Matters*. Chicago: University of Chicago Press, 2001.

Szymańska, Hanna. *Terres cuites d'Athribis*. Monographies reine Élisabeth 12. Turnhout, Belgium: Brepols, 2005.

Takács, Sarolta. "The Magic of Isis Replaced, or Cyril of Alexandria's Attempt at Redirecting Religious Devotion." *Poikila Byzantina* 13 (1994): 489–507.

Talbot, Alice-Mary. "Pilgrimage to Healing Shrines: The Evidence of Miracle Accounts." *Dumbarton Oaks Papers* 56 (2002): 153–73.

Tallet, Gaëlle. "Isis, the Crocodiles and the Mysteries of the Nile Floods: Interpreting a Scene from Roman Egypt Exhibited in the Egyptian Museum in Cairo [JE 30001]." In *Demeter, Isis, Vesta, and Cybele: Studies in Greek and Roman Religion in Honour of Giulia Sfameni Gasparro*, edited by Attilio Mastrocinque, 137–60. Stuttgart: Steiner, 2012.

Tambiah, Stanley J. "The Magical Power of Words." *Man* 3, no. 2 (1968): 175–208.

Taussig, Michael T. *What Color Is the Sacred?* Chicago: University of Chicago Press, 2009.

Teeter, Emily. *Baked Clay Figurines and Votive Beds from Medinet Habu*. Oriental Institute Publications 133. Chicago: Oriental Institute of the University of Chicago, 2010.

Tezgör-Kassab, Dominique, and Ahmed abd el Fattah. "La diffusion des tanagréennes à l'époque hellénistique: à propos de quelques moules alexandrins." In *Le moulage en terre cuite dans l'antiquité: Création et production dérivée, fabrication et diffusion*, edited by Arthur Muller, 353–74. Lille, France: Presses universitaires du Septentrion, 1997.

Thelamon, Françoise. *Païens et chrétiens au IVè siècle: L'apport de l'"Histoire Ecclésiastique" de Rufin d'Aquilée.* Paris: Études augustiniennes, 1981.
Thierry, Nicole. "Aux limites du sacré et du magique: Un programme d'entrée d'une église en Cappadoce." In *La Sciences des cieux: Sages, mages, astrologues*, edited by Rika Gyselen, 233–47. Bures-sur-Yvette, France: Groupe pour l'étude de la civilisation du Moyen-Orient, 1999.
Thissen, H.-J. "Koptische Kinderschenkungsurkunden: Zur Hierodulie im christlichen Ägypten." *Enchoria* 14 (1986): 117–28.
Thomas, Thelma K. *Late Antique Egyptian Funerary Sculpture: Images for This World and for the Next.* Princeton, NJ: Princeton University Press, 2000.
———. "Material Meaning in Late Antiquity." In *Designing Identity: The Power of Textiles in Late Antiquity*, edited by Thelma K. Thomas, 20–53. Princeton, NJ: Princeton University Press/Institute for the Study of the Ancient World, 2016.
———. "Silks." In *Byzantium and Islam: Age of Transition, 7th–9th Century*, edited by Helen C. Evans and Brandie Ratliff, 148–59. New York: Metropolitan Museum of Art, 2012.
Thompson, Deborah. *Coptic Textiles in the Brooklyn Museum.* Wilbour Monographs 2. Brooklyn: Brooklyn Museum, 1971.
Till, Walter. *Koptische Heiligen- und Martyrerlegenden.* Orientalia Christiana Analecta 108. Rome: Pontificium Institutum Orientalium Studiorum, 1936.
Timbie, Janet. "A Liturgical Procession in the Desert of Apa Shenoute." In *Pilgrimage and Holy Space in Late Antique Egypt*, edited by David Frankfurter, 415–41. Religions in the Graeco-Roman World 134. Leiden: Brill, 1998.
———. "Dualism and the Concept of Orthodoxy in the Thought of the Monks of Upper Egypt." Ph.D. diss., University of Pennsylvania, 1979.
———. "Jesus and Shenoute: From 'Christless Piety' to 'Those Who Have Christ.'" *Coptica* 13 (2014): 1–9.
———. "Once More into the Desert of Apa Shenoute: Further Thoughts on BN 68." In *Christianity and Monasticism in Upper Egypt: Volume 1: Akhmim and Sohag*, edited by Gawdat Gabra and Hany N. Takla, 169–78. Cairo and New York: American University in Cairo Press, 2008.
Timbie, Janet, and Jason Zaborowski. "Shenoute's Sermon *The Lord Thundered*: An Introduction and Translation." *Oriens Christianus* 90 (2006): 93–125.
Torallas Tovar, Sofia. "A New Sahidic Coptic Fragment: Sortes Sanctorum or Apophthegmata Patrum?" *Journal of Coptic Studies* 17 (2015): 153–64.
Török, László. *Coptic Antiquities I.* Bibliotheca Archaeologica 11. Rome: L'Erma di Bretschneider, 1993.
———. *Hellenistic and Roman Terracottas from Egypt.* Bibliotheca Archaeologica 15. Rome: Bretschneider, 1995.
———. *Transfigurations of Hellenism: Aspects of Late Antique Art in Egypt, A.D. 250–700.* Probleme der Ägyptologie 23. Leiden: Brill, 2005.
Torp, Hjalmar. "Leda Christiana: The Problem of the Interpretation of Coptic Sculpture with Mythological Motifs." *Acta Ad Archaeologiam et Artium Historiam Pertinentia* 4 (1969): 101–12.
Toynbee, J.M.C. *Death and Burial in the Roman World.* Baltimore and London: Johns Hopkins University Press, 1971.
Tran, Nicolas. *Dominus Tabernae: Le statut de travail des artisans et des commerçants de l'occident romain (Ier siècle av. J.-C. - IIIe siècle ap. J.-C.).* Bibliothèque des écoles françaises d'Athènes et de Rome 360. Rome: École française de Rome, 2013.
Tran Tam Tinh, V. "De nouveau Isis Lactans (Supplement I)." In *Hommages a Maarten J. Vermaseren*, edited by Margreet B. de Boer and T. A Edridge, 1231–68. Études préliminaires aux religions orientales dans l'empire romain 68. Leiden: Brill, 1978.
———. *Isis lactans: Corpus des monuments gréco-romains d'Isis allaitant Harpocrate.* Études préliminaires aux religions orientales dans l'empire romain 27. Leiden: Brill, 1973.

Traunecker, Claude. "Manifestations de piété personelle à Karnak." *Bulletin de la société française d'Égyptologie* 85 (1979): 22–31.
———. "Une pratique magique populaire dans les temples de Karnak." In *La magia in Egitto ai tempi dei faraoni: Atti, convegno internazionale di studi, Milano, 29–31 ottobre 1985*, edited by Alessandro Roccati and Alberto Siliotti, 221–42. Milan: Rassegna internazionale di cinematografia archeologica, Arte e natura libri, 1987.
Treffort, Cécile. "Vertus prophylactiques et sens eschatologique d'un dépôt funéraire du haut Moyen Âge: Les plaques boucles rectangulaires burgondes à inscription." *Archéologie médiévale* 32 (2002): 31–53.
Treu, Kurt. "Varia Christiana." *Archiv für Papyrusforschung* 24–25 (1976): 113–27.
Trombley, Frank, and J.W. Watt, eds. *The Chronicle of Pseudo-Joshua the Stylite*. Translated Texts for Historians 32. Liverpool: Liverpool University Press, 2000.
Trout, Dennis. "Christianizing the Nolan Countryside: Animal Sacrifice at the Tomb of St. Felix." *Journal of Early Christian Studies* 3 (1995): 281–98.
Tsafrir, Y. "The Christianization of Bet Shean (Scythopolis) and Its Social-Cultural Influence on the City." In *Die spätantike Stadt und ihre Christianisierung*, edited by Gunnar Brands and Hans-Georg Severin, 276–84. Wiesbaden, Germany: Reichert, 2003.
Tudor, Bianca. *Christian Funerary Stelae of the Byzantine and Arab Periods from Egypt*. Marburg, Germany: Tectum Verlag, 2011.
Turner, Victor. "Passages, Margins, and Poverty: Religious Symbols of Communitas." In *Dramas, Fields, and Metaphors: Symbolic Action in Human Society*, edited by Victor Turner, 231–71. Ithaca, NY: Cornell University Press, 1975.
———. "Pilgrimages as Social Processes." In *Dramas, Fields, and Metaphors: Symbolic Action in Human Society*, edited by Victor Turner, 166–230. Ithaca, NY: Cornell University Press, 1975.
Turner, Victor W., and Edith L. B. Turner. *Image and Pilgrimage in Christian Culture: Anthropological Perspectives*. New York: Columbia University Press, 1978.
Uhlenbrock, Jaimee Pugliese. "The Coroplast and His Craft." In *The Coroplast's Art: Greek Terracottas of the Hellenistic World*, edited by Jaimee Pugliese Uhlenbrock, 15–21. New Rochelle, NY: Caratzas Publishers, 1990.
Uljas, Sami. "The IFAO Leaves of the Life of Moses of Abydos." *Orientalia* 80, no. 4 (2011): 373–422.
Valantasis, Richard. "Demons and the Perfecting of the Monk's Body: Monastic Anthropology, Daemonology, and Asceticism." *Semeia* 58 (1992): 47–79.
Valbelle, Dominique, and Geneviève Husson. "Les questions oraculaires d'Égypte: Histoire de la recherche, nouveautés et perspectives." In *Egyptian Religion: The Last Thousand Years: Studies Dedicated to the Memory of Jan Quaegebeur*, edited by Willy Clarysse, Antoon Schoors, and Harco Willems, 1055–71. Orientalia Lovaniensia Analecta 85. Leuven, Belgium: Peeters, 1998.
Valensi, Lucette. *La fuite en Égypte: Histoires d'orient et d'occident: Essai d'histoire comparée*. Paris: Éditions du Seuil, 2002.
Van Dam, Raymond. *Saints and Their Miracles in Late Antique Gaul*. Princeton, NJ: Princeton University Press, 1993.
Van den Kerchove, Anne. "Le Livre du grand traité initiatique (Deux livres de Ieou: dessins et rites.)" In *Écrire la magie dans l'antiquité*, edited by Magali De Haro Sanchez, 109–20. Liège, Belgium: Presses Universitaires de Liège, 2015.
Van den Ven, Paul. *La vie ancienne de S. Syméon Stylite le Jeune*. 2 vols. Subsidia Hagiographica 32. Brussels: Société des Bollandistes, 1962–70.
Van der Horst, Pieter Willem. "Sortes: Sacred Books as Instant Oracles in Late Antiquity." In *The Use of Sacred Books in the Ancient World*, edited by Leonard V. Rutgers, 143–73. Leuven, Belgium: Peeters, 1998.
Van der Leeuw, G. *Religion in Essence and Manifestation*. Translated by J. E. Turner. New York: Harper & Row, 1964.

Van der Spek, K. "Feasts, Fertility, and Fear: Qurnawi Spirituality in the Ancient Theban Landscape." In *Sacred Space and Sacred Function in Ancient Thebes*, edited by Peter Dorman and Betsy M. Bryan, 177–87. Chicago: Oriental Institute of the University of Chicago, 2007.

Van der Veer, Peter, ed. *Conversion to Modernities: The Globalization of Christianity*. London and New York: Routledge, 1996.

———. *Gods on Earth: The Management of Religious Experience and Identity in a North Indian Pilgrimage Centre*. Monographs on Social Anthropology 59. London: Athlone Press, 1988.

———. "Introduction." In *Conversion to Modernities: The Globalization of Christianity*, edited by Peter Van der Veer, 1–21. London and New York: Routledge, 1996.

Van der Vliet, Jacques. "Bringing Home the Homeless: Landscape and History in Egyptian Hagiography." *Church History and Religious Culture* 86, no. 1–4 (2006): 39–55.

———. "Chenouté et les démons." In *Actes du IVè congrès copte*, edited by M. Rassart-DeBergh and J. Ries, 2:41–49. Louvain-la-Neuve, Belgium: Institut Orientaliste, 1992.

———. "The Coptic Gnostic Texts as Christian Apocryphal Literature." In *Ägypten und Nubien in spätantiker und christlicher Zeit: Akten des 6. internationalen Koptologenkongresses, Münster, 20.–26. Juli 1996*, edited by Stephen Emmel, Martin Krause, Siegfried G. Richter, and Sofia Schaten, 2:553–62. Wiesbaden, Germany: Reichert, 1999.

———. "The Copts: 'Modern Sons of the Pharaohs'?" *Church History and Religious Culture* 89, no. 1–3 (2009): 279–90.

———. "Demons in Early Coptic Monasticism: Image and Reality." In *Coptic Art and Culture*, edited by H. Hondelink, 135–56. Cairo: Shouhdy Publishing House, 1990.

———. "Les anges du soleil: À propos d'un texte magique copte récemment découvert à Deir-En-Naqloun (N. 45/95)." In *Études coptes VII: Neuvième journée d'études, Montpelliere 3–4 juin 1999*, edited by N. Bosson, 319–27. Louvain, Belgium: Peeters, 2000.

———. "Literature, Liturgy, Magic: A Dynamic Continuum." In *Christianity in Egypt: Literary Production and Intellectual Trends in Late Antiquity. Studies in Honor of Tito Orlandi*, edited by Paula Buzi and Alberto Camplani, 555–74. Rome: Institutum Patristicum Augustinianum, 2011.

———. "Spätantikes Heidentum in Ägypten im Spiegel der koptischen Literatur." In *Begegnung von Heidentum und Christentum im spätantiken Ägypten*, edited by Dietrich Willers, 99–130. Riggisberg, Switzerland: Abegg-Stiftung, 1993.

Van Esbroeck, Michel. "Three Hebrews in the Furnace." In *The Coptic Encyclopedia*, edited by Aziz Atiya, 7:2257–59. New York: Macmillan, 1991.

Van Lantschoot, Arnold. "Fragments coptes d'une homélie de Jean de Parallos contre les livres hérétiques." In *Miscellanea Giovanni Mercati, I: Bibbia–Letteratura Christiana Antica*, 296–326. Vatican City: Biblioteca apostolica Vaticana, 1946.

———. "Révélations de Macaire et de Marc de Tarmaqâ sur le sort de l'âme après la mort." *Le Muséon* 63 (1950): 159–89.

———. "Une collection sahidique de 'Sortes Sanctorum' (Papyrus Vatican Copte 1)." *Le Muséon* 69 (1956): 35–52.

Van Minnen, Peter. "Boorish or Bookish? Literature in Egyptian Villages in the Fayum in the Graeco-Roman Period." *Journal of Juristic Papyrology* 27 (1998): 99–184.

———. "The Greek Apocaypse of Peter." In *The Apocalypse of Peter*, edited by Jan N. Bremmer and István Czachesz, 15–39. Leuven, Belgium: Peeters, 2003.

Vikan, Gary. "Art, Medicine, and Magic in Early Byzantium." *Dumbarton Oaks Papers* 38 (1984): 65–86.

———. *Catalogue of the Sculpture in the Dumbarton Oaks Collection from the Ptolemaic Period to the Renaissance*. Washington, DC: Dumbarton Oaks Research Library and Collection, 1995.

———. *Early Byzantine Pilgrimage Art*. 2nd ed. Washington, DC: Dumbarton Oaks Research Library and Collection, 2010.

———. "Early Byzantine Pilgrimage Devotionalia as Evidence of the Appearance of Pilgrimage Shrines." In *Akten des XII. internationalen Kongresses für christliche Archäologie, Bonn 1991*, edited by Ernst Dassmann and Josef Engemann, 377–88. Münster, Germany: Aschendorffsche Verlagsbuchhandlung, 1995.

Villa, Silvia Alfayé. "Nails for the Dead: A Polysemic Account of an Ancient Funerary Practice." In *Magical Practice in the Latin West*, edited by R. L. Gordon and Francisco Marco Simón, 427–56. Religions in the Graeco-Roman World 168. Leiden: Brill, 2010.

Vivian, Tim. "The Bohairic Life of Maximus and Domitius." *Coptic Church Review* 26, no. 2/3 (2005): 34–63.

———. "Coptic Palladiana III: The Life of Macarius of Egypt." *Coptic Church Review* 21, no. 3 (2000): 82–109.

———. *Histories of the Monks of Upper Egypt and the Life of Onnophrius by Paphnutius*. Cistercian Studies 140. Kalamazoo, MI: Cistercian Publications, 1993.

Vivian, Tim, Kim Vivian, and Jeffrey Burton Russell. *The Lives of the Jura Fathers*. Cistercian Studies 178. Kalamazoo, MI: Cistercian Publications, 1999.

Volokhine, Youri. *La frontalité dans l'iconographie de l'Égypte ancienne*. Cahiers de la société d'Égyptologie 6. Geneva: Société d'Égyptologie, 2000.

———. "Les déplacements pieux en Égypte pharaonique: Sites et pratiques cultuelles." In *Pilgrimage and Holy Space in Late Antique Egypt*, edited by David Frankfurter, 51–97. Religions in the Graeco-Roman World 134. Leiden: Brill, 1998.

Vryonis, Speros, Jr. "The *Panēgyris* of the Byzantine Saint: A Study in the Nature of a Medieval Institution, Its Origins and Fate." In *The Byzantine Saint*, edited by Sergei Hackel, 196–226. Crestwood, NY: St. Vladimir's Seminary Press, 2001.

Wallace, Vesna A. "Mongolian Livestock Rituals: Appropriations, Adaptations, and Transformations." In *Understanding Religious Ritual: Theoretical Approaches and Innovations*, edited by John P. Hoffmann, 168–85. New York: Routledge, 2012.

Walsh, P. G. *The Poems of St. Paulinus of Nola*. Ancient Christian Writers 40. New York: Newman Press, 1975.

Walters, C. C. "Christian Paintings from Tebtunis." *Journal of Egyptian Archaeology* 75 (1989): 191–208.

Waraksa, Elizabeth A. *Female Figurines from the Mut Precinct: Context and Ritual Function*. Orbis Biblicus et Orientalis 240. Göttingen, Germany: Vandenhoeck & Ruprecht, 2009.

Ward, Benedicta. *The Desert Christian: The Sayings of the Desert Fathers*. New York: MacMillan, 1975.

Ward-Perkins, Bryan. "Reconfiguring Sacred Space: From Pagan Shrines to Christian Churches." In *Die spätantike Stadt und ihre Christianisierung*, edited by Gunnar Brands and Hans-Georg Severin, 285–90. Wiesbaden, Germany: Reichert, 2003.

Ward-Perkins, J. B. "The Role of the Craftsmanship in the Formation of Early Christian Art." In *Atti del IX congresso internazionale di archeologia christiana: Roma, 21–27 settembre 1975*, 637–52. Vatican City: Pontificio istituto di archeologia cristiana, 1978.

Warga, Richard G. "A Christian Amulet on Wood." *Bulletin of the American Society of Papyrologists* 25 (1988): 149–52.

Warner, Nicholas. "Architectural Survey." In *The Red Monastery Church: Beauty and Asceticism in Upper Egypt*, edited by Elizabeth S. Bolman, 49–77. New Haven, CT: Yale University Press/American Research Center in Egypt, 2016.

Wassef, Cérès Wissa. *Pratiques rituelles et alimentaires des coptes*. Bibliothéque d'études coptes 9. Cairo: Publications de l'IFAO, 1971.

Wasserman, Tommy. "P78 (P. Oxy. XXXXIV 2684): The Epistle of Jude on an Amulet?" In *New Testament Manuscripts: Their Texts and Their World*, edited by Thomas J. Kraus and Tobias Nicklas, 137–60. Leiden: Brill, 2006.

Watts, Edward Jay. *Riot in Alexandria: Tradition and Group Dynamics in Late Antique Pagan and Christian Communities*. Transformations of the Classical Heritage 48. Berkeley: University of California Press, 2010.

Weber, Max. *The Sociology of Religion*. Translated by Ephraim Fischoff. Boston: Beacon Press, 1963.

Weingrod, Alex. *The Saint of Beersheba*. Albany: State University of New York Press, 1990.
Weinryb, Ittai, ed. *Ex Voto: Votive Giving across Cultures*. New York: Bard Graduate Center, 2016.
Weiss, Lara. "The Consumption of Religion in Roman Karanis." *Religion in the Roman Empire* 1, no. 1 (2015): 71–94.
Wendrich, Willeke. "Entangled, Connected or Protected? The Power of Knots and Knotting in Ancient Egypt." In *Through a Glass Darkly: Magic, Dreams, and Prophecy in Ancient Egypt*, edited by Kasia Szpakowska, 243–70. Swansea, UK: Classical Press of Wales, 2006.
Werbner, Richard P. "Regional Cult of God Above." In *Ritual Passage, Sacred Journey: The Process and Organization of Religious Movement*, 245–98. Washington, DC: Smithsonian Institution Press, 1989.
———, ed. *Regional Cults*. Association of Social Anthropologists Monographs 16. London and New York: Academic Press, 1977.
Wessely, Charles. *Les plus anciens monuments du christianisme écrits sur papyrus*. Vol. 2. Patrologia Orientalis 4. Paris: Firmin-Didot, 1946.
Westerfeld, Jennifer. "Monastic Graffiti in Context: The Temple of Seti I at Abydos." In *Writing and Communication in Early Egyptian Monasticism*, edited by Malcolm Choat and Mariachiara Giorda, 187–212. Texts and Studies in Eastern Christianity 9. Leiden: E. J. Brill, 2017.
Wild, Henri. "Les danses sacrées de l'Égypte ancienne." In *Les danses sacrées*, 33–117. Sources Orientales 6. Paris: Éditions du Seuil, 1963.
Wilfong, Terry G. "Agriculture among the Christian Population of Early Islamic Egypt: Practice and Theory." *Proceedings of the British Academy* 96 (1999): 224–33.
———. "Western Thebes in the Seventh and Eighth Centuries: A Bibliographical Survey of Jême and Its Surroundings." *Bulletin of the American Society of Papyrologists* 26 (1989): 89–145.
———. *Women of Jeme: Lives in a Coptic Town in Late Antique Egypt*. Ann Arbor: University of Michigan Press, 2002.
Willis, R. G. "Instant Millennium: The Sociology of African Witch-Cleansing Cults." In *Witchcraft Confessions and Accusations*, edited by Mary Douglas, 129–40. Association of Social Anthropologists Monograph 9. New York: Routledge, 2004.
Wilson, Penelope. "Slaughtering the Crocodile at Edfu and Dendera." In *The Temple in Ancient Egypt: New Discoveries and Recent Research*, edited by Stephen Quirke, 179–203. London: British Museum Press, 1997.
Winroth, Anders. *The Conversion of Scandinavia: Vikings, Merchants and Missionaries in the Remaking of Northern Europe*. New Haven, CT: Yale University Press, 2012
Wipszycka, Ewa. "The Institutional Church." In *Egypt in the Byzantine World, 300-700*, edited by Roger S. Bagnall, 331–49. Cambridge: Cambridge University Press, 2007.
———. "La valeur de l'onomastique pour l'histoire de la christianisation de l'Égypte. À propos d'une étude de R. S. Bagnall." *Zeitschrift für Papyrologie und Epigraphik* 62 (1986): 173–81.
———. "Le degré d'alphabétisation en Égypte byzantine." *Revue des études augustiniennes* 30 (1984): 79–96.
———. "Le nationalisme a-t-il existé dans l'Égypte byzantine?" *Journal of Juristic Papyrology* 22 (1992): 83–128.
———. "Les formes institutionelles et les formes d'activité économique du monachisme égyptien." In *Foundations of Power and Conflicts of Authority in Late-Antique Monasticism. Proceedings of the International Seminar Turin, December 2–4, 2004*, edited by Alberto Camplani and Giovanni Filoramo, 109–54. Leuven, Belgium, and Dudley, MA: Peeters, 2007.
———. *Les ressources et les activités économiques des églises en Égypte du IVè au VIIIè siècle*. Papyrologica Bruxellensia 10. Brussels: Fondation égyptologique Reine Élisabeth, 1972.
———. *L'Industrie textile dans l'Égypte romaine*. Warsaw: Zakład Narodowy im. Ossolińskich, 1965.
———. "Textiles, Coptic: Organization of Production." In *The Coptic Encyclopedia*, edited by Aziz Atiya, 7:2218–21. New York: Macmillan, 1991.

Wiśniewski, Robert. "Pagans, Jews, Christians, and a Type of Book Divination in Late Antiquity." *Journal of Early Christian Studies* 24, no. 4 (2016): 553–68.
Wisse, Frederik. "Language Mysticism in the Nag Hammadi Texts and in Early Coptic Monasticism, I: Cryptography." *Enchoria* 9 (1979): 101–20.
Wong, Jun Yi. "Raze of Glory: Interpreting Iconoclasm at Edfu and Dendera." *Journal of Late Antiquity* 9, no. 1 (2016): 89–131.
Worrell, William H. "Coptic Magical and Medical Texts." *Orientalia* 4 (1935): 1–37, 184–94.
———. *Coptic Texts in the University of Michigan Collection*. University of Michigan Studies, Humanistic Series 46. Ann Arbor: University of Michigan Press, 1942.
———. "A Coptic Wizard's Hoard." *American Journal of Semitic Languages and Literatures* 46, no. 4 (1930): 239–62.
Yasin, Ann Marie. *Saints and Church Spaces in the Late Antique Mediterranean: Architecture, Cult, and Community*. Cambridge: Cambridge University Press, 2009.
———. "Sight Lines of Sanctity at Late Antique Martyria." In *Architecture of the Sacred: Space, Ritual, and Experience from Classical Greece to Byzantium*, edited by B. D. Wescoat and R. G. Ousterhout, 248–80. Cambridge: Cambridge University Press, 2012.
———. "The Pilgrim and the Arch: Paths and Passageways at Qal'at Sem'an, Abu Mena, and Tebessa." In *Excavating Pilgrimage: Archaeological Approaches to Sacred Travel and Movement in the Ancient World*, edited by Troels Myrup Kristensen and Wiebke Friese, 166–86. London and New York: Routledge, 2017.
Young, Allan. "Magic as a 'Quasi-Profession': The Organization of Magic and Magical Healing among Amhara." *Ethnology* 14, no. 3 (1975): 245–65.
Young, Dwight W, ed. *Coptic Manuscripts from the White Monastery: Works of Shenute*. Vienna: Hollinek, 1993.
———. "A Monastic Invective Against Egyptian Hieroglyphs." In *Studies Presented to Hans Jakob Polotsky*, edited by Dwight W. Young, 348–60. East Gloucester, MA: Pirtle & Polson, 1981.
Youtie, Herbert C. "Questions to a Christian Oracle." *Zeitschrift für Papyrologie und Epigraphik* 18 (1975): 253–57.
Zandee, Jan. *Death as an Enemy: According to Ancient Egyptian Conceptions*. Studies in the History of Religions 5. Leiden: Brill, 1960.
———. "Traditions pharaoniques et influences extérieures dans les légendes coptes." *Chronique d'Égypte* 91 (1971): 211–19.
Zanetti, Ugo, and Stephen J. Davis. "Liturgy and Ritual Practice in the Shenoutean Federation." In *The Red Monastery Church: Beauty and Asceticism in Upper Egypt*, edited by Elizabeth S. Bolman, 27–35. New Haven, CT: Yale University Press/American Research Center in Egypt, 2016.
Zeitler, Barbara. "Ostantatio Genitalium: Displays of Nudity in Byzantium." In *Desire and Denial in Byzantium*, edited by Liz James, 185–201. Aldershot, UK: Variorum, 1999.
Zuckerman, Constantine. "The Hapless Recruit Psois and the Mighty Anchorite, Apa John." *Bulletin of the American Society of Papyrologists* 32, no. 3–4 (1995): 183–94.

ILLUSTRATION CREDITS

PLATES

PLATE 1. Brooklyn, Brooklyn Museum, acc. # 16.160. Gift of Evangeline Wilbour Blashfield, Theodora Wilbour, and Victor Wilbour honoring the wishes of their mother, Charlotte Beebe Wilbour, as a memorial to their father, Charles Edwin Wilbour, 16.160. Creative Commons-BY (Photo: Brooklyn Museum [in collaboration with Index of Christian Art, Princeton University], CUR.16.160_view1_ICA.jpg).

PLATE 2. Kom Aushim magazine, FeG acc. #183. Photograph courtesy of Brigham Young University Egypt Exploration Project.

PLATES 3 and 4. Bibl.: Martens-Czarnecka, *Wall-Paintings*, 233–38. Archive PCMA, photo by D. Zielińska.

PLATE 5. Florence, Institute of Papyrology "G. Vitelli," Egyptian Museum. Bibl.: *Antinoe cent'anni dopo*, 101, ##89–98. Photo courtesy of Institute of Papyrology "G. Vitelli." Courtesy of Egyptian Museum, Institute of Papyrology "G. Vitelli," Florence.

PLATE 6. London, Victoria and Albert Museum, inv. 279-1891. © Victoria and Albert Museum, London.

PLATE 7. London, Victoria and Albert Museum, inv. 259-1890. © Victoria and Albert Museum, London.

PLATE 8. Providence, Rhode Island School of Design, Museum Works of Art Fund 59.030. Photography by Erik Gould, courtesy of the Museum of Art, Rhode Island School of Design, Providence RI.

PLATE 9. Bibl.: Clédat, *monastère . . . de Baouît* (1904), 80–81. Painting in public domain.

FIGURES

FRONTISPIECE. Map by Ancient World Mapping Center, Chapel Hill NC.

FIGURE 1. From Kaufmann, *Die Menasstadt*, taf. 73. Photo in public domain

FIGURE 2. London, British Museum, EA49530. Bibl.: Bailey, *Catalogue*, #3393EA. Photograph courtesy of British Museum.

FIGURE 3. University of Michigan, Kelsey Museum of Archaeology inv. 3432. Bibl.: Allen, "Terracotta Figurines," #96. Photograph courtesy of Kelsey Museum, University of Michigan.

FIGURE 4. British Museum PE 1924.10-06.42. Bibl.: Bailey, *Catalogue*, #3401PE. Photograph courtesy of British Museum.

FIGURE 5. Budapest, Szépművészeti Múzeum 84.16.A. Bibl.: Török, *Coptic Antiquities*, #G6. Photograph courtesy of Szépművészeti Múzeum.

FIGURE 6. Liebighaus Skulpturensammlung, Frankfurt am Main, inv.-No. 2400-1617. Bibl.: Kaufmann, "Archäologische Miscellen," 106–7; Bayer-Niemeier, *Bildwerke*, #262. Photo © Liebieghaus Skulpturensammlung, Frankfurt am Main.

ILLUSTRATION CREDITS

FIGURE 7. Musée des Beaux-Arts, Lyon, Inv. G 175, dépôt de l'Institut d'égyptologie Victor-Loret, Université Lyon 2. Bibl.: *Égypte romaine*, #120. © MBA Lyon.
FIGURE 8. By Peter Grossmann, used by permission.
FIGURE 9. Washington DC, Dumbarton Oaks, Byzantine Collection, acc. no. 40.61. Bibl.: Vikan, *Catalogue*, 58–60, #22; Frankfurter, "Binding of Antelopes." © Dumbarton Oaks, Byzantine Collection, Washington DC.
FIGURE 10. Brooklyn Museum, Charles Edwin Wilbour Fund, 38.753. Creative Commons-BY (Photo: Brooklyn Museum, 38.753_PS9.jpg)
FIGURE 11. New York, Metropolitan Museum of Art, acc. #89.18.123. Purchase by subscription, 1889. Photo courtesy of Metropolitan Museum of Art, Open Access for Scholarly Content.
FIGURE 12. Oxford, Ashmolean Museum, acc. #AN 1891.182. © Ashmolean Museum, University of Oxford.
FIGURE 13. New York, Metropolitan Museum of Art, Rogers Fund, 1909, acc. #09.50.1769. Photo courtesy of Metropolitan Museum of Art, Open Access for Scholarly Content.
FIGURE 14. New York, Metropolitan Museum of Art, Fletcher Fund, 1946, acc. #46.156.18a. Photo courtesy of Metropolitan Museum of Art, Open Access for Scholarly Content.

INDEX

Aaron (monk), 75, 84, 89, 90, 91, 94–95
Abgar correspondence, apocryphal, 97, 191, 199–200
Abraham of Farshut (monk), 82, 90, 98
Abydos: 240, 242–43, 246–47, 249
ACM (by reference #): **4**: 194; **25**: 62, 109; **26**: 61; **43**: 207–8; **47**: 57; **48**: 209–10; **49**: 1–2; **61**: 97; **63**: 98; **64**: 62; **66**: 218; **74**: 86; **75**: 86; **78**: 86; **79**: 86, 218; **81**: 204–5; **91**: 205–6; **92**: 218; **93**: 65; **98**: 218; **104**: 83, 98; **111**: 218; **113**: 203; **117**: 152; **119**: 218; **128**: 137; **133**: 204n79; **134**: 97; **135**: 204n79
Acts of Paul, 112–13
Acts of John, 224n139
Agency, 20–21, 23–24, 36, 52–54, 61–63, 68, 143–47, 149, 152, 154, 162–64, 176, 181, 183–85, 189–90, 192, 200, 228, 235, 237, 241, 245–47, 253, 256–57, 250–61
Alston, Richard, 38
Amente, 185, 211, 218–29, 231
Amulets and charms, 2–3, 14, 21–25, 27–28, 37, 40–41, 61–62, 96–98, 103, 109, 129, 154, 156–57, 177, 180–81, 184, 187, 195–96, 198, 200–201, 204, 206–11, 228–30, 232, 257, 258
Antinoë, cemetery of, 179. *See also* Colluthus, Shrine of St.
Antisyncretism, 18–19, 26, 28. *See also* Syncretism
Antony (monk), 82, 87–88, 99, 105. *See also* Athanasius of Alexander, *vita Antonii* by
Apocalypse of Elijah, 99, 104, 107, 212–15, 217, 224, 255, 259
Apocalypse of Paul, 225
Apocalypse of Peter, 192, 222, 225
Apocalypse of Zephaniah, 225
Apocalyptic texts and traditions, 30, 84, 87, 104, 157, 190–92, 197, 202, 212–15, 222–28, 230–31

Apollo of Hermopolis/Bawit (monk), 77, 78, 90, 154
Apollo the Archimandrite (monk), 96–97
Apotropaia, 48, 50, 112, 145–49, 151, 153, 155, 157, 175, 177, 199, 231, 245
Appadurai, Arjun, 148, 151n27
Apuleius of Madaura, 152
Archaisms and archaizing, 12, 19, 137, 208–9, 217, 222, 230, 250
Asterius of Amaseia, 172, 176
Athanasius of Alexandria, 105, 107, 141–42, 190–91; *vita Antonii* by: 82, 88, 105, 107, 178, 217, 254. *See also Homily on the Virgin*

el-Bagawat, cemetery of, 107
Barb, Alphonse, 10
Bauer, Walter, 190n28
Bawit, Monastery of, 93, 100, 153, 154n47, 169
Bell, Harold, 9
Bes (Egyptian god), 42, 55–56, 77, 85, 101, 131–32, 147, 168, 233, 242, 247
Bes (monk), 91, 172–73
Besa, abbot of White Monastery, 153
Blessings (*eulogia*): from monks and holy men, 47, 61, 64, 67–68, 70, 76, 80, 93–100, 109, 193, 195, 228, 260; from saints' shrines, 127, 132, 151, 164
Book of Bartholomew, 220–21
Books of Jeu, 223–25
Bourdieu, Pierre, 22, 38, 72–73
Boushēm, anonymous monk of, 89
Bovon, François, 190
Bowes, Kimberly, 47
Brakke, David, 82n41, 83n51
Brown, Peter, 5, 6, 26, 73–74, 75, 106
Burridge, Kenelm, 102
Bynum, Caroline Walker, 150

INDEX

Caesarius of Arles, 14, 18, 23, 28, 47, 112, 123–24
Carthage, Council of (419 CE), 106, 113, 142n157
Charakteres, 198–200
Child-donations, 63
Colluthus (martyr-saint), 126
Colluthus, Shrine of St. (Antinoë), 106–7, 109n26, 128–29, 131, 133, 186–88
Communitas, 109, 119, 124, 144
Conversion, xiii, 3, 6–7, 10, 234–35, 237, 257, 261
Cross, 5, 10, 15, 17, 21, 27–29, 48, 56, 70, 145–46, 155, 156–61, 171–73, 175, 180–82, 187, 200, 213, 231, 242, 249, 258, 260; in *ankh*-form (*crux ansata*), 157–59, 161; manual gesture of, 112, 122, 182
Cryptography, 198–99
Crypto-paganism. See Secret devotions
Curses and cursing, 65, 79, 82–83, 97–98, 101, 112, 205–6, 210, 228, 259
Cyril of Jerusalem, 112
Cyrus and John, Saints, Shrine of. See Menouthis

Däbtära (Ethiopian cantor-exorcist), 196–97
Damascius, 47, 208
Dance, 28, 52, 109, 114, 122–26, 144, 171
Davis, Stephen, 176
Death personified, 219–22
Demonology, 76, 79–82, 84, 143, 196–97, 218, 244–45
Demons, 27, 33, 40, 50, 56, 62, 76–87, 93–94, 99–101, 104–5, 112, 136, 139–46, 153, 157, 169, 230, 244–45; of Amente, 218–22. See also Spirits of the landscape
Denderah, 233–34, 237, 239, 241–42, 245
Dijkstra, Jitse, 4n6, 237n14, 244n52
Discourse on Abbadon, 221
Divination, 14, 41, 51–52, 55, 74, 87–90, 101–2, 114, 130–38, 184, 186–90, 259. See also Oracle; Ticket oracle

Egeria, 246, 248, 256
Elsner, Jaś, 148, 168, 244
Epiphanius, Monastery of (Thebes), 93, 96–97, 101, 177, 193n38
Eulogia. See Blessings
Evagrius Ponticus, 84
Evagrius Scholasticus, 124–25
Exorcism, 12, 33, 45, 51, 63, 67, 74, 77, 82–84, 87, 94, 99, 101–2, 106, 112, 134, 139, 169, 196, 239–43

Felix, Saint of Nola. See Paulinus of Nola
Festival, 8n27, 12, 14–15, 21–22, 28, 30, 108–25, 138, 140–41, 144, 155, 162–63, 171, 184, 189–90, 221–22, 249–50, 255
Figurines, terracotta, 24–25, 28, 34–37, 47–49, 58–60, 65–66, 68, 108, 127–30, 144, 152, 154, 162–67, 171, 182; *mater lactans* form of, 166–67
Firmilian of Caesarea, 139
Flood, Finbarr, 172–73
Frange (monk), 96n103, 97
Freedberg, David, 146, 155n50
Fromont, Cécile, 171
Frontality in iconography, 147, 168–69, 233–34

Gascou, Jean, 134
Gell, Alfred, 22, 129, 146–47, 153–54
Graf, Fritz, 136n141
Gregory I, Pope, 238, 240
Gregory of Nazianzus, 123
Gregory of Tours, 95
Gregory the Great, 18

Habitus, 22, 72–74, 87–88, 93, 102–3, 111–13, 120–22, 126, 128, 130, 132, 134, 136, 166, 183, 231, 236
Halbwachs, Maurice, 236
Hathor (Egyptian goddess), 155, 166, 168, 233–34
Hell. See Amente
Heresy and heretics, 44–46, 105, 110, 191
Historia monachorum in Aegypto, 88, 94, 107
History of Joseph the Carpenter, 178, 220
Holy Family, 216–17, 248
Homily on the Virgin by Pseudo-Athanasius, 3, 23, 37, 96, 195, 237, 244
Horus (Egyptian god), 1–2, 12, 42, 56–57, 61, 66, 92, 168, 207–10, 231, 243, 246; magical *cippi* of, 145, 231
Huebner, Sabine, 40

Iconoclasm and mutilation of images, xiii, 3, 18, 30, 33, 44–45, 77, 85–86, 101, 147, 159n63, 233–35, 241–42
Incubation, 28, 114, 130, 132–37, 144, 187
Isis (Egyptian goddess), 1–2, 12, 18, 42–43, 56–58, 66, 113, 120, 128, 134–35, 152, 166–68, 171, 207–10, 231, 241, 243, 246–47, 256

Jerome, 143
Jesus, 1–2, 5, 141, 157, 162, 178, 199–200, 258
John Chrysostom, 56, 123, 143
John of Ephesus, 45, 47

John of Lycopolis (monk), 88
John of Paralos, 191, 195–96
John the Little (monk), 76, 91, 140
Johnson, Paul, 46
Jorio, Andrea de, 111

Karanis, 36–37, 39, 165n80, 168
Krawiec, Rebecca, 173

Lamps and lamp-lighting, 13, 22, 26–27, 41–42, 47, 50, 54, 57, 81, 168, 182, 253
Leontius, Shrine of St. (Arsinoë), 131–32
Lévi-Strauss, Claude, 15
Liturgy, 63, 71, 84, 106–7, 109, 112, 118–19, 177, 182, 185, 192–92, 195–97, 201–6, 211, 218–22, 228, 230–31, 250, 255, 257, 260; mortuary forms of, 161, 180–81, 218–22
Lullaby, 56–57, 210, 231–32
Luxor, temple of (Thebes), 240–41

Macarius of Egypt (monk), 84, 89
Macarius of Tkow (monk), 77–78, 85, 99. See also *Panegyric on Macarius of Tkow*
MacMullen, Ramsay, xiv, 5
Magical texts, 1–2, 7, 29–30, 40–41, 47, 51, 56–58, 61–62, 65, 81, 86, 91, 97–98, 100, 136n138, 137, 151–52, 184–86, 190, 192–211, 218–19, 226, 228–30. See also ACM; Amulets and charms
Mamre, Shrine of (Palestine), 111–12, 121–22, 154
Martin of Braga, 14, 18, 47
Martyr, 30, 92, 99, 104–7, 109, 128, 148, 253–56
Martyrology, 30, 106, 109, 189–90, 253–55
Mary, Virgin, 34, 40, 53, 58, 88, 162, 170–71, 201, 216. See also Holy Family
Mathews, Thomas, 168
Mauss, Marcel, 22, 72–73
Menas, Shrine of St. (Apa Mena), 29, 34, 36–37, 40, 58, 60, 108, 111, 115–19, 128–30, 133, 136, 241; *ampullae* of, 108, 127, 154; figurines from, 127–30, 164; incubation practices at, 133, 136; workshops of, 154–55, 163–64, 166
Menouthis: shrine of Isis at, 45, 132, 134–36; shrine of Saints Cyrus and John at, 18, 65, 70, 108, 111, 127–28, 130, 133–36
Meyer, Birgit, 260
Michael, Archangel, 1, 78, 125, 191, 195, 205, 216, 221, 251, 254
Min (Egyptian god), 81, 236
Miracles of St. Menas, 119–20, 165
Monumentality and church building, 240–41

Moses of Abydos (monk), 71–72, 76, 85, 88, 240, 242, 244–45, 249
Mummification and the adornment of corpses, 29, 50, 155–56, 176–81, 260

Nag Hammadi Library, 190, 217–18, 224, 229
Names and naming, 5, 38–39
Naqlun, Monastery of (Fayyum), 177–78
Nile, 27, 79, 88–92, 99–100, 103–5, 107, 113, 213, 217, 237, 240, 243, 246, 248–51
Nomina sacra, 198–99

Oil, as sacred material, 3, 10, 28, 37, 61, 69–70, 94, 96–98, 108, 112, 127, 228, 257
Old Dongola, monastery of (Nubia), 124–25, 170–71
Oracle, 27, 30, 33, 105–6, 136–37, 242; holy men as, 87–88, 100; by the spirit-possessed, 138–44; ticket, 114. See also Divination; Ticket oracle
Orans gesture, 22, 34, 112–14, 164, 167
Oxyrhynchus, religion in, 36, 100, 118, 120, 131, 160, 178n137, 251. See also Philoxenus, St., shrine of

"Pagan"/"paganism," 2, 7–9, 14, 31–32, 37, 54
Panegyric on Macarius of Tkow, 26, 36, 45, 78, 99
Panel-paintings of Egyptian gods, 167–69
Papyrus Cologne 354, 215–17, 248, 255
Paulinus of Nola, 18, 113, 121–22, 143
Phib (monk), 60, 100, 154
Philae, religion in, 4n6, 234, 237, 241, 249
Philoxenus, St., shrine of (Oxyrhynchus), 131, 186–87
Pisentius (monk), 64, 88, 96, 105
Possession, by demons and spirits, 114, 139–44. See also Exorcism; Oracle
Pregnancy and conception, 34–36, 40–41, 49, 58–60, 62, 64–67, 93, 100, 126, 129–31, 163, 166–67, 182
Procession, 6, 17–18, 24, 28, 30–31, 77–79, 88, 99–100, 109, 111, 113, 118–20, 124, 144, 168, 220, 237, 248–52, 257–58

Ramsay, William, 11
Redfield, Robert, 228, 257–59
Religion in Roman Egypt, xiii, xiv, 3, 9, 37–38, 234n4, 244n52
Revelation, Book of, 104, 139, 212, 222, 225
Rufinus of Aquileia, 250

Sacrifice and festive animal slaughter, 8n27, 78, 81, 110, 112, 114, 120–22, 144
Sallnow, Michael, 23–24
Sanzo, Joseph, 201
Schatzki, Theodore, 24, 110
Secret devotions, 13, 21, 42, 44–46, 57, 135–36
Shai (Egyptian god), domestic veneration of, 13–14, 26, 41, 45, 54, 57
Shenoute of Atripe, 191, 212, 226–27, 235; church of, 75, 149, 241, 245; describing conflict with Gesios, 12–13, 42, 44, 46–47, 77, 83; in hagiography, 76–77, 79, 85, 94, 173, 217, 244; on heathenism, 81, 101, 134, 135n131, 169–70, 239, 259; as holy man, 83–85, 87–89, 91, 94, 101, 173; and the Nile, 217, 250–51; on popular religious practices and comportment, 13, 22, 26, 41–42, 55, 61, 69–70, 97, 107, 115, 119–20, 122–23, 125, 132, 134, 142, 165, 184, 195, 228, 253–54; posthumous cult of, 71, 94, 99–100, 118, 173, 217; *Vita* of, 77, 79, 85
Simeon the Stylite, 23, 72, 75, 99, 118, 124–25, 138, 148
Simeon the Younger, 168–69
Simon, Marcel, 9
Sissinios, St., 169, 171, 182
Smith, Jonathan Z., 49
Smith, Julia, 20
Socrates Scholasticus, 157–59
Sophronius of Jerusalem, 108, 111, 127, 133–36
Sortes-books, 188–89, 228, 230
Spirits of the landscape, 1, 80–81, 86, 89, 136, 142–43, 218, 236–37, 242–48, 256. *See also* Demons
Survivals, pagan, xiv, 7, 10–12, 15–16, 20, 23, 28, 30–31, 95, 132, 136, 144–45, 182, 185, 211, 222–23, 227, 230, 256

Syncretism, xiv, 6, 15–21, 24–29, 32, 54, 63, 66, 70–72, 76, 86–87, 90, 95, 100–103, 114, 122, 125–26, 130, 134, 138, 143–44, 148–49, 171, 181, 184, 210–11, 226–27, 230, 259–61. *See also* Antisyncretism
Swidler, Ann, 259

Taussig, Michael, 150
Testament of Abraham, 220, 222
Testament of Job, 173–74
Thecla, 112–13, 138, 154
Thelamon, Françoise, 159n63
Theodoret of Cyrrhus, 73
Theodosian Code, 44, 120, 238
Theophilus of Alexandria, 240–41, 252
Thomas, Thelma, 161
Three Hebrew Youths, Shrine of (Alexandria), 40, 45, 67, 107, 139–42
Ticket oracle, 19–20, 28, 130–32, 134, 185, 186–88, 228, 230
Török, László, 161
Traditional iconographic strategy, 145–46, 150–51, 157, 162, 165, 167, 182
Tran, Nicolas, 152
Turner, Victor, 119, 144

Votive offerings and deposits, 21, 28–29, 52, 63, 67, 109, 111–12, 114, 120–30, 132, 141, 144, 163–64, 167, 169

Weber, Max, 147

Yasin, Ann Marie, 238

Zachariah of Mytilene: 44–45

GPSR Authorized Representative: Easy Access System Europe - Mustamäe tee
50, 10621 Tallinn, Estonia, gpsr.requests@easproject.com